T0301516

"*Over the past 20 years, Tom Wilson has been a highly visible risk management practitioner in major financial services firms – both banks and insurance companies – as well as in leading advisory firms. The discussion of value management in banking and insurance in a single volume highlights that one of the major roles of financial services firms is risk-taking, risk transformation and risk management. Tom's unique experience in both sectors has allowed him to produce a most welcome integrated handbook.*

The clear exposition that risk-taking and strategic management in banking and insurance must be integrated in a value creation framework provides invaluable tools to address managerial issues such as risk identification, capital allocation, measurement of performance and risk governance. The sharing of Tom Wilson's vast experience is a gift to the profession."

Jean Dermine, Professor of Banking and Finance, Insead, author *of Bank Valuation and Value Based Management*

"*Much has been written on value and capital management, also for the financial services industry. But this handbook is truly different in a number of ways.*

First, it provides a solid conceptual basis to understand true value creation in banking and insurance. This may seem academic, but is indeed highly relevant in practice. As a long-standing practitioner in both industries, I have seen numerous situations where profit generation has been mistaken for value creation, often leading to the wrong decisions. This book clearly dispels some deeply embedded valuation myths in both the banking and insurance worlds, some of which are still being trained today!

Second, it provides a sound basis to understand and manage the value of risk-based, capital intensive businesses using a common set of practical tools, filling a void in the available literature.

Third, it covers the entire spectrum of finance and risk activities relevant for the CFO and CRO: From valuation to management information to management action. Real life examples from both banking and insurance are used to illustrate the various tools in practice, be that efficiency management, asset liability management, risk management, strategic planning, and many others.

I was forced to learn many of the themes covered in this handbook the hard way over several years, and I suspect the author has taken a similar journey. Much could have been easier if I had this book at hand earlier."

Jo Oechslin, CRO, Credit Suisse Group AG

"*Tom's book on risk and capital management is the most comprehensive in the field. It is not only well structured and thorough, it is an easy read. I particularly enjoyed the anecdotes throughout giving live examples in insurance and banking. Like minded CROs and CFOs will also find this book comforting in that it not only supports their beliefs, it conveys they are not alone in trying to get the fundamental point of true value measurement accepted and embedded in their own organizations. Lastly I wanted to compliment Tom on his description of the roles of the CFO and CRO in financial institutions. I have too often heard that CROs must remain fully independent of business decisions only being able to blow a whistle when there is a problem. The book clearly points to the CRO as a vital part of management decision making from strategy to execution and that CROs must remain objective, leaving independence to audit and supervisors.*"

Tom Grondin, CRO, Aegon Insurance

Value and Capital Management

A Handbook for the Finance and Risk Functions of Financial Institutions

THOMAS C. WILSON

WILEY

Library of Congress Cataloging-in-Publication Data

Wilson, Thomas C.,
  Value and capital management : a handbook for the finance and risk functions of financial institutions / Thomas C. Wilson.—1
      pages cm.—(The Wiley finance series)
   Includes bibliographical references and index.
ISBN 978-1-118-77463-2 (hardback)
1. Banks and banking. 2. Financial services industry. 3. Risk management. I. Title.
   HG1601.W558 2015
   332.1068′1—dc23   2015013221

A catalogue record for this book is available from the British Library.

ISBN 978-1-118-77463-2 (hardback)   ISBN 978-1-118-77438-0 (ebk)
ISBN 978-1-118-77462-5 (ebk)   ISBN 978-1-118-77435-9 (obk)

Cover Design: Wiley
Cover Image: © Iaroslav Neliubov/Shutterstock

Set in 10/12pt TimesLTStd-Roman by Thomson Digital, Noida, India
Printed in Great Britain by TJ International Ltd, Padstow, Cornwall, UK

To Kurt and Arlyn, with love and gratitude

Contents

List of Abbreviations

ABC	Activity-Based Costing
ADM	Application Development and Maintenance
AEP	Aggregate Exceedance Probability
ALCO	Asset Liability Committee
ALM	Asset/Liability Management
APE	Annualized Premium Equivalent
ATE	Absolute Tracking Error
AUM	Assets Under Management
BPO	Business Process Outsourcing
BPR	Business Process Re-engineering
CAPM	Capital Asset Pricing Model
CER	Capital Efficiency Ratio
CFO	Chief Financial Officer
CIO	Chief Investment Officer
CIR	Cost Income Ratio
CLV	Customer Lifetime Value
CNHR	Cost of Non-Hedgeable Risks
COC	Cost of Capital
CoR	Combined Ratio
CRM	Customer Relationship Management
CRO	Chief Risk Officer
CUO	Chief Underwriting Officer
DAC	Deferred Acquisition Costs
DJSI	Dow Jones Sustainability Index
EaR	Earnings at Risk
EC	Economic Capital
ECI	Economic Capital Intensity
EDP	Electronic Data Processing
EEV	European Embedded Value
EIA	Equity Indexed Annuity
EP	Economic Profit
EPS	Earnings Per Share
ERM	Enterprise Risk Management
ESG	Economic Scenario Generator
ESG	Environmental, Social and Governance
FASB	Financial Accounting Standards Board

FCF	Free Cash Flow
FCReC	Frictional Costs of Required Capital
FNAV	Fair Net Asset Value
FS	Free Surplus
FSB	Financial Stability Board
FTP	Funds Transfer Pricing
GAAP	Generally Accepted Accounting Principles
GIC	Guaranteed Investment Contract
GMAB	Guaranteed Minimum Accumulation Benefit
GMDB	Guaranteed Minimum Death Benefit
GMIB	Guaranteed Minimum Income Benefit
GMWB	Guaranteed Minimum Withdrawal Benefit
G-SIFI	Globally Systemically Important Financial Institutions
HRO	High-Reliability Organization
IBES	Institutional Brokers' Estimate System
IC	Invested Capital
ICT	Information and Communications Technology
IDR	Implied Discount Rate
IFRS	International Financial Reporting Standards
ILS	Insurance-Linked Securities
IRR	Internal Rate of Return
ITO	Information Technology Outsourcing
IV	Intrinsic Value
KPI	Key Performance Indicator
KRI	Key Risk Indicator
LCR	Liquidity Coverage Ratio
LH	Life and Health insurance business
Libor	London inter-bank offered rate
LLPO	Limited Liability Put Option
LTP	Liquidity Transfer Pricing
MBR	Monthly Business Review
MC	Market Capitalization
MCEV	Market-Consistent Embedded Value
MIS	Management Information System
MPL	Maximum Probable Loss
MREL	Minimum Required Eligible Liabilities
MVBS	Market Value Balance Sheet
MVE	Market Value of Earnings
NAV	Net Asset Value
NBM	New Business Margin
NDM	Net Deposit Margin
NFCL	Non-Financial Component of Liabilities
NI	Net Income
NII	Net Interest Income
NLM	Net expected Loan Margin
NOPLAT	Net cash Operating Profit Less Adjusted Taxes
NPS	Net Promoter Score

NSFR	Net Stable Funding Ratio
OAS	Option-Adjusted Spreads
OCF	Operating Cash Flow
OCI	Other Comprehensive Income
PAYD	Pay As You Drive
PC	Property and Casualty insurance business
PRE	Policyholder Reasonable Expectations
PVFP	Present Value of Future Premium
PVIF	Present Value In-Force business
PVNBP	Present Value of New Business Premium
QBR	Quarterly Business Review
RAC	Risk-Adjusted Capital
RAG	Red, Amber, Green
RAPM	Risk-Adjusted Performance Measures
RAROA	Risk-Adjusted Returns on Assets
RAROC	Risk-Adjusted Return on Capital
RARORAC	Risk-Adjusted Return on Risk-Adjusted Capital
RC	Required Capital
RCSA	Risk Control Self-Assessment
ROE	Return on Equity
ROIC	Return on Invested Capital
RoMVS	Return on Market Value Surplus
RORAA	Return on Risk-Adjusted Assets
RORAC	Return on Risk-Adjusted Capital
SLA	Service Level Agreement
SML	Securities Market Line
TDIs	Top-Down Indicators
TEV	Traditional Embedded Value
TNAV	Tangible Net Asset Value
TOM	Target Operating Model
TRA	Top Risk Assessment
TSR	Total Shareholder Return
TVA	Total Value Added
TVOG	Time Value of Financial Options and Guarantees
UL	Unexpected Loss
UL	Unit Linked investment product
VaR	Value at Risk
ViF	Value in Force
VNB	Value of New Business
VOBA	Value of Business Acquired
WACC	Weighted Average Cost of Capital

Creating value is challenging in any highly competitive industry, a daily battle to capture market share, defend margins and improve expenses. Managing value in financial services is even more challenging due to the unique role that risk and capital play in the economics of the business: whereas most industrial corporations actively avoid risk, there can be no return to shareholders – and no satisfied customers – if banks and insurers avoid risk, and taking risks requires capital. In banking and insurance, risk and capital management and value management are synonymous.

The role of the Chief Financial Officer (CFO) and Chief Risk Officer (CRO) has evolved and adapted to this economic reality. Modern finance and risk functions now have substantial influence on the strategy, operations and, ultimately, the value of their firms. This influence comes in part from being a business partner and in part through the financial and risk management activities directly within their responsibility.

This Handbook is intended as a practical but theoretically grounded reference for finance and risk professionals interested in managing value. The Handbook consists of three main sections.

Better information – Measuring value. What gets measured, gets managed. Accurately measuring value is a necessary precondition for managing it. This section develops a risk-adjusted valuation and performance measurement framework tailored to banks and insurers, reconciled with the way that our shares are actually valued by the market. The framework clearly links management actions to shareholder value creation and is the foundation for internal, value-based management initiatives.

Better insights – Managing value. Better information may be a necessary condition, but it is not a sufficient condition: ultimately, the "right" decisions have to be taken. Allocating capital to existing businesses and exploiting new growth opportunities requires insights beyond risk and capital; it also requires an understanding of the markets, the drivers of operating performance and the sources of profitable growth. This section presents corporate and segment-specific "rules of the game" (or strategies) as well as Key Performance Indicators (KPIs) tailored to banking and insurance and gives examples of value-enhancing initiatives. It is designed to give CEOs, CFOs and CROs concrete ideas for increasing the value of the individual businesses as well as the corporate portfolio.

Better decisions – Capital, balance sheet and risk management. In addition, CFOs and CROs contribute directly to value creation through their own areas of responsibility, especially through strategic planning and capital allocation; balance sheet, liquidity and asset/liability management; risk underwriting and risk management. This section provides insights into how CFOs and CROs can actively create value in these areas.

WHO SHOULD READ THIS BOOK?

This Handbook provides an accessible reference for professionals working within and around the financial services industry, targeted toward

- CFOs, CROs and other finance and risk professionals in banks and insurance who are interested in increasing the value of their company, especially those active in strategic planning and performance management; capital management, Treasury, balance sheet, liquidity management and asset/liability management; risk underwriting and risk management.
- CEOs and business unit heads who want to understand how the business and value creation look "through a finance and risk lens."
- Analysts who cover banks and insurers from a value and solvency perspective, including buy- and sell-side equity analysts, as well as analysts in rating agencies, regulators and supervisors.
- Graduate students in business, economics and finance who are interested in bridging the gulf between financial theory and the practical realities of managing value in banks and insurance companies.

Acknowledgments

T he intellectual foundations for this Handbook have been laid over the past 20 years while working with bank and insurance professionals in finance and risk. While too numerous to acknowledge individually, some warrant special mention.

COLLEAGUES AT WORK

At Allianz, a special note of thanks to Michael Diekmann, Oliver Baete and Dr Helmut Perlet for bringing me on board and supporting me in building a world-class risk function. I would also especially like to thank Dieter Wemmer for reinforcing active capital management within the Group. In addition, thanks to Max Zimmerer for discussions on asset/liability management; to Clem Booth for discussions on underwriting; and to Manuel Bauer, Helga Jung, Christoph Mascher, Jay Ralph, Axel Theis and Werner Zedelius for valuable business discussions.

For challenging my thinking, special thanks to Peter Etzenbach, Kamesh Goyal, Burkhard Keese, Thomas Naumann, Walter Reinl, Giulio Terzariol and Renate Wagner in Finance and Strategic Planning; Dirk Diederich and Stephan Theissing in Treasury and Capital Management; Oliver Schmidt in Investor Relations; Michele Gaffo, Andreas Gruber, Günther Thallinger and Axel Zehren in Investment Management. Also, to my Global Risk team at Allianz, especially Larisa Angstenberger, Blaise Bourgeois, Violeta Bondoc, Michael Buttstedt, Jean-Marc Cornet, Wolfgang Deichl, Doug Franklin, Marco Hauck, Andreas Graser, Erick Holt, Pierre Joos, Kathrin Meier, Sebastian Pichler, Sigurd Volk, Terry Watson and Andreas Wilhelm.

At ING, thanks to Cees Maas and especially John Hele and Koos Timmermans whom I consider as friends and mentors. Within the ING Risk team, thanks to Doug Caldwell, Bill Cokins, Emmanuel van Grimbergen and Francis Ruijgt in particular for challenging my thinking.

At Oliver Wyman and Company, special thanks to John Drzik, Thomas Garside, Andy Kuritzkes, John Paul Pape and Dylan Roberts, who challenged me to merge finance and risk into a coherent, value-oriented framework and supported my practice-building and client-oriented work. At Mercer Human Resources, thanks to Vicki Elliott, who helped me to understand the power of linking strategy, performance and incentives in changing the culture and, ultimately, the performance of a company.

At Swiss Re, special thanks to Walter Kielholz, John Fitzpatrick and Bruno Porro for giving me the opportunity to develop and implement many of the ideas for the first time in a "line capacity." In addition, thanks to Paul Huber, Adam Litke and Christoph Menn for helping me to make the theoretical, practical.

At McKinsey & Company, special thanks to Peter Wuffli, whose good common sense and mentorship during my early years encouraged me to dedicate myself to finance and risk. Thanks also to Kevin Buehler, Christian Casal, Arno Gerken, Wolfgang Hammes, Nils Are Lyso and Thomas Poppensieker for helping me to build the risk management practice so many years ago. Finally, to Tom Copeland for providing me with an early "apprenticeship" in valuation and value-based management.

COLLEAGUES IN THE PROFESSION

There is an old cliché, "A consultant is someone who borrows your watch in order to tell you what time it is . . . and then charges you for the 'service'!" While I believe my former clients will find much humor and little truth in this cliché, it is nonetheless fair to say that I have learned significantly from former clients and other industry professionals and professional bodies.

While too numerous to name individually, a special debt of gratitude is owed to Mark Abbot, Guardian Financial; Martin Blessing, Commerzbank; Michel Crouhy, CDC-Ixis; Ron Denbo, Algorithmics; Philipp Halbherr, Zuercher Kantonalbank; Tobias Guldimann, Credit Suisse Group; Tom Grondin, Aegon; Robert Gumerlock, Swiss Bank Corporation; Will Hawkins, KBW; Philipp Keller, Deloitte; Martin Kauer, Converium; Arno Kratky, Commerzbank; Bob Mark, Black Diamond; Dan Marinangelli, Toronto Dominion; Chris Matten, KPMG; Jean-Christoph Meniuex, AXA; Charles Monet, Morgan Stanley; Per-Göran Persson, UBS; Jo Oechslin, Credit Suisse; Bruno Pfister, Swiss Life; Professor Stuart Turnbull, University of Texas at Austin; Martin Senn, Zurich Financial Services; Walter Stuerzinger, Union Bank of Switzerland; Johnny Vo, Royal Bank of Canada; Bob Yates, Fox-Pitt, Kelton.

In addition, I would like to thank the European CRO Forum and PRMIA for creating a platform for the exchange of ideas and best practices between industry professionals.

RESEARCH AND EDITORIAL SUPPORT

I would like to thank Professor Andreas Richter, PhD candidates Dominik Lohmaier and Verena Jaeger and the students in the Ludwig Maximillian University 2014–15 Masters' Seminar on Managing Value in Financial Institutions who provided me with critical comments and challenged me to make the messages clearer. Thanks also to Yoanna Histrova, Master's Student at LMU, for research assistance on the value relevance of market-consistent approaches. Thanks to Jean-Fredrick Breton for illustrative calculations.

Further thanks to Tom Copeland, Mark Wagner, Jean-Fredrick Breton and Tom Grondin for reviewing an earlier draft, as well as to the editors at John Wiley who helped to bring this book to completion.

TO MY FAMILY

Finally, I would like to thank my family who supported and encouraged me. First and foremost, to my parents, Kurt and Arlyn Wilson, to whom I dedicate this book – their continued love and support through good weather and stormy seas provided a safe harbor. Second, to my wife, Nontaya Ekmonachai, for having the patience to see this project through to the end and for being the sweetest, most caring and special person I know. To my brothers, Marc and Kurt Wilson, for always being there when I needed them. Finally, with special love to my children, Paige, Christian and Lucas, who continually make me both very happy and very proud.

DISCLAIMER

Acknowledging my intellectual debts does not absolve me of the responsibility for any errors and omissions. In addition, the opinions and views expressed in this Handbook are mine alone and do not represent the opinions or views of any other individual or institution that I have worked with now or in the past.

About the Author

Thomas C. Wilson has over 20 years' experience in finance and risk with world-class financial institutions and advisory firms.

Since 2008, Tom has been the CRO for Allianz SE, one of the largest insurance companies and asset managers in the world. During the financial crisis of 2008, Tom also held the dual role of CRO for Dresdner Bank, then an Allianz subsidiary and the third largest bank in Germany, until it was sold. Tom helped Allianz earn the highest possible Enterprise Risk Management rating by Standard & Poor's in 2013 and was recognized as the Insurance Chief Risk Officer of the Year by *Risk Magazine* in 2009 and *Life & Pensions Magazine* in 2009.

Prior to joining Allianz, Tom was the CRO for ING's global insurance operations. During his tenure, Tom helped ING to achieve the highest possible Enterprise Risk Management rating granted by Standard & Poor's in 2007 and was recognized as the Insurance Chief Risk Officer of the Year by *Risk Magazine* in 2006 and *Life & Pensions Magazine* in 2007.

Prior to joining ING in 2005, Tom was Global Head of the Finance & Risk Practice at Oliver Wyman & Company (OWC), a consulting firm specializing in serving banks and insurers in risk, strategy and organization. This newly created position was designed to leverage and expand OWC's traditional risk expertise into an equivalent strength in finance and serving the CFOs of financial services firms.

Prior to joining OWC in 2002, Tom was the CFO of Swiss Re New Markets (SRNM), the alternative risk transfer and capital markets division of Swiss Reinsurance. While at SRNM, Tom was responsible for strategic planning, financial and management reporting, Treasury, back-office operations and risk management.

Prior to joining SRNM in 1998, Tom was Global Head of the Risk Management Practice at McKinsey & Company. Tom is credited as being the founder of McKinsey's risk management practice, making substantial contributions to the industry and clients in risk management and governance.

Tom began his career at the Union Bank of Switzerland (UBS) in Zurich as a swap and swap option trader.

Tom is a former Chair of the CRO Forum and on the Blue Ribbon Advisory Panel of PRMIA, the Professional Risk Management International Association.

Tom earned a BSc in Business Administration with honors from the University of California at Berkeley and a PhD in Economics from Stanford University.

Tom was born in San Francisco and has lived and worked in Munich, Amsterdam, New York, London and Zurich. Tom is a dual American/Swiss citizen.

Introduction

C hief Financial Officers (CFOs) and Chief Risk Officers (CROs) have significant potential to influence the value of their firm through three channels.

- First, by providing *better information* in the form of Risk-Adjusted Performance Metrics (RAPMs), which link management actions directly to shareholder value.
- Second, by challenging businesses to higher levels of performance through *better insights*, including segment-specific strategies and management actions.
- Third, by taking *better decisions* in their own areas of responsibility, especially corporate strategy and capital allocation, balance sheet management and risk management.

These three levers are so important for managing the value of banks and insurers that they form the organizing framework for this Handbook, illustrated in the figure below.

These responsibilities are also relatively new, representing an evolution in the roles of the CFO and CRO over the past 20 to 30 years. As banks and insurance companies evolved into larger, more complex, internationally diversified financial services groups, the roles of the CFO and CRO evolved in parallel. The result is a finance and risk "backbone" that helps diversified groups get the most from their corporate portfolio through strategic planning, performance management, capital allocation and balance sheet management. In order to understand the role of the modern CFO and CRO within a diversified financial services firm, you first have to understand how and why their roles have evolved in parallel.

The remainder of this Part I of the Handbook motivates the three levers – better information, better insights and better decisions – and the unique role of the CFO and CRO in applying them toward value creation.

Better Information – What gets measured, gets managed

- How to value risk-based, capital intensive businesses?
- How to link management actions, risk adjusted performance measures (RAPMs) and other, Key Performance Indicators to value?

Better Insights – How to create value through operations

- What "rules of the game" (or generic strategies) create value in each business segment?
- What core skills are required in each segment?

Better Decisions – How Finance & Risk creates value

- Strategic planning and capital allocation
- Balance sheet, asset/liability and liquidity management
- Risk management and risk underwriting

FIGURE P1.1   Managing for value from the finance and risk perspective

CHAPTER 1

Why is Value Management Important?

CFOs and CROs have significant potential to influence the value of their firm through three channels.

- First, by providing *better information* in the form of RAPMs,[1] which link management actions directly to shareholder value.
- Second, by challenging businesses to higher levels of performance through *better insights,* including segment-specific strategies and management actions.
- Third, by taking *better decisions* in their own areas of responsibility, especially corporate strategy, capital allocation, balance sheet management and risk management.

This chapter motivates the importance of these three levers in managing the value of the company from a CFO and CRO's perspective.

BETTER INFORMATION

The first objective of this Handbook is to develop a value and performance measurement framework which can be used by managers at all levels to set strategy and steer risk-based, capital-intensive banking and insurance businesses. The valuation framework, illustrated below, splits the value of the firm between its current net asset value (or the market value of its current assets less its liabilities) and its franchise value (reflecting future, profitable new business).

Figure 1.1 is used throughout the Handbook to represent the three value levers available to CFOs and CROs – better information, better insights and better decisions.

The top part of the figure represents better information in the form of a valuation framework suitable for risk-based, capital-intensive businesses. This framework explicitly links management actions to both traditional value drivers – including profitable growth and operating efficiency – and value drivers unique to banking and insurance – including

---

[1]Banks and insurers use different risk-adjusted metrics in practice, including RAROC (Risk-Adjusted Return On Capital), RORAC (Return On Risk-Adjusted Capital) and even RARORAC. By definition, not all of them will lead to the "right" answer. This Handbook defines RAPMs consistent with shareholder value.

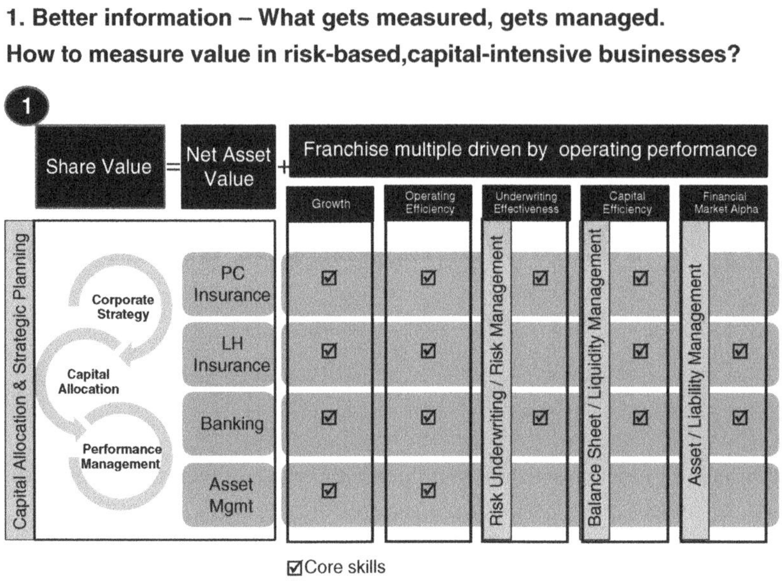

1. Better information – What gets measured, gets managed.

How to measure value in risk-based,capital-intensive businesses?

FIGURE 1.1 Better information – What gets measured, gets managed

underwriting effectiveness, capital efficiency and financial returns from asset/liability mismatches. Better information is covered in Part II of the Handbook.

The rows in the figure represent better insights, representing the strategies and core skills needed to create value in each business segment. It suggests, for example, that sales effectiveness and operating efficiency are critical for all segments, but that managing "alpha" through asset/liability management is core only for Life and Health (LH) insurance and banking. Better insights is the theme of Part III of the Handbook.

The columns in the figure represent better decisions taken by the finance and risk functions, focusing on strategic planning and capital allocation; risk management and underwriting; balance sheet and liquidity management; asset/liability management. The topic of better decisions is covered in Part IV of the Handbook.

Why It Is Important

There is an old saying, "What gets measured, gets managed." It is colorfully illustrated by the story of the chandelier factory in the old Soviet Union, where the Party had set production targets in gross tons of chandeliers. What did they get? Consistent with the incentives, the factory produced a dozen chandeliers, each weighing the equivalent of a small bus and capable of pulling down the roof of any building were they ever to be installed. The result: many tons of chandeliers, all twelve of them, but no light.

If we want to manage shareholder value and performance, we first need to measure it. If a company measures performance in terms of market share or sales growth then, guess what, market share and sales growth will be what it gets if successful. But does higher market share or growth create value? Not always. The international expansion of Japanese commercial banks and German Landesbanken in the 1990s illustrates strategies which arguably focused on growth but sacrificed shareholder value.

Similarly, a company focusing on risk-adjusted returns will achieve a higher return on capital if successful. But do higher percentage returns always translate into higher shareholder value? Even if the capital deployed is decreasing? Returns below the cost of capital obviously destroy value, but investing less and less capital at marginally higher risk-adjusted returns also represents an opportunity cost to shareholders.

Growth without adequate returns or risk-adjusted returns without growth. Both are bad strategies. Ultimately, the trade-off between growth, risk and returns needs to be understood and evaluated so that the right path can be taken. Providing clarity is one of the key levers that CFOs and CROs can "pull" to help create value.

Why It Is Challenging

Measuring the performance of financial services firms is inherently difficult given the duration, complexity and risks inherent in their products. How to measure the value created by products with highly uncertain cash flows far into the future? Although the standard corporate finance mantra "Cash is King!" works well for industrial corporations, anyone who has had to wade through the complexities of insurance and bank financial accounts knows how difficult it is to go from financial reporting to cash and from cash to value.

In response, banks and insurers have converged on internal RAPM and Economic Profit (EP) frameworks, which make the returns and risks of very different, highly complex financial businesses directly comparable. Unfortunately, RAPM frameworks can be complex, reflecting the complexity of the business, and in spite of the complexity, not all of them provide the "right" answer.

In addition, the inherent complexity can make the link between RAPMs and shareholder value seem so tenuous to senior managers that they revert to a simpler paradigm to manage value – one of accounting earnings, earnings growth and P/E (price/earnings) multiples – even though, by ignoring capital and risk, the simpler approaches will lead almost certainly to the wrong decisions.

I remember a conversation that I had with the CFO of a large bank in North America while conducting a survey on the role of the CFO and CRO (OWC, 2003). We quickly established that the bank used RAROC to evaluate individual credits and business unit strategies, that RAROC was accepted by management and used to set targets and incentivize performance.

"At last!" I thought to myself. "Here is the poster child for value management that I have been searching for!" And so, with growing enthusiasm and great expectations, I (naively) asked my final question of the interview, "So, RAROC has had a strong influence in terms of shaping your corporate strategy?"

The answer was dumbfounding: "Shaping corporate strategy? But why? The CEO and I drive strategy by looking at earnings, earnings growth and a P/E multiple – from a shareholders' perspective, isn't that all that we need to set the strategy of the bank?"

A lot of questions ran through my head: If the bank's internal metrics don't link to value and are not used to set corporate strategy, then why go through the effort? Looking at it from another angle, if P/E or M/B (market-to-book) ratios accurately reflect value, then what determines them? Why do some firms enjoy an M/B multiple of 2× tangible equity and others only 1× or less? And finally, isn't ignoring risk and capital, as P/E and M/B multiples seem to do, asking for trouble when managing risk-based, capital-intensive businesses?

During the remaining interviews, I asked the same question of other CFOs and CROs. A consistent picture emerged: even in the most "advanced" institutions, senior management relied more on a combination of revenue and earnings growth and market multiples to set strategy, ignoring internal performance metrics which were developed over many years and with great effort. This is not to say that RAPMs and EP didn't have an impact at the tactical and transaction level, just that they more often failed to impact the strategy of the firm.

The reasons cited most often were the complexity of the internal metrics, combined with lingering concerns regarding stability and accuracy. From my experience, however, the real issue was simpler: most CEOs, business unit heads and CFOs saw no clear link between the complex internal metrics and the external valuation multiples used in practice. During my career, I have seen more CEOs sketch their corporate strategy on the "back of an envelope" for equity analysts using P/E multiples than I have seen using RAPMs and EP!

Fortunately, there is a way to salvage RAPM frameworks, correcting the flaws and allowing them to be understood and more closely aligned with value creation. These are the themes developed in the more technical Part II of this Handbook.

BETTER INSIGHTS

Better information is necessary but not sufficient; ultimately, strategic and operational decisions have to be taken, including the allocation of capital, and this requires an in-depth understanding of the marketplace as well as business strategies, core competencies and management actions which can be implemented. See Figure 1.2.

Why It Is Important

An interview with the CFO of a mid-sized European bank illustrated the importance of better insights in terms of both business challenge and capital allocation. Like many of his peers, the

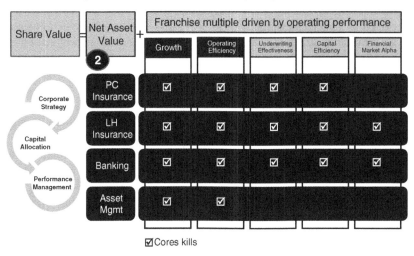

FIGURE 1.2 Better insights

CFO's role had evolved over time from the Head of Accounting and Reporting to a modern CFO, including responsibility for the strategic planning process.

Focusing on strategic planning, he explained the steps already taken in supplementing accounting information with an economic value framework and moving from a bottom-up, revenue- and expense-budgeting exercise to a process emphasizing strategy.

Even with this progress, the results were unsatisfactory: the plans, derived bottom-up, were anything but "strategic," being better characterized as "business as usual" or "last year plus 5%."

The firm had more than adequate information and a clearly defined planning process supported by extensive Gantt charts,[2] taking up significant resources and delivering a bulky end product. In spite of these, the CFO and CEO were left feeling that the company was missing opportunities which would have required a more fundamental rethink of where capital was allocated and that the business units should have – and could have – committed to much more in terms of results and tangible actions to address the real issues. Unfortunately, these commitments were simply not forthcoming and the businesses were allowed to grow, and capital was allocated, based on momentum and not on their potential.

This was frustrating, because the CFO and CEO (as well as the market!) knew that competitors were more aggressively re-dimensioning their commercial loan portfolio, building more profitable private client businesses and adjusting their cost base. As a consequence, the bank's share price lagged behind those of its peers, and analysts were playing Monday morning quarterback during every conference call, letting the CFO know what plays they should have run after the fact.

Why It Is Challenging

The portfolio of businesses in a large, diversified financial services firm is increasingly complex and international, limiting the effectiveness of market discipline on capital allocation decisions. The role of market discipline falls naturally on the corporate center, comprising the group's CEO, CFO and CRO: it is the corporate center's responsibility to allocate capital between competing interests and challenge business strategies based on an in-depth under-standing of the marketplace, competitors' strategies and relative business performance.

Returning to the interview, the CFO described how, working together with the CEO, they altered the role of the corporate center from that of a "financial investor" (focused on providing capital and consolidated financial reporting) to that of a "private equity firm," focusing relentlessly on value creation through a deeper understanding of the businesses and proactive capital management.

One important step was the creation of an "equity analyst" group within the finance function, which regularly performed a sum-of-parts valuation of the firm, defining and benchmarking key value drivers for each business and evaluating peer strategies. The end result was a clear understanding of which businesses were under- and over-performing and the value of the "performance gaps" in terms of potential share price appreciation.

As he explained it, these insights were fundamental in reshaping the dialog between the corporate center and the business units: during the next planning round it was much easier to set tougher targets, initiate greater change, reallocate capital and ultimately shake the business

---

[2]A Gantt chart is a type of bar chart used to illustrate a project schedule. It was developed by Henry Gantt in the 1910s.

units out of their strategic inertia, especially in areas where the company was producing bottom quartile results.

The interview reinforced the observation that *better insights* – with respect to markets, competitors and strategies – are critical for the CFO as a value manager.

Part III of this Handbook provides segment-specific insights into business strategies (or "rules of the game"), core competencies and management actions used by successful banks and insurers. It then continues by outlining strategies for profitable growth and operating efficiency applicable to all segments. It is useful for CEOs and business leaders when taking strategic and operational decisions as well as for the finance and risk functions when allocating capital and challenging line managers from a shareholder value perspective.

BETTER DECISIONS

CFOs and CROs also take important decisions in their own areas of responsibility. From a value management perspective, the most important decisions include corporate strategy and capital allocation; balance sheet, liquidity and asset/liability management; as well as underwriting and risk management. The third objective of this Handbook, highlighted in Figure 1.3, is to help CFOs and CROs take decisions in these three important areas.

Corporate Strategy and Capital Allocation: Why It Is Important and Challenging

Capital allocation is the tool used to implement corporate strategy, clearly defining which businesses you will harvest for cash, which you will invest in for profitable growth, which you will fix or exit and how much remaining capital will be returned to shareholders. These are the

**3. Better Decisions –
How to create value in Finance & Risk areas of responsibility?**

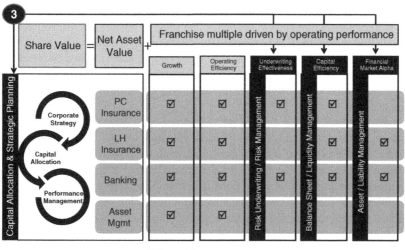

☑Core skills

FIGURE 1.3 Better decisions

most important decisions taken at the corporate center from a value management perspective. Getting it wrong represents at best a serious opportunity cost; in the worst case, it can destroy shareholder value.

An Anecdote from Banking

Consider another interview, this time with the CFO of a regional bank in North America. During the meeting, he outlined the corporate goal of doubling the share price in 5 years. Observing that "the P/E multiples for retail and commercial banking are relatively similar," they set the bank's 5-year strategy to invest retained earnings in commercial banking (which was easier to expand organically) at roughly 4× the rate in retail banking (which was more difficult to expand organically). For this company, earnings, earnings growth and the P/E multiple drove the bank's strategy to shift from retail to commercial banking.

Unfortunately, from a shareholder's perspective, the retail bank required significantly less capital per dollar of earnings, offering a 20% RoE (Return on Equity) and an implied M/B valuation multiple of 2× invested capital even without the prospect of significant growth. This was in contrast to the commercial bank, whose 10% RoE only just covered its cost of capital, generating an implied 1× M/B valuation multiple, with or without growth.

While each dollar of earnings from the retail and commercial bank were "worth" about the same based on the segment P/E multiples, the retail bank was throwing off more earnings per unit of invested capital. Given that both businesses required capital to grow, the opportunity cost of the bank's strategy was tremendous: there was an extra dollar of share value foregone for every dollar invested in the commercial bank rather than the retail bank.

An Anecdote from Insurance

LH and Property and Casualty (PC) P/E multiples can also be similar in mature markets. Looking only at P/E multiples, there may have been an historical bias to focus on LH businesses which can grow faster in a bull market, driven by higher account balances and higher investment margins.

This may be the wrong decision, however: even if P/E multiples are comparable, LH RoE and M/B multiples can lag those of a well-run retail PC franchise. The difference is due in part to the higher capital tied up over longer periods to support LH retirement and savings businesses and in part to the quality of earnings, with LH more dependent on investment margins than operating performance.

In 2012, the European LH segment was valued at an average M/B multiple 0.7–0.8× versus 1.2–1.4× for the European PC segment. As Table 1.1 illustrates, the relative differences are consistent independent of whether book value, tangible book value or embedded value is

TABLE 1.1 European Insurance Average Sector Multiples, 2012

Sector* Multiples	PC	LH
Market P/BV	1.12	0.78
Market P/NAV	1.36	0.88
Market P/EV	1.33	0.47

*Own analysis based on JPM 2012 Insurance Sector Report, June
BV = Book Value, NAV = Tangible Net Asset Value
EV = Embedded Value

used in the denominator. (The notable outlier is the price to embedded value for the LH segment; one can only conclude that the industry's embedded values are either naively optimistic or overly aggressive relative to the market's valuation of the business.)

One implication is that there may be an opportunity cost in growing traditional LH at the expense of PC businesses during this period. The second, more disturbing implication is that any incremental growth in LH may actually have been value destroying unless the new business was materially different from the business in force.

The moral of these stories? While growth in earnings may be a Siren's song, one cannot ignore risk and capital when setting strategies and allocating capital for risk-based, capital-intensive businesses.

Balance Sheet Management: Why It Is Important and Challenging

Balance sheet management encompasses three core disciplines, each of which can have a significant impact on value.

- *The capital and financing structure of the firm.* Capital structure and financial leverage directly influence the firm's return on equity and weighted average cost of capital; in addition, operational leverage is key to the banking business model. It is through these channels that the capital financing structure of the firm can influence share valuations.
- *Liquidity management.* The importance of liquidity management is easily illustrated by the list of firms forced into resolution during the 2008 financial crisis due to a lack of liquidity, including for example Bear Stearns, Lehman Brothers, Northern Rock and AIG.
- *Asset/liability management.* Both the banking and insurance industries have suffered spectacular, industry-wide failures due to poor Asset/Liability Management (ALM) decisions. Examples include the US savings and loan crisis in the 1980–90s and the Japanese insurance crisis during the late 1990s, with the current low interest rate environment not boding well for European and other global insurers.

Specifically related to ALM is another interview which I had with the CFO of a large European composite insurance company.

As you may recall, the European insurance industry was hit hard by the equity market correction in 2001–02.[3] The correction had an immediate balance sheet impact for firms heavily exposed to equities, prompting many firms to take drastic action: for example, Aegon, Allianz, Aviva, Hanover Leben, ING, Mannheimer Leben, Munich Re/Ergo, Royal Sun Alliance, Swiss Life, Winterthur, Zurich Financial Services, as well as many others, all did some combination of cutting dividends, recapitalizing the balance sheet, shedding non-core businesses, curtailing growth and radically reducing their risk exposures.

During the course of the interview it became clear that this insurance company had all the outward trappings of "best-in-class" finance and risk management analytics: their risk management function had been measuring and attributing economic capital since before the crisis, including to the equity positions. In addition, the numbers were delivered and accepted by senior management, including the Chief Investment Officer (CIO, who chaired the Asset/Liability Management Committee) and the head of the insurance business who was responsible for product design and pricing.

---

[3]See Wilson (2003b) and Chapter 16 for more details.

Once again, I ecstatically thought "Here is the poster child for strategic finance and risk: a company which has not only developed advanced risk models to shed light on the true economics of their business, but has also had them accepted by senior management, setting the stage for true impact!"

I was quickly brought back down to earth, however: on my way out the door, the CFO sat at his desk shaking his head and muttered the rhetorical question, "For years, we reported the risk of such a large equity position on our balance sheet and the potential cost of the guarantees – it wasn't as if it was subtle, more like the 900-pound gorilla sitting in the middle of the Board room. We saw the numbers and occasionally talked about the potential impact. Why-oh-why, didn't we *do* anything?"

As the door closed behind me, my last image was of him picking up the phone to his investment banker to arrange a new rights issue or the sale of a non-core business (does it really matter which?) that would stabilize the company's balance sheet and allow it to hobble forward and survive in the aftermath of the 2001–02 crisis.

As I went through the remaining interviews, I noticed a similar trend: "best practice" finance and risk functions in terms of measurement techniques which nonetheless were unable to address the 900-pound gorilla in their Board room. Put another way, even though a company's models and strategic analysis may have correctly identified the issues, many organizations seem incapable of taking the right decisions.

Risk Management: Why It Is Important and Challenging

Financial services create value for shareholders and clients by managing risk, either by underwriting and holding a diversified pool of risks or by intermediating and transforming risks between capital market participants or by providing risk advisory services. It should therefore not come as a surprise that Enterprise Risk Management (ERM) is a cornerstone of creating, and protecting, value in financial services.

With respect to risk underwriting, the cost of risk comprises a significant part of the economics of insurance and banking businesses and a significant source of earnings volatility even during "normal" times. For example, the "cost of risk" can be as high as 60–70% of revenues for a PC insurer as measured by the loss ratio; furthermore, a two to three percentage point variation in the loss ratio can be levered up to a 20–30% impact on operating profit, depending on the company's expense ratio and investment results. Risk has a similarly large impact on the fortunes of banks and LH insurers.

Better risk underwriting can lead to both *higher average* operating earnings and *lower volatility* in earnings. But the profitability advantage from better underwriting is not only defensive: it can also be used to attack the market by identifying niches where more profitable business can be written. In other words, good risk management is not only about applying the brakes; it is also used to give gas and grow profitable business.

"Good" risk decisions balance uncertain rewards potentially far in the future against revenues today. Achieving this balance on an institution-wide scale is challenging for a variety of reasons.

Risk underwriting. First, because it is difficult to accurately identify, assess, price and underwrite risks. The challenges arise frequently due to a lack of adequate data, models or experience or because the environment has changed, implying that the past is not a good indicator of the future. Unfortunately, the challenge just as frequently comes from a fundamental failure in the basic blocking-and-tackling needed to be a world-class underwriter.

Incentives and culture. Second, because it is difficult to align the incentives of those who take the decisions today with the interests of the shareholders, customers and regulators who may have to cover the adverse outcomes in the future. Aligning interests is challenging due to the complexity of the business, management's information advantage on the risks taken and the limited liability nature of managers' contracts, potentially leading to a "heads I win, tails you lose" proposition. Most important, it is impossible to fully align interests using only quantitative mechanisms, implying that risk culture plays an important but unquantifiable role in ERM.

Risk strategy and appetite. Third, because it is challenging to link business and risk strategy, answering fundamental questions such as the following.

- How much exposure to a market do we "need" and how much is "too much?" How high should limits be set during normal times? During bull markets or periods of "irrational exuberance?" Should we be "dancing while the music is playing" or be more prudent, occasionally sitting one out?
- Which risks are necessary for our strategy to create value and which are incidental, to be avoided if possible? Where do we create value by taking risks and where do we simply generate earnings?

WHY SHAREHOLDER VALUE?

In order to be successful in a highly competitive and dynamic environment, value managers need to have better information, better insights and take better decisions. But this presupposes that shareholder value is a key objective of the firm.

I firmly believe that if shareholder value is not your top priority, then it should be. My line of argument is simple: in addition to being in the best interests of shareholders, it is also in the long-run best interests of other stakeholders, including your customers, employees, regulators, society more broadly and even you as a manager of the firm.

Value Management, In the Interests of Shareholders . . .

Financial services represent a tough, competitive arena. Corporate Darwinism suggests that the fittest firms will survive and prosper in a self-reinforcing, virtuous cycle. It also suggests that sudden "mutations" and/or environmental disruptions – such as the rise of the Internet and mobile telephony – can create new opportunities as well as new competitors to threaten even the most successful incumbents. Given increased shareholder activism and the benefits of a higher valuation multiple in terms of making acquisitions both firms and management teams that are not able to successfully adapt are destined to pass by the wayside.

However, this is where the analogy breaks down. Whereas evolution breeds success in incremental changes over eons or through sudden, uncontrolled genetic mutations, the management of a bank or insurer has the capability to consciously redesign, adapt and improve itself.

Top-performing institutions *by definition* excel in the core areas of distribution, operations, underwriting and balance sheet management and allocate capital optimally to current and future profitable growth opportunities. These represent decisions taken, not decisions genetically preordained.

In short, bank and insurance management can influence the destiny of their firm, for good or ill, and a strong focus on shareholder value is a necessity if the firm – and the management team – is to survive in highly competitive and dynamic markets.

. . . And All Other Stakeholders

Focusing on shareholder value may not resonate in today's socially conscious world. Should the focus rest solely on shareholder interests, ignoring the interests of other stakeholders such as customers, employees, regulators and the broader society in which we operate? Isn't this too narrow minded? Shouldn't the modern corporation also focus on these other stakeholders' interests?

The role of the corporation in society is hotly debated, a debate which I do not want to open up here. Instead, I make a simple assertion: managing for *long-term* shareholder value requires that you consider the interests of *all* stakeholders, including employees, customers, regulators and the broader society. You cannot create shareholder value without selling products and services and you cannot produce and sell products in the long term without providing value to customers and employees, meeting their expectations regarding environmental and social objectives while satisfying the expectations of regulators.

Depending on what side of the debate you sit, this assertion is either "acting responsibly" or "enlightened self-interest." However, it doesn't matter what side of the debate you take, the results are the same – creating long-term, sustainable value for shareholders is also in the best interests of customers and employees and other stakeholders.

Allianz practices enlightened self-interest, taking comfort in the fact that our products provide value to our customers and they are designed and underwritten considering our customers' needs and the impact on the environment and society. We also take comfort in offering a fair and competitive wage and working conditions to our employees (all 145,000 of them); in the fact that we are compliant with all regulatory requirements at all times; that we support the broader society through other means, such as Allianz4Good, Finance Coach, etc.; that the taxes we pay represent a significant contribution to support other social objectives in the countries that we operate.

This enlightened view is also clearly reflected in the disclosures at our 2014 Annual General Meeting, explaining that in 2013 Allianz distributed €93 bn to clients, indemnifying them against the damages of floods and hailstorms and providing income in retirement, €12 bn to employees, €12 bn to distributers, €3 bn to governments in the form of taxes and €2 bn to shareholders in the form of dividends. In parallel, Allianz has been continuously included in the Dow Jones Sustainability Index (DJSI) since 2000 and in the "FTSE4Good" Sustainability Index since 2001; we also received the "Industry Leader and Gold Class Sustainability Award" in 2014.

Returning to the economic Darwinism analogy, Allianz could not create this value – value to customers, to employees, to society and to shareholders – unless we were in business, and remaining in business in such a competitive arena requires a continual focus on long-term value creation.

CHAPTER 2

How do CFOs and CROs Add Value?

The CFOs and CROs of large, diversified financial services firms have the potential to significantly influence the strategy, operating performance and value of their firms, primarily through three areas of responsibility:

- strategic planning, capital allocation and performance management;
- balance sheet, liquidity and asset/liability management;
- risk management and underwriting.

These responsibilities are relatively new, generally acquired only over the past 20 years, and represent an evolution from their more narrowly focused forbears – the head of accounting and controlling as predecessor to the modern CFO and the transaction-oriented chief credit officer/chief underwriting officer as predecessor to the modern CRO.

THE EVOLUTION OF THE CORPORATE CENTER AS "SHAREHOLDER SURROGATE"

The evolution in roles is tied to the broader evolution of the corporate center within financial services firms: simply put, the role of the CFO and CRO was forced to change as firms became larger, more diversified and more complex. If you want to understand how to manage the value of a large, diversified bank or insurer, you have to begin by understanding the role of the corporate center and the roles of the CFO and the CRO within the corporate center.

From "Monolith" . . .

Prior to the 1980s, most financial services firms were purely domestic in orientation, operated and organized as if they were a single "bank" or "general insurance company," which in many cases they were.

In such monolithic institutions, there was no "corporate center" because there was no need for a management layer different from line management: there was one business and one CEO covering strategy and operations. The forbear to the modern CFO was the financial controller or head of accounting, who focused on transaction accounting and financial reporting. Similarly, the forbear to the modern CRO was the head of credit, the head of treasury or the chief underwriting officer (and sometimes all three, depending on the segment), the person who had final signing authority for the largest transactions.

In addition, shareholder activism was also simpler: with only one "business" under the corporate umbrella, shareholders could "vote with their feet" by selling shares or exercising their rights to displace management if strategy and performance were deemed lacking.

. . . To "Diversified Financial Services"

During the 1980s, many financial institutions began to view their company not as a single, monolithic business but as a portfolio of distinct businesses. There were four factors influencing the "breaking up" of the monolithic company into distinct business segments.

Economies of scale and scope. The first factor was the attainment of sufficient scale within each segment, whether through natural growth or acquisition. Scale was a necessary pre-condition to support dedicated and tailored operations, management teams, strategies, systems and cultures. The fact that financial services firms have achieved scale in their component segments is obvious: companies such as Citigroup, Swiss Re or Allianz can be thought of as comprising three or more firms, each in the global top 10 in their own markets – a good indicator that scale economies have been potentially reached in each segment.

Conglomerate diversification strategies. The second factor was a trend toward corporate "diversification." In the 1980s, "corporate America" pursued conglomerate strategies, acquir-ing portfolios of (often unrelated) businesses under a corporate umbrella which benefited from cheaper access to financing, predominantly due to economies of scale. Famous examples of industrial companies following this strategy included General Electric, Litton Industries and United Technologies.

Banks and insurers also diversified internationally and entered product and customer adjacencies to achieve revenue synergies and access funding at lower cost. For example, revenue synergies were behind Citibank's "financial supermarket" strategy when it acquired Salomon Brothers and Travelers Insurance; it was also behind the bank assurance strategies of Credit Suisse/Winterthur, ING, Allianz/Dresdner Bank, etc. In addition, there is a long list of bank mergers arguably driven by diversification and access to lower-cost funding, with examples including the acquisition of British merchant banks and securities firms such as Barings, Morgan Grenfell, Kleinwort and SG Warburg, and even some US firms such as First Boston, Kidder Peabody, Dillon Read and Bankers Trust, by commercial banks and foreign players (Masaharu, 2008).

Increasing complexity. The third factor was the challenge presented by more focused competitors in each segment. Competing in retail financial services – including the manage-ment of different distribution platforms such as the Internet, financial advisors, brokers and brick-and-mortar or tied agents – against focused competitors is complex enough; intermin-gling this with running a global Fixed Income Currency and Commodity (FICC) sales and trading business competing against best-in-class global investment banks is impossible. More focused strategies and skills needed to be applied in order to remain competitive in each individual segment.

Internal capital market. The fourth factor was the need to create an "internal capital market" for funding profitable growth opportunities, for example retail banking businesses providing liquidity and funding to investment banking operations, domestic PC operations funding LH new business strains or domestic, home-market operations financing foreign expansion.

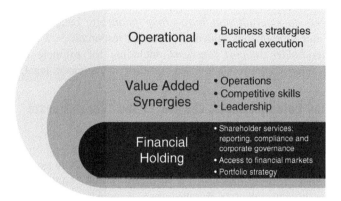

FIGURE 2.1   Corporate center role and value added

The Potential Value Added By the Corporate Center . . .

A direct by-product was the birth of the corporate center: after segmenting the institution into different businesses, some "glue" was needed to manage the portfolio of businesses. This glue was the corporate center. But what does the corporate center do and how does it add value?

As Figure 2.1 illustrates, there exists a continuum of roles which the corporate center can play, ranging from a pure "financial holding" role (e.g., narrowly focused on performing shareholder services and providing access to the capital markets) to a fully "operational" role (e.g., broadly focused, retaining near-complete operational responsibility for each business segment).

Somewhere in between is the *value-added synergy* model, often characterized by a matrix of customer (or product or regional) units crossed with functional units where operational synergies are deemed to exist (e.g., in operations, IT, human resources, etc.). This model was a natural step for firms coming from a monolithic starting point as they already had shared services in some sense to begin with.

It is generally agreed that there are only a handful of ways that the corporate center "adds value" in the sense that the corporate portfolio is worth "more than the sum of the parts" (Couto and Neilson, 2007; Baumgarten and Heywood, 2011). These include the following.

- *Operational synergies*, for example through the management of shared services such as purchasing, administration, transaction accounting, IT operations and data center, human relations, facilities, etc., and the leveraging of existing resources such as distribution networks with new products and services.
- *Capability-based or competitive advantage synergies*, through the development and dissemination of expert knowledge and best practices (e.g., in sales force management, distribution, product development, underwriting, administration, etc.), via centers of excellence, strategic initiatives, and so on.
- *Leadership synergies*, ensuring the depth and breadth of the leadership pool through personnel development and a common culture (e.g., through training, job rotation and international relocation, compliance programs, etc.).

- Ensuring *access to external and intra-group financing*, balance sheet and treasury management and appropriately allocating financial resources.
- Providing *shareholder support functions*, including for example investor relations, internal audit, financial consolidation and reporting, compliance, legal, etc.

. . . Offset By the Potential Costs, Leading To the "Conglomerate Discount"

Unfortunately, many diversified financial services companies suffer from a "conglomerate discount,"[1] a situation where the market value of the firm is markedly less than the sum of its parts. A conglomerate discount can occur if the relative value added from operational or financing synergies is outweighed by the increased complexity and weaker focus on value management inherent in large, complex firms.

In general, the financial discipline imposed by capital markets is less effective for financial conglomerates: it is impossible for shareholders to "vote with their feet" or change the management of an individual business within a diversified financial services group. In addition, in contrast to mono-line firms, financial conglomerates become more opaque with segment-level information generally less available.

Further, the distance between the corporate center and the businesses has increased, leading to a lack of meaningful challenge from within the firm. Hall *et al.* (2012) comment, "The independent, hard-nosed perspective that executives need to make decisions about a corporation's businesses is often elusive. It can't be delegated to the business units, whose managers have competing interests and may lack a corporate-wide perspective."

Recognizing these trends and following the financial crisis of 2008, activist shareholders and regulators have required the strengthening of corporate governance, the role of the corporate center and the Board, especially with respect to balance sheet and liquidity management, risk management and governance (for an excellent example, see FSB, 2013).

The "Shareholder Surrogate" Model of Firm Governance

As a consequence, some firms have put the corporate center more squarely in the shoes of the shareholders in an effort to address the conglomerate discount. They do this by adopting the management characteristics of a private equity firm, effectively becoming the shareholders' surrogate (Bright *et al.*, 2008; Couto *et al.*, 2012).

The *shareholder surrogate model of corporate governance* is one where the corporate center applies even more market discipline internally to each of the business segments, which is no longer feasible for external shareholders to apply due to the increased complexity, opacity and diminishing effectiveness of shareholder rights. The activities of a shareholder surrogate are summarized in Sidebar 2.1.

By reinforcing value management, the "shareholder surrogate" model can potentially reverse part of the conglomerate discount. However, if a large valuation gap persists in spite of these actions, it may be that the company is simply not the best owner of the entire portfolio of businesses and that the synergies are not sufficient to outweigh the increased complexity and opacity. It may be the case that "breaking up" the bank or insurance company in reality, as

---

[1]Research into the "conglomerate discount" was prevalent during the 1990s. A good survey article is that by Martin and Sayrak (2001). More directly relevant for financial services, see Laeven and Levine (2005).

SIDEBAR 2.1: IDEALIZED[2] SHAREHOLDER SURROGATE MODEL OF THE CORPORATE CENTER

The corporate center puts itself into the shoes of long-term shareholders, from an operational and strategic perspective, by:

- continuously reinforcing a value management culture focused on the long-term value creation of the company;
- setting corporate portfolio strategy, allocating capital and aligning incentives consistent with this goal, balancing short-term opportunities against investments to secure long-term profitable growth;
- understanding the economics of each business and challenging the strategies and operating performance, pushing for even greater performance and value creation;
- capturing scope and scale synergies across businesses where possible and leveraging core competencies in underwriting, distribution, compliance, leadership, operations, etc.

And from a corporate resource management perspective, by:

- ensuring access to the lowest cost of capital, leverage and liquidity, allocating these resources in a manner consistent with its strategy and optimizing the group's financing structure;
- ensuring that risks are appropriately underwritten and that the risk profiles of the group and the businesses are consistent with the group's risk appetite and risk strategy;
- providing cost-effective shareholder services, including consolidated reporting, tax optimization, legal services, investor relations and, increasingly, regulatory relations;
- developing a deep "bench" of experienced and capable managers and ensuring that the right people consistently occupy the right positions, especially in turnaround situations;
- managing and protecting the company's brand and reputation.

---

opposed to virtually, is in the best interest of shareholders. This is a tough call, but occasionally a necessary call to make as illustrated by the actions of Aviva summarized in the Portfolio Inertia Sidebar, Chapter 13, as well Goldman's (unasked-for) advice to JP Morgan, suggesting that[3] " . . . JP Morgan would be worth as much as 25% more if it were split into (four) different pieces . . . (and the) returns from a split would far outweigh the synergies that JP Morgan claim it gets from its current size."

It is interesting to note that *the three CFO and CRO levers for creating value – corporate strategy and capital allocation, balance sheet management and risk management – figure*

---

[2] I use the adjective "idealized" when discussing the shareholder surrogate model. This ideal is built on the (potentially romantic?) notion that shareholders are long-term investors, more resembling Warren Buffet than intra-day traders. Unfortunately, not all shareholders have a long-term orientation. Some institutional asset managers switch between firms or go long/short within the same industry driven by daily "news" flow or, even worse, using high-frequency algorithms to trade with no involvement at all. Often times, this active trading on the margin drives short-term share price fluctuations which do not reflect the underlying economics of the business.

[3] *Fortune*, January 5, 2015, Goldman Sachs says JP Morgan Chase should be broken up.

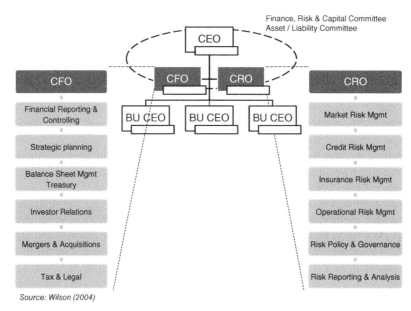

Source: Wilson (2004)

FIGURE 2.2   CFO and CRO responsibilities

prominently in the shareholder surrogate model of corporate governance. In other words, the CFO and CRO have a central role to play in the "shareholder surrogate" governance model. Figure 2.2 illustrates this, depicting the generic finance and risk structure for a typical bank or insurance company, described in greater detail in the remainder of this chapter.[4]

THE IMPLICATIONS FOR THE CFO

The role of the modern CFO has evolved in parallel with the role of the corporate center, from humble accounting origins to now include activities which have a strong potential to influence strategy and operating performance.

Figure 2.3 illustrates that a large majority of the CFOs have responsibility for strategic planning and investor relations, two functions which were historically "owned" by the CEO. In addition, CFOs typically "own" balance sheet and capital management as well as asset/liability management in most banks and insurers.

Not surprisingly, CFOs are eager to leverage these activities into impact. Whereas in the past, their aspirations may have been limited to "financial reporting, done well," today they unanimously aspire to become *business partners* and *value managers* in their own right, *identifying opportunities, providing financial information and analysis to support decision making, challenging the business and even leading key initiatives, for example in the areas of corporate development, company turnaround and expense management* (see also McKinsey, 2009).

---

[4]The remainder of this chapter draws heavily on conversations I had with industry professionals when conducting a survey while at Oliver Wyman & Company, summarized in OWC (2003).

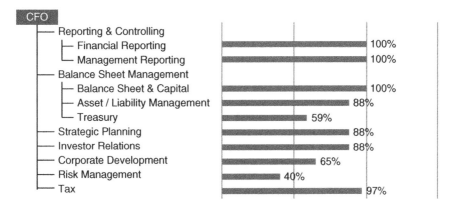

FIGURE 2.3 CFO responsibilities
Source: Wilson (2004).

The changing role of CFOs is being lauded by the investor community, suggesting that (G.A. Kraut & Company, 2008): "great CFOs . . . have a deep understanding of the business. They think like investors. They are viewed as key players strategically as well as operationally. They take charge of their relationships with investors . . . There is no spin to how they present the company. And they are hallmarks of trust."

A CFO's Job Description

Sidebar 2.2 gives an example job description for a bank or insurance CFO, representing a synthesis of the discussion so far and serving as a preview to the discussion on business steering and capital and balance sheet management in later chapters.

SIDEBAR 2.2: ENTERPRISE CFO JOB DESCRIPTION

RESPONSIBILITIES

The CFO has seven main responsibilities[5]:

- corporate portfolio strategy and capital allocation;
- challenging business unit strategy and performance;
- balance sheet, liquidity and capital management;
- financial and management reporting;
- tax optimization;
- managing external stakeholders;
- leadership of the finance network and promoting a value-oriented culture.

---

[5]The CEO of some companies retains the corporate portfolio management task but with a clearer separation between strategy and budgeting / performance management as discussed in Chapter 14. See Copeland *et al.* (2000) for a good description of the role of the CFO in an industrial corporation.

CORPORATE PORTFOLIO STRATEGY AND CAPITAL ALLOCATION

- Support the development of the firm's portfolio strategy through the strategic planning process, advising the CEO and business heads.
- Reinforce an institutional focus on:
  - shareholder value and capital management, in addition to revenues and earnings;
  - longer-term, horizon 2 and 3 growth strategies;[6]
  - the solvency and rating aspiration of the firm.
- Translate the portfolio strategy into action by:
  - allocating capital between existing businesses for organic/inorganic growth and strategic investments, returning any unused capital to shareholders;
  - aligning and allocating other financial resources, especially financial and operational leverage, liquidity and rating agency or regulatory capital;
  - setting performance targets against KPIs aligned with the corporate strategy;
  - restructuring the portfolio through disposals and executing strategic M&A activities to position the firm for long-term profitable growth.

CHALLENGE THE BUSINESS UNIT STRATEGY AND PERFORMANCE

- Advise and challenge business unit strategies through the strategic planning process.
  - Provide external and internal benchmarks as well as industry and market intelligence.
  - Critically challenge key assumptions, aspiration levels and management actions – are they realistic and aggressive enough?
  - Critically evaluate the plans from the perspective of shareholder value – why would *you* invest *your* money in the business?
- Help drive superior operating performance.
  - Define segment-specific KPIs against which performance is measured.
  - Challenge and agree on short-term operating activities, plans and budgets.
  - Translate plans into a balanced score card based on corporate and segment KPIs.
  - Regularly monitor, discuss and challenge operating performance with the CEO and business unit leaders through monthly/quarterly business reviews.
- Drive cross-divisional and corporate-level improvements in the areas of expense management, capital efficiency, corporate development, etc.

BALANCE SHEET, LIQUIDITY AND CAPITAL MANAGEMENT

- Optimize the capital financing structure and other financial resources against external constraints set by rating agencies and regulators and those set internally by the firm's own risk appetite.

---

[6]Horizon 2 and 3 growth strategies refer to McKinsey's three stages of growth framework introduced later in Chapter 14. Horizon 1 strategies are operational in nature, "getting the most out of what you have." Horizon 2 strategies are also operational, but are longer term with investments required and execution the key to success. Horizon 3 strategies are about "anticipating longer-term trends, disruptions and building options."

- Define the optimal target capital, financing and liquidity profile of the firm:
  - set the mix between Tier 1 and other forms of capital, the level of financial leverage, the allocation of operational leverage to the businesses and the desired liquidity profile of the firm;
  - keep within the solvency, leverage and liquidity constraints imposed by rating agencies and regulators;
  - define and keep within the risk appetite of the firm, especially with respect to the firm's target solvency, rating and liquidity profile.
- Manage the firm's capital, financing and liquidity profile, through:
  - capital market transactions, including financial debt issuance, capital raising, share repurchases, dividend policy, etc.;
  - cash and liquidity management, including cash pooling and corporate FX hedging, through treasury operations.
- Define and implement the high-level asset/liability management strategy of the firm:
  - chair the ALCO,[7] setting the firm's ALM strategy and funds transfer pricing policy and aligning with the individual business unit commercial strategies;
  - ensure execution of the strategy through the treasury, investment activities and business units.

FINANCIAL AND MANAGEMENT REPORTING

- Ensure a cost-efficient, well-controlled and error-free financial reporting process to meet all external reporting requirements.
- Develop an efficient and controlled management reporting process focusing on a limited number of corporate and segment KPIs required to steer the portfolio and evaluate performance.
- Discuss the efficient production of additional, operational KPIs required by each business, coordinating the development of reporting systems as appropriate.
- Ensure compliance with all required reporting standards, establishing the appropriate internal controls, evaluating their adequacy and testing their effectiveness.

MANAGE EXTERNAL STAKEHOLDER RELATIONS

Especially:

- regulators, supervisors and rating agencies on their perception of the capital required as well as the adequacy of the liquidity and leverage profile of the firm;
- financial analysts and investors on the performance of the firm and how value is created;
- politicians, regulators and industry associations to ensure that changing laws and regulations encourage, rather than discourage, good business practices in the industry.

---

[7]ALCO = Asset/Liability Committee.

LEADERSHIP AND DEVELOPMENT

- Inculcate a value management culture across the firm through training, incentives and setting the "tone at the top."
- Develop global leaders and personnel in the finance functional network through talent management, job rotations, cross-functional staffing, etc.
- Develop skills in the finance functional network, especially in terms of technical skills, business acumen and communication skills, through training, work experience, etc.

INTERNAL INTERACTIONS

- With the CEO and business leaders, develop strategies, allocate capital, set targets and review operating performance.
- With the CRO, integrate risk into strategy and balance sheet management activities and translate the business strategy into risk appetite, limits and policies.

SKILLS OR REQUIREMENTS

- In-depth understanding of the businesses combined with seasoned judgment, experience and a balanced view of the role of earnings, risk and capital in value creation.
- Technical skills in the areas of balance sheet transactions, treasury operations, asset/ liability management, accounting rules and tax.
- Personal gravitas, presence and communication skills needed to deal with regulators, financial analysts and investors.
- Strong communication, administration and leadership skills. The ability to work within a complex and dynamic organization and influence leaders.

MEASURES OF SUCCESS

- Financial benchmarks, especially long-term total shareholder returns relative to peers and the firm's short- and medium-term performance on growth, earnings and return on capital.
- Balance sheet performance measured against rating, solvency, leverage, liquidity and cost of capital targets.
- A strong internal "value management" culture. Internal and external stakeholders understanding the firm's strategy and acknowledgment of the firm as being value oriented.
- Adherence to functional budget and the cost-effectiveness of the function compared with peers.

THE IMPLICATIONS FOR THE CRO

A long time ago in a land far away, chief credit officers and chief underwriting officers focused on individual transactions, bringing large binders of transactions home on the weekend to prepare for a full-day Underwriting Committee on Monday, and the treasury and investment

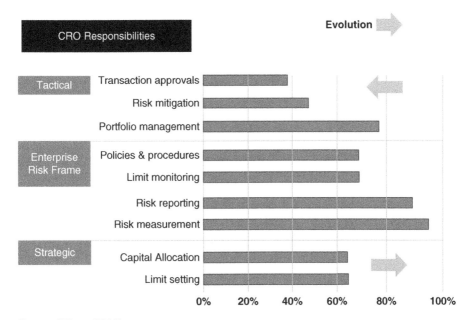

Source: Wilson (2004)

FIGURE 2.4   CRO responsibilities

functions both managed and controlled ALM positions. In general, the division between risk takers and independent risk managers was blurred and the risks were managed in silos.

Today, virtually all large financial services firms have an independent CRO with comprehensive, enterprise-wide risk responsibilities cutting across all risk categories. In addition, independent risk oversight responsibilities are more clearly delineated through the separation of risk taking and risk controlling. However, aspiration levels to have strategic impact have also increased in parallel with the expanded remit, as modern CROs seek to have a greater impact on strategy and performance through the alignment of risk and business strategies and supporting the capital allocation process. This rotation in roles can be seen in Figure 2.4.

According to the Ernst & Young (2014a) survey, more CROs are focusing on integrating risk into business decisions. In the words of one of the survey respondents, "The CRO is changing from being a 'brake' to being a 'copilot.' More knowledge of capital and financial management will be required . . . as they become a decision making member of the executive suite . . . (they) will be more forward looking and much more integrated with strategic decision making."

A CRO's Job Description

Sidebar 2.3 gives an example job description for an enterprise CRO, summarizing the discussion so far and serving as a preview to the discussion on capital, risk and balance sheet management in the following chapters. Chapter 21 discusses in detail the Risk Organization.

SIDEBAR 2.3: ENTERPRISE CRO JOB DESCRIPTION

RESPONSIBILITIES

The CRO has five broad responsibilities, described below:

- support daily business;
- anticipate emerging risks and market developments;
- integrate risk into business strategy and capital allocation decisions;
- communicate clearly with external stakeholders;
- lead the functional risk network and promote a strong risk culture.

SUPPORT DAILY BUSINESS

- Develop and maintain the company's ERM framework and proactively work with the business to achieve sustainable, profitable growth and shareholder value creation.
- Support the identification and evaluation of all risks, including those that are:
  - core to the business strategy (e.g., financial, credit, insurance, liquidity);
  - incidental to but critical for value creation, for example operational risks and reputational risks.
- Support risk underwriting and risk taking consistent with our business strategy and value management objectives, balancing risk-adjusted returns against growth potential:
  - support underwriting;
  - develop risk-adjusted technical pricing and capital allocation frameworks;
  - ensure that the limit system is comprehensive and robust to model failures;
  - review and approve new products and material transactions or exposures;
  - support the development of a comprehensive internal control system to mitigate operational and reputational risks.
- Evaluate the risk profile versus risk appetite and market opportunities.
- Recommend actions to take advantage of opportunities and avoid threats.
- Ensure that the risk profile is understood by management and that it remains within the risk appetite, delegated authorities and limits which have been set.
- Evaluate the appropriateness and limitations of the internal model and measurement frameworks and implement a controlled model change framework.

ANTICIPATE EMERGING RISKS AND MARKET DEVELOPMENTS AND REACT ACCORDINGLY

- Monitor developments (e.g., financial markets, underwriting, legal, regulatory and operational) and build early warning systems to anticipate emerging risk scenarios.
- Conduct stress tests, including historical, reverse and ad hoc scenarios based on current market conditions.
- Prepare for discontinuities and unexpected risks:
  - develop recommendations based on stress test results;
  - build institutional resilience (e.g., through capital and liquidity positioning, contingency planning, "war gaming," recovery and resolution planning);
  - dynamically respond to protect the net assets and franchise value of the firm.

INTEGRATE RISK INTO BUSINESS STRATEGY AND CAPITAL ALLOCATION DECISIONS

Align the risk strategy, appetite and limits accordingly:

- participate in and challenge the business strategy and capital allocation decisions, making the role of risk in value creation transparent;
- align the firm's business and risk strategy (e.g., with respect to top-line and return targets);
- align the firm's balance sheet and risk strategy (e.g., with respect to ratings aspiration and liquidity and funding risks);
- ensure that the risk strategy is translated into a clear and consistent risk appetite, delegated authorities/limits and risk policies.

COMMUNICATE CLEARLY AND EFFECTIVELY

Support the discussions, especially with external stakeholders, including:

- supervisors and rating agencies on their perception of the capital needed to support our business;
- equity analysts and shareholders on how we create value from active risk taking and mitigate those we do not want;
- politicians, regulators and industry associations to ensure that changing laws and regulations encourage, rather than discourage, good business practices.

LEADERSHIP, DEVELOPMENT AND CULTURE

Develop an effective risk network and a broader risk culture within the firm:

- develop individuals within the firm's functional risk network in terms of technical skills, business acumen and communication skills;
- develop sufficient "bench strength" behind each key position through job rotations and talent management;
- promote an effective risk culture across the firm, building risk awareness into the front-line operations and business awareness into the risk and control functions, through, for example, training, job rotations and setting the "tone at the top."

INTERNAL INTERACTIONS

- With the CFO, on integrating risk into the strategy and business plans, on balance sheet and capital management and on external stakeholder communication.
- With business leaders, the Chief Underwriting Officer (CUO) and management committees (including the ALCO) in the design of the ERM framework and in taking better decisions.
- With the CEO, Executive Board and Supervisory Boards, on the assessment of the firm's internal control and governance environment, on the firm's risk profile and on management's assessment of the risk profile and management actions.

SKILLS OR REQUIREMENTS

- An in-depth understanding of the business and strategy. A clear understanding of the role that active risk taking plays in creating sustainable value. Line experience directly taking risk/reward decisions.
- The technical and analytical skills in risk and finance to understand the risk profile of the firm and effectively challenge the models.
- Personal integrity and the willingness to constructively challenge the business, working toward a solution but stopping "bad" business as necessary.
- Strong communication and leadership skills. The ability to work within a complex and dynamic organization and influence business leaders.

MEASURES OF SUCCESS

- Long-term total share value relative to peers.
- Risk-adjusted performance of the different businesses through a cycle.
- Savings in the total cost of capital via the level of required capital and the cost of that capital.
- Adherence to functional budget and the cost effectiveness of the risk function compared with peers.
- The assessment by internal peers on personal integrity, ability to constructively influence and the ultimate effectiveness of the risk function in supporting sustainable profitable growth.

Two

Better Information – Measuring Value

In contrast to other industries, both banking and insurance are risk-based, capital-intensive businesses. Any attempt to manage the value of banks and insurers therefore needs to explicitly recognize both the risks taken as well as the capital deployed. Not surprisingly, RAPMs are now ubiquitous across both industries.

In spite of their prevalence, RAPMs are challenging to use for two reasons. The first is practical: while often used to take pricing decisions, RAPMs rarely influence corporate strategy; this is because the link between RAPMs and share price is not easily understood by management and external stakeholders.

As a consequence, RAPMs are frequently supplanted by simpler measures when setting corporate strategy. It is easier to "connect the dots" between sales or cost-cutting initiatives, earnings growth, the P/E[1] multiple and the growth in share price than it is between RAPMs and share value. Unfortunately, ease of use is not of much use if applied to risk-based, capital-intensive businesses where improvements in underwriting effectiveness and capital efficiency may have a much stronger influence on value but only an indirect influence on realized earnings and earnings growth.

The second challenge is technical: how to ensure that the RAPM gives the "right" valuation signals for complex financial businesses? More often than not, RAPMs confuse risk-based capital *constraints* with the *shareholder capital invested in the business*; furthermore, RAPM decision rules frequently fail to charge an appropriate cost for that capital. The net effect is that many firms destroy value by over-investing in high-risk businesses and by taking too much financial market risk in their asset/liability mismatch portfolio.

Fortunately, it is possible to "connect the dots" between correct RAPMs and share value, leading to a valuation framework that better matches the way that bank and insurer shares

---

[1]P/E = Price/Earnings multiple or the ratio of price per share to the projected earnings per share of the company.

actually trade in the market. More important, the RAPM-based valuation framework also makes clear how management actions in the areas of sales and distribution management, operating efficiency, underwriting effectiveness, capital efficiency and asset/liability mismatches affect the value of the company.

The remainder of this Part II of the Handbook summarizes the development of RAPMs by banks and insurers and discusses the practical and technical challenges in using them. It then develops a valuation framework for risk-based, capital-intensive businesses that better reflects the way that bank and insurer shares trade in the market and highlights the most important drivers of value for financial services firms – sales and distribution effectiveness, cost efficiency, underwriting effectiveness, capital efficiency and financial market earnings through the asset/liability mismatch portfolio.

CHAPTER **3**

RAPMs – The Industry Standard

Risk-adjusted performance metrics are now ubiquitous across both the banking and insurance industries. The reason is simple: in contrast to other industries, both banking and insurance are risk-based, capital-intensive businesses and therefore need performance measures which explicitly recognize both the risks taken as well as the capital deployed.

This chapter describes at a high level the evolution of RAPMs within the banking and insurance industries, differentiating between RAPMs used to support tactical applications such as loan or insurance pricing and those used to evaluate business unit performance.

WHAT MAKES FINANCIAL SERVICES UNIQUE?

No other industry has devoted so much effort to developing and using RAPMs.[1] This is because banking and insurance differ from other industries in four distinct ways.

Uncertain "Cost of Goods Sold"

We sell products whose ultimate profit contribution is uncertain at the time of sale, with the uncertainty stemming from risk underwriting and future market developments.

When a publisher or shoe manufacturer sells a book or a pair of shoes, the value created at the time of sale is reasonably easy to calculate and, once sold, the ties between buyer and seller are limited.[2] Because of this, value creation can be determined reasonably well at the time of sale by deducting the cost of goods sold from the sales price.

The products offered by financial services firms are different. First, they represent future commitments for one or both parties, commitments extending well beyond the initial sale date: borrowers repay loans in the future and insurers settle claims. Second, these future obligations are risky and may develop in unexpected ways: borrowers can default and an insurable event may or may not occur.

---

[1]With the possible exception of energy or commodity trading firms, which share some of the same characteristics with banks and insurers.

[2]Abstracting from estimates of customer lifetime value due to repeat purchases and any warranties, service programs or vendor financing, all of which can be considered additional products or services.

31

Some of this uncertainty depends on *underwriting decisions* and represents deviations from the company's estimate of the probability and severity of a loan loss or insurance claim at the time of sale. Some depends on future *market developments*, for example the level of interest rates or equity prices, claims inflation, etc. Valuing both of these sources of risk requires complex financial models and assumptions which differentiates financial services from other industrial activities.

Risk is Inherent in Our Value Proposition

These risks are inherent in financial products and play a defining role in how we create value for shareholders and customers.[3]

Whereas industrial corporations generally try to avoid risks,[4] banks and insurers create value by taking and managing risks using three strategies.

First, financial services firms create value by "intermediating" risks, matching buyers' and sellers' interests directly on their balance sheet or indirectly (e.g., by providing a gateway to exchanges or packaging risks and placing them in the capital markets). Intermediation activities are rewarded by fees, bid/offer spreads and product margins, depending on the channel. Some intermediation strategies are imperfect, however, leaving the bank or insurance company with a residual liquidity or mismatch risk on the balance sheet.

Second, financial services firms create value by "absorbing" non-hedgeable or non-traded risks into their balance sheet against adequate compensation. This is a core role of banks and insurers: by appropriately underwriting and holding a diversified portfolio of credit or insurance risks, they not only provide a service to customers, but also generate more stable results for their own account.

Risk diversification and pooling benefits society in two ways: first, by transferring individual uncertainty into a more stable aggregate form and second, by minimizing the origination, due diligence and underwriting expenses associated with opaque individual risks, costs which need to be borne only once by the firm which originates and holds the pooled risks.

Third, financial services firms create value by "advising" clients, for example on how best to invest to meet their future needs, and offering the financial services to execute those strategies.

Our Capital and Financing Structure is Driven By Risk

Because of these unique characteristics, our capital and financing structure is not a theoretical exercise in indeterminacy, as might be implied by the Modigliani–Miller theorem.[5] Rather, our capital structure is determined by risk considerations and our financing structure directly drives operating earnings.

---

[3]For a further discussion, see Casserly (1991).

[4]The exceptions to this rule, e.g. the financial arms of industrial corporations such as GE Capital, General Motors Acceptance Corporation (GMAC), etc., and the trading arms of resource companies such as Shell Trading or Carlyle Trading, prove the rule as they more resemble financial institutions than their industrial holding companies in strategies and business models.

[5]Modigliani and Miller won a Nobel Prize in economics for their work demonstrating the conditions under which the firm's value is independent of its capital structure (e.g., debt versus equity financing). Chapter 15 revisits the Modigliani–Miller theorem in the context of financial services firms.

Risk and Capital Requirements

Financial institutions can only engage in these activities if regulators and clients – especially depositors, policy holders and financial counterparties – have the confidence that the firm will be in business when it is time to honor its obligations. If that confidence vanishes, banks would find it impossible to attract deposits or other sources of funding and insurers would find it impossible to issue policies today against a (devalued) promise to pay tomorrow.

What gives customers the confidence that their obligations will be honored? Capital, to a large extent. In contrast to industrial corporations where capital is tied up in operating assets, the role of capital in financial institutions is to be unencumbered and highly liquid, sitting around on sunny days doing not a lot . . . until it is called on to cover losses following a windstorm or financial market crisis.

While many factors play a role, there is a simple rule: the more risk is taken, the more capital is needed.[6] As a consequence, capital and solvency ratios are one of the first lines of defense required by rating agencies and regulators in protecting the interests of depositors, policy holders and financial counterparties.

When evaluating the creditworthiness of a bank or the claims-paying ability of an insurance company, rating agencies such as Standard & Poor's, Moody's Investor Services, A.M. Best and Fitch begin with an evaluation of the company's capital position and then move on to other factors such as strength of earnings and growth, quality of management, etc. Similarly, bank and insurance regulators put great emphasis on minimum capital levels as the first pillar for prudential regulation.

Because capital should be held in relation to the risk assumed, measuring and attributing capital to financial businesses is more complicated than measuring the historical level of investment in an industrial corporation's property, plant and equipment. More specifically, in order to estimate the capital required by a financial services institution, one must understand and measure the institution's risk profile in detail, again differentiating financial services from other industrial activities.

Liabilities As Operating Profit Opportunities

The liability side of the balance sheet funds the firm's operating assets for industrial corporations, including property, plant and equipment, trade receivables, inventories and working capital. In principle, the franchise value of an industrial firm is driven by the future production of its operating assets, with its liabilities determining how that value is to be split between debt holders and shareholders.

The situation is more complex for financial services firms because liabilities generate shareholder value in their own right. For example, a bank which grows its consumer deposit base creates value, assuming that deposits are priced to deliver an appropriate margin net of expenses. Similarly, an insurance company issuing a policy also creates value, again assuming that the policies are structured, underwritten and priced appropriately. In short, a bank or insurer's liabilities represent profit opportunities and not just funding resources.

This observation helps to explain the relatively high level of leverage that financial services firms seem to have compared with industrial corporations. It also goes a long way to explain why managing solvency and leverage ratio constraints plays such a critical role in managing the value of a bank or insurer.

---

[6]This ignores explicit support mechanisms such as deposit insurance or implicit support from regulatory activities to support "too big to fail" institutions.

We Are a Heavily Regulated Industry

Finally, banking and insurance are among the most regulated industries, enjoying a higher degree of supervision and constraints on capital and leverage than any other industry.

This regulation not only affects our business models and capital structure but also our governance structure. It begins with how we interact with our customers, covering issues such as customer advice, sales practices, product documentation, design, pricing and fees. It continues with how we manage our business on a day-to-day basis, leading to hard standards for solvency, leverage, liquidity and public disclosures and soft standards for risk management and corporate governance. It ends literally with our end, with Resolution and Recovery Planning, or the so-called "living wills" being defined as part of the Financial Stability Board's Globally Systemically Important Financial Institutions (G-SIFI) work.

The regulation of the financial services industry is designed to promote public policy objectives, to mitigate micro-externalities[7] (e.g., protecting depositors and policy holders from losses due to misinformation or the failure of a bank or insurer) as well as macro-externalities and systemic risks (e.g., preventing a failure of the payments system or credit markets which are needed to support economic growth).

WHAT DO RAPMs DO AND HOW?

Financial institutions are different from industrial corporations, primarily due to the role that risk and capital play in creating value. Not surprisingly, banks and insurers have developed complex RAPMs and risk-adjusted Economic Profit (EP) metrics which explicitly incorporate risk, returns and capital in order to measure and manage their business. There are a wide variety of RAPM "flavors" used in practice, including RAROC, RAROA, RORAC, RORAA and even RARORAC.[8] Unfortunately, as we will see, only one can be "correct."

What Are RAPMs Trying to Achieve?

Banks and insurers achieve two primary objectives by implementing RAPMs.

Make risky returns directly comparable. Consider the challenge of comparing $100 mio earnings from corporate lending, proprietary trading or wealth management activities or from LH retirement and savings products versus PC personal and commercial lines. Each offers the same accounting returns ($100 mio), but each has a different risk profile. Which has created more value relative to the risk taken? One would hope that higher-risk businesses offer higher returns, but this is not always the case. RAPMs help to compare businesses by "normalizing" returns for the risks taken, making them directly comparable.

Measure value creation. If the returns can be directly compared, then it should be possible to also compare them against a common cost of capital or hurdle rate, identifying activities where incremental capital investment creates value and those that potentially destroy value. Ultimately, shareholders should be willing to pay a premium to the invested capital for

---

[7]An externality is defined as the situation where one person's actions influence another's wellbeing.

[8]RAROC (Risk-Adjusted Return On Capital), RAROA (Risk-Adjusted Return On Assets), RORAC (Return On Risk-Adjusted Capital), RORAA (Return On Risk-Adjusted Assets), RARORAC (Risk-Adjusted Return On Risk-Adjusted Capital).

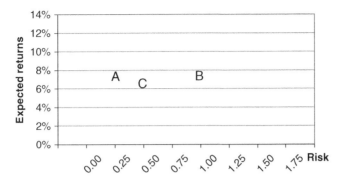

FIGURE 3.1 Comparing risks and returns

businesses consistently delivering excess returns, and an even higher premium if the business can be grown profitably. As the shareholders' agents, management needs to understand where the firm creates value and how they are doing it so that they can do more of the same.

How Is It Done?

Consider the two businesses represented by A and B in Figure 3.1. Both offer the same expected returns; however, A takes less risk. Any risk-averse decision maker[9] would prefer business A over business B.

The choice between A and B was simple, but how can we generalize the decision criteria when the answer is less obvious – for example, business C offering *both* less risk *and* less return compared with business B? Which is the better business from a shareholder's perspective?

One approach would be to *define a utility function for shareholders.*[10] Using a utility function, we know exactly how much expected return a shareholder would need to accept in order to take more or less risk. Unfortunately, different shareholders have different preferences and a common utility function representing the preferences of all possible shareholders does not make sense; the other possible shortcut, defining the manager's utility function, violates the principal–agent relationship that we like to believe in when thinking about corporate governance.

A more fruitful approach is to *assume that there exists a market relationship between risk and return, expressed in a common numeraire and inherent in market prices.* This assumption is illustrated by the solid line in Figure 3.2.

This market risk/return line is written as $R = R_f + \text{risk}^*R_p$, where R represents the expected returns, R_f is the risk-free rate of return and R_p is the risk premium that the market is willing to pay per unit of "risk." This relationship should be intuitive: you expect to earn at

---

[9]It is possible to ask why a firm (as opposed to an individual) should be risk averse in the first place and therefore have a preference for business A. As discussed later in Chapters 15 and 18, management's own preferences help to shape the decisions of firms. In addition, any asymmetry in generating profits and losses (e.g., caused by asymmetric taxes, a high proportion of fixed costs, any frictional cost of bankruptcy, etc.) will also make the firm naturally risk averse.

[10]A utility function is an abstraction used in the field of economics to compare the relative "value" of different choices for an individual. Ultimately, a utility function defines a person's willingness to pay different amounts for different goods or services, even when the outcomes are uncertain. One of the earliest discussions can be found in Marshall (1920).

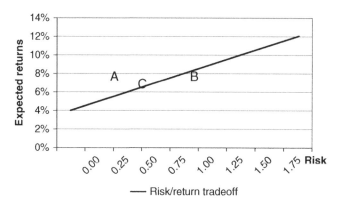

FIGURE 3.2   RAPM normalizing risk/return

least the risk-free rate of return plus a premium which increases with the "risk" taken – the higher the risk, the greater the expected return.

Using the "market price of risk," it is clear that business A creates excess returns, business C "breaks even" (lying directly on the market line) and business B destroys value, lying below the line.

Managing a portfolio of businesses is challenging even with a "market price of risk," because one has to think in three dimensions at the same time: risk, return and the market return appropriate for the risk taken. We can simplify this to one dimension by normalizing expected returns using the market price of risk, illustrated by the dashed line and normalized returns (A', B', C') in Figure 3.3.

This normalization is exactly what a RAPM is supposed to do: implicitly assume a (market) relationship between risk and return and use the relationship to normalize returns, making them directly comparable with one another and a common hurdle rate.

The normalization for this simple example is done by defining the required risk-based economic capital (EC) proportional to "risk" as $EC = a^*$ "risk" and adjusting the expected returns ($\hat{R}$) appropriately.

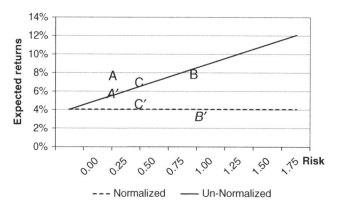

FIGURE 3.3   RAPM normalized and un-normalized risk/return

EQUATION 3.1:   Intuitive RAPM formula[11]

$$\text{RAPM} = \frac{\text{Adjusted Returns}}{\text{Adjusted Capital}} = \frac{\hat{R} - R_f}{\text{EC}} = \frac{\hat{R} - R_f}{\alpha^* \text{``risk''}} \geq R_f$$

Returning to Figure 3.3, the RAPM transforms A to A', B to B' and C to C'. These normalized returns can then be directly compared against a common hurdle rate, which in this instance is the risk-free rate of return, R_f.[12]

As is evident from this example, there is a unique definition of economic capital which correctly normalizes returns for any given market risk/return relationship. Put differently, RAPMs are uniquely defined by the underlying market relationships – one cannot simply assume any RAPM relationship and hope that it provides the right results. This raises an interesting point: if the RAPM is unique, why are there so many RAPMs used in practice (RAROC, RORAC, RARORAC, etc.)? Only one of them can be "right." This point is elaborated on later when we discuss the theoretical limitations of RAPMs.

THE RAPM (R)EVOLUTION

The use of RAPMs has by now become standard in the banking and insurance industries. The trend began in banking during the 1980s, leading Parsley (1995) to assert that "A RAROC . . . type system *will become a necessity for all banks.*" Although slower to adopt initially, the insurance industry has more than made up for lost time in the intervening years.

As illustrated by the case examples, the early adopters were not motivated by purely theoretical or intellectual interest – they needed to address compelling business issues forced upon them by dynamically changing markets, issues which could not be addressed using accounting-based performance metrics. This section discusses the evolution of RAPMs in both industries.

Early Adopter Profile: Bankers Trust

Bankers Trust is considered to be the pioneer of risk-adjusted performance measurement, developing its economic capital and RAROC approach in the early 1980s (Guill, 2009). Garbade (1986) outlined an approach to attribute economic or risk capital to trading and asset portfolios, with a parallel development allocating capital to portfolios of loans.

Bankers Trust was motivated by a pressing business issue: how to measure the profitability of an individual customer across different products, including corporate lending versus trading activities, given their very different risk profiles? Answering this question was of significant tactical importance to the bank: the margins and the profitability of corporate banking were

---

[11]Begin with the relationship $R \geq R_f + \text{risk}^* R_p$. Multiply both sides of the relationship by $\alpha = R_p / R_f$. Rearranging gives the equation.

[12]Note that the choice of the risk-free rate as the hurdle rate is somewhat arbitrary. One could just as easily have set the hurdle rate for measuring the excess returns from risk to be the market risk premium itself, R_p, in which case α would be set to $\alpha = 1$, or any other hurdle rate desired by the appropriate choice of α.

coming under intense pressure due to the commoditization of balance sheet lending and the disintermediation of bank loans by the capital markets for the largest borrowers. An alternative source of profits from trading and financial solutions was identified. Without the ability to measure and manage customer profitability across these two products, the transformation of the bank from a commercial lender to a trading powerhouse would not be possible.

Coupled with strong senior management commitment, the implications of RAROC were substantial: changes to standard commercial banking practices included a "zero-hold" policy on most new loans, a new, solutions-oriented approach to serving clients using derivatives and an aggressive trading culture, transforming Bankers Trust ". . . from a second rate, ill-focused, near insolvent commercial bank into a dynamic, well capitalized, highly profitable merchant bank" (Lee, 1991). In the words of Charles Sanford, then Chairman, "We're a bank, no question. But we don't like to be pigeon-holed. We're not exactly a traditional commercial bank. Nor an investment bank, really. It's, well, partially a trading house . . . but not with the stereotyped trading mentality" (Picker, 1992).

With perfect hindsight, many authors have commented that aggressive profit taking from clients through complex derivative products was ill-advised: ultimately, Bankers Trust was sold to Deutsche Bank following derivatives sales practice cases (e.g., Gibson Greeting Cards, Procter & Gamble), which severely damaged the bank's reputation and franchise.

Early Adopter Profile: JP Morgan[13]

Similar to Bankers Trust, JP Morgan also faced challenges in improving the economics of its commercial lending and trading businesses in the 1980s. Just like Bankers Trust, the senior management at JP Morgan came to realize that accounting performance measures were inadequate for measuring the contributions from both and that traditional risk and exposure limits were inadequate to control and monitor the risk of increasingly complex trading businesses.

As a consequence, in the late 1980s JP Morgan developed a firm-wide Value at Risk (VaR) system covering its market risk and comprising several hundred risk factors, their associated covariance matrix and a linear representation of the portfolio's exposure profile. VaR was ultimately used to replace exposure limits for the trading desks and, starting in 1990, VaR numbers were combined with the profit and loss information for each of the trading desks – the precursor to RAROC – in a report which was discussed daily at the Treasury meeting and ultimately forwarded to the Chairman, Dennis Weatherstone, with comments.

The development of JP Morgan's economic capital approach had a broader influence on the industry as a version of their VaR internal model for financial market risk was offered to the industry in the form of RiskMetrics™. The "toolkit" was expanded in the mid-1990s with the introduction of CreditMetrics™, a VaR-like approach applied to credit risk from loans, securities and derivatives.

Early Adopter Profile: Bank of America[14]

Bank of America faced the same business issues as Bankers Trust and JP Morgan. Prior to 1994, Bank of America used return on assets (net income/assets) as a key performance metric.

---

[13]This profile follows from Holton (2002).

[14]This profile follows from James (1996), Walter (2004) and Zaik et al. (1996).

In parallel, the bank attempted to replace return on assets with a return on regulatory capital metric (e.g., net income divided by regulatory capital), but with the cost of capital or hurdle rate differentiated by line of business to reflect the businesses' underlying risk profile.

Unfortunately, this attempt at risk-adjusted performance measurement was not accepted by management for two reasons: first, because it was difficult to reconcile regulatory capital with the economic capital the bank attributed to its businesses and second, because of the complexity of justifying differentiated hurdle rates based on regulatory capital.

In response, the bank launched a project in November 1993 to develop a comprehensive and consistent approach for attributing risk capital to its major business lines, including a first cut at the numbers, all within a 4-month period. The project was successful, ultimately attributing capital to each of the businesses to cover credit and country risk, market risk and business risk. This model was the cornerstone of Bank of America's RAPM framework.

Early Adopter Profile: Swiss Reinsurance[15]

During the 1980s and 1990s, the property reinsurance market was plagued by several adverse trends. First, there was a secular downward trend in risk premium as traditional, proportional covers became commoditized, overall growth stagnated and capital mobility into the reinsurance industry increased. Second, around the declining secular trend were highly volatile, "feast or famine" pricing cycles driven by ruthless competition, with prices hardening to risk-adequate levels only after a natural catastrophe or if the financial markets wiped out a significant part of the industry's capital. Third, there was a general trend away from quota share treaties and toward more complex structures such as excess of loss and facultative covers as primary insurers managed their capital and optimized their reinsurance purchasing more professionally. Finally, in the late 1990s there was a search for growth into new and more complex markets, including structured financial reinsurance, insurance-linked securities, weather and credit derivatives, etc.

Partly in response to these trends, Swiss Re launched an effort in the 1990s to calculate the risk-adjusted capital required by the group. The objective was to both ensure the solvency adequacy of the group but also to strengthen the group's discipline in terms of risk acceptance and pricing.

Between 1993 and 1996, Swiss Re's RAC (Risk-Adjusted Capital) model was used for a variety of important purposes including risk reporting, the determination of the group's economic solvency position and the allocation of risk capacity across the group for peak exposure risks (e.g., credit and financial risks, natural catastrophe exposures, etc.).

In parallel, Swiss Re began to develop its Group Performance Measurement (GPM) system, an attempt to put the earnings of different lines of business on a comparable basis. GPM required adjustments to income (e.g., the discounting of reserves, the separation of the underwriting result from investment decisions, etc.) as well as the explicit allocation of RAC to the different businesses. Until approximately 2003, GPM was calculated and reported together with statutory earnings, but was not used for planning, performance measurement or incentive purposes.

---

[15]This profile is primarily based on personal observations gathered while I was working for Swiss Reinsurance Company from 1998–2002 as the CFO of Swiss Re New Market, the alternative risk transfer and risk finance business of Swiss Re. See also Patrik *et al.* (1999) and Jameson (2001).

However, as early as 1999, Swiss Re New Markets (SRNM), the alternative risk transfer business, implemented RAROC-based pricing across its entire business, ahead of the group's implementation of GPM. This decision was taken based on the relative diversity of risks underwritten by the SRNM, including credit, financial, insurance, weather, residual value and other risks and the diversity of transaction types, including (re)insurance contracts, insurance-linked securities and derivatives.

The development of a RAPM was critical for SRNM to execute its strategy of providing solutions to corporations, banks and insurers which cut across insured and non-insured risks in any contractual form. By 2000, SRNM was pricing all of its transactions using a RAROC approach and reporting business unit performance on both an accounting and risk-adjusted basis, with the latter driving business planning.

The Current Status of RAPMs in the Industry

By now, most of the largest banks and insurers globally have implemented RAPMs and economic capital approaches.

Use in Banking

Economic capital models and RAPMs are ubiquitous in the banking industry: as early as 2004, a survey by Oliver Wyman indicated that 24 of the top 25 European and North American banks had implemented economic capital and some form of RAPM measure, at a minimum for loan pricing. RAPM approaches had also penetrated smaller banks as well by then; Nakada and Kapitan (2004) provide an overview of the use of economic capital and RAROC by smaller banks.

Use in Insurance

Although the insurance industry started later, it quickly caught up. As early as 2000, equity analysts at Lehman Brothers (Lehman Brothers, 2000) were extolling the virtues of RAPMs implemented by (re-)insurers, mentioning that "there are currently seven . . . companies using RAROC . . . Half of these are bancassurance companies . . . The other half include U.S.-based primary insurers and Bermuda-based reinsurers. We suspect that there are a couple of more insurers using risk adjusted capital models (as well) . . ."

A 2005 survey conducted by the CRO Forum indicated that all of its members had an internal economic capital model, including Aegon, Allianz, Aviva, AXA, Converium, Fortis, Generali, ING, Munich Re, Prudential UK, Swiss Re, Winterthur and Zurich Financial Services.

The rapid development in the insurance industry followed three broad waves. The first wave consisted of reinsurers and large-case, commercial PC companies – not a surprising development given the nature of the risks underwritten and the relatively egregious pricing cyclicals in the industry. Included in this group of early adopters were the market leaders, Munich Re and Swiss Re, as well as most of the rest of the top-10 firms, including SCOR, Converium, etc.

The second wave was led by the bancassurers such as Allianz/Dresdner, Fortis, Credit Suisse/Winterthur and ING: first, because the injection of banking "DNA" into the management team made the concepts of economic capital and RAPM more familiar and second, because putting risks and returns on a comparable basis was even more important for allocating capital across the two business segments, banking and insurance.

Having successfully penetrated these segments, economic capital and RAPM approaches began to be more broadly accepted and implemented by other insurance firms.

Use in Disclosures

In addition to being used to support internal management decisions, EC and RAPMs are also used for public disclosure purposes. For one, the disclosure of EC is hard-wired into the existing Basel Pillar III reporting requirements for banks (BIS, 2012) as well as the forthcoming Solvency II Pillar III requirements for insurers in Europe.[16]

In addition, the International Accounting Standards Board IFRS 4/7 reporting requirements hold firms to disclose their risk profile "through the eyes of management," including quantitative reporting on credit, liquidity, market and other price risk as well as qualitative narrative on risk management processes and policies. In addition, under IAS 1, companies must explain their objectives, policies and processes for managing capital. Most large financial institutions use their internal economic capital model as the basis for these disclosures.

THREE RAPMs FOR THREE DISTINCT PURPOSES . . .

As mentioned, there are a wide variety of RAPM "flavors" used in practice, including RAROC, RORAC and even RARORAC. Underlying this alphabet soup lie three generic RAPMs used in the industry, each focused on a very specific and important business objective.

- *New Business RAPMs* support underwriting and customer profitability management decisions by narrowly focusing on the value created by underwriting a new transaction, focusing only on underwriting risks (e.g., credit, insurance risk).
- *Investment RAPMs* focus narrowly on financial market risk, separating excess returns, or "alpha," from "luck" in trading and asset/liability mismatch portfolios. They accomplish this by comparing realized or expected returns against a risk-appropriate benchmark in the capital markets.
- *Business RAPMs* focus on the totality of a business's risk profile, measuring the value created from all risk sources and all sources of earnings (including underwriting and financial market risk), an ambitious objective when using a single cost of capital or hurdle rate.

As developed in the remainder of this Part II of the Handbook, there is a clear and direct link between New Business RAPMs, Investment RAPMs and value creation. Unfortunately, the same cannot be said for Business RAPMs. Table 3.1 summarizes, at a high level, the major differences between the three.

Like the illustrative example earlier, each of these RAPMs have a similar form and decision rule: they divide some measure of adjusted earnings by some measure of allocated capital, signaling value creation if the result is greater than an appropriate Cost of Capital (CoC).

---

[16]See EIOPA (2011) and the XBRL reporting taxonomies published thereafter (October 2013 and January 2014).

TABLE 3.1   Summary of RAPMs and business applications

	New Business RAPM	**Investment RAPM**	**Business RAPM**
Primary use	Risk-adequate pricing of loans and insurance policies.	Identifying excess returns or "alpha" from trading and investment portfolios.	Measuring risk-adjusted return on allocated capital for an entire business.
Risks and returns covered	Only risks and returns from underwriting, e.g. predominantly credit and insurance risks, occasionally business and operational risks.	Traded financial market risks, e.g. open interest rate, FX, equity, etc. positions.	All risks and returns managed by the business.
Cost of capital used	Market price of credit or insurance risk.	Market price of financial market risk based on the return for a risk-appropriate benchmark portfolio.	A single corporate weighted average cost of capital used across all activities.
Link to value	Direct link to value as the contribution of new loans and policies is recognized directly on a "mark-to-model" basis.	Direct link to value as portfolio returns are evaluated against a risk-appropriate benchmark which is achievable in the financial markets.	Often no direct link to value, relying on capital allocation alone to make returns comparable.

EQUATION 3.2:   Generic RAPM definition

$$\text{RAPM} = \frac{\text{Adjusted Earnings}}{\text{Adjusted Capital}} \geq \text{CoC}$$

RAPMs are converted into an EP measure,[17] translating a percentage RAPM into an absolute dollar amount of value created, by rearranging the decision rule.

EQUATION 3.3:   RAPM economic profit definition

$$\text{EP} = \text{Adjusted Capital}^*(\text{RAPM} - \text{CoC}) \geq 0$$

Consistent with the RAPM decision criteria, the business or individual transaction is considered to contribute (or destroy) shareholder value if its EP is greater than zero. The importance of recognizing the absolute amount of value creation is highlighted in Sidebar 3.1.

---

[17]EP is occasionally referred to as Economic Value Added (EVA^{TM}) or Economic Value Contribution (EVC) and is calculated. EVA is a trademark of Stern Stewart & Company.

SIDEBAR 3.1: RAPM OR EP?

The rationale for focusing on economic profit rather than RAPM is clear: RAPM is a percentage and not an absolute return amount. Focusing on transactions or businesses with higher and higher RAPMs may not be in the best interest of shareholders if it means that other, still profitable business is not accepted. Consider, for example, a business with a 50% RAPM but only $10 invested capital, yielding an economic profit of $4 (at a cost of capital equal to 10%). Now compare this with a business having a more modest 30% RAPM but $100 of invested capital, yielding an economic profit of $20. Clearly, shareholders would prefer both businesses, but *if* they could only choose one, they would prefer the latter, "lower-return" business.

To illustrate the importance of this distinction, consider the anecdote regarding the acquisition of JP Morgan by Chase in the late 1990s. It goes that JP Morgan was extremely disciplined in the application of RAROC at the transaction and business unit level. In part, this pervasive culture was driven by necessity as JP Morgan attempted to transform its business footprint from lower-return, commercial banking activities to higher-return, investment banking activities.

However, some analysts and industry pundits conjectured that JP Morgan's strong emphasis on RAROC caused it to scale back businesses which still potentially created shareholder value. As the story goes, although JP Morgan was successful in increasing its percentage returns, lower absolute earnings growth and market value compared with its competitors ultimately pushed it into the arms of Chase. While one might argue the veracity of the anecdote, the moral nonetheless remains valid: shareholders are interested in the absolute level of value creation, which depends on both the percentage return as well as the capital invested.

New Business RAPMs

New Business RAPMs measure the expected risk-adjusted returns from non-traded credit or insurance risk as if the loan or policy is held to maturity and financed/invested on a perfectly matched basis (e.g., excluding any financial market risks and returns).

Banks and insurers need to decide whether to write an individual loan or insurance policy and, if so, at what price. Writing the loan or policy entails risk – the borrower can default or the house can burn down – and it also binds the firm's capital for the duration of the contract. The firm needs to make sure that they are adequately compensated, both for the risks and for the use of its capital.

Since financial market risks can in general be hedged, this underwriting decision can and should be made independently of whether the firm chooses to take any financial market risk inherent in the contract. As a consequence, New Business RAPMs value only the underwriting risks (e.g., the risk of a loan default or a claim being filed). They explicitly exclude the potential risks and returns from leaving the loan or insurance policy with a funding or investment "mismatch."[18]

---

[18] A mismatch risk may occur if a long-term loan is funded by a short-term borrowing; if interest rates were to increase, then the bank would generate a market value loss on the combination because the long-term loan is more interest sensitive than the short-term funding. Asset/liability management is discussed in greater detail later.

Although the goal is complex, the calculation is intuitive: divide the mark-to-model value of the new transaction by the (present value of) capital required to support the credit or insurance risk of the transaction until its maturity. The numerator directly reflects the best estimate of the value of the loan or policy, priced at a cost of capital appropriate for the credit or insurance risk, implying a direct and unambiguous link to shareholder value.

The generic formula for New Business RAPMs is given below; the calculation of new business RAPMs specific to insurance and banking is described in detail later.

EQUATION 3.4:   Generic New Business RAPM

$$\text{New Business RAPM} = \frac{E\left[\sum_{t=0}^{T}\left(\dfrac{\text{CF}_t + r_f C_t}{\left(1 + r_f\right)^t}\right)\right]}{E\left[\sum_{t=0}^{T}\left(\dfrac{C_t}{\left(1 + r_f\right)^t}\right)\right]} \geq \text{CoC}_{uw}$$

The numerator represents the present value of all the transaction's expected cash flows *as if* it were completely hedged in terms of financial market risk and financed at the risk-free rate of return. This includes a deduction for expected loan losses and claims.

Also included in the numerator is a return from investing the required capital at the risk-free rate of return, often called the "capital benefit." The transaction value is calculated as if it is completely financed/invested at the risk-free rate of return,[19] leaving only credit or insurance underwriting risk. However, capital needs to be held to cover these underwriting risks. New Business RAPMs are calculated as if the capital does not finance the transaction but is held in a separate account and invested in risk-free assets until it is needed to cover unexpected losses; the returns on the risk-free assets backing capital represent the "capital benefit."

The denominator represents the present value of the capital expected to be bound over the life of the transaction. Since New Business RAPMs evaluate underwriting risks only, this capital is allocated for underwriting risks only based on the transaction's marginal contribution to the overall portfolio risk.[20]

In order to be consistent, the appropriate cost of capital should also reflect only underwriting risk. For much of this Handbook we assume that the appropriate cost of capital for underwriting risk can be expressed as the sum of the risk-free rate of return plus an underwriting risk premium, for example $\text{CoC}_{uw} = r_f + rp_{uw}$.

Investment RAPMs

Investment RAPMs measure risk-adjusted returns from taking traded financial market risk by using a cost of capital specific to the portfolio, based on a risk-appropriate benchmark portfolio in the market.

---

[19]Note that this simplified formula assumes that there are no options or guarantees embedded in the transaction. Examples of embedded options include prepayment options for mortgages or guarantees on LH savings products. If the transaction has embedded options, then option valuation techniques need to be used, as discussed in Chapter 17.

[20]Note that additional risk loadings may also be added, for example to cover operational risk, business risk, etc.

Banks and insurers take financial market risks as principals in different portfolios, the most prominent being their asset/liability portfolios. Earnings can be expected from the open positions, but value is created only if the earnings represent excess returns above a risk-appropriate benchmark.

Investment RAPMs indicate whether an investment or trading portfolio has produced excess returns relative to a risk-appropriate benchmark. By construction, they are directly linked to shareholder value: if a bank has an open market risk position, for example borrowing short and lending long, then the returns are evaluated against the market benchmark which reflects the interest rate and funding risk. Since the market benchmark is also available to the shareholder, the bank generates shareholder value only if the earnings are in excess of the benchmark. These excess returns are often called "alpha."

Because traded market risk positions can in principle be closed at any point in time, Investment RAPMs are measured on a single-period basis; this is in contrast to new business RAPMs, which measure the expected profitability from assuming non-traded loan or insurance risk over the transaction's lifetime.

EQUATION 3.5:   Investment RAPM

$$\text{Investment RAPM} = \frac{\left(\begin{array}{l} \text{Expected total returns on the portfolio}- \\ \text{Appropriate term funding cost for net investment}+ \\ \text{Risk-free return on risk capital} \end{array} \right)}{\text{Allocated risk capital}} \geq \text{CoC}$$

The numerator includes the expected total returns from the position less the net funding cost of the position where funding is assumed to be at the risk-free rate of return. Because capital is needed to support the position, similar to the New Business RAPM, the Investment RAPM adds a "capital benefit" defined by a risk-free return on allocated capital. The denominator is the position's required economic capital, based on the portfolio's risk profile and typically calculated using an internal economic capital model.

The key to an accurate Investment RAPM is in using an appropriate cost of capital which must be defined portfolio by portfolio even if the capital is allocated based on risk. Because Investment RAPMs focus on traded risks, the appropriate cost of capital is determined by a risk-equivalent benchmark portfolio, selected by management or derived from a model such as the Capital Asset Pricing Model (CAPM).[21] In the latter case, the required cost of capital is given by the CAPM Securities Market Line (SML), for example $\text{CoC}_i = r_f + \beta_i r p_m$, where $r p_m$ represents the financial market's risk premium and β_i represents the "beta" for portfolio i, a measure of the portfolio's systematic risk, adjusted appropriately for leverage. Both approaches are discussed in detail in Chapter 16.

Business RAPMs

Business RAPMs in principle measure the risk-adjusted return for an entire business, covering all sources of risk and return.

---

[21]See Morningstar Fund Course 205: "Alpha is the difference between a fund's expected returns based on its beta (a measure of systemic risk) and its actual returns (and) is interpreted as the value that a portfolio manager adds . . . If a fund returns more . . . , it has a positive alpha. If a fund returns less . . . , it has a negative alpha."

Business RAPMs are used by financial services firms in the same way that Return on Equity (RoE) is used by industrial corporations, to evaluate whether a business has generated returns in excess of the common hurdle rate. However, Business RAPMs adjust both returns and the capital allocated to reflect the risk inherent in the business.

EQUATION 3.6: Business RAPM

$$\text{Business RAPM} = \frac{\text{Adjusted Earnings}}{\text{Allocated Capital}} \geq \text{CoC}$$

Adjusted Earnings

There are two adjustments to accounting earnings typically made by financial services firms. The first is for *expected losses*, for example the expected loan losses or insurance claims over the period, creating a baseline which recognizes expected losses as part of "cost of goods sold." This in principle allows the allocated capital to do the "heavy lifting" in terms of the residual risk of unexpected losses.

The second set of adjustments are those required to translate accounting earnings into a comparable, economic basis. Examples include adjusting for unrealized gains/losses on assets, liabilities and off-balance sheet commitments, eliminating non-cash expenses such as goodwill and Deferred Acquisition Cost (DAC) amortization, etc.

Adjusted Capital

Virtually all Business RAPMs attribute capital in the denominator based on the overall risk profile of the business. Some firms attribute an internal measure of required capital, others based on the maximum of {internal model, regulatory and rating agency required capital} in order to ensure that the binding solvency constraint is always recognized.

Cost of Capital

Most companies use a common cost of capital for all businesses based either on the firm's actual weighted average cost of capital or the target return on equity that they want to achieve, rationalizing that to do otherwise would be to penalize riskier businesses three times – the first time for the expected losses in the numerator, the second time for unexpected losses via allocated capital in the denominator and the third time by using a differentiated hurdle rate. In a survey, over 75% of firms responded that they used a common cost of capital across all business activities, with a further 15% admitting to only minor differentiation (Wilson, 2004). Nonetheless some firms elect differentiated hurdle rates, a practice supported by the theoretical and practical considerations presented in Chapter 4.

. . . LINKING DIRECTLY TO SHAREHOLDER VALUE

The discussion so far has been generic. However, it is straightforward to make the link between generic RAPMs and the value-oriented KPIs managed by banks and insurers.

Motivated later, for now it is asserted that there are five drivers of value for a financial services firm. The first two, profitable growth and operating or cost efficiency, are also applicable to industrial corporations. The last three, underwriting effectiveness, capital efficiency and investment alpha, are unique to risk-based, capital-intensive financial services activities.

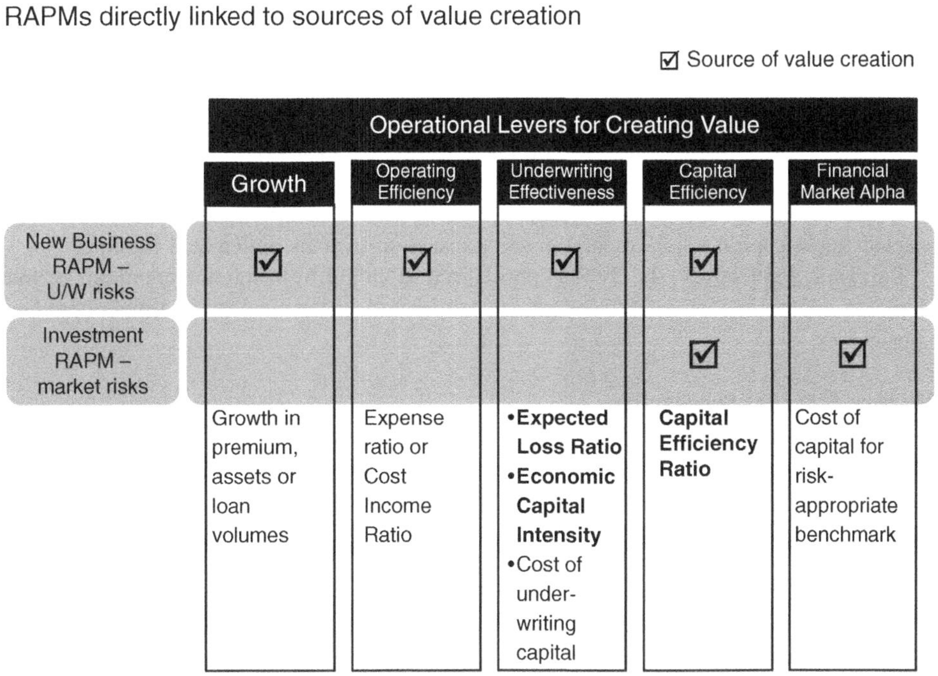

RAPMs directly linked to sources of value creation

☑ Source of value creation

Operational Levers for Creating Value					
	Growth	Operating Efficiency	Underwriting Effectiveness	Capital Efficiency	Financial Market Alpha
New Business RAPM – U/W risks	☑	☑	☑	☑	
Investment RAPM – market risks				☑	☑
	Growth in premium, assets or loan volumes	Expense ratio or Cost Income Ratio	•**Expected Loss Ratio** •**Economic Capital Intensity** •Cost of under-writing capital	**Capital Efficiency Ratio**	Cost of capital for risk-appropriate benchmark

FIGURE 3.4 RAPMs directly linked to sources of value creation

New Business and Investment RAPMs can be decomposed into KPIs which line up directly with each of these sources of value creation, as illustrated in Figure 3.4.

It is interesting to note that the two RAPMs combined cover all sources of risk and return that banks and insurers actively manage to create value, for example credit and insurance underwriting risk is covered by the New Business RAPM and financial market risk is covered by the Investment RAPM. Of further interest is that the RAPMs generally separate the two in terms of earnings, risk and capital utilization. This is an important intuition, which will be confirmed later when we value the firm by looking at the two sources of excess returns individually.

Underwriting Effectiveness, Capital Intensity and Capital Efficiency

Critical for the remainder of this Handbook are three KPIs which are specific to financial services firms but which may be new to the reader: underwriting effectiveness, capital intensity and capital efficiency.

KPIs from An Underwriting Perspective

A measure used to evaluate underwriting effectiveness is the Total Cost of Risk (TCR_{uw}), defined as the discounted sum of expected losses (e.g., expected loan losses or insurance claims) and the discounted cost of the minimum capital needed to cover unexpected losses with reasonable confidence.

Obviously, new business pricing has to cover the cost of the expected losses as this is a direct and predictable cost of doing business. In addition, pricing also has to be sufficient to cover the cost of capital required to protect against any additional, unexpected losses, determined by the minimum amount of required risk capital and the cost of that capital. Both of these are incorporated into the TCR:

$$\text{TCR}_{uw} = \sum \frac{\text{EL}_t}{\left(1 + r_f\right)^t} + rp_{uw} \sum \frac{\min C_t}{\left(1 + r_f\right)^t}$$

where EL_t represents the expected future losses or claims at time t, and C_t represents the expected future capital requirements for the transaction over its anticipated lifetime.

For some applications, the TCR is normalized, dividing by insurance premiums or loan volumes as appropriate, in order to compare the underwriting risk intensity of different products or businesses.

KPIs from A Capital Perspective

The TCR was calculated based on the minimum capital required to support the transaction over its lifetime. In general, firms hold more capital than the minimum economically required, implying a total cost of capital which is greater than the theoretical minimum. Two additional measures are useful for understanding the economics of the business: Economic Capital Intensity (ECI) and Capital Efficiency Ratio (CER).

ECI measures the discounted value of the *minimum* economic capital required for the policy or loan over its anticipated lifetime, divided by the premium received or the loan volume, for example $\text{ECI} = \left[\sum \min C_t / (1 + r)^t\right]/P$ or $\text{ECI} = \left[\sum \min C_t / (1 + r)^t\right]/L$. ECI is used in the total cost of risk defined earlier.

When entering into a new loan or insurance policy, banks and insurers are committing, or "locking up," capital over the duration of the transaction. Even if the position is later sold or the risk transferred through a derivative or reinsurance contract, whoever accepts the risk will ultimately have to hold the capital. As such, it is important to not only consider the theoretical value of the loan or insurance policy over its lifetime, but also the capital required over the same horizon.

ECI is important for evaluating new transactions and also for managing a portfolio of businesses. Looking only at a "slice of the business" by considering period earnings and period capital requirements, as is commonly done by Business RAPMs, unduly flatters businesses which lock up capital for longer durations; the fact that capital is locked up for long periods needs to be considered when allocating capital and setting dividend policy.

In general, ECI increases with maturity and with the annual expected capital requirement for the loan or insurance policy, as illustrated in Figure 3.5 where ECI is plotted on the

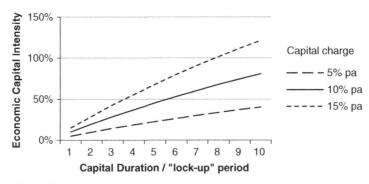

FIGURE 3.5 ECI, capital "lock-up" and period capital charges

vertical axis, the duration of the capital commitment on the horizontal axis and the lines represent ECIs for different levels of annual capital commitments as a percentage of premium or loan value.

CER is a measure of the *average capital actually held relative to the minimum capital required*, for example CER $= \left[\sum C_t/(1+r)^t\right]/\left[\sum \min C_t/(1+r)^t\right]$. It is rare that a bank or insurer will hold exactly the minimum required capital. The decision to hold more may be driven by management's risk appetite, reflecting a preference for greater security and resilience in the firm's capital structure; it can also be driven by regulatory and rating agency requirements, which force non-economic levels of capital or reserves. This excess capital can in principle be returned to shareholders if it can be unlocked. Making transparent the ratio of actual to minimum capital required is the first step toward actively managing that locked-up excess capital.

INSURANCE EXAMPLE

As an example, consider the PC new business EP illustrated in Table 3.2 using terms specific to the industry. (The link to shareholder value is easier to illustrate using EP, as it gives the absolute dollar contribution directly; the derivation of the associated RAPM is given in Chapter 24.)

Growth is trivially measured by the new business premium.

Operating efficiency is measured by the (discounted) *expense ratio*, or the discounted present value of expenses divided by premium.

TABLE 3.2 Insurance new business EP

Driver		Description
Growth	$P \times$ $[1 -$	*new business premium*
Operating efficiency	$ER_{pv} -$	*expense ratio* *(all future expected allocated operating expenses, present value basis)*
Underwriting effectiveness	$CR_{pv} -$ $rp_{uw} \times ECI_{uw} \times$	*claims ratio* (ultimate claims/premium) *(best-estimate claims, present value basis)* *cost of non-hedgeable risk capital* *(present value basis)* where rp_{uw} is the risk premium above the risk-free return for insurance risk $ECI = PVRC_{uw}/P$ where $PVRC_{uw}$ is the present value of all future minimum capital requirements, e.g. $ECI = \left[\sum \min C_t/(1+r)^t\right]/P$
Capital efficiency	CER]	CER = present value of actual capital divided by present value of minimum required capital $= PVAC_{uw}/PVRC_{uw} = \left[\sum C_t/(1+r)^t\right]/\left[\sum \min C_t/(1+r)^t\right]$

Underwriting effectiveness is measured by the TCR normalized by premium, $\frac{TCR_{uw}}{P} = CR_{pv} + rp_{uw}ECI$, where the first term represents the (discounted ex ante) claims ratio and the second the economic capital intensity of the transaction.

CER, defined as the ratio of the actual (discounted) capital divided by the sum of the (discounted) minimum required capital, is typically > 1 due to regulatory frictions.

Consistent with the role of the PC New Business RAPM/EP in supporting underwriting decisions, all capital and returns are measured relative to underwriting risks with no recognition of investment alpha or financial market risk taking.

BANKING EXAMPLE

As a further example, consider the loan new business EP in Table 3.3 using terms specific to the industry. (The link to shareholder value is easier to illustrate using EP, as it gives the absolute dollar contribution directly; the derivation of the associated RAPM is given in Chapter 24).

Growth is trivially measured by loan volume growth.

Operating efficiency is measured by the (discounted) cost income ratio with income measured by the loan's gross margin and fees.

Underwriting effectiveness is measured as the sum of the (discounted) loan loss ratio and the economic capital intensity.

Capital efficiency is measured by the capital efficiency ratio.

Consistent with the role of the loan New Business RAPM/EP in supporting underwriting decisions, all capital and returns are measured relative to underwriting risks with no recognition of investment alpha or financial market risk taking.

TABLE 3.3 Loan new business EP

Driver		Description
Operating profit and growth	$L \times$ $[(NIIM_{L\text{-}FTP} +$ $F/L)$ $\times$	*new loan volume* *net interest income margin, loans*[*][**] *fee income associated with loan as percentage of loan volume* * Based on FTP principles. ** Present value basis.
Operating efficiency	$(1 - CIR_{pv}) -$	*cost income ratio for lending business* *(all future expected allocated costs, present value basis)*
Underwriting effectiveness	$EL\%_{pv} -$ $rp_{uw} \times ECI_{uw} \times$	*expected loan loss percentage* (PVEL/L) *(present value basis)* $PVEL = \sum EL_t/(1+r)^t$ EL_t = expected loan loss at time t rp_{uw} is the risk premium above the risk-free return for insurance risk $ECI = PVRC_{uw}/L$ where $PVRC_{uw}$ is the present value of all future minimum risk capital requirements, e.g. $ECI = \left[\sum minC_t/(1+r)^t\right]/L$
Capital efficiency	CER]	CER = present value of actual held capital/ $PVRC_{uw} = \left[\sum C_t/(1+r)^t\right]/\left[\sum minC_t/(1+r)^t\right]$

CHAPTER 4

Two Challenges in Using RAPMs

In spite of being implemented broadly by both banks and insurers, using RAPMs is challenging for two reasons. The first is practical: while often used to take pricing decisions, RAPMs rarely influence corporate strategy. This is because the link between management actions, RAPMs and the share price is not easily understood by management and external stakeholders. As a consequence, RAPMs are frequently supplanted by simpler measures such as earnings, earnings growth and the P/E multiple when setting corporate strategy. Unfortunately, these simpler metrics fail to capture the important role of risk and capital for creating value in risk-based, capital-intensive businesses.

The second challenge is technical. How to ensure that the RAPM gives the "right" valuation signals for banking and insurance businesses? More often than not, RAPMs confuse risk-based capital *constraints* with the *shareholder capital invested in the business* and fail to charge an appropriate cost of capital. The net effect is that many firms destroy value by over-investing in high-risk businesses and taking too much financial market risk in their asset/liability mismatch portfolio.

This chapter discusses in detail both the practical and technical challenges in using RAPMs.

DO RAPMs INFLUENCE STRATEGY?

Most banks and insurers have developed complex RAPMs, building consensus amongst business managers and technical "gurus" and implementing them at great expense in their management reporting systems. Was the investment worth it?

While New Business RAPMs have achieved significant tactical impact, Business RAPMs have unfortunately failed to achieve strategic impact. One of my most memorable conversations was with the CEO of a major European bank who said, "Developing our economic profit framework has been a little like an elephant giving birth to a mouse – a long gestation period followed by lots of huffing and puffing and, in the end . . . not much." As the analysis later shows, this quote unfortunately reflects the situation at many firms.

The fact is that most firms put little emphasis on risk, capital and value when setting targets and incentivizing performance, choosing instead to focus on top-line revenue and earnings growth, implicitly assuming that the economics of the business will take care of itself if growth targets are met. If management does translate strategy into value it is typically through multiplying earnings by a P/E multiple as a shorthand to link management actions to value. In other words, Business RAPMs rarely seem to influence strategy.

Although there are many reasons for not using Business RAPMs strategically, one in particular stands out: the lack of a clear line of sight between Business RAPMs and shareholder value.

Significant Tactical Impact . . .

In my experience, New Business RAPMs and the economic capital models associated with them have had the most impact via three purely tactical avenues: reinforcing pricing discipline, setting risk limits and establishing internal solvency standards.

Reinforcing Pricing Discipline, Managing Customer Relationship Profitability

RAPM measures have had substantial tactical impact in instilling pricing discipline for risks which are not actively traded, for example SME loans or insurance policies, and in supporting relationship profitability management. They are used to define the technical price of the transaction, or the minimum, break-even price from a risk-adjusted perspective, with the actual price depending on the firm's commercial policy. (Going from technical pricing to value-added pricing is discussed in detail in Chapter 24.)

New Business RAPMs were originally developed specifically with this in mind as the "early adopter" case studies of Bankers Trust, JP Morgan, Bank of America and Swiss Reinsurance illustrate.

Delegating Limits and Authorities

The second area is the design and implementation of risk appetite and limit frameworks. Prior to the EC or VaR models at the heart (or in the denominator) of RAPMs, most trading limits were based on notional or equivalent values (e.g., 10-year swap or bond position equivalents in terms of interest rate risk) and single risk factors (e.g., DV01, deltas, gammas, vegas, etc.[1]).

This led to a complex set of constraints which were not directly comparable, preventing management from understanding how the delegated limit authority lined up with its risk appetite. In addition, because the limits were product- or risk-specific, they tended to lock risk capacity into rigid and non-fungible structures, thereby preventing the company from taking advantage of opportunities dynamically.

With VaR, two things became possible: first, it was possible to delegate a limit on the trading book consistent with management's overall risk appetite; second, because EC is in principle comparable across all risks, it was possible to implement limit structures with greater fungibility, allowing capacity to be shifted to where it was needed, when it was needed.

Virtually all banks and insurers currently use some form of EC or VaR metrics to set trading, asset/liability mismatch and investment portfolio limits.

---

[1] All of these are standardized measures of risk. DV01 is a measure of the dollar value of a 1 basis point increase in interest rates, delta is defined as the change in a security's or derivative's price for a small change in rates or the underlying ($\delta = \partial V/\partial r$), gamma is the rate of change or convexity of the value ($\gamma = \partial^2 V/\partial r^2$).

Establishing Capital Standards and Capital Attribution

Minimum capital levels for banks and insurers are to a great extent defined by external stakeholders, notably regulators and rating agencies. These external standards are typically based on commonly available information, allowing implementation across different institutions, both small and large, simple and complex. As a consequence, they also represent industry-average calibrations rather than being tailored to the specific risk profile and underwriting performance of the firm. As such, they represent the lowest common denominator in terms of data availability and generally a conservative calibration for well-managed firms.

Most banks and insurers use internal EC models to set their risk appetite, determine their target solvency levels and attribute capital to their business units. The internal models have the benefit of representing the specifics of the company, which the broader brushstroke approaches of standard models cannot do.

. . . But Limited Strategic Impact Due to No Clear Link to Shareholder Value

These three uses represent tactical, as opposed to strategic, uses: while institutions such as Bankers Trust and JP Morgan have fundamentally transformed themselves using New Business RAPMs, the fact is that the RAPMs were invented *to support* the desired strategic change and did not cause the change in strategy.

The lack of strategic impact is more challenging to explain for Business RAPMs, which are in principle designed to support strategic decisions. Table 4.1 illustrates this point: when asked what information is used to guide strategic decisions, almost all CFOs and CROs ranked return on economic capital a distant fifth, well below earnings, revenue and growth. Adding insult to injury, value measures ranked at the bottom of the list.

There are many reasons why Business RAPMs may not influence corporate strategy. As Table 4.2 illustrates, the most often cited include the level of management acceptance, the accuracy and complexity of the measures and the level of detail or granularity. (If cynical, I would also add whether or not management likes the answer.)

More importantly, Table 4.2 illustrates a fundamental paradox: although 90% of respondents believe that their internal metrics reflect the shareholder's perspective, only 27% clearly understand the link between those same metrics and shareholder value.

TABLE 4.1   RAPMs don't drive strategy

Which three measures are most used for strategic planning and decision making?
1. Earnings and earnings growth
2. Revenues and revenue growth
3. Cost or cost/income ratios
4. Return on book capital
5. Return on economic capital or economic profit
6. Market share
7. Other
8. Market or shareholder value, embedded value, intrinsic value

Source: Wilson (2004).

TABLE 4.2   RAPMs not linked to shareholder value

How satisfied are you with the following aspects of your current performance measurement framework?	
Accurately reflects shareholder perspectives	90%
Accepted within the organization	83%
Level of detail/granularity	67%
Transparency with respect to value drivers	58%
Accurate reflection of the business economics	58%
Link between internal metrics (e.g., RAPMs) and shareholder value	27%

Source: Wilson (2004).

TABLE 4.3   External stakeholders don't understand internal metrics

Do you feel that external stakeholders understand your business?	Rating agencies	Equity analysts	Regulators
Key business drivers	85%	82%	52%
Financial statements	95%	76%	71%
Economic performance and capital framework	33%	24%	33%

Source: Wilson (2004).

These results remind me of an American in London rooting for the champion cricket team or a European in the USA rooting for the National Football League champion – you are not going to get into trouble by rooting for the winner, even if you have no idea what the rules of the game are.

Apparently, other stakeholders also do not understand the rules of the game. As Table 4.3 illustrates, CFOs and CROs are very skeptical whether external stakeholders understand the link between Business RAPMs and value.

Only 24% believe that equity analysts understand internal economic performance and capital frameworks, well behind their understanding of the business drivers and financial statements (at 82% and 76%, respectively). Paradoxically, CFOs believe that rating agencies and regulators understand their internal frameworks better than equity analysts, likely due to the fact that economic capital inherently represents a debt holder's view on capital or solvency requirements.

The communication by CFOs of their corporate strategy is consistent with the perceived disconnect between internal metrics and shareholder value, putting Business RAPMs in a distant last place and earnings and growth in a clear first place (Table 4.4).

Put simply, for all the talk about Business RAPMs in the industry, very few CFOs and CROs seem to understand how they relate to shareholder value and even fewer use them to set and communicate strategy.

Note that this is not a question of accuracy – increasing the complexity of the RAPM or EC measures without addressing this fundamental issue will not help and may very likely exacerbate the problem. If RAPMs are to have an impact, the clear message is that we need to create a more direct and transparent link between them and shareholder value!

TABLE 4.4   Internal metrics not used for external communication

What is the most important financial information that you communicate externally?	
Earnings and earnings growth	83%
Return on equity	58%
Line of business information	58%
Capital or solvency ratio	58%
Exposure or risk information	42%
Revenue and revenue growth	42%
Earnings guidance	33%
Cost/income ratio	33%
Return on risk capital	17%

Source: Wilson (2004).

DO RAPMs GIVE THE RIGHT SIGNALS?

While Business RAPMs may have tactical impact in steering product and customer profitability, they typically do not drive business strategy, even for risk-based, capital-intensive businesses. This is not the only issue with Business RAPMs; the second issue is that, in spite of their complexity, Business RAPMs often do not give the "right" steering signals from a value management perspective.

Theoretical issues with Business RAPMs have been raised extensively in the literature (Wilson, 1992, 2003a; Froot and Stein, 1998a,b; Crouhy *et al.*, 1999; Turnbull, 2000), and the technical nature of the discussion may not appeal to everyone. For those with less appetite for equations using the Greek alphabet the next section introduces an intuitive example based on a levered investment portfolio to illustrate the issues. The main theoretical issues with Business RAPMs are:

- RAPMs based on risk-based capital allocations are wrong. The capital that matters is the actual net asset value invested in the company. Risk-based capital requirements and absolute leverage constraints are irrelevant except as a constraint to the leverage that the firm can achieve.
- Using a single cost of capital across all businesses is inappropriate and misleading, even if capital is allocated based on the risk of the business.
- Business RAPMs are single-period frameworks that fail to support decisions which entail trade-offs between current investments and future operating returns as well as the lifetime capital intensity of the business.

Following the intuitive example, a theoretically consistent Business RAPM based on the well-known CAPM is presented to illustrate the issues with more rigor. The CAPM framework is sufficiently rich to make all of the points in a technically rigorous manner and, because it is familiar to many, the results should be accessible.

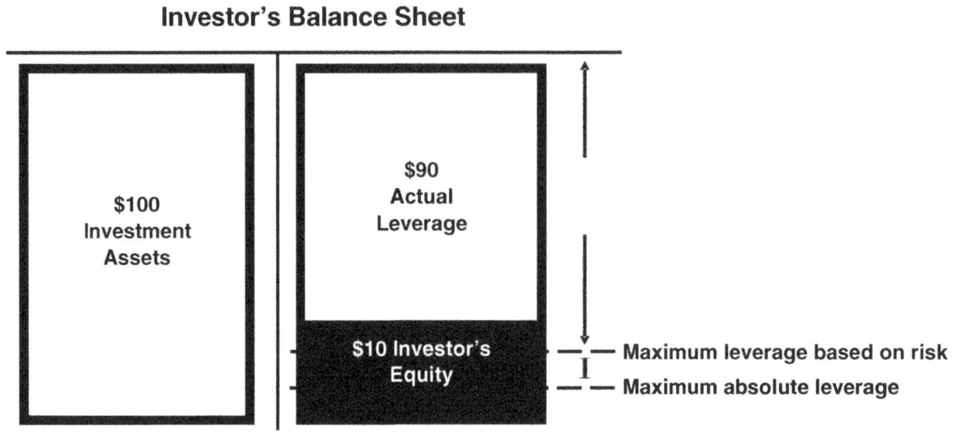

Investor's Balance Sheet

FIGURE 4.1   The shareholder's balance sheet

What are the Issues?

The issues with Business RAPMs can be illustrated with the simple investment portfolio in Figure 4.1: an investor holds a $100 portfolio in his securities account, funded with $90 of leverage and $10 of the investor's own money. We assume that the investor's *actual leverage* ($90 or 90%) is lower than the *maximum risk-based leverage* ($95 or 95%) allowed by the lender based on the quality of the asset portfolio, and less than the *absolute leverage constraint of $98 or 98%* regardless of the riskiness of the portfolio. The risk-based and absolute leverage constraints in this simple example are meant to represent the type of risk-based capital and absolute leverage constraints imposed, for example, under Basel III.

The Intuition

Putting yourself in the position of the investor, how you would answer the following questions?

What is the capital that you have invested in the business? If it was my account, the answer would be unambiguously $10, representing the value of my personal wealth tied up in the portfolio. It would not be $5, the minimum risk-based capital requirement allowed by the bank; nor would it be a multiple of the portfolio's earnings volatility (Matten, 2008); nor would it be the book value of the securities account (the "accounting perspective"). Very concretely, it would be the value that I could in principle take from the portfolio today and walk away with.

What about the leverage constraints? The lender in this example allows up to 95% leverage based on the riskiness of the portfolio and in all instances, no more than 98% absolute leverage. Both represent minimum capital requirements, or constraints, not capital.

What return do you expect on the portfolio? If it were my portfolio, the answer would depend on the assets held in the account. If the portfolio consisted of more equities than investment grade bonds, then I would expect a higher return than a portfolio with a higher proportion of bonds. And, if it was my account, I would not answer, "A constant expected rate of return which is independent of the portfolio composition because I have chosen to hold capital at or better than a risk-based minimum required capital ratio."

Making the Issues Precise

Now, replace the words "investor" with "shareholder," "portfolio of assets" with "portfolio of businesses," "maximum risk-based leverage" with "minimum economic capital" and "maximum absolute leverage" with "leverage ratio." We then get a feeling for how a Business RAPM should work intuitively and what goes wrong in practice.

Capital Attribution The capital that matters is the actual net asset value invested in the company, with risk-based capital requirements and absolute leverage constraints being irrelevant except as a constraint to the leverage that the firm can achieve.

Most Business RAPMs take a "debt holder's" perspective, attributing only the economic capital defined as the minimum capital required to ensure that the firm's obligations can be met with some level of confidence. In general, "debt holder" capital representing the minimum requirement is lower than the actual net asset value that shareholders have invested in the business.

You can see how silly the standard practice is by looking at the Business RAPM disclosures of banks and insurers: invariably, you see RAPMs well in excess of the actual RoE of the company, the reason being that attributed capital is often significantly lower than shareholder's equity. Touting a 20+% RAROC is silly when the actual RoEs are closer to 10%.

Shareholders require a return on their entire investment, not just on the minimum capital required to support the business from a risk perspective. Unfortunately, most RAPMs are based on minimum capital requirements and not on invested capital.

Cost of Capital Using a single cost of capital across all businesses is inappropriate and misleading, even if capital is allocated based on the risk of the business.

Most companies use a common hurdle rate under the assumption that the risk-based capital allocated to the business "normalizes" the risks. As the example illustrates, using a constant cost of capital may lead banks and insurers to over-invest in high-beta businesses (e.g., in investment banking or asset investment strategies for insurers) and under-invest in low-beta businesses (e.g., in retail banking or PC insurance).

This is a very general result in the literature,[2] illustrated by the example, proven rigorously for the CAPM-RAPM model discussed in the next section and substantiated by the empirical evidence at the end of this chapter.

Single-Period Perspective Business RAPMs are single-period frameworks that fail to support decisions which entail trade-offs between current investments and future operating returns, as well as the lifetime capital intensity of the business.

Management is confronted daily with such trade-offs – for example, deciding to invest in new branches or restructuring operations and systems: each requires cash today with the benefits in terms of revenue growth or expense reductions only in the future.

---

[2]See, for example, the comparable model of Crouhy *et al.* (1999) as well as the models which introduce agency costs based on asymmetric information or the cost of financial distress – such as those of Merton and Perold (1993), Froot and Stein (1998a,b), Stulz (1996), Stulz *et al.* (1999, 2000) and Perold (2001). This same conclusion was reached in a very general framework by Milne and Omato (2009) under limited assumptions on market processes determining equilibrium return.

Further, and more importantly, because they focus only on a period "slice" of returns and capital, Business RAPMs ignore the lifetime capital intensity of the business. This may lead to strategic decisions which lock in capital with very long pay-back periods, limiting capital management flexibility and overly relying on long-term assumptions which might be overly optimistic.

The Wrong Model Finally, it is highly likely that the market return model implicit in the Business RAPM is wrong. This is not surprising as all models are abstractions of reality and will be wrong when confronted with reality: since its inception, CAPM has generated a small cottage industry of academics throwing theoretical and empirical pineapples at the model.

While the criticism is valid, it is not constructive: the world is complex and any model will, by necessity, be an abstraction of reality. Nonetheless, management has the responsibility to interpret the returns from different businesses in light of the risks taken.

Although complex, this responsibility cannot be ignored or abrogated. Some framework must be used – throwing up one's hands in frustration is not an option. The relevant question is therefore not whether the model is wrong – they all are – but rather whether you take better decisions with or without the models. Models are an absolute necessity for risk-based, capital-intensive businesses.

The CAPM–RAPM: A Theoretically Grounded Example

This section develops a Business RAPM based on the CAPM in order to illustrate the issues.[3] The goal is to use a familiar framework to gain insights into how the "normalization" of returns should work in a theoretically consistent framework.

Risk, Return and Excess Returns in the CAPM World

CAPM is an equilibrium model which produces an explicit relationship between risk and return called the Securities Market Line (SML), under simplifying assumptions.[4] For a direct investment in security or portfolio i, the SML is written as follows.

EQUATION 4.1: CAPM – securities market line

$$R_i = R_f + \beta_i (R_m - R_f) = R_f + \beta_i R_p$$

where R_i is the expected return on security i, R_f is the risk-free rate of return, R_m is the expected return on the market portfolio, $R_p = (R_m - R_f)$ is defined as the market risk premium (or the expected return on the market portfolio above the risk-free rate of return). β_i is the systematic or non-diversifiable risk of security i, defined by the following equation.

---

[3]This section builds on Wilson (1992). It is similar to the models cited in the previous footnote. The extensions in the other papers add to, rather than alter, the general observations drawn from the simpler CAPM-RAPM example.

[4]The assumptions are that either investors have quadratic utility functions or asset returns are normally distributed; there are no transactions costs and no restrictions on short sales or lending and borrowing; the risk-free lending rate is the same as the risk-free borrowing rate; there are no tax distortions and no private information. For an overview, see Brealey et al. (2011). For original references, see Sharpe (1964).

EQUATION 4.2: CAPM – beta

$$\beta_i = \frac{\sigma_{i,m}}{\sigma_m^2} = \frac{\sigma_i \rho_{i,m}}{\sigma_m}$$

where $\sigma_{i,m}$ is the covariance between security i and the market portfolio; σ_i, σ_m are the standard deviation or volatility of returns for security i and the market portfolio, respectively, and $\rho_{i,m}$ is the correlation between security i and the market portfolio.

The interpretation of the SML is straightforward: if you invest in security i, then you should expect to receive the risk-free rate of return *plus* an additional return which depends on the risk of the security. In equilibrium, the market only compensates investors for the systematic or non-diversifiable risk of the portfolio measured by its "beta" or covariance with the market portfolio, not for the idiosyncratic risk which can be diversified away.

In the CAPM world, markets are efficient and no security or portfolio is expected to generate excess returns compared with the SML. In other words, you can't beat the market and there is no excess investment returns or "alpha" (α).

In order to make it interesting in the context of shareholder value creation, we deviate from the CAPM assumptions and assume that some securities or portfolios can outperform the market, generating excess expected returns or alpha. In this case, the SML for some asset i can be rewritten as follows.

EQUATION 4.3: CAPM – securities market line with expected excess profit

$$R_i = \alpha + R_f + \beta_i R_p$$

The Shareholder's Perspective: Invested Capital and Leverage

As noted earlier, the SML is applicable for both investments in individual securities as well as portfolios without leverage. However, both banks and insurers use leverage, for example through deposits and policy holder funding, securities lending and borrowing contracts, derivatives, etc. The SML can be adapted for leverage.[5]

EQUATION 4.4: CAPM – security market line with excess returns for levered positions

$$\hat{R}_i = \left[\alpha + R_f + \beta_i^* R_p\right] - dR_f$$
$$\hat{R}_i = \alpha + \gamma R_f + \beta_i R_p$$

where $\hat{R}_i$ is the expected return from the *levered* portfolio i, the total portfolio is financed by equity (e) and debt (d), dR_f represents the cost of leverage and $\gamma = \frac{e}{e+d}$ is the percentage of equity financing of the total portfolio. The returns on shareholder's equity are given by $\hat{R}_i/e$ due to the leverage.

---

[5]The derivation of Equation 4.4 assumes that the investor can borrow and lend at the same risk-free rate of return, an obviously unrealistic assumption which is shared by the CAPM. More importantly, it assumes that the absolute cost of debt financing does not increase with leverage, implying that the borrowing rate does not reflect any risk of default. For a model which includes the cost of default, see Merton (1974) as well as Cooper *et al.* (2008).

The Debt Holder's Perspective: Economic Capital in the CAPM World

Typical RAPMs allocate capital to each business unit according to its absolute or stand-alone risk profile (with some companies "downstreaming" part of the group's diversification benefit). This capital allocation reflects a "debt holder's perspective." Economic capital is defined as the amount of capital that would be required to meet the firm's obligations to its senior creditors, primarily depositors and policy holders, within a given confidence interval defined by management's rating aspirations. This method of capital attribution is risk based, implying that a higher rating aspiration will lead to a higher level of required capital.

In the CAPM world, the *absolute* risk from a security or portfolio is measured by its standard deviation, σ_i. The absolute risk can be split between systematic (non-diversifiable) and idiosyncratic (diversifiable) risk using $\sigma_i = \beta_i \sigma_m + \sigma_{Ii}$, where σ_m represents the standard deviation of the market portfolio returns, β_i is the portfolio's beta and σ_{Ii} is the portfolio's idiosyncratic risk.

Following standard practice, EC in the CAPM world is defined by the following equation.

EQUATION 4.5: CAPM – EC

$$EC_i = \eta(e + d)\sigma_i$$

or

$$EC_i = \eta\sigma_i \text{ if } (e + d) = 1$$

where η is a constant set by management in a manner consistent with management's rating aspiration or risk appetite. For example, if management desired to capitalize to a double-A rating's average 0.03% probability of default, then it would set η equal to 3.43, representing the one-sided confidence interval z-score for a normal random variable with mean 0 and standard deviation 1. If management had a higher risk appetite (or, equivalently, a lower rating aspiration), then it would choose a lower η.

In general, financial services firms hold more than the capital required from a debt holder's perspective (e.g., $e \geq EC$). The rationale is discussed in detail in Chapter 15.

The CAPM–RAPM, Appropriate Cost of Capital and Decision Rule

In this section, we assume that the firm is over-capitalized relative to minimum requirements (e.g., $e > EC$).

CAPM–RAPM is defined by dividing the expected portfolio returns by the CAPM EC definition, after first adjusting for the "equity funding benefit" discussed in the previous chapter, leading to the following equation.

EQUATION 4.6: CAPM–RAPM

$$E[\text{RAPM}] = \left[\frac{\hat{R}_i - \gamma R_f}{EC_i}\right] = \left[\frac{\alpha + \gamma R_f + \beta_i{}^* R_p - \gamma R_f}{EC_i}\right] = \left[\frac{\alpha + \beta_i R_p}{EC_i}\right]$$

Looking at the equation, one might conclude that the CAPM-RAPM gives an incentive to take more systemic risk since it is increasing in β. While this first observation ignores the fact that EC is also increasing in β, the intuition is correct.[6] In other words, in spite of normalizing returns by dividing by EC, CAPM-RAPM is biased toward higher-risk portfolios.[7]

The Appropriate Cost of Capital or Hurdle Rate   Assuming that we do not want to give incentives (and pay bonuses) simply for taking higher-beta positions, we have to define the cost of capital appropriately when using RAPM. The only way to do this is to make the cost of capital depend on the portfolio's risk profile, in spite of normalizing returns using EC.

The appropriate cost of capital in the CAPM-RAPM is tautological: it is the hurdle rate which isolates excess returns, or alpha. Recognizing this, the appropriate cost of capital for the CAPM-RAPM is given below.

EQUATION 4.7: CAPM-RAPM appropriate cost of capital

$$\text{CoC}_i = \left[\frac{\beta_i R_p}{\eta \sigma_i}\right] = \left[\frac{\rho_{i,m} R_p}{\eta \sigma_m}\right] = \left[\frac{\beta_i R_p}{\text{EC}_i}\right]$$

Using this definition of the cost of capital, the economic profit from the position, $\text{EP}_i = \text{EC}_i[\text{RAPM}_i - \text{CoC}_i]$, reduces to $\text{EP}_i = (e + d)\alpha$, leading to the following decision criterion.

EQUATION 4.8: CAPM-RAPM decision criterion

Accept if $E(\text{RAPM}_i) \geq \text{CoC}_i$ or, equivalently, $\dfrac{(e + d)\alpha}{\text{EC}_i} \geq 0$.

Associated economic profit and economic return definition:

$\text{EP}_i = \text{EC}_i[\text{RAPM}_i - \text{CoC}_i] = (e + d)\alpha$ in absolute terms and $\dfrac{(e + d)\alpha}{e}$ on an excess return to shareholder's invested capital perspective.

By design, economic profit reduces to a measure of the portfolio's dollar excess returns relative to the SML, $(e + d)\alpha$, often called investment or market "alpha." This leads to two interesting observations.

Observation 1. Excess returns to shareholders do not depend on risk-based capital but rather on the actual capital invested in the business (unless risk-based capital is a binding constraint).

Observation 2. The appropriate RAPM cost of capital will depend on the business's risk profile, even if risk capital is used to normalize returns.

Value Creation and Solvency or Leverage Constraints

In the last section, we assumed that the debt holder's perspective was not binding (e.g., $e > \text{EC}$). This section analyzes how a binding risk-based capital and/or absolute leverage restriction affects shareholder economics in this simplified world.

---

[6]To see this, consider that $\frac{\partial E[\text{RAPM}]}{\partial \beta} = \frac{R_p}{\text{EC}}(1 - \rho_{im}) > 0$, where we have made use of the definition $\sigma_i = \beta_i \sigma_m + \sigma_{Ii}$ and $\beta_i = \sigma_i \rho_{im}/\sigma_m$.

[7]A similar result was derived by Milne and Omato (2009). They developed the result in a more general framework and, in the special case of CAPM assumptions (e.g., multivariate normal returns or quadratic utility functions), concluded that a constant hurdle rate can only be theoretically justified if ρ_{im} is constant for all assets, clearly an unrealistic assumption which would imply that σ_i is proportional to capital requirements for all assets and portfolios.

TABLE 4.5   Economic capital and leverage constraints

Constraints	Traditional form	Expressed in terms of constraint on debt	Comments
Risk-based capital constraint	$e \geq EC_i$ $e \geq (e + d)\eta\sigma_i$	$d \leq e\left(\dfrac{1 - \eta\sigma_i}{\eta\sigma_i}\right)$	Limits the amount of risk that can be assumed per unit of equity, or equivalently the leverage that can be used to fund risky assets.
Financial leverage constraint	$\dfrac{d}{d + e} \leq x$	$d \leq e\left(\dfrac{x}{1 - x}\right)$	Limits the absolute amount of leverage that can be assumed, regardless of the riskiness of the portfolio.

An Incentive to Increase Leverage Assuming positive expected excess returns (e.g., $\alpha \geq 0$), it is clear that shareholders should "locally" prefer more leverage to less since their economic profit increases with leverage – for example, $EP_i = EC_i[RAPM_i - CoC_i] = (e + d)\alpha$ implies $\partial EP_i / \partial d = \alpha \geq 0$. In other words, in the absence of constraints or impact on the cost of debt, increasing leverage allows shareholders to capture additional excess returns at the absolute rate of α and at a relative return on equity of $\alpha(e + d)/e$.

    Observation 3. If the business generates excess returns, then marginally more leverage used to grow the business increases economic profit, all else being equal.

Solvency and Leverage Constraints Unfortunately, life is not so easy. First, because "all else" is seldom equal: it is reasonable to expect that the cost of debt financing will increase as leverage is increased, reflecting a higher probability of default on the debt.

    More important in the context of this discussion, banks and insurers also face balance sheet constraints which limit the amount of leverage they can take. Generally speaking, there are two types of constraint which debt holders or their surrogates (e.g., rating agencies and regulators) impose on financial services firms. The first is the risk-based or economic capital constraint ($e \geq EC$) discussed earlier. The second represents an absolute limit on portfolio leverage, regardless of the riskiness of the portfolio. Representative constraints in the context of the CAPM world are given in Table 4.5.

    The first column represents the constraints as they are typically expressed (e.g., equity greater than risk capital requirements, debt limited to $x\%$ of the financing structure of the firm); the second column expresses both constraints as the maximum amount of debt allowed within the constraints.

    Both of these constraints must be met simultaneously. Since shareholders strictly prefer more leverage to less on the margin in this simple model, the minimum constraint will be binding, implying that we can combine the constraints.

EQUATION 4.9:   Risk-based solvency and leverage restrictions on debt

$$d(e, \sigma_i) \leq e \times \min\left[\left(\frac{x}{1 - x}\right), \left(\frac{1 - \eta\sigma_i}{\eta\sigma_i}\right)\right] \text{ with } \frac{\partial d}{\partial e} > 0 \text{ and } \frac{\partial d}{\partial \sigma_i} \leq 0$$

The comparative statistics are intuitive: the firm can raise more debt if it raises more equity first and, for any level of equity, the firm may have to reduce its debt if it chooses a riskier portfolio.

Many in the industry argue that the economic solvency constraint is both appropriate and sufficient because it defines the maximum leverage in a manner consistent with the risk of the business. And, in the past under Basel II, international regulators agreed, imposing no additional absolute leverage constraints. However, high levels of bank leverage prior to the 2008 financial crisis led bank regulators to impose an additional, absolute leverage constraint under Basel III; this new leverage constraint is independent of the business's risk profile (see Chapter 15 for a further discussion).

Economic Profit Under Leverage Constraints   Given that one of the constraints will be binding, we can substitute the leverage constraint into the EP equation to get the following.

EQUATION 4.10:   Maximum CAPM – economic profit under leverage constraints

$$
EP_i = EC_i[RAPM_i - CoC_i] = (e + d(e, \sigma_i))\alpha = e\left(1 + \min\left[\left(\frac{x}{1-x}\right), \left(\frac{1 - \eta\sigma_i}{\eta\sigma_i}\right)\right]\right)\alpha
$$

It is clear from Equation 4.10 that the leverage constraint limits economic profit: once the firm is levered up to the maximum allowed under the constraints, the only way to increase economic profit is to invest more shareholder capital. Put differently, we have the following observation.

Observation 4. Risk-based capital and leverage constraints only matter if they are binding. If the business is generating excess returns, a binding constraint represents a constraint on shareholder value.

Differentiated Cost of Capital: Empirical Evidence[8]

As illustrated in the previous section, it is a general result of theoretically correct RAPMs that a differentiated cost of capital should be used depending on the business, even after bringing the businesses to a common rating or solvency standard. Unfortunately, it is common industry practice *not* to differentiate the cost of capital.

How big of an issue is this? Would using a differentiated cost of capital give radically different management signals? The remainder of this section presents empirical evidence suggesting that it is in fact a big issue, leading firms to over-value high-risk businesses (such as investment banking) and under-value low-risk businesses (such as retail banking and personal lines insurance).

Phrasing the Questions
In order to provide empirical support, we first have to ask questions which can be answered empirically. The three questions we answer in this section are:

---

[8]This section follows Wilson (2003a).

- First, is there evidence that shareholders require different hurdle rates for different businesses, even if each is capitalized to a common rating standard? We call this the "Differentiated Cost of Capital Effect" and it is strongly supported by the data.
- Second, is there evidence that shareholders require a higher return from firms with higher leverage, but in the same business? We call this the "Leverage or Default Effect" and it is strongly supported by the data.
- Third, is there evidence that shareholders place a premium on firms that have less idiosyncratic risk, for example due to diversification, and can therefore afford greater leverage? We call this the "Idiosyncratic Risk Effect" and it is weakly supported by the data.

The differentiated cost of capital and leverage effects can be directly supported with a very simple analysis in Table 4.6.

Differentiated Cost of Capital   The left side of Table 4.6 gives the average betas for insurers and investment banks which had public ratings between AA and A+. If we believe that public ratings reflect the default risk of a firm, then each of these firms was arguably capitalized to a comparable confidence interval.

The table indicates how absurd the common cost of capital assumption is: investment banks had levered betas which are 2-3x insurers, implying a cost of capital 6–10 percentage points greater (based on a market risk premium of 3–5%), even after "adjusting" to a common probability of default by comparing similarly rated institutions.

Why is this the case? Shareholders value the residual profits after meeting debt holders' obligations and these residual cash flows depend on the systematic risk of the business. The fact that each business is capitalized to a common rating standard *does not change the systematic risk characteristics of the residual cash flows, it only changes the leverage ratio*. For the same rating, the cost of capital is higher for investment banking than for insurance because the residual cash flows have more systemic risk than the residual cash flows from insurance operations.

Leverage Effect   The right side of Table 4.6 gives the average betas for selected "universal" banks, sorted by rating allowing us to isolate the impact of rating or capital confidence. As the table indicates, the average levered beta increases as the probability of default increases (as measured by the firm's rating class). The table indicates how strong the leverage effect is: a +0.8 difference in beta between the AA+ and A+ institutions leads to a +2.4–4 percentage point difference in the firms' cost of capital, depending on the market risk premium. The intuition? A firm in the same business with higher leverage should have a higher cost of levered capital.

Idiosyncratic Risk Effect   The third proposition is that, all else being equal, shareholders require a premium from firms that have more idiosyncratic risk. The most direct rationale is that firms with more idiosyncratic risk cannot leverage as much, implying a lower return on equity. This intuition is not lost on rating agencies: Standard & Poor's (1999) explicitly recognizes a company's diversification as one of the criteria when assigning a financial

TABLE 4.6 Comparison of betas[*]

	(A) Differentiated Cost of Capital[**]		(B) Leverage Effect[**]				
	AA to A+ firms	Beta range	Rating	AA+	AA	AA –	A+
Insurance	AEG, CGNU, AXA, AS	0.81–1.29 (1.03)	**Universal banks**	DB – 0.94	DRB – 1.01 NBA – 0.92 COM – 0.72	BHV –0.93 SG –1.23 BBVA – 1.22 BSCH – 1.25 FB –1.19	BNP – 1.56 JPM – 1.95 RBS – 1.70 BA –1.76
Investment banking	ML, MS, GS, LB	2.34–3.78 (2.90)	**Average**	0.94	0.88	1.16	1.74

[*] Average domestic betas and blended public rating (Moody's, Standard & Poor's) when available, 1990–2001.
[**] MR = Munich Re, SR = Swiss Re, AL = Allstate, PRU = Prudential UK, AEG = Aegon, ML = Merrill Lynch, AS = Allstate, MS = Morgan Stanley, GS = Goldman Sachs, LB = Lehman Brothers, DB = Deutsche Bank, DRB = Dresdner, NBA = National Bank of Australia, COM = Commonwealth Bank of Australia, BHV = Bayerishe Hypo-Vereinsbank, BSCH = Banco Santander Central Hispanoamerica, FB = FleetBoston, BNP = Banque National de Paris, JPM = JP Morgan, RBS = Royal Bank of Scotland, BA = Bank of America.

TABLE 4.7 Differentiated Cost of Capital: Impact for AA-US/UK representative firms

Representative Firm	Share	Levered Beta	Cost of Capital	P/E Multiple
Regional Bank				
Retal banking	60%	1.05	9.30%	24.6
Commercial banking	40%	1.58	12.20%	14.62
Average	100%	1.26	10.40%	19.32
Multiline Insurance				
Life insurance	40%	0.90	8.40%	30.56
P&C insurance	40%	0.99	9.0%	26.44
Asset management	20%	1.55	12.0%	14.99
Average	100%	1.07	9.4%	24.06
Investment bank				
Asset management	20%	1.55	12.0%	14.99
Equity investment banking	40%	3.9	25.0%	5.26
Fixed income investment banking	40%	1.77	13.3%	12.72
Average	100%	2.58	17.7%	8.27
Universal bank				
Retail banking	40%	1.05	9.3%	24.6
Commercial banking	30%	1.58	12.2%	14.62
Asset management	10%	1.55	12.0%	14.99
Equity investment banking	5%	3.9	25.0%	5.26
Fixed income investment banking	15%	1.77	13.3%	12.72
Average	100%	1.51	11.8%	15.44
Diversified financial services firm				
Retail banking	25%	1.05	9.3%	24.6
Commercial banking	20%	1.58	12.2%	14.62
Asset management	15%	1.55	12.0%	14.99
Life insurance	15%	0.9	8.4%	30.56
P&C insurance	5%	0.99	9.0%	26.44
Equity investment banking	10%	3.9	25.0%	5.26
Fixed income investment banking	10%	1.77	13.3%	12.72
Average	100%	1.56	12.1%	14.81

Underlying assumptions for the table: risk free = 3.5%, risk premium = 5.5%, growth = 5%
Source: Wilson 2003a, *Overcoming the hurdle*

TABLE 4.8 Default/leverage effects

Business	European						US/UK					
	Beta			P/E Multiple			Beta			P/E Multiple		
	AAA	AA-	A	AAA	AA-	A	A	AA-	A	AAA	AA-	A
Retail	1.03	1.11	1.31	25.1	22.7	18.4	1.01	1.09	1.29	25.8	23.3	18.8
Commercial	1.20	1.30	1.52	20.5	18.7	15.2	1.53	1.64	1.94	15.2	13.9	11.5
Asset Mgmt	1.19	1.29	1.51	20.7	18.8	15.4	1.49	1.61	1.9	15.6	14.3	11.8
Life insurance	0.98	1.05	1.24	27.2	24.5	19.8	0.87	0.94	1.1	32.1	28.8	23.1
P&C insurance	1.01	1.09	1.29	25.8	23.3	18.9	0.96	1.04	1.22	27.7	25.0	20.2
Equity I-banking	1.68	1.81	2.13	13.6	12.4	10.3	3.77	4.07	4.78	5.5	5.0	4.2
Fixed income I-banking	1.26	1.35	1.59	19.4	17.7	14.5	1.71	1.85	2.17	13.2	12.1	10.0

Underlying assumptions for the table: risk free = 3.5%, risk premium = 5.5%, growth = 4%

Source: Wilson, 2003a, *Overcoming the hurdle*

TABLE 4.9 Impact of idiosyncratic risk

| | Avg Idiosyncratic risk | | | Avg R-squared - 1.65sd | | | |
Representative firm	Leveraged beta	Cost of Capital	P/E Multiple	Leveraged Beta	Cost of Capital	P/E Multiple	P/E diff
Regional bank	1.26	10.4%	19.32	1.24	10.3%	19.73	2.1%
Multiline insurance	1.07	9.4%	24.06	1.05	9.3%	24.51	1.9%
Investment bank	2.58	17.7%	8.27	2.49	17.2%	8.59	3.8%
Universal bank	1.51	11.8%	15.44	1.48	11.6%	15.81	2.4%
Diversified financial services firm	1.56	12.1%	14.81	1.53	11.9%	15.17	2.5%

Underlying assumptions for the table: risk free = 3.5%, risk premium = 5.5%, growth = 4%
Source: Wilson, 2003a, *Overcoming the hurdle*

strength rating.[9] A.M. Best (2006) also includes diversification as an important criterion when evaluating an insurance company's ability to leverage.

The Results

Wilson (2003a) developed a model that can be empirically estimated based on Merton (1974) and Crouhy *et al.* (1999), recognizing business mix, leverage and idiosyncratic risk effects. The following results are based on that model using data from 1995–2003.

Using a Common Cost of Capital Can Lead to Bad Decisions Table 4.7 (p. 66) gives an indication of how large an impact using a constant cost of capital can have. It lists the levered beta, cost of capital and theoretical P/E multiple for representative AA-rated firms and their standalone businesses.[10]

For example, a double-A, US regional bank with a 60%/40% split between retail and commercial banking would have had an average beta of 1.26, a cost of capital of 10.4% and an implied P/E multiple of 19×. Note, however, that these averages hide the fact that shareholders expect a much lower cost of capital for the retail versus the commercial bank (e.g., 9.3% vs. 12.2%), and therefore a much higher implied P/E multiple. This 3% difference in the cost of capital for the retail versus commercial bank implied a 10 point difference in implied P/E multiples (e.g., 24.6 vs. 14.6)! Clearly, using the corporate average cost of capital to evaluate both businesses would have led the firm to over-invest in commercial banking and under-invest in retail banking.

This is because the differences are compounded for market multiples, where we used the steady-state P/E multiple, derived in a later chapter, and given by $P/E = d/(\text{CoC} - g)$, where d is the dividend rate and g is the growth rate. Focusing on the denominator, a small error in the cost of capital leads to a large change in the implied P/E multiple as it is used to discount all future dividends. This, in turn, leads to a dramatic difference in relative valuations.

Impact of Leverage or Default Effect Holding the business mix constant, how important is financial leverage or rating? In Table 4.8 (p. 67), the difference in P/E between AAA- and A-European retail banking operations was 6.7 points (e.g., 25.1 − 18.4) due to the AAA's lower beta. In other words, the market expects lower absolute returns from more highly rated companies.

Impact of Idiosyncratic Risk After adjusting for the differentiated cost of capital and leverage effects, how much more impact will managing idiosyncratic risk have on the firm's value? In other words, does further diversification help in lowering the company's cost of capital? Not much, it turns out.

Comparing the P/E multiples in Table 4.9 (p. 68), the benefit from reducing idiosyncratic risk from an average level to 1.65 standard deviations below the average translates to less than

---

[9]Other important criteria recognized by Standard & Poor's include economic risk, industry risk, market position, management and strategy, credit risk, market risk, funding and liquidity, capitalization, earnings, risk management and financial flexibility.

[10]Where the levered betas are determined by the estimated relationships in Figure 5 of the original article, the cost of capital is determined by the SML (e.g., $R_E = R_f + \beta R_p$ with ($R_f = 3.5\%, R_p = 5.5\%$)), and the P/E multiple calculated using $P/E = d/(\text{CoC} - g)$ with a growth rate of 5%.

0.5 points in the P/E multiple, with higher systematic risk firms benefiting more. Clearly, this is not meaningful from a corporate strategy perspective, and is probably due to the fact that each institution in the sample is already a highly diversified, globally active financial institution. In other words, diversification for diversification's sake does not bring much value in terms of lowering the firm's cost of capital.

CHAPTER 5

Valuing Financial
Services – The Theory

The last two chapters made the case that Business RAPMs are not generally used for strategic decision making, in large part due to the lack of a clear link with share value, and that they often do not make theoretical sense, especially in the way that capital and the cost of capital are measured. Both issues can lead to wrong decisions, including over-investing in value-destroying businesses and under-investing in businesses which create value.

Counterbalancing these criticisms is the observation that New Business RAPMs continue to have a substantial tactical impact on some firms' pricing and underwriting decisions and that both New Business and Investment RAPMs are directly linked to shareholder value.

This leads to an obvious question. Can we integrate New Business and Investment RAPMs into a valuation framework that makes sense for banks and insurers, with a direct link to shareholder value? The answer is yes, if we go back to fundamentals.

WHAT DETERMINES SHARE VALUE? MARKET MULTIPLES, RoE AND GROWTH . . .

As Figure 5.1 illustrates, the difference between Total Shareholder Return (TSR) of top-quartile and bottom-quartile firms can be substantial. During the period from 1995 to 2002, the top quartile of the largest 50 banks in the USA managed to quadruple their market value in a little over 5 years, while the bottom-performing firm did not even double its market value over the same period.

What drives the differences between the top and bottom quartile? As illustrated in Figure 5.2, it is tautological that there are only three factors which determine a firm's market capitalization if it funds growth out of retained earnings.

- The RoE, which determines how much book equity can potentially grow through retained earnings.
- The dividend rate,[1] which determines how much of the return is retained and reinvested in the business and how much is returned to shareholders.

---

[1]For simplicity, we ignore share buybacks which play a similar role in determining the evolution of retained earnings. The differences between regular dividends, special dividends and share buybacks is discussed in Chapter 13.

Different Performance

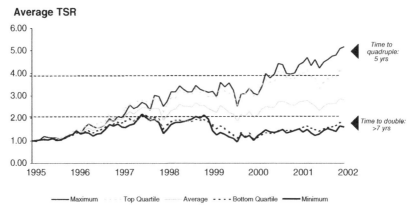

FIGURE 5.1   US bank TSR, 1995–2002

▪ The M/B multiple, which gives the "price" (premium or discount) the market is willing to pay for the book equity invested in the company.

Consider a firm which has a 12% RoE and a dividend rate of 33%. This implies that retained earnings are growing and reinvested at a rate of 8% per annum. If the reinvested earnings are valued at an M/B multiple of 1.0×, then the company would double its value in a little over 10 years. If the company enjoyed a 1.5× M/B multiple, then the share price would double in a little over 8 years; the reason being that each increment to retained earnings reinvested in the company is valued at 1.5× as opposed to 1.0×. If the company is earning and reinvesting even more retained earnings (e.g., in the case of a 15% RoE), then it would double its share value in an even shorter amount of time (e.g., in a little over 6 years).

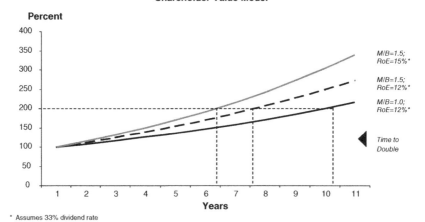

Source: Wilson (2004)

FIGURE 5.2   Role of RoE, M/B and dividend rate

This is a useful exercise because it highlights the major drivers of total shareholder return: *invested capital, the return on that capital, its reinvestment or growth rate* and *the multiple the market is willing to pay for capital invested in the business.*

Most have a clear understanding of the drivers of RoE and growth. Less clear is what drives the firm's M/B multiple. Logically, the valuation "lift" implied by a 1.5× M/B multiple is also driven by returns and growth, and these are in turn driven by operating efficiency, underwriting effectiveness and capital efficiency. Unfortunately, these fundamentals of the firms' economics are "hidden" in the M/B multiple.

If we are to develop a coherent and practical framework for managing value, we must first understand the connection between a firm's M/B multiple and the fundamental economic drivers (e.g., cost efficiency, underwriting performance and capital KPIs), in addition to growth.

Understanding this link is even more critical in today's "new normal" (Gross, 2009): generations of managers have grown up to expect growth as the norm, as firmly engrained as the dauphin's expectation of his birthright. Unfortunately, the new reality may be less accommodating due to a wide variety of unfavorable headwinds: the deleveraging of consumer, bank, government and trade account balance sheets; government fiscal and monetary policy "crowding out" productive investment; deglobalization of trade patterns; increased regulation, to name but a few.

All these changes lead me to believe that, if we are looking to grow our share price, we may find more potential in a multiple expansion through operating efficiency, underwriting effectiveness and capital efficiency than through the historical focus on growth, especially for those with businesses more firmly entrenched in mature markets.

. . . BUT WHAT DETERMINES MARKET MULTIPLES?

There is a vast corporate finance literature dedicated to valuing industrial corporations,[2] but less on valuing banks and insurers due to their unique characteristics and complexities. All of the approaches calculate the present value of future cash flows distributable to shareholders (or the financiers of the firm), including those from both the existing portfolio and from new business. They differ only in terms of their accounting basis. The different approaches fall into four broad categories.

- *Accounting approaches.* These project accounting-based measures of earnings, capital and returns to derive future dividend streams and then discount these back to today's present value using an appropriate cost of capital. The starting point for the projection is the accounting or book value of equity.
- *Distributable Free Cash Flow (DFCF) approaches.* These follow the "Cash is King!" mantra. They begin by reformulating accounting earnings and balance sheets to track the free cash flows which can be distributed to the financiers (typically, debt and equity holders) of the firm. These are then discounted at an appropriate weighted average cost of capital.[3] The starting point for the projection is the *adjusted* book value of equity.

---

[2]See Appendix B for a summary.

[3]For those in the LH insurance industry, this is equivalent to an embedded value approach to valuing the current portfolio. See Chapter 7 for a discussion.

TABLE 5.1   Comparison of valuation approaches

		Starting capital	Excess returns from existing portfolio	Excess returns from future business
Approach	Value	Closed-block, going-concern value		"Franchise value"
Accounting	$V =$	E_0+	$\displaystyle\sum_{t=1}^{\infty} \frac{E_t^{EP}\left(\text{RoE}_t^{EP} - \text{CoE}\right)}{(1 + \text{CoE})^t} +$	$\displaystyle\sum_{t=1}^{\infty} \frac{E_t^{NB}\left(\text{RoE}_t^{NB} - \text{CoE}\right)}{(1 + \text{CoE})^t}$
DFCF	$V =$	IC_0+	$\displaystyle\sum_{t=1}^{\infty} \frac{\text{IC}_t^{EP}\left(\text{RoIC}_t^{EP} - \text{CoIC}\right)}{(1 + \text{CoIC})^t} +$	$\displaystyle\sum_{t=1}^{\infty} \frac{\text{IC}_t^{NB}\left(\text{RoIC}_t^{NB} - \text{CoIC}\right)}{(1 + \text{CoIC})^t}$
Business RAPM	$V =$	EC_0+	$\displaystyle\sum_{t=1}^{\infty} \frac{\text{EC}_t^{EP}\left(\text{RoEC}_t^{EP} - \text{CoEC}\right)}{(1 + \text{CoEC})^t} +$	$\displaystyle\sum_{t=1}^{\infty} \frac{\text{EC}_t^{NB}\left(\text{RoEC}_t^{NB} - \text{CoEC}\right)}{(1 + \text{CoEC})^t}$
Market-consistent	$V =$	MVS_0+		$\displaystyle\sum_{t=1}^{\infty} \frac{\text{MVS}_t^{NB}\left(\text{RoMVS}_t^{NB} - \text{CoMVS}\right)}{(1 + \text{CoMVS})^t}$

- *Market-consistent approaches.* These adjust both earnings and balance sheets to a mark-to-market basis.[4] The starting point for the projection is the current market value surplus or net asset value.
- *Business RAPM approaches.* These are not as widely discussed in the valuation literature. They are based on economic capital as the measure of invested capital and can be derived in an analogous manner as the three more common valuation approaches mentioned above.

Under certain conditions,[5] the different approaches yield valuation formulae which are comparable in structure but different in implementation, as illustrated in Table 5.1.

In Table 5.1, the starting capital and excess returns are measured on a comparable basis – for example, E = accounting book value of equity, IC = adjusted book value (removing goodwill and other intangibles, including pension obligations, etc.), EC = "debt holder's" version of economic capital driven by the risk of the business and MVS = Market Value Surplus, equal to the mark-to-market value of existing assets and liabilities.

From Discounted Free Cash Flows to Theoretical Market Multiples

Each of the valuation formulae reduce to a familiar form if one is willing to assume a steady state (e.g., constant expected return on capital, dividend rate, growth rate and cost of capital)

---

[4]For those in the LH insurance industry, this is equivalent to the CFO Forum's original market-consistent embedded value approach to valuing the current portfolio. See Chapter 7 for a discussion.

[5]One condition is that anything which impacts the balance sheet under each approach first has to go through the income statement consistent with that approach. This assumption is violated by other comprehensive income, to the extent that it impacts shareholder equity without going through the income statement. The second condition is that dividends are based on whatever measure of period income is used, for example accounting income under the accounting approach, mark-to-market income under the market-consistent approach, etc.

TABLE 5.2 Generic "M/B" formulae following different valuation approaches

Approach	Theoretical "M/B"	Starting capital	Excess returns from existing portfolio and new business
Accounting	$\dfrac{V}{E_0} =$	$1+$	$\dfrac{(\text{RoE} - \text{CoE})}{(\text{CoE} - g_E)}$
DFCF	$\dfrac{V}{\text{IC}_0} =$	$1+$	$\dfrac{(\text{RoIC} - \text{CoIC})}{(\text{CoIC} - g_{IC})}$
Business RAPM	$\dfrac{V}{\text{EC}_0} =$	$1+$	$\dfrac{(\text{RoEC} - \text{CoEC})}{(\text{CoEC} - g_{EC})}$
Market-consistent	$V =$	MVS_0+	$\dfrac{(\text{new business EP} + \text{investment EP})}{(\text{CoEC} - g_{EP})}$

and if the expected excess returns from new business and the existing portfolio are added together. Using the accounting metric as an example, the steady state M/B multiple can be written as follows.[6]

EQUATION 5.1: Accounting M/B multiple

$$\frac{V}{E_0} = 1 + \frac{(\text{RoE} - \text{CoE})}{(\text{CoE} - g_E)}$$

where RoE and CoE are the steady-state expected return on equity and cost of equity, respectively, and g_E is the steady-state growth in shareholder's equity (equal to $\text{RoE}(1 - d)$, where d is the dividend rate). Intuitively, the formula suggests that the market value of the firm is equal to its current book equity plus the growing perpetuity of excess returns generated by reinvesting returns net of dividends to grow the business.

Under steady-state assumptions, the valuation formulae are transformed into similar M/B multiples, as illustrated in Table 5.2.

Why M/B is a Better Multiple to Focus on Than P/E

Each of these identities can also be used to derive a steady-state P/E multiple, again in a similar form. Using the accounting basis as an example, the P/E multiple can be written as follows.

EQUATION 5.2: Accounting P/E multiple

$$P = \frac{Ea \times d}{(\text{CoE} - g_E)} \text{ or } \frac{P}{Ea} = \frac{d}{(\text{CoE} - g_E)}$$

---

[6]We have used the fact that the present value of a growing perpetuity paying $c(1 + g)^t$ at period t, where g is the rate of growth and r is the discount rate, is equal to $\sum c(1 + g)^t/(1 + r)^t = c/(r - g)$ so long as $r > g$.

where *Ea* are the accounting earnings and *d* is the rate at which dividends are paid out of accounting earnings. The interpretation is also straightforward: the theoretical price of a share is equal to the present value of its growing dividend stream, the cash ultimately distributed to the shareholder.

Comparing the M/B and P/E multiples, the P/E multiple would appear to be the easier to use for management: there are not as many moving parts and what few moving parts there are tell a simple story – higher earnings, higher value. While this is true, *unfortunately, the P/E multiple focuses on earnings and ignores the capital required to generate the earnings (except implicitly through the dividend rate). More specifically, the P/E multiple does not tell whether the marginal capital invested for growth creates or destroys value by generating earnings in excess of the risk-adjusted cost of capital.*

To see this, consider a €10 marginal capital investment which yields only 0.01% return. The P/E multiple formulae would say that the share price should increase by the present value of a growing perpetuity cash flow equal to €10 × 0.01% × *d* (representing the investment, the return on investment and the dividend rate). Assuming a 100% dividend rate for the marginal investment (and therefore no further incremental growth) and a 10% CoE, the increase in share value would be €0.01. Under the P/E multiple approach, higher earnings do indeed lead to a higher share value.

Unfortunately, shareholders have put up an additional €10 worth of capital in the business, capital which could also have been distributed directly to shareholders. Put simply, shareholders traded €10 in cash they could have received for an investment worth only €0.01. This is clearly not a good deal.

The P/E multiple focuses on earnings only, correctly suggesting that value increases as earnings increase, but unfortunately ignoring the capital required. The fact is that the P/E multiple is opaque with respect to risk, capital investment and capital efficiency considerations. This is a fatal flaw which prevents P/E multiples from being a useful "shorthand" for managing the value of a financial services company.

The Theory Works in Practice . . .

According to the theory, shareholders should place a premium on firms with superior operating performance and capital efficiency, using the RoE as a surrogate, as well as profitable growth opportunities. Casual empirical evidence supports this view. In Figure 5.3, the relationship between M/B and RoE represented by the regression line in the figure has above 60% adjusted R^2 (a measure of the goodness of fit between the data and the regression line).

This observation is supported generally. For example, in the author's previous study,[7] the correlations between M/B ratios and analysts' expected RoE and growth were 57% and 43%, respectively. Table 5.3 summarizes the results of regressing M/B ratios with the firms' rolling average 3-year RoE and IBES growth estimates as explanatory variables using the underlying data in Wilson (2003a).

The regressions "explain" a significant amount of the variability in M/B multiples across the firms in the sample: about 85% for the combined bank and insurance samples and for the banks alone and 79% for insurers alone. Furthermore, all the coefficients have the anticipated sign and all are statistically significant at a confidence level greater than 95%. Looking at the

---

[7]Based on research conducted for Wilson (2003a), for a cross-sectional, time series panel of over 40 banks and insurers.

What drives value?

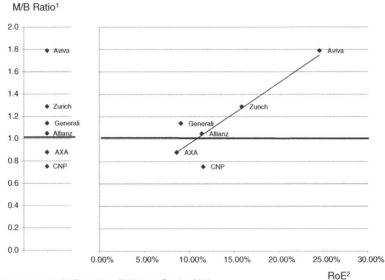

Author's analysis, (1) Bloomberg, (2) Ycharts, October 2014

FIGURE 5.3 What drives value?

TABLE 5.3 Linear M/B regressions – banks and insurers

$$\frac{M}{B}_{i,t} = \beta_0 + \beta_1 \mathrm{ROE}_{i,t} + \beta_2 g_{i,t} + \varepsilon_{i,t}$$

M/B multiple	Adjusted-R^2 (F-statistic)	Constant β_0	RoE β_1	Growth β_2
All firms	84.5% (60.64 ***)	−0.39 (−0.37)	16.84 (1.81 ***)	5.76 (0.79 ***)
Banks only	85.4% (67.37 ***)	−1.08 (−0.42 **)	19.16 (2.07 ***)	6.57 (0.87 ***)
Insurers only	78.9% (4.36**)	1.33 (0.77*)	10.97 (3.72**)	3.13 (1.89*)

*Significant at the 95% level.
**Significant at the 99% level.
***Significant at the 99.9% level.

results, it is fair to conclude that a firm's fundamentals, at least in terms of RoE and growth, go a long way toward explaining its valuation multiple.

WHY A MARKET-CONSISTENT APPROACH?

The four different approaches yield remarkably similar M/B ratios, at this level leading to observations equally relevant for an automobile manufacturer, a fast food restaurant or a financial services firm. But there are two important reasons why using a market-consistent approach is better when valuing financial services firms.

First, because *market-consistent approaches produce values better aligned with actual share price developments*. If we aspire to manage shareholder value, then we need a framework which explains share value and the market-consistent framework is the best for this purpose. Chapter 6 is devoted exclusively to supporting this claim.

Second, because *market-consistent frameworks are better aligned with the economics of banks and insurers, especially recognizing the role of risk and capital, and therefore bring more useful management insights*. More specifically, market-consistent valuation approaches:

- deliver the theoretical market value surplus directly, without the need to project and discount earnings from the existing book of business;
- use New Business RAPMs and Investment RAPMs directly to measure the value contribution of new business.

Better Alignment, Value of Existing Portfolio

The first benefit of using a market-consistent approach is in valuing the existing portfolio of assets and liabilities. Table 5.4 is an excerpt from Table 5.1 which excludes future business and focuses only on valuing the firm's existing assets and liabilities from a closed-block, going-concern approach (e.g., including reasonable expenses for the maintenance and administration of the portfolio).

You will notice that I inserted an additional line into the table, the line labeled "Identity." Why? Because if each approach is correctly calibrated and applied then all four of the approaches should in principle give the same value for the existing book of business. This unique value, the one that we are looking for, is the market value surplus by definition.

All approaches should give the same value, the MVS. The market-consistent approach gives it directly; unfortunately, the other approaches do not because they use different capital measures – book equity, adjusted book equity, economic or risk capital – and have to project and discount different "excess returns" to balance out the difference from MVS.

TABLE 5.4 Equivalence between going-concern values

Approach	Starting Capital	Excess returns from existing portfolio
		Closed block, going-concern value
Accounting	E_0+	$\sum_{t=1}^{\infty} \dfrac{E_t^{EP}\left(\text{RoE}_t^{EP} - \text{CoE}\right)}{(1+\text{CoE})^t}$
DFCF	IC_0+	$\sum_{t=1}^{\infty} \dfrac{\text{IC}_t^{EP}\left(\text{RoIC}_t^{EP} - \text{CoIC}\right)}{(1+\text{CoIC})^t}$
RAPM	EC_0+	$\sum_{t=1}^{\infty} \dfrac{\text{EC}_t^{EP}\left(\text{RoEC}_t^{EP} - \text{CoEC}\right)}{(1+\text{CoEC})^t}$
Identity	$=$	
Market-consistent	MVS_0	

Discounting excess returns using accounting or distributable free cash flow approaches and a constant cost of capital will *not* deliver the mark-to-market value of the firm's current assets and liabilities. Equivalence can only be achieved if you calculate the MVS first and then set the cost of capital by back-solving for the "right" answer (see Sidebar 5.1). Given the identity, why would you go through the effort if you can calculate the MVS directly?

SIDEBAR 5.1: ON THE EQUIVALENCE OF THE APPROACHES

Each of the approaches gives the same MVS in principle, but only if the "appropriate," unique cost of capital or discount rate is used. This equivalence is illustrated in a practical manner by the CFO Forum's European- and Market-Consistent-Embedded Value principles (EEV and MCEV).

In 2004, the CFO Forum introduced its EEV Principles defining a DFCF approach based on management's best-estimate cash flows and a risk discount rate set typically at the firm's cost of capital (CFO Forum, 2004a). EEV was criticized because it depended on management's expectations, implying that the results could not be compared across firms; because management's expectations with respect to future investment returns were often optimistic, resulting in aggressive valuations; and because EEV did not even correctly value simpler products such as bonds or equities (the "1=1" test), let alone the complex embedded options and guarantees of LH products. As a consequence, in 2009 the CFO Forum introduced its MCEV Principles, a market-consistent approach, for the existing business (CFO Forum, 2009).

The EEV and MCEV approaches can be aligned in principle by selecting the appropriate cost of capital used to calculate EEV. The unique cost of capital which aligns EEV and MCEV is called the Implied Discount Rate (IDR). For example: "In the valuation of a block of business, the implied discount rate (IDR) is the rate of discount such that a traditional embedded value for the business equates to the MCEV." The IDR is determined by *back-solving* for the "appropriate" discount rate such that the EEV/DFCF value is equal to the MCEV value. Since the DFCF value depends on management's expectations and the financial characteristics of the business, each sub-portfolio (and, in fact, each individual bond and equity and insurance line of business) will generally have a different IDR. Finding the unique, correct IDR has to be done by calculating MCEV for the portfolio of interest and then back-solving such that the EEV and MCEV are aligned.

Better Alignment with New Business, or "RAPM Revisited"

The second benefit is in measuring the contribution of new business and financial market risks. This is seemingly a complex calculation under all approaches, leading to a complex formula as the excerpted section in Table 5.5 of the previous tables illustrates.

While seemingly complex, the numerator of the market-consistent franchise value reduces to a much simpler form. This is because, in the market-consistent framework, the expected risk-adjusted contribution of each new loan or policy is recognized on the day that it is written, implying that the value is fully recognized in that year with no trailing effects into future years.

TABLE 5.5 Measuring contribution of new business and financial market risk

Approach	Theoretical "M/B"	Starting capital	Excess returns from existing portfolio and new business
Market-consistent	$V =$	$MVS_0 +$	$\displaystyle\sum_{t=1}^{\infty} \frac{MVS_t^{NB}\left(RoMVS_t^{NB} - CoMVS\right)}{(1 + CoMVS)^t}$
Market-consistent	$V =$	$MVS_0 +$	$\dfrac{(\text{new business EP} + \text{investment EP})}{(CoEC - g_{EP})}$

In addition, the franchise value is measured on a risk-adjusted basis split between new business EP and investment "alpha," only possible because each is measured relative to its own, unique cost of capital, as argued in earlier chapters.

The new business franchise value reduces to the future new business contributions measured using New Business RAPM and Investment RAPM – but only if the appropriate (and differentiated) cost of capital is used to evaluate new business and investment alpha!

Recognizing the value of new business when it is underwritten is a tremendous benefit in terms of both calculations and transparency. These models are complex enough without having to carry a long tail of "emerging profits" from each year of new business which is exactly what happens for all other approaches except for the Market Consistent approach. For example, the accounting approach will have loan and insurance policy "excess contributions" emerge over the product's lifetime as a stream of accounting earnings, as opposed to recognizing the value of new business on the day that it is underwritten.

VALUE: WHERE IT COMES FROM AND HOW TO CREATE MORE OF IT

The market-consistent approach suggests an intuitive way to think about a bank or insurance company's value, as the sum of two components – highlighted in Figure 5.4.

- *Net asset value of the existing portfolio*, representing the accumulated value that shareholders have "invested" in the firm from prior years' business.
- *Value created from future new business*, often called the franchise value, determined by the *new business contribution* of future products and growth measured using New Business RAPM and Investment RAPM.

Increasing Value Through Multiple Expansion

This result is intuitive . . . but not very helpful. The following question is still open. *How can we increase the value of our company?* The market-consistent approach reinforces the message of this section, that a firm's market capitalization can grow through only one of two channels:

- *either* the net asset value of the firm grows, trivially accomplished through retained earnings;
- *or* the premium that the market is willing to pay for the current net asset value increases, leading to a re-rating of the company's multiple.

1. Better Information – What gets measured, gets managed

How to measure value in risk-based, capital-intensive businesses?

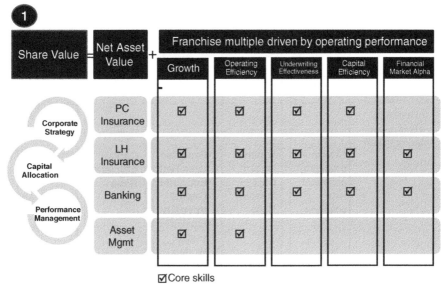

FIGURE 5.4 Better information

In a market-consistent framework, a multiple greater than 1 is driven entirely by the *prospect of profitable new business measured on a risk-adjusted basis relative to the risk-appropriate costs of capital or by lowering the firm's cost of capital.* If the current portfolio is valued correctly, future earnings from existing assets and liabilities are just appropriate for their risk profile: as such, you can expect *earnings* to emerge from the existing portfolio but not *value*, which warrants an immediate re-rating of the share price. Both the prospect of profitable new business relative to the firm's cost of capital and lowering the firm's cost of capital can drive a market value multiple greater than 1×.

Re-rating the firm's multiple is not an easy task and it does not happen overnight. Part of the challenge is that it takes fundamental improvements in the company's growth prospects, operating performance and/or capital efficiency. The other challenge is that a higher multiple today is by definition based on value which is delivered in the future. In order to re-rate the share price today, management needs not only to make promises about the future, but also to back these up with a strong track record of delivering on the promises.

Operating Value Levers and KPIs

Figure 5.5 illustrates that there are five levers for getting a multiple expansion: four operating levers – *operating efficiency, underwriting effectiveness, capital efficiency* and *profitable growth* – and one non-operating lever – *investment alpha*. Why these drivers and not some others? Because these value drivers not only make intuitive sense, but they are also aligned with the theoretical valuation framework. This link was first introduced in Chapter 3 and is illustrated in Figure 5.5.

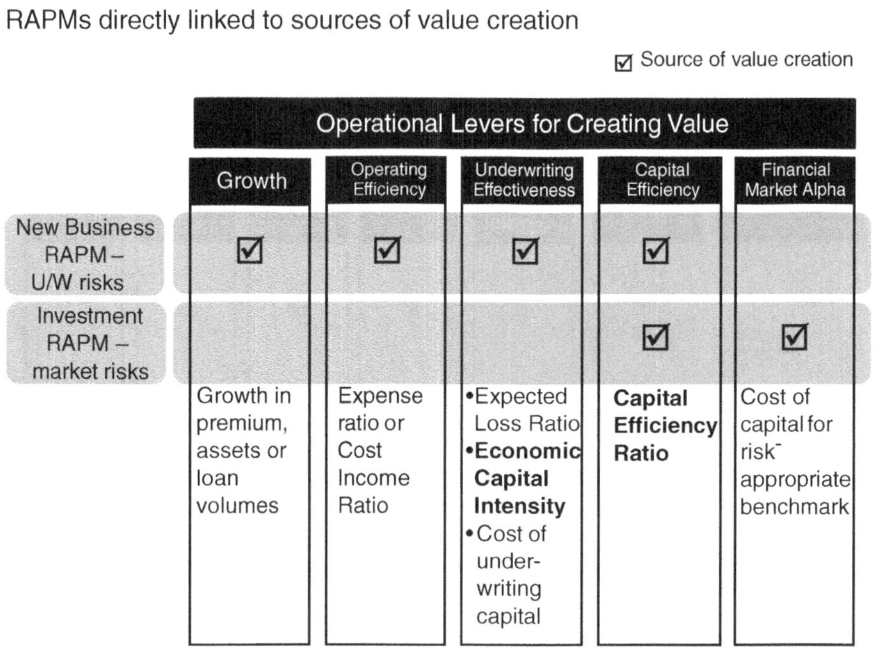

RAPMs directly linked to sources of value creation

☑ Source of value creation

Operational Levers for Creating Value				
Growth	Operating Efficiency	Underwriting Effectiveness	Capital Efficiency	Financial Market Alpha

	Growth	Operating Efficiency	Underwriting Effectiveness	Capital Efficiency	Financial Market Alpha
New Business RAPM – U/W risks	☑	☑	☑	☑	
Investment RAPM – market risks				☑	☑
	Growth in premium, assets or loan volumes	Expense ratio or Cost Income Ratio	•Expected Loss Ratio •**Economic Capital Intensity** •Cost of under-writing capital	**Capital Efficiency Ratio**	Cost of capital for risk⁻ appropriate benchmark

FIGURE 5.5   Operating levers for value creation

Profitable Growth

This is the one area which probably does not need definition or motivation: it is generally accepted that growth is one of the most powerful drivers behind a firm's valuation multiple.

Unfortunately, what is occasionally left out of this statement is the word *profitable* – revenue growth from businesses which do not return their cost of capital on a sustainable basis destroys value, even if it does increase earnings. The better alternative to investment in economically unprofitable new business is to return the capital to shareholders.

Operating Efficiency: Expense Ratio, Cost Income Ratio

Following industry practice, *operating efficiency* is *measured by operating expenses divided by the level of operating revenue or income*. The result is a metric measuring how much it costs on average to generate a dollar of revenue or operating income.

The exact measures differ by industry. For example, in PC insurance, operating efficiency is measured by the *expense ratio*, defined as the ratio of operating expenses to net earned premium. In banking and asset management, it is measured by the *cost income ratio*, or the ratio of operating expenses to operating income.

All else being equal, the lower the expense ratio, the better. Improvements in operating efficiency not only impact the value of new business but also the value of the in-force portfolio by lowering the effective expense margin applicable to the business on a going concern basis.

Underwriting Effectiveness: Total Cost of Risk

Although there is no standard practice, we define *underwriting effectiveness* as *the ratio of the TCR divided by revenues or operating income*. This is a measure of how much risk cost is borne on average to generate a dollar of revenue or net income. As discussed in Chapter 3, the TCR comprises two elements: *expected losses* and *a charge for capital based on the capital intensity of the portfolio*.

Expected Losses   Risk underwriting is all about taking the right risk at the right price. All else being equal, lower expected losses imply a higher risk-adjusted margin. *Expected losses* are a good starting point for defining underwriting efficiency because they recognize and reward the ability to select lower risks from a pool of otherwise identical borrowers or policy holders.

Economic Capital Intensity   However, expected losses are only one component: we also need to include some measure for *unexpected losses*, for example stemming from low-frequency but high-severity natural catastrophes or the systemic impact of a recession on loan losses. If we judge underwriting efficiency based only on expected losses, we give the incentive to write out-of-the-money credit default options or high-attachment, excess-loss insurance policies. This strategy would yield lower expected losses, but at a much higher relative capital intensity per unit of premium due to the remote but severe loss potential.

Economic Capital Intensity (ECI), defined as the minimum capital required to be held over the lifetime of the commitment per unit of revenue or income, is the second component needed to measure underwriting effectiveness.

ECI is defined by segment. For PC insurance, ECI is calculated as the present value of minimum required capital over the lifetime of the new business divided by the net earned premium for the new business, that is, $\text{ECI}_{uw} = \text{PVRC}_{uw}/P$. ECI measures the minimum amount of underwriting risk capital tied up, from inception until the transaction runs off the book, per unit of premium earned. Underwriting effectiveness for PC insurance is defined as the sum of expected losses and the cost of capital to cover unexpected losses, that is, $\text{CR}_{pv} + rp_{uw} \times \text{ECI}_{uw}$, where CR_{pv} is the discounted claims ratio.

For lending businesses, underwriting efficiency is defined in a similar manner, that is, the discounted value of the expected losses plus the cost of the minimum capital needed to cover unexpected losses, measured in terms of the loan portfolio's ECI:

$$\text{Underwriting efficiency} = \left[\text{PV(EL)} + rp_{uw} \times \text{PVRC}_{uw}\right]/L = \text{PV(EL)}/L + rp_{uw} \times \text{ECI}_{uw}$$

ECI recognizes that capital is tied up over the entire life of the transaction, rather than looking only at the capital required over a single period. ECI provides better steering impulses for long-term businesses: once the capital is bound, for example in long-term LH retirement and savings products or illiquid structured finance loans, it cannot be reallocated or used to support other lines of business. ECI helps support better capital management by making transparent not only the capital needed to be held today but also the capital committed in the future.

Capital Efficiency

Capital management can strongly influence the value of the firm through two channels: first, by minimizing the quantum of capital required to support the same business (e.g. improving capital efficiency) and, second, by minimizing the weighted average cost of capital.

Capital efficiency is defined as *the ratio of capital actually held to the theoretical minimum capital required.* The theoretical minimum capital required for underwriting businesses is defined by their ECI. The CER is the *actual* capital held divided by the minimum capital requirement; in general, CER > 1. The two multiplied together give the actual capital held over the life of the transaction or portfolio per unit of premium or loan value.

Effective capital management attempts to minimize CER and bring it closer to 1. However, it may be impossible to bring CER $= 1$. For example, local regulatory reserve and capital requirements may be uneconomic, resulting in an unwarranted degree of prudence, or there may be restrictions which prevent the full recognition of diversification across an international group, effectively locking excess capital in local operating units. Alternatively, the firm may choose to hold additional capital based on their risk appetite, preferring a more conservative and resilient capital structure. In any case, CER > 1 implies that more shareholder value is tied up in the business than the theoretical minimum warranted economically.

Effective capital management not only minimizes CER subject to external constraints and management's risk appetite, it also simultaneously minimizes the firm's weighted average cost of capital (WACC) within the same constraints. Financial leverage, comprising equity, hybrid capital, subordinated and senior debt issued by the parent company, is used to finance the capital invested in operating businesses. In general, WACC decreases as more hybrid, subordinated or senior debt is issued, giving management a valuable lever for managing the value of the firm.

Investment Alpha

Again, with no industry standards to rely on, we define investment alpha as the excess financial market returns from an asset/liability mismatch, investment or trading portfolio relative to a risk-appropriate comparable benchmark portfolio.

Financial market earnings come from a variety of sources, including the asset/liability mismatch portfolio, the portfolio of investment assets backing capital and from trading businesses. Value is created only if the earnings are in excess of what a passive investor can earn from a portfolio with similar risk characteristics.

It may be difficult to "beat the market" consistently unless there is something else about the business which provides the bank or insurer with a source of sustainable competitive advantage. Three potential sources of competitive advantage are often cited in the literature, including: better market or individual asset information, leading to better asset selection and/or timing; having a cheaper cost of funding, increasing the returns from carry for any trading inventory; and having a better customer trading franchise, capturing more customer fees and the bid–offer spread between buyers and sellers through market-making activities and tailored solutions which better meet the clients' needs. Chapter 16 outlines the debate on whether alpha exists and whether shareholders are likely to pay a premium for it.

Plus One

Multiple expansion through profitable new business is one way to increase share value. The other is to improve the value of your existing assets and liabilities. This is accomplished through operating actions which improve the going-concern value of the existing book, for example by improving cost efficiency (e.g., lowering payment, settlement or administration expenses, etc.); underwriting effectiveness (e.g., managing claims or loan workouts, behavioral scoring and customer relationship management, crediting strategies for LH traditional products); capital efficiency (e.g., through capital relief transactions lowering the quantum of required capital, optimizing the firm's financing structure lowering its WACC and better asset/liability management).

Trivially, market value surplus can also be increased by retaining earnings and "parking" the money in risk-free bonds or financial assets which do not generate excess returns, as opposed to operating businesses which potentially do generate excess returns. While this will increase the market value surplus and future expected earnings, shareholders would likely prefer a higher dividend pay-out ratio, especially if the company is already trading at a conglomerate discount.

CHAPTER 6

Valuing Financial Services – The Evidence

Market-consistent frameworks address the theoretical and practical challenges of valuing risk-based, capital-intensive businesses. In spite of this, they are not universally embraced.

Some in the industry characterize market-consistent valuations as "too volatile" and not reflective of the long-term economics of the business. But what if market-consistent approaches better reflect the way that our shares are actually valued? In this case, value managers who do not like either the volatility in the measures or in their share price should address the underlying business model rather than shoot the messenger.

Others blame mark-to-market accounting for procyclical behavior, such as the forced sale of assets or capital raising at distressed prices during a crisis. A contrary view is that forced actions are the result of poor capital and risk management practices: crises occur with amazing regularity, so why aren't we prepared? Again, rather than shooting the messenger, management should build a robust and resilient capital structure and risk appetite if it doesn't like being forced to take action during the next crisis.

This chapter presents compelling evidence that market-consistent approaches reflect actual share price developments far better than other, more stable accounting approaches. The implication for value managers? Don't shoot the messenger – read the message, understand what influences share value and manage accordingly.

EVIDENCE FROM THE INSURANCE INDUSTRY[1]

Is there evidence that market-consistent approaches better reflect share values than other approaches? The answer is clearly yes. This section begins with a review of the literature and then provides compelling evidence from the insurance sector.

---

[1]This section summarizes results from Wilson and Hristova (2014).

A Review of the Literature

There is a substantial literature concerning the value relevance of Embedded Value (EV) disclosures.[2] Information or disclosures are deemed to be *value relevant* if they have "a predicted significant relation with share prices . . . if the amount reflects information relevant to investors in valuing the firm and is measured reliably enough to be reflected in share prices" (Barth and Beaver, 2001).

One of the first studies to document the incremental value relevance of EV disclosures examined a sample of 10 UK life insurers and banks with life insurance operations in the period 2000 2004 (Horton, 2007), before market-consistent approaches were adopted, and concluded that EV disclosures were value relevant. The same conclusion was reached in the study of Almezweq and Liu (2012), which investigated nine British life insurers during the period pre- and post-mandatory adoption of IFRS in 2005 (from 2000 to 2009). It concluded that EV disclosures had informational content relevant to share valuation over and above statutory accounting information, even after the mandatory adoption of IFRS.

Value relevance has also been documented outside the UK. For example, Prefontaine *et al.* (2009, 2011) found that EV disclosures by Canadian life insurers in the period 2000–2008 provided information relevant to share price development.

A more recent study by El-Gazzar and Jacob (2013) covers the period 2000–2008 but considers a larger sample of 53 insurance companies from various countries, investigating whether EV represents a superior valuation metric relative to Earnings Per Share (EPS) and Book Value (BV). The results indicate that EV disclosures are more strongly correlated with share price developments and that they provide incremental information for assessing share price developments after controlling for EPS and BV. The results also suggest higher value relevance for UK insurers, where EV reporting has evolved into industry standard practice. This finding is in line with prior research, including Bartov *et al.* (2001).

Despite providing useful insights, the existing studies cover the period prior to the global financial crises of 2008 and 2012, which had significant influence on European insurers' EV disclosures; as such, they do not incorporate the most important events to test the question of whether EV approaches are "too volatile" relative to actual share price developments. More importantly, the literature does not address whether *market-consistent* measures specifically are value relevant compared with both the more stable accounting and traditional EV metrics.

The hypothesis that should be tested is whether Market-Consistent Embedded Value (MCEV) measures are "the best" metrics for explaining share price developments of insurers, in spite of (or because of) their inherent sensitivity to current market conditions. The null hypothesis, confirmed by the data, is that market-consistent approaches are in fact better. More specifically, we demonstrate the following.

1. Market-consistent approaches are better at reflecting the *absolute level* of share values and the *changes* in market value over time compared with more stable IFRS net asset values and European embedded values.
2. Reported market-consistent sensitivities (e.g., to equity indices and interest rate levels) provide valuable information in predicting future share price changes and explain a large amount of actual share price volatility.

---

[2]EV is a discounted free cash flow approach developed specifically for the insurance industry. Both EV and MCEV are described in detail in Chapter 7.

3. Attempts to dampen the volatility of market-consistent measures, for example using long-term assumptions under traditional embedded value approaches or including illiquidity premium, actually worsen the relationships, artificially driving a wedge between MCEV disclosures and share price developments.

Empirical Evidence: Event Study, 2008 Financial Crisis

Some might argue that the European insurance industry has "shot itself in the foot." By making market-consistent information available, we may have inadvertently influenced how the market values our shares. Put the other way around, banks and insurers might experience more stable valuations if we simply did not disclose market-consistent information!

This relies on the "ignorance is bliss" view of shareholders – the less they know, the better off they are. I personally believe that this argument is bunk. The period between 2007 and 2009 offers a unique opportunity to compare market-consistent valuation against more stable accounting approaches. As Figure 6.1 illustrates, the period was characterized by high volatility in equity markets, interest rates, credit spreads and implied market volatilities.

These market developments represented a "perfect storm" for LH retirement and savings businesses as declining equity markets reduced free surplus, lower interest rates put guarantees closer to the money and lowered implied reinvestment rates on asset/liability mismatch positions, higher bond spread levels reduced asset values relative to claims obligations and free surplus even further, and higher implied volatilities made embedded options and guarantees more expensive. Table 6.1 gives an overview of average valuation results for a sample of European insurers from year-end 2007 to year-end 2008.

How Did Firms Reporting MCEV Fare?

The first group of companies in Table 6.1 reported under the MCEV principles and includes Allianz, Aviva, AXA, Ergo, Swiss Life and Zurich Financial Services. The average decline in IFRS shareholder equity for these companies was −24% from year-end 2007 to year-end 2008. The change in IFRS equity is "less volatile" or more stable, below the average decrease in the disclosed MCEV values, −32%.

The average decrease in MCEV would have been closer to −40% without the application of the illiquidity premium (the so-called "clean" or adjusted MCEV). The illiquidity premium was applied for the first time by some of the firms in the industry in 2008 in order to counteract the harsh crisis market conditions. The introduction of the illiquidity premium helped to dampen the effects of financial market developments, as seen by comparing the average disclosed MCEV values with the estimated clean MCEV changes (e.g., −32% vs. −40%).

Of the different measures, the unadjusted or "clean" market-consistent values best reflected both the analysts' Sum of Parts (SoP) valuation (−50%) and the actual average share price development (−45.5%) for the firms from year-end 2007 to 2008.

How Did Firms Reporting More Stable EEV Fare?

The second set of firms, including Aegon, Generali and ING, reported under European EV (EEV) principles. EEV tends to be more stable and more flattering as it depends on management's long-term expectations of financial market returns as opposed to the harsh reality of crisis market conditions. In fact, the EEV figures (−13.3%) were much more stable and flattering than the actual change in IFRS equity (−28.6%). It was also substantially much, much more flattering than the average decline in analyst SoP valuations (−64.4%) and the actual average share price decline (−57.7%) for the companies in this group.

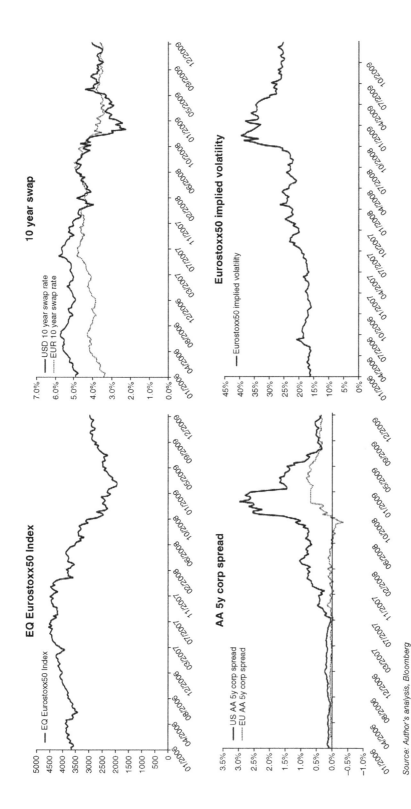

FIGURE 6.1 Financial market developments (2007–2009)

Source: Author's analysis, Bloomberg

TABLE 6.1   European insurance valuations (2007–2008)

	Metric	% Change, 2007–08	Comments
MCEV reporting companies: Allianz, Aviva, AXA, Ergo, Swiss Life, ZFS	Shareholder equity* MCEV*	−24.2% −32.0% −39.8%	"Clean" or adjusted MCEV estimated, w/o illiquidity premium used by AXA, Aviva
	SoP valuation** Share price change	−50.0% −45.5%	
EEV reporting companies: Aegon, Generali, ING	Shareholder equity* Traditional EEV*	−28.6% −13.3%	
	SoP valuation** Share price change	−64.4% −57.7%	
European insurance industry	Euro Stoxx insurance index***	−62.5%	

*Change in shareholder equity, MCEV and EEV based on annual disclosures, 2007 and 2008 year-end.
**Merrill Lynch, "Not out of the woods" (22 May 2008); "Pausing the roller coaster to look at valuations" (23 June 2009). Total firm SoP for AXA, Aegon, Aviva, Generali, ING, Swiss Life.
***Euro Stoxx insurance index level, average values, August 2008 to March 2009.
Source: Author's analysis.

This event study provides evidence supporting the hypothesis that equity markets generally "look through" more stable disclosure measures such as IFRS equity and EEV as well as attempts to stabilize MCEV measures (e.g., the inclusion of the illiquidity premium) and that disclosing MCEV information does not seem to "create" higher volatility in share prices (as the firms reporting under MCEV had a lower change in both average SoP valuation and share price).

Empirical Evidence: 2009–2013 Panel, Time Series Data[3]

The event study conclusions are also supported by broader panel and time series data of European insurance companies over the period 2009–2013. The following analysis compares three metrics – reported MCEV, "clean" or adjusted MCEV (i.e., without illiquidity premium) and IFRS Tangible Net Asset Value (TNAV)[4] – and asks which metric better reflects the way that the share prices actually developed.

The sample of insurers – Allianz, Aviva, Axa, CNP, Generali, Prudential plc and Zurich Financial Services – includes some of Europe's largest insurers and is thus broadly representative of the industry. All these firms are members of the CFO Forum and provided supplementary MCEV disclosures compliant with the CFO principles; all of them also report the illiquidity premium used and MCEV sensitivities, necessary for the calculation of a "clean" MCEV.

---

[3]This section summarizes the results of Wilson and Hristova (2014).
[4]TNAV represents IFRS equity less intangibles such as goodwill, from Bloomberg.

Two analyses are conducted. First, a *level test*, comparing the reported MCEV, "clean" MCEV and TNAV to see if one metric is consistently closer than the others to the firm's actual Market Capitalization (MC). The null hypothesis is that the "clean" MCEV is closer to the firm's market capitalization than either reported MCEV or TNAV values.

Second, a *roll-forward test*, comparing actual changes in market capitalization against changes in TNAV and predicted MCEV changes calculated using disclosed MCEV sensitivities and market developments. The null hypothesis is that MCEV roll-forward based on disclosed sensitivities better reflects share price changes, implying that MCEV sensitivities are highly relevant for both explaining and predicting a meaningful part of share price developments. Put the other way around, it suggests that share price volatility accurately reflects the underlying business and actual market changes as seen through a market-consistent lens – the higher the MCEV sensitivities or risk taken, the more the share price reacts to financial market developments.

The Level Test

Figure 6.2 illustrates the average MC as a percentage of reported MCEV and TNAV over the entire 5-year period for each company as well as an index of all companies calculated as a simple average.

The average index MC/MCEV ratio (91%) is much closer to 100% than the index MC/TNAV ratio (292%), implying that the firms in the sample traded on average at a slight discount to MCEV and a large premium to TNAV over this period. Inspection indicates MCEV better matches the MC for Allianz, Axa, CNP, Generali, Prudential and Zurich Financial Services over the period (e.g., average MC/MCEV is closer to 100%), with only Aviva being "better" represented by TNAV over the period.

The results may be misleading, however, as they represent averages over 5 years. In Table 6.2, the absolute differences are compared on an annual basis; there is a "check" in the table if MCEV is closer than TNAV to MC at year-end, which was the case in **80% of cases**. In other words, reported MCEV was a better predictor of share value than the more stable IFRS TNAV in 80% of cases.

In order to examine the value relevance of the illiquidity premium, the same comparison between the reported and the adjusted or "clean" MCEV values is undertaken. Figure 6.3 presents an overview of the average MC/MCEV and MC/adjusted MCEV ratios over the period.

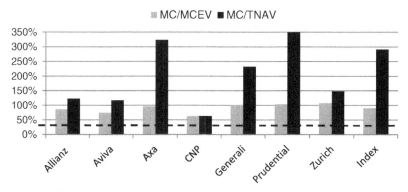

FIGURE 6.2 MC vs. MCEV and TNAV (average ratios for the period 2009–2013)
Source: Wilson and Hristova (2014)

TABLE 6.2   Comparison, MCEV vs. TNAV and MC

Company	2009	2010	2011	2012	2013
1. Allianz	✓	✓			✓
2. Aviva	✓			✓	✓
3. Axa	✓	✓	✓	✓	✓
4. CNP			✓	✓	
5. Generali	✓	✓	✓	✓	✓
6. Prudential	✓	✓	✓	✓	✓
7. Zurich	✓	✓	✓	✓	✓

✓ MCEV closer than TNAV to the MC of the firm at year-end.
Source: Wilson and Hristova (2014).

Looking at the figure, the average index MC/adjusted MCEV ratio (93%) is slightly closer to 100% than the corresponding average MC/MCEV index ratio (91%). Also interesting is that, in general, MCEV tends to be higher than the actual market capitalization, with the "clean" MCEV values being less flattering than reported MCEV values.

Analogous to the previous analysis, Table 6.3 compares the absolute differences between the two metrics and MC for each year. As the table shows, the "clean" MCEVs better reflect the firms' MC in **63% of observed cases**.

One interesting observation is that in 2009 the adjusted MCEV of almost all companies (except Generali) was closer to the MC than the unadjusted value. This was the year that the illiquidity premium was introduced by most companies in order to offset the dramatic increase in bond spreads observed during 2008 (with AXA and Aviva having already introduced the illiquidity premium in 2008). The large number of "checks" in 2009 may indicate that, while the illiquidity premium was effective in dampening the impact of financial markets on reported MCEV values, it did so at the expense of driving a wedge between MCEV and the actual MC of the firms.

A caveat in interpreting the results: MCEV does not value future new business, or franchise value, but focuses only on the value in-force. MC should theoretically exceed the reported MCEV if new business is thought to be profitable. However, during this period most of the insurers in the sample were trading on multiples which put limited weight on profitable

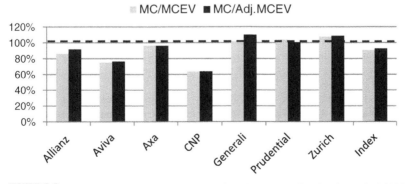

FIGURE 6.3   MC vs. MCEV and adjusted MCEV (average ratios for the period 2009–2013)
Source: Wilson and Hristova (2014)

TABLE 6.3   Comparison of adjusted MCEV vs. reported MCEV and MC

Company	2009	2010	2011	2012	2013
1. Allianz	✓	✓	✓	✓	
2. Aviva	✓	✓	✓	✓	
3. Axa	✓		✓		✓
4. CNP	✓	✓	✓	✓	✓
5. Generali		✓			
6. Prudential	✓				✓
7. Zurich	✓			✓	✓

✓ "Clean" MCEV closer than unadjusted MCEV to MC.
Source: Wilson and Hristova (2014).

growth due to their strong focus on Western European markets; the exception to this rule was Prudential plc, which had a strong Asian growth story.

MCEV Roll-forward Test

In this section, we ask the question whether disclosed MCEV sensitivities help to explain share price movements. Since in most cases embedded values are calculated and reported only annually, a roll-forward[5] methodology based on published sensitivities is used to generate MCEVs during the year. This analysis allows us to increase the number of observations and also test the joint hypothesis that disclosed MCEV sensitivities "explain" share price developments. The MCEV roll-forward is calculated using the formula[6]

$$\text{Normalized MCEV RF} = 1 + \frac{|EQ_{sensi}|^* \Delta \text{Euro Stoxx } 50_t}{10\%^* MCEV_{t-1}} + \frac{IR_{sensi}^* |\Delta \text{Euro Swap}_t|}{100\, \text{bps}^* MCEV_{t-1}}$$

---

[5]In accounting, a roll-forward is the systematic establishment of a new accounting period's balances using (rolling forward) prior accounting period data.

[6]Description of the approach. The normalized MCEV roll-forward deviates from 100% based on the reported sensitivities to equity changes (EQ_{sensi}) and interest rate changes (IR_{sensi}) and actual financial market movements. The reported EQ sensitivities represent the change in MCEV for a −10% fall in all equity prices and are converted into a sensitivity for a 1% change in equity prices by dividing by 10%. Two interest rate sensitivities are typically disclosed: one for a +100 bps (basis points) parallel increase in interest rates and one for a −100 bps parallel decrease. For the roll-forward, the +100 bps sensitivity is used when the change in the Euro Swap rate is positive and the −100 bps sensitivity is applied when it is negative. The up- and down-sensitivities reflect the negative convexity to interest rates often associated with long-dated guarantees.

Insurers report embedded value sensitivities only annually. The sensitivities are held over four consecutive quarters (Q1–Q4) until the next reporting event; after the annual disclosure, the sensitivities are updated. Finally, $MCEV_{t-1}$ represents last period's Group market-consistent embedded value. For example, in Q1, the disclosed MCEV at the end of the previous year is used. For quarters where no MCEV is published, the estimated change in the respective period is multiplied by the most recent available embedded value – e.g., $MCEV_t = MCEV\ RF_t^* MCEV_{t-1}$. Three of the companies in the sample (Aviva, Prudential and Zurich) report MCEV semi-annually, in which case the reported values are used in the roll-forward of the following quarter (Q1 and Q3).

MCEV / Economic Capital as Driver of Value?

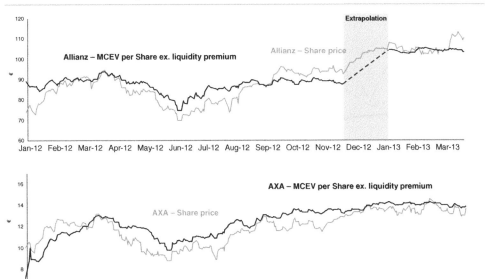

Source: Capital IQ, Bloomberg, disclosed MCEV sensitivities and RBC estimates

FIGURE 6.4 Share price vs. MCEV roll-forward, AXA and Allianz 2012
Source: Vo (2013)

Note that this does not *estimate* the "best relationship" between market indices and share price movements – that would be too easy. Rather, it uses disclosed sensitivities and actual financial market developments to see if they can *explain* share price movements.

Examples A similar roll-forward approach is conducted by equity analysis. For example, Figure 6.4 from Vo (2013) compares share price and MCEV roll-forward values for Allianz and AXA during 2012–2013.

It demonstrates that "clean" MCEV and associated sensitivities do a very good job of representing how share prices react to changing market conditions. As noted, the "gap" for Allianz in 2012 is attributed by Vo to the introduction of yield curve anchoring using Solvency II's ultimate forward rate, another assumption to dampen MCEV volatility. Visual inspection leads to the conclusion that MCEV sensitivities explain a substantial amount of share price changes!

Another interesting question is whether MCEV or IFRS values provide a "better" explanation of share price movements? Some firms also disclose IFRS equity sensitivities, Allianz being one of them. We conducted a similar exercise for Allianz over 2011 in Figure 6.5, but also added the roll-forward IFRS value based on our disclosed IFRS sensitivities. All information to conduct the analysis can be found in public disclosures.

It is interesting to note that the MCEV roll-forward does a better job of tracking our actual share price development than does the IFRS roll-forward. What is also interesting is that, while

IFRS NAV, Share Price, *MCEV roll-forward based on disclosed sensitivities*

AZ share price vs. economic & IFRS roll-forward[1] (EUR)

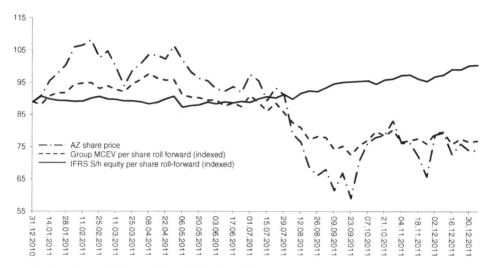

1) Roll-forward based on 2010 year-end Group MCEV and IFRS S/h equity and disclosed sensitivities (i.e. equities & rates) but without quarterly rebalancing.

Source: Allianz analysis

FIGURE 6.5 Explaining share price changes based on disclosed sensitivities

the correlation between MCEV roll-forward and share price was significant and above 70% during the period, the correlation between IFRS and share price developments was insignificant and *negative* (−5%!).

A Broader Sample and Longer Period   The following represents a multi-company, multi-year extension of the roll-forward analysis.

In Figure 6.6, we compare a simple average of the differences between adjusted MCEV and TNAV changes across all companies to the average change in share price.

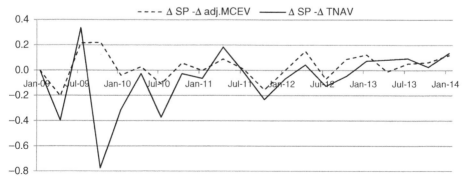

FIGURE 6.6 Comparison of Δadj MCEV and ΔTNAV with Δshare price (index)
Source: Wilson and Hristova (2014)

TABLE 6.4   Comparison of adjusted MCEV roll-forward vs. ΔTNAV and Δshare price

Company	2009	2010	2011	2012	2013
1. Allianz		✓	✓		✓
2. Aviva	✓	✓	✓	✓	✓
3. Axa	✓	✓	✓	✓	✓
4. CNP	✓	✓	✓	✓	✓
5. Generali		✓		✓	
6. Prudential	✓	✓	✓	✓	✓
7. Zurich	✓	✓	✓	✓	✓

✓ Adjusted MCEV roll-forward closer to Δshare price than ΔTNAV.
Source: Wilson and Hristova (2014).

During the period, the average changes in adjusted MCEV were generally closer to the actual share price changes than were the changes in IFRS TNAV. This can be seen in the figure by comparing the absolute deviations of the adjusted MCEV line (which is closer to 0) with the TNAV line. The correlation between the results is a further indicator for the superiority of adjusted MCEVs relative to IFRS measures, with the correlation between the adjusted MCEV roll-forward and the index being significantly higher (0.77) than the correlation with the TNAV (0.25). Not surprisingly, the adjusted R^2 (a measure of the how well a regression "fits" the data) from regressing share value developments against the MCEV index is high (57%) compared with the adjusted R^2 using ΔTNAV as the explanatory variable (8.7%).

The results for the individual companies are summarized in Table 6.4. A "check" in the table indicates that the adjusted MCEV roll-forward is closer than the TNAV to Δshare price, a result which held in **86% of cases!**

We can also test whether adjusted or unadjusted MCEV is a better reflection of share price developments. Table 6.5 shows that in **75% of cases** the "clean" MCEV dominates the reported MCEV value.

TABLE 6.5   Adjusted MCEV roll-forward vs. unadjusted MCEV roll-forward

Company	2009	2010	2011	2012	2013
1. Allianz	✓	✓	✓		✓
2. Aviva	✓	✓	✓	✓	✓
3. Axa	✓			✓	✓
4. CNP	✓	✓		✓	✓
5. Generali	✓	✓		✓	✓
6. Prudential	✓	✓		✓	
7. Zurich	✓		✓	✓	

✓ Adjusted MCEV roll-forward closer to Δshare price than unadjusted MCEV roll-forward.
Source: Wilson and Hristova (2014).

What is interesting from the table is that the "clean" MCEV dominates MCEV in 93% of cases during 2009 and 2012, the two years when the illiquidity premium had a strong impact due to the higher spread levels caused by the financial crisis. This might imply that the illiquidity premium, designed to dampen MCEV volatility, dampens it so much relative to credit spreads that it becomes disconnected with actual share values. Put another way, the markets seem to "look through" the illiquidity premium when valuing an insurer's shares.

Note that there is still a significant 83% outperformance if we include the years immediately following the turmoil in the financial markets, 2010 and 2013. It is only during the "calm in the eye of the storm" – 2011, with lower and stabilized levels of credit spreads, that the MCEV with the illiquidity premium better matched share price developments.

The first conclusion is that "clean" MCEV better reflects share price developments than TNAV and reported MCEV. The second conclusion is that MCEV sensitivities give an accurate representation of the way that the share price will develop as interest rate and equity prices change.

EVIDENCE FROM BANKING

The evidence that market-consistent or "fair" values better track market capitalization is also compelling for banks. The following provides an overview of research on the subject, as well as a similar analysis based on the period 2009–2013.

A Direct Comparison of Levels: Fair Values Versus Tangible Net Asset Values

The closest analog to MCEV for banks can be found in the notes of bank financial statements. While the bank "trading book" is on fair value already, the "banking book" is not; however, SFAS 107[7] requires banks to disclose all financial instruments at fair value, including loans in their "banking book." Using this information, we compared:

- the TNAV of the bank, calculated as IFRS equity less intangible assets such as good will, and
- the Fair Net Asset Value (FNAV) of the bank, calculated as the TNAV plus the fair value adjustment for the banking book as published in the footnotes to the annual accounts, against
- the actual market capitalization of the bank.

The results are summarized in Table 6.6, where a check indicates that the fair value of the bank (including the fair value adjustment for the banking book) is *closer* (measured in absolute value deviations) to the actual market capitalization than was the IFRS TNAV. In summary, the fair value was closer in **78% of the sample**.

---

[7]FASB (1991). SFAS defines fair value as "the amount at which the instrument could be exchanged in a current transaction between willing parties, other than in a forced or liquidation sale."

TABLE 6.6 Comparison of (TNAV + adjusted fair value) vs. TNAV, 2009–2012

Bank	2009	2010	2011	2012
Barclays	✓	✓	✓	✓
BBVA		✓	✓	
Citi	✓		✓	✓
Commerzbank	✓	✓	✓	✓
JPM		✓	✓	✓
Lloyds		✓	✓	✓
RBS	✓	✓	✓	✓
Société Générale	✓		✓	

✓ (TNAV + adjusted FV) closer to MC than TNAV.
Source: Author's analysis.

Consistent with Other Empirical Research

These conclusions are confirmed by more detailed investigations. There have been a number of studies[8] investigating whether fair value information is share price "relevant," with relevance defined by a relationship between incremental fair value accounting information and share price developments.

Barth *et al.* (2000) provide an excellent summary of the "value relevance" research and cite an extensive literature providing, ". . . evidence that financial instruments' fair values are value relevant. The conclusions apply to pension and other post-retirement liabilities,[9] debt and equity securities,[10] bank loans and core deposits.[11] There is also evidence that the fair values of derivatives are value relevant.[12]"

Especially interesting in the context of market-consistent bank valuation is the conclusion of Barth *et al.* (1996), which "provides evidence that fair value estimates of loans, securities and long term debt disclosed under SFAS No. 107 provide significant explanatory power for

---

[8]For example, most studies concentrate on investigating the strength of the relationship between EVA™ measures and shareholder value relative to other, standard accounting measures such as Net Income (NI) and Operating Cash Flow (OCF). See, e.g., Peterson and Peterson (1996), Bacidore *et al.* (1997), Chen and Dodd (1997), Biddle *et al.* (1999), Sandoval (2001) and O'Brien (2005).

[9]For a generic discussion of pension liabilities and impact on company valuation see, e.g., Landsman (1986), Amir (1993) and Choi *et al.* (1997).

[10]For a specific discussion of debt and equity securities on bank and insurance company valuation, see e.g., Barth (1994), Barth *et al.* (1996, 1997), Petroni and Wahlen (1995), Eccher *et al.* (1996) and Nelson (1996).

[11]For a specific discussion of bank loan disclosures, see for example, Barth *et al.*, 1996, *Value relevance of banks' fair value disclosures under SFAS 107* Eccher *et al.*, 1996, *Fair value disclosures of bank holding companies*, and Nelson, 1996, *Fair value accounting for commercial banks: an empirical analysis of SFAS 107*

[12]For a specific discussion of bank derivatives disclosures, see, for example, Venkatachalam, 1996, *Value-relevance of banks' derivatives disclosures* and Schrand, 1997, *The association between stock-price interest rate sensitivity and disclosures about derivative instruments*

bank share prices beyond that provided by related book values . . . (and) we consistently find incremental explanatory power for loans' fair value."

There is another branch of literature linking share price development with measures of the structural interest rate mismatch (or asset/liability mismatch) position of the bank. Flannery and James (1984) provide empirical evidence supporting the conclusion that the share price of banks with greater asset/liability mismatches is more sensitive to interest rate developments. This result is confirmed by English *et al.* (2012), who reference many other authors confirming the result.

More recent research after the 2008 crisis has highlighted some issues, however. It is well known that fair valuation is subjective and offers the potential for manipulation, as summarized by Chee (2011): "Loans are especially controversial as they are usually not actively traded in the market and thus are measured with a model based on banks' assumptions. The estimation process involves considerable subjectivity with respect to the methods and assumptions . . . and the resulting estimates will contain intentional and/or unintentional errors."

Various authors, including Chee (2011), have found evidence that banks may be taking advantage of that subjectivity: "the aggregate fair values of loans considerably lag the market values of loans during the credit crisis. Finally, financially distressed banks overstate both the fair values and the carrying amounts of their loan portfolios." Landsman (2005) summarizes similar results from Barth *et al.* (1996), who report that loan fair values are incrementally informative to book values but that investors discount loan fair value estimates made by less financially healthy banks.

Not surprisingly, shareholders generally respond more strongly to fair value disclosures for assets traded in deep and liquid markets with directly observable prices (so-called Type 1 assets), as opposed to those whose values are inferred by proxy or calculated using models and market data (so-called Type 2 and 3 assets; see, e.g., Petroni and Wahlen, 1995; Carroll *et al.*, 2003; Khurana and Kim, 2003; Lim *et al.*, 2011) and for banks with a higher perceived risk profile (see, e.g., Hirst *et al.*, 2004; Hodder *et al.*, 2006; Lim *et al.*, 2011). The first observation in particular is often cited as a reason why further fair value disclosures may not be beneficial on the margin for the readers of bank disclosures (Shaffer, 2012).

IS IT JUST ME OR ARE OTHERS THINKING THE SAME THING?

Most analysts follow a similar path for calculating the intrinsic value of a bank or insurer. In the early 1990s, the prevalent practice within the analyst community was to use industry average market multiples (e.g., P/E, M/B). Now, virtually all equity analysts use corporate finance approaches based on firm-specific returns and adjusted earnings to bring accounting values closer to economic reality.

Firm-specific Approach Based on Economic Fundamentals

The rationale for doing so is obvious: while average market multiples may provide an indication of the average industry valuation, they do not explain the premium (or discount) put on high-performing (or low-performing) firms within the industry, nor do they make transparent the drivers of that premium for each of the firm's major business segments.

The trend in using the firm's fundamentals is reflected in BT Alex Brown analysts' comments made several decades ago, "For an insurance stock to be a long-term outperformer, four basic criteria are required: a growth profile, efficient use of capital, an attractive ROE and a strong management profile." Virtually all analysts now value banks and insurers using three broad principles.

- First, they value each of the businesses independently, with the value of the firm represented by the sum of its parts.
- Second, they use some form of discounted free cash flow approach (or steady-state formula) to calculate each business's intrinsic value.
- Third, they value each business unit as the sum of its current net asset value (including the capital needed to support the business) and its future earnings streams.

This is supported by a quick review of analyst methodologies. For example, for valuing banks, BNP Paribas (2003) ". . . used the SOTP (sum of the parts) as a central valuation method. This involves valuing the various business lines of each bank using the equation $P/\text{NBV} = (\text{RoE} - g)/(\text{CoE} - g) = 1 + (\text{RoE} - \text{CoE})/(\text{CoE} - g)$, where g is the long-term growth and CoE is the cost of equity."

Focusing on the insurance industry, Morgan Stanley has ". . . tried to get closer to economic reality by introducing a new valuation metric, Enhanced Embedded Value (EEV) capturing the value of the in-force book of business . . . which (addresses) . . . some of the shortcomings of the traditional approach, most notably policyholder option costs and mismatches." A similar approach is taken when valuing non-life operations, "we estimate a normalized return on equity, that is, the return we expect to be achieved over the cycle, allowing for average combined ratios and investment returns, using the formula $V/B = \text{normalized RoE/CoC}$."

Intrinsic Values Based on Market Value Adjustments

Analysts are often forced to make adjustments to earnings and capital to bring them closer to market-consistent values. These adjustments are necessary because traditional accounting figures do not adequately reflect the underlying economics of the business.

For banks, most of the adjustments are made in the "banking" book as the trading book is ostensibly already carried at fair market values. The clearest example of adjustments is in the area of credit losses: during the higher-default periods of 2001–2003 and 2008–2009, virtually all analysts critically reviewed loan loss provisions for additional, unreported losses which would likely materialize.

Analysts covering the insurance industry have historically been hindered by the lack of transparency in spite of (or because of?) insurers' disclosures. The CFO Forum issued its MCEV principles in 2007 in order to proactively address the perceived "opacity discount" suffered by the industry, believing that the broader adoption of MCEV principles will deliver the following.

- "A shareholder's perspective on value, being the present value of future cash flows available to the shareholder, adjusted for the risks of those cash flows.
- A market-consistent approach to financial risk.
- A greater focus on disclosing cash emerging from covered business."

These approaches have been adopted and supported by some, but not all, sell-side analysts. For example, Morgan Stanley (2011a) believes that MCEV ". . . is a reasonable guide to value: (it values) options and guarantees in life insurance policies in a manner that is consistent with how markets value similar instruments . . . We think this is the right way to look at these companies."

CHAPTER 7

Market-Consistent
Valuation for Insurers

Core to a market value framework is the ability to value all assets and liabilities on a market or "fair value" basis. Because market prices do not exist for all elements of a bank or insurer's balance sheet, mark-to-model standards have been developed to fill the gaps. Given the complexity of the financial products offered by banks and insurers, these standards can be complex. This chapter provides an overview of market or fair valuation techniques used in the insurance industry to value insurance liabilities.

INTRODUCTION TO FAIR VALUATION FOR INSURERS

A fair value standard was introduced in 2006 by the Financial Accounting Standards Board (FASB) under Statement 157, entitled *Fair Value Measurements*. The statement defines fair value, establishes a framework for measuring fair value in Generally Accepted Accounting Principles (GAAP) and expands disclosure about fair value measurements.

Fair Valuation of Assets

Under the rules, fair value is an exchange price in an orderly transaction between market participants to sell the asset or transfer the liability. The price is an exit price, not the price for the entity to purchase the asset or assume the liability (an entry price). Consequently, fair value is not an entity-specific measurement.

In order to increase consistency, the FASB standard provides a hierarchy of preferred methods for calculating the fair value based on the available market data.

1. Quoted prices in active markets for the identical asset or liability. In this situation, the price is determined without serious analysis and is not to be adjusted for size ("Type 1").
2. Observable data or market prices that are usually interpreted during the course of an appraisal. This includes (i) market transactions for similar assets, (ii) data from small/inactive markets and (iii) inputs that directly correlate with economic data affecting the items being valued ("Type 2").

3. Unobservable data that comes from the entity's own data or economic models, requiring an experienced or skilled appraiser for its interpretation and application ("Type 3").

These standards are generally applied to the assets held in the general and segregated accounts of insurers. They are not generally applied to the insurer's liabilities, except for some categories of benefits associated with variable annuities and equity indexed annuities; rather, most liabilities are carried on an amortized cost basis.

The Focus on the LH Insurance Liabilities

The fact that fair values are not generally applied to the liability side of the balance sheet is unfortunate, because the liabilities are exactly "where the action is" for LH insurers and where improvements need to be made: while amortized cost accounting for the PC industry may provide a reasonable basis for understanding the economics of the business (because of the typically shorter run-off profile and the absence of financial options and guarantees), accounting in the LH insurance industry is notoriously opaque, potentially obscuring the underlying economics which depend heavily on financial market developments.

So dire is the situation for the LH industry that some industry executives and equity analysts believe that the industry trades at a discount relative to other industries and will continue to do so until disclosure frameworks better reflect the economics of the business. As a consequence, the industry has worked hard to provide supplemental disclosures to eliminate the discount. The following is a brief history of market-consistent embedded value approaches for LH insurance businesses (see also Wilson and Hristova, 2014).

Embedded Value (EV)

EV approaches have a long history driven by a noble objective: to better reflect the value creation of long-term life businesses. EV became popular in the late 1980s in the UK, driven by increasing demand from investors for more accurate and reliable information about the value generated by life insurers and spurred by the ongoing deregulation and restructuring of the insurance industry through takeovers and demutualization.

Managers were concerned that existing GAAP accounting did not properly reflect the value of the in-force and future new business; in order to provide a more realistic measure of their company's value, especially in the face of potentially hostile takeovers, many UK insurers began to systematically disclose embedded values.

Traditional Embedded Value (TEV)

The first attempt to harmonize EV reporting is often referred to as Traditional Embedded Value and was made in December 2001, when the Association of British Insurers published guidelines referred to as the *Achieved Profits Method* covering key aspects of the EV calculation. All UK insurers followed these rules, although they were not formally required to do so.

In spite of the advances, the TEV methodology was criticized as it allowed for a large degree of management discretion in best-estimate assumptions, especially financial market assumptions, leading to results that were generally not comparable across firms. In addition, the results were viewed as often too optimistic, substantially flattered by the assumptions of higher equity returns or higher future interest rates.

Finally, TEV approaches did not explicitly consider the risk from embedded options and guarantees as they were based on these optimistic best estimates – guarantees rarely come in-the-money if a high enough reinvestment rate is assumed – and used a single risk discount rate to discount all future best-estimate cash flows.

European Embedded Value (EEV)

In order to address these issues, European insurance CFOs proposed principles to improve TEV, beginning with the CFO Forum's EEV framework in 2004–2005. These principles represented a tremendous advance over TEV and appraisal value approaches by being more prescriptive with regard to financial market assumptions and disclosure standards, as well as introducing stochastic cash flow models for the valuation of options and guarantees embedded in life insurance products.

However, they did not go far enough, leaving the EEV framework exposed to many of the same criticisms as the original EV framework, albeit at a more complicated level. Merrill Lynch[1] expressed concerns, saying that the introduction of EEV has been ". . . of little or no assistance in gaining clarity on valuations. In some respects EEV has turned out to be the antithesis of what it was intended to be – complexity has increased, visibility has reduced and comparing the embedded values of different companies is even more challenging than before."

"Clean" Market Consistent Embedded Value (MCEV)

Responding to the criticism, the European insurance industry developed principles for a fully market-consistent valuation framework – MCEV – in 2009.[2] This standard corrected the issues inherent in TEV and EEV by prescribing that financial risks embedded in LH policies should be valued using techniques similar to the approaches used for valuing cash flows, options and guarantees in a bank's trading book.

The Market Value Balance Sheet Approach

Following (or at least influenced by) the industry's lead, the MCEV framework was later adapted to a Market Value Balance Sheet (MVBS) framework which can be applied to both LH and PC segments. This final step was implicit in the CRO Forum's Market Value Liability (MVL) approach (CRO Forum, 2009) and explicitly forms the basis for the European Solvency II risk-based solvency framework.

Solvency II and Subsequent, Non-economic Adjustments

The "clean" market-consistent approach was developed before the 2008 financial crisis. During the crisis, the results were seen by many as too volatile and not reflective of the "long-term" economics of the business.

Since Solvency II was based on market-consistent principles, any volatility in available financial resources directly translates into volatility in solvency ratios. In this context, the desire

---

[1] Quote attributed to Merrill Lynch in a presentation to the Society of Actuaries by Todaro (2007). Presenting a more colorful criticism, Merrill Lynch is credited with providing the following answers. What does EEV stand for? "(a) Excuse to Embellish Valuation; (b) Evil, Elusive and Volatile; (c) European Embedded Value." Does every EEV have a similar cost of capital? "(a) Of course; (b) Not quite; (c) You must be joking." What is FOG? "(a) Financial Options and Guarantees; (b) Something that descends over you when an insurance analyst starts talking about EEVs; (c) All of the above."

[2] For EEV, see CFO Forum (2004a,b, 2005). For MCEV, see CFO Forum (2008, 2009). For the precursers to MCEV, see Swiss Re (2001, 2005), Tillinghast-Towers Perrin (2004, 2005) and O'Keeffe *et al.* (2005).

to "stabilize" solvency ratios became a discussion point between the industry, regulators and academics.[3]

In spite of the fact that "clean" MCEV better reflects share prices, the CFO Forum and Solvency II subsequently adapted the definition of market consistency in ways which were decidedly non-economic. Two of the most important adjustments,[4] discussed later in detail, include:

1. defining an anchor or ultimate forward rate for long-term interest rates beyond the last observable liquid bond market;
2. the inclusion of bond spreads in discounting the firm's liabilities (e.g., the illiquidity premium, countercyclical premium, matching adjustment or volatility adjustment).

In addition to these, the Solvency II framework introduced a third significant economic distortion:

3. sovereign bonds from the Eurozone are treated as if they are risk free.

This is a characterization which has clearly proven inaccurate given the restructuring of Greek sovereign debt in 2011–2012, the challenges to the sovereign debt of Cyprus and the fragility of other sovereign issuers, including Spain, Italy, Portugal and Ireland during the 2012–2013 European sovereign crisis.

CALCULATING TRADITIONAL EMBEDDED VALUE

The TEV and appraisal value concepts[5] measure the value of shareholders' interest in the *existing portfolio* by valuing the *distributable free cash flows to shareholders* after allowance for the aggregate risks in the business. The TEV calculation begins with the decomposition of the insurance company's balance sheet into two parts, the present value of future profits and net asset value, as described in Figure 7.1.

Present Value of Future Profits (PVFP)

The present value of future profits represents the present value of statutory liabilities and the assets backing statutory liabilities. It represents the discounted value of the profits expected to emerge from the covered portfolio, calculated in the following manner.

EQUATION 7.1 Embedded value

$$\text{PVFP} = \sum_{t=0}^{\infty} \frac{\text{CF}_t}{(1 + rdr)^t}$$

---

[3]See, e.g., www.voxeu.org/article/countercyclical-regulation-solvency-ii-merits-and-flaws and www.voxeu.org/article/prudential-regulatory-issue-heart-solvency-ii.

[4]For a discussion on the market consistency of the illiquidity premium, see Keller (2010), Groupe Consultatief Actuariel Europeen (2012) and Wüthrich (2011).

[5]In the remainder of this discussion, I will use the term "embedded value" to also include PC appraisal value techniques unless there are specific differences which need to be highlighted.

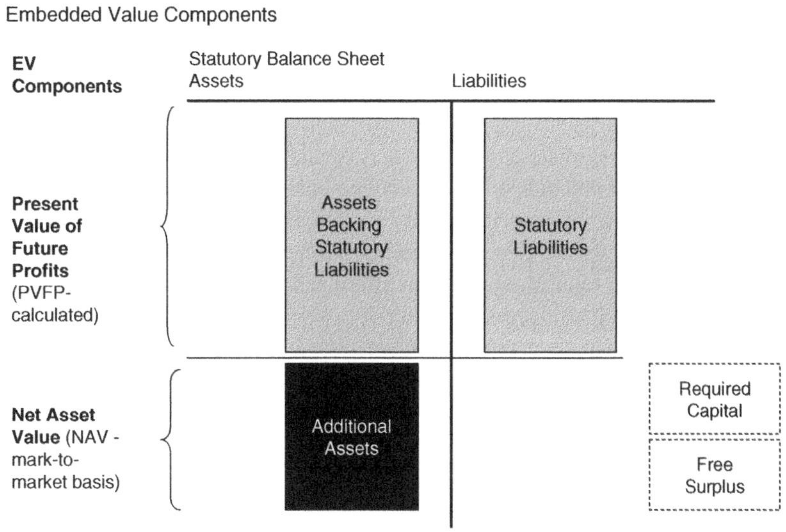

Embedded Value Components

FIGURE 7.1 EV statutory balance sheet decomposition

where CF_t represents the best-estimate statutory profits generated by the existing book of business which are distributable to shareholders at time t and rdr is the appropriate risk discount rate. Generically speaking, the statutory profits at any point in time are represented by the following equation.

EQUATION 7.2 Best-estimate statutory cash flows from covered business

$$
\begin{aligned}
CF_t = &\ P_t && \text{Premium received at } t^6 \\
+ &\ R_{t-1} - R_t && \text{Change in reserves} \\
- &\ C_t && \text{Policy holder claims} \\
- &\ E_t && \text{Expenses} \\
+ &\ I_t && \text{Investment income} \\
- &\ T_t && \text{Taxes}
\end{aligned}
$$

where all values represent management's best estimates. Even though the TEV is calculated for the business as if it was in "run-off," that is with no new business, the expense allocations are done on a "going-concern" basis with an appropriate assumption regarding wage or expense inflation. Also, policy holder claims include all claims arising from insurable risks (e.g., mortality, morbidity, property or liability claims, etc.), any contractually defined minimum investment returns and an estimate of the additional investment returns which policy holders can reasonably expect (PRE, or Policyholder Reasonable Expectations).

The TEV framework is applied to PC businesses as well as LH businesses. However, for LH businesses, the best-estimate projected cash flows depend on assumptions regarding future

---

[6]Future premiums may arise in the context of the existing, closed block of business for regular premium asset accumulation products or for products which allow for optional top-ups at contractual rates.

financial market developments, future management decisions – such as crediting or bonus strategies – and policy holder decisions such as customer lapses or additional, non-obligatory top-up premium payments. Under the TEV framework, each of these are set to best-estimate values.

Once the future best-estimate cash flows are calculated, the final step is to select a risk discount rate appropriate for the risk of the underlying business to calculate the present value of the best-estimate cash flows. Given its "roots" in DFCF corporate finance models, the risk discount rate typically consists of two components: a long-term risk-free yield (e.g., a 10-year government bond or swap rate) plus a risk premium reflecting the company's actual cost of capital (e.g., using the CAPM discussed earlier).

Net Asset Value (NAV)

The second part consists of the mark-to-market value of any additional assets above and beyond those backing statutory liabilities; this is the Net Asset Value (NAV). Since the TEV is an after-tax value, the NAV is net of an allowance for future taxes on unrealized capital gains.

For disclosure purposes, the NAV is also decomposed into two parts: the Required Capital (ReC) needed to support the business above reserve assets (taking into account both external and internal requirements) and any residual Free Surplus (FS) which is not strictly required and could in principle be distributed immediately to shareholders.

Following this decomposition, the embedded value of an insurance company is expressed in the following manner.

EQUATION 7.3   Traditional embedded value

$$TEV = PVFP + NAV$$
$$= PVFP + ReC + FS$$

Criticisms of TEV

Discounting best-estimate free cash flows from complex financial products is challenging, especially for LH products which include embedded options and guarantees. Three issues in particular are worth reiterating. First, TEVs depend on management assumptions regarding financial market developments, making them incomparable and often overly optimistic. Second, TEV fails to correctly value embedded options and guarantees because it is based on best estimates. Finally, although the risk discount rate can ostensibly compensate for these shortcomings, the reality is that the use of a single risk discount rate will be inappropriate for any portfolio of complex financial products.

EUROPEAN EMBEDDED VALUE

Given these shortcomings, the CFO Forum extended the EV framework in 2004–2005 by publishing the EEV Principles (CFO Forum, 2004a,b, 2005) and associated guidance (see

Sidebar 7.1). The CFO Forum, consisting of the CFOs from 19 sponsoring, predominantly European insurers, had three primary objectives for developing the EEV Principles.

- First, to improve the consistency and transparency of life insurance supplemental reporting.
- Second, to ensure that the disclosure accurately reflects the economics of long-term life insurance business, explicitly recognizing the value of financial options and guarantees (which were not explicitly accounted for under TEV approaches).
- Third, to define a minimum level of disclosure, allowing analysts to compare the results across companies.

SIDEBAR 7.1: CFO FORUM EEV PRINCIPLES

The European embedded value framework consists of 12 general principles. These principles are summarized at a very high level here; for the complete text, readers are referred to CFO Forum (2004a,b, 2005).

Principle 1: Embedded value is a measure of the consolidated value of share-holders' interests in the covered business.

Principle 2: The business covered should be clearly identified and disclosed.

Principle 3: EV is the present value of shareholders' interests in the earnings distributable from assets allocated to the covered business after sufficient allowance for the risk. The EV consists of free surplus, required capital, less the cost of required capital plus the present value of the in-force covered business (PVIF).

Principle 4: Free surplus is the market value of assets not required to support the in-force covered business at the valuation date.

Principle 5: Required capital includes the assets above that are required to back liabilities whose distribution to shareholders is restricted. EV should allow for the cost of holding required capital.

Principle 6: The value of future cash flows from the in-force business is the present value of future cash flows projected to emerge from the assets backing liabilities of the in-force covered business (PVIF). This value is reduced by the value of financial options and guarantees, as defined in Principle 7.

Principle 7: Allowance must be made in the EV for the potential impact on future shareholder cash flows of all financial options and guarantees in the in-force business. This allowance includes the time value of options and guarantees based on stochastic techniques consistent with the assumptions used in the underlying embedded value.

Principle 8: New business is defined as the sale of new contracts during the reporting period. The value of new business includes the value of expected renewals on the new contracts. The EV should reflect the in-force business, which excludes future new business.

Principle 9: Assumptions for future experience should reflect past, current and expected future experience and any other relevant data. Changes in future experience should be allowed for in the value of the in-force business when

> sufficient evidence exists and the changes are reasonably certain. The assumptions should be actively reviewed.
>
> *Principle 10:* Economic assumptions must be internally consistent and should be consistent with observable market data. No smoothing of market data, account balances, unrealized gains or investment returns is permitted.
>
> *Principle 11:* EV must make assumptions for participating business about future bonus rates and the profit allocation between policy holders and shareholders. These assumptions should be consistent with projection assumptions, established company practice and local market practice.
>
> *Principle 12:* Embedded value results should be disclosed at consolidated group level using a business classification consistent with the primary statements.

Important Improvements

The EEV Principles contained three significant advances relative to the TEV. First, whereas TEVs were based on management's *best-estimate* cash flows, the EEV Principles discounted simulated, *real-world stochastic* cash flows under different financial market scenarios (Principle 7). This was significant because it helped to capture some of the possible adverse developments in falling markets when guarantees might become binding and shareholder funds are required to make up the difference.

The second, related advance was the requirement that management and policy holder behavior regarding options be explicitly modeled within the stochastic framework. This increases the complexity of the calculations as behavior needs to be explicitly modeled in three areas.

- The *investment strategy*, consisting of a target asset allocation and the dynamics of future (re-)investment decisions. These strategies are defined either as static proportions or dynamic functions (e.g., allocation rules which depend on realized returns, the level of statutory solvency or hidden reserves, the pricing of competitive products, etc.). In order to provide controls around the valuations, the Principles require that the assumptions should be supported by business plans, must conform to contractual, legal or regulatory requirements and be evidenced over time by actual management behavior.
- The *crediting or bonus strategy* for profit participation products, which should reflect regulatory and contractual rules and be consistent with PRE. Most firms define complex relationships between realized and unrealized investment returns, competitors' crediting rates, new product pricing, free surplus in the fund and the ability of management to "smooth" returns intertemporally. These rules likewise need to be evidenced by the firm's business plans and by actual management behavior over time.
- Finally, *customer behavior* (including dynamic policy lapses, annuitization rates, options to pay in additional premiums, etc.) also needs to be documented and evidenced. These assumptions take the form of equations relating customer behavior to realized crediting rates offered by the firm, current pricing of competitors, and so on.

The final important advance was the additional guidance on setting financial market assumptions (Principle 10) and their disclosure with the goal to promote consistency and transparency across the industry.

The Market's Reception

Although a significant improvement over TEV, unfortunately three major concerns remained.

First, Principle 10 was sufficiently loose to still allow a wide variation across firms due to management discretion in setting valuation assumptions. For example, Tillinghast-Towers Perrin (2004) commented that a major problem was "the degree of subjectivity in setting the assumption, which can have the biggest single impact on the valuation result."

Second, even with the refinements under Principle 7, the EEV approach did not ensure that the assets backing life businesses or the options and guarantees embedded in life insurance products were valued in a manner consistent with comparable valuations in the financial markets. Tillinghast-Towers Perrin (2004) again commented that, "the EEV Principles . . . give answers that are very different from the market value of the options concerned, which could be calculated using 'risk neutral' projections."

Third, the risk discount rate still had to do some "heavy lifting" as the use of a single, top-down risk-adjusted discount rate would not likely value portfolios with different risk characteristics correctly. Tillinghast-Towers Perrin (2004) concluded that a major issue was the "lack of a direct link between the RDR and the risks within the business (and) the use of a single measure to reflect all areas of risk to which shareholder cash flows are exposed."

MARKET CONSISTENT EMBEDDED VALUE (MCEV)

In order to address the issues of consistency and the valuation of options and guarantees, the CFO Forum refined the EEV Principles and issued the MCEV Principles in 2009, summarized in Sidebar 7.2. MCEV represented a logical extension of the EEV framework toward a fully market-consistent framework, correctly valuing all assets, options and guarantees and substantially removing differences in economic assumptions between reporting firms.

SIDEBAR 7.2: 2009 CFO FORUM MCEV PRINCIPLES

The MCEV framework consists of 17 general principles, summarized at a high level here. For the complete text, readers are referred to CFO Forum (2009).

Principle 1: MCEV is the consolidated value of shareholders' interests in the covered business. Group MCEV measures the value in covered and non-covered business.

Principle 2: The business covered by the MCEV should be clearly identified and disclosed.

Principle 3: MCEV represents the present value of earnings distributable from the covered business after allowance for risk. The allowance for risk should be calibrated to match the market price for risk where reliably observable. MCEV consists of free surplus, required capital and the value of the in-force business (ViF). The value of future new business is excluded from the MCEV.

Principle 4: Free surplus is the market value of any assets allocated to, but not required to support, the in-force covered business at the valuation date.

Principle 5: Required capital is the market value of assets, attributed to the covered business over and above that required to back liabilities, whose distribution to shareholders is restricted.

Principle 6: The value of the in-force covered business (ViF) consists of the following components: PVFP (where profits are post-tax shareholder cash flows from the in-force covered business), time value of financial options and guarantees (TVOG), frictional costs of required capital (FCReC) and cost of residual non-hedgeable risks (CNHR).

Principle 7: MCEV recognizes all financial options and guarantees within the in-force covered business. The allowance for the time value of financial options and guarantees must be based on stochastic techniques using methods and assumptions consistent with the underlying embedded value. All projected cash flows should be valued using economic assumptions such that they are valued in line with the price of similar cash flows that are traded in the capital markets.

Principle 8: An allowance should be made for the frictional costs of required capital, independent of the allowance for non-hedgeable risks.

Principle 9: An allowance should be made for the cost of non-hedgeable risks, including the impact of non-hedgeable non-financial risks and non-hedgeable financial risks. Sufficient disclosures should be provided to enable a comparison with a cost of capital methodology.

Principle 10: New business is defined as the sale of new contracts and in some cases increases to existing contracts during the reporting period. The value of new business includes the value of expected renewals on those new contracts. MCEV should only reflect in-force business.

Principle 11: The assessment of appropriate assumptions for future experience should be based on past, current and expected future experience and any other relevant data. The assumptions should be considered separately for each product group and be best-estimate and entity specific, representing a going-concern approach, rather than based on the assumptions a market participant would use. Changes in future experience should be allowed for in the ViF when sufficient evidence exists. The assumptions should be actively reviewed.

Principle 12: Economic assumptions must be internally consistent and be determined such that projected cash flows are valued in line with the prices of similar cash flows traded on the capital market. No smoothing of market or account balance values or unrealized gains is permitted.

Principle 13: ViF should be discounted using discount rates consistent with those that would be used to value such cash flows in the capital markets.

Principle 14: The reference rate is a proxy for a risk-free rate for the currency, term and liquidity of the liability cash flows. Where the liabilities are liquid the reference rate should, wherever possible, be the swap yield curve appropriate

Principle 15: Stochastic models and parameters should be appropriate, internally consistent and based on recent market data. Volatility assumptions should be based on those implied from derivative prices rather than the historical observed volatilities.

Principle 16: For participating business, assumptions need to be made about future bonus rates and the profit allocation between policy holders and shareholders. These should be consistent with the projection assumptions, established company practice and local market practice.

Principle 17: MCEV results should be disclosed at consolidated group level using a business classification consistent with the primary statements, with a clear description of what business is covered and what is not. Except where they are not considered material, compliance with the MCEV Principles is compulsory and should be explicitly disclosed.

MCEV Framework Changes

The MCEV approach is similar to the EEV and TEV approaches in the sense that all three attempt to value the net distributable profits to shareholders starting from statutory assets and liabilities. MCEV begins with the same decomposition of the statutory balance sheet as for TEV and EEV, that is, into:

- the ViF – the discounted value of future profits embedded in the statutory assets and liabilities, an analog to the EEV-PFVP component but based on the risk-neutral forward rate scenario; and
- the NAV – or the mark-to-market value of all assets in excess of statutory reserve requirements.

The NAVs under both the MCEV and EEV frameworks are in principle identical. It is only in the ViF/PVFP where the two approaches differ materially.

In order to generate market-consistent values for hedgeable risks (where market prices exist) and mark-to-model valuations for non-hedgeable risks, the MCEV approach further decomposes the ViF into four components, illustrated in Figure 7.2 and discussed in greater detail below.

Present Value of Future Profits (PVFP) is calculated in a similar manner as the EEV-PVFP with two important exceptions:

- first, real-world expected asset returns are replaced by risk-neutral, risk-free expected returns for all assets consistent with the implied risk-free forward rates;
- second, cash flows are discounted at the risk-free term structure of interest rates, ensuring in principle that the market value of all current *linear* assets and liabilities (e.g., without embedded options) are correctly reflected in the MCEV.

Market Consistent Embedded Value Components

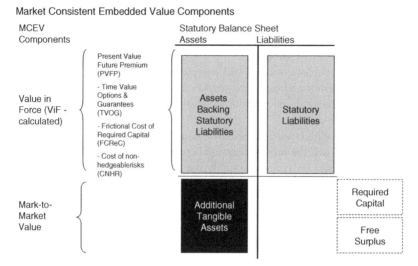

FIGURE 7.2 MCEV statutory balance sheet decomposition

Time Value of Options and Guarantees (TVOG), calculated as the difference between the deterministic PVFP described above and a full stochastic PVFP calculated using financial option pricing techniques.

By construction, the combination of PVFP and TVOG fully captures the mark-to-*market* value for traded risks. More specifically, if MCEV is applied to a traded option, the combined PVFP and TVOG would be equal to the market value of that option. This is tautological in the construction of TVOG and PVFP, for example

PVFP − TVOG

= deterministic DFCF − TVOG

= deterministic DFCF − (deterministic DFCF − risk-neutral stochastic DFCF)

= risk-neutral stochastic DFCF

Cost of Residual Non-Hedgeable Risk (CNHR), which represents the "mark-to-model" price of non-traded financial and non-financial risks such as mortality and longevity risks, operational risks, expense risks, etc.

Frictional Cost of Required Capital (FCReC), which measures the frictional cost to shareholders of capital "locked" into the business, is typically calculated as the projected corporate taxes and the investment management expenses for the assets backing the locked-in capital. This component, "new" to the MCEV framework, is discussed later.

The significant advances made by the MCEV framework in the area of financial market risk valuation are found in the differences between EEV-PVFP and MCEV-PVFP/TVOG. The advances in the area of non-hedgeable risk valuation are found in the new MCEV-CNHR component. Both are explained in detail below.

MCEV Valuation of Financial Market Risks

One of the criticisms of the TEV and EEV approaches was that they did not accurately value financial risk positions, primarily due to the use of management's best-estimate investment returns combined with a potentially inappropriate risk discount rate.

Valuing Assets: The 1=1 Test

In order to address this issue, the 2009 CFO Forum's MCEV Principles mandate that all financial risk positions, both those arising from assets and those embedded in liabilities, be valued using financial market approaches *as if* they were actively traded on financial markets.

For the asset side of the balance sheet (including traded derivatives), this requirement manifests itself in the "1=1 test," for example the requirement that the discounted present value of the stochastic future cash flows from the assets and traded instruments such as options, swaps, futures, forwards, etc. be valued in such a way that their *calculated value is equal to their traded market value*. This straightforward and intuitive requirement was frequently violated under TEV and EEV.

For simple fixed-income instruments, this 1=1 test can be found, for example, in the Guidance under CFO Forum Principle 14, which states that "Where a company invests in fixed-income assets which have a yield different to the reference rates, the company should make appropriate adjustments to the projected asset cash flows to ensure that the asset cash flows, discounted at the reference rates, equal the market value of the assets."

Valuing Liabilities

Valuing insurance liabilities is more challenging because they contain both financial elements, which can in principle be valued using observable market rates (e.g., a mark-to-*market* approach) and insurance risks, which need a mark-to-*model* approach.

Splitting Liabilities into Financial and Non-financial Components Insurance liabilities can be thought of as comprising two elements, a Financial Component of Liabilities (FCL) and a Non-Financial Component of Liabilities (NFCL), where the FCL is valued using mark-to-market techniques and the NFCL is valued using a mark-to-model approach (see, for example, CRO Forum, 2009). This is intuitively represented for PC claims in Figure 7.3.

As illustrated, the financial component of a PC liability is defined as the zero-coupon cash flow equal to the best-estimate future claims and expenses. By discounting with the current risk-free market rates,[7] the FCL is valued using a mark-to-market approach.

The NFCL of the PC liability represents the residual uncertainty surrounding the best-estimate cash flow. This residual comes from any uncertainty regarding the timing and ultimate amount of the claim and is represented by the light gray bar in the Figure. This is a non-traded risk, implying that mark-to-market approaches cannot be used; rather, a mark-to-model approach needs to be used to value the NFCL.

Valuing the FCL for LH Products In the example, the FCL for PC products was a zero-coupon cash flow representing the best-estimate claims. Similarly, the FCL cash flows for LH products are projected based on the best estimates for mortality, longevity, lapsation, etc.

---

[7]This simplistic representation does not allow for traded inflation. See Chapter 17 for a discussion on how to include inflation in PC FCLs.

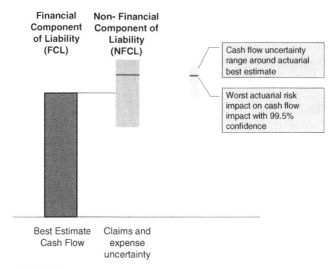

FIGURE 7.3   Financial and non-financial components of PC insurance liability

Even with this simplification, the application of the 1=1 test for LH liabilities is more complicated because of the embedded options and guarantees. MCEV Principle 13 provides the following guidance for valuing options embedded in assets: "Where cash flows contain financial options and guarantees such that they do not move linearly with market movements, all cash flows (should be) discounted using risk-neutral stochastic models" This is reinforced by Principle 15, which states that "The calibration of the model should be based on market values such as option implied volatilities and the initial swap rate curve for market-traded contracts (and . . .) the model should reproduce these values to a high degree of accuracy."

Principles 13–15 ensure that MCEV reproduces market values for traded securities, options and guarantees, giving some comfort that the approach can be applied to the more complex financial cash flows from LH insurance liabilities.

Mark-to-model for NFCL   The second area where MCEV improved on the EEV Principles was in developing a mark-to-*model* approach for non-hedgeable risks, found in Principle 9. There are many different sources of uncertainty in insurance liabilities, beyond financial market uncertainty, including but not limited to the following.

- *Insurance claims risk:* The uncertainty surrounding the best-estimate level and timing of claims, including claims inflation.
- *Expense risk:* The uncertainty surrounding future expenses relative to best-estimate expense assumptions in the cash flow model.
- *Behavioral risk:* The uncertainty surrounding management's assumptions about policy holders' decisions to lapse the policy, convert into an annuity, etc.

These risks can be significant. As such, they also need to be reflected in the "market value" of the liability.

Although markets have developed for some actuarial risks (e.g., insurance-linked securities and insurance derivatives), in general they are limited in scope and, even when they do exist, they are not actively traded. The lack of traded markets implies that a mark-to-*model* framework needs to be developed.

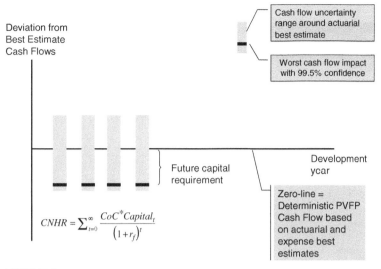

FIGURE 7.4 Cost of non-hedgeable risks

The CFO Forum's mark-to-model framework for non-hedgeable risks is based on a cost of capital approach. It defines CNHR as the cost of the economic capital necessary to support the non-hedgeable risk over the life of the transaction,[8] as illustrated in Figure 7.4: the gray bars indicate the uncertainty range around future claims and the thick black lines represent the level of capital held against the uncertainty.

This calculation is defined in Principle 9, with the guidance further defining the specifics for the calculation – including a 99.5% confidence interval for the capital calculation, the types of diversification benefit which can be included in the calculation, etc.

HOW IS MCEV CALCULATED IN PRACTICE?

Owing to the complexity of LH products, the FCL cannot be calculated using standard financial market-building blocks such as zero-coupon cash flows, traded put and call options, etc. which can be valued using closed-form or analytical formulae. As a consequence, numerical or simulation approaches must be used.

As the name implies, simulation approaches simulate the future contractual cash flows under different financial market scenarios and then discount the cash flows from each scenario to a present value. The value of the liability is the mean or average value over all simulations, illustrated by the following formula:

$$\text{FCL} = \frac{1}{N} \sum_{n=1}^{N} \sum_{t=1}^{T} \frac{\text{CF}(t, S_t, \text{BE}_t)}{\prod_{s=1}^{t} (1 + r_t)}$$

---

[8]An alternative approach, typically used by property and casualty insurers, is to add a margin (often called the Market Value Margin, MVM) based on a higher confidence interval around the firm's best-estimate claims development. For example, some firms use best-estimate (or 50th percentile) cash flows for the FCL and set the MVM to the difference between the 70th and 50th percentiles.

Process

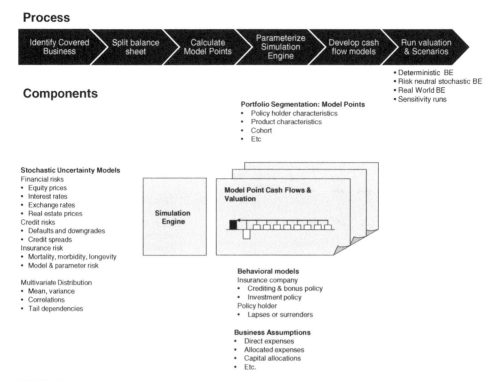

FIGURE 7.5 Components of an MCEV calculation framework

where N is the number of simulations, T is the maximum maturity of the cash flows, S_t represents the set of all simulated market prices up until date t, BE_t represents management's best estimate of future non-hedgeable risks, $CF(\cdot)$ represents the cash flow at time t (which depends on S_t and BE_t) and r_t represents the simulated one-period discount rate.

In order to meet the 1=1 test when applied to traded assets and options, a "risk-neutral" Economic Scenario Generator (ESG) is used. The ESG is calibrated for future interest rates, equity prices and other financial market developments such that the values calculated using the simulation approach are identical to the values found in the capital markets for the same instruments. While a detailed discussion of option valuation approaches is beyond the scope of this book, the general approach can be described at a high level using Figure 7.5.[9]

Defining the Scope

1. Identify the scope of the covered business, consistent with Principles 1–3 and 10.
2. Split the statutory balance sheet into assets and liabilities to be included in the NAV and ViF calculations according to Principles 4–6.

---

[9]The simulation approach is not appropriate for options which are path dependent, including for example options with American features, which can be exercised at any time, options such as Asian or averaging options, clique or high-water market options or options on risks which might "jump" and therefore might not be able to be dynamically hedged using underlying, traded instruments. In spite of these theoretical considerations, simulation is still the most widely used technique for calculating MCEV.

3. *(Optional)* To avoid seriatim or policy-by-policy valuation (which may take significant run time), segment the liability portfolio into a finite number of "model points," with each model point representing a homogenous pool and all model points collectively representing the portfolio. Typically, model points are defined by factors which segment the portfolio into groups whose future cash flows are "similar," for example client characteristics (age, gender, customer behavior, etc.), product features or conditions (guarantees), contract cohort date, etc.[10]

Define and Parameterize the Uncertainty

4. Develop and parameterize a risk-neutral ESG consistent with Principles 7 and 12–15 for all market risk factors which affect the policies' future cash flows.
   a. The ESG needs to characterize the full distribution of potential future financial market developments, including the paths, expected values, volatilities, correlations, etc. for interest rates, equities, credit spreads, foreign exchange rates, and so on.
   b. It must satisfy the 1=1 test for all assets as well as a broad range of instruments which behave "similarly" to the liability cash flows, including any embedded options and guarantees. The 1=1 test is satisfied if the simulated value of a traded instrument is equal to its observed market price A_j, for example $A_j = \dfrac{1}{N} \sum_{n=1}^{N} \sum_{t=1}^{T} \dfrac{CF_j(t, S_t)}{\prod_{s=1}^{t}(1 + r_t)}$ for a wide set of traded assets $j = 1, ..., J$.
   c. The ESG must be multi-period in nature, extending to the maturity of the longest contract date in the portfolio.
5. *(Optional)* Define and parameterize a real-world scenario generator for financial market projections centered around management's best estimates, included anticipated risk premia earned on holding bonds and equities. This is used for calculating real-world values, including the distribution of statutory profits and internal rates of return.
6. Define and parameterize distributions for the non-hedgeable risks (e.g., mortality/longevity risk, reserve risk, expense risk, etc.). These will be used to calculate the NFCL, with the best estimates used to "anchor" the FCL.

Define and Parameterize the Liability Cash Flows

7. Develop cash flow models for each product. These cash flow models produce cash flows at each date in the future which depend upon the realization of the exogenous, financial market variables and insurance/business risks, including the impact of contractually defined options and guarantees, management and policy holder behavior, and so on.
8. Develop behavioral models for each model point which describe the endogenous behavior of policy holders and the company consistent with Principles 7 and 11. Example behavioral assumptions include the following.

---

[10]This same segmentation or model point approach is used when valuing a portfolio of retail mortgages, including those within a Mortgage-Backed Security (MBS) structure. See Fabozzi (2012) for an example.

    a. *Profit participation behavior:* How will accounting investment returns be realized? How will crediting rates be set given investment returns, the strength of the balance sheet, etc.? How will they be credited to policy holders, split between terminal and periodic bonuses, and what is the residual for shareholders?

    b. *Investment decisions:* How are current assets invested? How will future premia be invested and assets rolled over? How will this change depend on market dynamics, the firm's balance sheet strength, etc.?

    c. *Policy holders' behavior:* How many policies will lapse or be surrendered as a function of bonus and crediting policy? Financial market developments? How will future, discretionary future premiums evolve? And so on . . .

Simulate and Discount

  9. Simulate and discount the modeled cash flows under different, risk-neutral scenarios generated by the ESG and calculate the mean value. The more simulations, the less error in the estimated value and the more stable the estimate.

    a. A single scenario is used to calculate PVFP, setting all actuarial and expense assumptions at their best-estimate values, projecting financial cash flows based on implied market forward rates and discounting using the appropriate risk-free rate.

    b. To calculate the FCL (PVFP and TVOG), simulate risk-neutral financial market developments, recalculating the present value under each scenario.

    c. Calculate CNHR: for each future year, set each individual non-financial risk (actuarial, business and expense risk) to its worst-case scenario within a 99.5% confidence interval and recalculate the stochastic PVFP after each shock. The difference between the original PVFP before and after the shock is equal to the risk capital needed for each future year. These are then multiplied by the cost of capital for non-hedgeable risks and discounted to their present value.[11]

  10. *Calculate sensitivities:* Revalue the portfolio under different, standardized scenarios, including for example a 10% immediate drop in equity values, a 10% drop in expense rates, a 5% increase in the base mortality table, and so on.

Side Comment on Calculating Risk Capital

The steps described earlier explain how to calculate the value of the portfolio and its sensitivities. If one also wants to use these cash flow models directly for calculating risk capital, then a nested simulation is required.

For risk capital calculated over a 1-year horizon, first simulate K (real-world) scenarios of market prices over the 1-year time horizon; in order to value the portfolio under each of these real-world scenarios, simulate N risk-neutral scenarios for each of the real-world scenarios for valuation purposes. In aggregate, this requires $K \times N$ scenario sets. If you had M products and

---

[11]Note that this approach for calculating the risk capital associated with non-hedgeable risks is not entirely appropriate as it shocks each risk variable individually and therefore does not capture the potentially strong interplay (or cross-gamma effects) between the different risk factors. One alternative is to generate stochastic-within-stochastic projections (e.g., for the first year, generate a simulation set of X thousand scenarios, for each of these, generate a further set of X thousand scenarios for year 2, and so on); while this may be more accurate in theory, it is practically more challenging and much more expensive to implement.

each product had P model points with maximum duration T, then you would have $K \times N \times M \times P \times T$ sets of cash flows to simulate and value.

Depending on your confidence interval, K will need to be very large because the simulation error for risk capital is higher than for the mean. Taking $K = 25,000, N = 5000, M = 10, P = 5$, the total number of simulated cash flows you would need to calculate is on the order of 6.25 billion sets of cash flows over T years. If you are a large international group, M might be more on the order of 250, implying a number on the order of 156 billion.

Calculating risk capital using nested simulations can be computer intensive. It is not unheard of to use 100+ quad-processor PCs in order to run calculations within a reasonable time (e.g., under 48 hours) for a large book of variable annuities. Given the high computational expense and the fact that you also need to have all liability models in one central library, you can see why large groups use portfolio reduction techniques such as portfolio replication, interpolated splines or regression techniques to calculate risk capital.[12]

Implementation Challenges

Implementation can be challenging both from a systems and a technical perspective. In addition, there is also the need to establish quality controls and discipline around the financial reporting process. The most challenging aspects include the following.

1. The development and calibration of the financial and actuarial models, including:
   a. the dynamic cash flow models and model point compression techniques for each product;
   b. the multi-currency, multi-asset-class, risk-neutral economic scenario generators calibrated to current option prices and the real-world economic scenario generators for sensitivity analysis;
   c. the distribution assumptions for actuarial risks such as mortality, longevity, reserve and expense uncertainty, etc.
2. The implementation of a robust, efficient and controlled systems environment.
   a. The implementation, documentation and independent validation of the models, parameters and assumptions, including a model governance framework outlining model and parameter documentation standards, validation standards and approval processes. In addition, a model change calendar, outlining when models can be changed during the year.
   b. Implementation in an overall business application and data architecture linking administration systems, cash flow projection systems, Treasury databases for valuation curves, etc. and separating and securing the production systems from the development and testing environment.
   c. Ensuring that the data flows and operational steps between all of the host-based administration systems and end-user computing applications are well controlled, efficient and robust.
   d. Ensuring that sufficient computing capacity is available to ensure that the run time fits within the closing period, including the need to rerun to correct for data errors, parameter updates, etc.
   e. In general, the design, implementation and testing of suitable Internal Controls Over Financial Reporting (ICOFR) to give management the confidence to rely on the numbers.

---

[12]See Chapter 17 for a detailed discussion of replicating portfolios.

FROM MCEV TO MVBS

The last step in the evolution is toward a Market Value Balance Sheet (MVBS) representation. In general, the MVBS yields similar results to the MCEV approach but begins from an entirely different conceptual starting point.

A Different Heritage

MCEV has in effect "evolved" from traditional EV calculations, both reflecting the net business to shareholders and making refinements for the valuation of hedgeable and non-hedgeable risks along the way. In this sense, TEV is to MCEV as Cro-Magnon man is to modern Homo sapiens: they represent different points along an evolutionary tree but share a common origin. As a consequence, despite the evolutionary advances, TEV, EEV and MCEV all share common calculation and representational features which are "inherited" from their common ancestor. For example:

- all start from the same statutory balance sheet, taking a "horizontal" slice for the ViF/PFVP and another for the net asset value;
- all take a shareholder's valuation directly, including corporate taxes and (in the case of MCEV), a frictional cost of capital;
- finally, all rely on deterministic "best-estimate" calculations to calculate the PVFP, an artificial split for representational purposes.

Suppose, however, that we started on a completely different planet with a completely different predecessor. More specifically, suppose that we started not from statutory accounts and the shareholder's perspective but from the desire to get the corporate balance sheet "right," the MVBS approach. On this alternative planet, the results would be slightly different in several important respects, as depicted in Figure 7.6.

- In contrast to MCEV, which takes a "horizontal slice" of the balance sheet, the MVBS approach takes the more traditional *vertical or "double-entry" approach*, putting a high emphasis on the accurate valuation of the assets and liabilities, separately.
- In contrast to MCEV, which incorporates all aspects of the shareholder's valuation directly, the MVBS only attempts to calculate the economic balance sheet *of the corporation*. Very concretely, this means that the Market Value of Assets (MVA) and the Market Value of Liabilities (MVL) entries are *pre-tax and there are no "frictional costs" applied*.
- Finally, consistent with the double-entry balance sheet, the MVBS would have a different representation and disclosure basis, providing transparency by directly calculating a separate market value of assets and market value of liabilities as opposed to a net number which is challenging to reconcile with either.

Calculation of the MVBS is straightforward from MCEV: the MVA is taken directly from the accounting systems as the fair value of current assets (e.g., excluding intangibles). In order to calculate the MVL, in a first step, calculate the MCEV *without taxes and without the frictional cost of capital*, and in a second step, deduct this value from the MVA.

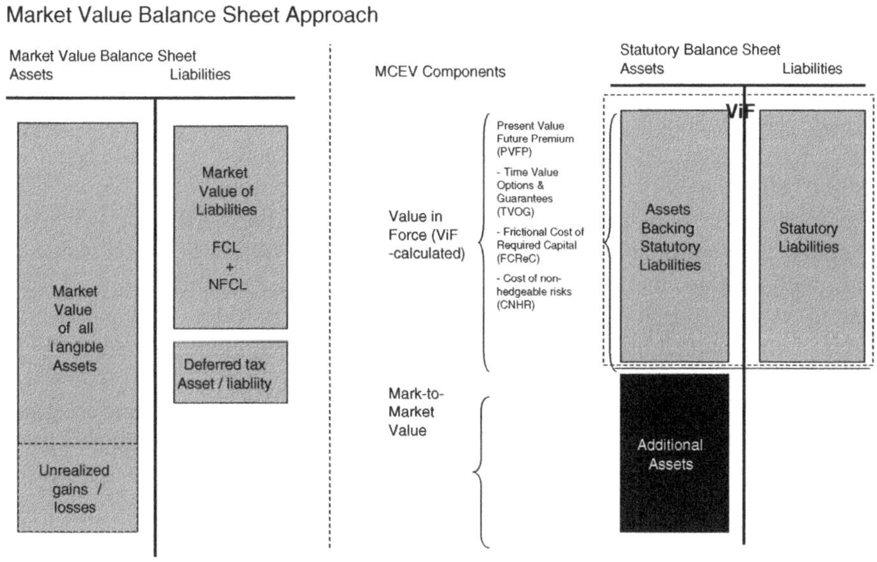

Market Value Balance Sheet Approach

FIGURE 7.6 EV statutory balance sheet decomposition

On the Exclusion of Frictional Costs

MCEV attempts to value all cash flows to the shareholder, from a shareholder's perspective. Because of this, MCEV deducts a frictional cost of required capital, FCReC. In contrast, the MVBS calculates a fair value balance sheet and does not apply a frictional cost of required capital. The frictional cost comprises four components, motivated in Swiss Re (2001, 2005), Tillinghast-Towers Perrin (2004, 2005), and O'Keeffe *et al.* (2005).

Limited Liability Put Option (LLPO). Given the limited liability nature of stock companies, shareholders are not obligated to make up any deficit if the firm's assets prove insufficient to cover its liabilities. The option to default has value to shareholders and in principle reduces the value of liabilities; as such, it impacts the value of all of the firm's obligations, including the value of its insurance liabilities.

Cost of double taxation. Corporate taxes have to be paid on corporate income (e.g., coupons and gains) generated by assets backing required capital; shareholders also have to pay taxes on corporate distributions (through dividends) or share capital gains if earnings are retained. Double taxation represents the additional corporate taxes compared with those payable if the assets were distributed today.

Agency costs. The managers of a firm may not always take decisions in the best interests of shareholders. For example, ego may drive M&A activity or a sense of entitlement may drive higher, non-salary perks such as the use of private jets, etc. Normally, incentives cannot be perfectly aligned between shareholders and managers due to contracting inefficiencies or asymmetric information.

Cost of financial distress. When firms go into insolvency proceedings, they often incur additional costs which dilute the value available to settle policy holder, debt holder and shareholder claims. For example, legal costs may dissipate a large fraction of the estate. In addition, the future franchise value may be lost.

During the period 2003–2008, these four elements were often used to justify the addition of a frictional cost of capital component in the MCEV calculation. Notwithstanding these theoretical arguments, for practical purposes the final MCEV Principles reduced the four categories to only the double taxation on investment returns (income and gains) and associated investment management charges (see CFO Forum, 2009b) based on projected capital which needs to be held.

The frictional cost of capital has no role to play in the MVBS for two reasons. First, because asset and liability values are carried as "exit values" (e.g., the value that a company with similar characteristics would be willing to pay for the assets or need to be paid to assume the liabilities). In general, the market value of the assets to a purchaser is not reduced by agency costs, the cost of financial distress and the benefits of the LLPO.

Second, and more important, *all* stock companies theoretically face the same costs and yet no other industry reports them in their accounts! Why the insurance industry should want to be unique in discounting its value explicitly when no other industry does so is beyond my understanding, especially if we are trying to combat an opacity discount: while of theoretical interest, it is not clear to me that discussing the LLPO as part of our voluntary disclosures is going to make our business more understandable or well liked by equity analysts, regulators and rating agencies.

It can be argued that the inclusion of such "frictional" costs in MCEV is to the detriment of our industry, increasing the challenge in communicating our value to an already confused analyst community. Apparently, the CFO Forum agreed (CFO Forum, 2009b), stating that "Consideration was given to include agency costs and cost of financial distress under frictional costs. However, the CFO Forum believed that these are general corporate risks that individual investors should assess rather than general business risks that management of the company should assess."

FINAL COMMENTS: WHITHER MCEV?

The CFO Forum's MCEV Principles were developed during 2003–2007, in parallel with the European Solvency II requirements, with the industry strongly supporting the integration of market-consistent approaches into a risk-based capital regime. The reasoning was simple: the industry wanted to remove the perceived "opacity discount" for LH businesses through more consistent and objective disclosures. In addition, MCEV offered more flattering valuations during the bull market of 2002–2007 when it was developed.

From the regulatory perspective, MCEV was also acceptable as it is natural to assume that policy holder claims can eventually be settled as long as there is sufficient value in the firm, either by putting the business into run-off or shifting the portfolio (and associated embedded value) to another insurance company.

The Wake-up Call, 2008 Market Volatility

Unfortunately, the global crisis of 2008 and the subsequent European sovereign debt crisis in 2012 have shown that market-consistent values are highly volatile – a volatility which was not appreciated earlier given that MCEV was developed during 5 years of benign (and, in retrospect, bubble) financial markets.

Volatility is not necessarily desirable in a solvency regime, being more likely to trigger supervisory intervention and resolution "fire drills" during times of crisis. Banks had the benefit of the "banking book" held at amortized cost during the 2008 crisis, with the market-value "trading books" contributing materially to solvency volatility during the crisis. It is fair to say that most, if not all, of the world's banks would have been put into insolvency if they also had to mark-to-market their banking book using observable mortgage and credit spreads.

While one could argue that more capital should be held to prevent these fire drills, the reality is that short-term fluctuations in market risk aversion and the associated "flight to quality" can cause major dislocations which do not reflect the underlying viability or cash-flow solvency of the business. In addition, shareholders will demand capital to be repatriated during long, sustained periods of favorable market developments as opposed to leaving the capital "locked" into the firm, apparently doing very little for shareholders.

The Paradox

On the one hand, the volatility inherent in "clean" MCEV figures mirrors the volatility of our share price. In addition, most of this volatility is "self-inflicted." Traditional LH savings and retirement businesses generally take interest rate mismatch and credit risk positions with an eye toward higher earnings; if this is our business model, then we should be prepared for the consequences when financial markets move against us.

On the other hand, it is also clear that short-term market fluctuations may *not* reflect the ultimate security of policy holders' claims. For example, as long as the liabilities are backed with a diversified portfolio of high-quality, cash-flow-viable bonds and are reasonably matched from an asset/liability perspective, then policy holder interests will remain secure even in the face of sudden changes in market risk aversion adversely impacting bond spreads.

The point that is worth making (and the lesson that is supported by experience through the last few crises) is that the two issues, shareholder value and policy holder security, are not as perfectly aligned as originally thought when Solvency II was being developed.

Let me illustrate this with a concrete example. Suppose that in 2006 you were offered two life portfolios:

- pay-out annuities perfectly matched with Italian government bonds or
- the same pay-out annuities matched with German government bonds.

In 2006, most in the industry would have paid the same for both portfolios because there was little or no difference between Italian and German government bonds. Fast forward and ask the same question. Which portfolio would you pay more for in 2012, at the height of the European sovereign bond crisis? Clearly, the business backed by the German bond portfolio would have a higher value because the Italian sovereign bonds lost significant market value relative to the Bunds while the value of the liability cash flows remained the same for any company aspiring to maintain a solid financial rating.

Does this necessarily mean that the obligations backed by the Italian sovereign bonds are any less secure? The answer depends on your perception of the cash-flow viability of Italian sovereign bonds. If you believed that Italy was certain to repay its debt, then policy holders would be no less secure than before, even though shareholders would have clearly lost significant value. In short, while they are related, policy holder security and shareholder value are not identical.

The Challenge

Unfortunately, the Solvency II framework is based on market-consistent principles, cast in stone before the 2008 crisis and offering limited ability to incorporate such a simple insight gleaned through practical experience.

One way to resolve the paradox is to offer a "banking book" for solvency purposes for some of the general account assets matching the liabilities, neutralizing bond spread movements when they are not due to changing credit quality. This is equivalent to the matching adjustment, which has only limited applicability under Solvency II.

The matching adjustment and other "dampeners" – such as the inclusion of an illiquidity premium or volatility adjuster and yield curve extrapolation to an Ultimate Forward Rate (UFR) – are attempts to dampen the effects of changing market conditions on solvency requirements while retaining some semblance of market consistency; a challenging task. These are also changes which take the CFO Forum's principles further and further away from an economic perspective and further away from the way our shares are actually valued in the market.

Conclusions

Three conclusions can be drawn from these experiences and the discussion of the last three chapters.

- First, "clean" market-consistent metrics are the best at explaining the value of our company and should therefore play a prominent role in managing the value of our company.
- Unfortunately, pure market-consistent approaches make a horrible basis for solvency rules, especially for well-managed and well-matched books of business.
- If we make adjustments to stabilize market-consistent approaches for solvency calculations, then we should clearly recognize that the two sets of measures serve different purposes and we should not confuse them.

Three

Better Insights – Managing Value

W hat gets measured, gets managed. If we want to manage shareholder value, we first have to measure it.

The previous part of the Handbook argued that value managers should use market-consistent approaches combined with New Business and Investment RAPMs to measure value because they better reflect share values than accounting-based approaches and because they provide better insights for managing risk-based, capital-intensive businesses.

While better information is necessary, it is not sufficient: ultimately, the right decisions have to be taken. How, then, to translate better information into better management? In the interests of simplicity, we define *management* as the set of:

- *strategies*, defining high-level goals;
- *actions*, needed to achieve those goals; and
- *metrics*, used to determine whether the goals have been attained.

CFOs and CROs can create value in their companies by challenging and shaping the strategies, actions and metrics used to manage the business. Strategies and actions are unique to the firm. However, it is possible to define *rules of the game*, or generic strategies, and core competencies generically used in creating value.

Challenging and influencing management decisions takes better insight. As illustrated in the following figure, this part of the Handbook outlines the rules of the game, core competencies and management actions used in the PC and LH insurance and banking segments. It represents a type of shorthand describing what is important for creating value in each segment and why. It then describes two core competencies required by all segments – sales and distribution to support profitable growth and operating efficiency to lower cost-to-income ratios.

2. Better Insights –
What strategies, initiatives and KPIs by segment?

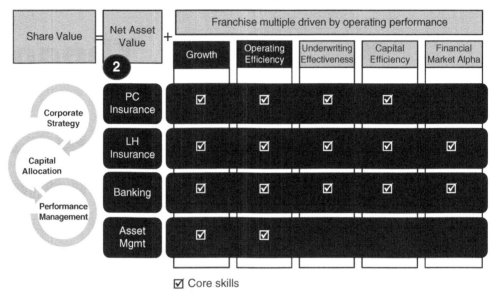

☑ Core skills

FIGURE P3-1   Structure of the following chapters

CHAPTER 8

Property and Casualty Insurance

This chapter outlines the "rules of the game" (or generic strategies) and core competencies for creating value in PC insurance, beginning with a brief history and economic rationale of the industry.

HISTORY AND ECONOMIC RATIONALE[1]

The concept behind property and casualty insurance – sharing risks across a larger collective so that the burden is made manageable for an individual – is as old as human society; for example, early agrarian societies often committed to rebuild the home of a member in the event of fire or other catastrophe. Through such commitments, risks which were infrequent but catastrophic to an individual become manageable to the collective.

Modern insurance involving an upfront payment to protect against potential future losses is recorded in early history, especially with risks arising from commercial, maritime activities. One contract is recorded as early as 1750 BC in the Babylonian Code of Hammurabi: a merchant financing a shipment could pay the lender an additional premium to cancel the loan should the shipment be stolen or lost at sea. Similarly, in Athens c. 400 BC, a "maritime loan" provided merchant financing but repayment was cancelled if the ship was lost; the rates on these loans differed according to the time of year, evidence of risk-based underwriting and pricing.

Coverage of personal losses is also recorded very early: during the period of Achaemenian monarchs in Persia (550–330 BC), upon receipt and registration of a payment by the court, the "insured" could receive up to twice the amount of the payment during a time of personal need.

Insurance policies not bundled with loans or other contracts were introduced in Genoa in the 14th century, allowing insurance risk decisions to be separated from investment decisions. Lloyds of London originated in the 1680s in a London coffee house owned by Edward Lloyd, where parties would meet to exchange information. Eventually, it evolved into a marketplace where merchants and ship owners could find "names," or individuals willing to underwrite maritime risks. Early Lloyds' names and syndicates differed from modern insurance companies in that they had unlimited personal liability, backing the ventures with their entire personal wealth; limited liability partnerships were introduced at Lloyds only in 2007.

---

[1]For more information, see Prudential Insurance Company of America (1915), Vaughn (1997), Trenerry (2009).

Insurance provided by limited liability companies can be traced to the Great Fire of London in 1666, which destroyed more than 13,000 houses. Afterwards, private insurance was promoted as a matter of public policy and, in 1681, Nicholas Barbon and 11 associates established England's first fire insurance company, the "Insurance Office for Houses," initially insuring 5000 homes.

The first insurance company in the United States was formed in Charleston, South Carolina, in 1732, also focusing on fire insurance. Later, in 1752, Benjamin Franklin helped to popularize insurance and founded the "Philadelphia Contributionship for the Insurance of Houses from Loss by Fire," the first company to promote risk engineering and risk-based underwriting: the company advised policy holders how to mitigate certain fire hazards and refused to insure certain buildings, such as wooden houses, where the risk of fire was too great.

Economic Rationale

PC insurers receive a premium upfront in compensation for indemnifying the policy holder against covered losses in the future; the goal of the contract is to restore the policy holder to their original financial position following the event.

Benefits to the Contracting Parties
The policy holder benefits by being protected against potential losses against a premium which they deem reasonable given their personal risk aversion and financial circumstances.

The insurance company benefits if the premium is appropriate for the policy's risk, both in terms of expected claims and the policy's contribution to the risk of the overall portfolio. PC insurers build reserve assets to cover the policy's expected losses and hold capital to cover any unexpected losses at the portfolio level.

The policy holder and the insurance company can mutually agree on a premium because of *risk pooling* and *diversification*. In general, insurers underwrite a large pool of similar risk exposures. The aggregate portfolio benefits from diversification because individual risks are not perfectly correlated; in other words, it is not likely that the insurer will see a loss on each and every contract at the same time.

Diversification implies that the ratio of the *uncertain losses relative to the expected losses will be lower for the portfolio than for each individual risk*. Put simply, the insurance company needs less capital to support the portfolio than the original policy holders would need in order to achieve the same level of security. Even if they face the same cost of capital and the same level of risk aversion, an insurance company will be able to offer coverage at a price which individuals find attractive because of this diversification.

Benefits to Society
In addition to the benefits to the contracting parties, society also benefits as private insurance reduces negative externalities associated with insurable events. A negative externality is said to occur if the actions or behavior of one person impact another. For example, the decision to speed while driving or to build a home in an earthquake zone may cause an externality if the losses from a traffic accident or earthquake are implicitly or explicitly covered by the broader society through public support mechanisms.

In addition to mitigating the externality, private insurance more closely aligns the cost of coverage with the benefits of the coverage. Externality considerations help to explain why some forms of insurance are mandatory as a matter of public policy, for example, third-party motor liability and health insurance.

Insurable Risks

Not all risks can be insured. "Insurable risks" are defined by the following characteristics.[2]

1. *Risks which diversify to some extent when pooled with other risks.* Insurance works because of risk pooling and diversification. In general, home owner or automobile property coverage diversifies because individual loss events (e.g., fire, theft, damage, etc.) are largely independent of one another. The exceptions are losses triggered by natural catastrophes such as earthquakes, floods, hailstorm, etc., which can simultaneously affect many automobiles or homes in the same area. Nonetheless, even natural catastrophe risks can be diversified if the portfolio is broad enough, as it is not likely that a major Californian earthquake will occur at the same time as an earthquake in Japan or windstorms in Europe or Asia, and so on.

2. *There is a loss to the policy holder which can be calculated and is definite in terms of time, place and cause.* Insurance *indemnifies* the policy holder for covered losses, implying that the policy holder has a direct interest in the loss and not a speculative interest in the outcome. These characteristics (indemnification, direct loss interest and clear definition of the loss event) are what separates an insurance contract from a financial derivative or a bet on a football game.[3]

3. *A loss which is accidental or outside the control of the policy holder.* An insurable risk should not be influenced by the policy holder as this could cause moral hazard. Shavell (1979) defines moral hazard as "the tendency of insurance protection to alter an individual's motive to prevent loss." Moral hazard causes the interests of the insured and the insurer to diverge. For example, if a driver were to drive recklessly because of insurance and more conservatively if they had none, then this could be a non-insurable risk due to moral hazard; fortunately, there are mechanisms for limiting moral hazard and better aligning interests, for example through deductibles, co-insurance, policy limits, bonus/ malus or "good driver" premium adjustments, etc.

4. *A meaningful or material loss to the policy holder which can be covered at a premium deemed acceptable as a substitute for self-insurance.* In other words, the insurance has to make economic sense for the two parties involved.

Examples
PC insurance provides coverage to individuals and corporations covering a broad spectrum of risks. Table 8.1 gives a flavor of the diversity of perils covered.

---

[2]For further discussion, see Mehr *et al.* (1985).

[3]The IMF differentiates between insurance and financial derivatives along the two dimensions of indemnification and loss event triggers: "Insurance is not a form of financial derivative. Insurance contracts provide individual institutional units exposed to certain risks with financial protection against the consequences of specified events, many of which cannot be expressed in terms of market prices" (IMF, 1998).

TABLE 8.1 PC insurance products/perils

Type	Description
Property	Protection against loss or damage to real or personal property from a variety of perils, including fire, lightning, business interruption, glass breakage, tornado, windstorm, hail, water damage, explosion, riot, civil commotion, rain, damage from aircraft or vehicles.
Crops	Protection against loss or damage to crops from a variety of perils, including fire, lightning, loss of revenue, tornado, windstorm, hail, flood, rain or damage by insects.
Flood	Standalone or supplementary coverage for loss or damage to real or personal property from flood.
Farm owners	Insurance package for farms and ranches similar to home owners, including farm dwellings and contents, barns, stables, other farm structures, inland marine, mobile equipment and livestock.
Home owners	Insurance package combining real and personal property with liability coverage. Coverage can include dwelling, appurtenant structures, unscheduled personal property and additional living expenses. Sub-categories include condominiums, owner occupied, tenants and mobile homes.
Commercial multiple peril	Insurance package covering two or more property or liability risks. In addition to general property and liability risks, may also include builders' risk (during the course of construction), e-commerce, business owners (for small/medium-sized apartments, offices and retail stores), commercial package policy (broader package of perils), commercial farm and ranch, etc.
Mortgage guarantee	Indemnification of a lender for a loss upon borrower foreclosure.
Ocean marine	Coverage for ocean and inland water transportation exposures, including goods or cargoes, ships or hulls, earnings and liability.
Inland marine	Coverage for property that may be in transit (e.g., cargo) or goods which are at different locations (e.g., off-road construction equipment) or scheduled property (e.g., home owner's personal property). Also included are transportation and communication infrastructure, including bridges, tunnels, piers, wharves, docks, pipelines, power and phone lines, television towers, etc. Special categories may include animal mortality, electronic data processing (EDP), pet insurance, communication equipment, event cancellation and travel coverage for trip cancellation/interruption, lost baggage, etc.
Financial guarantee	Indemnification for a loss associated with the failure of a third party to perform a financial obligation.
Medical malpractice	Indemnification of a licensed health care provider or facility against liability resulting from the death or injury of any person due to misconduct, negligence or incompetence in rendering or failure to render professional services. Sub-categories include acupuncture, ambulance services, anesthetist, assisted living facility, chiropractic, community health centers, dentists and dental hygienists, home care, hospitals, nurses, ophthalmic, optometry, osteopathy, pharmacy, physical therapy, physicians and surgeons, podiatry, psychiatry, psychology, speech pathology.
Earthquake	Indemnification for property losses resulting from sudden trembling or shaking of the earth, including that caused by volcanic eruption.

(continued)

TABLE 8.1 (*Continued*)

Type	Description
Workers' compensation	Indemnification for employer's liability for injuries, disability or death of persons in their employment, without regard to fault, as prescribed by compensation laws or other statutes.
Other liability categories	Indemnification for legal liability resulting from negligence, carelessness or failure to act resulting in property damage or personal injury to others. Can include completed operations (defective work), contractual liability, day care centers, directors and officers, elevators and escalators, employment practices, employee benefits, environmental pollution, fire legal liability, kidnap and ransom, liquor, municipal acts, nuclear energy, personal injury (discrimination, false arrest, illegal detainment, libel, malicious prosecution, slander, mental anguish, violation of privacy), premises and operations, professional errors and omissions, veterinarian, Internet liability.
Product liability	Coverage for losses or injuries caused by defect or malfunction of the product.
Automobile	Personal lines coverage of property and liability coverage for private passenger automobiles, motorcycles and recreational vehicles. Commercial lines for any vehicle engaged in commerce.
Mobile homes under transport	Property and liability.
Aircraft	Property coverage for aircraft (hull) and contents as well as aircraft owners' and manufacturers' liability to passengers, airports and other third parties.
Fidelity	Coverage of an employer's loss resulting from an employee's dishonest act.
Surety	Insurer agrees to pay a third party compensation if the insured should fail to complete their obligation due to default, acts or omissions.
Burglary and theft	Indemnification for property taken or destroyed by break-in, entering the insured's premises, burglary, theft, forgery or counterfeiting, fraud.
Boiler and machinery	Coverage of losses due to a failure of boilers, machinery and other electrical equipment, including property damage, temporary repairs and liability damage.
Credit – commercial	Coverage purchased by manufacturers, merchants, service providers and others extending credit for losses or damages resulting from non-payment of debts owed to them.
Credit – personal	Indemnification for losses due to non-payment of debts owed. Most important categories include the coverage of debts used to finance homes, automobiles and other personal property used as collateral as well as protection against involuntary unemployment and the total destruction of the collateral asset.
Title	Indemnification if the title to real and personal property has undiscovered defects.

Note: This list is a highly summarized and condensed version of the NAIC (2007) Uniform Property & Casualty Product Coding Matrix.

Products

PC insurance is generally characterized along three dimensions. The first is the differentiation between *property* insurance, providing indemnification for damage to or loss of the insured's own property, and *casualty or liability* insurance, which provides indemnification for injury or damage to the property of a third party caused by the insured.

The second dimension is the *customer segment* to which the policies are sold, with *personal lines* sold to individuals or small business owners and *commercial lines* sold to larger companies.

The third is the difference between the contracting parties, with *primary insurance* representing a contract between the policy holder and an insurance company and *reinsurance* representing a contract to transfer risk from the primary insurer to another (re)insurance company.

Primary Insurance

Most PC insurance is annually renewable, able to be re-priced every year based on actual loss experience; however, some policies are written on a multi-year basis, securing capacity at a known and predictable premium.

Important contract features of a primary insurance policy include *deductibles or retention levels* (the first loss amount to which the policy holder is exposed before the insurance policy begins to pay), *policy limits* (the maximum amount of the insurance coverage), *exclusions* (the perils which are not covered in the contract) and the *co-insurance rate* (the proportion of the loss retained by the policy holder between the deductible and the limit). All these features can be used to align the interests of the insured and the insurer and mitigate moral hazard. In order to better align incentives, policies may also have an explicit *bonus/malus system*, whereby customers with a low claims experience pay lower premium rates in the future and those with a high claims experience are charged more.

Reinsurance

Reinsurance contracts transfer risk between an insurer and a (re)insurance company. Reinsurance is used primarily for one of three purposes.

- First, as a capital substitute by lowering exposure to risk concentrations and decreasing the volatility of results. For example, a regional insurer may find itself quickly over-exposed to local earthquake losses and therefore restricted by its capital base in writing more profitable home owners' business. By purchasing reinsurance, some of the peak risk is transferred to a reinsurer, allowing the primary insurer to continue underwriting profitable business. A directly related benefit is that the reinsurance also leads to lower earnings volatility.
- Second, as a balance sheet management tool, mitigating the effects of uneconomic reserve or capital requirements and/or monetizing the embedded value of the portfolio.
- Third, to take advantage of the underwriting capabilities of the reinsurance company, especially for unusual risks or in new or developing markets.

Reinsurance contracts are differentiated along two dimensions. The first dimension is between treaty and facultative reinsurance: *treaty reinsurance* is a contract negotiated in advance to cover specific business that the primary insurer has underwritten or intends to underwrite; in contrast, *facultative reinsurance* is negotiated and priced separately for each insurance contract covered. Often the two are used in combination; for example, facultative reinsurance is purchased when the primary policy represents a large exposure not adequately covered by a reinsurance treaty in terms of size or in terms of coverage.

The second dimension is between proportional and non-proportional reinsurance. *Proportional reinsurance* transfers a fixed percentage of the covered business, starting from the ground up (*quota share* reinsurance) or after a fixed deductible (*surplus* reinsurance). *Non-proportional coverage* indemnifies the insurer only if the loss is above a specific threshold, called the retention level, and up to a specific limit. Non-proportional reinsurance includes *excess of loss* (XL) reinsurance, which can be defined on a *per risk* basis (providing coverage and eliminating the risk of a single, large commercial exposure), *per event* basis (providing coverage for catastrophic events such as hurricanes, earthquakes, etc.) or *aggregate portfolio* basis (providing coverage for a larger than expected number of large losses combined, sometimes called a *stop-loss* cover).

FROM PRINCIPLES TO RULES OF THE GAME

The economics of PC businesses are the easiest to understand and manage because there is a reasonably direct relationship between value creation and cash: the premiums and a significant part of the claims uncertainty are resolved during the underwriting year, with the remainder of the claims emerging after only a few more years.[4]

Principles for Managing a PC Insurer

The fact that value and cash are largely synchronized has three benefits. First, operating performance and underwriting results become clear very quickly, over quarters and years as opposed to decades, allowing management to make course corrections earlier and with more confidence. Second, it is more difficult to fool oneself by using accounting gimmicks and the valuation chicanery often associated with longer-term financial products such as LH retirement and savings products and financial derivatives. Third, shareholders like to see dividends rather than paper profits and sustainable dividends can only be paid out of cash.

As a consequence, the underlying principles for successful PC insurance businesses are relatively straightforward: superior execution in sales, expense management and underwriting and the preservation of capital to support profitable underwriting. As illustrated in Figure 8.1, this requires core skills across the board, except in financial market risk taking.

While it might be taken for granted that excellence in sales, expense management and underwriting is required, the principle of preserving capital and the limitation of financial market risk warrants some explanation.

Invested capital is what allows a PC company to underwrite profitable business: capital does not do much during sunny weather, but it definitely has to be there after the storm in order to cover unexpected claims. It may seem a paradox that invested capital can earn a premium

---

[4]The obvious exception is long-tailed insurance lines such as product liability, construction and environmental liability (e.g., asbestos) and workers' compensation where claims uncertainty emerges over longer periods. For these lines especially, self-delusion through inadequate reserving can be sustained longer.

PC Insurance – What strategies, skills and KPIs by segment?

Managing the Economic Profit of a PC Insurer

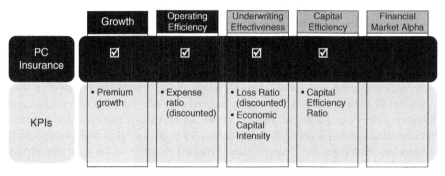

☑ Core skills

FIGURE 8.1 PC insurance economic profit sources and core skills

from shareholders while "sitting idle in the sunshine" most of the time. In fact, it is working hard to earn that premium: it is supporting the company's profitable underwriting activities.

Some occasionally suggest levering the capital in a PC insurer by taking more financial market risk through higher risk assets. This is an unwise strategy: if the insurer suffers a loss in capital due to financial market developments, then it not only loses the net asset value directly associated with the investment, but also the profits and franchise value from future underwriting activities which can no longer be supported due to the diminished capital base.

This is an important point. Consider a successful PC insurer valued at 1.5× invested capital due to its underwriting expertise, expense management and growth prospects, dedicating its capital to support its underwriting activities. Suppose it takes additional financial market risk: any market losses will have a direct 1× loss in net asset value. Unfortunately, it will also have an additional 0.5× impact if the capacity to underwrite profitable business in the future becomes constrained relative to expectations. On the contrary, a financial market gain will generate earnings but not excess value, implying a multiple of 1×. The higher valuation multiple enjoyed by a successful PC insurer is derived from its core underwriting activity and puts a very high price on financial market losses, one of the few downsides to having a higher market multiple.

For this reason, the investment strategy of PC insurers is generally conservative, with the goal of earning a reasonable return but preserving the firm's net asset value to support its core underwriting activities. The assets backing reserves and capital are typically well-diversified, investment grade, duration-matched fixed-income assets with few derivatives or structured products. Real asset positions are taken only with funds in excess of reserve and capital requirements, if at all.

Equity analysts reinforce this conservative investment strategy by removing capital gains from the PC insurer's results when evaluating the long-term operating profitability of PC insurers. In other words, earnings from financial markets do not influence the market multiple or the premium (or discount) that analysts are willing to pay for the firm's invested capital.

From Principles to "Rules of the Game"

Keeping these principles in mind, there are three rules of the game that should be kept in mind for creating value in PC insurance.

RULES OF THE GAME: PC INSURANCE

- Focus on risk-adjusted profitability and growth.
  - Grow the top-line through superior sales and distribution capabilities.
  - Convert top-line into excess bottom-line returns. Keep the combined ratio below 100% and ensure a positive new business economic profit through
    - operating efficiency/expense management
    - underwriting excellence
    - claims management.
- Preserve capital so that you can continue to underwrite profitable new business.
  - Hold reserves and capital appropriate for the risk of your portfolio.
  - Invest assets backing reserves and capital in low-risk assets which closely match the duration and liquidity characteristics of your liabilities.
- Manage your capital efficiently.
  - Minimize uneconomic capital or reserve requirements through balance sheet management.
  - Invest as much free capital as possible in profitable growth opportunities, returning excess capital to shareholders if retained earnings are in excess of profitable growth opportunities.

FROM RULES TO THE VALUATION OF PC BUSINESSES

The first-best solution for measuring and managing the value of a PC insurer is to use PC new business Economic Profit (EP) information. While available internally, it is not generally available externally, neither to analysts evaluating your company nor for peer comparisons. As a consequence, an "outside-in" valuation has to rely on financial statements and supplemental disclosures as well as assumptions to translate accounting information into economics.

The value of a PC insurer is equal to its current net asset position (e.g., the value of all assets and liabilities as a closed block of business using ongoing business expense assumptions) plus its franchise value (e.g., the value of the company's future new business). In general, it is easier to value a PC franchise value based on its historical financial statements if the following conditions are met:

1. the business is in a steady state in terms of business mix, rate of growth and underwriting and expense performance;
2. the asset portfolio is conservative and matches the duration and liquidity characteristics of the liabilities;
3. the capital supporting the business is appropriate, with no excess or surplus capital.

If these conditions are met, then past performance may be a good indicator of future performance and the valuation of a PC insurer proceeds in three steps, described below. If these conditions are not met, then the analyst will have to use their judgment and adjust historical figures as appropriate to better reflect the value of future business.

TABLE 8.2 PC net asset value

Balance sheet items	Generic adjustments
+ Assets	Adjust assets to fair or market value. Deduct non-tangible assets – e.g., goodwill, capitalized deferred acquisition costs (DAC) or value of business acquired (VOBA).
– Liabilities	Assess reserve adequacy relative to best estimate, ultimate reserve requirements and adjust as necessary. This can be challenging for long-tail liability lines such as product liability or workers' compensation, which can be materially impacted by changing litigation precedents and the late emergence of latent developments. Discount the best-estimate, ultimate reserves to a fair value basis,* offset by an appropriate market value margin reflecting the cost of capital needed to support the portfolio in run-off.
+/– Off-balance sheet commitments	Deduct any underfunded pension obligations. Deduct the value of guarantees or other off-balance sheet commitments.
= TNAV	

*As a rule of thumb, the discount effect will be similar to the risk margin for diversified primary insurers, an assumption implicit in the CFO Forum's 2009 MCEV Principles governing the calculation of Group MCEV for multi-line insurers.

Step 1: Determine the Current Net Asset Value of the Insurer

The first step is to calculate the current net asset value of the business. This is done by adjusting the balance sheet for intangible assets, revaluing assets and liabilities to fair value where necessary and adding/deducting off-balance sheet obligations. These adjustments are described in Table 8.2.

Step 2: Determine the Normalized Value of Next Period's New Business

The second step is to calculate the normalized value of new business using the PC new business EP formula. Compared with other financial services segments, the PC industry generally provides sufficient disclosures to understand new business economic profit if the firm is in a steady state. Table 8.3 gives an example of net income information generally disclosed by firms in financial statements or in supplementary disclosures.

There are four primary differences between PC new business EP (PC.EP) and the net income from financial disclosures,[5] as described above.

---

[5]The tables and discussion in this chapter are net of reinsurance. Reinsurance is used as a risk management and a capital management tool and will generally affect the firm's financials as follows.

- Net premiums will be lower than gross premiums as premium is ceded to the reinsurer.
- The combined ratio will likely be higher, reflecting that business is ceded at rates sufficient to cover the reinsurer's expected claims as well as its cost of capital.
- Non-proportional reinsurance will typically provide more stable loss ratio and limit downside risk.
- Acquisition expense ratios may improve if ceding commission is paid by the reinsurer. The ceding commission and associated "over-ride" defrays the direct and indirect acquisition costs of the primary insurer.

TABLE 8.3 PC net income

+ Operating income

   + Underwriting results

   = + Premium

     ×(1

     − Combined Ratio)

     o/w^* − Expense ratio (calendar year)

         + Acquisition expense ratio

        o/w + Commission

           + Other acquisition

        + Administration expense ratio

     o/w − Loss ratio (calendar year)

        o/w + Accident year ratio

          o/w + NatCat

             + Attritional & large losses

         + Run-off ratio

  + Risk free or normalized investment returns

    + Average assets

    o/w + Assets backing reserves

       + Assets backing capital, free surplus

    × "Low risk" rate of return

+ Non-operating income

  + Investment income beyond normalized returns, realized & unrealized gains

  + Non-operating items

    − Head office expenses

    − Cost financial leverage - interest on double leverage & Tier 2 capital

    − Restructuring charges, net investment in new businesses, projects, etc.

= Net income before tax

    − Tax

= Net income after tax

---

* o/w = of which

Operating efficiency. In general, the calendar year expense ratio is reported, which differs from the discounted expected accident year expense ratio used in PC.EP by the discounting effect and any unexpected expense developments leading to expense over-/under-runs relative to long-term expectations. *Except for the discounting effect, the two should be similar in a steady state.*

Underwriting effectiveness. Using the definition of the Total Cost of Risk (TCR) defined in Chapter 3, underwriting effectiveness comprises two elements: the *discounted expected accident year loss ratio* plus the *cost of underwriting risk capital needed to support the business over its expected lifetime.*

Financial disclosures report a calendar year loss ratio. The primary difference between the calendar year loss ratio and the discounted expected accident year loss ratio is the discounting effect and the fact that calendar year loss ratios reflect developments from past underwriting years (calendar and accident year loss ratios are described later in this chapter). *Except for the discounting effect, the two will be similar in a steady state.*

In addition to the loss ratio, the capital used in PC.EP to reflect underwriting effectiveness differs from disclosed capital measures in three respects:

- First, PC.EP should represent the present value of all future capital requirements needed to support the slice of *new business* over its expected lifetime, represented by the new business economic capital intensity $\left(\text{ECI} = \left[\sum \min C_t/(1+r)^t\right]/P\right)$. The disclosed capital represents the "slice" of capital needed to support *all* current and past business *in this year only. In a steady state, the two should be similar except for the discount effect.*
- Second, PC.EP deducts the cost of capital only for *underwriting* risk capital, whereas financial disclosures reflect the actual capital held in the business, including capital held to cover financial market risks. *The two measures of capital will be similar if the company follows a conservative investment strategy* (e.g., underwriting risk clearly dominates financial market risk taking) and *if they use capital efficiently* (e.g., there is no excess capital which could in principle be paid out as a dividend).
- Third, the disclosed capital figures may reflect excess capital, represented by a steady-state capital efficiency ratio $\left(\text{CER}\left[\sum C_t/(1+r)^t\right]/\left[\sum \min C_t/(1+r)^t\right]\right)$ significantly greater than 1. The analyst may have to adjust historical capital levels when attributing capital to new business in order to remove any excess capital, but only if the analyst believes that the actual capital intensity will be more aggressively managed in the future (e.g., through the firm's dividend policy).

Investment returns and the discount effect. PC.EP does not recognize any investment returns except for the risk-free return on capital supporting underwriting risks; this is because PC.EP discounts expected future claims and expenses at the risk-free interest rate and represents a present value perspective.

However, realized investment income can be a good proxy for the discounting effect on reserves and the risk-free return on assets backing capital *if* the investment and asset/liability management strategy is "conservative," *if* the firm does not have "too much" excess capital and *if* the business is in a "steady state." In other words, under these conditions, *the EP discount effect plus risk-free return on capital is roughly comparable with reported investment income in a steady state.*

Finally, the disclosed *net income does not consider the cost of capital*, which must be deducted in order to evaluate economic profit from a shareholder's perspective.

Nonetheless, one can use historical operating profit to estimate the new business economic profit after suitable adjustments, as illustrated in Table 8.4.

Step 3: Project PC.EP into the Future and Discount to Today

The franchise value of the firm represents the present value of the economic profits from future new business. As such, the future stream of new business needs to be projected and discounted to a present value.

TABLE 8.4 PC insurance new business economic profit – the value of one period's new business

Driver	Description		Comments
Growth	New business premium	$[P \times$	Adjust the projected new business premium for the point in the economic cycle and expected GDP growth, for business mix, etc.
Operating efficiency	Normalized expense ratio	$(1 -$ ER $-$	Adjust the expense ratio as appropriate, e.g. for expected efficiency gains, business mix, channel mix (tied agents, direct, bancassurance, etc.).
Underwriting effectiveness	Normalized claims ratio	CR)	Adjust the loss ratio as appropriate, e.g. by replacing actual catastrophe losses with a normalized level of "nat cat" losses, for anticipated changes in business mix and for cyclical pricing effects.
Investment returns	Normalized investment returns	$+ \text{I}]$	Remove any capital gains/losses. Alternatively, replace investment income with a rolling average "risk-free" return consistent with the duration of reserves times the average capital and reserve level.
Taxes	Normalized taxes	$\times (1 - t)$	Adjust the tax rate as appropriate.
	Normalized net income contribution before cost of capital	$= \text{NI}$	
Underwriting effectiveness and capital efficiency	Cost of capital	$- \text{CoC}$	Adjust the firm's cost of capital for leverage, if significant.
	Economic capital intensity	$\times \text{ECI}$	In a steady state, undiscounted capital intensity is estimated by dividing the calendar year premium by the actual capital held.
			Adjust the attributed capital if CER is greater than 1: actual capital $= P^*\text{ECI}^*\text{CER}$, attributed capital $= P^*\text{ECI}$, but only if management is able and committed to becoming more capital efficient.
			Adjust the ECI to reflect historical growth (e.g., ECI will be under-estimated for fast-growing books).
PC economic profit		$= \text{PC.EP}$	

Steady state. If we assume a steady state into perpetuity, then the franchise value can be written in the following manner:

$$\text{Franchise value} = \frac{\text{PC.EP}}{\text{CoC} - g}$$

where g is the assumed steady-state growth rate.

Non-steady state. If a steady state assumption is not appropriate, then PC.EPs need to be projected for different periods into the future using assumptions regarding operating performance which are appropriate for the forecast period. Common practice is to divide the future into an explicit projection period, for example the next 3 or 5 or 10 years, with an associated terminal value determined by steady-state assumptions:

$$\text{Franchise value} = \sum_{t=1}^{T} \frac{\text{PC.EP}_t}{(1 + \text{CoC})^t} + \frac{1}{(1 + \text{CoC})^{T+1}} \frac{\text{PC.EP}_T}{\text{CoC} - g}$$

The first term represents the present value of the PC.EP during the explicit projection period at time T and the second term represents the terminal value after the explicit forecast period, or the present value of a growing perpetuity which begins in period T.

PC KPIs: UNDERSTANDING AND MANAGING VALUE

Based on the arguments outlined above, we can create PC-specific KPIs from generically available financial information.

The only PC KPI focused on the current net asset value of the firm is the run-off result, defined as the additions to or release from reserves covering prior accident years. This is primarily because PC insurers do not focus on generating extraordinary earnings through risky investments and because reserves should reflect best estimates, implying that there should generally be no "surprises" in terms of reserve developments. Any unanticipated variation in the run-off result may imply problems in reserve adequacy or, if consistently positive, a conservative approach to reserving.

The most important PC KPIs are geared toward the franchise value of the firm, focusing on premium growth and the drivers of new business economic profit, especially the expense ratio, the claims ratio and the actual capital intensity.

Growth KPIs

The first important PC KPI is premium growth. The level of premium changes from year to year for many reasons, some directly influenced by management (e.g., marketing campaigns) and others influenced more by market developments (e.g., industry pricing cycles, anticipated claims inflation).

Table 8.5 gives some key diagnostic indicators used in the PC industry for analyzing premium development and monitoring the impact of management actions; these indicators are typically reported at a more granular level by line of business, distribution channel, etc. for internal management and performance measurement purposes.

TABLE 8.5   PC premium growth diagnostic indicators

Premium/Premium growth		Line of Business/Region/Distribution Channel			
		1	2	...	Total
–	Portfolio management activities	Volume effects			Internal growth
–	Lapse of existing customers				
+	New customers				
+	New business from existing customers				
+/–	Price effects	Price effects			
o/w	+/– Expected inflation				
	+/– Discounts and rebates				
	+/– Pure price effects				
	+/– Terms and conditions				
+/–	FX effects	External growth			
+/–	Acquisition/divestiture/internal restructurings				
Total					

The definition of many of these generic growth performance indicators and associated management levers is discussed in Chapter 11. However, there are four price effect KPIs specific to the PC insurance industry which are worth commenting on here.

- *Expected claims inflation.* Current-year pricing should reflect management's best estimate of future claims inflation. Because premium is collected today to cover claims in the future, a price increase today will not necessarily lead to an improved combined ratio in the future; a price increase today will only improve tomorrow's combined ratio if the increase is above the level of expected claims inflation. In other words, a 2% price increase today will have no effect on the long-term calendar year loss ratio if average claims are expected to increase by 2% due to inflation and would only represent an improvement in future combined ratios if expected claims inflation was below 2%. Without understanding the level of expected inflation, price "improvements" could be reported year after year which will never show up in lower future combined ratios.
- *Pure price effects.* These are defined as the change in targeted premium level, net of expected claims inflation, all other terms and conditions being equal. Targeted price effects may be caused by active pricing decisions, for example to capture more surplus in segments exhibiting inelastic demand. Alternatively, they can be caused by a hardening or softening market generally. Both may lead to an improvement or deterioration in the combined ratio.
- *Discounts and rebates.* These reflect deviations from the targeted price levels. Discounts are often given at the discretion of the sales channel in order to meet competitive threats and retain the best clients. Without close management, discounting can lead to a significant source of leakage. Discounts and rebates are discussed in greater detail in Chapter 25.

■ *Terms and conditions.* The final category of price effects is terms and conditions, reflecting other, non-price factors influencing the economics of a PC insurance contract. For example, coverage can be expanded for important clients during soft markets in order to retain business; similarly, the level of deductibles or limits can be altered. Both reflect a change in the economic value of the insurance contract. This category of price changes cannot be understood by looking at financial reporting results and requires a detailed analysis based on information in the policy administration systems.

A Management Information System (MIS), which provides this information on a granular basis (e.g., by line of business, distribution channel, region, customer segment, etc.) is absolutely necessary for internal performance evaluation and business steering purposes.

As Figures 8.2(a) and 8.2(b) illustrate, some of this information is also externally communicated in order to help analysts better understand and value the company. The figures are taken from Allianz's 2012:Q4 analyst presentation and 2012 Annual Report. Figure 8.2(a) groups Allianz's PC operations into growth clusters based on internal premium development, isolating price and volume effects; Figure 8.2(b) provides greater information with respect to the price developments in individual markets.

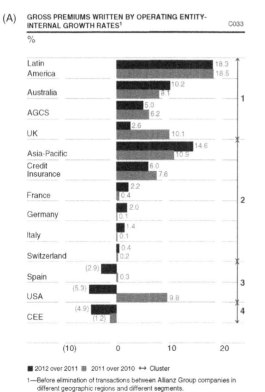

Cluster 1:
Overall growth–both price and volume effects are positive.

Cluster 2:
Overall growth–either price or volume effects are positive.

Cluster 3:
Overall decline–either price or volume effects are positive.

Cluster 4:
Overall decline–both price and volume effects are negative.

FIGURE 8.2(a)   Example disclosures, PC premium development. Reproduced by permission of Allianz SE.

(B)   B. Group financial results 2012 – Property-Casualty   **Allianz ⑪**

Price effects on renewals

Pricing overview for selected operating entities[1] (in %)

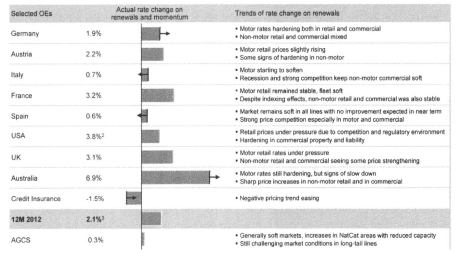

Selected OEs	Actual rate change on renewals and momentum	Trends of rate change on renewals
Germany	1.9%	• Motor rates hardening both in retail and commercial • Non-motor retail and commercial mixed
Austria	2.2%	• Motor retail prices slightly rising • Some signs of hardening in non-motor
Italy	0.7%	• Motor starting to soften • Recession and strong competition keep non-motor commercial soft
France	3.2%	• Motor retail remained stable, fleet soft • Despite indexing effects, non-motor retail and commercial was also stable
Spain	0.6%	• Market remains soft in all lines with no improvement expected in near term • Strong price competition especially in motor and commercial
USA	3.8%[2]	• Retail prices under pressure due to competition and regulatory environment • Hardening in commercial property and liability
UK	3.1%	• Motor retail rates under pressure • Non-motor retail and commercial seeing some price strengthening
Australia	6.9%	• Motor rates still hardening, but signs of slow down • Sharp price increases in non-motor retail and in commercial
Credit Insurance	-1.5%	• Negative pricing trend easing
12M 2012	**2.1%[3]**	
AGCS	0.3%	• Generally soft markets, increases in NatCat areas with reduced capacity • Still challenging market conditions in long-tail lines

1)   Estimates based on 12M 2012 survey as communicated by our operating entities; coverage of P/C segment 77%
2)   Figure excludes crop business. Rate change on renewals including crop business at 1.8%
3)   Total actual rate change on YTD renewals also including Ireland

© Allianz SE 2013

B 22

FIGURE 8.2(b)   Example disclosures, PC premium development. Reproduced by permission of Allianz SE.

Loss Ratio, Expense Ratio and Combined Ratio

The other important PC KPIs reflect the development of the business's technical underwriting performance and operating efficiency. The highest-level operating KPI is the Combined Ratio (CoR or CR), which is further decomposed into the Loss Ratio (LR) and the Expense Ratio (ER), discussed in Sidebar 8.1.

SIDEBAR 8.1: A DIGRESSION ON THE PC LOSS RATIO, EXPENSE RATIO AND COMBINED RATIO

The CoR is the sum of the ER, defined as the sum of non-claims operating expenses divided by premium, and the LR, defined as the sum of claims and claims adjustment expenses divided by premium.

Businesses with a combined ratio below 100% are often deemed profitable, as the sum of claims and expenses is less than the premium earned. However, this quick rule of thumb does not reflect the time value of money as the value of future claims and expenses is not comparable with the premium received today, nor does it reflect the uncertainty of future claims, as the economic capital intensity and cost of capital for the business is likewise ignored. These observations imply that, while a CoR less than 100% may be a good rule of thumb, it is not sufficient to steer the business. Instead, businesses should be steered based on PC.EP or a risk-adjusted CoR (defined in Chapter 25).

LOSS RATIO

At any point in time, the expected claims from any underwriting or accident year can be divided into three components.

- Those that have already been paid.
- An estimate for those that have already been reported but not yet paid.
- An estimate for those that have been incurred but not yet reported (IBNR, Incurred But Not Reported).

Estimated reserves are built for the latter two categories. Various statistical and actuarial methods are used to set reserves, making specific assumptions about the distribution of claims.[6] Nonetheless, judgment is still one of the primary determinants of setting reserves given data limitations and the underlying dynamics of claim developments (Houltram, 2003).

Claims and estimates form *loss triangles*, illustrated in Figure 8.3, which reflect the actual and estimated claims development from each accident or underwriting year in the past and in the future. The *accident or underwriting year* (along the vertical axis) is defined as *the year when the insurer was "at risk" on the policy and when the loss event took place*. The *development year* (along the horizontal axis) is defined as *the year in which the claim is paid*.

As Figure 8.3 illustrates, the loss ratio can be calculated on three bases.

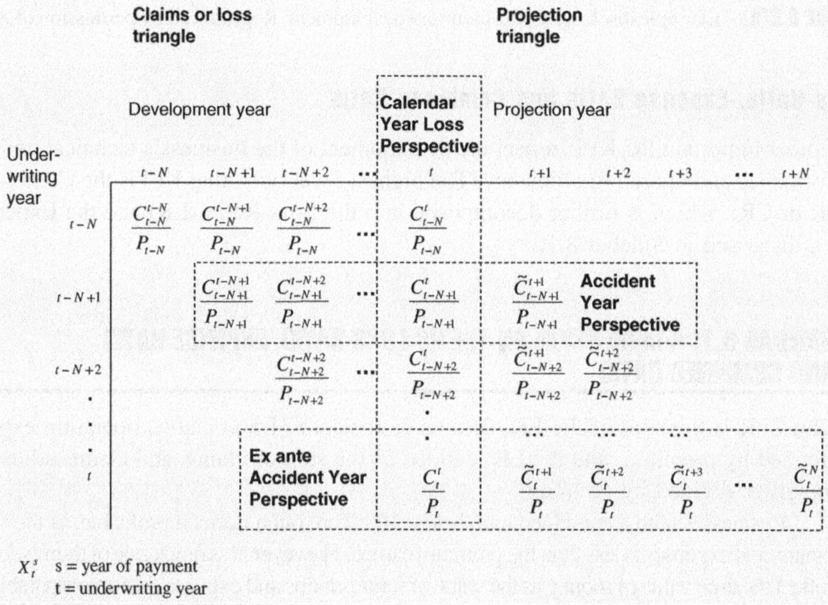

X_t^s s = year of payment
          t = underwriting year

FIGURE 8.3 Loss triangle

---

[6]For a good overview of stochastic reserving techniques, see England and Verral (2002). Also Institute and Faculty of Actuaries (1997), Taylor (2000), Wüthrich (2003).

Ex-ante Accident Year Loss Ratio

This ratio is calculated as $E_0 \left[\sum_{t=0}^{N} C_0^t / P_0 \right]$, where $E_0 \left[C_0^t \right]^7$ represents the expectation at time 0 of claims to be paid at time t associated with the policy underwritten at time 0. P_0 is the premium received at time 0.

The ex-ante accident year loss ratio is used to evaluate the *expected* profitability and rate adequacy at the time of underwriting and should be used in calculating PC.EP for new business.

Calendar Year Loss Ratio

This ratio is calculated as $\left(\sum_{s=-N}^{t} C_s^t + \sum_{s=-N}^{t} \sum_{m=s+N+t}^{N} \left[E_{t-1}\left(C_s^m\right) - E_t\left(C_s^m\right) \right]_t \right) / P_t$, where

$\sum_{s=-N}^{t} C_s^t$ is the sum of all actual claims paid at time t originating from previous underwriting years, $\sum_{s=-N}^{t} \sum_{m=s+N+t}^{N} \left[E_{t-1}\left(C_s^m\right) - E_t\left(C_s^m\right) \right]$ represents the change in best-estimate reserves for expected future claims from the existing book of business based on information at time t (called the *run-off* result) and P_t is the premium earned in year t.

The calendar year loss ratio is used to evaluate the performance of the underwriting function as if it was "in a steady state." There are two sources of uncertainty in the calendar year combined ratio: first, the current year's contribution to the loss ratio may be impacted by natural catastrophes, pricing cycles, etc. and second, changes in reserves for prior years may be required, with a positive (negative) run-off indicating better (worse) than expected developments relative to historic reserving levels.

In addition to these sources of inherent uncertainty, the calendar year loss ratio will also change predictably as year-on-year growth rates, claims inflation or business mix changes over time.

Accident Year Loss Ratio

This ratio is calculated as $\left(\sum_{m=0}^{t} \left(C_s^{s+m}\right) + \sum_{m=t+1}^{N} E_t\left(C_s^{s+m}\right) \right) / P_s$ for business written in year s being evaluated at date t. The accident year loss ratio is used to evaluate the performance of the underwriting function for business written in year s; a comparison of accident year loss ratios helps to understand the effects of the pricing cycle, changes to the underwriting or claims management processes, etc., all of which can impact the combined ratio over time.

EXPENSE RATIO

The expense ratio is defined as *the operating, non-financial/non-claim expenses divided by the premium earned.* It is typically calculated on a calendar year basis or projected on an ex-ante basis for new business pricing purposes. Operating or non-

---

[7]The formula represents the combined ratio for a single period contract where the premium is paid upfront. Suitable adjustments would need to be made for multi-year contracts or for contracts where premium is received periodically over the coverage period.

financial expenses include acquisition and administration expenses but exclude claims and claims handling expenses,[8] financial interest payments and unallocated corporate expenses.

COMBINED RATIO

The combined ratio is defined as the sum of the loss ratio and the expense ratio.

In order to understand and steer the business internally, both the loss ratio and the expense ratio are in turn decomposed into more granular information, as illustrated in Table 8.6.

As discussed in Sidebar 8.1, the calendar year loss ratio can be split into the contribution from the *current accident year* and claim developments from prior years, called the *run-off results*. Additional information on current accident year claims is often provided, including the following.

- For non-catastrophic losses during the accident year, the average claims frequency and severity for policies underwritten during the year. This information is useful for

TABLE 8.6   PC combined ratio diagnostic indicators

		Line of Business/Region		
Calendar Year Combined Ratio	**1**	**2**	**. . .**	**Total**
+ Loss ratio				
+ Losses				
o/w + Non-cat losses, accident year				
o/w Average Frequency				
×Average Severity				
+ Cat losses, accident year				
+/ − Run-off, previous years				
/ Premium				
+ Expense ratio				
+ Expenses				
o/w + Administration expenses				
+ Acquisition expenses				
o/w Commissions				
Other acquisition expenses				
/ Premium				
Total				

---

[8]Claims handling expenses are typically reported with claims. The rationale is that the decision whether to investigate and/or defend a claim materially affects the expected claim amount and is in some sense inseparable from the cost of the claims.

determining if the accident year results were influenced by a higher frequency of large losses stemming from, for example, large industrial clients.

▪ A split between catastrophe and non-catastrophe losses is useful for distinguishing between "normal," more predictable developments versus less predictable "acts of God" or "acts of man" (e.g., terrorism). Catastrophe loss thresholds are defined by each firm, with the cause of the loss categorized following standard practices for specific, named perils such as earthquakes, flooding, windstorms, fires, etc.

▪ The influence of pricing changes on the loss ratio, defined crudely as the average premium per policy, may also be reported.

Reserve run-off. This represents "unexpected" claims developments from prior years relative to the carried reserves. A positive run-off means that prior year reserves were set "too high" relative to actual developments, a negative run-off means that reserves were insufficient and need to be strengthened. Most firms have a positive run-off on a fairly consistent basis, indicating that reserves are set conservatively.

As Figures 8.4(a) and 8.4(b) illustrate, that some of this information is externally communicated to analysts in order to help them better understand and value the company. The figures are taken from Allianz's 2012:Q4 analyst presentation and 2012 Annual Report. Figure 8.4(a) gives the combined ratio, loss and expense ratio loss developments and the impact of natural catastrophes on the results, by country. Figure 8.4(b) gives further information on the development of the accident year loss ratio, including the natural catastrophe and run-off results as well as a decomposition between frequency, severity and price effects for "non-cat" losses.

(A) B. Group financial results 2012 – Property-Casualty   **Allianz** ⑪

Improved combined ratio driven by lower NatCat …

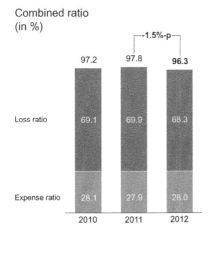

Combined ratio (sel. OEs)		2010	2011	2012	NatCat impact in 2011[1]	NatCat impact in 2012[1]
German Speaking Countries	Germany	100.8	102.9	96.8	3.9%-p	1.3%-p
German Speaking Countries	Switzerland	94.6	95.4	92.0	3.3%-p	1.7%-p
Western & Southern Europe	France	102.7	97.9	96.9	0.9%-p	0.0%-p
Western & Southern Europe	Italy	99.6	93.2	85.0	0.0%-p	0.8%-p
Iberia & Latin America	Spain	90.3	87.9	91.0	0.0%-p	0.0%-p
Iberia & Latin America	Latin America[2]	96.6	96.6	98.4	0.0%-p	0.0%-p
Global Insurance Lines & Anglo Markets	Reinsurance	93.2	108.2	92.7	27.0%-p	3.7%-p
Global Insurance Lines & Anglo Markets	AGCS	93.1	92.9	96.3	11.4%-p	5.4%-p
Global Insurance Lines & Anglo Markets	UK	96.0	95.7	96.4	0.0%-p	0.0%-p
Global Insurance Lines & Anglo Markets	Credit Insurance	71.7	74.0	80.2	n/a	n/a
Global Insurance Lines & Anglo Markets	Australia	96.1	97.6	95.1	4.2%-p	0.4%-p
Growth Markets	Asia-Pacific	91.2	93.8	91.3	0.0%-p	0.0%-p
Growth Markets	CEE	102.0	96.6	96.9	0.0%-p	0.0%-p
USA	USA	102.4	115.5	129.5	4.1%-p	9.7%-p
Global Assist.	Allianz Global Assistance	95.6	96.1	95.2	0.2%-p	0.1%-p

Combined ratio (in %)

-1.5%-p

97.2   97.8   **96.3**

Loss ratio   69.1   69.9   68.3

Expense ratio   28.1   27.9   28.0

2010   2011   2012

1) Without reinstatement premiums
2) South America and Mexico

© Allianz SE 2013

B 18

FIGURE 8.4(a) Example disclosures, PC loss ratio development. Reproduced by permission of Allianz SE.

(B) B. Group financial results 2012 – Property-Casualty   **Allianz** (ⅼⅼ)

... and positive development in underlying a.y. loss ratio
(in %)

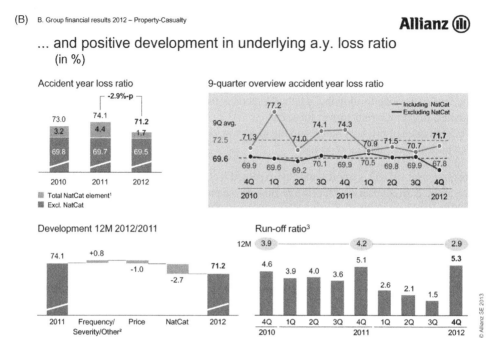

1) NatCat costs (without reinstatement premiums): EUR 1.3bn (2010), EUR 1.8bn (2011) and EUR 0.7bn (2012)
2) Including large claims, reinsurance, Credit Insurance
3) Positive values indicate positive run-off; run-off ratio is calculated as run-off result in percent of net premiums earned

B 19

FIGURE 8.4(b)   Example disclosures, PC loss ratio development. Reproduced by permission of Allianz SE.

B. Group financial results 2012 – Property-Casualty   **Allianz** (ⅼⅼ)

Expense ratio stable
(EUR mn)

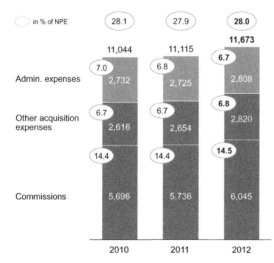

B 20

FIGURE 8.5   Example disclosures, PC expense ratio development. Reproduced by permission of Allianz SE.

Expense ratio. As described in Sidebar 8.1, the calendar year expense ratio is defined as the total operating or non-financial expenses of the firm (e.g., excluding claims and interest expenses as well as unallocated corporate overheads) for the calendar year divided by the premium earned in the calendar year. In order to understand and steer the business, the expense ratio is typically decomposed into two parts:

- the *acquisition expense ratio*, including commissions paid to brokers, agents or intermediaries, as well as any other, non-commission acquisition expenses such as marketing, advertising, branding, etc.;
- the *administration expense ratio*, defined as total operating expenses excluding acquisition expenses.

Figure 8.5 gives an example of expense ratio reporting, splitting the expense ratio between administration and acquisition expenses and further decomposing acquisition expenses between commissions and other acquisition expenses such as network support, and so on.

CHAPTER 9

Life and Health Insurance

This chapter outlines the "rules of the game" (or generic strategies) and core competencies for creating value in LH insurance, beginning with a brief history and the economic rationale for the LH insurance industry.

HISTORY AND ECONOMIC RATIONALE

Life and health insurance helps individuals to meet the challenges of three distinct "life events."

- By providing *protection* or indemnification in the event of illness, disability or death ("protection products").
- By facilitating *savings and asset accumulation*, predominantly in preparation for retirement but also for major expenses such as children's college education ("savings" or asset accumulation products).
- By providing a *steady and predictable income* after retirement over the individual's remaining lifetime ("annuities" or decumulation products).

While protection products emerged very early, retirement and savings products represent a relatively more recent development.

History of Protection Business[1]

Protection products provide support in the event of death (mortality), illness (health) or disability (morbidity), all of which can generate unexpected expenses or loss in income.

Similar to property and casualty insurance, the roots of protection products can be traced to social arrangements common in early societies prior to 2000 BC. These arrangements took the form of implicit or explicit commitments by a group to support its members or their survivors in the event of death or illness. As a substitute for insurance, such social commitments carried on for millennia, an example being the formalized social arrangements found in the Brehon Laws

---

[1]For more information, see Stone (1947), Hendrick (1907), Lewin (2004), Swiss Re (2012). Also www
.myceisonline.com/courses/thelifeinscourse/book.doc and www.investopedia.com/articles/08/history-of-
insurance.asp.

of 8th-century Medieval Ireland, which imposed a legal responsibility on the extended family group, or "kin," to take care of its members who were aged, blind, deaf, sick or insane.

One of the earliest references to a formal arrangement obliging non-related parties to make a payment upon the death of an individual goes back to 2500 BC when stonemasons in Egypt formed funeral cooperatives to pay for their members' burial expenses. Similar arrangements, referred to as "burial clubs," were common in India in 1000 BC. In 100 BC, Roman military leader Caius Marius created a burial club for his troops, with the expense shared by the surviving members of the "club." Burial clubs spread from the military to include other sectors of society, including free people and slaves, and also expanded in some cases to include a payment for the survivors of the deceased.

Later, trade and craft guilds organized similar arrangements. In ancient Greece and Rome, some guilds formed "benevolent societies" which cared for the families and paid funeral expenses for members upon their death. In the Middle Ages, guilds in the rest of Europe performed similar activities, occasionally with an even wider remit including support in the case of fire, robbery, death, ill health or disability. Especially the latter formed the basis for today's "group" health insurance.

Formal mechanisms for replacing income for the benefit of surviving family members began in the 1600s. Widows' funds were introduced by Duke Ernest the Pious of Gotha, first for the widows of clergy in 1645 and later for teachers in 1662. These schemes were established across Europe around the start of the 18th century for the widows of ministers against a payment of a premium. In 1759, the first life insurance company in America was set up for the benefit of the spouses of Presbyterian ministers. The Episcopalians organized a similar fund approximately 10 years later.

In 1752, the first mutual life insurance company was formed, the Equitable of London. Between 1787 and 1837, more than two dozen life insurers were started but less than six of them survived the financial crisis of 1837. Immediately afterwards, there was a shift toward mutual structures with 17 mutual societies chartered between 1838 and 1849 in the USA versus only one new insurance company.

During this period, anyone could purchase a life insurance policy on anyone else, including a complete stranger. This had the unintended and unfortunate consequence of increasing the likelihood of being murdered. Also, speculative interests in life insurance contracts flourished, a financial innovation bordering on the macabre: for example, life insurance contracts on King George II were offering 3:1 odds on his survival at the start of the Battle of Dettingen in June 1743. As another example, the premium for a life insurance contract for Admiral Byng fluctuated dramatically during his court martial, ultimately paying off when he was executed on March 14, 1757. In order to stop the practice of life insurance as a speculative adventure, the English government stipulated in the Life Assurance Act of 1774 that the purchaser of a policy had to have a legitimate interest in the insured (Applebaum, 2012).

The modeling of mortality also has a long history. In 1662, John Grant of London recognized that longevity and mortality patterns in a defined group of individuals were more predictable than for any individual in the group. In 1693, the astronomer Edmund Halley developed the first mortality table allowing an actuarial basis for life insurance pricing. In 1756, Joseph Dodson adapted Halley's mortality table by allowing the premium to be age dependent.

This rich history points to the role of life and health protection business: to indemnify expenses associated with death or illness and to replace income lost from such events. As with PC insurance, the risks covered by LH protection contracts have to be "insurable" in order to prevent moral hazard and limit adverse selection (see Chapter 8 for a definition of insurable risks).

History of Savings and Retirement Business

"Retirement" has emerged as another significant life event, but only much more recently. Unlike mortality, morbidity and illness, retirement is not necessarily a bad thing – as long as there is a suitable income available during retirement. In principle, sufficient assets need to be built up prior to retirement (the *accumulation phase*) and these assets then need to be converted into a secure income during retirement for the remainder of the individual's lifetime (the *decumulation phase*). The risk that assets are depleted before death is called *superannuation*.

Demographic Changes Make Retirement Relevant

While protection products date back millennia, the emergence of retirement products such as annuities has been a relatively recent phenomenon, dating back just a couple of centuries.[2] This is because retirement itself has been a relatively recent phenomenon for the majority of the population.

Prior to the Industrial Revolution in Western economies during the 19th century, retirement was not an option for the majority: most individuals worked in agriculture or in crafts and trades and typically worked as long as they were able to. For the vast majority, lifespans were too short and incomes too low to support an extended period of leisure without income derived from active participation in the labor force.

Instead, security in the limited period of old age was provided by children who took over the farm or trade, allowing parents to stay in their own homes alongside multiple generations of family. For many societies this structure represented an implicit contract between the older and younger generations. In some cases the contract was made explicit; for example, some wills in Colonial America stipulated the level of care to be provided to surviving parents, for example in terms of the weight of food or firewood to be periodically received.

Three significant developments in the 19th century created the need for individuals to secure independent financial resources for old age as opposed to relying on the traditional, inter-generational family support mechanisms.

- First, Western societies generally moved from an agrarian to an industrial economy. This trend broke the implicit contract between generations as children left the farm and migrated to cities and industrial centers in search of employment. Individual saving and securing a predictable income for retirement became a necessity, both for those left behind and for the new generation of factory workers.

---

[2]Specialized forms of annuities were developed earlier, but targeted at a narrow segment of the population or not primarily designed to support retirement. The earliest forms of annuities come from the Roman Empire, with "annua" meaning an annual stipend in Latin. They were associated with a very narrow range of individuals, Roman soldiers, who were paid an annuity as part of their compensation for military service. In AD 225, the Roman judge Gnaeus Domitius Annius Ulpianis was credited with creating the first actuarial life table to support the determination of annuity payments.

During the Middle Ages, annuities called tontines were used by kings and feudal lords to raise funds to cover the cost of wars, with large pools of cash being generated and paying out a fixed return, often increasing as the number of survivors declined until the surviving members could claim the rest.

■ Second, life expectancies increased, driven by better nutrition and health care, potentially leaving more time for leisure – assuming that a sufficient level of savings had been accumulated. Whereas the average life expectancy at the beginning of the 20th century was 47 years in the USA, it is now 77 years and increasing, with similar trends seen in other Western societies.

■ Third, a middle class emerged which enjoyed incomes during their working lifetime sufficient to accumulate enough assets to fund a steady income for an extended period of leisure in retirement.

The resulting demographic change has been dramatic: it is estimated that the labor force participation of men over the age of 65 in the USA has decreased from 78% in 1880 to less than 20% in 1990, and this on the back of increasing life expectancy.

Public and Private Solutions

In response, industrial firms and governments developed private and public pension schemes. These schemes were designed in part to mitigate the negative externalities of an aging population driven into poverty in the absence of such arrangements and in part as a "paternalistic" measure to ensure the security of existing and retired workers.

In terms of public sector solutions, Otto von Bismark introduced the Old Age and Disability Insurance Bill in Germany in 1889. The old age pension program provided an annuity for workers who reached the age of 70 (later lowered to 65 in 1916) and was funded by a tax on current workers. Although the average life expectancy during this period was estimated at around 45 years of age, this included high infant and maternal mortality rates; the Act was somewhat more effective for those actually attaining the age of 65, as this group had an additional 5 years of average life expectancy.

In the United States, public pensions began with implicit and explicit promises made to the veterans of the Revolutionary and Civil wars. They expanded to state and local government employees and later, in 1920, to federal employees under the Civil Service Retirement System (CSRS), which provided retirement, disability and survivor benefits for most federal employees.

In 1935, Roosevelt extended public pensions beyond civil servants by signing into law the Social Security Act, which paid retired workers 65 years or older and disabled people a monthly fixed income for life. In 1935, the social security system was funded by a 1% tax on both employers and employees for the first $3000 of earnings; today, the rate is 7.65%.

Private sector alternatives also emerged. For example, the American Express railroad company established the first private pension plan in America in 1875. American Express was copied by other companies, with mostly employer-funded private pension contributions. Similar practices developed in Europe. Most of these private and public pension schemes were *defined benefit* schemes, that is, the benefits paid to the retiree or survivors were defined upfront.

Recent Trends: Defined Benefit to Defined Contribution

Owing to the same demographic trends, the cost of defined benefit pensions has increased and the certainty of benefits to retirees has decreased as the accumulated obligations become harder and harder to meet. In some instances, private (and public) pension obligations have had to be restructured during insolvency and retirement ages have had to be increased.

When combined with the positive trend toward higher economic development, the responsibility of achieving security in retirement is increasingly falling on the shoulders of the retiree, with self-funded and voluntary *defined contribution* schemes becoming much more common. Recognizing the negative externalities of poverty in old age, governments often support retirement savings through tax advantages on retirement savings products.

Today, life insurers offer a variety of products to support retirement savings, including for example *universal life*, *endowment policies*, *whole of life* and *unit-linked* products (described in Sidebar 9.1), as well as *annuities* to provide a predictable income over the retiree's remaining life, regardless of how long they live. Some products, including *variable or fixed-income deferred annuities*, combine the two, accumulation and decumulation elements.

The distinction between protection and retirement products is not always black and white: some savings products offer benefits in the case of death or illness (many are required to if they are to receive beneficial tax treatment), and some protection products offer savings elements. An early example of such a blended product was the modified tontine offered by the Equitable Life Assurance Society in 1868 in the USA. This policy split premiums between a protection component that paid a death benefit and an investment component that deferred dividends until 10 or 20 years later, at which point the investment returns would be paid out to the survivors of the pool either as a lump sum or as an annuity.

Products

The resulting product landscape for the LH insurance segment is quite diverse, as illustrated in Sidebar 9.1.

SIDEBAR 9.1: LH INSURANCE PRODUCTS

LH insurance products are more varied than PC insurance products, predominantly because they have developed to cover three very different customer needs – protection, retirement savings or asset accumulation, and decumulation.

Although the lines are blurred, a general rule is that the majority of the premium paid for protection products is used to provide coverage for mortality, morbidity or health events. In contrast, the majority of the premium for asset accumulation and decumulation products goes to purchasing assets and future financial pay-outs on the policy holder's behalf.

PROTECTION PRODUCTS

Term insurance provides a payment to the policy's beneficiary upon the death of the individual covered by the policy. Premiums are paid and the policy pays a claim only during the term; the policy has no residual value after the term has expired. Term policies often require a medical examination as part of the underwriting process. They tend to be annually renewable at premium levels which can be adapted over time and which are specific to the individual covered. Various exclusions (e.g., for suicide, war, terrorism, etc.) are standard.

Health, accident and disability insurance indemnify the beneficiary in the event of illness, accident or disability during the coverage period. As with term life insurance, medical examinations may be required and exclusions (e.g., for pre-existing illnesses) are standard. Typically, these are annually renewable contracts with premium levels specific to the individual covered.

Protection products can be sold to *individuals or offered to groups*, for example as an employment benefit paid for by an employer. Although occasionally also sold by banks, banks do not generally "manufacture" protection products, preferring to source them from insurers to leverage distribution synergies (e.g., term life or disability insurance aligned with a home owner's mortgage obligations, etc.).

SAVINGS, INVESTMENT OR ASSET ACCUMULATION PRODUCTS

Savings and investment products come in two forms: *single premium* products for those who want to invest and *regular premium* products which support savings by collecting premiums at regular intervals during the accumulation phase. Both can be *general account* or *separate account* products.

General Account Products

The assets backing general account savings or investment products are held on the balance sheet of the insurance company, with returns credited by the insurance company to the policy holder's "account." The crediting rate is often at the discretion of the insurance company, subject to a minimum guaranteed crediting rate, and an insolvency of the insurance company may reduce the value that the policy holder receives relative to their account balances.

Guaranteed Investment Contracts (GICs) offer a guaranteed investment return, either fixed or floating, over the term of the contract. They are more often sold to institutional clients and offer direct competition for bank deposits and certificates of deposit.

Universal life insurance combines death benefits and a savings component where the cost of the death benefit insurance, as well as other expense loadings, is deducted from the premium every period and any remaining premium is credited to the cash value of the policy. The premium charged for protection is reset annually. The cash value of the policy grows with investment returns credited by the insurance company, subject to a minimum guaranteed level of return.

Whole life insurance products are similar to a universal life product but the premiums, as well as death benefits and cash surrender values, are set in advance for the whole life of the individual. As such, there is more mortality risk for the insurer.

Endowment policies are designed to pay a lump sum upon maturity or on the death of the policy holder. Maturities can range from 3 years up to 20 or more years. Shorter-term endowment policies compete directly with bank deposits.

Equity Indexed Annuities (EIAs) or *Fixed Index Annuities (FIAs)* are general account savings products whose crediting rate is based on an equity index return, subject to a minimum guaranteed rate of return, or *floor*, and a maximum return, or *cap*, with the value of the cap helping to defray the value of the guarantee. After the accumulation phase, the policy holder often has the option to take the account value as a lump sum or to convert it into an annuity. During the accumulation phase, the EIA or FIA "looks" similar to a mutual fund, albeit with some form of guarantee, or a structured investment note issued by a bank.

Most universal life, whole life and endowment policies are *participating* (*par* in the USA or *with-profits* in the UK), where the policy holder participates in any investment returns or profits above the minimum guaranteed return level earned by the assets. Partially in compensation for the guarantee, the insurance company also participates in the returns if they are in excess of the minimum guaranteed return level.

Separate Account Products

Separate account products hold the assets backing the account balance in a separate, segregated account on behalf of the policy holder; an insolvency of the insurer generally does not influence the separate account value. The returns to the policy holder are determined to a large extent by the returns on the separate account assets, typically invested in mutual funds or other investment funds, subject to any additional fees or guarantees provided by the insurance company.

Unit-linked products invest the premium in a segregated investment fund such as a mutual fund after the deduction of any fees. In the absence of any guarantees, the return on the policy holder's account directly matches the return on the fund less any applicable expense loadings or asset management fees. Unit-linked products typically do not offer a guarantee beyond a Guaranteed Minimum Death Benefit (GMDB) in order to qualify as insurance for tax purposes. Unit-linked products compete directly with mutual funds.

Variable annuity products are separate account products, like unit-linked products, but allow the client to select from a variety of different fund alternatives and offer a wider range of guarantees or "riders," including: GMDB; Guaranteed Minimum Accumulation Benefit (GMAB), based on return of premium, roll-up of premium at minimum rate of return, maximum anniversary value, etc.; Guaranteed Minimum Income Benefit (GMIB), upon conversion into a pay-out annuity; Guaranteed Minimum Withdrawal Benefit (GMWB), similar to an income benefit but without triggering conversion into an annuity. Variable annuities compete directly with mutual funds and other managed asset funds and, in fact, many of the underlying funds offered to a variable annuity purchaser are supplied by banks or asset management firms.

Decumulation Products

Lifetime or immediate annuities are products purchased by the payment of a single, upfront premium in order to receive regular, fixed payments over the policy holder's remaining lifetime, or the joint lifetime with their spouse, or until the contract matures. Immediate annuities are designed to provide protection against insufficient funds in retirement.

Deferred annuities are blended products – initially, they are savings and investment products which allow the account value to appreciate during the accumulation phase; later, the policy holder can either elect to take a lump sum payment or convert the account into an immediate annuity. Examples include FIAs and variable annuities.

Economic Rationale: The Insured's Perspective

The economic rationale for the insured depends on the specific needs being met.

Protection Products

The economic rationale for LH protection products is basically the same as for PC insurance: they provide security against insurable events, in this case events related to an individual's life or health, for example premature death (mortality), disability (morbidity) or illness (health), helping to defray expenses and replace lost income. Policy holders receive this protection against a premium they deem reasonable based on their situation and risk aversion.

Retirement Savings and Annuity Products

In contrast, retirement products have a different economic rationale. While often including protection elements such as death benefits and health care riders, the primary reason for purchasing retirement savings products is to save for the future and the primary reason to purchase decumulation products is to provide predictable income throughout retirement. Although the longevity risk can be large, in both instances most of the premium goes toward purchasing income-generating assets and not toward the coverage of insurable risks.

This puts LH retirement and savings products directly in competition with products offered by banks and asset managers. In spite of the similarities, there are three primary reasons why customers might prefer an LH insurance product to a banking or asset management product.

- First, there are often *tax benefits* from an insurance product. For example, some retirement savings products are funded through pre-tax income (the German Riester voluntary pension product[3] and US 401(k) contributions) and the returns on other insurance products delay the taxes on investment income or capital gains to the maturity of the policy, as opposed to taxing investment income every year as it accumulates in the insurance account. These tax benefits can be substantial but also often require a minimum investment horizon in order to differentiate them from shorter-term investment products offered by banks or asset management companies.
- Second, because insurance retirement and savings products often offer *guarantees*, providing greater certainty in financial planning. In contrast, most bank and asset management savings products do not offer guarantees. Some of the most common guarantees include the return of premium, annual or terminal minimum returns, portfolio high-water marks, the right to convert savings into an annuity at a predetermined rate, etc.
- Third, because insurance products also offer *protection benefits* linked to mortality, morbidity and health, including for example death benefits, health care riders, etc. This is also often a requirement in order for a savings product to be eligible for beneficial tax treatment.

In short, in contrast to a banking or asset management product, a well-designed and fairly priced LH retirement or savings product can provide the policy holder with a tax-advantaged, guaranteed savings vehicle combined with protection in life and in retirement.

---

[3] http://schlemann.com/altersvorsorge/riester-rente/riester-pension-english/#

Economic Rationale: The Insurer's Perspective

The insurer creates value for shareholders in one of three ways depending on the underlying customer needs.

Technical Underwriting Profits from "Protection Products"

First, by *appropriately underwriting and pricing* the mortality, health, morbidity and longevity risk embedded in the contract or sold as riders to the base contract. Success in LH protection businesses requires similar skills as those required to be successful in PC insurance where sales and expense management, combined with underwriting excellence, are critical.

Asset Management Fees from "Capital Light Products"

Second, by earning a margin on Assets Under Management (AUM) and profits from expense loadings, especially for "capital light" savings and investment products such as Unit Linked policies. As a consequence, the business model and success factors for these products are similar for asset managers: keeping expenses under control, growing AUM by gaining new customers or a higher share of wallet, and retaining the assets of existing customers.

Just like an asset management business, the value of the in-force business will increase as the existing accounts increase in value; however, asset growth driven by capital market appreciation is generally already incorporated in the firm's valuation multiple. The multiple can only be increased by generating new net asset inflows. In this sense, it matters how AUM grows, with expected market appreciation already factored into the multiple and only net new asset accumulation leading to a higher multiple.

Participating in Investment Returns from "Guaranteed Products"

Third, the insurance company is compensated *by participating in general account asset returns that are above the guaranteed rates promised to policy holders*, a source of earnings for most general account products including universal and whole of life products, traditional European participating products, endowments and annuities.

Because earnings are tied in part to investment returns, there may be an incentive to increase financial market risk taking. It is argued that shareholders should generally not assign a multiple greater than 1 to capital used to support financial risks in the absence of a clear ability to generate "alpha," a position argued in Chapter 16.

In addition, taking financial market risk to increase earnings may actually destroy shareholder value: in general, higher financial market risk increases not only expected earnings but also the value of policy holder guarantees to the detriment of shareholders' interests.

Guaranteed products generally have high Economic Capital Intensities (ECI), driven by financial market risk and the longer tenor of the policies, with each slice of new business tying up large amounts of capital for a significant and extended period. Capital intensity for LH products is discussed in detail later, given its importance in managing value.

Least Capital Intensive – Hedged Products   Products which are accounted under fair value rules such as equity index and variable annuities typically require less capital in spite of the fact that they may contain complex embedded derivatives. This is because insurers hedge these products in order to minimize volatility in accounting earnings.

Financial Accounting Standards FAS 133 (American Academy of Actuaries, 2010) stipulates the embedded derivatives which must be recognized on the balance sheet at their fair value, applying to certain benefits embedded in variable annuity contracts (e.g., GMWB and GMAB, respectively) while leaving other benefits to be accounted using more stable amortized cost accounting (e.g., GMDB and GMIB, respectively). In addition, FAS 133 can also apply to the equity return component of the EIA or FIA. All benefits accounted under fair value rules will generate significant accounting volatility if they are not hedged.

In theory, it is possible to hedge the FAS 133 riders completely and lock in a predictable and secure margin, just as if they were an asset management product. In practice, however, insurers may be unable or unwilling to fully hedge the financial market risk and lock in the margin.

- The embedded options may be too complex to hedge using exchange traded instruments or Over-The-Counter (OTC) derivatives with small bid–offer spreads.
- The hedge ratios may be affected by *biometric or behavioral risk* causing hedge slippage if actual behavior (e.g., lapsation, annuitization, mortality events, etc.) deviates from the predicted behavior.
- The exposure may be to illiquid indices or managed funds which can only be hedged by proxy, implying significant *basis risk* between the hedge and the account value.
- The embedded derivatives may have a maturity that extends beyond the hedge instruments available in the capital markets.
- The insurer may simply decide to hedge only part of the risk, for example dynamic hedging to neutralize the local "Greeks" such as delta, gamma, vega and rho[4] but leaving unhedged the more obscure risks such as rotations in the volatility surface, changes in the volatility smile, etc. This is often done based on the argument that market prices for hedging more obscure risks are "too rich" due to limited supply.

Regardless of the reason, the insurer cannot lock in the margin and has to take some financial market risk, implying that they also have to hold capital. Because insurers prefer to minimize P&L volatility, they will hedge most of the financial market risk, lowering the overall capital requirements for these products and leading to a lower capital intensity.

More Capital Intensive – Spread Products   Consider the immediate pay-out annuity which guarantees a fixed payment for life against an upfront premium payment. Typically, pay-out annuities are cash flow matched with a diversified portfolio of investment grade bonds. If matched, the insurer's margin will not be materially affected by changing interest rates, credit spread levels or bond rating changes and will be secure as long as:

- the bonds are held to maturity and remain cash flow viable (e.g., no defaults) and
- the policy holder does not surrender the contract, creating a call on the insurance company's liquidity and the forced sale of the bonds at current market prices.

This predictable and stable margin must be balanced against the default risk of the assets backing the contracts. Following strict asset/liability matching, the required capital is generally "low" during any given period. However, spread products, especially annuities, tend to have very long tenors, implying that the limited capital per period will be tied up for a very, very long

---

[4]Delta is a sensitivity measure, expressing the change in price for a small change in the underlying risk index (e.g. $\partial = \partial P / \partial \tau$); gamma is the change in delta for a change in the risk index (e.g. $\gamma = \partial \delta / \partial \tau = \partial^2 P / \partial \tau^2$) and measures convexity; vega is the change in price for a change in implied volatilities used to value options (e.g. $v = \partial P / \partial \sigma$); and, rho is the change in price for a change in interest rates (e.g. $\rho = \partial \Pi / \partial r$).

time. Further increasing the economic capital intensity of these products are the reinvestment risks caused by long-dated obligations which cannot be matched.

It is important to note that stable earnings do not necessarily indicate stable net asset value or shareholder value. Consider a 10-year liability paying 3% exactly matched by 10-year assets paying 4%; if the assets remain cash flow viable, the resulting gross margin will remain constant at 1%. Assume further that bond spreads increase by 1% due to time-varying risk or liquidity premia, with no implications for the cash flow viability of the bonds (e.g., no increase in default risk). If the liability discount rate is held constant, then the net asset value of the firm will decrease by the full asset value change, approximately $-1\% \times 10$ years $= 10\%$ of the asset value.

This volatility in shareholder value may be dampened if the liability discount rate changes partially in "sympathy" with the asset spreads (e.g., by using an illiquidity premium or Solvency II's MAVB); however, it is difficult to see why the value of our obligations has changed due to a change in bond spreads, especially if our obligations are backed by the value of our global franchise. Even with a discount rate which moves "in sympathy," there can still be a substantial change in the shareholder's net asset value due to credit spread movements.

Most Capital Intensive – Structural Mismatches and "Chasing Market Returns"   The most capital-intensive products offered by LH insurers are those products which:

- cannot be managed from an asset/liability perspective, for example cash flows which extend beyond the maturities offered in local financial markets or
- any product if the company decides to take an investment risk position by opening an asset/ liability mismatch.

Both represent a "large naked bet" on financial markets, one forced by the characteristics of the product and the other voluntary. Both require significant shareholder capital.

As the case studies in Chapter 16 illustrate, structural mismatch positions represent significant risk to sustained low interest rates and have led to crisis in several markets. The only way to mitigate the risk is to *design products which can be matched from an asset and liability perspective and then to actually match them.*

A similar risk profile occurs if the insurance company decides not to match a general account, guaranteed product – only in this case the risk taken is voluntary. This is also "capital intensive" for the insurer: the company may take financial market risk in order to participate in the higher expected investment returns *but* any shortfall below the guaranteed rate of return has to be made up out of shareholders' funds, representing an asymmetric pay-off.

Creating value from LH guaranteed products depends critically on product design and asset/liability strategy, in addition to its technical underwriting capabilities and the ability to accumulate assets under management. An interesting example of guaranteed product business strategy is given in Sidebar 9.2.

Economic Rationale: Benefits to Society[5]

Beyond the benefits to the signatories of an insurance contract, society benefits from an active and robust LH insurance market in several important ways.

---

[5]See, for example, Hoppe (2012).

SIDEBAR 9.2: GUARANTEED PRODUCTS – EXAMPLE BUSINESS STRATEGY

Athene Holding was founded in 2009, sponsored in part by the Apollo Hedge Fund, to take advantage of the upheaval in the US life annuity market following the 2008 financial market crisis. By 2013, Athene had acquired several companies, including Liberty Life Insurance, Investors Insurance Corporation, Presidential Life Insurance and the US subsidiary of Aviva.

Athene Holding (2013) characterizes its business strategy, saying that it is effectively a spread business, earning ". . . the difference between its investment(s) . . . and the rate on its liabilities . . . capturing today's spreads based on low-cost, stable funding matched by an outperforming asset management portfolio. This spread can be leveraged due to a business model that requires 7–10% capital/reserve ratio (which translates to ~10–14× leverage)."

Athene's asset management philosophy is a study in contradictions, being for example both *buy and hold* but also *total return focused*, ". . . adjust(ing) allocations as markets change . . . (and viewing) realized gains as an important part of earnings." Its investment strategy includes more interesting asset classes such as hedge funds and private equity, as well as assets offering a premium for complexity and illiquidity. "Athene is a patient, long-term investor that is comfortable with difficult to understand products and situations (and) is able to take advantage of opportunities often overlooked by others."

According to Mider (2013), this investment strategy is not without risk. Before Liberty Life was acquired by Apollo in 2011 it had "a 'squeaky clean' portfolio: bonds backed by state governments and blue chip corporations. Now the unit's holdings include securities backed by subprime mortgages, time-share vacation homes and a railroad in Kazakhstan . . . 'they're substantially increasing the risk, sooner or later . . . that has to come home to roost . . . All the upside would go to Athene if it worked out. And the downside would go to the annuity holders if it didn't.'"

This shift has attracted the attention of regulators. In a 2013 speech, B. Lawsky, New York superintendent of financial services, said "New York State may need to modernize its regulations to deal with the increased presence and 'troubling role' of private equity firms in selling annuities. 'The risk we're concerned about . . . is whether these private equity firms are more short-term focused, when this business is all about the long haul'" (Mider, 2013).

First, LH insurance helps to mitigate negative externalities and the potential burden on social support mechanisms caused by individual disability, illness, death and poverty in old age. In addition, private insurance aligns the cost of these externalities directly with the source. In this sense, private insurance is an economically useful substitute or complement to public support mechanisms.

Second, LH companies intermediate between policy holders who want long-term savings and corporations who want to invest in long-term productive assets (e.g., insurers purchasing corporate bonds and equities). This supports economic development and wealth generation for society.[6] Intermediation through an LH insurance company may be better for society

---

[6]Assuming that the investment is in real, productive asset formation as opposed to government bonds which might "crowd out" real investment.

than through a bank or asset management company because LH insurers typically have a longer-term investment horizon suitable for less liquid real assets such as infrastructure, real estate, etc.

FROM PRINCIPLES TO "RULES OF THE GAME"

In comparison with PC insurance, the underlying principles for LH insurance are more challenging to summarize for two reasons.

- First, because LH insurance actually comprises three very different businesses – protection, asset management and guaranteed products – and each requires specific skills to create value and specific metrics to measure value creation.
- Second, because it is difficult to separate earnings from value creation for products which rely on investment margins, a fact that can lead to a muddled strategy and the sacrifice of value for earnings.

Nonetheless, there are some general principles which guide the "rules of the game" for LH insurers:

- have a clear strategy and build differentiated skills for each of the protection, asset management and guaranteed product segments;
- remain brutally objective and value-oriented when deciding how to participate in the savings and retirement profit pool, balancing asset management and guaranteed products;
- especially for retirement and savings products which are long term and capital intensive, focus on the capital investment and cash generation, not just on earnings;
- emphasize managing the in-force book of business, ensuring that the returns expected at the time of sale actually emerge.

Have a Clear and Differentiated Strategy for Each Product Family

LH insurance comprises three distinct businesses. All three require sales and distribution capabilities to grow the top-line profitably and all three require expense discipline to convert the top-line into a bottom-line contribution. However, each business also requires unique skills (see Figure 9.1). For example, protection products require strong underwriting skills and guaranteed products require disciplined asset/liability and capital management.

Aligning institutional skills to the products requires greater focus and differentiation – in strategy, in planning, in reporting and in execution. *In short, LH insurers must explicitly recognize that they are in three distinct businesses and build the distinct strategies and skills to manage each appropriately.*

This inherent complexity is recognized by analysts and may lead to the "opacity discount" for LH businesses. A recent industry working group of CFOs in Europe (CFO Forum, 2012) summarized analysts' perceptions by saying that "Fund managers (are) frustrated with their ability to understand the (LH insurance) business and comparability with other industries . . . issues identified principally related to perceived excessive business model complexity and the need to sharpen strategic focus."

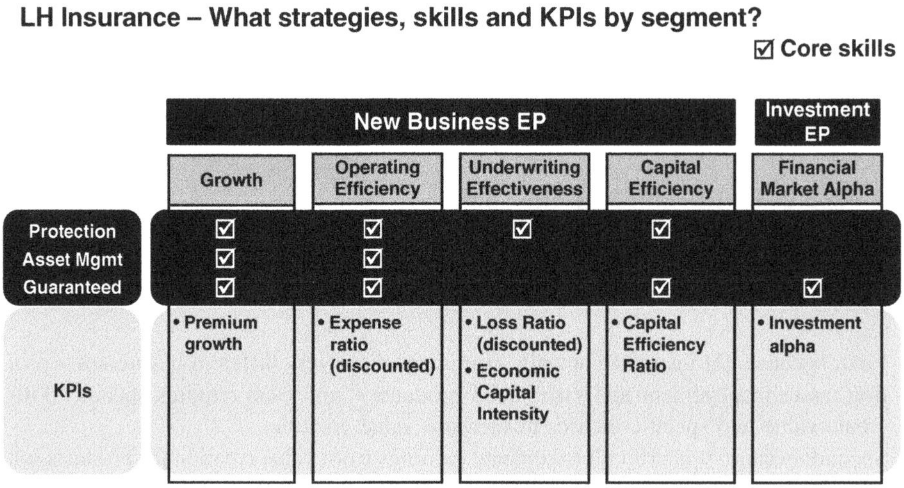

LH Insurance – What strategies, skills and KPIs by segment?

☑ **Core skills**

	New Business EP				Investment EP
	Growth	Operating Efficiency	Underwriting Effectiveness	Capital Efficiency	Financial Market Alpha
Protection	☑	☑	☑	☑	
Asset Mgmt	☑	☑			
Guaranteed	☑	☑		☑	☑
KPIs	• Premium growth	• Expense ratio (discounted)	• Loss Ratio (discounted) • Economic Capital Intensity	• Capital Efficiency Ratio	• Investment alpha

FIGURE 9.1 LH economic profit sources and core skills

Have a Clear Strategy for the Savings and Retirement Profit Pool

The opportunity. The pool of potential customers with retirement needs will continue to grow over the coming years due to the aging demographics of developed economies and the emerging middle class in developing economies, leading to higher penetration rates and asset accumulation.

The challenges. Tapping into the retirement profit pool is not without challenges. First and foremost, a growing customer pool itself does not necessarily translate into an attractive profit pool.

Consider the core retirement need during the decumulation phase: an annuity paying a guaranteed income. At its core, this need is relatively easy to meet by providing fixed cash flows of long duration, something that low-cost, fixed-income alternatives can easily meet. As a consequence, the core income component of decumulation products is inherently commoditized and low margin. The value added of insurance is the promise of an income for life, or the assumption of longevity risk, a risk which does not seem to generate significant excess returns in practice. The same can be said for the guarantees embedded in asset accumulation products: if the guarantee is transparent and easy to replicate in the capital markets, then it is not likely that the capital to back the guarantees will earn more than the appropriate risk-adjusted cost of capital, implying zero "alpha" and at best a multiple of 1× on invested capital.

The message? Just because there is a high dollar premium attached to a growing customer base does not mean that the profit pool will be rich for shareholders.

Second, in the search for higher earnings to compensate commoditized economics, the insurer may be incentivized to take additional investment risk. In the best of cases, this investment risk generates earnings but not value because shareholders can generally make similar investments.

Unfortunately, the pursuit of higher investment earnings may actually destroy value given the asymmetric pay-offs to shareholders: while participating in a fraction of the upside from investment returns, shareholders bear the full downside risk through the guarantees.

Third, in order to compete with banks and asset management firms, insurers may be tempted to offer products with non-hedgeable options and guarantees in order to attract investment dollars.

As discussed in Chapter 16, earnings from asset/liability mismatch results are generally not rewarded with a higher multiple because shareholders can take similar positions in a more straightforward manner through their own account; in fact, they may even be valued at a discount if they represent structural risks which cannot be managed at all.

The decision. Some firms compete in the retirement space with asset management products which require limited capital, others with guaranteed products which are more capital intensive. The fundamental strategic question LH insurers have to answer is how they want to participate in the long-term retirement and savings profit pool and what the optimal mix is between capital intensive and capital light solutions?

The Disconnect Between Earnings, Cash, Capital and Value

The link between earnings, cash capital and value creation for guaranteed products is confusing at best: accounting earnings reflect only a slice of the product's value whereas value, estimated based on assumptions, emerges as cash only years or decades later. While the future cash earnings may be subjective, these products require a very real and significant cash strain upfront to cover acquisition expenses and capital requirements, with the capital "locked in" for significant periods. As a consequence, there is a significant disconnect between earnings, cash, capital and value creation.

This disconnect is recognized by analysts who are focusing more and more on cash and capital rather than earnings. Morgan Stanley (2011b) believes that "earnings analysis is of limited use . . . We prefer composites that i) generate strong cash flow after 'maintenance capex' . . . , ii) have high growth capex that supports future earnings and iii) . . . surplus cash generation, driving financial flexibility and the ability to redeploy capital for growth." In other words, don't show us accounting earnings, show us the cash that you actually generate and how you are using that cash.

Barclays (2011) reinforces this view, stating that investors should understand ". . . how the capital . . . is spent . . . we are supportive of investment in new business . . . (if it generates) IRRs above the company's cost of capital and with reasonable payback periods . . . (but) business at or sub 9% IRRs which takes 9 years to break even . . . is not a viable source of value for shareholders."

Value creation is possible if management focuses on capital efficiency, as emphasized by Redburn (2012): "Most life insurers have significantly improved new business (capital) efficiency . . . Put simply insurers are delivering much greater new business value for the same level of investment. This has been accomplished through a combination of selling more sensible products, taking advantage of market conditions to increase prices and redesigning products."

From a shareholder's perspective, "Cash is King!" Whereas earnings are not sufficient to measure the long-term value of the business and value estimates can "lie" or be overly optimistic, cash does not. Managing the value of long-term retirement products requires that firms focus less on earnings and more on aligning cash, capital and value creation.

Managing the Back Book

In contrast to PC insurance, managing the value of LH savings and retirement products also requires a focus on managing the back book equal to or greater than on new business. Why?

First, given upfront acquisition costs, the value created from long-dated products typically emerges far into the future, with payback periods approaching 10+ years and based on critical assumptions about market returns and management actions. Ignoring the in-force book of business and focusing only on chasing after new premium may lead to the expected value never emerging.

Second, as opposed to short-tail PC business, new business represents only a fraction of the value tied up in the in-force book of business since most of the value creation is back-ended: if the capital duration of new business is 10 years, then the value and capital embedded in the in-force book will be approximately 10× the value of new business in a steady state.

Third, it is possible to influence the value of in-force business: through better asset/liability management, deciding which risks to take in the pursuit of higher earnings; through the crediting strategy of the firm, deciding how much of the investment earnings to credit to the benefit of policy holders versus shareholders; and, finally, through lapse and retention management, ensuring that the profits expected to emerge from the existing portfolio actually do emerge.

Rules of the Game

These considerations lead to the following "rules of the game" for LH insurance.

RULES OF THE GAME: LH INSURANCE

- Focus on risk-adjusted, profitable growth.
  - Grow the new business top-line through strong sales and distribution.
  - Have a clear strategy for tapping the savings and retirement profit pool:
    - set the primary focus on "capital light" asset management and protection products;
    - offer limited "capital intensive" guaranteed products, and then only if designed and priced to be actually hedged.
  - Convert new business top-line into attractive risk-adjusted returns:
    - ensure positive LH new business EP;
    - reduce economic capital intensity and payback periods, putting more focus on the cash investment requirements and future cash generation;
    - develop underwriting excellence for protection products;
    - drive lower costs through operating efficiency for all products.
- Manage the back book so that the profits expected to emerge at the time of sale actually do emerge.
  - Rigorously match "capital intensive" guaranteed products to lock-in stable profit margins promised at the time of underwriting.
  - Ensure that the crediting strategy is optimal from a shareholder's perspective and represented accurately when considering new business profitability.
- Manage your capital:
  - make the sources of capital generation and investment transparent to shareholders and management, applying a return on capital perspective rigorously;
  - invest as much free capital as possible in profitable organic or inorganic growth, returning any remaining capital to shareholders.

LH VALUATION

The value of an LH insurer is equal to its current market value surplus (e.g., the value of all assets and liabilities as a closed block of business based on ongoing business expense assumptions) plus its franchise value (e.g., the value of the company's future new business).

The first-best solution for valuing an LH insurer is to directly use market-consistent information, available for some European firms in the form of voluntary MCEV disclosures, and removing any uneconomic distortions including the impact of yield curve anchoring to an ultimate forward rate or the inclusion of an illiquidity premium.

Relevant but more challenging is the case where only statutory or accounting information is available, especially if amortized cost accounting is used for liabilities. Almost useless are EV disclosures which rely on management discretion over key parameters such as the risk discount rate, future financial market returns, etc.

Given the challenges in valuing LH businesses from the outside-in, it is recommended to use a combination of approaches whenever possible and then triangulate to an appropriate valuation.

Valuation Using MCEV Information

Many firms disclose supplementary EV or MCEV information. According to Towers Watson (2013), in 2012 insurance companies globally reported over USD 900 billion of EV, including USD 395 in Europe, USD 161 in Japan, USD 145 in China/Hong Kong, USD 122 in the rest of the Asia–Pacific region and USD 70 in Canada, South Africa and Israel.

However, the industry tends to be somewhat aggressive in valuing LH businesses using EV; earlier, evidence was presented suggesting that European LH firms were trading at a 0.47× multiple to their reported EV figures, implying that the average EV reported by the European industry in 2012 was 200% of the market valuation of their firm, implying that EV information may need to be taken with a grain of salt.

However, we have demonstrated that *adjusted* MCEVs more accurately represent the value of the business. Assuming that MCEV information is available, the valuation of LH insurers proceeds in three steps.

Step 1: Determine the Current Market Value Surplus of the LH Insurer

The first step is to calculate the current market value surplus of the LH business based on MCEV disclosures, as described in Table 9.1.

TABLE 9.1   LH net asset value

Embedded value reporting	Generic adjustments
+ MCEV + adjustments to MCEV	Remove non-economic elements of MCEV: ■ the impact of the illiquidity premium, volatility adjuster or matching adjustment based on published sensitivities; ■ the yield curve anchoring to an ultimate forward rate based on published sensitivities.
= MVS	

TABLE 9.2   LH normalized value of next period's new business

New business economic profit	Generic adjustments
+ VNB	
+ Adjustments to VNB	Remove non-economic elements impacting VNB: ■ the illiquidity premium, volatility adjuster or matching adjustment based on published sensitivities; ■ the yield curve anchoring to an ultimate forward rate based on published sensitivities; ■ (less critical) the FCReC. Normalize historic reported VNB: ■ adjust New Business Margin (NBM) to reflect expected levels under current market conditions, including the effects of any re-pricing or product changes; ■ adjust for predictable changes in product and geographic mix.
= Adjusted LH.EP	

Step 2: Determine the Normalized LH New Business Economic Profit

The second step is to calculate the normalized value of new business economic profit contributions, as illustrated in Table 9.2. As Sidebar 9.3 illustrates, reported MCEV Value of New Business (VNB) will be "close" to LH new business EP if there is no asset / liability mismatch risk taking or, alternatively, if there is no "investment alpha" earned on the mismatch, with the only differences being in:

■ Non-economic assumptions (e.g. illiquidity premium, ultimate forward rate, etc.), which can be material.
■ The frictional cost of required capital, which is less material.

As indicated in Table 9.2, the reported VNB should be adjusted for these two differences, especially the first which can lead to substantial overstatement of value.

It is worthwhile highlighting two additional observations about Table 9.2. First, there is no explicit deduction for the cost of capital; this is because VNB is calculated by deducting a capital charge for non-financial risk based on the projected lifetime capital requirements for the product. Second, there is no addition for Investment EP or "alpha"; this reflects my own view (described in Chapter 16) that it is challenging to consistently generate investment returns in excess of the risk-appropriate benchmark and even more difficult to expect shareholders to pay a premium for such returns.

Step 3: Discount Future Projected LH.EP to Today's Value

The franchise value of the firm represents the present value of all future new business. As such, the future stream of new business contributions needs to be projected and discounted to a present value.

Steady state. If we assume a steady state into perpetuity, then the franchise value can be written in the following manner:

$$\text{Franchise value} = \frac{\text{adjusted LH.EP}}{\text{CoC} - g}$$

where g is the assumed steady-state growth rate.

Non-steady state. If a steady-state assumption is not appropriate, then the LH.EP may need to be projected for different periods into the future using assumptions regarding operating performance which are appropriate for the forecast period. Common practice is to divide the future into an explicit projection period, for example the next 10 years, with an associated terminal value determined by steady-state assumptions:

$$\text{Franchise value} = \sum_{t=1}^{T} \frac{\text{Adjusted LH.EP}_t}{(1 + \text{CoC})^t} + \frac{1}{(1 + \text{CoC})^{T+1}} \frac{\text{Adjusted LH.EP}_T}{\text{CoC} - g}$$

The first term represents the present value of the explicitly projected LH.EPs up until the end of the explicit projection period at time T and the second term represents the terminal value, or present value of a growing perpetuity which begins in period T.

Valuation Based on Accounting Information

Valuation becomes more challenging if the company does not report MCEV, in which case the valuation will have to be based on accounting information. Even if the company does report MCEV, this is a useful approach for triangulating the results.

It is challenging because there is no separate estimate of the current market value surplus; instead, accounting book values have to be used as the starting point and these can deviate strongly from market-consistent values, especially for long-term guaranteed business. Consistent with this, accounting earnings have to be projected, earnings which are derived both from existing and new business combined as opposed to representing solely the value of new business.

Information is generally needed at the product level, for example split between guaranteed, protection and unit-linked products, because of their different characteristics (illustrated in Table 9.3). Unfortunately, although disclosure practices are improving, not all companies provide a sufficiently granular view by product. Swiss Re (2012) observes that "There is limited disclosure of performance at the product level and few insights into a product's risk profile and its consequences for future earnings." This is an area that insurance companies need to work on.

Using accounting or statutory information, the valuation of an LH insurer proceeds in three steps.

Step 1: Define (An Arbitrary) Valuation Basis

The starting point can be the accounting or statutory capital or the traditional EV attributed to the product segment, represented by the first row in Table 9.3. The attributed capital provides the baseline for calculating the appropriate valuation multiple. In practice, it does not matter which basis is used – in the end, earnings are compared relative to the attributed capital and the cost of capital in order to determine the appropriate multiple. An overly optimistic initial starting capital value requires higher earnings in order to meet the cost of capital.

TABLE 9.3   Valuation of LH insurers based on accounting information

	Total Portfolio	Guaranteed Products	Protection & Health Products	Unit linked w/o Guarantee
1) Attributed capital				
2) Normalized excess returns				
+ Loadings & fees		Adjust for changes in product		
+ Technical margins		pricing and mix, predictable		
+ Investment margin		expense improvements, etc.		
− Expenses				
= Operating profit before DAC				
+ Change in DAC				
= Operating profit				
− Taxes				
= Net operating income				
− Cost of Capital				
= Normalized excess returns				
3) Implied multiple				
Growth				
Cost of capital				
PV excess book returns				

Step 2: Determine Normalized Excess Returns

The next step is to determine the normalized expected excess returns, represented by the second section in the table. Earnings should be normalized (e.g., for any anticipated changes in business mix and the impact on investment margin from changing financial market conditions, pricing initiatives, etc.). The total cost of capital is determined by the capital attributed to the business times the appropriate cost of capital.

If the normalized earnings fall below the cost of capital, then excess returns will be negative, implying a valuation multiple less than 1x relative to attributed capital. There are two possible explanations for negative normalized excess returns, implying a valuation multiple less than 1× relative to attributed capital.

- First, in the best-case scenario, the allocated capital is economically too high, representing a CER >> 100%. The valuation multiple can be improved if the excess capital can be extracted from the business, for example by monetizing the value in-force through an embedded value securitization or reinsurance arrangement.
- Second, in the more common case, if the CER is close to 1, then the combination of the legacy and new business is not expected to generate returns sufficient to meet the firm's cost of capital.

Step 3: Project Excess Returns into the Future and Discount to Today

The addition to book value is calculated as the present value of all excess book returns, including those from existing and new business.

Steady state. If we assume a steady state into perpetuity, then the addition to book value can be written in the following manner:

$$\text{Additional value} = \frac{\text{Excess returns}}{\text{CoC} - g}$$

where g is the assumed steady-state growth rate.

Non-steady state. If a steady-state assumption is not appropriate, then excess book returns may need to be projected for different periods into the future. Common practice is to divide the future into an explicit projection period, for example the next 10 years, with an associated terminal value determined by steady-state assumptions:

$$\text{Additional value} = \sum_{t=1}^{T} \frac{\text{Excess returns}_t}{(1 + \text{CoC})^t} + \frac{1}{(1 + \text{CoC})^{T+1}} \frac{\text{Excess returns}_T}{\text{CoC} - g}$$

The first term represents the present value of the excess returns up until the end of the explicit projection period at time T and the second term represents the terminal value, or present value of a growing perpetuity which begins in period T.

UNDERSTANDING VALUE CREATION: CAPITAL INTENSITY AND FINANCIAL RISK TAKING

In contrast to PC insurance, the LH industry offers long-term guaranteed products which require significant capital tied up for long periods of time. Because of this, new business metrics based only on underwriting returns which do not explicitly recognize the aggregate capital intensity of the products are not appropriate. Unfortunately, the industry standard KPIs for new business (e.g., MCEV NBM and Internal Rates of Return (IRRs) or payback periods) either do not recognize the capital intensity of the business or are unduly influenced by management's optimistic assumptions.

This section begins by describing why the LH New Business RAPM is superior to MCEV NBM (e.g., because New Business RAPMs recognize the inherent capital intensity of the product). It then continues by motivating and developing the LH Investment Margin RAPM, which also recognizes financial market returns and risks. It concludes by comparing these measures against other measures often used, including IRR and payback periods.

Why the LH New Business RAPM is Better Than NBM – Capital Intensity

Many companies manage and report MCEV NBM instead of the LH New Business RAPM.[7] This focus leads to the wrong management decisions: *LH New Business RAPM is clearly superior to MCEV NBM for steering long-term, capital intensive businesses.* Why? Because NBM is not useful in managing capital-intensive businesses.

More specifically, the same NBM can represent very different returns on shareholders' capital depending on the capital intensity of the product. Consider the three unit-linked

---

[7]The differences and similarities between NBM and the LH New Business RAPM are discussed in detail in Sidebar 9.3.

NBM versus LH New Business RAPM
Unit Linked Product

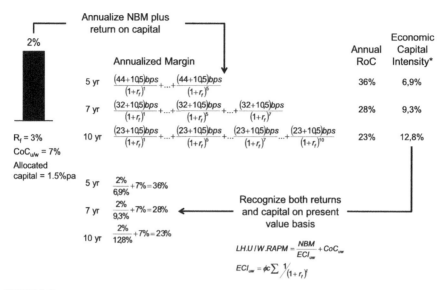

FIGURE 9.2 NBM versus LH New Business RAPM – unit-linked product

products illustrated in Figure 9.2, each offering a 2% NBM and all three requiring capital equal to 1.5% of the premium per annum. The only difference between the three is that they bind capital for different durations – 5, 7 and 10 years, respectively.

The 2% NBM (and associated real-world profits, including the return on capital) are going to emerge faster and stronger for the 5-year product than for the 10-year product, implying a higher annual operating margin and therefore a higher return on the annual capital required.

Referring to Figure 9.2, the same 2% NBM emerges as a 44 bps p.a. annuity for the 5-year unit-linked policy versus 23 bps p.a. for the 10-year alternative. The additional 10.5 bps p.a. in the numerator reflects the return on underwriting risk capital (1.5% p.a. required capital times 7% cost of underwriting capital), which is subtracted when calculating NBM and therefore needs to be added back when calculating the total return on capital. Because the 2% NBM emerges faster and stronger for the 5-year product, this leads to an annualized return on capital equal to 36% for the 5-year unit-linked product versus 23% for the 10-year product.

Equally, we can also compare the product returns on an ex-ante, present-value basis (equivalent to the LH New Business RAPM) by dividing the present value returns to capital by the product's ECI, illustrated in the lower half of the figure. ECI is defined as the present value of all future minimum capital requirements. All else being equal, the 10-year product will have an economic capital intensity about 2× that of the 5-year product, implying that it uses approximately twice as much capital over its lifetime in present value terms; the 10-year product is potentially more dependent on long-term assumptions. The ex-ante, present-value return on capital is identical to the periodic return on capital calculated earlier, for example 36% for the 5-year product but only 23% for the 10-year product.

It is understandable why shareholders prefer the 5-year product over the 10-year product: although both offer the same NBM, but the 5-year product requires significantly less cumulative capital over its lifetime. As illustrated in Sidebar 9.3, under certain conditions the LH New Business RAPM and NBM measures are related by the following formula:

$$\text{LH New Business RAPM} = \left(\frac{\text{NBM}}{\text{ECI}_{uw}} + \text{CoC}_{uw} \right)$$

SIDEBAR 9.3: RELATION BETWEEN LH NBM AND LH NEW BUSINESS RAPM

Both MCEV-VNB/NBM and LH New Business RAPM reflect *only* the contributions from underwriting risks. They are closely related *if the same valuation and capital attribution basis is used*, in which case LH New Business RAPM can be expressed as a function of MCEV-NBM:

$$\text{LH New Business RAPM} = \frac{\text{NBM}}{\text{ECI}_{uw}} + \text{CoC}_{uw}$$

where ECI_{uw} is the economic capital intensity ratio for the new business reflecting underwriting risks only and CoC_{uw} is the total cost of underwriting capital (e.g., $\text{CoC}_{uw} = r_f + rp_{uw}$).

MCEV-VNB

MCEV-VNB is equal to the present value of future profits from new business plus the time value of options and guarantees minus the cost of non-hedgeable risk minus the frictional cost of capital:

$$\text{MCEV-VNB} = \text{PVFP} + \text{TVOG} - \text{CNHR} - \text{FCReC}$$

(Market consistent) Present value future premiums, claims and expenses	Present value of future risk premium for future capital requirements

PRESENT VALUE OF PREMIUMS, CLAIMS AND EXPENSES

PVFP + TVOG represents the market-consistent present value of future premiums, claims and expenses for the new business, including the value of options and guarantees. This is identical to part of the LH underwriting RAPM numerator *if the same discount rates and valuation techniques are used*.

Without loss of generality, PVFP + TVOG can be expressed as a constant, annualized operating margin on the capital tied up in the new business:

$$\text{PVFP} + \text{TVOG} = m_{uw}{}^* \varphi c_{uw}{}^* d_{cuw}$$

where m_{uw} is the constant expected technical return margin for the new business without taking any financial market risk, ϕc_{uw} is the average capital needed per annum to support the underwriting contribution and d_{cuw} is a factor which reflects both the duration and discounting of the capital tied up by the product – e.g., $d_{cuw} = 1/(1 + r_f)$ for a product which ties up the capital for 1 year, $d_{cuw} = \left(1/(1 + r_f) + 1/(1 + r_f)^2\right)$ for a 2-year product, etc.

COST OF REQUIRED CAPITAL

FCReC should represent the frictional cost of total required capital in MCEV calculations, often set at 1% times the total required capital to reflect double taxation and additional asset management expenses which the company could avoid by returning the capital to shareholders (see CFO Forum, 2009b). As noted in Chapter 7, FCReC should *not* be recognized when valuing insurance liabilities; this is especially the case if the required capital is primarily driven by financial risk taking which is not explicitly recognized under NBM/VNB or LH New Business RAPM. It is therefore set to zero when calculating the LH New Business RAPM.

The term CNHR reflects *the cost of capital above the risk-free rate* needed to compensate capital for underwriting risks. Defining the *total* cost of capital for underwriting risk as the risk-free return plus the underwriting risk premium (e.g., $CoC_{uw} = r_f + rp_{uw}$), CNHR can be expressed as

$$\text{CNHR} = rp_{uw}{}^{*}\varphi c_{uw}{}^{*}d_{cuw}$$

Combining the two, we get

$$\text{VNB} = (\text{PVFP} + \text{TVOG}) - (\text{CNHR} + \text{CREC}) = (m_{uw} - rp_{uw})^{*}\varphi c_{uw}{}^{*}d_{cuw}$$

NBM is defined as VNB divided by the present value of new business premium. Using consistent notation, we define the PVNBP as

$$\text{PVNBP} = \varphi p^{*}d_p$$

where ϕp is the average premium to be received over time and d_p is a factor which represents discounting of the accumulated average premiums – e.g., $d_p = 1$ for a single-premium product, $d_p = 1 + 1/(1 + r_f)$ for a product with two premium payments, etc.

Using the definition of NBM and substituting, we get

$$\text{NBM} = \frac{\text{VNB}}{\text{PVNBP}} = (m_{uw} - rp_{uw})^{*}\frac{\varphi c_{uw}{}^{*}d_{cuw}}{\varphi p^{*}d_p} = (m_{uw} - rp_{uw})^{*}\text{ECI}_{uw}$$

where the economic capital intensity for underwriting risks is given by

$$\text{ECI}_{uw} = \frac{\varphi c_{uw}{}^{*}d_{cuw}}{\varphi p^{*}d_p}$$

ECI_{uw} is the sum of the discounted average capital requirements divided by the sum of the discounted average premiums; for a single-premium product, the economic capital intensity ratio is nothing more than the discounted average capital divided by the premium – e.g., $\text{ECI}_{uw} = \varphi c_{uw}{}^{*}d_{cuw}/p$.

LH New Business RAPM and EVA

Using the same notation, we can rewrite LH New Business RAPM in simplified form

$$\text{LH New Business RAPM} = \frac{m_{uw}{}^*\varphi c_{uw}{}^*d_{cuw} + r_f{}^*\varphi c_{uw}{}^*d_{cuw}}{\varphi c_{uw}{}^*d_{cuw}} = m_{uw} + r_f$$

This relationship is intuitive: it says that the LH New Business RAPM is equal to the excess technical contribution margin (which should be sufficient to compensate for the underwriting risks taken), plus the risk-free return on the capital needed to support the product. The LH New Business RAPM can be converted into an absolute EP contribution:

$$\text{LH new business EP} = (\text{LH New Business RAPM} - \text{CoC}_{uw})^*\varphi c_{uw}{}^*d_{cuw}$$

$$= (m_{uw} - rp_{uw})^*\varphi c_{uw}{}^*d_{cuw}$$

This relationship is also intuitive: it says that the new business will only create value if the technical operating margin is sufficient to cover the cost of the risk premium for the capital deployed.

Relation Between NBM and LH New Business RAPM/EP

If calculated on the same basis (and removing the FCReC from the VNB calculation), the MCEV-VNB and LH New Business EP equations above are identical. Setting the two equal and rearranging, we can also express the LH underwriting RAPM in terms of NBM:

$$\text{LH-EP}^* \frac{1}{\varphi p^* dp} = (\text{LH-RAPM} - \text{CoC}_{uw})^*\varphi c_{uw}{}^*d_{cuw}{}^* \frac{1}{\varphi p^* dp} = \frac{\text{VNB}}{\varphi p^* dp} = \text{NBM}$$

$$(\text{LH New Business RAPM} - \text{CoC}_{uw})^*\text{ECI}_{uw} = \text{NBM}$$

Implying that

$$\text{LH New Business RAPM} = \frac{\text{NBM}}{\text{ECI}_{uw}} + \text{CoC}_{uw}$$

This relationship is also intuitive: it says that the LH New Business RAPM is equal to the NBM adjusted for the product's capital intensity plus the cost of capital. The translation of NBM by the capital intensity makes sense since RAPM represents the returns relative to the product's minimum lifetime capital requirement whereas NBM represents the returns relative to premium. The inclusion of the CoC_{uw} term is necessary since RAPM measures the total return on capital whereas NBM measures only excess return, above the cost of capital. They both yield the same decision rule in the end: whereas new business creates value if NBM > 0 and destroys value otherwise, it creates value if LH New Business RAPM > CoC and destroys value otherwise.

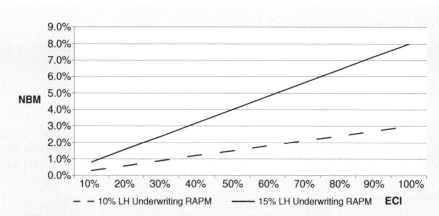

FIGURE 9.3   Relation between NBM and LH New Business RAPM

As Figure 9.3 indicates, it takes a higher NBM to provide the same LH New Business RAPM if the product's capital intensity increases (the figure is based on a 7% cost of capital for underwriting risks).

ECI_{uw} for underwriting risk is generally increasing for longer-duration retirement and savings products (because capital is tied up for longer periods) or if there is more non-hedgeable risk such as mortality or morbidity per period of exposure. Generally, long-duration products with high longevity risk have the highest capital intensity ratios.

Why the LH Investment Margin RAPM is Better – Financial Risk Taking

While the LH New Business RAPM better reflects capital efficiency for protection and asset management products, it is less well suited for guaranteed retirement products. This is because the New Business RAPMs look at the underwriting risks only, *as if the financial elements were perfectly matched* (e.g., as if there were no returns from financial market risk positions and no capital requirements to support any open asset/liability mismatch).

Unfortunately, the majority of the capital required for long-term, guaranteed retirement and savings products is used to cover financial market risk. This makes both NBM and LH New Business RAPM incapable of evaluating long-term guaranteed products which take substantial financial market risk in the normal course of business. This section motivates and develops a metric, the LH Investment Margin RAPM, which gives the right steering impulses for long-term, capital-intensive retirement savings products.

NBM and LH Investment Margin RAPM in the Absence of Alpha

Consider three *guaranteed* unit-linked products, illustrated in Figure 9.4. Like the last example, these products also offer a 2% NBM and tie up capital for 5, 7 and 10 years, respectively.

NBM versus LH Investment Margin RAPM
Unit Linked with Guarantee, no alpha*

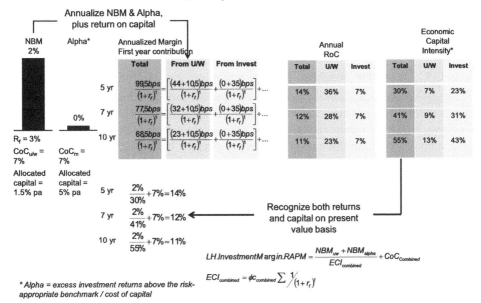

FIGURE 9.4 NBM versus LH Investment Margin RAPM – unit-linked product with guarantee, no alpha

However, these are guaranteed products and it is assumed that the insurer does not hedge the financial market risk of the guarantees, choosing instead to take the financial market risk in order to avoid the cost of hedging the guarantee.

In order to illustrate the economics of the product, we first consider the case where the insurer earns only its cost of capital from providing the guarantee and does not earn any "alpha," or an excess return relative to the appropriate financial market cost of the guarantee. This is represented in the figure by setting the value creation from "alpha" equal to 0; the capital required to back the financial market risk of the guarantee is assumed to be 5% p.a. and the real-world returns reflect the 7% expected return on financial market risk capital.

The figure is identical to the previous one, except for the addition of returns and capital requirements for financial market risk taking. In order to make the economics transparent, the sources of profit and the relative capital intensity from underwriting versus financial market risk are presented separately and in total.

As seen in the figure, taking financial market risk increases real-world earnings, represented by the 35 bps additional spread per annum (e.g., 7% expected returns from taking financial market risk times 5% p.a. capital requirements). However, *in the absence of alpha, taking financial market risk actually lowers the return on capital for the product! This is because financial market risk adds a lot of capital but brings no excess returns or alpha, diluting the underwriting excess returns measured by the NBM.*

Because financial market returns can be a substantial contributor to the sources of earnings, the expected real-world returns and the cost of financial market risk capital need to be recognized. The LH Investment Margin RAPM depends on the amount of "alpha" expected to be generated:

$$\text{LH Investment Margin RAPM} = \frac{\text{NBM}_{uw} + \text{NBM}_{alpha}}{\text{ECI}_{comb.}} + \text{CoC}_{comb.}$$

where $\text{CoC}_{comb.}$ is the weighted average return on capital, for example $\text{CoC}_{comb.} = \frac{1.5\% \times 7\% + 5.0\% \times 7\%}{1.5\% + 5.0\%}$ and $\text{ECI}_{comb.}$ is the weighted average ECI (where both are calculated assuming that underwriting risk and financial market risk share the same capital profile but with different intensities). NBM_{alpha} represents the present value of the stream of excess returns, a type of "alpha annuity" – e.g., in this example 0 bps p.a. because NBM_{alpha} is assumed to be 0%.

NBM and LH Investment Margin RAPM With Alpha

The story does not change qualitatively with the inclusion of alpha, defined as excess returns above the risk appropriate benchmark cost of the guarantee. Figure 9.5 shows the same unit-linked products with guarantees, but this time assuming that the company can earn a 1% "alpha margin" above the appropriate required return on capital for taking financial market risk by leaving the guarantee unhedged. As can be seen in the figure, a 1% alpha margin is equivalent to 22 bps, 16 bps and 12 bps p.a. investment outperformance relative to the cost of the guarantees for the 5-year, 7-year and 10-year product, respectively.

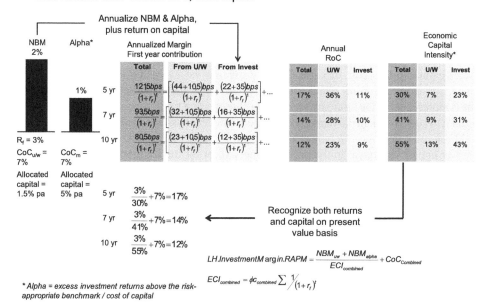

FIGURE 9.5 NBM versus LH Investment Margin RAPM – unit-linked product with guarantee, with alpha

The existance of alpha increases real-world returns as well as the LH Investment Margin RAPM, however not by that much. This is because the capital intensity for the financial market risk tends to be relatively high in terms of the per annum charge on reserves. As an aside, it is challenging to create alpha; it is even more courageous to count on it when pricing products and taking risk/return decisions.

A Comparison of Measures Used in Practice

LH products which combine financial market and underwriting profits are challenging to evaluate due to the complexity of evaluating the two sources of risk appropriately.

Why LH Investment Margin RAPM is Superior

The LH Investment Margin RAPM, defined by the following formula, is the correct way to evaluate such products:

$$\text{LH Investment Margin RAPM} = \frac{\text{NBM}_{uw} + \text{NBM}_{alpha}}{\text{ECI}_{comb.}} + \text{CoC}_{comb.}$$

where $\text{CoC}_{comb.}$ and $\text{ECI}_{comb.}$ are the weighted average costs of capital and economic capital intensities for the combined underwriting and financial market risk taking. NBM_{alpha} represents the present value of the stream of excess returns from taking financial market risk, a type of "alpha annuity."

The LH Investment Margin RAPM has several advantages over other LH profitability measures.

First, it is superior to MCEV NBM in that it explicitly recognizes the *economic capital intensity for both technical underwriting and financial market risks*. In contrast, NBM does not recognize the capital intensity from financial risk taking.

Second, the LH Investment Margin RAPM has a significant advantage over other real-world return measures such as the IRR in that it only values alpha, representing financial market outperformance, and does not ascribe value creation to the total real-world financial market gains. This is important as it is far too easy to be seduced by expected earnings from taking market risk when in reality shareholders will only pay a premium for "alpha" or excess returns relative to a risk appropriate benchmark return. Separating the two will lead to better discussions on the sources of value creation versus the sources of earnings.

Third, LH Investment Margin RAPM does not depend on your belief regarding the real-world benchmark returns from taking financial market risk. While an expected 6% or 10% or 20% expected benchmark return will increase real-world earnings, the appropriate cost of capital for financial risk is increased or decreased in line with your expectations, neutralizing the assumed real-world returns. LH Investment Margin RAPM recognizes that the only thing that matters in terms of value creation is alpha, or how many basis points you think you can create above and beyond the risk-appropriate benchmark returns for the guarantee.

This helps tremendously to focus the discussion on "value added." Instead of talking conceptually about an illiquidity premium or equity risk premium which can be "earned" by even a passive investor, the conversation is instead turned to the *excess* returns "above the 7-year duration Barclays bond index" or "above the Eurostoxx 50" or "above the value of the guarantees left unhedged" your investment team is committing to earn while staying within their risk budget.

Other Performance Metrics Commonly Used[8]

Another metric often used is the Internal Rate of Return (IRR). It is defined as the discount rate for which the discounted present value of all expected cash flows, from the premium inflow and initial capital investment to the claims outflow and return of capital, is identically equal to zero. In general, the higher you set your real-world return assumptions, the higher your IRR. Note that this is not the case with the LH Investment Margin RAPM because the cost of capital mirrors the real-world benchmark return assumptions, effectively isolating alpha outperformance.

Another metric often used is the *payback period*, defined as the time it will take the product's real-world expected earnings to just cover or break even relative to the initial capital investment in terms of acquisition costs and capital strain to support the new business.

Both IRRs and payback periods suffer from theoretical issues well documented in corporate finance textbooks; for example, the cumulative cash flows can turn positive and then negative again, implying that there may be multiple IRRs, with some representing negative present values.

However, the most important issue with IRRs and payback periods is that they depend on management's assumptions with respect to future financial market developments: the more optimistic the assumptions, the higher the IRR and the shorter the payback period.

Table 9.4 gives a complete overview of various metrics used to steer LH businesses.

Some of these diagnostic indicators are also disclosed in order to aid financial analysts and shareholders in interpreting the business. An example of these disclosures from Allianz's analyst presentation on 2013 results is given in Figure 9.6.

LH KPIs: Capital and Surplus Development

In contrast to PC insurance, LH KPIs include information on the development of the market value surplus and free capital. This is because capital is tied up over much longer time horizons, so tracking the sources and uses of capital during any single period becomes more critical, and because there is significant value embedded in the LH in-force business which needs to be managed if it is to be realized through earnings.

Understanding MVS Movements

The movement in LH MVS is reported as part of the overall MCEV developments using a standardized movement analysis is defined in the CFO Forum (2008) Principles, illustrated in Table 9.5. The movement in MCEV is split between free surplus, required capital and ViF, in order to demonstrate the impact on capital flows. In principle, free surplus could be distributed to shareholders if it can be unlocked from the ViF, for example through an embedded value securitization, or more free surplus can be created by lowering required capital, for example through de-risking the investment portfolio.

The line items in the movement analysis are described in the CFO Forum MCEV Principles, summarized at a high level here.

- Opening and closing adjustments are limited to "Capital & Dividend flows," "Foreign Exchange variance" and "Acquired/Divested Business" when appropriate.

---

[8]A good overview of market-consistent and real-world pricing metrics can be found in Junus *et al.* (2012).

TABLE 9.4 Additional LH diagnostic indicators for growth and profitability

Profitability diagnostic indicators	Description
LH New Business RAPM	Represents the ratio between the present value of future profits from underwriting to the present value of capital tied up in the product, where profits and capital are measured *as if* no financial market risk is taken. Represents the majority of earnings for protection and asset management products. This metric is preferred over NBM for protection and asset management products because it explicitly recognizes the capital intensity of the product. Under specific assumptions (described in Sidebar 9.3), the LH New Business RAPM can be expressed as a function of $\text{MVEC-NBM: RAPM}_{uw} = \left(\frac{\text{NBM}}{\text{ECI}_{uw}} + \text{CoC}_{uw}\right)$
LH Investment Margin RAPM	Represents the ratio between the present value of future profits from all sources to the present value of all capital tied up in the product, where profits and capital are measured *including* financial market risk taken. Represents the majority of earnings and capital requirements for long-term, guaranteed retirement and savings products. This metric is preferred over NBM and New Business RAPM because it explicitly recognizes the capital intensity of the product, including the capital tied up in financial market risks (which are excluded from MCEV-NBM and the LH New Business RAPM). Under specific assumptions (described in Sidebar 9.3), the LH Investment Margin RAPM can be expressed as a function of NBM and the NBM "alpha" or financial market outperformance expected to be earned: $\text{RAPM}_{comb.} = \left(\frac{\text{NBM}_{uw} + \text{NBM}_{alpha} +}{\text{ECI}_{comb.}} + \text{CoC}_{comb.}\right)$
MCEV-NBM	Represents the ratio between the present value of future excess profits to shareholders (after deducting the cost of underwriting capital) divided by the present value of future premiums, where profits are measured *as if* no financial market risk is taken. Represents the majority of earnings for protection and asset management products. It is a less useful measure for managing capital as it is broadly insensitive to the capital intensity of the product and substantially under-represents the earnings and capital strain of guaranteed products which rely on financial market returns.
IRR	A measure of the expected return on invested capital (including upfront capital and expense strains) under "real-world" financial market assumptions. It does not reflect value creation unless an appropriate cost of financial market risk capital is used: in general, higher expected financial market returns will increase the IRR *and* also the appropriate cost of capital simultaneously. The appropriate cost of capital needs to be increased in lock step if the company does not create "alpha" and the benchmark returns can be replicated in the market by shareholders and investors directly.
Payback period	The expected time required to recoup the capital and expense strain of new business under real-world return assumptions.
ECI	Used in RAPM, a measure of the initial capital and expense strain of new business relative to the PVNBP. ECI is defined as the present value of all future capital requirements divided by the present value of new business premium: $\text{ECI} = \sum C_t / (1 + r_f)^t / \sum P_t / (1 + r_f)^t$
Investment intensity	Analysts occasionally calculate an intensity ratio based on public disclosures. For example, some analysts calculate the ratio of net investment (acquisition and capital strain) relative to premium or value: $\text{Intensity} = \frac{\text{Capital and expense strain}}{\text{PVNBP}}$ or $\frac{\text{Capital and expense strain}}{\text{VNB}}$

(A) A. Group financial results 2013 – Additional information on Life/Health   **Allianz ⑪**

L/H: value of new business[1]
(EUR mn)

Region	Value of new business 12M 2012	Value of new business 12M 2013	New business margin 12M 2012	New business margin 12M 2013	Present value of new business premium 12M 2012	Present value of new business premium 12M 2013	Δ %[2]	Recurring premium 12M 2012	Recurring premium 12M 2013	Single premium 12M 2012	Single premium 12M 2013
German Speaking Countries	453	406	2.8%	2.7%	16,017	14,815	-7.4%	795	636	5,367	6,340
Germany Life[3]	415	354	3.2%	2.8%	12,905	12,501	-3.1%	620	486	4,712	5,983
Europe	135	202	1.0%	1.2%	12,952	16,192	+25.1%	576	652	8,412	10,756
France	80	81	1.1%	0.8%	7,263	8,361	+15.1%	308	331	4,232	4,544
Italy	46	100	1.0%	1.7%	4,666	6,026	+29.1%	211	192	3,630	5,202
Iberia & Latin America	48	55	3.8%	3.5%	1,276	1,566	+23.0%	81	107	733	929
Growth Markets	196	166	3.2%	3.0%	6,082	5,485	-6.4%	765	732	2,852	2,415
Asia-Pacific	132	108	2.8%	2.4%	4,646	4,478	+0.6%	616	575	2,135	2,073
CEEMA	64	57	5.2%	6.4%	1,234	889	-26.5%	149	157	515	224
USA	44	219	0.6%	3.0%	7,212	7,279	+2.7%	50	55	6,772	6,818
Total[4]	790	952	1.8%	2.1%	43,540	45,337	+4.4%	2,263	2,182	24,134	27,258

1) After non-controlling interests, including holding expenses and internal reinsurance. All values using F/X rates as of valuation date
2) Internal growth (adjusted for F/X and consolidation effects)
3) The single premium for Germany Life does not include Parkdepot business (12M 2012: EUR 890.4mn, 12M 2013: EUR 1.319bn)
4) Total including holding expenses and internal reinsurance

© Allianz SE 2014

A 69

FIGURE 9.6(a)   LH supplementary disclosure – capital intensity measures. Reproduced by permission of Allianz SE.

- The expected existing business contribution to MCEV earnings represents management's expectations based on real-world return assumptions, but should include the expected change in the cost of options and comprising two elements:
  - earnings assuming assets earn the beginning of period reference rates;
  - plus the additional earnings consistent with management's real-world return expectations.
- Analysis and explanations should be provided:
  - for any significant variance between actual and expected experience (variance analysis);
  - for any significant change to the method or approach – which should also be quantified and disclosed (model changes);
  - for any significant impact resulting from changes in experience assumptions – which should be disclosed and explained (assumption changes);
  - if management has made changes to crediting strategies – these should be included in "Other operating variances."
- Economic variances include the impact of financial market conditions being different at the end of the reporting period from the real-world expected conditions.

Given the strong role that modeling and assumptions play in MCEV, financial analysts pay particular attention to operating variances caused by model and assumption changes. For example, one analyst conducts a "Peacocks and Squirrels" analysis (Redburn, 2012), accumulating the company's reported MCEV variances over time and labeling those with

(B) A. Group financial results 2013 – Additional information on Life/Health   **Allianz ⓘ**

L/H: new business profitability by region

	Value of new business (EUR mn)[1,2]					New business margin (in %)[1,2]					Capital return 4Q 13 (in %)[3]	
	4Q 12	1Q 13	2Q 13	3Q 13	4Q 13	4Q 12	1Q 13	2Q 13	3Q 13	4Q 13	IRR	Payback period (yrs)
German Speaking Countries	172	140	74	87	105	3.0%	2.7%	2.8%	2.8%	2.7%	16.2%	5.9
Western & Southern Europe	30	39	44	47	72	0.8%	0.9%	0.9%	1.6%	1.8%	9.9%	7.6
Iberia & Latin America	12	11	13	13	18	2.8%	3.3%	2.7%	4.2%	4.2%	9.2%	9.3
Growth Markets	50	47	44	32	43	3.3%	3.1%	3.0%	2.8%	3.2%	14.1%	5.9
USA	7	24	41	62	92	0.5%	1.5%	2.3%	3.8%	4.1%	13.8%	5.5
Total[4]	256	238	190	215	310	2.0%	1.8%	1.7%	2.3%	2.6%	11.9%	6.9

1) After non-controlling interests. All values using F/X rates as of each valuation date
2) Based on beginning of quarter economic assumptions. For the USA we use point of sale assumptions
3) Both IRR and payback period are real world metrics, using an expected over-return on certain assets and capturing risks in the discount rate
4) Including holding expenses and internal reinsurance

© Allianz SE 2014

A 70

FIGURE 9.6(b)   LH supplementary disclosure – capital intensity measures. Reproduced by permission of Allianz SE.

negative net cumulative changes as "Peacocks" (e.g., reported MCEVs deemed overly optimistic, more for show and not being able to be maintained over time) and positive cumulative net changes as "Squirrels" (e.g., hiding nuts for winter through more conservative MCEV assumptions which then show positive developments over time).

However, the "economic variances" tend to dominate MVS movements for long-term, guaranteed retirement and savings products during volatile financial markets. While there are many channels through which market turbulence can impact the MVS, experience during the 2008 and 2012 financial crises suggests that the major impact comes predominantly through four channels.

- First, any increase in credit spreads due to heightened risk aversion, flight to quality and/or higher probability of defaults decreases the market value of assets directly. While these asset spread movements may be dampened by mechanisms which transfer some of the changes into a higher-liability discount rate (e.g., the illiquidity premium, matching adjustment or volatility balancer), the evidence presented in Chapter 6 suggests strongly that these are not recognized in the share price, presenting an overly optimistic view of the business during times of crisis.
- Second, any decrease in interest rates will negatively impact MVS for long-dated retirement and savings business with a substantial asset/liability mismatch, with assets of shorter duration relative to liabilities representing a reinvestment risk. While the impact of lower long-term rates may be dampened by yield curve anchoring to an ultimate forward

TABLE 9.5 MCEV movement analysis

MCEV movement analysis	Free surplus	Required capital	Value in force	MCEV
Opening MCEV				
Opening adjustments				
Adj opening MCEV				
Value of new business				
Expected existing contribution				
At reference rate				
In excess of reference rate				
Transfers from ViF and required capital to free surplus				
Experience variances				
Assumption changes				
Other operating variances				
Operating MCEV earnings				
Economic variances				
Other non-operating variances				
Total MCEV earnings				
Closing adjustments				
Closing MCEV				

rate, the evidence presented in Chapter 6 suggests strongly that these are not recognized in the share price, presenting an overly optimistic view of the business during times of crisis.

- Third, any increase in implied volatilities will increase the value of embedded options and guarantees.
- Fourth, any decrease in equity values will directly impact the market value of assets held in the general account. In addition, the guarantees on equity-linked products can increase substantially, depending on a company's hedging strategy and the size of the market movement.

The 2008 event study in Chapter 6 suggested that the market value of LH insurers can be substantially impacted by these factors, leading to a reduction in "clean" MCEV of between 40% and 60% for LH businesses at the height of a financial crisis, and that their share prices mirror this impact. The conclusion to be drawn is that, if management is unhappy about the resulting share price volatility, then it should make changes to the product mix and asset/liability strategy.

Information on the movement of market value surplus is not only used internally, but also disclosed externally. An example of supplementary disclosures related to MCEV movement analysis can be found in Figure 9.7, taken from Allianz's analyst presentation on 2013 fiscal year results.

The CFO Forum Principles also specify that additional information be provided, including a Group MCEV calculation (including non-covered business such as PC insurance activities,

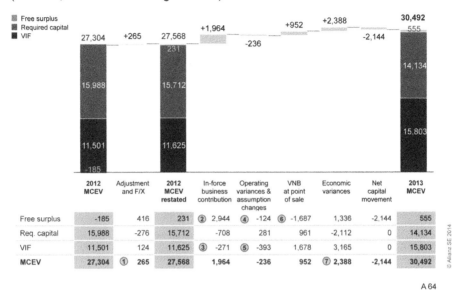

Allianz ⑪

L/H: MCEV development (1/2)
(EUR mn, after non-controlling interests)

■ Free surplus
■ Required capital
■ VIF

	2012 MCEV	Adjustment and F/X	2012 MCEV restated	In-force business contribution	Operating variances & assumption changes	VNB at point of sale	Economic variances	Net capital movement	2013 MCEV
Free surplus	-185	416	231	② 2,944	④ -124	⑥ -1,687	1,336	-2,144	555
Req. capital	15,988	-276	15,712	-708	281	961	-2,112	0	14,134
VIF	11,501	124	11,625	③ -271	⑤ -393	1,678	3,165	0	15,803
MCEV	27,304	① 265	27,568	1,964	-236	952	⑦ 2,388	-2,144	30,492

A 64

FIGURE 9.7(a) MCEV movement analysis. Reproduced by permission of Allianz SE.

Allianz ⑪

L/H: MCEV development (2/2)
(EUR mn, after non-controlling interests)

① 265 — Mainly correction of Life vs Non-Life split of the shareholders' equity France +410mn, acquisition of Yapı Kredi +172mn, offset by negative F/X effects, incl. -206mn for US, -89mn in Indonesia

② 2,944 =
- 1,477 Projected release of risk free profits from VIF in the reporting period
- 708 Projected release of in-force capital
- 148 Projected risk free return on Net Asset Value
- 610 Expected over-returns earned in the year, mainly from US and Italian spreads

③ -271 =
- -1,477 Projected release of risk free profits from VIF in the reporting period
- 582 Projected unwinding of VIF at the risk free rate and release of Options and Guarantees
- 624 VIF increase from higher asset base due to expected over-return, mainly US, Germany and France

④ -124 — Small negative impact from increase in Required Capital in Korea from adjusted methodology, partly offset by positive experience variances in France and Germany Life

⑤ -393 =
- 120 Assumption changes and experience variances
- -513 Other operating variances, mostly Germany (new treatment of Going Concern Reserve)

⑥ -1,687 =
- -961 New business capital strain
- -726 New business cash strain

⑦

(EUR mn) Estimates based on sensitivities	German speaking countries	Western & Southern Europe[1]	Iberia & Latin America[2]	Growth markets	USA[3]	Total[4]
Economic variances	**1,008**	**891**	**320**	**102**	**78**	**2,388**
Driven by changes in interest rate	543	552	316	54	54	1,517
Driven by changes in equity value	347	238	1	6	9	591
Driven by changes in volatilities	119	101	3	42	15	280

1) Includes EUR 242mn effect of reduced spread on Italian government bonds in changes in interest rate
2) Includes EUR 272mn effect of reduced spread on Spanish government bonds in changes in interest rate
3) Includes EUR 42mn effect of increased credit spreads in the US in changes in interest rate
4) Total includes holding expenses and reinsurance

A 65

FIGURE 9.7(b) MCEV movement analysis. Reproduced by permission of Allianz SE.

(A) A. Group financial results 2013 – Additional information on Life/Health

Allianz ⅀

L/H: MCEV sensitivity analysis
(EUR mn, after non-controlling interests)

2013 Region	Base case	Drop in equity value by 20%	risk free assumptions -100bp	risk free assumptions +100bp	volatilities +25% swaption	volatilities +25% equity	Credit Risk Spreads +100 bp	-10% expense	+15% mortality death risk	-20% mortality longevity risk	-10% lapse
					Economic factors				Non economic factors		
German Speaking Countries	13,736	-858	-1,316	514	-468	-141	-473	216	-117	-542	348
thereof: Germany Life	*9,340*	*-716*	*-1,087*	*365*	*-308*	*-143*	*-223*	*90*	*-39*	*-557*	*302*
Europe	9,376	-560	-493	250	-144	-36	-747	344	-147	-262	67
thereof: France	*5,351*	*-281*	*-45*	*35*	*7*	*4*	*-332*	*208*	*-76*	*-235*	*49*
thereof: Italy	*2,415*	*-179*	*-370*	*168*	*-134*	*-31*	*-343*	*80*	*-29*	*-20*	*-15*
Iberia & Latin America	798	-7	-7	-7	-10	-1	-266	23	-59	-136	36
Growth Markets	1,646	-86	-650	378	-12	-21	-350	110	-115	-128	66
thereof: Asia-Pacific	*651*	*-75*	*-693*	*425*	*6*	*-18*	*-241*	*79*	*-98*	*-128*	*41*
thereof: CEEMA	*974*	*-11*	*43*	*-47*	*-18*	*-3*	*-109*	*30*	*-17*	*0*	*25*
USA	5,303	-125	45	-163	-43	-393	-1,565	97	-19	-230	19
Total[1]	30,492	-1,635	-2,412	968	-677	-591	-3,400	795	-494	-1,303	539

- Still high sensitivities due to decreases in interest rates
- Especially in Germany Life, Taiwan and Korea where the duration mismatch is highest, but also Italy as low rates are close to guaranteed rates
- Sensitivity to interest rates in Germany Life relatively low from yield curve extrapolation after 20 years
- High sensitivity to volatilities in Germany Life, US and Italy due to high O&G value
- Sensitivity to Credit Risk Spreads is highest in the US, with a large share of corporate bonds
- Significant exposure to longevity risk in Germany Life, France, Korea and the US

© Allianz SE 2014

1) Total includes holding expenses and reinsurance

A 66

FIGURE 9.8(a)   MCEV sensitivities. Reproduced by permission of Allianz SE.

asset management businesses, etc.), a reconciliation to IFRS net asset value and sensitivities to key assumptions or financial market developments.

The CFO Forum mandates that sensitivities be reported to ±100 bps parallel change in the risk-free discount rate curve, a −10% change in the value of equities and real estate, a +25% increase in the implied volatilities for rates, equities and real estate. In addition, it is common practice to also include sensitivities to credit spread movements.

If the MCEV representation remains economic, these sensitivities are sometimes used for asset/liability management purposes. For example, the ±100 bps interest rate sensitivities can be used to calculate the dollar duration and convexity of the existing asset/liability mismatch this implies that the sensitivity long-dated cash flows is being artificially dampened, hiding the full extent to which the firm has an asset/liability mismatch.

Information on market value sensitivities is not only used internally, but also disclosed externally. An example of supplementary disclosures related to MCEV and VNB sensitivities can be found in Figure 9.8, taken from Allianz's analyst presentation on 2013 fiscal year results.

From MVS to Capital Movements
It is easy to have a capital problem in LH businesses: significant investments are made today in new business, investments which will only pay back years or decades later with the IRRs and

(B) A. Group financial results 2013 – Additional information on Life/Health   **Allianz ⓘ**

L/H: value of new business[1] sensitivity analysis
(EUR mn)

	Base case[2]	Economic factors						Non economic factors		
		Drop in equity value by 20%	risk free[3] assumptions		volatilities		-10% expense	+15% mortality death risk	-20% mortality longevity risk	-10% lapse
			-100bp	+100bp	+25% swaption	+25% equity				
German Speaking Countries	406	-12	-76	24	-22	-9	17	-5	-14	31
thereof: Germany Life	*354*	*-12*	*-70*	*18*	*-22*	*-10*	*13*	*-3*	*-21*	*22*
Europe	202	-31	-50	25	-5	-2	22	-19	-3	34
thereof: France	*51*	*-8*	*-41*	*25*	*0*	*0*	*13*	*-12*	*-2*	*24*
thereof: Italy	*100*	*-17*	*-3*	*-4*	*-5*	*-1*	*5*	*-5*	*0*	*6*
Iberia & Latin America	55	0	10	-11	-1	0	-1	-9	-9	7
Growth Markets	166	0	-15	-2	-1	-1	13	-12	0	20
thereof: Asia-Pacific	*106*	*0*	*-15*	*1*	*1*	*-1*	*8*	*-8*	*0*	*13*
thereof: CEEMA	*57*	*0*	*0*	*-2*	*-2*	*0*	*4*	*-3*	*0*	*7*
USA	219	-6	12	-14	1	-23	7	-1	-12	5
Total[4]	952	-50	-115	24	-28	-35	59	-49	-38	98

1) After non-controlling interests
2) Sensitivity analysis for new business in 2013 is assessed relative to the VNB calculated using parameters as of 31.12.13
3) The ultimate forward rate for yield curve extrapolation is unchanged for interest sensitivities
4) Total including holding expenses and internal reinsurance

© Allianz SE 2014

A 71

FIGURE 9.8(b)   MCEV sensitivities. Reproduced by permission of Allianz SE.

payback periods heavily dependent on management's assumptions. As a consequence, focusing on the actual capital flows is becoming more and more important.

Reflecting this, Barclays (2011) comment that the European insurance industry ". . . is a prolific capital generator . . . However, . . . much of this has historically been hidden due to traditionally high spending habits. More recently, a focus on cash flows . . . has resulted in better new business spending controls and better overall capital management, ultimately boosting shareholder cash flows and dividend growth optionality . . ."

TABLE 9.6   Sources and uses of capital for LH businesses

Starting free surplus

+ Net cash flows

   + In-force cash earnings ⟵————————Capital generated

   − New business cash strain ⟵————————**Capital invested**

+ Net capital flow s

   + In-force capital release ⟵

   − New business capital strain ⟵

− Net dividends or capital injections

= **Free surplus before economic and operational variances**

+ Net change due to economic and operational variances

= **Ending free surplus**

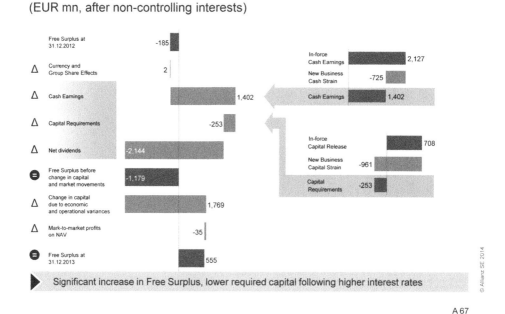

FIGURE 9.9   Earnings and investments. Reproduced by permission of Allianz SE.

One important question is how much capital is actually generated by the business? A general framework for analyzing the sources and uses of capital is supplied by the MCEV analysis of free surplus development in Table 9.6.

Cash earnings reflect the actual local P&L effect in the current accounting year and the new business cash strain reflects acquisition expenses paid upfront.

This information is also disclosed, as Figure 9.9 illustrates. According to this figure, Allianz LH businesses generated about EUR 2.8 bn worth of capital during 2013 (through cash earnings and the release of capital from the in-force book of business) and invested about EUR 1.7 bn in new business (including both acquisition and capital strains of new business).

CHAPTER 10

Banking

This chapter outlines the "rules of the game" (or generic strategies) and core competencies for creating value in retail and commercial banking, beginning with a brief history of the industry and a summary of its economic rationale.

HISTORY[1]

The earliest bank-like activities included deposit taking, lending and payment services. These services were often motivated by "merchant banking" or (commercial trading) on behalf of the "bank's" own account but later morphed into services provided by institutions which did not have a direct commercial interest in the underlying transactions.

Around 2000 BC in Assyria and Babylonia, wealth in the form of commodities (e.g., grain and metal) was deposited in temples and treasuries against a fee. From this wealth, loans were made, for example in the form of seed-grain to be repaid with interest following the harvest. These agreements were documented in clay tablets called *tokens*, later replaced by ledgers to record production and exchanges. Deposit taking and lending reached a level of maturity sufficient to be regulated in the *Code of Hammurabi* in circa 1750 BC. Similar practices are found in Egypt around the 18th century BC.

Later, the role of temples extended to include payment services, either through an account in a banking network or through letters of credit or bills of exchange. Beginning with the reign of the Greek Ptolemy I (305–284 BC), government granaries were transformed into a network of grain banks centralized in Alexandria where the main accounts from all the state banks were recorded. This was the first recorded government bank network, providing a trade credit system that transferred payments between accounts without physically passing money. The development of private banks was not far behind: Xenophon the Greek is credited with suggesting the creation of a joint-stock bank in *On Revenues*, written c. 353 BC.

This trend continued in the Roman Empire, with deposits gradually moving from temples to private depositories. Money lenders set up stalls in the middle of marketplaces on a long bench called a *bancu* (from which "banco" and "bank" are derived), and there they would take deposits, make loans and convert foreign currency into Roman currency. During this period, the Roman Empire formalized the administration and regulated banking activities. By the 2nd

---

[1] For further information, see Hoggson (1926), Hildreth (2001), Kindleberger (2006), Beattie (n.d.).

century AD, a debt could be settled by paying an appropriate sum into a bank with the transaction being officially notarized.

After the fall of Rome, trade effectively collapsed, taking with it most of the associated banking activities in Europe. Banking was later revived during the time of the Crusades.

Further limiting the development of modern banking was the ascent of Christianity, Judaism and Islamism around the same time as the fall of Rome, religions which deemed the charging of interest or "usury" as immoral. This development, in combination with the fall of Rome, materially affected the further development of the nascent banking industry.

Re-emergence to Finance the State

In the 12th century, the need to transfer large sums of money to finance the Crusades stimulated the re-emergence of banking in Western Europe. In 1162, Henry II of England levied his first tax to support the crusades. The Templars and Hospitallers acted as Henry's bankers in the Holy Land. From 1100 to 1300, the Templars would take local currency against a demand note which could then be exchanged at any of their castles across Europe, allowing the movement of money without the usual risk of robbery while traveling.

In parallel, money changers at medieval trade fairs in locations such as Hamburg issued documents in exchange for hard currency. These documents could be cashed at another fair in a different country or at a future fair in the same location. If redeemable at a future date, they would be discounted by an amount comparable to a rate of interest. Eventually, these documents evolved into bills of exchange, which could be redeemed at any office of the issuing banker.

The first European bank was established in 1157 in Venice, with a guarantee from the State. The Bank of Venice acted in the interests of the Crusaders of Pope Urban the Second. With an initial capital of 5 million ducats, it continued until the French invasion of 1797. In addition to supporting the Crusades, the bank also financed the expansion of Duke Vital Mitchel II's empire and war efforts through a forced loan paying 4% interest and backed by specific public revenues. With the benefit of this backing, the Bank of Venice began to discount letters of exchange, settle payments through its own accounts and take deposits. Later, every merchant in Venice was obliged to open an account with the Bank of Venice and all payments on bills of exchange were to be made through the bank. The Table of Exchange at Barcelona and the Chamber of St. George in Genoa were later copied after the Bank of Venice.

Financing the intrigues of monarchies continued for centuries. Edward III of England financed a war with France through Italian banks and subsequently defaulted in 1345, bringing down the famous banking houses of Bardi and Peruzzi in Florence. Between 1481 and 1525, the Fuggers in Germany built a dynasty by lending to the Habsburgs, taking as collateral interests in mines in Tirol, feudal rights in two Austrian counties and the revenues of the Spanish orders of knighthood.

Although the Bank of England began as a joint-stock company in 1694, its entire capital was tied up in a 1.2 million pound loan to the government made in order to gain its banking franchise. Because of a lack of own, liquid funds, instead of buying and selling bills of exchange against coin that it did not have, the Bank of England paid with its own bank notes, effectively ushering in paper money. The Bank of England later organized the sale of government bonds and acted as a clearing bank for government transactions and other London banks.

The "Renaissance" of Banking

The resurgence of banking in the modern sense can be traced to medieval and early Renaissance Italy. The original banks were "merchant banks," focused on trading for their own account and ultimately financing grain production and trade in Northern Italy. The lending of money at an explicit interest rate reemerged, spurred by the increase in trade and commerce. The general prohibition against usury was circumvented by an interpretation which allowed Jews to lend money to new-Jews, but not to Jews; the difference in interpretation created a unique niche in banking for those of the Jewish religion during the 12th through the 15th centuries. Nascent merchant banks lent money to farmers against crops in the field at rates which would have been considered usurious by the Church; through the loans they secured the right to sell the grain once harvested. They also advanced payment (at a discount) against the future delivery of grain shipped to distant ports. In addition, the merchant banks also provided insurance, guaranteeing the delivery of the crop to the buyer through alternative sources – grain stores or alternate markets, for instance – and insured farmers against crop failure.

Soon, there arose a class of merchants who were trading more grain *debt* than physical grain. This then progressed from financing trade on their own behalf to settling trades for others and holding deposits for the settlement of notes written by those who traded the physical grain. And so the merchant's "banca" in the great grain markets became centers for holding money against a bill (*billette*, a note or letter of formal exchange, later a bill of exchange and later still a check).

These deposited funds were intended to be held for the settlement of grain trades. However, they were also used to leverage the bench's own trading activities. The term "bankrupt" comes from the Italian *banca rotta*, or broken bench, which is what happened when someone lost the traders' deposits.

In 1587 the Banco della Piazza Rialto opened in Venice, once again backed by the State of Venice; while mimicking the practices of earlier money lenders, the backing of the State of Venice provided greater security to depositors. But in 1617, history repeated itself and the Banco della Piazza Rialto also ran into problems due to unsecured loans.

Modern Investment Banking and the Capital Markets

The financing of most corporate and government activities was met by private banks in the more mature Europe. The rise of Protestantism helped to further weaken Rome's usury laws and Protestant merchant families began to undertake more and more banking activities in the UK (Barings), Germany (Schroders, Berenbergs) and the Netherlands (Hope & Company). Originally focused on trading for their own accounts, the new merchant banks extended their activities beyond traditional deposit, loan and payment services and included the underwriting of bonds and originating foreign loans to finance governments. The Rothschilds in particular were known for bullion trading and bond issuance and, in 1803, Barings joined Hope & Comapny in financing he Louisiana Purchase. Ultimately, banking dominated merchange activities for these family enterprises.

Unfortunately, private banks in the United States could not meet the financing needs of the new, developing continent which required massive investments to support the development of railroads, mining and heavy industries. In order to satisfy their financing needs, governments and corporations had to tap into the emerging but potentially deeper "capital markets."

The capital markets, loosely defined as the placement of securities across a broader spectrum of retail customers, began in the USA during the Civil War, which was in part financed by the selling of Treasury securities to the general public. Jay Cooke acted as the Treasury's agent and organized thousands of sales personnel to place bonds directly with the general public, ultimately raising approximately USD 1.5 billion for the war effort.

After the Civil War, "investment banks" were formed to help companies issue debt and equity securities; in addition, they continued to act as agents to place US Treasury securities. In addition to acting as brokers or intermediaries, the investment banks also engaged in more traditional commercial banking activities of deposit taking and lending. At the time, there was no legal requirement to separate commercial and investment banking operations, with deposits from the commercial banking activities used as capital for the investment and merchant banking operations of the firms.

Many of the prominent investment banking firms emerged during the late 1800s, including Goldman Sachs, Lehman Brothers, Salomon Brothers, Kidder Peabody & Company, Drexel and JS Morgan (the predecessor to JP Morgan founded in 1854). These firms played a leading role in the financing of railroads, the automobile industry (including General Motors and Studebaker), retailers (Woolworth, Sears, Gimbels, Macy's) and helped to develop the New York Stock Exchange. Because of their financing activities, bank directors often sat on the Boards of the companies they helped to finance.

Following the financial market panic of 1907, the Pujo Committee of the House Committee on Banking and Currency concluded that a small cadre of financiers had gained disproportionate control of American industry; as an example, officers of JP Morgan sat on the Boards of 112 corporations representing close to 85% of the New York Stock Exchange's USD 26.5 billion market capitalization. Part of this control was affected directly through their banking operations and part through directorships in Trust companies which held the shares of industrial companies, including Banker's Trust, Guaranty Trust, Chase National Bank and the National Bank of Commerce.

The Great Depression caused the collapse of the commercial banking system in the United States, with depositors demanding their money back and causing a "run on the bank." Soon afterwards, the Glass–Steagall Act of 1933 was passed, forcing the separation of commercial and investment banking activities. Around the same time, the Federal Deposit Insurance Corporation (FDIC) was mandated. Both acts were designed to protect depositors, on the one hand by separating riskier merchant and investment banking activities from commercial banking activities and, on the other hand, by providing a guarantee on deposits.

As a consequence of the Glass–Steagall Act, many of the banks split into separate entities; for example, JP Morgan was split into three – a commercial bank of the same name, the investment bank Morgan Stanley and the British merchant bank Morgan Grenfell.

The Great Depression also prompted more stringent regulation of the securities market in the form of the 1933 Securities Act, which required the registration of any inter-state offer or sale of securities, and the Securities Exchange Act of 1934, which governed secondary trading of securities and established the Securities Exchange Commission (SEC), the Federal agency primarily responsible for the enforcement of securities law in the United States.

The Glass–Steagall Act was later reversed by the Graham–Leach Act of 1999, once again allowing commercial and investment banking activities within the same company. History again repeated itself, with the recession of 2008 (the worst since the Great Depression) being blamed in part on the Graham–Leach Act for allowing high-risk investment and merchant banking activities to coexist with commercial banking activities. Coming complete circle, the Volcker Rule of the US Dodd–Frank Act, the European Liikanen Report and the UK's Vickers

Report all propose once again a similar form of separation of riskier investment banking from commercial banking activities.

The Forces of Disintermediation

Bank-like activities are not unique to banks, and the role of banks in providing these services is coming increasingly under threat from non-bank competitors.

Disintermediation of Corporate Financing

Historically, banks raised deposits from savers and, with the exception of merchant banking activities,[2] provided capital to borrowers in the form of loans. Over the past 100 years, the chain from depositor to bank to borrower has been increasingly "disintermediated"[3] by the debt capital markets and financial innovation.

Especially in the United States, large corporations have for decades been able to borrow long-term funds directly from the capital markets by issuing debt securities, thereby circumventing the bank balance sheet. The threshold for issuing debt securities has become lower and lower due to declining information costs, the lower cost of public ratings, improved securities regulation and greater standardization in the form of issuing rules, documentation and workout mechanisms. In addition to longer-term financing, shorter-term working capital and trade receivable financing are increasingly met by (asset-backed) commercial paper programs, effectively cutting the bank out of the financing loop except for providing a liquidity support to the commercial paper conduits.

The gradual disintermediation of corporate financing by banks is illustrated in Figure 10.1 by the share of corporate financing gradually decreasing over time in the USA, effectively being replaced by corporate bonds and equity financing.

The process of disintermediation has been stronger in the United States than in Europe, where bank lending still representing the lion's share of corporate debt financing, as illustrated in Figure 10.2. The difference between bank disintermediation in the USA and Europe is attributable to a variety of factors, including differences in industrial structure (e.g., with the US industrial landscape dominated by larger companies which have better access to the capital markets), differences in the consistency and effectiveness of securities regulation and bankruptcy proceedings in the USA compared with Europe.

Disintermediation of Savings Activities

Disintermediation is not only driven by the way that companies raise money, but also by a change in the way that savers save.

Money market funds were first introduced in 1971 as a result of Regulation Q, which limited interest rates on bank deposits (Markham, 2002). The first money market fund, the Reserve Fund founded by B.R. Brown and B.R. Bent, was soon followed by other funds including Fidelity and Dreyfus. In 1976, money market funds held $3 bn, rising to $80 bn in

---

[2]According to Craig (2001), "the term merchant banking is generally understood to mean negotiated private equity investment by financial institutions in the unregistered securities of either privately or publicly held companies." More recent regulatory developments (e.g., the Dodd–Frank Act) may limit the scope of merchant banking activities.

[3]Disintermediation in this context refers to the removal of the bank in the chain from depositor to bank to borrower, for example with the depositor investing in instruments issued by the ultimate user of the funds.

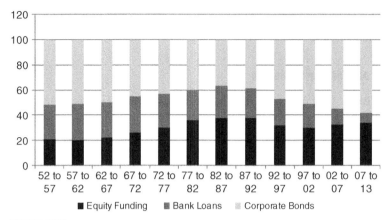

FIGURE 10.1 Bank versus bond and equity financing by non-financial corporations in the USA, 1952–2013
Source: Data from the Financial Accounts of the United States, Board of Governors of the Federal Reserve System. Adapted from Contessi *et al.* (2013).

1980 and over \$230 bn in 1982 – representing a 30+% CAGR over the 16-year period and becoming within two decades the most popular form of investment in the United States.

Most of this money came from bank savings accounts, which were prohibited from paying competitive rates due to Regulation Q. Some of the funds remained within the banking system, for example by linking money market funds to other banking services such as the cash management accounts of Merrill Lynch, which swept excess cash into a money market account while also providing checking and payment services.

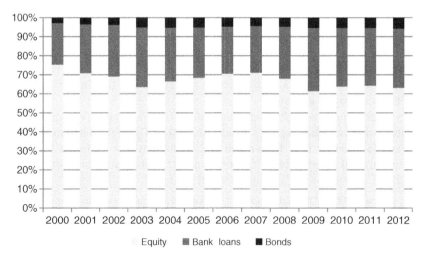

FIGURE 10.2 Bank versus bond and equity financing by non-financial corporations in Europe
Source: Adapted from Deutsche Bank (2013).

Disintermediation of Payment Services

Payment services have been less affected by disintermediation, with many of the advances building on, rather than replacing, the banking sector's legacy payment infrastructure. According to the Federal Reserve Bank (2013), payment systems should meet several general conditions.

1. They should be ubiquitous, connecting all potential parties at low cost. Specialized or narrowly defined payment networks (including person-to-person transfers, online merchants, etc.) may make it "inconvenient or impossible for in-network end users to make or receive payments to or from out-of-network end users."
2. They should cover payments from end to end, beginning at the source of payment instruction to the point of receipt, including notifications and reconciliations.
3. They should ensure the availability and finality of payment.
4. They should be as near to real time as possible as well as cost efficient.

Cash meets all these requirements; however, cash is cumbersome and does not offer security against theft or accidental loss.

The legacy payment infrastructure of banks, consisting of transaction accounts accessed by various media, meets most of these criteria except for the last one – bank transaction accounts are nearly ubiquitous, with over 90% of US consumers having a transaction account. These accounts have access to different payment media including checks, fund transfers such as the Automated Clearing House (ACH) and ATM transfers as well as debit and bank-sponsored credit cards (Federal Reserve Board, 2013). Many of these methods ensure the availability and finality of payment directly (e.g., funds transfer, ACH and debit cards) or through the sponsor. However, many of these are inefficient, especially checks and ACH, relying on paper and batch processes, rather than offering real-time settlement.

Other, innovative forms of non-bank payment services rely to a great extent on this legacy payment infrastructure: credit card companies temporarily substitute a line of credit for a stock of funds held in a bank account needed to cover payment obligations; however, they more often than not rely on access to the banking system's payment services to ultimately pay off the credit. Similarly, while money market mutual accounts may offer similar services, they still participate in bank clearing systems.

As an example of the more incremental "evolution" as opposed to "revolution" in payments, consider the conclusions of Bowyer (2014) following the announcement of the partnership between Bitcoin (a digital currency which could in principle replace existing payment mechanisms) and PayPal, suggesting that the 'Bitcoin Revolution' ". . . could be less explosive, more incremental, and far more reliant on existing processes . . . Bitcoin is a disruptive technology with the capacity to bring about huge changes . . . However, these changes look likely to come with the help and blessing of today's commercial giants, rather than by a process of immediate disintermediation."

PRODUCTS

As detailed in Table 10.1, retail and commercial banking products can be characterized into four broad categories: lending/financing, savings/investments, payments and other services, third-party products to leverage revenue synergies.

TABLE 10.1 Overview of retail and commercial banking products

Category	Product	Description
Lending/financing	Uncollateralized personal and business loans	Financing to support:
	Mortgages	▪ immediate consumption;
	Other collateralized finance (e.g., leasing, lending against securities account, etc.)	▪ investment in real or productive assets; ▪ short-term liquidity/working capital requirements.
	Credit cards	
	Overdrafts	
Savings and investments	Savings accounts	Short-term investments with implicitly or explicitly "protected" principal.
	Money market accounts	Investment accounts for holding listed securities, the trading of which generates commission revenue.
	Certificates of Deposit	
	Securities accounts and trading services	Investment and financial planning advice to earn asset management fees and trading commissions.
	Wealth management advisory	
Payment and other services	Current accounts	Accounts and services offering instant access to funds and payment services.
	Debit cards	
	Wire and direct transfers	
	Remote deposit	
	Payroll services	
	Treasury services (payment, receipt, liquidity, fraud, cash management)	
Third-party products	Payment protection insurance (e.g., in case of death, illness or unemployment)	Products distributed through the bank's distribution network generating commission income.
	Property insurance for collateral assets	
	Life retirement and savings insurance policies	
	Third-party mutual funds, investment funds, retirement products	

ECONOMIC RATIONALE

Banks fulfill several important roles in society, illustrated by the previously cited historical anecdotes and summarized by Cassidy (2010): "Since . . . Hammurabi's Code . . . no advanced society has survived without banks and bankers. Banks enable people to borrow money, and, today, by operating electronic-transfer systems, they allow commerce to take place without notes and coins changing hands. They also play a critical role in channeling savings into productive investments." More concretely:

1. bank deposits provide an (ostensibly) *safe and secure store of wealth*, made safer by deposit insurance schemes;
2. bank deposits and the payment system, including checks, paper and electronic transfers, debit and credit cards and other mechanisms, *facilitate commerce by providing payment connectivity which is near ubiquitous, secure and final*;
3. banks support economic development by *financing productive investment in corporations* (in the form of loans and private equity through merchant banking activities, as well as by facilitating the issuance of securities in the capital markets);
4. banks *finance immediate consumption* by individuals (financing "lifecycle" consumption patterns through, e.g., personal loans, automobile and home financing, reverse mortgages, etc.) and governments against future repayment;
5. finally, banks facilitate trade and risk transfer between individuals by *intermediating exposures between counterparts and providing liquidity to financial markets*.

Banks' Unique Position

Banks currently enjoy a unique position in performing some of these tasks. Especially with respect to intermediating between savers and investors and providing payment services, banks have at least a partial advantage as they engage in the following.

1. *Liquidity transformation.* Banks maintain the liquidity of individual deposits, making them immediately available to satisfy payment obligations. However, they also transform the pool of small, liquid deposits into larger, less liquid loans. This liquidity transformation works well as long as not all the liabilities are called at the same time. The dark side of liquidity transformation is a liquidity crisis, for example if depositors lose confidence, causing a "run on the bank," or if short-term funding sources dry up.
2. *Maturity transformation.* Relying on the same principle, banks convert short-term deposits into long-term, committed financing. Maturity transformation not only meets the needs of depositors and borrowers, but also allows the bank to "ride the yield curve" – if the yield curve is upward sloping, the bank will earn a higher nominal yield on their assets than they pay for their funding. The dark side of maturity transformation is the economic and net interest income losses if interest rates should rise or become inverted, forcing the bank to pay higher funding rates than they are earning on their long-term loans.
3. *Availability and finality of payments.* Regardless of the medium, ultimately a temporary stock of wealth needs to be available to a ubiquitous payment network for meeting payment demands. Bank deposits and the bank payment system generally fulfill these requirements.

Other savings and investment alternatives do not share these properties. For example, investments in individual securities may be subject to minimum lot sizes and are generally illiquid, requiring a discount in order to monetize the asset into a more fungible form necessary to make payments. Money market funds are often considered close substitutes for bank deposits and also ultimately fund industrial activities; however, they are less able to engage in liquidity and maturity transformation as they are prevented from investing in longer-term, opaque and illiquid assets.

According to Investopedia,[4] money market funds keep from "breaking the buck"[5] by avoiding liquidity and maturity transformation, with their asset portfolios characterized by debt which is short term ("with a weighted average portfolio maturity of 90 days or less"), of high credit quality ("typically AAA rated") and well diversified, with explicit limitations on issuer concentration.

In addition to being more flexible in engaging in liquidity and maturity transformation, banks also have an advantage over money market funds in that they face looser restrictions on underwriting and holding credit-risky assets. In addition, banks have the following advantages.

4. *Information and management advantage.* Evaluating the credit risk of borrowers can be expensive, requiring initial due diligence as well as costly, ongoing monitoring. It may be prohibitive for individual investors to pay this cost and collect information individually as it represents a duplication of effort to society. Also, banks can leverage payment and account information gleaned from the overall bank relationship, using the information to monitor and manage the credit after it is originated. As a consequence, banks have an advantage in making loans to smaller, less transparent firms.

5. *Risk transformation advantage.* Just like a PC insurer, by pooling a large number of risks, banks can support more lending while requiring less risk capital.

   These natural advantages are echoed by Federal Reserve Board Governor Kevin Warsh (Warsh, 2007): ". . . banks finance relatively opaque entities, such as private companies and households. They raise funds primarily by issuing demand deposits. They deploy capital by underwriting loans, monitoring borrowers, and retaining some loans in portfolio as long-term investments . . . internalize(ing) the costs of their own underwriting standards, and so have strong incentives to screen borrowers and enforce contractual covenants, as appropriate."

6. *Risk intermediation.* Finally, banks also intermediate between individuals and corporations who want to transfer or exchange risk positions, leveraging the bank's private and proprietary client network and the bank's willingness to put capital to work in meeting short-term differences in supply and demand for traded assets.

Regarding the banking sector's risk intermediation activities, Cassidy (2010) comments that "Some kinds of trading serve a useful economic function. One is market-making, in which

---

[4] http://www.investopedia.com/articles/mutualfund/08/money-market-break-buck.asp

[5] "Breaking the buck" is defined as a situation where the net asset value of a money market fund becomes less than $1. Before the 2008 financial crisis, this occurred only one time since money market funds were first introduced in 1971: in 1994, a small money market fund lost value holding an adjustable-rate security in a rising interest rate market. During the 2008 financial crisis, many funds would have similarly found themselves in trouble, facing a potential run on the fund, but the US Treasury announced a program to protect covered funds.

banks accumulate large inventories of securities in order to facilitate buying and selling on the part of their clients."

FROM PRINCIPLES TO "RULES OF THE GAME"

At first blush, the economics of a retail and commercial bank are straightforward to understand and manage. Joseph Strumpf, Chairman of Wells Fargo, describes the economics of banking succinctly by using the income statement to "tell a story" – as adapted in Table 10.2.

Some of the principles of value creation in retail and commercial banking are straightforward, lining up against this simple income statement representation.

- *Banks need to have superior execution in sales and distribution, supporting profitable growth.* As summarized in Strumpf (2012), "The ability to grow profits consistently is based on sustainable revenue growth. It's the most important measure of service, sales and customer satisfaction. It's the vote our customers cast every day with their pocketbooks."
- *Banks need to have superior execution in expense management.* As summarized in Strumpf (2012), "We are making expense management a competitive advantage . . . (helping) us grow market share when many of our competitors are struggling. Remaining competitive also means investing wisely, such as our multiyear investment in expanding our international operations . . . Managing our resources wisely is good for us (and) good for our customers."
- *Banks need to have superior credit underwriting skills.* As summarized in Strumpf (2012), "To be the best in our industry, we have to be the best in credit and risk management . . . Our time-tested lending discipline has made it possible for us to grow and prosper through many economic cycles. It's helped us avoid many of the credit traps experienced by others."

Unfortunately, the simplified income statement representation masks three critical drivers of value creation (or value destruction) in banking, which can only be seen by looking at the balance sheet.

- *Banks need to manage the asset/liability mismatch arising from maturity transformation.* (e.g., converting short-term funding into longer-term, committed financing). As a

TABLE 10.2   Economics of retail and commercial banking

What banks do	. . . how it shows up in the income statement
Make loans and investments	+ Interest income
Take prudent risks	− Provision for loan loss/charge-offs
Receive deposits and borrow money	− Interest expense
Provide products and advice	+ Non-interest or fee income
Invest in our people	− Salary/benefits expense
Our people need systems, space, computers	− Non-interest expenses
Uncle Sam gets his share	− Tax expenses
	= Net income

Source: Adapted from Strumpf (2012).

consequence, their natural asset/liability position is long assets, short financing; if left open, this natural position exposes the bank to rising or flattening interest rate scenarios. These can negatively impact the bank's net asset value immediately, but flow through the income statement only slowly over time. According to OWC (2013), the ALM margin for European retail banks in 2012 was ". . . generally small and has a contribution which ranges from −10% to +10%," illustrating that "riding the yield curve" can produce returns, but also entails risk.

■ *Banks need to manage liquidity funding risk arising from liquidity transformation.* (e.g., converting short-term, immediately callable customer and wholesale funding into less liquid loans). In a worst-case liquidity scenario, banks may be exposed to a "run on the bank" or be unable to tap traditional funding sources, leaving them unable to fulfill their obligations although they may remain economically solvent.

■ *Banks need to proactively manage their capital base and cost of financial leverage.* Bank lending is capital-intensive and banking is generally a heavily regulated industry, with binding capital requirements imposed both by supervisors and rating agencies. As a consequence, banks can create value by optimizing the level and mix of capital and financial leverage,[6] increasing RoE and lowering the firm's weighted average cost of funding for their operations while staying within the constraints imposed externally and by management's risk appetite.

Executing against these principles requires core skills across the board, as summarized in Figure 10.3.

Rules of the Game

With these principles in mind, there are three "rules of the game" that are important for creating value in retail and commercial banking.

RULES OF THE GAME: RETAIL AND COMMERCIAL BANKING

- Focus on risk-adjusted profitable growth
  - Grow top-line net interest income and non-interest fees through *superior sales and distribution capabilities.*
  - Convert the top-line into excess bottom-line returns:
    - maintain a top-quartile cost income ratio (CIR) through operating efficiency/ expense management;
    - ensure a positive new business EP through underwriting excellence.

---

[6]There is no industry standard definition of financial versus operational leverage. In this Handbook, financial leverage generally meets two criteria. First, it is issued by the holding company in the form of senior and subordinated bonds, "bail-in" bonds and Tier 2 capital, etc., to fund participations in operating businesses. Second, the cost of financial leverage is generally not deducted when calculating the operating profit of a business; rather, it is considered as part of the Weighted Average Cost of Capital (WACC) used as the hurdle rate to determine whether the operating businesses are creating value. This is in contrast to operational leverage, which is used to fund operating assets and whose cost is directly deducted when calculating operating profits.

- Manage the risks inherent in maturity/liquidity-transformation activities
  - Maintain an asset/liability mismatch profile within prudent risk limits from an economic perspective; stabilize the net interest income dynamics through product design and commercial (re)pricing actions.
  - Strictly maintain a liquidity funding profile robust to idiosyncratic and systematic liquidity scenarios.
- Manage capital efficiently
  - Minimize uneconomic capital requirements through balance sheet management.
  - Invest as much free capital as possible in profitable growth opportunities.
  - Return excess capital to shareholders if retained earnings exceed profitable growth opportunities.

Commercial and Retail Banking– What strategies, skills and KPIs by segment?

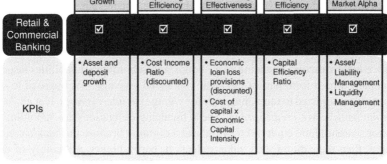

FIGURE 10.3 PC insurance economic profit sources and core skills. Reproduced by permission of Allianz SE.

FROM "RULES" TO VALUE

The value of a retail and commercial bank is equal to its current net asset value (e.g., the value of all assets and liabilities as a closed block of business using on-going business expense assumptions for administering the portfolio) plus its franchise value (e.g., the value of the company's future new business).[7] The valuation of a bank proceeds in three steps based on publically available information.

---

[7]For a theoretical discussion see Dermine (2015), who also develops a valuation framework for banks comprising two elements: the net asset value of the bank (or liquidation value in Dermine's terminology) and a franchise value consisting of future loan and deposit product margins where the margins are calculated based on a market-oriented funds transfer pricing approach. See also Dermine (2010).

Step 1: Determine Current Net Asset Value

The first step is to calculate the current net asset value of the bank on a market-consistent or fair value basis. Because part of the bank balance sheet is carried at amortized cost (e.g., the "banking book"), there are several adjustments to the balance sheet which may need to be done, as illustrated in Table 10.3.

First, assets and liabilities carried at amortized cost in the "banking book" are brought to fair values. This can be done using information provided in the Notes to the financial statements which give "fair values" for loans, deposits and securities not held available for sale (including own bonds issued) based on current interest rates and credit spread levels. However, the following caveats should be kept in mind.

First, asset values may need to be adjusted further to the extent to which the analyst believes that:

- non-performing loans are not adequately recognized (e.g., due to less conservative rules determining non-performing loans and/or insufficient loan loss provisions);
- the credit spreads used by the bank for fair valuation of performing loans do not reflect current market conditions but rather are more stable, through the cycle cost of credit or consumer lending rates;
- fair valuations in the trading book are deemed to be optimistic (e.g., during times of market dislocation, especially for Type 2 and Type 3 positions where valuations are based on assumptions and models).

Second, capital structure financing (e.g., bonds and subordinated liabilities issued by the holding company which form part of the bank's financial leverage – as opposed to operating leverage) should be adjusted to fair values *only for changes in interest rates*, if at all, and *not for changes in the bank's own credit spread*. These financing obligations are subordinate to and substitutes for shareholders' equity; if they trade at a discount because the bank's credit spread has increased, then their diminished value reflects in part a higher probability of default. It would be a paradox if the net asset value attributable to shareholders should benefit when there is a higher probability of default.

This view is supported by Chasteen and Ransom (2007), who comment that liabilities reported at fair value are controversial: "The primary controversy centers on the counterintuitive results of an entity's recording of a loss if its credit standing improves or a gain if its credit standing deteriorates." As a solution, they suggest a similar treatment as recommended here, for example that liabilities be reported using risk-free rates, a proposal which " . . . recognizes the default risk portion of a debt's fair value as a distribution to shareholders when the liability is incurred."

Finally, provisions for litigation and conduct issues may be adjusted to the extent to which the analyst believes that they are not sufficient. These adjustments are becoming more relevant given the steadily increasing regulatory fines and litigation imposed on the sector.

Step 2: Normalized New Business Value

The second step is to calculate the normalized value of new business, the building block for the firm's franchise value. The first-best solution is to use new business EP information. This is difficult for two reasons.

TABLE 10.3 PC net asset value

Balance sheet items	Generic adjustments
+ Assets	For financial assets measured at amortized cost (e.g., "banking book" assets including loans and advances to banks and customers and reverse repurchase agreements and other secured lending): ■ replace amortized carrying value with fair value from the Notes to the financial statement; ■ make adjustments to the fair values as appropriate (e.g., adjusting for non-performing loans, etc.). For financial assets measured at fair value (e.g., trading portfolio assets, derivatives, available for sale assets, investments), make adjustments to fair values if appropriate based on disclosed fair valuation sensitivities to key unobservable parameters. Deduct non-tangible assets (e.g., goodwill).
– Liabilities	For financial liabilities measured at amortized cost (e.g., "banking book" liabilities): ■ replace deposits from banks and customers and repurchase agreements and other similar secured lending with the fair value from the Notes to the financial statement; ■ do not replace amortized cost values for financial leverage and capital substitutes (e.g., debt securities and subordinated liabilities issued by the bank or bank holding company which forms part of the bank's financial leverage). For financial liabilities measured at fair value (e.g., trading portfolio liabilities, financial liabilities designated at fair value and derivative financial liabilities), make adjustments to fair values deemed appropriate based on disclosed fair valuation sensitivities to key unobservable parameters. Adjust other provisions, especially litigation reserves, as deemed necessary.*
+/– Off-balance sheet commitments	Deduct under-funded pension obligations. Adjust for valuation differences due to guarantees, other off-balance sheet commitments and contingent liabilities.**
= TNAV	

*Provisions are defined as present obligations arising as the consequence of past events where it is probable that a transfer of economic benefit will be necessary to settle the obligation and where it can be reliably estimated. These may include charges for restructuring and redundancy, conduct remediation and litigation.
**Contingent liabilities reflect possible obligations whose existence will be confirmed only by uncertain future events and present obligations where the transfer of economic benefit is uncertain or cannot be reliably measured. Contingent liabilities are not recognized on the balance sheet but are disclosed when the possibility of an obligation is not remote. Contingent liabilities may include guarantees and letters of credit pledged as collateral, performance guarantees and endorsements, standby facilities and credit lines.

First, new business EP is not generally made available externally. As a consequence, an "outside-in" valuation has to rely on financial statements, supplemental disclosures and assumptions to translate period accounting information into information on the economics of the business. Second, the risk-adjusted contribution from new business lending is only part of the story – banks also generate shareholder value by taking appropriately priced deposits as well as by providing payment and other fee- and commission-based services.

It is easier to project new business EP using information from the financial statements if the following conditions are met.

1. The bank is in a steady state in terms of business mix, rate of growth and underwriting and expense performance.
2. The asset/liability mismatch and capital required to cover the associated financial market risk is limited.
3. The capital supporting the business is appropriate, with no excess or surplus capital.

If these conditions are met, then past financial information may be a good indicator of future performance. If these conditions are not met, then the analyst will have to make adjustments to historical information to better reflect expected future performance.

Retail and commercial banks generally provide disclosures sufficient to understand the drivers of franchise value. Table 10.4 gives an example of net income information generally disclosed by firms, either in financial statements or through supplementary disclosures.

Translating net income into an economic profit contribution for future new business can be challenging for a variety of reasons. For example, banks report net interest income calculated as the total interest income on loans and securities held backing capital, less the total interest expense for the bank, including both financial and operating leverage; this is related to new business EP for loans and deposits but is different in two important respects.

Net Interest Income Includes Financial Market Risk

First, net interest income includes not only the operating profit contribution from loan and deposit product margins, but also the contributions from financial market risk taking as part of an asset/liability mismatch or "riding the yield curve." As illustrated in the left-hand panel of Figure 10.4, net interest income will be equal to gross loan and deposit margins *if and only if* all *loans and deposits have the same interest rate maturity **and** if loans are 100% financed by deposits or other forms of operating leverage.*

In this restrictive case, the marginal cost of financing the loan in the market and the marginal opportunity rate for placing deposits in the market are identically equal (the Funds Transfer Price (FTP) for loans equals the FTP for deposits, $FTP_L = FTP_D$) and "cancel out." In this case, we can rewrite the Net Interest Income Margin ($NIIM = r_L - r_D$) as the sum of the gross loan margin ($r_L - FTP_L$) and the deposit margin ($FTP_D - r_D$), where $FTP_L = FTP_D$.

The right-hand panel of Figure 10.4 represents the more typical case of a bank engaging in maturity transformation or "riding the yield curve." In this case, the NIIM includes a third component – the difference between the marginal market price of funding loans and placing deposits ($FTP_L - FTP_D$) – in addition to the gross loan and deposit margins (($r_L - FTP_L$) and ($FTP_D - r_D$)).

TABLE 10.4   Bank net income

Net income	Additional information
+ Net Interest Income	
+ Interest income	
+ Return on Assets	Additional metrics (used to calculate margins relative
× Interest bearing assets	to funds transfer price)
− Interest expenses	− Margin on loan assets
+ Interest on interest bearing liabilities	− Deposit rate or margin on deposits
× Interest bearing liabilities	
− Change in loan loss provisions	
	Additional information by source of fees
	+ Deposit service charges
+ Fee based revenues	+ Mortgage banking origination and service fees
	+ Brokerage, trust and investment management fees
	+ Commissions on insurance
	+ Other commissions and fees
− Expenses	Expressed as Cost Income Ratio or Expense Ratio
+ Personnel expenses	(non-interest operating expenses/(net interest income
+ Non-personnel expenses	plus non-interest income))
Total operating profit	
Non-operating items	
− Head office expenses	
− Restructuring charges, IT projects etc.	
Net income before tax	
− Tax	
Net income after tax	

The future franchise value of the bank should not include earnings from "riding the yield curve" since this does not represent a source of excess returns, only earnings commensurate with the open risk positions. In general, no "alpha" or excess returns are generated by "riding the yield curve" and shareholders can easily recreate a similar open interest rate risk position for their own account at no or low cost.

Rather, the franchise value and economic profit generated by new business should only reflect the product margins calculated using an appropriate funds transfer price. Unfortunately, information on product margins is not uniformly provided by banks.

Net Interest Income Includes Returns on Assets Backing Capital

Second, net interest income also includes the interest earned on assets backing capital. In reality, loans are not solely financed by deposits or operating leverage; they are at least in part financed by equity.

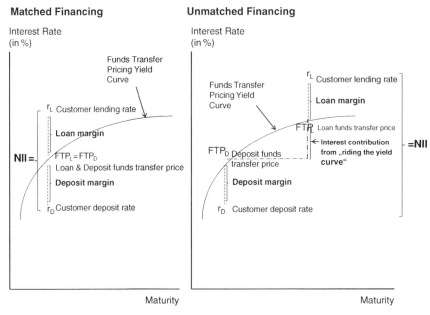

FIGURE 10.4 Reconciling net interest income and product margins

As discussed in Chapter 16, banks often hold assets backing regulatory required capital in a strategic portfolio comprising highly rated, very liquid securities; this is done in order to preserve capital to support future profitable new business.

As a consequence of this practice, a more capital-intensive loan book should produce higher net interest income through three channels: first, due to higher loan margins to compensate for the greater risk; second, due to higher levels of equity financing for the loans, the cost of which is not deducted from operating profit; third, due to higher interest income on the assets backing capital which are invested in fixed-income securities.

From Period Contribution to steady-state Present Value

Another important difference is that net income reflects this period's contribution from the entire portfolio of new and existing loans and deposits as opposed to the expected present value contribution of a single year's new business.

Adjusting and normalizing historic, single-period net income information into future new business contributions can be challenging. However, viewing the business "in a steady state" (e.g., with constant loan and deposit volumes, business mix, cost of credit, etc.) can provide some insights valuable for translating net income into new business economic profit.

- In terms of revenue, net interest income will be roughly equal to the present value of new business loan and deposit margins plus return on required capital to support the new business, except for the discounting effect. (Unfortunately, it also includes the contribution from "riding the yield curve," if any.)

- In terms of cost efficiency, the cost income ratio represents the expenses for acquiring new business during the year and the expenses for administering both new business and all previous cohorts of business. This differs from the discounted expenses associated with a slice of new business used to calculate economic profit contribution. *Except for the discounting effect, the two should be similar in a steady state.*
- In terms of underwriting effectiveness, the current loan loss provisions and economic capital requirements are set based on the existing portfolio and are typically not discounted. *Except for the discounting effect, the two should be similar in a steady state.*

The Appropriate Level of Capital

A final difference between the new business EP calculation and reported net income is that the cost of capital is deducted when calculating EP. In general, banks provide sufficient disclosures regarding capital to make this deduction, except that the capital used for new business EP should reflect only loan *underwriting* risk capital whereas the capital reported in the financial statements reflects the capital to cover other risks, including asset/liability mismatch risk, and the actual capital held in the business, including any excess capital. *The two will be similar if the company follows a conservative asset/liability management strategy* (e.g., loan underwriting risk dominates financial market risk) and *if it uses capital efficiently* (e.g., there is no excess capital which could in principle be paid out as a dividend, implying that the CER is minimized and close to 1).

Economic Profit Contribution of One Period's New Business

As discussed, under steady-state assumptions historical operating profit can be used to estimate the value of a single slice of new business. Although greater granularity may be desired (e.g., split between assets and liabilities, by lending or funding source, etc.), it may not be supported by publically available information (see Table 10.5).

Step 3: Project Economic Profit and Discount to Today

The franchise value of the firm represents the present value of economic profits from future new business. As such, new business economic profit contributions need to be projected and discounted to a present value.

Steady state. If we assume a steady state into perpetuity, then the franchise value can be written in the following manner as a function of bank economic profit:

$$\text{Franchise value} = \frac{\text{B.EP}}{\text{CoC} - g}$$

where g is the assumed steady-state growth rate.

Non-steady state. If a steady-state assumption is not appropriate, then B.EPs need to be projected for different periods into the future using assumptions regarding operating performance which are appropriate for the forecast period. Common practice is to divide the future into an

TABLE 10.5 Bank economic profit – the value of one period's new business

Driver		Description	Comments
Operating profit and growth	$(L + \Delta L) \times [(NIIM + F/L) \times$	Total loan volume Net interest income margin (e.g., NII/L) Fee and commission income as a percentage of loan volume	Total steady-state loan volume plus net new loans in excess of those which have run off. Normalize historical net interest income margin to reflect recent changes to yield curve, margins and business mix. Adjust ratio of fee and commissions to loan balances as appropriate.
Operating efficiency	$(1 - CIR) -$	Cost income ratio	Adjust cost income ratio to reflect new business mix as well as acquisition and administration expense levels.
Underwriting effectiveness	$EL\%]$	Expected loan loss % (EL/L)	Normalize expected loan loss as a percentage to reflect new business mix and point in the cycle.
Taxes	$\times (1 - t)$ $= NIC$	*Normalized taxes* *Normalized total net income contribution*	Adjust tax rate as appropriate.
Underwriting effectiveness and capital efficiency	$- CoC \times ECI]$	*Cost of capital* *Economic capital intensity*	Adjust the firm's cost of capital for leverage, if significant. In a steady state, undiscounted capital intensity is estimated by dividing the loan volume by the actual capital held. ■ Adjust attributed capital if CER is greater than 1, e.g. actual capital = $P*ECI*CER$, attributed capital = $P*ECI$. ■ Adjust ECI to reflect historical growth (e.g., ECI will be under-estimated for fast-growing books).
	$= B.EP$	Bank Economic Profit	

explicit projection period, for example the next 3 or 5 or 10 years, with an associated terminal value determined by steady-state assumptions:

$$\text{Franchise value} = \sum_{t=1}^{T} \frac{\text{B.EP}_t}{(1 + \text{CoC})^t} + \frac{1}{(1 + \text{CoC})^{T+1}} \frac{\text{B.EP}_T}{\text{CoC} - g}$$

The first term represents the present value of the B.EP during the explicit projection period at time T and the second term represents the terminal value after the explicit forecast period, or the present value of a growing perpetuity which begins in period T.

CHAPTER 11

Achieving Profitable Growth

Profitable growth is one of the five KPIs driving the franchise value of the firm (as illustrated in Figure 11.1). Joseph Strumpf of Wells Fargo says (Strumpf, 2012) that revenue growth is ". . . the most important measure of service, sales and customer satisfaction. It's the vote our customers cast every day with their pocketbooks. When they rave about our service, they'll give us more of their business, increasing revenue. They'll refer new customers to us. They'll stay with us for life."

This chapter describes the "rules of the game" for generating profitable growth, highlighting the importance of long-term growth opportunities in addition to excellence in day-to-day sales and distribution activities in the current business footprint.

RULES OF THE GAME AND KPIs

Bankers measure it in terms of revenues or net interest income; insurers in terms of premium or new business value; asset managers in terms of net new in-flows or AUM. Although each segment uses a different metric, everyone is talking a lot about growth. This is not surprising since profitable growth is one of the key drivers of a bank or insurer's valuation multiple.

Top- or Bottom-line Growth?

Before discussing growth strategies and metrics, it is important to agree on the type of growth that is important. More specifically, should you be focusing on growth in top-line revenues or in bottom-line profits?

Some companies put the emphasis on top-line growth, paying less attention to the development of the bottom line. You can tell these companies by looking at the way performance is measured and incentivized, primarily driven by revenue, market share or position in league tables rather than by operating profit and risk-adjusted returns.

A strong focus on top-line growth is natural when engaging in the guerrilla warfare common to mature, highly competitive markets: defending market share is challenging in any case and taking share from competitors even more so. In developing markets, solidifying a leading position early on can lead to sustainable excess returns through scale advantages in the future.

Not all business is equal, however, and a myopic focus on the top line can lead to lower (or even negative) marginal contributions; the net effect may be unprofitable incremental growth

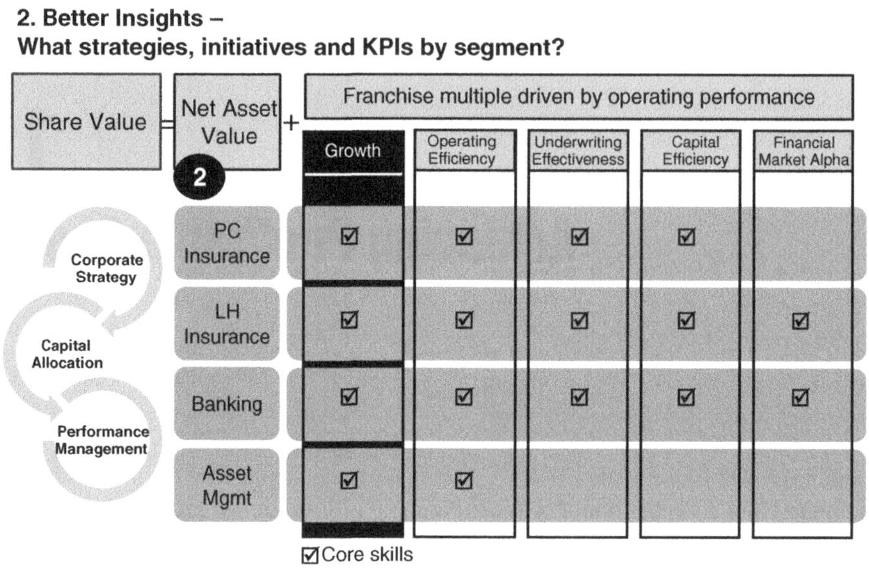

**2. Better Insights –
What strategies, initiatives and KPIs by segment?**

FIGURE 11.1   Growth as a key driver of franchise value. Reproduced by permission of Allianz SE.

that actually destroys shareholder value. Typical issues from a myopic focus on top-line growth include an incentive to chase large-ticket corporate business or distribution agreements which offer a lot of revenue but very, very thin risk-adjusted margins; an implicit cross-subsidization between products or customer segments, with some segments creating value and others destroying it; and, finally, destructive price wars as firms attempt to take share from competitors using only price as a weapon.

Shareholders would rather have capital returned than deployed at margins below the cost of capital. Even growing at the cost of capital doesn't necessarily help: while it may give a sense of progress to take market share at break-even risk-adjusted margins, like a hamster running on a wheel in its cage it is an interesting sense of progress. At best, growth at the cost of capital will accumulate capital resources but not improve your multiple; while accumulating capital may not sound too bad, it can be if the company trades at a conglomerate discount, implying a valuation penalty on accumulated capital. As a consequence, a stronger focus on the bottom line – on *profitable* growth – is required.

"Rules of the Game" for Profitable Growth

At a high level, the "rules of the game" for profitable growth are straightforward.

RULES OF THE GAME: PROFITABLE GROWTH

Value managers should focus on *growing risk-adjusted profits* through three distinct initiatives.

First, continuously improve core sales and distribution capabilities in your existing business. Part of your corporate DNA should include continuous improvements in the following areas.

- Acquiring new customers through:
  - sales force productivity improvements, leveraging technology, providing support and strengthening sales force management;
  - building multi-channel distribution capabilities, accommodating customer buying habits through a coordinated approach to optimize growth and improve cost of service.
- Getting more out of existing customers, e.g. through cross-sell and share of wallet initiatives, customer relationship management, improved service and customer satisfaction.
- Increasing average risk-adjusted contribution per unit of revenue through:
  - product design and product portfolio management;
  - product pricing, improving margins above the technical cost of production;
  - managing the customer portfolio in terms of cross-subsidization.
- Increasing transparency on business profitability:
  - improving internal reporting systems to ensure that the customer/product/channel economics are transparent and well understood;
  - using "big data" and other analytical tools to ensure underwriting effectiveness and efficient sales campaigns.

Second, invest in strategic initiatives to secure growth in the medium term by extending your business footprint. More specifically, invest in initiatives to exploit the following.

- Mega-trends such as aging demographics, the emergence of a middle class in emerging and developing markets, the trend toward mega-cities, technological changes such as mobile telephony, etc.
- Product/market/customer adjacencies.
- Industry consolidation through bolt-on acquisitions.

Third, invest in potentially "game-changing" innovations in order to secure your company's dominance over a longer time horizon. For example, take bets using new technologies such as telematics, disintermediate existing distribution channels, etc.

Growth KPIs and Management Actions

Managing profitable growth requires a granular understanding of where revenues and profits come from. As Figure 11.2 illustrates, banks and insurers generate *top-line revenues* by selling *different financial products and services* to *different customer segments* in *different regions or markets* through *different channels*.

The revenue from the {customer, product, market, channel} combinations will make a positive *bottom-line contribution* if the risk-adjusted contribution margins cover all costs, including the cost of capital.

Trivially speaking, *revenue* growth can come from several sources: growth in the number of customers (N) or in the average number of transactions or services sold to each customer (T) or in the average notional volume of each transaction (V).

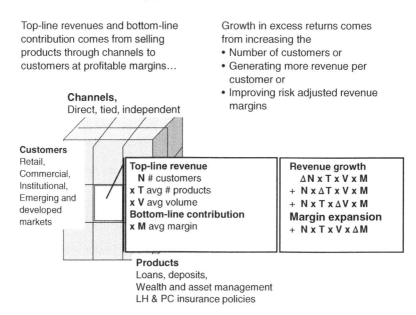

Top-line revenues and bottom-line contribution comes from selling products through channels to customers at profitable margins...

Growth in excess returns comes from increasing the
- Number of customers or
- Generating more revenue per customer or
- Improving risk adjusted revenue margins

Channels,
Direct, tied, independent

Customers
Retail,
Commercial,
Institutional,
Emerging and
developed
markets

Top-line revenue
  N # customers
  x T avg # products
  x V avg volume
Bottom-line contribution
  x M avg margin

Revenue growth
  $\Delta N \times T \times V \times M$
  $+ N \times \Delta T \times V \times M$
  $+ N \times T \times \Delta V \times M$
Margin expansion
  $+ N \times T \times V \times \Delta M$

Products
Loans, deposits,
Wealth and asset management
LH & PC insurance policies

FIGURE 11.2 Understanding top- and bottom-line growth: the contribution cube

Growth in the bottom line can come from any of these sources as well if contribution margins are positive and remain stable. In addition, growth in the bottom line can also come through an improvement in the average risk-adjusted contribution margin (*M*).

In summary, profitable growth comes from three sources: the net acquisition of new customers; growth in revenue per customer (driven by the number of transactions or volume per transaction); and an expansion of the average risk-adjusted margins per unit of revenue.

Figure 11.2 illustrates the sources of growth using a granular {customer, product, market, channel} cube. This level of granularity is not necessary for taking corporate portfolio decisions, but it is absolutely necessary at the business unit level: deciding where and how to grow depends on knowing the relative economics and behavior of individual customer segments, sales channels, products and markets at a very granular level.

Table 11.1 outlines a comprehensive set of KPIs which are useful for understanding and monitoring the sources of top- and bottom-line growth. It is divided into the three drivers outlined earlier – net customer acquisition, growth in revenue per customer and the change in the average risk-adjusted contribution margin.

Because of their importance in understanding and steering the business, some of these growth KPIs are in focus for strategic planning and MBRs (Monthly Business Reviews, discussed in Chapter 14) as well as external analyst disclosures. The remainder of this section provides more details on each of the KPIs.

A comment on foreign exchange effects. Real, underlying growth trends can be obscured by foreign exchange translations used for consolidated reporting: an appreciating foreign currency can give the impression of a growing business even though local market share and absolute volumes have deteriorated; likewise, a depreciating foreign currency can give the perception of a shrinking business which has not occurred in reality. For this reason, the growth analysis should be done before currency translation for business steering purposes.

TABLE 11.1   Profitable growth, KPIs and DIs

Profitable Growth Value Tree/Waterfall

Starting operating profit

+ Change in operating profit due to number of customers (x avg revenue/customer x avg margin)

    – Customer attrition

    + Newly acquired customers

    – Portfolio management activities

    +/– Inorganic growth, including M&A or internal restructuring

+ Change in operating profit due to revenue per customer (x # customers x avg margin)

    + Change in average transactions or products per customer

    + Change in average volume per transaction

+ Change in operating profit due to average margin (x # customers x avg revenue/customer)

    + Due to changes in product or channel mix

    + Due to changes in pricing conditions

    + Due to changes in product design or features

+/– FX effects

Growth KPI

KPIs for Net Customer Acquisition

The following KPIs are relevant for measuring growth in risk-adjusted operating profit due to net new customer acquisition.

Newly acquired customers, defined as *new customers for which no previous business relationship exists*, are often the primary focus of sales-oriented companies and an important driver of revenue growth. However, new customers may be less profitable than customers with a mature relationship with your firm.

Customer attrition, defined as *customers ending their relationship with the firm.* Counterbalancing new customer acquisition is the loss of existing customers, a loss which may occur for a variety of reasons: customers can become dissatisfied with the company's products or services; they can be enticed away by a competitor's pricing; customer losses can be triggered by a major event independent of your company (e.g., a change in job, relocation, divorce, death, etc.); and, finally, some attrition occurs naturally as part of the product lifecycle, for example as loans and LH savings products reach maturity.

Dormant customers are like attrition, representing a loss in revenues, but more expensive in terms of ongoing administration costs. Dormancy occurs when customers leave a limited amount in a savings account without other compensating business or when they discontinue regular premium payments. Dormant accounts, especially dormant new accounts triggered by aggressive sales campaigns, may look impressive in terms of number of customers but they are misleading in terms of the average quality of the customers and the potential for actual bottom-line growth, representing a drag on average contributions and destroying value if the cost of account administration is higher than the marginal revenues earned.

Portfolio management activities, defined as *active decisions by the firm to severe a customer or sales channel relationship or de-emphasize a product or line of business.* These decisions are driven by profitability considerations.

Inorganic growth, including *new customers acquired through mergers or acquisitions, the loss of customers due to divestitures and any gains/losses for a specific business unit due to the internal transfer or restructuring of the business*. Note that internal restructuring should in principle be a zero-sum game: customers transferred from one business unit to another still remain customers of the firm; however, it may not be zero sum if customer attrition increases due to the transfer or if the new combination of customers and products leads to higher customer acquisition synergies.

KPIs for Average Revenue Per Customer

The following are KPIs measuring growth in risk-adjusted operating profit from changes in average revenue per customer.

Number of transactions per customer, which can increase if you successfully *cross-sell* products or increase the number of transactions for the same product with an existing customer.

Notional value of average transactions. Absolute revenue per transaction will generally increase if notional values increase. Economic development will trigger some of this growth: assuming no change in margin, both the absolute interest income from a mortgage loan as well as the insurance premium for home owners' protection will increase with the value of the home.

Both the number of transactions and the value per transaction are influenced by the *share of wallet*, a term used to indicate how much of your customer's total activity takes place with your institution. Increasing your share of wallet can drive growth from the existing customer base substantially.

KPIs for Risk-adjusted Contribution Margin

The following are KPIs for measuring growth in risk-adjusted operating profit coming from changes in average risk-adjusted contribution per product or transaction.

Changes in product/channel mix. Contribution margins are not equal across all products and channels. The same product may have a different contribution margin depending on whether it is sold through an independent or tied sales channel due to differences in sales commissions or if the channel influences the product's lifecycle characteristics through churn. Similarly, the average contribution of a given channel may change as the product mix sold by the channel changes.

Pricing conditions also influence contribution margins. Pricing conditions are influenced by decisions at the micro-level, with good underwriting practices capturing more of the consumer surplus by setting the price higher than the technical cost of production. Pricing conditions are also influenced by macro-level decisions as the firm finds the optimal trade-off between volume, price and total profitability based on the elasticity of demand for the product and segment. Finally, prices are also influenced by external factors, for example a hardening or softening of the market generally as seen in PC pricing cycles or in the compression of loan spreads associated with low interest rates.

Non-price terms and conditions. Economic contribution margins may change even if the "price" does not change due to non-price terms and conditions. For example, PC insurance coverage can be extended or deductibles lowered in order to retain the best customers during a soft cycle. Similarly, underwriting standards for bank loans may change (e.g., no documentation loans) or because of loosening terms and conditions (e.g., covenants). All these terms and conditions impact risk-adjusted contribution margins but not necessarily top-line revenues directly.

MANAGEMENT ACTIONS – THREE HORIZONS OF GROWTH

It is useful to think of growth initiatives which yield results over different time horizons, beginning with tactical initiatives to get more out of your existing business in the short term and ending with strategic "bets" which may only produce growth years or decades later. This multiple-horizon perspective is motivated by the observation (Baghai and Chan, 2000) that a ". . . snapshot of any company that has managed fast profitable growth for over a decade . . . will reveal a pipeline of businesses at different stages of development from large core businesses, to emerging businesses, to options for future businesses . . . (over) three horizons." See also Mehrdad *et al.* (1999).

McKinsey's three horizons of growth framework, illustrated in Figure 11.3, is useful for characterizing the continuum between tactical and strategic initiatives.

Horizon 1: Get the most out of what you have. Horizon 1 activities focus on growing profits from your existing business footprint, including both acquiring new customers as well as increasing the revenue from existing customers. Horizon 1 initiatives include improving sales activities to increase efficiency and effectiveness as well as "cross-sell" or "share of wallet" programs.

Horizon 1 initiatives can deliver a step-change in growth with visible results coming over a 6- to 18-month horizon. Success requires superior execution capabilities. Because they are so fundamental to long-term value creation, Horizon 1 initiatives should represent a continuous stream of activities, undertaken as part of your company's DNA, as opposed to being seen as one-off initiatives.

Horizon 2: Investment required, execution capabilities a must. Horizon 2 initiatives require a higher investment over longer time horizons. Typical Horizon 2 activities include expanding the business footprint into product or market adjacencies and capturing growth from predictable, long-term trends or industry consolidation through bolt-on acquisitions.

These sources of growth require a greater investment, both in terms of cash (as revenues will likely lag the investment) and in terms of management capacity. Success for Horizon 2 initiatives is also about superior execution, made more complicated by the longer payback

Horizon 3

Create options for future business, anticipating new sources of demand and the effects of disruptive technologies

Focus on building options, invest in controlled experiments

Horizon 2

Expand from existing businesses into new, adjacent markets, products and services and along the value chain; invest to meet long term, predictable trends

Focus on top-line growth but with a clear long-term return target

Horizon 1

Grow and defend current core businesses, managing for value as they mature

Focus on sales effectiveness as well as bottom-line performance, especially cost efficiency and underwriting effectiveness

Source: Author's adaptation of Baghai, et al.

FIGURE 11.3 McKinsey's three horizons of growth framework

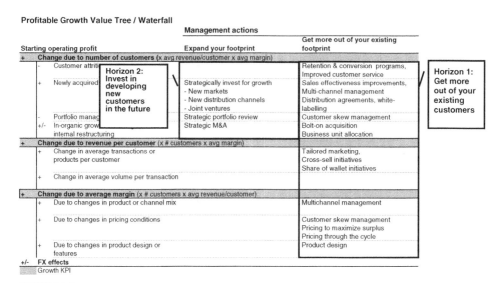

FIGURE 11.4   Management actions for profitable growth

periods, typically 2–3 years as opposed to within the next 6–18 months. These initiatives therefore require a longer-term commitment and continuity of focus, which unfortunately can become derailed by short-term developments or management changes.

Horizon 1 and 2 growth initiatives, discussed in greater detail in the remainder of this section, can easily be mapped into the KPI framework, as illustrated in Figure 11.4.

Horizon 3: Anticipating disruptions, building options. Horizon 3 initiatives focus on long-term options or "bets" which may be less clear, more speculative and, by definition, further off on the horizon. They may be associated with a vision regarding how technology can be used to disrupt existing business models or provide new products and services. Examples include the role of mobile communications in telematics and usage-based insurance, the role of electronic currencies such as Bitcoin in facilitating payments, etc. Success in Horizon 3 initiatives requires not only making the right bet on the "next big thing" but also shaping the industry and contributing to make it happen.

HORIZON 1 – INCREASING SALES PRODUCTIVITY

Banks and insurers undertake a variety of growth initiatives to drive more profits from their existing franchise. These initiatives focus on increasing the customer base and improving the contribution per customer. As Table 11.2 illustrates, the four generic initiatives include those focused on sales force productivity, multi-channel distribution, "share of wallet" programs and managing the portfolio of customers.

When asked which levers were the most important for generating short-term growth, senior executives ranked "expansion into new markets," "finding new customers in existing markets" and "selling more to existing customers" as the top three (Proudfoot Consulting, 2009). Two out of three is not bad – managers generally believe that getting more out of their existing business footprint is critical for profitable growth.

TABLE 11.2 Growth rules of thumb and initiatives

Areas for action	Generic observations	Initiatives
Increase sales productivity	Sales forces are not spending enough time actually selling and effectiveness of time spent can be increased.	Leverage technology and front-office support in the sales process. Improve productivity through sales force management: ■ recruitment and training ■ design of uniform "sales process" ■ target setting, incentives and sales force management.
Go multi-channel	The customer chooses when, where and how to interact with your company.	Multi-channel management, accommodating and shaping customer behavior through coordinated channel approaches to optimize growth potential and minimize cost of service.
Get more out of existing customers – "share of wallet"	Existing customers are an under-exploited source of growth. Easier to sell to an existing customer than to acquire a new customer. Satisfied customers are your best advertisement, positively influencing sales through referrals.	Leverage technology and front-office support in the sales process. Cross-sell, up-sell, share of wallet, retention and loyalty programs. Implement "big data" to support customer relationship and customer lifetime value management. Improve service and the overall customer experience to increase positive referrals.
Manage the customer portfolio	Generic rule of thumb: 80% of the contribution comes from 20% of the customers.	Manage customer profitability skew, focusing more on the most profitable customers and upgrading or shedding those that are not. Engage in value-oriented pricing and product design.

Financial services already invest significantly in new business generation, with acquisition expenses often being more than 50% of their expense base. Given this substantial investment, is it simply a question of "more of the same"? Is a step change in sales as simple as getting more sales people and agents and opening more branches, especially in mature markets? Apparently not: only 6% of the executives said that increasing the sales force size is the answer.

In contrast, 40% mentioned that improving *sales force productivity* was the key, focusing the sales force more on sales and less on unproductive activities. The remaining 55% said that *better management of the sales force* was the most critical.

Improving Productivity

In general, sales people spend only a limited amount of time on client-focused activities (only 20% based on the survey). This is significantly below their perception (34%) and their goal (50%). The remaining time is spent on less productive activities, including administration (31%), problem solving (18%), downtime (16%) and travel (15%).

What are the implications? If one could shift a marginal 5% of their time from other activities to the 20% already spent on sales, then the top line could grow in principle by 1.25×! While it is unreasonable to expect this kind of impact in practice, it nonetheless indicates the leverage one can get from getting sales people to focus more on sales and less on other activities. As a consequence, banks and insurers invest heavily in enabling sales personnel to focus more on sales, including:

- leveraging sales personnel through front-office support or centralized services for lead generation, prospecting and qualifying, scheduling, administration and problem-solving activities;
- encouraging customers to use online and call center channels for simple queries and problem solving;
- streamlining quoting, data entry and administration processes, for example through mobile technologies, intelligent/fast quoting processes and single-entry, straight-through processing.

These activities are win/win, leading potentially to double-digit improvements in effective sales capacity, combined with lower costs as well as quicker turnaround times and more transparent decisions for customers.

Better Manage the Sales Force

It is not uncommon to see a 3–4× performance gap between the top and bottom quartiles in the sales force, whether measured in terms of number of contracts, revenues, closing rates per call or number of calls per sales agent.

The disparity between the best and worst sales personnel represents untapped potential: there is tremendous leverage from increasing the average productivity by bringing the bottom quartile up to the average. Toward this end, sales managers focus on initiatives designed to:

- improve recruitment processes and implement structured "apprenticeship" programs, combined with ongoing training and coaching of the sales force and an exit plan for consistently low performers;
- develop and continually refine standardized, "best" sales practices along each step of the sales chain from identifying needs, preparation, customer dialog or "scripts," closing and follow-up;
- support the sales chain with the appropriate tools, for example more effective marketing materials, time management systems and real-time Customer Relationship Management (CRM) systems providing an overview of the relationship with the bank or insurer, recent sales, contacts and service requests and prompting additional questions and cross-sell ideas;
- improve the management of the sales force, for example by freeing up managers' time for setting account priorities, setting explicit revenue and margin targets reinforced by aligned incentives, regular coaching and oversight by senior sales professionals and an optimal allocation of accounts and prospects to the most successful sales agents;
- improve the measurement of activities (e.g., time allocation, number of calls, etc.) as well as results (total sales, closing rates, etc.), helping to identify improvement potential and supporting remedial action earlier.

In addition to boosting the average performance across all the horses in the stable, many sales programs "bet" more heavily on their proven producers, for example providing their best sales people with more support through "silver, gold, platinum" programs, preferential lead generation and the allocation of new territories or accounts, etc.

The diagnostic indicators needed to improve sales effectiveness will logically differ by channel. Table 11.3 gives an indication of the KPIs used in practice.

HORIZON 1 – GOING MULTI-CHANNEL

Traditional sales channels such as branches and agents are an important source of revenue for banks and insurers; however, their relative importance is declining. While PC insurance sales in Europe in 2009 were still dominated by tied agents in Italy (~80%) and Germany (~60%), they were led by direct channels in the Netherlands (~50%) and France (~35%) and the rate of direct penetration continues to increase all across Europe (CEA, 2009).

Similar trends are found in banking. According to one study (McKinsey, 2010), over 55% of transactions in the US banking industry are conducted either online or via call centers, with a compounded annual growth rate in 2008–2012E of 12.6% for online, 4.3% for call centers but under 0.5% for both branches and ATMs.

These figures may actually underrepresent the importance of non-traditional distribution channels as customers increasingly engage in ROPO (Research Online, Purchase Offline) activities. Binder (2014) comments that "Consumers often engage in research-online-purchase-offline (ROPO) behavior . . . particularly for search products . . . or for customers with technology anxiety and high purchase risk perceptions . . . Furthermore, a majority of consumers still prefers to make the actual transaction in a physical store . . . (using the) Internet to search and compare products but purchase offline."

These trends are driven by three factors.

- First, by the technological developments and higher utilization rates of Internet and mobile technologies by consumers generally.
- Second, by evolving consumer preferences. According to Maklan and Wilson (2006), "Customers make channel choices alongside their product-service choices and expect suppliers to offer sales, marketing and service across multiple channels – online, telephone and physical presence . . . For many companies, channel strategy is now every bit as critical to their success, as are brand and product range policies." These preferences are reinforced by Generation Y (born between 1982 and 1995), who put a higher emphasis on practicality, convenience and fees and who view Internet and mobile technologies as a natural way to acquire information, conduct transactions and share experiences.
- Third, by banks and insurers in an attempt to improve sales and service levels as well as improve cost efficiency. For example, Internet websites can not only generate direct sales, but also bring valuable leads to be followed up by sales professionals. Also, cost savings can be achieved by encouraging the use of call centers, online service portals and ATMs for simple enquiries, problem solving and transactions.

These distribution trends represent a threat as well as an opportunity – a threat as the franchise value of traditional distribution channels becomes eroded, but an opportunity for acquiring and servicing more customers in a more cost-effective manner.

TABLE 11.3 Sales management KPIs

KPIs from lead generation to sales – direct/e-commerce

Visits	New, unique, total, page views, time on site per visit, page views per visit, referral sources (from search, direct, email, pay-per-click, other)
To revenue	Checkout abandonment, cart abandonment, new customers, total orders per day/week/month, average order value, return rate
Cost effectiveness	Pay-per-click cost per conversion, per acquisition
Social media	Facebook new likes, "talking about this"; Twitter retweets, new followers; Amazon ratings, response and order turnaround time
Service	Customer service open cases

KPIs from lead generation to sales – agent/branch/call center

Sales pipeline
Leads/prospects, contact, qualification, negotiation, offer stage
Conversion rates, new, closed
Offer acceptance, renegotiation, cancellation rates
Performance
New sales – mix and by number, notional, value contribution
Number of products/customer (cross-sell)
Percentage at recommended pricing, above, below
Average customer retention/attrition rate, length of relationship
Percentage of customers using call center, Internet support for after-sales service
Service levels
Average customer waiting time
Average time to make offer, process transaction, enter system, complete billing
Percentage of process exceptions/referrals
Error rate capture/completeness/verification/compliance information

KPIs for sales force efficiency

Summary, per agent/branch
Customers
Product – number, volume, value, cross-sell
Expense per customer, product
Contribution per customer, product
Sales staffing
Personnel mix

- Sales, underwriting, transaction support, supervisor
- Within sales – senior/junior sales, "platinum," "gold," "silver" status, licensed, unlicensed, part/full-time

Employee turnover per category
Recruitment/training – intake, average time/expense, completion rate
Allocation of time
New leads/prospecting
Existing client
Underwriting/pricing
Supervision, management activities
Administration

Source: Adapted from Traxler (2013).

From Multiple Channels . . .

One possible response to these trends is to build multiple distribution "silos," continuing to manage the branch or agent sales force independently from the new Internet direct channel and separate from other intermediary channels such as banks, brokers, comparison websites, independent financial advisors, etc.

As with many things, the most direct response may not be the best response. There are many issues with offering customers multiple points of contact in an uncoordinated manner, including the following.

- The unnecessary cannibalization of one channel by another, accompanied by the adverse effects on relationships if one channel feels threatened by another or by your own, direct contact with the customer.
- The risk of presenting an inconsistent face to the customer, who ultimately chooses which channel to use and when, in terms of the different channels' "look and feel," differences in quotations for the same product and inability to access all the customer's own information.
- The opportunity cost of foregone revenues by not leveraging customer access points to increase sales completion rates, failing to offer tailored proposals based on a comprehensive relationship view or missing out on up-sale and cross-sell opportunities.

. . . To a Multi-channel Strategy – More Than the Sum of Its Parts

Rather than building silo-oriented channels, banks and insurers are responding in the same way that other retailers are responding – by implementing an *integrated, multi-channel* strategy of interacting with their customers.

Rangaswamy and van Bruggen (2005) note that customers increasingly ". . . choose the times and the channels through which they deal with firms for different aspects of their interactions," from research to sales to queries and problem solving. This observation leads naturally to the definition of multi-channel marketing as ". . . simultaneously offering customers and prospects information, products, services and support (or any combination of these) through two or more synchronized channels."

In their report, McKinsey (2010) elaborate, characterizing a multi-channel platform as one that provides customers with products and services "in a seamless and always available fashion across all channels . . . a consistent experience (where consumers) can see the full view of their relationship, can shift at will (e.g., mobile to online), and can pick up an interaction where they left off (e.g., part-way through the application for a product) . . . at any time of day."

Achieving the Goal

Building multi-channel capabilities requires management actions in five interrelated areas: systems, processes, products, organization and monitoring.

Build the systems needed to support a multi-channel approach, focusing on three dimensions.

- First, capturing, storing and providing access to comprehensive customer data consistently across all channels, not only in terms of static customer information but also the history of their transactions, telephone or Internet inquiries, service and sales contacts, offers and responses, etc.
- Second, ensuring consistent pricing and acceptance criteria across all channels – beyond the risk of arbitrage, getting different answers from different channels can be frustrating for the consumer.

■ Third, ensuring that customer touch points are leveraged to increase sales completion rates and to promote customer-specific up-sale and cross-selling opportunities. This includes tailored messaging and offers, the ability to interact with sales personnel via telephone or Internet messaging during a visit to the website, etc.

Redesign the sales process and the interaction between sales channels, to resolve potential channel conflicts as well as improve sales completion, cross-sell and up-sale success rates. Maklan *et al.* (2008) illustrate how the sales process can be transformed with both of these objectives in mind, where the Internet "feeds" field sales agents and central desks can be used to make agents more effective.

Redesign products and services so that they can be sold through the different channels simultaneously if desired. Standardize and modularize retail products so that they are easy to understand and communicate. Modular products also allow for mass customization, allowing you to meet specific customer needs in a cost-effective manner. Finally, an additional benefit of standardized products is that they will also be easier and more cost efficient to administer using straight-through processing.

Redesign the organization to ensure a comprehensive and consistent approach across all channels and products for the same customer. This requires coordinating across product or customer silos, each of which may have their own marketing, sales and service agendas. In addition, incentive systems need to be aligned to encourage the optimal treatment of customers who switch between different channels at different times for different products.

Monitor, manage and improve performance of the different sales and service channels. This includes understanding the cost and success rates of converting inquiries into qualified prospects, prospects into offers and offers into closed transactions. In addition, monitor the level of customer satisfaction and complaints.

Finally, it also requires a strategy of continual improvement and innovation, deciding whether and where to invest in new products and delivery approaches. Not all multi-channel initiatives will be successful; while some improvements may be obvious, representing a win/win from the company and customer's perspectives, others may be better tackled by selective test trials or by finding partners to provide the required services.

HORIZON 1 – GETTING MORE OUT OF EXISTING CUSTOMERS; CROSS SELL, BIG DATA AND CUSTOMER LOYALTY

The "management guru" Tom Peters talks about "the customer as (an) appreciating asset," citing the anecdote of Stew Leonard, a grocer in Connecticut who is quoted as saying (Peters, 1987) "'When I see a frown on a customer's face, I see $50,000 about to walk out of the door. ($100 worth of groceries a week, over ten years . . .)' We all agree that repeat trade is the key to business success . . . (and a satisfied customer is) obviously any firm's principle vehicle for word-of-mouth advertising."

This simple anecdote supports three well-accepted "truths" about the value of existing customers.

■ *It costs more money to acquire a new customer than to do more business with an existing customer.* For example, in terms of advertising, marketing and sales expenses as well as lost time chasing unproductive leads. A simple rule is that it costs up to 5–10 times more to acquire a new customer than it does to retain and grow revenues from existing customers.[1]

- *A satisfied customer will have a positive multiplier effect on revenues through "word-of-mouth" referrals.* With the penetration of social media increasing, satisfied customers and word-of-mouth referrals are fast becoming the most effective means of advertising.
- *Existing customers are more likely to be better customers* , exhibiting lower price sensitivity, lower switching rates and increased repeat purchases than new customers – they have, after all, already taken the critical first step by deciding to buy from your firm as opposed to buying from one of your competitors.

Acting on these observations can lead to higher revenues and profitability, as emphasized by F.F. Reichheld (1993): "When a company consistently delivers superior value and wins customer loyalty, market share and revenues go up, and the cost of acquiring and servicing customers go down."

But how to take advantage of these simple "truths"? There are three initiative often used to exploit the potential of the existing customer base: enhanced sales programs, relationship management programs and improving the customer experience.

Enhance Sales Programs

The most direct approach is through programs designed to increase and retain revenue from existing customers. While similar in intention and overlapping in practice, these programs differ in focus.

- *Cross-sell* programs focus on increasing the number of products sold to the customer, for example by offering an auto or home owner's policy to an existing life insurance customer, coverage "riders" to a base policy, or home insurance and investment products to a mortgage customer.
- *Share of wallet* programs focus on increasing your share of the customer's business for products you have already sold, in terms of investable assets or deposits, loan financing, personal and commercial property insurance, etc.
- *Up-sale* programs focus on offering higher value-added products and services, for example moving a customer from a "normal" savings or investment account to a "platinum" account, increasing the range or amount of coverage on an insurance policy, etc.
- *Retention and loyalty programs* focus on developing your most valuable customers. *Retention* programs may include meeting or beating a competitor's offer, contacting the customer prior to key events such as the maturity of the loan, etc. *Loyalty* programs are designed to increase business from customers with high potential and include special offers, discounts, bonus "points" or special status.

Executing these initiatives requires improvements across many dimensions, such as the following.

- *Leverage all touch points.* Sales activities are not limited to sales channels: every point of customer interaction is an opportunity to sell, for example transaction services or account inquiries through call centers or branch networks, mailings, online, etc.

---

[1]http://thecustomerinstitute.blogspot.de/2008/11/real-impact-of-customer-complaints.html. See also Hart *et al.* (1990), Goodman (2009).

- *Adjust incentives.* Monitoring and incentivizing cross-sell, up-sale and share of wallet at all touch points is a prerequisite for success. However, the incentives must balance successful sales against product profitability by providing higher incentives to sell a more profitable combination of products.
- *Improve product design.* Consider offering modular products that are easy to understand and complementary in their components, increasing the ability to cross-sell and up-sell; alternatively, design product bundles which offer combined services at a discount.
- *Improve systems.* Similar to the support needed for multi-channel, provide access to all customer information at each interaction point, including information on existing products, recent offers and inquiries.

Big Data, CRM and Lifetime Value Added

Each of the sales enhancement initiatives can in principle be executed independently. However, there is benefit from a holistic approach to maximizing the profitability of a customer relationship. The most obvious benefit is to ensure that your offers are made to those clients who are most likely to accept them, thereby increasing success rates and lowering costs.

Equally as important is the ability to make the offers to those customers who *you want*. It may seem counterintuitive, but there are some customers that you may not want, for example, customers who ultimately use a disproportionate level of services, who prepay or lapse their contracts opportunistically, or who are simply bad risks (Shah and Kumar, 2012).

Customer Relationship Management   CRM frameworks are implemented by many commercial and investment banks. The goal is to increase profits from large corporate clients. The challenge is that these clients can behave opportunistically, taking only loss-leading, relationship "entry" products such as loans or credit lines with limited use of higher-margin products such as treasury services, trading or capital markets products.

The solution is to create a CRM function which ties together the product offerings and optimizes the contribution per customer and, if it is not possible to make a profit from the customer, manages out of the customer relationship.

Implementing a CRM model requires information on customer profitability by product; clear priorities and rigorous planning how to improve the profitability of the relationship; and the organization and incentives needed to bring different product specialists together to meet the customer plan.

Customer Lifetime Value Management   Not all customers can support the expense of a relationship manager, especially retail or mass-market customers where profit improvement activities have to be designed and targeted at customer segments as opposed to individual customers.

Lifetime value added tools are used to segment customers and support more efficient and successful acquisition, retention and cross-selling initiatives. Typically, customer lifetime value added management proceeds in three steps.

Step 1: Develop the Customer Lifetime Value (CLV) metric. Gupta *et al.* (2006) define lifetime value added as ". . . the present value of all (expected) future profits obtained from a customer over his or her life of relationship with a firm. CLV is similar to the discounted cash flow approach used in finance . . . estimated at an individual customer or segment level rather than simply examining average profitability."

Step 2: Understand product profitability and customer behavior. The building block for CLV calculations is the product-level, risk-adjusted contribution margin, or New Business

RAPM. These building blocks are tied together into an overall, expected lifetime profit estimate. This requires assumptions about the future business relationship – the probability and cost of *acquiring* the customer in the first place, the probability of *retaining* the customer over different time horizons, the propensity of the customer to *increase their contribution* through cross-sales, up-selling and volume increases in the future and, finally, the *underwriting "quality"* of the customer (e.g., the customer's loan default or claims filing propensities).

Step 3: Segment customers and prioritize actions based on customer data. The final step is to use customer data ("big data") to estimate these relationships and segment customers into actionable groups. The results take the form of acquisition, retention, cross-sell and under-writing "scorecards" which are then integrated into the company's sales and service platforms.

Gupta *et al*. (2006) discuss many approaches for segmenting customers including heuristic approaches, probabilistic models, econometric models and persistence models, depending on the data available; similar approaches are used in evaluating the "quality" of the customer (e.g., the probability of default or the propensity to file a claim), as discussed in detail in Chapter 24. Very often, different models are estimated and used for each purpose; while this approach may not capture cross-effects, it does reduce the complexity of estimating, maintaining and using the models.

Improve Customer Satisfaction and Loyalty

The final activity for increasing business with existing customers is to increase customer loyalty and satisfaction. In addition to a stronger relationship, customer loyalty will have positive knock-on effects as satisfied customers ultimately drive growth through positive "word-of-mouth" endorsements, made increasingly powerful through social media.

One of the tools used to systematically monitor and improve customer satisfaction is the Net Promoter Score (NPS) developed by F.F. Reichheld (2003). The NPS is derived from a customer questionnaire and is seen as highly correlated with growth – the higher the NPS, the higher the growth rate of the company. Reichheld says, ". . . it's about customers' willingness to recommend a product or service to someone else. In fact . . . the percentage of customers who were enthusiastic enough to refer a friend or colleague—perhaps the strongest sign of customer loyalty—correlated directly with differences in growth rates among competitors."

The NPS is used by many financial services firms, including Charles Schwab, American Express and Allianz (Markey and Reichheld, 2011). The NPS is calculated by asking customers a simple question: How likely are you to recommend our company to a friend or colleague? Responses are elicited along a 10-point scale (Satmetrix, 2013): scores in the 9–10 range are characterized as "promoters," or *loyal enthusiasts who will keep buying and refer others, fuelling growth*; scores in the 7–8 range are "passives," or *satisfied but unenthusiastic customers who are vulnerable to competitive offerings*; scores in the 0–6 range are "detractors," or *unhappy customers who can damage your brand and impede growth through negative word-of-mouth*.

The company's NPS score is calculated by subtracting the percentage of detractors from the percentage of promoters, with the NPS lying in the range of [−100%, 100%]. An NPS above zero is considered "good" and an NPS above 50% excellent. Customers are additionally asked for comments, used to better understand the scores.

Customer satisfaction can be influenced at every touch point, beginning with the customer's buying experience, extending to the quality of the product or service in use and the periodic contacts for account updates, and culminating in after-sales service if something goes wrong.

Because of the multiplicity of touch points, improving the management of NPS scores tends to focus less on a specific, targeted "program" and more on building a process to understand and resolve the issues they develop, called "closing the loop." Markey and Reichheld (2011) define closing the loop as "sharing feedback from a customer as soon as possible . . . with the employees most responsible . . . contacting customers . . . so that you can probe deeper . . . (and) remedy individual problems where possible and begin to address systemic issues."

Other authors have focused on specific elements of the value chain in promoting customer loyalty. For example, Goodman (2009) was an early promoter of customer service in "delighting the customer," advocating strategic customer service as a management prerogative. Goodman emphasizes that ". . . when something goes wrong, customers don't call the director of product development, the manager of operations, or the vice president of marketing. They call customer service. When they do, customer service must preserve the relationship, gather information, and improve the process, wherever the problem originated."

However, care must be taken: not all customer service and loyalty initiatives are value adding – especially if the cost of providing customer "delight" is higher than the value added.[2]

HORIZON 1 – MANAGING THE CUSTOMER PORTFOLIO SKEW

There is a general management rule that 80% of the profits come from 20% of the customers. This "rule" is an application of the so-called Pareto management principle[3] – a generalized observation that in most business contexts 20% of the effort generates 80% of the results – but applied to the skew of the customer profitability distribution.

In principle, one should focus more resources on the 20% "vital few" at the expense of the "trivial many," looking for growth through retention programs, higher service levels and sales efforts.

The strategy for the remaining 80% is less clear: while the middle 60% may not bring much value added, they nonetheless make a contribution to the firm's fixed expenses. Unfortunately, the bottom 20% may actually destroy value, even on a marginal cost basis. Given this complexity, the appropriate management strategy is to grow, harvest or divest customers selectively as appropriate, illustrated in the 3×2 matrix in Figure 11.5.

The horizontal axis represents current profitability, divided into three regions: negative, low and high. The vertical axis represents future profitability, divided into two regions: low and high. It is important to increase profitability for customers with low or negative current profitability, while focusing on retention and loyalty for customers with high current profitability.

Not all customers can be made profitable. Some will simply do too little business with your firm, others will have the wrong use or risk profile. For these, there are two specific actions worth discussing in detail: redesigning and re-pricing products such that the low value added customers are moved into products with more appropriate profiles and/or exiting relationships that will remain negative.

---

[2]For a good summary of some of the pitfalls in focusing myopically on customer loyalty, see Seschadri (2011).

[3]In 1906, Italian economist V. Pareto observed that 80% of the wealth (land) was owned by 20% of the people in Italy. Observing similar relationships in many business applications – 80% of profits or complaints come from 20% of customers, 80% of sales come from 20% of sales staff, etc. – Juran (1951) generalized the notion of the "vital few and the trivial many."

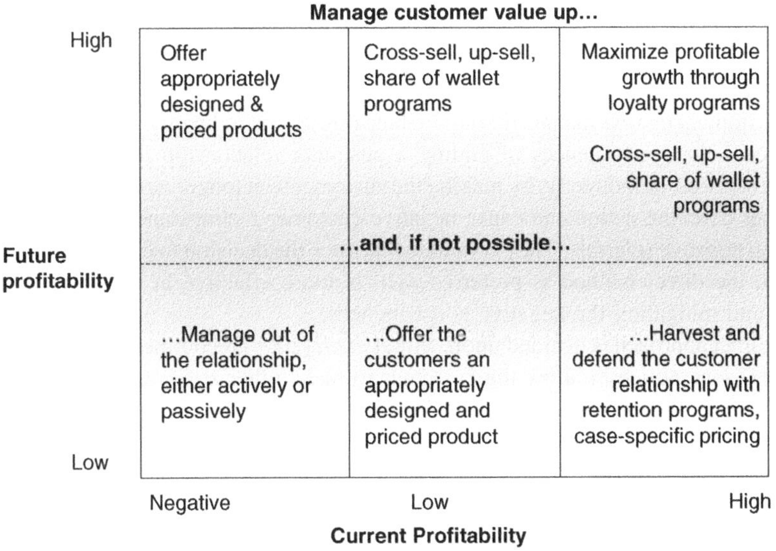

Manage customer value up...

	Negative	Low	High
High	Offer appropriately designed & priced products	Cross-sell, up-sell, share of wallet programs	Maximize profitable growth through loyalty programs Cross-sell, up-sell, share of wallet programs
Future profitability		...and, if not possible...	
	...Manage out of the relationship, either actively or passively	...Offer the customers an appropriately designed and priced product	...Harvest and defend the customer relationship with retention programs, case-specific pricing
Low			

Current Profitability

FIGURE 11.5 Manage the customer profitability skew management

Design and Price Products so that Customers can self-select

Some customers are unprofitable because they are not charged the right price based on their risk profile; risk-based technical pricing tools, discussed in Chapter 24, can help in these situations.

However, other customers are not charged the right price given their service or use profile. For example, they may "over-use" the call center or branch or agent for information or problem solving, or they may not keep sufficient credit card, deposit or investment balances to make the account profitable after administration costs. Some of these customers may, however, become profitable if they are encouraged to use lower-cost channels or services or to pay for the services they have used.

One solution is to educate and encourage the customer to alter their behavior. For example, Mittal *et al.* (2008) provide an anecdote that "Fidelity Investments identified low-margin customers who were frequently phoning service reps. Instead of divesting them, Fidelity taught them to use its other (lower-cost) troubleshooting options, such as automated phone lines and company Web site."

Another solution is to encourage the customer to shift into products or services whose price depends on the customer's behavior, for example by offering checking accounts with fees depending on usage (e.g., one with a monthly fee and a charge per check and another, premium account, with free checking and a higher rate if the balance remains over a specific level). In this way, less profitable, service-intensive customers are encouraged to select, and pay for, the appropriate services.

Another solution is to divert the customer to a different distribution or service channel (e.g., the Internet) or to a partner whose offering and pricing may be better suited to the customer's needs.

Manage Unprofitable Customers Out

It may seem counterintuitive to actually wish that some of the customers that we worked so hard to acquire would simply go away and do business with one of our competitors.

Nonetheless, there may be some customers who remain unprofitable no matter what we do. The last option in such instances is to manage the customers "out," a strategy discussed in Mittal *et al.* (2008).

The customers can be managed "out," either directly or indirectly. Haenlein and Kaplan (2011) discuss the consequences of ending a customer relationship directly, by cancelling accounts or services, or indirectly, by making the customer wait longer on customer service lines.

In either case, the action can cause negative customer feelings and potentially harm the firm through negative referrals. They conclude that once the decision to end the relationship has been taken, the direct method is preferred as it is more effective in shedding unprofitable customers and mitigating the negative consequences.

If the direct approach is decided upon, Mittal *et al.* (2008) recommend that it be done with sufficient advance notice to allow the customer to make other arrangements, and communicated by a person rather than by email or letter.

Horizon 2 – Strategic Growth Initiatives

In addition to getting more out of your existing footprint, other sources of growth include anticipating trends, expanding into adjacencies and industry consolidation. These are Horizon 2 growth strategies because they require a longer time horizon and greater investment.

HORIZON 2 – ANTICIPATING MEGA-TRENDS

There are some "mega-trends" which will impact financial services firms over the coming decade, representing both threats and opportunities. Some of the most important trends include:

- *Growth in emerging and developing markets*, with demand triggered by the emergence of a middle class and increasing penetration rates for risk and savings products, ultimately converging to developed market levels. It is estimated that banking revenues from the emerging markets of China, India, Brazil, Russia, Mexico, Indonesia and Turkey could eclipse the revenues from G7 economies by a factor of 1.25–1.75× by 2050 (PriceWaterhouseCoopers, 2007). The typical industry response is to "plant flags," to develop joint ventures and sign agreements with distribution partners in Asia Pacific, Central and Eastern Europe and Latin America.
- *Changing demographics and an aging population*, driven by low birth rates and increased life expectancy. For the first time in history, the number of senior citizens worldwide will be greater than the number of children under five: seniors represented 8% of the population in 1950, 10% in the year 2000 and, by 2050, an estimated 20%. This naturally leads to greater demand for retirement savings, income security in old age and long-term care products. The typical industry response is to develop new products covering both savings and annuity pay-out phases (e.g., variable annuities in the USA), reverse mortgages and long-term care products, and services needed by an aging population.
- *Changing demographics and mega-cities*, characterized by an increasing concentration of wealth and economic activity in larger, more concentrated cities. In the 1800s, only 3% of the world's population lived in cities; 30% in the 1950s, 50% today and an estimated 66% by the year 2030 (Euramet, 2013). These trends have the possibility to influence employment, housing, transportation, health care, infrastructure and transfers of wealth, thereby affecting borrowing and savings patterns, payment mechanisms, etc.

- *Increased regulation*, in terms of solvency requirements, systemic interlinkages, consumer protection, lending and retirement products, to name a few (Deloitte, 2014). These trends will have a substantial impact on the products offered as well as distribution channels and sales practices, with an increasing emphasis on the transparency of fees and commissions and a higher standard for independent advice.
- Changing *consumer behavior*, spurred by the Internet and mobile telephony, for example in terms of multi-channel access, price comparison websites and the influence of social media.
- *Big data*, presenting opportunities to better and more quickly tailor offers, products and prices to individuals, but presenting the threat of adverse selection or lost opportunities for those too slow off the mark.

These are predictable, slow-moving trends, developing over years or decades. However, in spite of their predictable development, the consequences in terms of business models and strategies are not always clear. In addition, capturing the opportunities requires investments well in advance of demand if a leading position is to be built and defended. Given the long time horizon, successfully exploiting Horizon 2 initiatives requires:

- a vision regarding how the trend will develop;
- a clearly defined strategy how to build a sustainable and defendable competitive advantage in the future;
- a significant investment in terms of management capacity and financial resources to build that advantage;
- a sustained focus on execution over decades, not disrupted by short-term factors.

To illustrate the need for both commitment and the right strategic vision, consider that there are many firms which have made the investment in successfully building emerging market franchises, enjoying some of the highest multiples in their industry before the emerging market volatility in 2013–14. Examples including HSBC and Standard Chartered in banking and AIA and Prudential plc in insurance (see Sidebar 11.1). However, there have been many other firms which have planted flags but did not achieve the same level of multiple expansion.

SIDEBAR 11.1: PRUDENTIAL UK ASIA PACIFIC STRATEGY

Consider the relative success of Prudential plc in building its Asia Pacific franchise. For years, Prudential used its UK "cash cow" to successfully fund its Asian growth strategy. Ultimately, this investment paid off, summarized in a 2013 news article (Pratley, 2013): "(T)wo-thirds of the Pru's outperformance can be explained by its extraordinary rate of growth in Asia. The time has come to retire the old caricature of a cash-cow UK business funding an Asian operation with uncertain medium-term prospects."

Prudential's success is apparently due to two factors: distribution and the right product. According to *Insurance News* (Lai, 2012), Prudential's competitive advantage in Asia rests on ". . . a multi-channel strategy, which maximizes market access and minimizes channel conflict . . . (and a) focus on products meeting Asian customers' savings and protection needs . . . while delivering shareholders value with high returns and short payback periods."

> The demographic changes in Asia have been anticipated for decades. The Pru's investment in building a sustainable and defendable source of competitive advantage – specifically, a network of over 300,000 agents and 77 bancassurance partnerships in 11 Asian countries, leading to a top-three position in eight markets and a leading position in Indonesia, Malaysia, Singapore, the Philippines, Vietnam and India in 2011 – started years ago and is difficult to replicate. This distribution advantage also allows the Pru to have a greater control over the products offered.
>
> As of September 2013, Prudential plc was trading a little over 3× book value, a multiple that very few European LH companies could dream of, primarily driven by its Asian businesses.

HORIZON 2 – EXPLOITING ADJACENCIES

Profitable adjacencies represent a second Horizon 2 growth initiative. According to Zook and Allen (2003), adjacencies allow companies to grow up to three times faster than their competitors, even in a mature market. The idea is to expand along one of the company's {product, market, customer, value chain} dimensions, in a manner consistent with the core capabilities which made the company successful in the first place. According to Allen and Zook (2001), some of the most common adjacencies include the following.

- *Existing products, new customers* or "interlocking customer and product adjacencies," with an existing product sold to new customers and then adapted over time to the new segment's unique needs.
- *Existing customers, new products* or "cross-sell adjacencies," offering a broader pallet of related products to a customer that you know intimately, for example offering insurance products to a bank's clients.
- *Existing competence, leveraged into new products and services or* "capability adjacencies," leveraging core skills in production or along any step in the value chain into new products or services for new markets.

Some adjacencies represent incremental steps along a consistent and coherent path. Concrete examples in insurance include the provision of health riders on asset accumulation products or the bundling of assistance coverage with home or auto policies. In banking, examples include offering third-party investment alternatives and auto or life insurance with auto or home financing arrangements.

Exploiting an adjacency is not without risk. As Allen and Zook suggest: "The average company succeeds only 25% of the time in launching new initiatives . . . That's because growing a business is normally a complex, experimental and somewhat chaotic process." There are two risks to implementing an adjacency strategy.

The first is that the strategy takes the firm further and further away from its core competencies, diminishing the value of whatever made it successful in the first place. The second is not having a clear idea about the strategy and core skills required to capture value in the adjacency. An example of both can be found in the bancassurance models of the 1990s, as outlined in Sidebar 11.2.

SIDEBAR 11.2: BANCASSURANCE, AN ADJACENCY TOO FAR?

Citibank and Travelers Insurance jumped with both feet into a "customer adjacency" strategy when they merged in 1998 to form Citigroup. Citibank was one of the largest banks in the world with an enviable international presence and the number one credit and debit card issuer in the USA. Travelers was the second largest commercial PC insurance company in the USA and owned Smith Barney brokerage firm and Salomon Brothers investment bank. Together, they covered virtually everything financial – from retail and commercial banking to brokerage and investment banking, credit cards and insurance, both in the USA and internationally.

The idea behind the merger was to create a "financial services supermarket" with "one-stop shopping," which could cater to their customers' every need, whether it be for insurance, banking, brokerage or investment products. Ostensibly, consumers would pay for this convenience through higher fees as well as greater loyalty and greater share of wallet, representing revenue synergies (Nabi and Saeed, 2012).

Citigroup was not alone in this aspiration: other financial services firms also jumped in with both feet, for example the merger of Credit Suisse and Winterthur Insurance in 1997, Allianz and Dresdner Bank in 2002, as well as ING and Fortis Group's dual banking and insurance platforms, to name just a few of the higher-profile combinations.

What is interesting about all these "adjacent" growth strategies is that absolutely none of them exist in the same form today, only slightly more than a decade later. Citigroup announced the sale of Travelers in 2001, Allianz sold Dresdner in 2009, Credit Suisse sold Winterthur in 2006, and ING and Fortis Group had to split up their banking and insurance operations following the 2008 crisis.

Why the reversal? One hint can be found in the prescient comment by Lukas Mühlemann, then CEO of Credit Suisse, which acquired Winterthur as a "White Knight" in order to save it from a corporate raider. Just prior to the acquisition, Mühlemann is quoted (*Economist*, 2002) as saying "Why buy a cow when all you want is a glass of milk?"

It is true that capturing the value of the adjacency – specifically, leveraging the existing bank and insurer customer base with new products and services – required new products. However, as Mühlemann suggested, it is not clear that you have to make the product yourself. In retrospect, it is commonly held that more of the value was in the distribution than in providing the capital backing and administering the insurance products.

To reinforce this point, it is interesting to note that while there are virtually no Bancassurance conglomerates (capital "B") in existence today, there are a growing number of bancassurance agreements (small "b") in place: it is more common for banks and broker dealers to form distribution relationships and offer "shelf space" to insurers, some on an exclusive basis and some with a panel of preferred insurers, for the provision of life insurance, home owner or auto policies or credit-linked life insurance.

This bancassurance model (with a small "b") is especially strong in emerging markets, especially those in Asia Pacific and Central and Eastern Europe. Increasingly, insurers have to make upfront payments in order to access the bank distribution channel, highlighting where value is created in terms of the value chain. Nonetheless, these relationships can be beneficial to both parties if managed correctly.

HORIZON 2 – TRANSFORMATIONAL AND BOLT-ON ACQUISITIONS

Reflecting on industry trends over the past 20 years, I am compelled to add a third category to Horizon 2 growth strategies: transformational and bolt-on acquisitions.

As Sidebar11.3 illustrates, bank mergers have contributed substantially to the growth of virtually all the largest banks in the USA. They have also spurred the growth of many non-US banks and insurers, including such prominent examples as ABN Amro, BNP Paribas and Lloyds TSB (as the names imply), but also transformational deals including the Union Bank of Switzerland (acquired by Swiss Bank Corporation); Deutsche Bank's acquisition of Bankers Trust, Morgan Grenfell, etc.; Credit Suisse's acquisition of First Boston and DLJ; the acquisitions which fundamentally changed the footprint of the Royal Bank of Scotland and so on. In insurance, mergers and acquisitions played a key role in the growth of Allianz, AXA, Prudential plc, Royal and Sun Alliance, CGU and Norwich, and so on.

Not all acquisitions are ultimately successful. Industry consolidation involves M&A, which can be a dirty word. Common wisdom suggests that M&A transactions fail at a high rate, estimated as high as 90% across all industries (CNN, 2009). If one were to do a detailed study of the insurance and banking industry, the success rate is probably a little but not much better. Some of the more obvious cases include firms put under duress by the timing and price of their acquisitions, for example, Bank of America's acquisition of Merrill Lynch and Countrywide Financial and Royal Bank of Scotland's acquisition of ABN Amro just prior to the 2008 financial crisis.

The success rate also suffers as firms expand into areas outside their core expertise and into areas which, in retrospect, were either strategically or operationally challenging for them to manage. Examples include the acquisition of investment banking businesses by retail and commercial banks – such as Dresdner's acquisition of Kleinwort Benson and Wasserstein Parella, Union Bank of Switzerland's acquisition of SG Warburg, Pain Webber and (as SBC) Dillon Read, as well as acquisitions in pursuit of bancassurance strategies, including those already mentioned – for example, Citibank and Travelers Insurance, Credit Suisse and Winterthur, Allianz and Dresdner Bank, ING, Fortis, etc.

Nonetheless, there have also been a large number of firms which have been successful in growth through acquisitions. Looking at the list of US banks in Sidebar11.3, the "regionals" and "super regionals" in the USA, including Wells Fargo, BB&T, US Bancorp, PNC Bancorp, Fifth Third, Regions Financial and UnionBanCal, stand out in particular; all of these firms grew substantially through acquisition but managed to retain a focused strategy, eschewing transformational deals for those that played to their core strengths in regional retail and commercial banking. Most of these firms enjoy a healthy valuation premium to other banks today, in part because they "stuck to their knitting" and learned how to knit very well.

What conclusions can be drawn? Profitable growth is more likely to be achieved through bolt-on acquisitions in or near the company's core product and market segment: although typically paying a premium, the valuation premium is based more on concrete expense synergies rather than more nebulous revenue synergies; there are fewer cultural challenges to be resolved and the underlying business is well understood. All these factors bode well for a successful acquisition and later integration.

The view that "bolt-on" and adjacent acquisitions can add value and have a higher success rate compared with transformational deals is also shared by others. Nolop (2007) writes in the *Harvard Business Review*: "Adjacent moves yield better results . . . because they capitalize on the company's tacit strengths and are brand consistent in the eyes of customers. Rather than focusing on big, game-changing deals, it's better to make many smaller acquisitions. This approach poses less risk and produces more predictable financial results over time."

SIDEBAR 11.3: GROWTH THROUGH ACQUISITION, US BANKING

Acquisitions have fuelled the growth of many banks and insurers. Consider the list in Table 11.4 of the top 25 banks and bank holding groups in the USA in 2012.[4]

From the top to the bottom of the list, virtually all have grown significantly through acquisition. As the names imply, JP Morgan Chase and Bank of New York Mellon are the direct products of mergers; but hidden behind these names and the others are a significant track record of acquisitions, as illustrated in Table 11.5 providing an incomplete listing of transactions after 1990 (Hardak, 2012).

TABLE 11.4 2012 Top 25 US banks by asset size, USD bn

	Bank	Value		Bank	Value
1	JP Morgan Chase	2265.8	14	Capital One Financial Corp.	206.1
2	Bank of America Corp.	2136.6	15	TD Bank US Holding Company	201.1
3	Citigroup Inc.	1873.9	16	ALLY Financial Inc.	184.1
4	Wells Fargo	1313.9	17	SunTrust Banks, Inc.	176.9
5	Goldman Sachs Group	923.7	18	BB&T Corporation	174.6
6	Metlife, Inc.	799.6	19	American Express	152.3
7	Morgan Stanley	749.9	20	RBS Citizens Financial Group, Inc.	129.8
8	Taunus Corp.	354.7	21	Regions Financial Corp.	127.1
9	U.S. Bancorp	340.1	22	BMO Financial Corp.	117.4
10	HSBC North America Holdings Inc.	331.4	23	Fifth Third Bancorp	116.9
11	Bank of New York Mellon Corp.	325.8	24	Northern Trust Corp.	100.2
12	PNC Group	271.4	25	UnionBanCal Corp.	89.7
13	State Street Corporation	216.4			

---

[4]banksdaily.com, http://www.banksdaily.com/topbanks/USA/2012.html

TABLE 11.5   Selected US bank mergers since 1990

	Acquired bank	Acquiring bank	Ultimate parent		Acquired bank	Acquiring bank	Ultimate parent
1990	First Pennsylvania Bank	CoreStates Financial Corp.	Wells Fargo	1999	BankBoston Corp.	FleetBoston Financial Corp.	Bank of America
1990	Florida National Bank	First Union Corp.	Wells Fargo	1999	Bankers Trust Corp.	Deutsche Bank AG	Deutsche Bank
1990	Sovran Financial Corp.	C&S/Sovran Corp.	Bank of America	1999	Republic New York Corp.	HSBC Bank USA	HSBC Bank USA
1991	Bank of New England	Fleet/Norstar Financial Group, Inc.	Bank of America	1999	Mercantile Bancorp., Inc.	Firstar Corp.	U.S. Bancorp.
1991	C&S/Sovran Corp.	NationsBank Corp.	Bank of America	1999	First American National Bank	AmSouth Bancorp.	Regions Financial
1991	United Bank of Denver	Norwest Corp.	Wells Fargo	2000	JP Morgan & Co., Inc.	JP Morgan Chase & Co.	JP Morgan Chase
1991	The South Carolina National Bank	Wachovia	Wells Fargo	2000	Bank United Corp.	Washington Mutual	JP Morgan Chase
1991	Southeast Banking Corp.	First Union Corp.	Wells Fargo	2000	First Security Corp.	Wells Fargo & Co.	Wells Fargo
1991	Summcorp.	NBD Bank	JP Morgan Chase	2000	Paine Webber	UBS AG	UBS AG
1991	Ameritrust Corp.	Society Corp.	KeyBank	2001	U.S. Bancorp	U.S. Bancorp	U.S. Bancorp
1991	Madison National Bank	Signet Banking Corp.	Wells Fargo	2001	Wachovia	Wachovia	Wells Fargo
1992	Security Pacific Corp.	BankAmerica Corp.	Bank of America	2001	Old Kent Financial Corp.	Fifth Third Bancorp.	Fifth Third Bank
1992	Puget Sound National Bank	Keycorp.	KeyBank	2001	Michigan National Bank	Standard Federal Bank	Bank of America
1992	First Florida Bank	Barnett Banks, Inc.	Bank of America	2001	Summit Bancorp.	FleetBoston Financial Corp.	Bank of America
1992	Manufacturers Bank	Comerica	Comerica	2002	Golden State Bancorp.	Citigroup	Citigroup
1992	INB Financial Corp.	NBD Bancorp.	JP Morgan Chase	2002	Dime Bancorp., Inc.	Washington Mutual	JP Morgan Chase
1992	Manufacturers Hanover Trust Co.	Chemical Bank	JP Morgan Chase	2002	Household International, Inc.	HSBC Bank USA	HSBC Bank USA
1993	Colorado National Bank	First Bank System, Inc.	U.S. Bancorp.	2003	1st Virginia Banks, Inc.	BB&T Corp.	BB&T
1993	The Valley National Bank of Arizona	Banc One Corp.	JP Morgan Chase	2003	Allfirst Bank	M&T Bank	M&T Bank
1993	South Shore Bank, Mechanics Bank, First Agricultural	Bank of Boston Corp.	Bank of America	2004	Savings Bank of Manchester, Tolland Bank	NewAlliance Bank	NewAlliance Bank
1993	Dominion Bank	First Union Corp.	Wells Fargo	2004	The Trust of New Jersey	North Fork Bancorp., Inc.	Capital One Financial

(continued)

TABLE 11.5 *(Continued)*

	Acquired bank	Acquiring bank	Ultimate parent		Acquired bank	Acquiring bank	Ultimate parent
1993	First American Bankcorp.	First Union Corp.	Wells Fargo	2004	FleetBoston Financial Corp.	Bank of America Corp.	Bank of America
1993	Maryland National Bank	NationsBank Corp.	Bank of America	2004	Bank One	JP Morgan Chase	JP Morgan Chase
1993	American Security Bank	NationsBank Corp.	Bank of America	2004	Quaker City Bank	Banco Popular	Banco Popular
1994	Keycorp.	Keycorp.	KeyBank	2004	Union Planters Corp.	Regions Financial Corp.	Regions Financial
1994	Pioneer Financial Corp.	Signet Banking Corp.	Wells Fargo	2004	National Commerce Financial	SunTrust	SunTrust Banks
1994	Continental Illinois National Bank	BankAmerica Corp.	Bank of America	2004	SouthTrust	Wachovia	Wells Fargo
1995	Deerbank Corp.	NBD Bank	JP Morgan Chase	2005	Riggs Bank	PNC Bank	PNC
1995	NBD Bank	First Chicago NBD	JP Morgan Chase	2005	Hibernia National Bank	Capital One Financial	Capital One Financial
1995	Southern National Corp.	BB&T Corp.	BB&T	2005	MBNA Corp.	Bank of America Card Services	Bank of America
1995	Shawmut National Corp.	Fleet Financial Group, Inc.	Bank of America	2006	Westcorp Inc.	Wachovia	Wells Fargo
1996	First Interstate Bancorp.	Wells Fargo Corp.	Wells Fargo	2006	Cornerstone Bank	NewAlliance Bank	NewAlliance Bank
1996	Bank of California	Union Bank of California	Union Bank N. A.	2006	North Fork Bank	Capital One Financial	Capital One Financial
1996	Chase Manhattan Corp.	Chase Manhattan Corp.	JP Morgan Chase	2006	Golden West Financial	Wachovia	Wells Fargo
1996	Meridian Bancorp., Inc.	CoreStates Financial Corp.	Wells Fargo	2006	AmSouth Bancorp.	Regions Financial Corp.	Regions Financial
1996	BayBanks, Inc.	BankBoston Corp.	Bank of America	2007	Republic Bancorp.	Citizens Republic Bancorp.	FirstMerit Bank
1996	First Fidelity Bank	First Union Corp.	Wells Fargo	2007	Compass Bancshares	BBVA Compass	BBVA Compass
1996	Center Financial Corp.	First Union Corp.	Wells Fargo	2007	LaSalle Bank	Bank of America	Bank of America
1996	National Westminster Bancorp.	Fleet Financial Group, Inc.	Bank of America	2007	Investors Financial Services Corp.	State Street Corp.	State Street Corp.
1996	Citizens Bancorp. (Laurel, MD)	Crestar Financial Corp.	SunTrust Banks	2007	Mellon Financial Corp.	Bank of New York Mellon	Bank of New York Mellon
1997	First Bank System, Inc.	U.S. Bancorp.	U.S. Bancorp.	2007	World Savings Bank	Wachovia	Wells Fargo
1997	Boatmen's Bancshares	NationsBank Corp.	Bank of America	2007	U.S. Trust Corp.	Bank of America	Bank of America
1997	Great Western Financial Corp.	Washington Mutual	JP Morgan Chase	2007	Partners Trust Financial Group	M&T Bank	M&T Bank

(continued)

TABLE 11.5 (*Continued*)

	Acquired bank	Acquiring bank	Ultimate parent		Acquired bank	Acquiring bank	Ultimate parent
1997	Signet Banking Corp.	First Union Corp.	Wells Fargo	2008	Commerce Bancorp.	TD Bank, N.A.	TD Bank, N.A.
1997	First Bank of America Bank	National City Corp.	PNC	2008	Bear Stearns	JP Morgan Chase	JP Morgan Chase
1997	First USA	Bank One Corp.	JP Morgan Chase	2008	Merrill Lynch	Bank of America	Bank of America
1997	California Federal Bank	California Federal Bank	Citibank	2008	Wachovia	Wells Fargo	Wells Fargo
1998	Barnett Banks, Inc.	NationsBank Corp.	Bank of America	2008	Washington Mutual	JP Morgan Chase	JP Morgan Chase
1998	CoreStates Financial Corp.	First Union Corp.	Wells Fargo	2008	First Charter Bank	Fifth Third Bank	Fifth Third Bank
1998	BankAmerica Corp.	Bank of America Corp.	Bank of America	2008	National City Corp.	PNC	PNC
1998	First Nationwide Holdings, Inc.	Golden State Bancorp.	Citigroup	2008	Downey Savings and Loan	U.S. Bancorp.	U.S. Bancorp.
1998	Wells Fargo Corp.	Wells Fargo Corp.	Wells Fargo	2009	Provident Bank of Maryland	M&T Bank	M&T Bank
1998	Firstar Holdings Corp.	Firstar Corp.	U.S. Bancorp.	2009	Bradford Bank	M&T Bank	M&T Bank
1998	First Chicago NBD	Bank One Corp.	JP Morgan Chase	2011	Wilmington Trust	M&T Bank	M&T Bank
1998	First Commerce Corp.	Bank One Corp.	JP Morgan Chase	2011	ING Direct USA	Capital One	Capital One
1998	Citicorp.	Citigroup	Citigroup	2012	RBC Bank	PNC	PNC
1998	Crestar Financial Corp.	SunTrust Banks, Inc.	SunTrust Banks	2013	Citizens Republic Bancorp.	FirstMerit Bank	FirstMerit Bank
1998	H.F. Ahmanson	Washington Mutual	JP Morgan Chase				

HORIZON 3 – CREATIVE DISRUPTIONS

Horizon 3 focuses on longer-term options or "bets," which may be less clear, more uncertain and further off on the horizon. Often, they are associated with a vision of how technology can be used to disrupt existing business models or provide new products and services – in other words, not only betting on the "next big thing" but also contributing to making it happen.

Examples can be found in McKinsey's (2013a) list of 12 potentially disruptive technologies, including mobile Internet, intelligent software, Internet-linked network sensors, the "cloud," advanced robotics, self-driving vehicles and next-generation genomics. Other potential sources of change include nanotechnology and synthetic biology.

Each of these has the potential to impact insurance and banking in profound ways. Focusing narrowly on the insurance industry: the combination of the mobile Internet, GPS and sensor technologies is already leading to a change in how automobile insurance is provided and priced through telematics, with Pay As You Drive (PAYD) premium rates in principle being adjusted based on real-time driving behavior, weather conditions and location of the vehicle. They also create the possibility to provide tailored, short-term, context-specific insurance offerings, for example covering specific and short-term travel and assistance needs. These technologies also have the possibility to change health insurance and assisted care by allowing remote monitoring and diagnosis through wearable wireless devices.

The flipside of every opportunity is risk. Just as the Internet was disruptive to traditional sales channels, telematics will adversely impact those companies that are not prepared. And some technological advances – such as self-driving vehicles – will open up new legal uncertainties as society comes to grips with who is at fault for an accident: the "driver" or the manufacturer?

Banks and insurers who have vision and a strategy to exploit that vision have the potential to change an industry and create new opportunities for themselves, opportunities that others may have a hard time following.

Success in Horizon 3 initiatives requires taking manageable, long-term bets and a commitment to not only build the capabilities, but actually change the way the market operates.

CHAPTER 12

Achieving Operating Efficiency

Bankers and asset managers use cost/income ratios, insurers use expense ratios. Although each industry uses a different metric, each is used to help understand, compare and manage the cost of producing the next euro of revenue or income. As such, they all represent a measure of operating efficiency, one of the five KPIs which have a direct and material impact on the franchise value of the firm, as illustrated in Figure 12.1.

A balanced discussion of operating efficiency is timely: in lieu of any real growth prospects in developed economies, operating efficiency and expense management was the lever of choice for many banks and insurers during the 2008–2013 turbulence and subsequent weak economic recovery.

Some banks and insurers reacted to the crisis with broad-based cost savings programs – for example, across-the-board expense and FTE reductions, delaying critical IT investment, squeezing suppliers in an effort to "share the pain" – all of which were designed to deliver

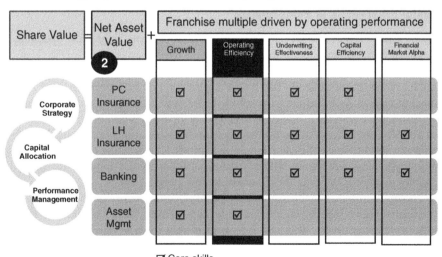

2. Better Insights –
What strategies, initiatives and KPIs by segment?

☑ Core skills

FIGURE 12.1 Operating efficiency as key driver of franchise value

short-term benefits (Accenture, 2008; BCG, 2013; McKinsey, 2013b). According to Price-waterhouseCoopers (2009), "Combating the worst financial crisis in living memory was never going to be easy, and immediate survival and associated cost reduction have therefore been the primary priorities for most financial services organizations."

Unfortunately, some of the short-term benefits may come at the expense of long-term potential value creation. While it is important to tighten the belt during lean periods, it is much better to address expense and efficiency issues continuously rather than being forced into sporadic action by market circumstances. On the one hand, some short-term cost improvement "programs" may cut more than fat, going through to the bone and impairing the company's long-term potential. On the other hand, some of the most important levers for improving cost efficiency require careful preparation, initial investment and time to implement.

Some of the most important strategies and management actions for improving operating efficiency, discussed in greater detail in this chapter, include the following.

- Improving procurement practices.
- Reorganizing service and administration activities through business process re-engineering (e.g., centralization and shared services, near-shoring, off-shoring) and deciding whether you are the best "manufacturer" for the re-engineered business processes (e.g., outsourcing).
- Re-engineering the product portfolio (e.g., portfolio complexity reduction as well as product standardization and modularization).
- Better leveraging information technology to improve the business system (e.g., digitalization, automation and straight-through processing).

THE IMPORTANCE OF OPERATING EFFICIENCY

Operating efficiency is important for three reasons.

Meaningful Differences in Performance

First, *because there is a wide difference in productivity across firms*, even those operating in the same segment and following the same strategy.

As an example, consider the European banking industry. According to one study (Little, 2008), the average European bank had a cost/income ratio of 59% between 2004 and 2006, with the best bank at 38% and the worst above 80%. Across Europe, there were pronounced national differences, with the average German bank at 73.5% and the average Spanish and UK bank at 50.5%. This means that the average German bank had to generate roughly 50% more top line if it wanted to make the same bottom-line profit, all else being equal! These averages naturally mask large variations within each country, with the top-quartile firms being substantially more efficient than their bottom-quartile peers.

As another example, consider the US PC industry over the period 2009–2011. A 2012 study compared the average expense ratios of the largest, medium and smallest PC insurers in the USA, which were 29%, 32% and 35%, respectively (StoneRidge Advisors, 2012). By definition, these averages mask variations within each category. However, even at the average expense ratio, the difference between the largest and smallest firms translates into an average 6 cent benefit on every dollar premium, which is significant.

Important Value Implications

The second reason is because *differences in cost efficiency represent a "currency" that can be converted into shareholder value*, either directly in terms of higher distributable cash or indirectly in terms of supporting a virtuous cycle of profitable growth.

Returning to the US PC industry, a 6% difference in expense ratios is equivalent to a $30 potential difference in price for a $500 automobile insurance policy. This is pricing power, which can be used to grow the business (e.g., in segments with higher price elasticity) or to improve the underwriting result by offering lower rates to segments with better driving performance. In the end, the cost advantage can lead to greater market share or better underwriting results or both, creating a virtual cycle of profitable growth.

Alternatively, the difference can be returned to shareholders. In the US PC market, the 6% difference in expense ratio materially explains the difference in average combined ratios and return on surplus for the largest versus the smallest firms, 101% vs. 105% and 8.1% vs. 0.3%, respectively. To state the obvious, higher cost efficiency directly contributes to higher profitability and shareholder returns; not a surprising result. And, while the average US PC market was not spectacular from a technical underwriting perspective during this soft market period, the difference in returns is nonetheless noteworthy for shareholders.

Management Influence

The third reason is because *you determine the result – management decisions and commitment are the key to cost efficiency*. Put differently, the actions that you take (or do not take) determine whether your firm will be in the top or the bottom quartile.

Factors Which Influence Operating Efficiency

Beyond differences in cost allocation methodologies, there are three commonly recognized factors which influence a firm's operating efficiency: scale, strategy and local specifics.

Differences in scale. All else being equal, firms with higher market share may have a structural cost advantage relative to other firms as they leverage their fixed costs over more volume, driving average cost down.

In addition, greater scale improves negotiation power with distributors (lowering acquisition costs) and suppliers (lowering the cost of goods sold, e.g. for IT and consulting services). Evidence for a scale effect can be found in the US PC example earlier, with the largest firms on average enjoying a 6% lower expense ratio relative to the smallest firms.

Differences in business strategy. These also drive structural cost differences. Some differentiated strategies which typically impact cost efficiency ratios include the following.

- *Higher service offerings versus "no frills" execution.* All things being equal, higher service quality costs more to deliver. Not surprisingly, Swiss private banking and wealth management businesses are likely to have higher relative expense levels compared with Charles Schwab retail brokerage and ING Direct deposit savings products. Similarly, direct auto insurers such as Geico will have a per policy cost advantage compared with companies focusing on high net worth or mass affluent individuals such as Chubb, Travelers or Fireman's Fund.
- *High returns to human capital.* Some businesses require skilled labor, which commands a higher share of the firm's profits. For example, investment banks have higher employee

cost ratios than commercial and retail banks, ostensibly because of the higher skill level required to generate revenues and the competitive market for those skilled resources.

■ *Product complexity.* Generally, more complexity translates into more costs. One key driver of complexity, with implications from sales to back-office administration, is the diversity of products offered and the degree of product standardization.

Local market specificities. Some markets simply have different cost characteristics than others. For example, labor markets across Europe are differentiated by the flexibility of employment conditions, working hours, minimum wage levels and mandated benefits. In addition, penetration and usage rates for the Internet and mobile devices may differ, making lower-cost forms of product delivery and after-sales service more or less feasible. Also, local regulations, especially those focused on consumer protection (e.g., transparency on commissions and fees, documentation requirements for informed consent, etc.), may drive structural cost differences across countries. Finally, the maturity and dominance of competitive intermediary channels may also drive differences.

The Most Important Factor – Management Action

These three factors – scale, strategy and local specificity – help to explain a large amount of the differences in operating efficiency. However, they do not explain *all* of the differences.

In fact, the most important differentiating factor between top- and bottom-quartile firms is that *some firms are simply more efficient than others, even after normalizing for scale, strategy and local specificity.* The simple fact is that some firms can get more sales time and higher closing rates out of a similar sales force than other firms, thereby lowering acquisition costs. Some firms are able to administer the same transaction or policy at a lower average unit cost, but for the same volume of contracts, due to automation, straight-through processing, lower error rates and/or better sourcing and utilization of labor.

There is ample evidence that cost efficiency is heavily driven by management focus and execution. In fact, there is evidence that the major differences in productivity across financial services firms in the same industry are better explained by differences in execution, and not by differences in scale (potentially a type of cost synergy) or scope (potentially a type of revenue synergy).

Berger and Humphrey (1994) state: "Scale and scope economies in banking are not found to be important, except for the smallest banks. X-Efficiency, or the managerial ability to control costs, is of much greater magnitude – at least 20% of banking costs." Taking it one step further, Berger et al. (1993) conclude that the inefficiencies in US banking are large, ". . . the industry appears to lose about half of its potential variable profits to inefficiency. Not surprisingly, technical inefficiencies dominate allocative inefficiencies, suggesting that banks are not particularly poor at choosing input and output plans, but rather are poor at carrying out these plans."

In summary, cost efficiency is not something that is uniquely determined by your products, markets and strategy in some fatalistic process of predetermination – *cost-efficient firms are cost efficient because they manage their costs and execute better and cheaper than their peers.*

A Digression on Cost Allocation

Expenses are typically aggregated, reported and compared as KPIs in three broad categories – *acquisition expenses*, *administration expenses* and *general overhead expenses*. Comparing acquisition or administration expense ratios across firms can be challenging because the methodologies for allocating costs across business segments and products or between overhead versus operating expenses may not be comparable across firms or even across products within the same firm. Comparability issues arise due to different definitions of line of business or product, the definition of allocated and overhead cost categories and the keys used to allocate the costs.

Operating expenses come from different sources, representing different *factor costs*, defined as *the cost per unit of input or factor of production*; for example, wages and benefits paid to employees; IT non-wage expenses including cost of data, software licenses, personal computers, other hardware and communication infrastructure; expenses for facilities – offices for own use – and services; other expenses such as travel and entertainment, consulting services, materials, etc.

Some of these factor cost categories are directly managed. For example, it is not uncommon for firms to have explicit initiatives limiting external consulting expenses or own-use office expenses.

Unfortunately, managing expenses based on factor cost categories is not always useful: wages are paid along every stage of the value chain, from front-office sales to back-office administration. If management blindly sets out to cut wage expenses without having some idea of what value you get for the wages paid – is it top-line revenue, back-office operations, customer service, etc.? – the results will be similar to swinging a bat at a piñata: you might get lucky, but you might also hit an innocent bystander.

In order to intelligently manage expenses, you first need to understand what value you get for the expenditure and why. Ultimately, this requires an expense allocation framework along the {customer, product, market, channel} dimensions in addition to distinguishing between factor costs and acquisition, administration and overhead categories. A granular level of cost allocation is a prerequisite for understanding whether a customer relationship is profitable, whether some customers or products are cross-subsidizing others, and whether some products and services are not more profitably sold through one channel or another.

While there are many approaches to cost allocation, the most useful is Activity-Based Costing (ABC). Allocating costs within a complex organization is an art and, with all things artistic, some firms seem to go more for realism and others seemingly for more abstract or even surreal. Sidebar 12.1 provides some insights into cost allocation approaches.

SIDEBAR 12.1: COST ALLOCATION APPROACHES

This sidebar outlines at a high level the main underlying concepts of a cost allocation framework.[1]

Cost Categorization

Direct costs are defined as "costs which can be accurately traced to a cost object with little effort. A cost object may be a product, a department, a project, etc. A particular cost may be direct cost for one cost object but indirect cost for another cost object." Examples include sales commissions for products and personnel expenses for a department.

---

[1] http://accountingexplained.com/managerial/costs/direct-and-indirect-costs

Indirect costs are defined as "costs which cannot be accurately attributed to specific cost objects. These typically benefit multiple cost objects and it is impracticable to accurately trace them to individual products, activities or departments, etc." Examples include call center personnel expenses.

Cost Allocation Principles

The objective is to allocate most or all direct and indirect costs along the {customer, product, market, channel} dimensions, a task made complicated by overhead departments or internal service providers such as IT, operations, call centers, etc. There are two approaches to allocating total costs to {customer, product, market, channel} couples: the traditional approach and the ABC approach.

Traditional Approach

The traditional approach to allocating costs is to follow a three-step process (Mabberley, 1996; CIMA, 2008):

1. Aggregate direct production costs by production unit. The production unit is typically defined along the product dimension (e.g., mortgages or insurance policies, etc.).
2. Aggregate non-production, overhead and service center costs (indirect costs) and allocate to production units based on a combination of high-level allocation keys (e.g., personnel expenses, transaction volumes, IT expenditure, etc.).[2]
3. Allocate the sum of direct production and allocated in-direct costs to {customer, product, market, channel} based on high-level allocation keys (e.g., the planned or actual number of transactions produced).

The decision to allocate costs based on plan or actual volumes is a key determinant of who bears the risk of a sales shortfall relative to plan and who bears the risk of an expense over-run due to an unexpected increase in factor costs.

There are three primary issues with this traditional cost allocation approach. The first is that the final allocation to {customer, product, market, channel} becomes increasingly arbitrary as the percentage of overhead expenses increases and as the number of products produced by the production unit increases. The second is that it is impossible to disentangle marginal versus full costs. The final issue is that it is possible to "game" the system, reallocating expenses between products or channels in order to flatter returns of one at the expense of the other. All these issues can lead to incorrect decisions as some products implicitly subsidize others.

---

[2]Note, this is the *direct or one-to-one approach*, drawing a direct line between overhead or service centers and production departments. For more complicated organizations with interim service centers, one might also consider a *sequential approach* (e.g., start with one service center, allocate to other services without reversing, then continue sequentially along the chain until you hit the production department) or a *simultaneous allocation* (e.g., allocate to production and services simultaneously, all at once).

Activity-based Cost Allocation

ABC addresses these issues by replacing the allocation keys with keys based on activity units and rigorous analysis. For example, the indirect costs might be broken down into activities such as procurement, policy or contract administration, claims or cash flow settlement, etc. Based on these activities, costs are allocated using more granular keys (e.g., the number of purchase orders, number and/or complexity of contracts administered, number of settlement operations, etc.).

ABC provides more accurate information on product economics and more transparency on where costs occur along the value chain. However, it can be challenging if taken to an extreme, leading to a very large activity inventory and definitions which are not stable as organizational units change.

ALLOCATION BASIS

There are three bases for evaluating a product's costs once the allocation has been done: the marginal approach; the direct, variable-cost approach; the fully loaded cost approach.

- *Marginal basis.* This approach allocates only those incremental expenses which are caused by each incremental transaction, limited to variable expenses directly attributable to the transaction. These expenses might include, for example, variable sales commissions, variable contract administration expenses, etc.
- *Average, direct basis.* This approach allocates only expenses which are directly related to the transaction or business, including both variable and fixed expenses. Under this approach, the fixed sales and administration expenses associated with the business are also allocated to each transaction based on an allocation key. The allocations are set such that the planned direct expenses are fully allocated if the planned volumes are met. In case planned volumes are not achieved, an expense overrun occurs.
- *Fully loaded basis.* This approach fully allocates both direct and indirect expenses. Indirect expenses include all corporate expenses not directly attributable to the business or product, for example the expenses associated with corporate reporting and shareholder services.

Most companies operating in mature markets set technical pricing benchmarks based on average, direct expense loadings. In some cases, a cost overrun based on higher targeted volumes may be acceptable in segments where rapid and material growth is planned, generating a predictable cost overrun until volumes catch up with long-run plans.

Marginal pricing may be allowed in special circumstances but should require explicit approval and an explicit limit or budget. The rationale is that marginal cost pricing does not guarantee that the firm will generate sufficient revenue to cover all its costs. In other words, the company can fail even though the products may look profitable "on the margin."

Fully loaded expense allocations are not often used as they tend to put local operating subsidiaries at a disadvantage relative to purely local players.

RULES OF THE GAME

Efficiency[3] can be defined as "a measure of whether the right amount of resources have been used to deliver a process, service or activity. An efficient process achieves its objectives with the minimum amount of time, money, people or other resources."

Following industry practice, I characterize operating efficiency in terms of a bank's cost/income ratio or an insurer's expense ratio. These are the most common measures of operating efficiency, putting all inputs and all outputs in a common numeraire – the euro costs needed to generate a euro of income or revenue.[4] These measures of operating efficiency are influenced by three factors.

Equation 12.1: Decomposition of cost income ratio

$$CIR = \frac{Cost}{Input} \times \frac{Input}{Output} \times \frac{Output}{Income}$$

- The *cost per unit of input* (e.g., the average cost of personnel, per square meter of office or branch facilities, of a workstation or gigabyte of memory, etc.).
- The *translation of inputs into the output* (e.g., how much labor or retail space is required for the products and services sold).
- The *income per unit of output*, reflecting both product pricing as well as product mix and channel strategy.

This decomposition is useful. It suggests that improvements in the cost/income or expense ratio are going to come from:

- decreasing the *average cost of the resources employed* (e.g., personnel, facilities, IT, materials, etc.) while maintaining the same level of quality;
- decreasing the *average amount of resources* used for the delivery of a given product or service, reflecting efficiency gains and scale.

In other words, either pay less for the resources used or use less resources, but more efficiently. These observations lead to the following "rules of the game" for managing operating efficiency, discussed and motivated in the remainder of this chapter.

RULES OF THE GAME: MANAGING OPERATING EFFICIENCY

Improving operating efficiency requires a culture of continuously focusing on the details in terms of costs and processes and undertaking specific initiatives.

Pay less and decrease the average cost of inputs by:

- improving procurement practices while maintaining quality;
- relocating support and services to less expensive locations or service models, including *on-shoring*, *off-shoring* and *outsourcing*.

[3]Information Technology Infrastructure Library (ITIL) v3, http://www.itil-officialsite.com/home/home.asp

[4]From a value management perspective, it might be better to define efficiency measures as the cost per unit of risk-adjusted operating profit, however this is not done in practice.

> *Use less* but get more out if it by:
>
> - re-engineering the entire value chain, increasing the efficiency and effectiveness of processes, through
>   - business process re-engineering and centralizing support and administrative processes,
>   - reducing product portfolio complexity through product standardization, modularization and active product portfolio management,
>   - digitalization, leading to increased automation and straight-through processing;
> - making individual, standalone processes efficient and effective, especially in sales, administration and IT development and maintenance;
> - continually challenging non-operating expenses, especially head office expenses and corporate overheads.

Management actions to improve efficiency fall into two categories: pay less for resources used or use less resources, but more efficiently.

PAY LESS: OPTIMIZE PROCUREMENT

Procurement is the business function which optimizes the acquisition of goods and services, taking into consideration the cost, quality and intended purpose or use.

In a recent survey (KPMG, 2012), the average benefit from improving procurement practices was between 4% and 9% for indirect spend (e.g., spend which does not flow directly into the manufacturing process and includes, e.g., consulting services, IT support and services, materials, etc.).

Professional procurement practices can create value in two ways: first, by consolidating purchasing power for products and services, increasing your leverage in negotiations with suppliers; second, by professionalizing the purchase of more complex products and services.

Consolidating purchasing power is done by:

- centralizing the purchase of materials or services (especially those that are more "commodity-like") across the company into a single procurement unit, thereby increasing the firm's negotiating position vis à vis suppliers;
- narrowing the supplier base so that the spend is increasingly relevant from the suppliers' perspective;
- using the purchasing power to directly negotiate preferred supplier relationships (or joining purchasing or buying groups if the company does not have the requisite scale);
- entering into longer-term contracts with suppliers, further consolidating purchasing power over time.

In most banks and insurers, the purchasing of all materials, IT services, travel and other services is centralized and governed by preferred supplier relationships.

Professionalizing negotiation for more complex products and services can create value by bringing a better understanding of the firm's needs and how they can be met when negotiating with vendors. For example, negotiating software licenses and maintenance agreements can lead to savings as you pay only for the services you need and structure the service and maintenance agreement accordingly (e.g., in terms of the number of users, the definition of use-based payment keys, systems availability requirements, on-site or remote service provision, etc.).

Success in procurement is not always about negotiating the lowest price. It is also about ensuring that quality levels are appropriate and that the lifetime costs are optimized, including the costs and ease of interfacing with the suppliers as well as the ongoing procurement expenses.

In addition, successful procurement programs should minimize the risks of using too small a panel of suppliers for critical services. The procurement function should use a balanced scorecard and critically assess whether the supply can be disrupted as well as whether the balance of power in a negotiation can flip as you turn from a large purchaser to a tied purchaser.

PAY LESS: FROM BUSINESS PROCESS REDESIGN TO OUTSOURCING

Financial institutions have historically had a strong presence on Wall Street due to their role in financing the economy and capital development. They have also had a strong presence on Main Street in serving retail and SME customers. These locations tend to be expensive, both in terms of physical space and the all-in cost of labor. In addition, physically locating *all* activities in each individual location can lead to differences in processes and productivity and a failure to capture economies of scale and knowledge.

Not all activities along the bank or insurer's value chain need to be physically located on Wall Street or Main Street. Given the advances in information and communications technology (ICT), banks and insurers can physically decouple back-office and other support, service and administration activities from front-office sales and service activities, allowing greater flexibility in terms of location.

In addition, not all activities along the value chain need to be "owned" and managed by the bank or insurer. Some might be better provided by a third party if the supplier can achieve increased scale and impose greater standardization and process discipline.

Reflecting these facts, banks and insurers improve operating efficiency by working along three dimensions, as illustrated in Figure 12.2:

- Business Process Re-engineering (BPR) to develop standardized, automated, efficient processes while simultaneously decoupling and centralizing selected activities into shared service centers, using IT to create a seamless process in the eyes of customers;
- relocating activities to lower-cost locations, including *near-shoring* (locating outside the broader metropolitan area where the customer is being served) and *off-shoring* (sourcing services from outside the country where the end customer is being served) (Sako, 2005);
- deciding what to produce yourself ("make") versus what to purchase from a service provider ("buy"), leading to *outsourcing*.

Business Process re-engineering

The first dimension involves getting your house in order. BPR is the analysis and redesign of workflows and business processes to improve costs and customer service. IT, especially telecommunication and wireless networks, shared databases and expert/decision support

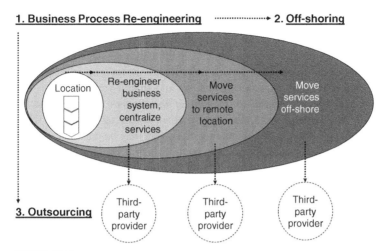

FIGURE 12.2 Off-shoring and outsourcing in context

systems (Hammer and Champy, 1993), supports BPR by enabling new ways of organizing work and collaborating across organizational and physical borders. This allows some activities and processes to be extracted and centralized either virtually through automation or physically into shared service centers.

However, the full benefits of BPR come not just from automating what you currently do – it is more about fundamentally rethinking what you are doing, why you are doing it and how it is getting done. Hammer (1990) suggests that a key benefit of BPR is in eliminating activities that are not value adding in the first place.

Corbett (2004) cites an interesting anecdote about General Electric, which re-engineered its accounting (payables, payroll and accounts receivable) activities in two steps. The first step in 1988 was to re-engineer and centralize processes, reducing costs by 60% and employees by a more modest 17%. The second step, in 1989, was to outsource those activities, leading to a further cost reduction of 20%.

The point is that BPR is *not only a prerequisite for the near-shoring, off-shoring or outsourcing of various re-engineered processes, it can also be the most significant contributor to operating efficiency in its own right* (BCG, 2004). Near-shoring, off-shoring and outsourcing will not work without a foundation of well-defined and well-engineered business processes, physically decoupled, optimized and centralized, and this is a valuable objective in its own right.

Hall et al. (1993) posit in the *Harvard Business Review* that there are three factors which make BPR projects successful.

- First, BPR will not *"move the dial"* if the scope is too narrowly defined (called "breadth" by the authors). The authors cite examples of finance functions which enjoyed a 34% cost reduction and an insurer which improved claims processing times by 44%, none of which had a meaningful impact on earnings simply because the cost contribution was relatively small to begin with. In addition to focusing on processes and expense blocks which "matter," focus BPR efforts broadly enough, looking "up and down, left and right" in order to capture efficiency gains in up- and downstream activities, in the hand-offs between functional areas as well as combining steps which span functions.

■ *Second, BPR has to actually change something* (called "depth" by the authors). Put succinctly, you should not expect significant impact if you simply relabel and move existing processes or activities unchanged. BPR initiatives will not deliver meaningful results unless they materially impact more than one of six critical areas, including structure, skills, IT systems, roles, incentives and shared values.

■ *Third, because of the breadth and depth of the change, management had better be committed!* The challenges are the same whether we are talking about BPR and shared service centers, off-shoring or outsourcing: managers may be reluctant to lose control over the processes, it represents a significant change which is not always appreciated, and the relationship between the service provider and the business has to be well defined, integrated and managed. These challenges cannot be overcome without significant commitment by all.

Whether for service centers, off-shoring or outsourcing, this last point is especially important: in order to capture the value, the relationship between the business and service provider must be both at the working level, to get things done, and at the most senior level, to break log-jams when necessary.

In addition, the relationship needs to be governed by concretely defined objectives, service levels and change management processes, all contained within an explicit Service Level Agreement (SLA). Finally, the performance under the SLA needs to be made transparent and managed through regular reporting, scorecards and escalation procedures.

Most companies begin with re-engineering lower value added, repetitive activities such as back-office transaction processing, product administration and service and support call centers. Over time, these have expanded to include higher value added, knowledge-intensive processes such as underwriting, claims management, finance and accounting, corporate actuarial, compliance and risk management as well as legal, contracting and other professional services. Finally, virtually all companies decouple IT support, administration, Application Development and Maintenance (ADM).

Near-shoring, Off-shoring

Once some of the redesigned activities are centralized, the second dimension is: *How far to relocate?* As illustrated in Figure 12.2, relocation can be thought of in terms of concentric circles around Wall Street or Main Street. The first circle represents a move from the city center to the suburbs, often leading to a reduction in facilities and personnel costs. The second represents a move from the immediate metropolitan area to a more remote city or possibly out of state, leading to a greater potential reduction in direct expenses.

The third and final circle, called off-shoring, encompasses locations outside the country with even lower cost base. Off-shoring to developing economies can be associated with up to 30–50% savings in all-in labor costs and also brings greater flexibility in terms of resource management to meet variable demand conditions.

Nonetheless, off-shoring is controversial, engendering a broader, societal discussion centered on job displacement. In addition to this important debate, there are several challenges which must be overcome in order to capture the expected value from off-shoring. More specifically, productivity and quality levels must be managed carefully to ensure that the labor cost benefits are not eroded by inefficiencies. In addition, data security must be carefully managed, especially with respect to client data. Finally, a long-term off-shoring strategy should recognize that labor cost differentials are likely to narrow as developing economies continue to develop.

These considerations have led some companies to re-shore their activities (Levine, 2012), eschewing the potential for direct labor cost savings but continuing to capture the benefits from centralized service centers and business process redesign.

Outsourcing

After activities have been physically decoupled from (but nonetheless fully integrated into) the bank or insurer's business system, one logical question is whether you are still the best "owner" of the activities?

There are many reasons why a company might consider outsourcing the activities to a third-party service provider. Corbett (2004) cites a survey suggesting that cost reduction is the primary benefit (49% of respondents). Cost savings can come from the service provider's greater economies of scale and skill, the need to define and enforce rigorous standards and change management processes with an arm's-length relationship and the service provider's increased focus and management attention. An additional 17% said that outsourcing helped their company to focus on core activities which actually provide a competitive advantage. An additional 12% said that the benefits came from a more variable cost structure.

In terms of business processes, whatever can be put into a service center can in principle be outsourced. For example, banks and insurers outsource payroll, accounts payable and receivable activities. In addition, Third-Party Administration (TPA) for claims processing is offered for on-going business, run-off portfolios and corporate plans in the insurance industry. According to the 2012 FSOkx survey,[5] 37% of the Business Process Outsourcing (BPO) by banks and insurers focused on the middle office, including trade support, risk management and reporting solutions, with a further 30% coming from banking or product administration processes.

However, IT Outsourcing (ITO) dominates the landscape. According to the same survey, ITO was 2× the volume of BPO in banking and 10× the level for the insurance industry, with the bulk of ITO in the form of applications support and operations (70%), application architecture (11%) and network management (8%).

USE LESS, BUT MORE EFFECTIVELY: DIGITIZE AND AUTOMATE

In addition to extracting processes, banks and insurers also think about how to leverage IT to make processes more efficient. Some common levers include the following.

- Leverage technology – digital entry, optical character recognition, "fast quote" and entry at point of sale using mobile telephony – to increase the percentage of transactions which undergo straight-through processing.
- Simplify and standardize all processes, including underwriting approval, administration and workout/claims processes, and automate those that pass risk, complexity and materiality criteria (e.g., automated underwriting, compliance checks, fraud detection, etc.).
- Centralize all client data, including transaction data, contacts and offer history, and make it available to all sales and service channels (e.g., branches, agents, Internet, call centers, etc.) to increase service and sales success rates.

---

[5] http://www.fsokx.com/Deal-Analytics/2012-Annual-Outsourcing-Deal-Analytics-Report

- Offer customers multiple channels to meet their needs (e.g., branch/agent, call center, Internet, mobile, ATM) and actively direct them to the best channel, providing the support they need in the most cost-efficient manner.

These steps not only improve cost efficiency, they also lower turnaround times, improve error and exception rates and generally improve customer service levels and satisfaction.

USE LESS, BUT MORE EFFECTIVELY: RE-ENGINEER THE PRODUCT PORTFOLIO

Another important avenue for improving efficiency is through the redesign of products and services, balancing the cost and complexity of product proliferation against the need to provide "customized" products to better meet customer needs.

It is clear that product and channel proliferation drives expenses and complexity, not only in the back office (as different contracts, terms and conditions have to be supported) but also at customer touch points (including the point of sale and customer service) as transaction details and how each serves customers' needs must be fully understood and communicated. Gounaris (2005) observes that "In the financial services sector . . .deregulation has led to intense and quite diverse competition . . . to new product launches and the proliferation of their product line . . . As a result, the amount of resources required to support increases and, consequently, issues of both effectiveness and efficiency in managing the product line rise."

Against the higher cost of product proliferation is the fact that tailoring products to meet specific customer needs and offering them through multiple channels increases the probability of making the sale and capturing a higher margin.

How to reconcile these seemingly inconsistent objectives, pitting operating efficiency against commercial considerations? One direction is hinted at in Kratochvil and Carson (2005): ". . . the recent leap towards component-based products and Mass Customization is still only beginning (and represents) . . . both a cost saving investment and a market-share investment at the same time." More specifically, the product portfolio is re-engineered by:

- *modularizing* products into component parts so that the consumer can select à la carte the individual features that appeal or choose a predefined "package" tailored to specific lifestyles or needs;
- *standardizing and automating* the components so that they are easier to understand and administer;
- *processing* the components *independently of channel and location*, ensuring consistency within a multi-channel strategy and capturing further operating efficiencies;
- *managing the product portfolio* in terms of new offerings as well as the back book or in-force book of business, to further reduce complexity. For the in-force portfolio, consider outsourcing the administration of legacy products or converting them into products that will continue to be offered.

Case Example

Sidebar 12.2 provides a case study focused on operating efficiency improvements, from process re-engineering to product portfolio redesign.

SIDEBAR 12.2: FROM PROCESS RE-ENGINEERING TO PRODUCT PORTFOLIO OPTIMIZATION

Allianz Germany launched a BPR program called Target Operating Model (TOM) in 2006 with the objective of creating a leaner, more cost-efficient and effective organization.

Using BPR, the TOM project implemented a functional organization which integrated historically disparate, regional operations and distribution functions across the PC and LH insurance operations, leading to "FTE reduction and cost cutting."

Having successfully completed the new organization in 2009, in 2011 Allianz Germany launched a five-pillar strategy with the goal of achieving sustainable market leadership and profitable growth (Allianz, 2013).

One of the pillars focused on further improving the operations, consisting of four sub-projects. The names of the sub-projects were self-explanatory:

- use of service companies;
- automation;
- reduce complexity of products and tariffs;
- improve process efficiency.

Some interesting results are illustrated in Figure 12.3, which shows a market-leading use of digital entry, straight-through processing and optical character recognition to generate productivity gains of 8% and improve customer service.

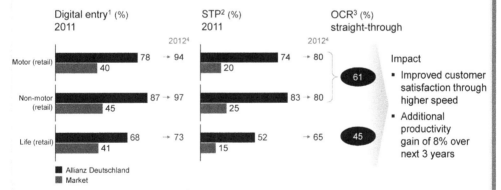

G. Operations   **Allianz** (iii)

3 Automation

Digital entry[1] (%) 2011	STP[2] (%) 2011	OCR[3] (%) straight-through

Allianz Deutschland / Market

Motor (retail): 78 → 94 / 40 | 74 → 80 / 20
Non-motor (retail): 87 → 97 / 45 | 83 → 80 / 25
Life (retail): 68 → 73 / 41 | 52 → 65 / 15

61 · 45

Impact
- Improved customer satisfaction through higher speed
- Additional productivity gain of 8% over next 3 years

■ Allianz Deutschland
■ Market

Additional measures

- Design new products for STP[2] (especially in individual business), e.g. new product "PrivatSchutz" with >90% STP rate for new contracts
- Improvement of digital entries for all channels (e.g. broker through BiPro[5])
- Modularity of ABS[6] product modeling allows for higher automation rates (e.g. to be applied in upcoming corporate product "FirmenSchutz")

1) Source: Verdi report 2011 (data Allianz Deutschland) / BCG "IT-Benchmarking in deutschen Versicherungen 2012" (market data)
2) STP = straight-through processing, source: Verdi report 2011 (data Allianz Deutschland) / BCG "IT-Benchmarking in deutschen Versicherungen 2012" (market data)
3) OCR = optical character recognition; OCR-STP: automatic recognition and routing to employee; no manual routing required; data for 2012
4) Source: Verdi report 2012 (data Allianz Deutschland)
5) BiPro = Brancheninstitut Prozessoptimierung = industry institute for process optimization
6) ABS = Allianz Business System

FIGURE 12.3 Productivity gains through automation. Reproduced by permission of Allianz SE.

4 Products: successful implementation of modular product design of MeinAuto

May 2011: „MeinAuto"

FIGURE 12.4 Modular products: MeinAuto, FirmenSchutz. Reproduced by permission of Allianz SE.

Another pillar of the 2011 strategy focused on "strong products" with the objective of moving from "Single product offerings ('one size fits all')" to "Specific tailor made solutions ('Needs depending on individual situation and access channels')" supported by the "Use of multiple channels and access modes ('Where, when and how I want it')."

4 Products: modular design enhances growth, profitability and customers satisfaction

Key feature	Customer	Allianz
Modular product design	• Flexible cover / costs based on demand	• Customer satisfaction • Growth • Profitability
Clean-up of remaining product portfolio	• Complexity reduction • Higher transparency	• Complexity reduction for operating and distribution • Economies of scale
Independent pricing of modules	• No cross-subsidization	• Better technical results through refined and positive risk selection
Bundle discount	• Better value for money	• Customer retention • Cross-selling
One policy and one in voice	• Complexity reduction • Higher transparency • Convenience	• Complexity reduction • Economies of scale
Ongoing enhancement of modules	• Upgrade guarantee	• Protection of our competitive advantage • Complexity reduction

FIGURE 12.5 Benefits of modularization product strategy. Reproduced by permission of Allianz SE.

The result in PC insurance was a "modularized" product strategy called MeinAuto ("My Auto"), PrivatSchutz ("Private Protection," a personal policy) and FirmenSchutz ("Firm Protection," a policy for SMEs). As Figure 12.4 illustrates, these products are modular in design, comprising highly standardized components which can be configured by the customer.

Ultimately, the "modularization" strategy should enhance growth, profitability and customer satisfaction while remaining cost efficient in serving the customer, as described in Figure 12.5.

The results from the introduction of MeinAuto suggest that the objectives were met: by the end of 2012, over 1.5 million MeinAuto policies were sold, the average premium per policy increased by over 17% and over 80% of the motor third-party liability customers bought an additional liability add-on. In addition, there was an improvement in the claims ratio, retention ratio and overall customer satisfaction.

USE LESS, BUT MORE EFFECTIVELY: MANAGING ACQUISITION EXPENSES

Acquisition expenses are defined as the *direct and indirect costs of selling, underwriting and initiating a product or service.*[6] Acquisition expenses include sales commissions and sales staff expenses (salaries, facilities and equipment costs), advertising and underwriting expenses (including appraisals and contract issuance expenses).

Managing acquisition expenses is challenging for two reasons. First, because improving sales activities is not just about *efficiency* (e.g., increasing the number of calls per sales personnel) but also about *effectiveness* (e.g., converting the calls into hot leads, the leads to offers and the offers ultimately to sales). Second, a multi-channel strategy makes it more complicated due to the need to manage and coordinate different sales channels, some of which you do not directly control.

As Figure 12.6 illustrates, there are three different "levels" for managing acquisition expenses under a multi-channel strategy:

- managing the proprietary sales force (agents, branches), for example by improving lead generation, conversion rates, sales time management, number of productive sales personnel, etc.;
- managing the channels, whether proprietary or independent, in order to get the most out of each;

---

[6]This is broadly consistent with FASB Accounting and Reporting by Insurance Enterprises, No. 60, paragraph 28, which defines acquisition costs "as those costs that vary with and are primarily related to the acquisition of and renewal of (insurance contracts, including) commissions and other costs (for example, salaries of certain employees involved in the underwriting and policy issue functions, and medical and inspection fees)." However, it differs from other definitions which are used when discussing the possible deferral of acquisition expenses, e.g. IAS 39 which defines transaction costs as "incremental costs that are directly attributable to the acquisition, issue or disposal of a financial asset or financial liability. An incremental cost is one that would not have been incurred if the entity had not acquired, issued or disposed of the financial instrument." IASB Meeting Staff Paper, Insurance contracts: Acquisition costs, April 2009.

Managing acquisition expenses, from product to customers, for a multi-channel strategy

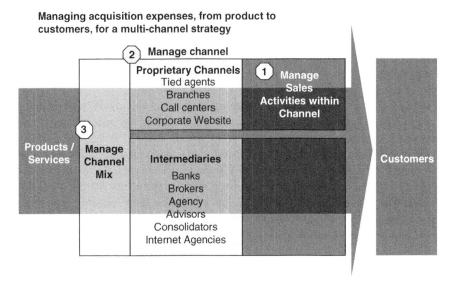

FIGURE 12.6   Managing acquisition expenses

■ managing the mix of product delivery and customer service between the different channels to ensure cost and revenue synergies and to minimize cross-channel cannibalization.

Managing direct sales activities was discussed in detail in Chapter 11. The remainder of this section focuses on ways to influence a sales channel even if you do not directly manage it. The most important levers for managing the channel relationship include the following.[7]

■ *Aligning the interests of the product provider and the distribution channel*, providing the incentives to focus sales on:
   ■ products and services with the highest value contribution;
   ■ acquiring customers with the highest potential value contribution;
   ■ extracting the most through cross-selling, up-selling and retention.
■ *Tailoring products, pricing and services to the channel* while simultaneously maintaining operating efficiency. Key dimensions to consider include an understanding of the customer needs, the product's complexity and its influence on the sales process, the qualifications of the sales force, the ease of understanding and communicating the product, the ease of benchmarking the products' features and pricing and the confidentiality of some data (e.g., medical history).
■ *Optimizing the interface between the product provider and the sales channel*, including:
   ■ integrated, fast ("real-time") and easy to use systems, combined with standardized application forms and limited referrals or escalations for the creation of offers, underwriting and administration of contracts;
   ■ for the distribution partner, integrated customer databases to increase closing rates, facilitate cross/up-selling and support a multi-channel architecture.
■ *Ensuring senior and working-level interaction and commitment* to get agreement on the product strategy, financial plans and targets and the management actions to reach

---

[7]For a generic discussion of channel management using bancassurance as an example, see SCOR (2005).

those targets; to design products and sales campaigns tailored to the channel; and to provide training to the sales and distribution staff in terms of products and administration systems, etc.

■ *Rigorously monitoring the relationship* (e.g., relative to plan in terms of volumes, products and margins, productivity and service calls, complaints, etc.) and meeting frequently to take mid-course corrections.

Four

Better Decisions – Capital, Balance Sheet and Risk Management

"**W**hat gets measured, gets managed." Recognizing this, Part Two: Better Information defined a value-based measurement framework tailored to risk-based, capital-intensive businesses. The framework makes a clear link between risk-adjusted performance measures, management actions and shareholder value, focusing attention on what is important for value managers in the financial services sector: profitable growth, operating efficiency, underwriting effectiveness and capital management.

While good information is a necessary condition for success, it is not a sufficient condition. Ultimately, tactical and strategic decisions need to be taken and this requires not only better information but also an in-depth understanding of successful business strategies and management actions by segment. Recognizing this, Part Three: Better Insights summarized successful business strategies, or the "rules of the game," and concrete management actions for creating value in each segment. These insights are useful for business leaders in refining operating strategies and for the finance and risk functions to effectively challenge those strategies.

In addition to providing better information and better insights, the finance and risk functions also create value by taking better decisions in the three critical areas directly under their responsibility, as illustrated in Figure P4.1.

- *Strategic planning, capital allocation and performance management.* Deciding where to grow, where to harvest and what businesses to fix or exit and then allocating capital and incentivizing performance accordingly.
- *Balance sheet, liquidity and asset/liability management.* Securing a long-term, sustainable financing structure for the firm and delivering stable earnings by managing the firm's structural asset/liability mismatch.

3. Better Decisions –
How to create value in Finance & Risk areas of responsibility?

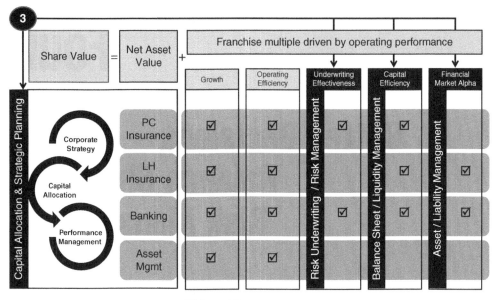

☑ Core skills

FIGURE P4.1 Better decisions

- *Risk management and underwriting.* Improving the firm's technical underwriting performance and building the enterprise risk management framework within which good risk/return decisions are taken on a daily basis.

This part of the Handbook describes how CFOs and CROs take better decisions and create value in these three areas.

CHAPTER 13

Corporate Strategy and Capital Allocation

C orporate strategy and capital allocation determine which businesses you grow, which you harvest, which you fix or exit and where you take strategic investments to secure for future, profitable growth. These are some of the most important decisions taken at the corporate or holding company level. In the best case, wrong decisions at this level represent an opportunity cost; in the worst case, they destroy shareholder value.

CORPORATE STRATEGY, CAPITAL ALLOCATION AND PERFORMANCE MANAGEMENT

As Figure 13.1 illustrates, corporate strategy, capital allocation and performance management represent a continuous cycle.

Actions on all three levels are necessary. Developing a long-term strategic vision while the underlying business flounders is a bit like Nero playing fiddle while Rome burned: it may provide some short-term intellectual stimulation, but the priorities are misplaced. Conversely, myopically focusing on the last basis point at the expense of strategic thinking may lead to top-quartile returns for many years but runs the risk of waking up like Rumpelstiltskin to a dramatically changed, increasingly unfamiliar market.

With this in mind, value managers need to be prepared to answer the following questions regarding corporate strategy.

- What businesses do we choose to be in based on sustainable competitive advantage? What are our aspirations? How do we communicate them?
- Where should we position ourselves in 10–20 years given the predictable market, technological and demographic developments?
- How do we respond in the interim to unexpected disruptions?

- Where are we now?
- Where do we want to be in the future?
- How will we get there?

- Defining the Capital Budget: What are the sources and uses of capital?
- Capital Allocation: How is capital allocated for growth?
- Alignment: Is the internal capital allocation aligned with external constraints?

- What value should we be targeting?
- What actions to deliver?
- What operational targets to set?

FIGURE 13.1   Corporate strategy, capital allocation and performance management

Capital allocation is one of the most important levers for implementing corporate strategy, supporting the decisions where to grow and how to rebalance the portfolio. With regard to capital allocation and the capital budget, value managers have to be prepared to answer the following questions.

- Where is the capital generated, which can be reinvested for growth or returned to shareholders?
- What is the allocation of capital between requirements to maintain and grow earnings, longer-term strategic initiatives and uses which improve our financing, liquidity and funding profile?
- How is the capital earmarked for the existing business portfolio allocated, deciding which to grow, which to harvest and which business to fix or divest?
- How is the capital allocation aligned with other financial constraints, especially regulatory and rating agency constraints on solvency ratios, dividends, leverage, liquidity?

Following capital allocation, performance management makes sure that the capital is used effectively in reaching the strategic goals. With regard to business performance, value managers have to be prepared to answer the following questions.

- What is the value that we can expect from each of our businesses? What are the risks to this valuation?
- How do we express our aspirations in terms of business-specific KPIs and targets?
- What short- and medium-term actions are required to capture the value?
- Which businesses have the most significant performance and valuation gaps? Where are the "turnaround" cases and what actions are required?
- How do we monitor, evaluate and incentivize performance? More importantly, how do we drive higher performance?

It is clear that all these questions, from the strategic to the operational, are interrelated: corporate strategy drives business portfolio decisions just as the building of a defendable competitive advantage in a business will drive corporate strategy. However, each area is also distinct, requiring a different "mindset" and thinking over different time horizons, involving different stakeholders and undertaking different analysis in order to be addressed effectively. As such, while they need to be answered in a *coordinated* fashion, the company may be ill served if they are answered in the *same* fashion.

CAPITAL ALLOCATION: THE CAPITAL BUDGET, FROM SOURCES TO USES OF CAPITAL

Capital allocation is one of the most important tools used by the corporate center to implement corporate strategy, leading to the rebalancing of the corporate portfolio, growing profitable businesses, shrinking less profitable ones and funding strategic investments to secure the company's future.

Following from a clear corporate strategy, capital allocation proceeds in three steps: defining the capital budget, optimizing the corporate portfolio and aligning financial constraints – as illustrated in Figure 13.2. Each of the steps is discussed in detail in the remainder of this chapter.

Financial services firms generate free capital through earnings and then decide how much to "recycle" or reinvest to maintain or grow their business and how much to return to shareholders.

This decision cycle is so fundamental to value management that the CEO and CFO of a financial services firm should be able to clearly and concisely explain to any and all stakeholders what the group's sources of capital are and the strategy for deploying that capital. The end result is a capital budget. Figure 13.3 provides a conceptual representation of the capital budget.

Sources of Capital
For this discussion, "capital" is considered as the aggregate financial resources used by the group to finance its operating businesses, maintain the group's balance sheet and solvency ratio and make strategic investments.

Define the Capital Budget
- Generate capital from earnings, maturing business and the capital markets
- Decide how much to reinvest into the businesses and how much to invest in strategic and financing initiatives
- Return excess capital to shareholders

Optimize corporate portfolio
- Allocate the capital not set aside for strategic and financing initiatives across the existing portfolio of businesses
- Maximize value, focusing on growth and excess returns
- Balance short- and long-term horizons

Align financial constraints
- Identify potential constraints, especially regulatory or rating agency definitions of capital, leverage and liquidity
- Align constrained resources consistently with the internal capital allocation
- Iterate optimization based on binding constraints

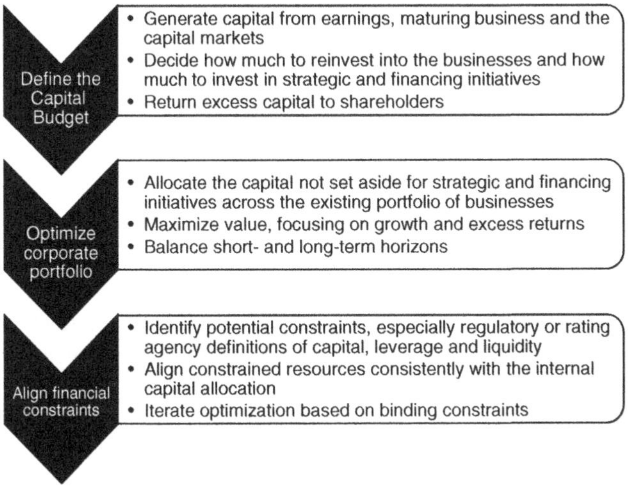

FIGURE 13.2 Capital allocation

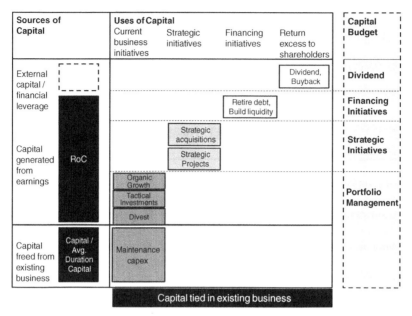

FIGURE 13.3 The capital budget: From sources to uses of capital

This definition of capital is different from regulatory – or rating agency – definitions, both of which are better viewed as *constraints* on capital allocation decisions. It is also different from accounting definitions, where intangibles such as goodwill and deferred acquisition costs may distort the link to cash resources which are actually available to be invested in the business.

As illustrated in Figure 13.3, there are three sources of capital available to the firm. First, capital is generated through earnings[1]; second, it is released as existing business matures or lapses. Most firms reinvest maturing capital and finance growth internally through retained earnings: a 15% RoE can support a compounded annual growth rate in excess of 10% as well as a 33% dividend pay-out ratio, a level of investment which is more than sufficient to finance the growth of most companies.

Finally, capital can be raised externally – for example, by issuing shares, hybrid equity or financial leverage. Assuming that leverage capacity is available, external debt can be used to finance large acquisitions or to fund cash dividends if there is a disconnect between the timing of accounting earnings and cash flow. Less common is raising equity; because it is dilutive to existing shareholders, it is usually reserved for financing the largest strategic acquisitions or to bolster solvency ratios following periods of stress.

Uses of Capital

The next step is to allocate free capital across four broad categories: to grow existing businesses, to finance strategic investments, to alter the financing structure of the firm and, finally, to be returned to shareholders.

---

[1]Note that this assumes all earnings translate into fungible capital. This will not be the case if accounting earnings are affected non-cash items such as building of a deferred acquisition cost asset, etc.

The capital which can be freely allocated in any period is not equal to the total capital in the firm and is often significantly less. In some businesses, only a tiny fraction of the capital can be reallocated to other purposes in any given period.

Flexibility is reduced by two factors. First, free capital is limited if the capital duration for existing business is long. For example, only 1/10th of the existing stock of capital is available in any year for a 10-year product in a steady state. Conceptually, there is a "sweet spot" for the capital duration of a portfolio of businesses: too short and the earnings generated will not have sufficient momentum to weather pricing or demand cycles; too long and capital flexibility is greatly reduced.

Second, regulators and rating agencies may impose non-economic constraints which limit capital flexibility (e.g., non-economic reserves or capital requirements, asset coverage ratios, etc.). Within these constraints, capital can be allocated to the following four broad categories.

Invested in the business. There are four ways that capital can be invested in the existing business.

1. Capital can be reinvested to *maintain* the current value-in-force (*maintenance capex*, because it "maintains" the current net asset value of the firm). This investment takes the form of initial acquisition expenses and the capital strain of the replacement business.
2. Capital can be invested to *grow* the existing businesses (*organic growth*) in order to participate in an expanding market at constant share or take share from competitors.
3. Capital can be invested through *tactical investments* (e.g., bolt-on acquisitions,[2] super-charging existing distribution networks or acquiring distribution rights from a third party).
4. Paradoxically, capital can also be deployed by *divesting a business*. Suppose that a legacy block of business generates steady, predictable losses. In this case, paying someone to take over the portfolio or funding a run-off vehicle or "bad bank" may be a good investment: while it won't lead to top-line growth, it will lead to earnings growth by eradicating the losses. It may also be the best investment opportunity available as the legacy block is typically well understood.

Capital to fund maintenance and organic growth is steered through the annual planning cycle, implicit in the growth of the business funded by the difference between earnings and dividends paid to the group. However, tactical investments and divestitures are typically highlighted for capital funding by the business unit during the planning process.

Strategic, transformational investments. There are two ways that capital can be deployed to transform the corporate portfolio with consequences beyond the existing business franchise.

1. Investments in transformational growth opportunities such as strategic acquisitions, joint ventures and "flag planting" in developing markets, etc.
2. Projects to fundamentally improve operations (e.g., building a multi-channel distribution platform, radically expanding the proprietary sales network, restructuring business processes or replacing of turnkey administration systems).

---

[2]Tactical, bolt-on acquisitions are defined as acquisitions which fall within a business's current product/market/geographic footprint, conducted by an experienced management team and executed in order to gain synergies.

These investments are more material, both in terms of investment dollars and strategic impact. In addition, they are often associated with implementation challenges which need to be monitored over much longer horizons. As a consequence, the business cases for strategic investments need to be explicitly discussed and agreed during the strategic planning round and performance against those plans is monitored separately from "business as usual" plans.

Alter the group's financing structure. An alternative to investing capital in operating businesses is to alter the firm's financing structure. For example, excess capital can be used to buy down external debt, lowering financial leverage; it can be kept to build up the group's liquidity or strategic M&A buffer; or it can be kept simply to improve the firm's solvency position. These decisions are typically taken by the Finance or Asset/Liability Management Committee and executed by the treasury function.

Return to shareholders. If there is no better use, capital can and should be returned to shareholders, either in the form of dividends or share repurchases.

Many firms focus on growing the balance sheet and earnings; however, bigger is not always better. Mauboussin (2011) cites research showing that corporate actions which ". . . contract assets, including spin-offs, debt prepayments and dividend initiations are followed by good shareholder returns . . . (and) higher dividend pay-out ratios have been associated with higher earnings growth rates . . . These studies broadly suggest that capital markets tend to reward companies that do not pursue asset growth for the sake of growth." See also Cooper *et al.* (2008), Li *et al.* (2010), Nissim and Ziv (2001), Arnott and Asness (2003).

Given the importance of dividends in capital management and signaling to shareholders, Sidebar 13.1 provides some insights into the relative attractiveness of dividends versus buybacks.

SIDEBAR 13.1: ON DIVIDENDS AND BUYBACKS

Returning capital to shareholders is done through dividends and share buybacks. Theoretically, the two should be equivalent under the assumption of efficient markets, equal borrowing terms, equivalent taxes on capital gains and dividends and perfect information (Mauboussin, 2006; CFA Institute[3]). However, because capital gains taxes tend to be lower than taxes on dividend income, share buybacks are often seen as a more tax-efficient method of returning capital to shareholders.

Ignoring tax considerations, an important difference between dividends and buy-backs is in *signaling*. In general, investors prefer regular, steadily increasing dividends that will not retreat except under exceptional circumstances. From a corporate finance perspective, committing to steadily increasing dividends is a clear signal of management's confidence in the strength of earnings and earnings growth (Brav *et al.*, 2005; Leary and Michaely, 2011). Once the commitment has been made, it is difficult to go back: retreating from a progressive dividend policy is almost exclusively associated with extraordinary events, including periods of solvency distress or for the funding of strategic investments.

---

[3]http://www.cfainstitute.org/learning/products/publications/inv/Documents/corporate_finance_chapter6.pptx

Dividend.com (2012) summarizes the popular perception that a higher dividend pay-out ratio ". . . shows the firm is confident in its future cash flows. The company is comfortable in its ability to afford ongoing payouts . . . Higher dividend payments prevent companies from retaining too much cash, which can then be wasted on foolish ventures . . . Instead, the company is focused on executing its business . . ."[4]

In contrast, there is no perceived commitment with a share buyback or a special, one-off dividend; the main message being that there is excess capital in the firm which could not be invested at rates above the cost of capital. Still, a share buyback also signals that management sees its shares as undervalued; in this case, buying shares from more pessimistic shareholders is in the best interests of the remaining shareholders. Warren Buffet (1984)[5] comments that "When companies with outstanding businesses and comfortable financial positions find their shares selling far below intrinsic value in the marketplace, no alternative action can benefit shareholders as surely as repurchases."

As a consequence of these considerations, dividends tend to be much less volatile and increase gradually compared with buybacks (Mauboussin, 2011). In addition, both share buybacks and an increase in regular, progressive dividends generally have a positive effect on share prices.

The most important factor for deploying capital should be the long-run excess returns generated by the investment. The fact that capital can be returned to shareholders creates an absolute minimum hurdle rate for investing capital and this hurdle rate must be respected. This implies relatively simple rules of the game.

RULES OF THE GAME: ALLOCATING CAPITAL WITHIN THE CAPITAL BUDGET

- Allocate capital between financing initiatives, strategic initiatives and the existing business portfolio in a manner consistent with your corporate strategy.
- Never invest in businesses or strategic initiatives with long-run returns below the cost of capital.
- Deploy as much capital as possible in initiatives which generate long-run excess returns, even considering raising additional capital if internal sources prove insufficient relative to the opportunities.
- Maintain a secure and resilient capital structure, always respecting regulatory constraints, in a manner consistent with your firm's risk appetite.
- Return any excess capital to shareholders.

---

[4]Note that there may be a principal–agent issue if managers' performance is judged based on earnings per share, in which case share buybacks would be inappropriately preferred by management over dividends.

[5] http://www.berkshirehathaway.com/letters/1984.html

Optimizing the corporate portfolio is covered in the next section; optimizing the financing structure of the firm is discussed in Chapter 15. With regard to strategic investments, these simple rules often prove challenging in practice due two behavioral considerations, discussed in Sidebar 13.2.

SIDEBAR 13.2: TWO BEHAVIORAL ISSUES AFFECTING STRATEGIC INVESTMENT DECISIONS

While having tremendous potential to transform the company, strategic investments are not without risk. Getting the balance right is critical: too little strategic investment and the company will shrink from relevance in a dynamically changing market; on the other hand, one too many investments– for example, an ill-timed acquisition – can ruin a company just as surely and far more quickly. Finding the right balance is challenging due to two very human behavioral traits: over-optimism and short-termism.

OVER-OPTIMISM

The world is uncertain, making investments with long payback periods especially challenging to evaluate. It seems as if, more often than not, there is a natural bias toward optimism. For example, assumptions about the revenue synergies used to justify an acquisition more often turn out to be too optimistic, as are the cost savings from replacing a turnkey system or the growth needed to achieve scale economies in a green-field start-up.

This bias toward optimism – called the *positivity illusion* – is described in Business Week (2009): "The basic idea is that when people judge their chances of experiencing a good outcome . . . they estimate their odds to be higher than average. But when they contemplate the probability that something bad will befall them . . . , they estimate their odds to be lower . . ."

The bias toward optimism is exacerbated by investments with long payback periods, with the current generation of managers applauded for taking bold moves but the adverse consequences materializing only for the next or later generations of managers.

Not surprisingly, optimism is often cited for the high failure rate of transformational acquisitions, joint ventures (Rankine, 2001) and business expansions outside the company's core footprint. Faulkner *et al.* (2012) state that "Strategies may often be expressed in grandiloquent terms based on excessive optimism about the world, the economy, the industry and the firm's own prospects."

Some optimism is good, but failures can be very costly. Additional steps should be taken to counteract "harmful" optimism, especially when evaluating long-term, capital-intensive investments, while nonetheless promoting productive risk taking.

First and foremost, implement a simple, common-sense rule. Don't get excited about significant investments which yield an IRR slightly above the cost of capital at payback periods 10 years in the future. It is reasonable to expect that the upside is substantially built into the plan, leaving only downside surprises. Aligned with this common-sense rule are more technical rules, including the following.

- Give preference to investments with shorter payback periods over those with longer periods.[6]
- Require all but Horizon 3 initiatives to be cash flow accretive in the first year(s).
- Give preference to businesses which have a lower capital intensity.[7] Put simply, if two investments both create €10 mio of value, but one requires capital which is a multiple of the other, then go for the investment with the lower capital intensity.
- Carefully consider investments with break-even IRRs. If even the most optimistic assumptions only get you to the point where you are preserving shareholder value, then it may well be better to return the capital.

Second, evaluate strategic investments in a balanced manner. For example, assign an experienced manager to argue the contra-investment case, helping to break a cycle of overly optimistic "group-think." Also, ensure that clear guidance and critical challenge/ triaging of deals is done early in the process rather than thinking you can reject a marginal deal after significant efforts and personal "capital" have already been invested in promoting it.

Finally, explicitly track the performance of strategic investments over time and make those responsible for the decisions also accountable for the long-term results, even if the individual changes jobs in the interim.

SHORT-TERMISM

Alternatively, management may have too short a perspective, avoiding longer-term investment opportunities. This may be because managers are too risk averse (Cotteleer and Gorman, 2013) or, more likely, because they are too focused on short-term earnings to make the investments needed to position the company for the next phase of growth.

According to Rappaport (2005), management's focus on earnings is in part fuelled by the investment community, "Companies delay or forgo value-creating investments to meet consensus earnings expectations. Although such actions improve the current period's reported earnings, they reduce the company's earnings potential and value." Rappaport cites the survey of Graham *et al.* (2005), which reports that 80% of the respondents would decrease discretionary spending on research and development, advertising, maintenance and hiring to meet earnings targets and more than half would delay initiatives, even if it entailed a loss in long-term value (see also Graham *et al.*, 2006).

In addition, short-termism is also reinforced by frequent CEO rotations at the business unit level: the incumbent may have an incentive to delay investments in operations which are drastically needed but have a longer payback period than his/her

---

[6]The payback period is the number of years in the future at which you expect to recoup the initial capital invested, e.g. the date at which the accumulated sum of earnings exceeds the initial capital investment.

[7]Capital intensity is measured here as the ratio of the discounted sum of all future expected capital requirements to the value created.

expected tenure, leaving an accumulated, deferred investment for his/her successor. This concern is very real given the increasing velocity of CEOs.

Short-termism can be combatted by better aligning managers' incentives to the long-term value of the firm (Rappaport, 2005; CFA, 2006). In addition, better communication and expectations management can help, for example by reforming earnings guidance, putting a higher emphasis on long-term objectives and giving ranges rather than point estimates (CFA, 2006); by making clear and emphasizing the long-term strategy; by better aligning financial disclosures with the strategy.

Finally, it can also be combatted by making the investments (or lack of investments) in operations explicit, separating and monitoring the results of the investment and aligning overall incentives to accommodate and promote required investment.

Increasingly, the sources and uses of capital are being explicitly discussed with analysts, both as a basis for understanding the company's economics and strategy and as a form of commitment to value and capital management. The commitment and conceptual capital management process was communicated to investors during our Capital Markets Day (Allianz, 2014b) and later formalized into an explicit Capital Budget. Figure 13.4 is an illustration of a uses of capital disclosure from Allianz's third-quarter 2014 analyst presentation (Allianz, 2014a), when Allianz committed to a progressive regular dividend with a pay-out ratio of 50% of net income. Allianz also explained how the remainder of the net income would be invested,

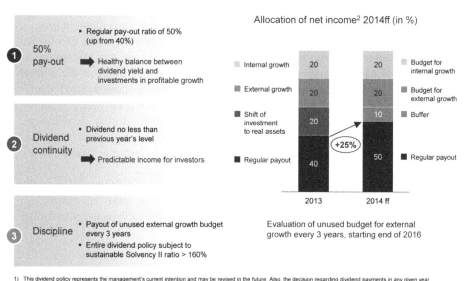

FIGURE 13.4 Allianz's uses of capital, 2014. Reproduced by permission of Allianz SE.

supporting internal growth (20%), external growth (20%) and a buffer (10%), in part to support the progressive element of the dividend policy in years when net income decreased. Additional examples can be found in other companies' disclosures. The announcement had a positive impact on Allianz's share price, in part because it demonstrated a commitment to shareholder value and capital management.

CAPITAL ALLOCATION: OPTIMIZING THE CORPORATE PORTFOLIO

Once the capital budget has been determined, the capital to grow existing businesses has to be allocated across the existing portfolio of businesses. Once again, the rules of the game are simple and straightforward.

RULES OF THE GAME: CORPORATE PORTFOLIO LEVEL

Develop your portfolio of profitable businesses by:

- growing faster than the market where you make excess returns, investing in organic growth and market adjacencies;
- fixing the businesses where you are not making excess risk-adjusted returns;
- exiting the businesses that you cannot fix or where you are not the best owner.

Note: While the discussion focuses on the allocation of capital across businesses in the corporate portfolio, the same thinking and approach can and should be used *within* a business for the allocation of capital across lines of business, products or customer segments.

While simple, these rules are not always followed in practice. In particular, many companies (and businesses) suffer from portfolio inertia, continuing to fund activities which are not generating value. The root causes and possible remedies for portfolio inertia are described in Sidebar 13.3.

SIDEBAR 13.3: PORTFOLIO INERTIA

Many companies suffer from portfolio inertia, always accumulating businesses and failing over extended periods to shrink or exit businesses which destroy value. In addition to the value destroyed, inertia also has an opportunity cost – the cost of profitable investment opportunities foregone. Inertia can have many causes:

- there may be no easy way to turn around a business and make it profitable, creating a defensive and entrenched management team;
- decisions may be delayed "just for another year," with current underperformance offset by unrealistic "hockey stick" projections during planning;
- the management mantra that "no one ever shrinks to greatness," seeming to imply that bigger is better even if it comes by sacrificing shareholder value;

- a naive emphasis on growth, especially in the top line, even if growth in the bottom line does not follow;
- the challenge of disentangling revenue or cost synergies, with some value-destroying businesses contributing to fixed costs or to the "feeding" of the sales and distribution network.

While comfortable in the short term, sustained inertia can trigger chaotic upheavals, or a revolution, which is far more disruptive than a steady, controlled and evolutionary value management approach to the corporate portfolio.

Consider the revolution at Aviva, which up until 2012 suffered lackluster returns from a portfolio of businesses which did not all create value. A shareholder revolt was triggered when the company's solvency came under pressure due to the 2011–12 crisis; ultimately, the revolt saw the exit of the CEO and a radical restructuring program was put in place, including stripping out management layers, the classification of 50 divisions into "core, in need of improvement or for sale" and leading to the decision to exit up to 15 of the divisions (Lobo, 2012).

One could argue that a steady, evolutionary process of pruning and shaping the corporate portfolio over time might have avoided the shareholder revolution and subsequent chaos, a view echoed by Copeland *et al.* (2000) who comment that "Management can avoid the need for cataclysmic change in the future by embracing the second aspect of the managing value process: developing a value-oriented approach to leading and managing their companies . . ."

It is difficult to counteract inertia. Nonetheless, some things can be done.

- First, make the value of existing businesses – and the cost of marginal investments in underperforming business – fully transparent. Most companies do not explicitly value their businesses, in part because valuations are likely to highlight "inconvenient truths." However inconvenient, these truths need to be recognized and acknowledged.
- Second, change discussions from revenues and earnings to value creation. Reinforce the message that lower revenues and earnings can actually lead to a higher share price if capital can be freed up from businesses which do not cover their cost of capital.
- Third, monitor performance against plans over several years, making it clear where "hockey sticks," rather than reality, are the basis for business projections.

KPIs for Portfolio Optimization

Reflecting the corporate value driver tree, these management rules are often expressed in the form of a four-quadrant matrix,[8] as illustrated in Figure 13.5.

The size of the "bubble" indicates the capital to be (re)invested in the business. All businesses located on the right-hand side create value as returns are greater than the hurdle rate; all businesses in the upper half by definition exceed growth targets.

---

[8]This 2×2 matrix is similar to the BCG "Star–Dog" matrix or the GE/McKinsey 3×3 matrix but uses information more directly tied to value and the corporate KPIs measuring value creation. See the discussion in Chapter 14.

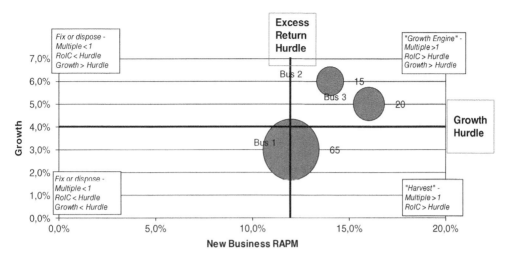

FIGURE 13.5 Standard business portfolio KPI analysis

The "best" businesses are those represented by a large circle in the upper right of the matrix: the business is generating excess returns and offers the opportunity to (re)invest a substantial amount of capital. In contrast, the "worst" businesses would be represented by a large circle in the upper left corner, signifying that there is substantial capital investment in activities which are destroying shareholder value.

Defining the Quadrants *Cost of capital hurdle.* The vertical line (which separates value-creating businesses from value-destroying businesses) is often set based on a constant hurdle rate across all businesses. As discussed in Part Two of the Handbook, the use of a common hurdle is inappropriate if the businesses have a materially different cost of capital.

An alternative is to define the vertical line so that excess returns are shown relative to the business's unique cost of capital; in this case, businesses which rely on financial market returns for a significant amount of their earnings will generally be placed exactly on the hurdle line, reflecting the inherent challenge in generating alpha in efficient capital markets.

Growth hurdle. For the dividing line along the vertical or growth dimension, firms often use a common rate such as 0% or 5%, useful in comparing absolute growth rates or the contribution to the company's overall growth target. However, two other variants are also used in practice – for example, setting the growth hurdle rate relative to:

- the plan growth rate for each business, useful for comparing over/underperformance *relative to plan*;
- the actual growth rate for each market, useful for comparing over/underperformance relative to the *change in market share*.

Differentiating the growth hurdle may be important: holding a constant volume in a shrinking market can be a remarkable success, while achieving only marginal growth in a fast-growing market may indicate poor performance as well as a loss of market share.

Different Perspectives   The matrix can be either forward or backward-looking.

- A backward-looking analysis, using the actual invested capital and realized returns, is useful for *performance evaluation* purposes. The analysis can be done based on the most *recent reporting period* for short-term performance evaluation or on a *rolling average* to eliminate short-term fluctuations and give a perspective on longer-term, sustainable performance.
- A forward-looking analysis, based on *current planning assumptions, forecast or scenarios*, including changes to the business strategy and improvements in operating performance, is useful in evaluating potential value creation.

Both perspectives are important: managing a business only looking backward is like driving a car while looking in the rear view mirror: it may be easy to measure how far you have come, but you run the risk of missing the turn in the road directly ahead of you. In contrast, looking forward allows you to adapt to a changing environment, but at the risk of delaying actions to address current sub-standard performance.

It is especially important to critically evaluate businesses where there is a large delta between the backward and forward-looking perspectives in order to avoid overly optimistic, hockey stick projections. This can be supported by a value improvement "waterfall," attributing the improvement to specific and concrete actions needed to reach the future state. Such a "waterfall" provides a sanity check for "hockey stick" projections, clearly identifies and isolates the management actions needed to turn the situation around and forms a baseline for measuring and monitoring performance against plans.

Allocated capital. If forward looking, the bubbles in the matrix should represent the (absolute or marginal) capital to be allocated to the business; if backward looking, the bubbles should represent the market value of capital currently embedded in the business, even though that capital may be locked in for many years to come. However, there are two cases where care must be taken.

- First, it may be useful to measure performance based on *historically* invested capital, *including goodwill* (as opposed to the current net asset value) for businesses which have grown rapidly through acquisition. Acquisition decisions are often based on revenue or cost synergies which may not materialize; measuring performance based on historic investment helps to promote accountability.
- Second, where the business unit is "under-capitalized" relative to required capital. This situation can arise in groups which implicitly support subsidiaries operating in countries with low local regulatory minimum requirements. In such instances, required capital should be used for performance measurement (including an imputed risk-free return on that capital) rather than the current market value surplus. This does not mean that the capital needs to be physically held by the business, just that performance should be measured relative to the capital consumed from the group's perspective.

From KPIs to Value
Ostensibly, you could do a "back-of-the-envelope" sum-of-parts franchise valuation based on this information *if* you used forward-looking estimates of returns and growth and *if* you were

Business Unit Performance

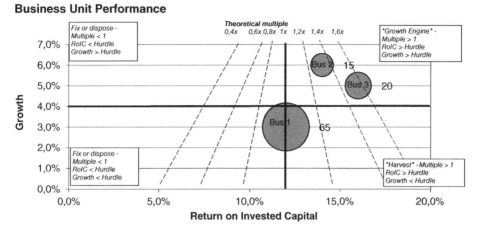

FIGURE 13.6 Incorporating the multiple for profitable growth

willing to define a multiple for new business based on the forward-looking return and growth estimates.

For example, under steady-state assumptions, the multiple would be defined by $V/\mathrm{IC} = 1 + (\mathrm{RoIC} - \mathrm{CoIC})/(\mathrm{CoIC} - g)$, where IC is the invested capital, V is the theoretical value of the business, RoIC is the steady-state return on invested capital and g is the steady-state growth rate.

Using this shorthand, Business 1 in Figure 13.6 has a theoretical valuation multiple of 1× invested capital regardless of its growth rate because its risk-adjusted returns are just equal to its cost of capital. Businesses 2 and 3 would enjoy theoretical multiples of 1.33× and 1.6×, respectively, due to their higher risk-adjusted returns and growth rates. In aggregate, the company is theoretically valued at approximately 1.15× based on where the capital is invested, the average expected returns on the investment and the average growth rate.

Figure 13.6 plots different "iso-value lines," defined as *the combination of expected returns and growth which give the same implied multiple under steady state assumptions.* These iso-value lines illustrate the break-even trade-off between growth and excess risk-adjusted returns which give the same valuation multiple. They depend on the starting point for the business: if the business moves east of the iso-value line, it creates incremental value; if it moves west, it destroys incremental value; and if it moves along the iso-value line, it retains the same multiple.

For example, in Figure 13.6, further growth in Business 1 yields additional earnings but not a multiple expansion. However, growth in Businesses 2 and 3 at the same RoIC would lead to a multiple expansion and, for Business 2, you would even be willing to accept a 0.3% decrease in growth as long as it was compensated by a 0.3% increase in RoIC, leaving the valuation multiple constant.

There are two important uses of iso-value lines.

- First, when combined with an understanding of the business's demand elasticity, iso-value lines represent a powerful tool for taking decisions which require a trade-off between growth and returns or pricing.

■ Second, the multiple "magnifies" excess over- and under-performance, helping to combat portfolio inertia and reinforcing the need for change. For example, while it might not sound all that bad to invest capital in a 10% RoIC business, doing so at a 12% cost of capital in perpetuity destroys 20 cents for every euro invested. Even worse, growing the same business at 7% compounded average growth rate would destroy 40 cents for every euro invested! This "magnification" effect helps to focus attention on the problem cases and the high performers.

The iso-value lines in the figure are based on steady-state assumptions. Alternative assumptions, for example a high growth phase followed by lower growth, imply different multiples. Applying a common multiple or even a common steady-state assumption across all business units can be misleading. An alternative is to lengthen the explicit planning horizon to 3 or 5 years and then use a steady-state multiple for the residual value, capturing the short- and medium-term dynamics explicitly. Another way is simply to apply the same, steady-state multiple approach for all businesses and discuss the implications of different growth paths qualitatively during strategic planning.

CAPITAL ALLOCATION: ALIGNING FINANCIAL RESOURCES WITHIN CONSTRAINTS

Capital allocation is not as simple as deciding where to invest free capital: the decision will be hindered by capital, leverage and liquidity constraints imposed externally by regulators and rating agencies. Some of these will be binding if the firm manages for value and the binding constraints will in turn limit value creation: firms facing no constraints can do at least as well and could most likely do better.

Added Complexity

Solvency, leverage and liquidity constraints are imposed by rating agencies and regulators. For good or for ill, external constraints are becoming more complex and more binding: the new Basel III rules have already fundamentally changed the economics of investment banking (Morgan Stanley & Oliver Wyman, 2011), just as Solvency II has the potential to fundamentally impact the product and investment strategies of European LH insurers. Unfortunately, there is more regulation on the horizon for both industries.

An Alphabet Soup of External Constraints   The multiplicity of constraints imposed externally is illustrated in ING's (2013) analyst presentation on capital and balance sheet management, which discusses no less than four constraints driven by Basel III – an absolute leverage constraint (including off-balance sheet items), the Liquidity Coverage Ratio (LCR), a Minimum Requirement for Eligible Liabilities (MREL, representing funds which can be "bailed in" as part of a recovery plan or resolution proceedings) and minimum Tier 1 Common Equity (CET1) requirements.

The regulatory landscape becomes even more complicated for large groups which are designated as a Global- or Domestic-Systemically Important Financial Institution (G-/D-SIFI) or as an Internationally Active Insurance Group (IAIG), in which case Higher Loss Absorbency (HLA) requirements and the new International Capital Standard (ICS), respectively, may also be applied.

Further complicating the task are the parallel constraints imposed by rating agencies, also focused on solvency, leverage and liquidity but using completely different measurement approaches.

Unfortunately, this alphabet soup of constraints is measured using different and non-comparable metrics, which differ from management's assessment of the capital allocated to the business; see, for example, Pfetsch *et al.* (2011).

A Dynamic or Static Problem, Depending on the Business Model   While the trade-offs between management's view of capital and external constraints are relatively static for insurers and retail and commercial banks, they are more dynamic for investment banks whose business model offers greater latitude to shift risk, leverage and liquidity resources over short time frames.

Retail and Commercial Banks and Insurers Are Less Complex   Retail and commercial banks, as well as insurers, face a complicated but reasonably static constrained optimization problem due to their business profile: in general, it is not possible to dramatically reallocate capital across lines of business or increase the firm's risk profile, funding risky assets through operating leverage, in the short term.

As a consequence, the overall solvency and leverage intensities for insurers and retail and commercial banks do not change dramatically over time; as discussed in Chapter 15, having solved for the optimum trade-offs initially, firms in both segments typically target a stable capital funding structure as well as solvency and leverage ratios and manage toward these targets over time.

This observation is confirmed for commercial banks by Shin and Adrian (2008), who find no relationship between a change in assets and a change in leverage, leading to the conclusion that commercial banks target a fixed leverage ratio.

Investment Banking Introduces More Dynamic Considerations   In contrast, the investment banking business model offers greater opportunities to dynamically utilize free regulatory capital resources, increasing the use of leverage and liquidity resources to purchase assets whenever risk-based capital constraints are relaxed.

For example, Shin and Adrian (2008) demonstrate that investment banks have historically allowed balance sheet leverage to expand and contract to fund asset growth, implying very dynamic leverage ratios compared with commercial banks (and insurers). The conclusion that investment banks historically have financed changes in total assets almost entirely from leverage is confirmed by Adrian and Shin (2008).

Historically, investment bank leverage increased to fund additional trading assets during benign market conditions: because risk-based regulatory capital requirements are typically determined using information from the last 250 trading days, they tend to decrease as a percentage of notional assets if market volatility is low. As evidence, Adrian and Shin (2008) demonstrate that the ratio of VaR (a measure directly related to Basel II/III capital consumption for the trading book) to equity is kept reasonably stable by investment banks, more stable than any notional measure of leverage.

Shin and Adrian (2008) comment that "The difference is accounted for by the active management of leverage by intermediaries, especially the active shedding of risks through deleveraging during times of market stress . . . consistent with the rule of thumb that Value-at-Risk normalized by equity is kept constant over the cycle, even at the height of the crisis." In other words: risk off, leverage on and risk on, leverage off.

Combining these two observations, it is fair to conclude that an investment bank has traditionally faced a far more dynamic and complex constrained capital allocation decision.

SIDEBAR 13.4: A NOTE ON THE LIQUIDITY PROVIDED BY BANK TRADING ACTIVITIES

It is commonly argued that bank trading activities provide valuable liquidity to financial markets, helping to buffer the impact of turbulent market conditions and thereby providing a service to society. For example, Eurofi (2012) suggests that market makers help ". . . to bridge the gap between buyers and sellers . . . The comfort of knowing that you can sell is crucial to having the confidence to buy in the first place. Thanks to . . . market makers, that confidence is there to allow for investment, the fuel of economic growth . . ."

This line of thought has been used to argue against the increased regulatory restrictions and higher capital requirements imposed on the proprietary trading activities of banks since the 2008 crisis. For example, according to Volcker (2012),[9] one of the four primary concerns raised about the Volcker Rule limiting bank proprietary trading was that the "needed liquidity in trading markets will be imperilled."

Similar concerns have been raised by hedge funds, with Bloomberg (2014) reporting that the market turbulence during 2014 ". . . sparked questions about whether bank regulations implemented after the 2008 financial crisis exacerbated price declines by limiting the ability of Wall Street banks to make markets . . . some hedge-fund managers said higher capital requirements had curbed Wall Street trading desks' ability to cushion the declines by stepping in to buy securities." The article continues by noting that the primary dealers' inventory of bonds had dropped from $285 billion in 2007 to only $38 billion in 2014, often cited as evidence for lower liquidity provision.

The (intuitive) reality is that leveraged investors actually take liquidity from markets during a crisis and only long-term investors, with limited leverage, can ultimately provide liquidity in turbulent markets.

The evidence from Shin and Adrian (2008) cited earlier suggests that the liquidity provided by bank trading activities during times of market turmoil is illusory at best and may actually exacerbate financial crisis: the evidence suggests that banks build asset inventories through leverage in bull markets and rapidly deleverage, selling the same assets, during times of market turbulence.

This view is further supported by anecdotal evidence. For example, the Bloomberg article comments that even when banks had the higher inventory in 2007, ". . . they failed to provide liquidity in the corporate bond markets when the 2008 crisis hit. Illiquidity – measured by how long it would take to sell all outstanding bonds at daily trading volumes – peaked at 550 days in late 2008 . . . Since 2010, it has fluctuated between 300 and 425 days."

An earlier empirical study pointed to similar conclusions while raising a more significant concern. Chae and Wang (2003) observed that dealers receive privileges in return for supposedly providing liquidity through market making. These privileges include access to order flow information, direct connections to exchanges, lower transaction costs and higher transaction execution speeds. However, they hypothesized

---

[9]The remaining three concerns were that proprietary trading was not, in fact, a high-risk activity for banks, that any further restrictions would hurt the competitive position of US-based banks and that the regulation is too complicated and costly.

that the privileges can be misused in the pursuit of an information-based, proprietary trading advantage and that the provision of market liquidity may be at odds with value maximization from proprietary trading profits. Their empirical research concludes that "Contrary to theory and intuition . . . dealers do not provide liquidity . . . (but do) earn significant excess returns . . . driven by information profits, rather than by market-making profits. (The results highlight) . . . the magnitude of the costs of allowing dealers institutional trading advantages."

A similar result was found for hedge fund trading activities. Franzoni and Plazzi (2012) find evidence that hedge funds, which are highly reliant on operating leverage, are also forced sellers during times of financial market turbulence. They conclude that "(H)edge funds that are more exposed to funding constraints because of their leverage, lack of share restrictions, asset illiquidity, low reputational capital, and trading style (are particularly impacted). Value-based trading strategies demand liquidity in bad times, whereas momentum strategies provide liquidity."

Optimization in the Face of Constraints: A Marginal Approach

Dynamically allocating capital in the face of the diverse constraints on solvency, leverage and liquidity imposed by rating agencies and regulators is a complicated problem.

There have been attempts to frame this capital allocation problem as a formal, mathematical optimization problem. This can be done by defining an objective function (such as the risk-adjusted value of the firm), which is maximized by allocating financial resources to one business or another subject to the solvency, leverage and liquidity constraints imposed by regulators and rating agencies. Examples are Kruger (2011), Pokutta and Schmaltz (2012) and Puts (2012) and, focusing only on liquidity constraints, Balasumgramanyan and Van Hoose (2012).

Each of these is successful in the sense that a tractable problem is formulated, mathematical or numerical techniques are applied and a solution is found in the form of "invest $X\%$ more in corporate lending or retail banking, $Y\%$ more in trading activities, etc." This is in itself no small feat.

However, these optimization problems often give "knife-edge[10]" solutions. Worse, they can represent substantial shifts away from the current business profile of the firm. And herein lies the problem: the fact is that corporate strategy depends on sources of competitive advantage which have been built up over years or decades, for example in terms of a strong customer franchise or distribution network, underwriting skills or operating efficiency. Rotating that strategy dramatically requires building new capabilities, which takes time and investment and is not without its own risk. While the theoretical analysis is useful, the actual solution space is limited in the near term by the practical realities of building capabilities and the history of how your firm got where it is today.

A more pragmatic approach is to understand the value of constrained financial resources "on the margin" and to explore the implications of incremental moves for the portfolio. While

---

[10]Knife edge refers to solutions which are unstable, e.g. a small change in the initial conditions can cause a dramatic change, as if the solution is on the edge of a knife and can fall to one side or another with a small push.

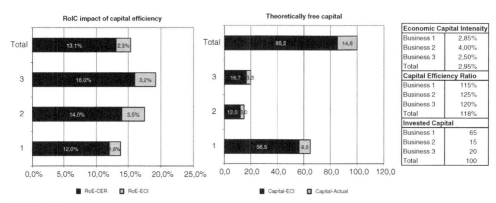

FIGURE 13.7   Capital efficiency metrics

this marginal approach runs the risk of yielding local maxima, the benefit is that it implicitly recognizes the current sources of the firm's competitive advantage.

Capital Efficiency KPIs   Unfortunately, the average and marginal solvency, leverage and liquidity intensity of businesses are expressed using different metrics defined by rating agencies, regulators and management's own risk appetite. It is not uncommon for rating agency capital to be binding but not regulatory capital, or regulatory leverage ratios but not the ratios defined by rating agencies.

Nonetheless, Chapter 3 defined two metrics which are useful for characterizing a business's marginal solvency and leverage intensity.

- ECI, defined as the *minimum capital required* to support the business from an economic perspective.[11] This metric reflects management's assessment of the capital required.
- CER, defined as the ratio of *actual capital to the minimum required capital*. Normally >1, the CER also reflects the capital and leverage constraints imposed by regulators and rating agencies or excess prudence.

Figure 13.7 uses these metrics to illustrate the average economic capital efficiency of different businesses. The graph on the left gives the difference between the actual RoIC and the theoretically achievable RoIC, where the latter is calculated as if you earned the same returns but used the minimum capital required (= actual RoIC * CER). The graph on the right gives a measure of the excess capital invested in the business based on the CER (= IC * (1 − IC/CER)). For example, although Business 1 has a realized RoIC of 12.0%, it could theoretically increase to 13.8% if it could free up the excess capital of 8.5 mio.

This information gives an indication about the capital intensity of the business relative to volumes and risk-adjusted returns. It also indicates where excess capital is currently tied up, leading to discussions on how to unlock the capital or relax the binding constraint.

---

[11] In the context of New Business RAPMs, ECI = PVRC/L for banks, where the present value of required capital is normalized by total loans, and ECI = PVRC/P for insurers, where the present value of risk capital is normalized by the net earned premium.

It is important to note that the source of the capital inefficiency is not transparent from the CER. For example, the CER could be higher because risk-based regulatory requirements are higher than management's view, representing a binding solvency constraint. Alternatively, the firm could have to hold more capital in order to meet a binding nominal leverage constraint. Regardless of the source, the implications for RoIC are equivalent.

Leverage Efficiency KPIs As discussed in Chapter 15, leverage is a fundamental and necessary ingredient for a bank's operating model: limited leverage = limited loans and trading positions = limited operating profits.

In contrast, leverage in excess of policy holder reserves is *not* a fundamental value driver for an insurance company.[12] While some operating leverage in the investment portfolio (e.g., in the form of repurchase agreements or sold Credit Default Swaps, CDS) may add basis points to the investment result, this is generally done "on the margin" and is not core to an insurance company's value proposition and operating model.

In light of the increasing emphasis on leverage constraints, the capital efficiency framework described above can be transformed to also explicitly recognize leverage. The first step is to define economic capital intensity relative to total bank assets and not just loans (e.g., $ECI_{Assets} = PVRC/Assets$). With this change, we can express the return on invested capital for a bank directly in terms of return on assets, leverage, capital intensity and capital efficiency, as in the following identity.

EQUATION 13.1: Leverage, return on assets and return on capital[13]

$$ROIC = net\ RoA^*Leverage + r_f$$
$$= net\ RoA^*\frac{Assets}{Capital} + r_f$$
$$= net\ RoA^*ECI_{Assets}^{-1}\ ^*CER^{-1} + r_f$$

where net RoA is the net return on assets less financing costs, where we assume that all net asset finance is done at the risk-free rate (e.g., net $RoA = (RoA - r_f)$).

The second equality follows from the identity below.

EQUATION 13.2: Leverage ratios for asset-based businesses

$$Leverage = \frac{Assets}{Capital} = \frac{Assets^*}{PVRC}\frac{PVRC}{Capital} = ECI_{Assets}^{-1}\ ^*CER^{-1}$$

This reformulation is intuitive for businesses which use levered assets to create operating returns: the return on capital depends on the return on assets (net of funding) and the amount of leverage used to purchase the assets.

---

[12]With the exception of double leverage at the holding company level used to mitigate the effects of uneconomic capital restrictions at the legal entity level. See Chapter 15 for a discussion.

[13]Total earnings are equal to $RoA^*A - RoL^*L$, which can be rearranged to $(RoA - RoL(1 - Leverage^{-1}))^*A$. Under the assumption that all financing is at the risk-free rate of return, this reduces to $(RoA - r_f)^*Leverage + r_f$ or net $RoA^*Leverage + r_f$.

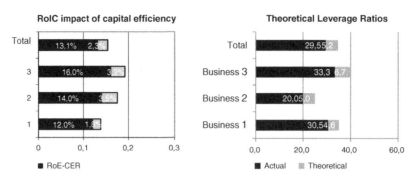

FIGURE 13.8 Leverage efficiency metrics for banks

The associated leverage ratios can be calculated in two ways: on an actual basis, including the excess capital required to support the assets (e.g., $ECI^{-1}_{Assets} * CER^{-1}$) and on a theoretical basis, without the excess capital (e.g., ECI^{-1}_{Assets}). The gap between the actual and theoretical, illustrated in Figure 13.8, gives an indication of where leverage constraints are binding.

The implications in terms of RoIC are identical with those reported earlier, illustrating that, in the end, it does not matter whether it is a risk-based solvency constraint or a nominal leverage constraint which is binding, only that a constraint prevents you from achieving the optimum capital efficiency ratio measured by ECI.

This information complements the capital or solvency view by giving an indication which business is the most leverage intensive, where leverage is artificially constrained either by risk or absolute leverage constraints, and the return on the leverage in the form of a risk-adjusted return on assets.

CHAPTER 14

Strategic Planning and Performance Management

S trategic planning and performance management together are defined as the process of setting goals, defining actions to achieve the goals, allocating and motivating resources to execute the actions and directing and monitoring performance to ensure successful execution. The strategic part describes which goals are set and how they are to be achieved, the performance management part ensures that resources are allocated and used effectively in reaching the goals.

CFOs run the strategic planning/performance management processes in most banks and insurers. In exercising these responsibilities, CFOs play an important role in value management by helping the company and the business units to define strategy, allocate capital, set targets and drive performance.

This raises a paradox. Given that all CFOs are "doing it," why is strategic planning rarely "strategic" in practice? Very often, what passes for "strategic" planning is a cumbersome, internally focused, bottom-up process primarily focused on negotiating incentive compensation targets and not on the initiatives which will fundamentally improve shareholder value. Dye and Sibony (2007) paraphrase some of the common symptoms well: "For the better part of a year, (corporate planners) collect financial and operational data, make forecasts, and prepare lengthy presentations . . . about the future direction of the business. But at the end of this expensive and time-consuming process, many participants say they are frustrated . . ." by the lack of impact on strategy or tactics.

This chapter begins by describing the typical strategic planning and performance management processes and then concludes with four recommendations to put the "strategic" back into strategic planning.

WHAT IS STRATEGIC PLANNING?

Strategic planning and performance management as corporate disciplines are not new. The theory of strategic planning has been developed, evolved and refined over the past 50 years by generations of academics and management gurus and, in practice, by generations of industry professionals.

As with the progeny of any evolutionary process, one can expect a wide variation of actual practices; nonetheless, because all share common roots and objectives – to set strategy, allocate capital and drive performance – the variations share some common characteristics.

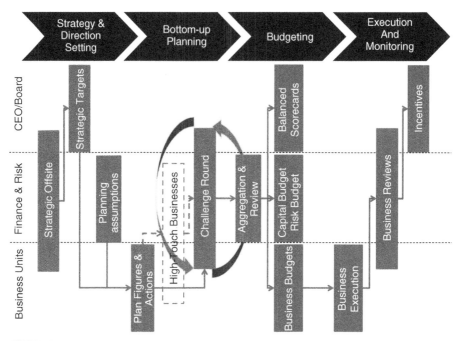

FIGURE 14.1   Generic strategic planning process

The Generic Strategic Planning Process

The generic strategic planning and performance management process is an annual process comprising four steps and involving different protagonists within the company. The four generic steps are illustrated along the horizontal axis in Figure 14.1.[1]

- Strategic direction setting, defining the corporate portfolio strategy and giving guidance consistent with that strategy to the business units.
- Bottom-up planning, with business units taking the guidance and developing detailed strategies and action plans.
- Dialog and budgeting, with the individual financial plans critically challenged by the corporate center. Once agreed, capital and other financial resources are allocated and the plans are translated into detailed financial budgets as well as balanced scorecards for measuring performance.
- Business performance monitoring and management, including regular business performance reviews and corrective actions as required.

The Generic Roles in Strategic Planning

Looking at the vertical dimension, there are three generic protagonists in the strategic planning and performance management process: the CEO/Board, the finance function and the business units.

---

[1]This discussion follows Wilson (2004).

Business Unit Management

Business units know the most about their local markets, competition, business system and, ultimately, how they create value. As a consequence, business units are often put at the center of the strategic planning process, responsible for the "heavy lifting" in terms of developing the detailed strategies, action plans and associated financial plans.

CEO/Board

By definition, diversified financial services companies have multiple businesses within their corporate portfolio. This represents two distinct challenges.

First, the *long-term composition of the corporate portfolio needs to be managed*, answering such questions as: Where will we invest for growth, where will we harvest and where will we divest? How will we finance the investment? How will we manage the group's scarce financial, risk and liquidity resources? Most importantly, how will we optimize the value of the portfolio so that it is more than the sum of its parts?

These are important questions, with the answers implemented through the firm's capital budget and capital allocation decisions. They are also difficult questions to answer because some will inevitably lead to "zero-sum" decisions,[2] with trade-offs between business units required.

Second, the *performance of each business unit needs to be challenged from a shareholder's perspective.* It is unrealistic to assume that each and every business is running optimally at any point in time: not all students can be in the top quartile and some may require additional attention and tutoring. Even if all businesses are well managed, there is always room to set "stretch targets" to encourage additional outperformance. Just like a private equity firm,[3] the corporate center as the "shareholder surrogate" needs to challenge the strategies and performance of the business units and take remedial action for those that are lagging.

The role of the CEO and Executive Board is to take these difficult decisions, setting the corporate portfolio strategy, balancing the requests for the group's limited resources and taking remedial action as necessary.

Finance Functions

The strategic planning and performance management cycle involves many people over an annual cycle. Success is determined in part by how well the process is managed, coordinating decisions and, ultimately, leading to actions.

Success is also determined by the quality of analysis and information used to support the decisions, including information from the financial accounts, operational KPIs, competitor benchmarking and market analysis. The CFO and finance function play an important role both in coordinating and supporting the process.

Step 1: Strategic Direction Setting

The process begins by confirming the strategic direction of the company and giving general guidance to the business units to be used for their bottom-up planning. Here, I take for granted

---

[2]"Zero sum" is a term used in game theory to describe situations where one of the players can improve their situation only at the expense of another. As a simple example, consider two players and one pie: if one of the players gets more pie, then it is at the expense of the other player. In a business context, if financing is limited, then investment decisions to grow one business may come at the expense of growth in another.

[3]See the discussion of the role of the corporate center in Part Two: Better information.

Objectives of the meeting
Looking backward: A review of performance and capabilities
- Did we do what we said we would do?
- How did we stack up relative to peers?
- How are our businesses and the portfolio valued by analysts?
- What are the opportunities and critical issues that we face?
Looking forward: Market developments, opportunities and threats
- Are there any short-term, emerging risks?
- What is the mid-term economic outlook?
- What are the long-term trends affecting our industry?
- What scenarios are relevant for our strategy and planning?
Discuss and review corporate strategy and its implications
- Does the strategy need refinement?
- What are the implications in terms of the Capital Budget and business portfolio?
Next steps, including communication

FIGURE 14.2   Illustrative agenda for the strategic offsite

that a corporate strategy is already broadly defined and requires only minor adaptation in order to align it with current market conditions and opportunities; some thoughts on formulating a more fundamental corporate strategy are given at the end of this chapter.

In order to adapt or refine the strategy, most firms conduct a strategic offsite early in the year prepared by the CFO and finance function. An illustrative agenda for a strategic offsite is outlined in Figure 14.2.

The agenda is designed to give comfort to those who appreciate linear thinking: looking backward to critically review the strategy and recent performance; looking forward to understand the factors which might influence strategy and future performance; discussing the alternatives; deciding on course corrections and implications for the capital budget and corporate portfolio.

The internal communication following the strategic discussion summarizes the conclusions and gives high-level guidance for bottom-up planning, typically including the following.

- High-level financial goals at the corporate and business unit levels, including top-line revenue and bottom-line operating profit, growth, risk-adjusted returns and dividend targets.
- An indication of the financial resources available to the business units, for example capital for acquisitions or organic growth, as well as risk limits to support investment risk, natural catastrophe risk retention, etc.
- Identification of the two to four specific issues each business will need to explicitly address during the bottom-up planning process.
- The designation of "high-touch" business units requiring additional management attention. This designation can be triggered by, for example, poor historical performance or extraordinary anticipated market developments.

Step 2: Bottom-up Planning

Based on the guidance, business units engage in an iterative, bottom-up planning process during Q2 and Q3. The objective is to reach agreement between the business unit and the corporate center on the unit's plan, financial goals and activities needed to achieve the goals.

Scenario Guidance

Different planning assumptions regarding, for example, interest rates, equity market developments or GDP would make business unit plans impossible to compare. As a consequence, a consistent *"baseline" scenario* covering external, macro-economic and financial variables needs to be used by the business units.

The baseline scenario can be set based on management's best estimate of future market conditions, although this might introduce spurious optimism into the planning assumptions and increasing the complexity as best estimates are negotiated. Another approach is to set the baseline scenario in a mechanistic manner based on market conditions at the end of Q2. In either case, the baseline scenario may be updated later in the year if markets change materially; however, this should be avoided as any update triggers a new analysis which increases the already heavy burden of the planning process.

Because reality will be different from the baseline scenario with absolute certainty, *sensitivity scenarios* representing moderate changes in the baseline scenario are defined and used to measure the plan's risk and to develop contingency actions. Sensitivity scenarios can be defined along single dimensions, for example, changes in interest rates or cyclical pricing conditions. Additional scenarios can be constructed by combining individual sensitivities through interpolation, extrapolation and aggregation, assuming that the direct effects are linear and that the cross-effects are negligible. In addition, "good" or "bad" scenarios can also be defined. In any case, the number of scenarios should be limited as each scenario can trigger a complete, new financial plan.

Bottom-up Planning

Armed with high-level guidance and planning assumptions, business units develop draft, multi-year plans for discussion. These plans typically include the following elements.

- *Summary.* An overview of the incremental value created under the plan, by line of business, and the associated action plans. The value should be estimated and communicated along with core KPIs, for revenue and operating profit growth, operating efficiency (e.g., expense ratios), underwriting effectiveness (e.g., loss ratios or loan loss provisions) and capital efficiency (e.g., actual capital intensity, solvency ratios), capital needed and anticipated cash dividends.
- *Market context.*[4] An overview of the "profit pool," including market demand, growth and profitability, as well as the business's competitive positioning, including relative growth rate, profitability and industry-specific operating KPIs covering operating efficiency, underwriting effectiveness and capital efficiency.
- *Plan.* A summary of the unit's financial plan, including the following.
  - Income or operating profit statements for the next 3 years, including operating KPIs.
  - Balance sheets and associated balance sheet KPIs for the next 3 years, including the development of assets and reserves, regulatory and rating agency available and required capital, liquidity and leverage resources and ratios, distributable free capital and planned dividend payments.

---

[4]Later in this chapter, we suggest splitting strategy development from annual planning and target setting; the "market context" is more logically placed in the strategic discussion.

- ▩ A deep dive on new business economics by line of business, including revenue/growth, technical underwriting/New Business RAPMs, any deltas between plan and return targets, etc.
- ▩ Key planning assumptions (e.g., market growth, pricing margin increases, retention rates, etc.).
- ■ *Actions.* A description of the three to five key new initiatives for extracting value from in-force and new business, expenses, investments or projects.
- ■ *Risks and contingency planning.* Identification of key risks to the baseline.
- ■ *Update on multi-year strategic initiatives.* A specific update on the status of multi-year strategic projects affecting distribution, operations, systems, etc.

The Challenge Round

As a final step, the business plans are discussed and challenged by the corporate center. The challenge is typically concluded with a formal presentation by the business to the CEO, CFO and CRO of the group late in Q3, similar to the "Capital Markets Day" presentations made by the group to analysts.

The analogy to a Capital Markets Day is not so far-fetched – at the end of the process, the center will decide on the capital budget and allocate capital resources across the corporate portfolio and strategic initiatives, just as investors decide whether to put a buy, hold or sell recommendation on your shares and how much they want to invest in the group relative to other opportunities. The most important questions to be answered during the challenge round include the following.

- ■ Do the plans meet the strategic objectives and top-down indicators set earlier? If not, why not?
- ■ Are the plans aggressive enough? Are they overly optimistic? Do they represent a "stretch target," a "hockey stick" or a "walk in the park"/"momentum plus" strategy?
- ■ Are the actions focused on the right priorities? Are they realistic, in terms of implementation challenges and potential impact? Is there sufficient commitment to execute?

In reality, the presentations tend to be more for ceremony, with the real discussions and negotiations happening beforehand through an iterative loop with the corporate center, including Finance, Risk and Treasury. This ensures "no surprises" – that they are pre-syndicated and agreed and, if not, then the issues are understood in advance and anticipated.

This iterative process is sufficient for well-performing businesses in a stable environment. Businesses not performing well or those strongly impacted by external factors may need a "high touch," involving more formal meetings more frequently during the planning process and when monitoring performance afterwards.

Step 3: Target Setting and Budgeting

Three distinct activities take place in the third phase, typically in Q3. At the corporate level, a balanced scorecard is defined for the leaders of each of the business units using measures and targets linked to value creation. Balanced scorecards are discussed in greater detail in Step 4 below.

Within the finance and risk functions, the individual plans are aggregated and translated into the firm's capital budget or top-down resource allocation framework. More specifically, risk limits and solvency, liquidity and leverage resources are allocated to the businesses. Given that risk, financing and liquidity have been discussed in the planning process, this last step should be without contention or surprises.

At the business level, the plan is translated into more granular budgets and specific targets for each functional area. These targets need to be aligned with those committed to by the business leadership: for example, holding the business unit CEO to value-based performance targets will not be effective if only revenue targets are set within the business unit.

Step 4: Performance Management

The performance management cycle consists of business reviews where performance is monitored regularly (monthly, quarterly) and course corrections implemented as necessary. At the end of the year, performance is evaluated and incentive-linked compensation is determined.

Business Reviews

Business performance is monitored on a monthly/quarterly basis through Monthly Business Reviews (MBRs) or Quarterly Business Reviews (QBRs), respectively. MBRs represent the most important performance control mechanism available to the group; they also represent an important opportunity for sharing insights on strategic and emerging issues. Sidebar 14.1 provides a skeleton of the business review process.

SIDEBAR 14.1: MBRs AND QBRs

Objectives. The primary objectives of periodic business reviews are to:

- manage expectations (especially of the "shareholders," the corporate center) with regard to current operating performance and outlook;
- assess the progress of key strategic initiatives and transversal projects;
- discuss emerging issues and course corrections in response;
- exchange ideas on group strategy (quarterly).

The objective of a business review is *not* to solve issues during the meeting, nor to engage in operational decision making: business unit management should have already identified the relevant issues and developed proposals for resolution. If they have not, or if they come to the business review unprepared, then you have the wrong management in place.

Information. MBRs focus on understanding the operating performance of the business, the forecast for the year and the position vis-à-vis planning. QBRs include a discussion on strategy and external benchmarking.

More important than tables and figures, a business review should focus on the MD&A (Management Discussion and Assessment), which summarizes the performance and actions, trends, issues and risks to achieving the forecast and plan. Information to support the business review should include value and operating KPIs relevant for the business:

- including a comparison – actual, plan and updated forecast;
- granular enough to indicate support for a root cause analysis;
- presented in a common format (across businesses where appropriate), consistent with the format used in planning;
- calculated consistently, using the same data source and approaches with sufficient controls in place to ensure quality.

Businesses should *not* be allowed to introduce alternative metrics or use data sources which are not reconciled and suitably controlled.

Process and ownership. The business review is "owned" by the business unit. This "ownership" needs to be demonstrated: participation is mandatory, management is responsible for ensuring that the relevant issues and actions are discussed and management is prepared to be challenged on current performance, outlook and actions. The materials for the business review should be provided in advance of the meeting, allowing sufficient time for questions to be raised beforehand.

Performance and Incentives

At the end of the year, incentive compensation is determined. A "good" incentive system accomplishes three goals:

- it reinforces the firm's strategic and tactical priorities;
- it aligns managers' and shareholders' interests, focusing on long-term value creation;
- specifically for financial services firms, it aligns managers' interests with broader stakeholders by minimizing excessive risk taking.

Specific objectives are communicated in the form of a *balanced scorecard* based on *SMART objectives* (described in Sidebar 14.2). The scorecard is then embedded into an incentive structure (e.g., base salary, cash bonus, deferred bonus, etc.), which rewards long-term, risk-adjusted value creation and includes mechanisms to counter potentially excessive risk taking (e.g., deferral with claw-backs).

SIDEBAR 14.2: ON INCENTIVE SYSTEMS FOR BANKS AND INSURERS

BALANCED SCORECARDS

Balanced scorecards include a combination of financial and non-financial measures used to evaluate performance. The concept was popularized in the early 1990s by Kaplan and Norton (1992, 1993, 1996).

Scorecard measures should align with and reinforce the strategic and tactical objectives of the firm. They need to include both measures of short-term business results as well as longer-term shareholder value, including value management KPIs such as risk-adjusted returns/New Business RAPMs, profitable growth, measures of cost efficiency, underwriting effectiveness and capital efficiency.

SMART TARGETS

Scorecard targets should be "SMART" (Doran, 1981): Specific, Measurable, Attainable, Realistic and Time-related.[5] They should balance individual objectives with the performance of the entire company, especially in situations where cooperation and alignment between activities is required to achieve the corporate objectives.

Scorecard measures are generally defined in a three-step process: first, define the firm's high-level objectives; second, define measures which evidence success (or failure) in meeting those objectives; third, set concrete targets for each measure. The interconnections and consequences of the high-level objectives can be mapped into a strategic map across different departments in order to align scorecards across functions (Lawrie and Cobbold, 2004).

There are three common criticisms of SMART balanced scorecards.

- First, they often include too many measures. A general rule of thumb is that any more than three to five measures dilutes focus, reduces autonomy in deciding how to achieve the objectives and may lead to evaluations which are "on average" meeting expectations but missing the truly important points.
- Second, there is too high an emphasis on measurable targets and not enough on judgment when evaluating performance; this may lead managers to optimize the specific target, or to "manage" the numbers, at the expense of common sense and long-term value creation.
- Third, even a series of well-designed short-term targets may be insufficient to fully align managers' and shareholders' interests.

ALIGNMENT WITH SHAREHOLDER INTERESTS

Ultimately, interests need to be aligned in order to address the "agency problem." If decisions and outcomes are difficult to monitor, managers may take decisions which maximize their own interests at the expense of shareholders. SMART balanced scorecards are a key element in aligning incentives; the second is a properly designed incentive structure used to align interests comprising base salary, cash or short-term incentives and longer-term deferred compensation.

Especially deferred, equity-based incentives[6] are used to align interests; they do so by converting managers into partial owners (Jensen and Meckling, 1976). The deferral period should be sufficient to ensure that the consequences of actions taken today can

---

[5]Other acronyms for SMART or SMARTER are possible, for example (significant, simple, sustainable), (motivational, manageable, meaningful), (appropriate, agreed, actionable, ambitious, aspirational, acceptable), (results-based, results-oriented, realistic, reasonable), (trackable, tangible, timely, time-oriented), (evaluated, ethical, enjoyable, engaging, evidenced), (re-evaluated, rewarded, revisited).

[6]Equity-based or equity-like incentives can include Non-Qualified Stock Options (NQSOs), Incentive Stock Options (ISOs), restricted stock, phantom stock, performance shares, performance units and stock appreciation rights. The different alternatives may have different consequences for taxes, expensing, dilution, retention, etc. See, e.g., Coleman and Fortier (2002).

impact compensation. However, over-reliance on equity-based incentives has been criticized for three reasons.

- Equity reflects the value of a portfolio of businesses and not individual performance; in this respect, "stock and stock options (granted to management) are like issuing only one report card for a whole class of students" (Bennett, 2002). This effect can be counterbalanced by adding business unit specific metrics linked to long term performance into long term compensation plans.
- The value of equity reflects many factors, not all of which are under the control of managers. "The uncertainty a manager faces about future bonuses should be limited to whether the targets will be achieved; it should definitely not include any uncertainty about the monetary value the bonus will have" (McTaggert *et al.*, 1994). This may lead to a preference for cash or cash equivalents over equity-based pay-outs.
- Managers may be tempted to manipulate earnings, giving the illusion of value by meeting Wall Street expectations but not actually creating value.

In general, measures tied to short-term business results are used to fund the annual, cash incentive plan whereas measures tied to shareholder value drive the longer-term, deferred compensation plan.

Combined, these considerations help to explain the most common elements of an incentive compensation structure. Cai *et al.* (2010) outline how bank and insurer inventive systems comprise the base salary, short-term cash incentives and longer-term, equity-based incentives including restricted stock grants, option grants and LTIPs (Long-Term Incentive Payments). The different relative proportions of each are interesting, depending on sector (Figure 14.3).

ALIGNING WITH STAKEHOLDER INTERESTS: PREVENTING EXCESSIVE RISK TAKING

One concern about incentive compensation structures is unique to financial services – it has to do with the potential for excessive risk taking. Given limited liability, both managers and

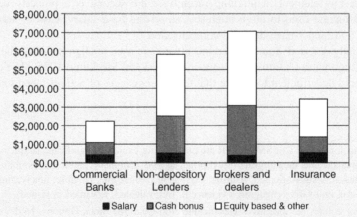

FIGURE 14.3 Compensation structure of various financial sectors
Source: Adapted from Cai *et al.* (2010).

shareholders may have an incentive to take higher risks, a "heads I win, tails you lose" bet, which increases the value of shares and managers' incentives at the expense of depositors, policy holders, bond holders and potentially taxpayers if the firm is deemed by the government to be "too big to fail."[7] This behavior can go unnoticed during bull markets as the risk profile of the firm may be complex and managers may have more information.

These considerations lead naturally to incentive systems with hold-back and claw-back features, originally recommended in the Squam Report (French, 2010) and synthesized by Small (2013): ". . . institutions should be required to hold back a substantial share – perhaps 20% – of the compensation of employees who can have a meaningful impact on the survival of the firm." The holdback would be forfeited if the firm's solvency ratio dropped below a specific threshold, set well in excess of minimum regulatory solvency requirements; beyond forfeiture, the pay-out would not depend on the firm's performance, eliminating any upside potential, and could not be hedged by the manager. The deferral period, for example 5 years, should be long enough for the impact of the manager's decisions to be clear. Other recommendations include setting caps on the ratio between incentive compensation and the base salary.

Implementation requires the identification of *material risk takers*, defined as individuals who – through decisions or influence – can expose the organization to material risk. Typically included in the list of material risk takers are traders and underwriters as well as those who design and implement the models used to measure risk and risk-adjusted performance.

Equally as important, it is necessary to use judgment in evaluating performance: results are not all that count, but also how the results are achieved. For example, the effect of "windfalls" should be capped and the achievement of stretch goals through inappropriate behavior needs to be forcefully discouraged.

Finally, an appropriate governance structure should be used to design and implement incentive compensation structures as well as to monitor and evaluate performance. This governance structure should balance quantitative and qualitative aspects and seek input from the second and third line of defense, including risk, compliance and audit.

WHY DOES STRATEGIC PLANNING FAIL AND WHAT CAN BE DONE ABOUT IT?

Strategic planning and performance management have evolved over the last 50 years, both as a management science and a corporate discipline. In all fairness, the results do a serviceable job in defining the budget for the next 12 months and setting incentive targets consistent with the budget.

The Issues and High-level Solutions

However, not everyone is universally enamored with the process or the results. Only 45% of the respondents to a recent survey said that they were satisfied with the strategic planning process and

---

[7]For a good overview, see Cai *et al.* (2010), Beal *et al.* (2013), Small (2013).

- Focus on value,
- Separate strategy from tactical decisions, bringing in an external view
- Make the firm's strategy explicit and communicate it
- Resource and structure the Finance Function appropriately

- Strategic inertia caused by the process, an internal focus and lack of challenge
- Limited focus on value, more focus on revenues, growth and earnings
- Significant investment with limited returns

FIGURE 14.4   Improving the strategic planning process

only 23% said that major strategic decisions were actually taken (McKinsey, 2006). It seems as if many strategic planning processes are in reality very expensive and time-consuming negotiations for next year's incentive targets, triggering very little strategic thinking.

In my experience, there are three root problems with the typical strategic planning exercise, as illustrated in Figure 14.4.

- First, it rarely delivers strategic insights and may actually contribute to strategic inertia (see Sidebar 14.3).
- Second, it does not focus on value creation – but rather on earnings and growth – and so it should come as no surprise that it does not deliver value.
- Third, it generates a tremendous amount of work which is disproportionate to the benefits delivered.

As mentioned, the typical strategic planning process does a serviceable job at producing annual budgets and targets but fails at driving strategy and performance. Rather than throwing

SIDEBAR 14.3: STRATEGIC PLANNING AND STRATEGIC INERTIA

"Strategic" planning may actually promote strategic inertia, both by design and lack of sufficient challenge.

BY DESIGN: THE BIRTH OF AN ELEPHANT

Consider the generic planning process. The Executive Board gives guidance in Q1; businesses plan bottom-up in Q2/Q3, employing many resources, choreographed into a complex interactive and iterative dance with the corporate center; finally, in Q4, approximately seven to nine months after the start,[8] the Executive Board approves the detailed business unit plans and ratifies the (amended? refined?) corporate strategy for the following year.

This planning cycle and the birth of an elephant have two things in common: first, the gestation periods are both long and protracted and second, it takes proportionally the same amount of commitment, effort and huffing-and-puffing before the results emerge. At least at the end of one you get a baby elephant.

In the case of strategic planning, consider what happens a mere three months later – the whole process begins again! How much appetite would you have to consider a bold new strategy after having just given birth to a baby elephant? How much appetite would you have to radically change direction with this year's bonus, carefully negotiated, on the line? It is no wonder that, in the absence of an external shock, most "strategic" plans are incremental and evolutionary.

Now add external dynamics to the mix: suppose that yours is a cyclical industry suffering from deteriorating (or improving) conditions. How will you react to the changing conditions?

In case of an improving market, your bonus for the year is secured after the first six months; instead of adjusting the plan upward, why not take the windfall? Also, if the bar is raised this year, there is no guarantee that you can negotiate a lower target for next year when the favorable tail winds disappear.

In case of a deteriorating market, if you choose to write less, less-profitable business, you will not meet your targets with absolute certainty; however, there is always a chance that the market could improve after you write the (bad?) business. The bonus for this year is already sunk, so why not take the call option on an improving market situation?

Both scenarios assume that targets are not adjusted, which is a reasonable assumption: raising the bar requires renegotiating targets with implications for bonuses; lowering the bar is not looked upon favorably by shareholders and the Board, especially if it is seen as a way to keep bonuses high while shareholders suffer. Another, more important, reason not to adjust target levels during the year is that business leaders may come to the conclusion that it is easier to renegotiate targets than to work hard and meet the plan.

LACK OF EFFECTIVE CHALLENGE

The corporate center can help drive value by challenging plans and performance. Getting the balance right is critical: too much challenge at too tactical a level can lead to a bureaucratic process that constrains entrepreneurial initiative. However, too little challenge can lead to "low-ball" or "current-year-plus" plans, consciously negotiated to preserve upside potential in bonuses; or to overly optimistic, "hockey stick" plans designed to buy time for business units with lackluster performance.

Hall *et al.* (2012) say that few finance functions are organized and resourced to play a meaningful role in challenging the business: "Some are more strategy focused but primarily prepare board papers and support special initiatives for the CEO, the chairman, or the board . . . Too often missing are the intense reviews, debates, and challenges that lie at the core of value-creating corporate strategy decisions."

---

[8]A recent survey of over 50 (predominantly) UK insurance companies had 77% of the financial planning processes lasting over four months, and of these 37% lasting over eight months (IncisiveMedia, 2014).

the baby out with the bath water, there are four actions which can improve the strategic planning and performance management process.

- *Focus on value at every step in the process*, from strategy to capital allocation to performance management. Actively benchmark the strategies and value against peers, bringing in an external focus.
- *Disentangle and elevate the strategic capital allocation discussions from the more frequent discussions on operating performance*, benchmarking strategy and performance against peers.
- *Make the strategy, objectives and implications for capital allocation explicit, both internally and externally*, in order to reinforce commitment.
- *Resource the finance function appropriately for business analysis and challenge.*

Focus on Value

Strategic planning focuses on many things; unfortunately, value is not often one of them. According to the OWC (2003) survey cited earlier, the top three things large banks and insurers focus on are earnings and earnings growth, revenue and revenue growth and cost or cost income ratios, in that order. Shareholder value, embedded value and intrinsic value were at the bottom of the list, even below market share!!

Unfortunately, success in risk-based, capital-intensive businesses requires an even stronger focus on value and specifically on the role of capital and risk in creating value. *Value, capital and risk need to be put center stage at every step in the strategic planning–capital allocation–performance management cycle.*

Changing the nature of the dialog can be eye opening: every 1 billion invested at 9% RoIC throws off 90 million in expected earnings, which sounds pretty good if revenue and earnings growth are the primary targets. However, at a 10% cost of capital, every 1 billion invested is only worth 900 million, a 100 million loss in terms of shareholder value. Put this way, the investment sounds absolutely horrible!

It may be easy to ignore and excuse a 10 million earnings shortfall relative to an amorphous concept such as the cost of capital for a single year, especially if driven by more concrete revenue and earnings targets; it is much more difficult to ignore a 100 million hole created by an investment which destroys value or a share valuation multiple of 0.9×. Explicitly valuing businesses and investment alternatives will raise "inconvenient truths," but these are truths that need to be addressed.

Here are some things to think about in order to build a "focus on value."

- *Explicitly value your company and its businesses.* Conduct a sum-of-parts valuation and make the excess returns (or losses) generated by incremental investments transparent *before* you allocate capital. Use this information to "explain" your actual share valuation to reinforce the message.
- *Make value the "headline" and the "baseline" in your strategic plan and your balanced scorecards*, transparently linking value creation, invested capital and return on capital and drilling down to the operating value drivers, including profitable growth, operating efficiency, underwriting effectiveness and capital efficiency.
- *Be explicit about where capital is generated, where that capital is invested and at what returns.* Do not let momentum carry under-performing businesses forward.

■ *Run your planning dialog as if it was an internal "Capital Markets Day,"* with businesses competing for investment dollars and the corporate center a well-informed investor eager to invest in the right business, but just as eager to return capital to shareholders if the returns from growth are not compelling.

Disentangle Strategy and Capital Allocation from Tactical Decisions

Strategy often gets shortchanged in favor of tactics during the planning process. Golsby-Smith (2011) suggests that "When the two activities are conflated, the strong, data-driven budgeting process can overwhelm the more fragile (but equally important) strategy-making process." This unfortunate reality is in part because setting bonus targets is more interesting to management and in part because capital allocation and portfolio optimization can be threatening.

Although the typical strategic planning process bundles strategy and tactics, in reality they are distinct – strategy focuses on where and how to compete in the long run and points the direction for capital allocation across businesses; tactics take the quantum of capital as given and focus instead on operating performance within a business over a shorter-term horizon.

If strategy is being shortchanged by tactics in the "strategic" planning round, the solution is to disentangle the strategic discussions from the operating discussions. Golsby-Smith (2011) continues by asserting that every business leader has two jobs, "to run the operation as it exists today, and to rethink the organization so that it can survive and thrive into the future. These are two distinct jobs. The budgetary and business planning system helps the organization manage today's operations . . . The strategic system . . . confronts an uncertain, further-off future." The distinction between the two roles can be reinforced.

■ Narrow the focus of the bottom-up planning process and MBRs on near-term performance, making both processes shorter, "lighter," more streamlined and more focused on operating performance.
■ Separate strategic discussions from the budgeting process and the MBRs/QBRs. While strategic issues can be earmarked during the QBRs, they should be tabled and only discussed at length during a separate strategy discussion, along with strategic investments and capital allocation over a 3- to 5-year horizon.
■ Emphasize an outside-in view, by benchmarking your company against the market and competitors in terms of strategies, actions and valuations.

Finally, consider whether the discussions on corporate portfolio optimization are not better done first within a smaller, more senior group of leaders. These discussions can be intense and threatening. Building a consensus within the Board on the issues and possible solutions before further refinement and syndication more broadly may make the task easier.

Make Your Strategy and Objectives Explicit

It is challenging for some firms to explain their corporate strategy, primarily because their strategy is nowhere explicitly stated but rather implicit or "emergent" in the actions taken by management. As a consequence, the same firms generally give only minimal guidance on financial targets. Other companies make their corporate strategy, capital budget and financial objectives explicit, using them as a communication and commitment device both internally and externally.

Why Make Strategy and Objectives Explicit?

There are four reasons why you should explicitly formulate and communicate the firm's strategy and financial objectives.

Enable leadership. Good leaders communicate the direction they want to go and communicate it often. If you can't tell people where you want to go, don't be surprised if they won't follow you.

From vision to reality. Knowing where you are going is only half the battle; the other half is getting there. Wicks (2010) comments that "A poor strategy can't be expected to produce good results. But is a good strategy enough . . . ? . . . the ability to implement strategy is more important . . . suggesting that more time and effort must be devoted to making a strategic decision work than to making the perfect strategic decision."

Clear communication of both strategy and objectives is critical for implementation. Collis and Rukstad (2008) question, "Can you summarize your company's strategy in 35 words or less? . . . Conversely, companies that don't have a simple and clear statement of strategy are likely to fall into the sorry category of those that have failed to execute their strategy or, worse, those that never even had one."

Maintain operational focus. A well-defined and communicated strategy also adds value by sharpening focus. For example, Collins and Rukstad (2008) suggest that "In an astonishing number of organizations, executives, frontline employees and all those in between are frustrated because no clear strategy exists for the company or its lines of business." According to Collins and Rukstad, the frustration arises when projects are shut down after significant investment because they "don't fit strategy" or when there are mixed messages sent with respect to the attractiveness of a market segment or product.

Combat the conglomerate discount. Many large banks and insurers suffer from a "conglomerate discount," with the intrinsic, sum-of-parts value higher than the firm's market capitalization. A discount can arise from many sources, for example due to complexity, a lack of apparent synergies, increased costs in the form of additional management layers, limited transparency and/or a reduced emphasis on shareholder value (see, e.g., Heppelmann and Wrona, 2009).

These issues are echoed by Kaye and Yuwono (2003): "The prejudice of analysts and investors against the conglomerate model is understandable . . . (as many are) obsessed with empire building, sacrifice value for growth, overpay for acquisitions, hang on to businesses that will never prosper . . . and fail to develop structures, impose disciplines and create cultures that sustain value growth."

It is straightforward to imagine how better communication, both in terms of strategic intent and financial reporting, may help to address many of the factors which presumably cause a conglomerate discount.

But let me try a different argument. Let's assume that your firm has a well-formulated strategy outlining where, why and how it creates value. Why wouldn't you explain this clear and powerful message to analysts and investors? If analysts are as disenchanted with financial conglomerates as Kaye and Yuwono suggest, it seems that you have an obligation to communicate your strategy clearly and effectively.

An example is the recent case of Vivendi, which came under tremendous pressure from shareholders to break up the company. According to Bloomberg (Mawad *et al.*, 2012): "While analysts estimate the shares should trade at between a 10 percent and 20 percent discount to the sum of Vivendi's parts, the disparity has been growing. Last month Chairman Jean-Rene Fourtou said the 'conglomerate discount has become gigantic, close to 40 percent.'" In their defense, "In a March 27 letter to shareholders, Fourtou and Levy said, *it's a misconception that Vivendi is a portfolio of businesses that have no connection*" (emphasis added).

If it was such an important misconception, leading to a 40% discount and pressure to break up the firm, why wasn't management clear in communicating the strategy and the synergies in the first place? There is a big difference between telling a story to fit the facts afterwards versus clearly articulating upfront where you are going and why. Analysts are not mind readers, and they do not have crystal balls.

Clear communication can be a powerful weapon in combating a conglomerate discount. However, to be effective, the company has to walk-the-walk as well as talk-the-talk, actually living the strategy in terms of dividend policy, acquisitions and divestitures. Clearly communicating both the strategy and the financial consequences helps to reinforce the commitment.

How to Make It Explicit?

Collis and Rukstad (2008) and Johnson *et al.* (2008) suggest that the communication takes the form of a hierarchy of statements – on mission, values, vision, strategy and balanced scorecard. Unfortunately, these statements end up seeming formulaic and "textbooky." From a hard-nosed analyst perspective, I believe that *management should at a minimum make explicit:*

- what businesses and markets are important, today and in the future as "strategic bets";
- what makes the company uniquely positioned to extract value from these markets and from the sum of the portfolio;
- expectations with respect to earnings growth, return on capital and dividends;
- the firm's capital budget, e.g. where cash is generated, where it is invested and how much is expected to be returned to shareholders.

Resource Finance Appropriately

Putting the "value" back into "value management" requires a significant investment in experienced Finance personnel:

- to conduct and analyze the sum-of-parts valuation, in-depth peer comparisons and industry benchmarking;
- to play the "buy-side analyst," covering and challenging the businesses from a tactical and strategic perspective;
- to make recommendations with regard to the capital budget and its allocation across strategic initiatives and operating businesses;
- to negotiate short-term performance targets and conduct regular business reviews;
- to run the strategic planning and business review processes.

Best practices would suggest that a *dedicated team in the finance function* undertake these activities and that this team should:

- *be separate and distinct from financial and management reporting* or other activities to ensure that the team does not focus on numbers generation, but rather on driving impact;
- *parallel the way that the business is segmented or organized* in order to ensure alignment on strategic and operational discussions;

- *have sufficient "segment specialists"* (e.g., for LH or distribution, which cut across the organization) in order to ensure that technical sectoral themes and challenges are appropriately addressed;
- *be staffed predominantly with senior executives with a strong business and financial background, supported by talented, high-potential associates;*
- *combine analytical and problem-solving skills with excellent communication and persuasion skills.*

CORPORATE STRATEGY

The discussion has assumed that a corporate strategy exists, either implicitly or explicitly, and that the annual planning process focuses at most on the review and potential refinement of that strategy. This section discusses what a corporate strategy might "look like" and some considerations for defining it.

What is a Corporate "Strategy" and How is It Decided?

It is fair to say that financial services firms face a variety of important, dynamic issues.

- We offer highly complex products which require multidimensional operational, capital and knowledge-intensive expertise in very competitive and highly regulated markets.
- Our industry is not immune to "game-changing" external forces, including regulation run rampant, technological changes which influence established cost and distribution paradigms, the emergence of non-traditional entrants (e.g., Google, Amazon, supermarkets, etc.) and the (potentially irrational) behavior of established competitors.
- Finally, the competitive landscape in the future will likely be very different from the current landscape, in part due to predictable but slow-moving "mega-trends" (e.g., globalization, digitalization/Internet, demographic trends, etc.) as well as more rapid and unpredictable factors such as regulatory and technological change.

Positioning the company in this complex environment is challenging – a Gordian knot[9] to be cut in order to claim the prize. At the risk of over-simplification, there are three strategic questions which banks and insurers need to address.

- First, what are the businesses we choose to be in today?
- Second, how should we position our portfolio over the next 10–20 years, allocating resources appropriately?
- Third, how do we respond dynamically in the interim to industry disruptions?

From this perspective, corporate strategy can be defined as the answer to why you do what you do today, where you want the firm to be a decade from now and how you will respond to

---

[9]"Gordian knot" refers to an intricate knot tied by King Gordius of Phrygia and cut by Alexander the Great with his sword after hearing an oracle promise that whoever unraveled the knot would be the next ruler of Asia.

unexpected bumps in the road along the way. This definition of "strategy" is broadly consistent with the more detailed definitions found in the academic literature.[10]

For those who believe in linear thinking, corporate strategy is based on fundamental analysis and developed through a well-defined strategic planning process. The reality is very different, however, with the development of corporate strategies rarely following a linear path. Mintzberg (1973) suggests that corporate strategies emerge in one of three ways: a planning mode, "a highly ordered, neatly integrated one, with strategies explicated on schedule by a purposeful organization"; an adaptive mode, "in which many decision makers with conflicting goals bargain among themselves to produce a stream of incremental, disjointed decisions"; and an entrepreneurial mode, where "a powerful leader takes bold, risky decisions."

This matches my own experience: if strategy defines where resources are allocated, then over the past 20 years I have seen it variously set by strong, entrepreneurial CEOs, through well-structured planning processes and as the result of consensus building or bargaining processes – and often all three in the same organization at different points in time! Which approach is taken depends on the situation, the company, its culture and its leadership.

What is the Role of Fundamental Analysis?

Regardless of how strategy is set, it is not set in a vacuum. Such an important decision requires analysis . . . and, typically, lots and lots of analysis. The most common analysis falls into two broad areas.

- "Market attractiveness," or understanding the potential "profit pools" defined by the market/product/customer segment, the trends affecting the market over time and the risks to each.
- "Competitive capabilities," understanding the source of the business's competitive advantage and its potential relative outperformance.

Market Attractiveness

One critical dimension influencing a firm's strategy is the relative attractiveness of the markets in which the company chooses to compete. The analysis most often considered when setting strategy includes the following.

- *"Profit pool" analysis*, including current market conditions and a forecast of future growth rates, pricing and profitability characteristics and competitor behavior.[11]
- *Long-term trends, risks and opportunities.* Specific examples include predictable changes in demographics such as age, income, penetration, etc., predictable trends in local or regional economic development, demand patterns, technological factors influencing the economics of distribution or production, etc.
- *Short-term discontinuities, risks and opportunities.* Specific examples include potential regulatory changes (e.g., Basel III/Solvency II, Dodd–Frank, Volker Rule, etc.), adverse

---

[10]An integrative definition of corporate strategy can be found in Johnson *et al.* (2008), who state that a *corporate strategy* should comprise a clear view on "The long-term direction of an organization; the scope of an organisation's activities; gaining advantage over competitors; addressing changes in the business environment; building on resources and competences (capabilities); values and expectations of stakeholders."

[11]See, e.g., https://solutions.mckinsey.com/globalbankingpools/cms/

macro-economic scenarios affecting consumer demand and/or net asset value (e.g., recession, equity market crash, etc.), and so on. Given the unpredictable nature of some discontinuities, this is often done using scenarios.

Digression on Industry Fundamentals   The attributes used to analyze market attractiveness – current profitability, growth, long-term predictable trends and potential short-term discontinuities – are intuitive, easy to understand and pragmatic.

Unfortunately, there is a risk that the analysis remains focused on the current situation without asking a more fundamental question: *Why* is the market attractive and what *will ensure that it stays this way* in the future? Frameworks such as the Porter five-forces framework, described in Sidebar 14.4, are often used to answer this more fundamental question.

SIDEBAR 14.4: PORTER'S FIVE-FORCES FRAMEWORK[12]

Michael Porter's five-forces framework, first published in the *Harvard Business Review* in 1978 (Porter, 1978), is designed to answer the questions: Why is the market attractive and is it likely to stay that way? It posits five industry-specific factors grounded in industrial economics which explain whether an industry is capable of sustained excess profits and the threats to this profitability. These five forces are described in Figure 14.5.

- *Threat of new entrants.* Factors which might affect this dimension include high absolute cost advantages; proprietary products, patents, knowledge or experience; unique access to inputs or distribution; restrictive government policy; high economies of scale, potentially driven by high capital or investment requirements; strong influence of brand on demand behavior; or, high consumer switching costs.

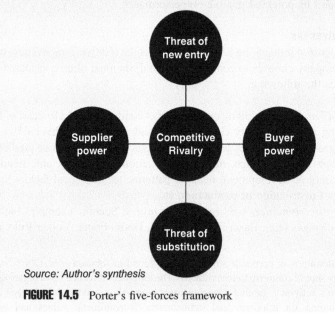

Source: Author's synthesis

FIGURE 14.5   Porter's five-forces framework

---

[12] http://hbr.org/2008/01/the-five-competitive-forces-that-shape-strategy/ar/1

- *Threat of substitutes.* Factors affecting this dimension include high consumer switching costs or low propensity to switch; availability of close substitutes; sensitivity of consumer choice to changing attributes such as price, performance, features, etc.
- *Supplier power,* allowing them to capture more of the economic surplus from downstream products or services. Relevant factors include supplier concentration; substitutability and differentiation of inputs; impact of inputs on cost or other product attribute, as well as contribution to total product cost; input switching costs; threat of forward integration.
- *Buyer or distributor power,* allowing them to capture more of the economic surplus at the point of sale. Relevant factors include high bargaining power and buyer volume, concentration; price sensitivity; low product differentiation and high availability of substitutes.
- *Degree of rivalry.* Relevant factors which influence how existing competitors will likely react if their position is challenged include high exit barriers; high industry concentration; low industry growth rates; high fixed costs and high occasional overcapacity; low switching costs; importance of market for individual competitors.

"Competitive Strength": Relative Performance

The second area of analysis concerns the relative strengths and performance of the individual businesses. One of the most important tools for comparing relative strengths is through *internal and external benchmarking.*[13] Benchmarking has three prerequisites: the definition of a relevant peer group; the definition of attributes which distinguish firm performance; and, finally, a deeper understanding of the business drivers which differentiate the best from the worst firms based on those attributes.

Definition of Peers   The peers selected should be relevant for your business and sufficiently diverse to offer insights. External peers should include firms operating in the same products/markets/regions; they should include large, diversified competitors but also specialized or regional competitors, especially since the top quartile in any market may well be dominated by local or niche players. In addition, it is likely that your business segments will be compared against the best in class in each segment, especially with large financial conglomerates trading at a discount and increasing shareholder activism.

You might also include firms offering close substitutes or in adjacent customer segments (e.g., if they are deemed to present a potential threat or have transferable business practices), as well as potential "game changers" (e.g., firms with radically new distribution models or technological platforms should also be on the radar).

Finally, internal peers within your own portfolio are extremely useful, both due to the more granular information available as well as the opportunity to directly transfer best practices in the process.

Definition of Benchmarks   The second step is to define those facts, figures or attributes which are to be compared across the peer group. Qualitative attributes may include strategy, management

---

[13]American Productivity and Quality Centre (1997): "Benchmarking is the process of improving performance by continuously identifying, understanding (studying and analyzing), and adapting outstanding practices and process found inside and outside the organization and implementing the results."

strength, etc. More common are quantitative benchmarks, which fall into two categories: *operational benchmarks* and *value benchmarks*.

Operational benchmarks link to specific activities within a value chain. For example, sales and distribution benchmarks may include market share, position in the league tables, measures of customer satisfaction, customer retention rates or growth in agents or distribution points. Similarly, transaction processing may be benchmarked based on scale and efficiency metrics.

Value benchmarking focuses on measures which directly drive valuations. These include metrics which can be compared across businesses (e.g., growth, cost income ratios and return on capital), as well as profitability measures specific to the industry (e.g., new business margins, combined ratios, net interest income margins, etc.).

The selection of benchmarks will depend on the availability of comparable data: while it may be desirable to measure the personnel or capital intensity of a specific business, such data may not be available in the public domain. Even if available, it may be difficult to compare if firms report on different accounting bases or if the company uses different cost or revenue allocation principles. In this case, assumptions need to be made in order to make the data comparable.

Most benchmarks are sourced from financial statements, voluntary supplementary disclosures (e.g., analyst presentations, MCEV reporting for the insurance industry), industry associations and surveys sponsored by individual companies or the industry.

From Benchmarks to Understanding Performance   The final step is to analyze and understand what the top-performing firms are actually doing differently. According to Jarrar and Zairi (2010), benchmarking is the process of ". . . learning lessons about how best performance is accomplished. Rather than merely measuring best performance, benchmarking focuses on how to improve any given business process by . . . discovering the specific practices responsible for high performance, understanding how these practices work, and adapting and applying them to the organization."

A Digression: Combining Market Attractiveness and Competitive Strength

The direct comparison of PC and LH insurance businesses is challenging; a comparison of insurance against asset management and banking activities becomes even more challenging. Some tool for making comparisons across disparate segments is needed.

One of the most useful approaches for comparing the attractiveness of balance sheet-oriented businesses is along the growth and risk-adjusted return dimensions, illustrated earlier in Chapter 13.

In addition, corporate portfolio frameworks can be used to integrate market attractiveness and competitive capabilities. These frameworks were developed during the 1970–1980s, coinciding with the emergence of the corporate conglomerate. The results include the two-dimensional "attractiveness/capabilities" matrices (e.g., the BCG stars–dogs and the GE/McKinsey 9-box analysis), as well as the more qualitative SWOT analysis, described in Sidebars 14.5 and 14.6.

SIDEBAR 14.5: TWO-DIMENSIONAL "ATTRACTIVENESS/CAPABILITIES" MATRICES

Condensing the two dimensions of market attractiveness and competitive capabilities so that the results can be compared across businesses and communicated quickly and intuitively is not an easy task. However, this was exactly the challenge that the management of many industrial companies faced in the 1970s and 1980s when the "conglomerate" model was at the height of its popularity. The BCG star–dog and GE/McKinsey 9-box matrices were both developed during this period.

THE BCG STAR–DOG–CASH COW MATRIX

The BCG star–dog matrix is often considered the "grandfather" of corporate portfolio frameworks. The matrix plots businesses along two dimensions: market share and growth. According to Bruce Henderson of BCG,[14] the rationale for focusing on these two dimensions is because:

- The value of a product depends on its obtaining a leading share of its market before growth slows.
- Every product should eventually be a cash generator; otherwise it is worthless.
- Only a diversified company with a balanced portfolio can use its strengths to truly capitalize on growth opportunities.

As is illustrated in Figure 14.6, "stars" are defined as businesses which have high market share in high-growth markets; they are attractive because they offer growth, but require investment. In contrast, "cash cows," characterized by high share but low growth, throw off more cash than they can invest. "Question marks" require investment but their ultimate attractiveness is not yet determined, while "dogs" require investment to build share but are not in growth markets.

In the absence of a well-functioning capital market, the "optimal" corporate portfolio is one which has sufficient "cash cows" to fund its "stars" and develop its "question marks," with management shedding its "dogs." This broadly translates into a corporate strategy where each business is assigned to a category – Grow, Hold, Harvest and Divest.

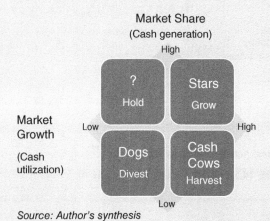

Source: Author's synthesis

FIGURE 14.6 BCG star–dog–cash cow matrix

---

[14] https://www.bcgperspectives.com/content/Classics/strategy_the_product_portfolio/

The common criticisms of the BCG matrix is that market share does not always equate to value creation (let alone cash generation), that industry growth is not the only determinant of market attractiveness and that external financing is also available.

GE/McKinsey 9-box Matrix[15]

Enter the GE/McKinsey 9-box matrix,[16] illustrated in Figure 14.7, a "second-generation" corporate portfolio framework. It is similar to the BCG matrix in that the two dimensions are related to industry attractiveness and corporate performance or ability to compete; the difference is that it is more complicated, taking into account multiple criteria along each dimension.

For industry attractiveness, factors include market or profit pool size and growth, industry profitability, degree of competitive rivalry, barriers to entry, influence of macroeconomic and other factors on demand variability and asset values, etc. (e.g., many of the same criteria used in Porter's five-forces framework).

For business unit competitiveness, factors might include market share, relative growth and profit margins, advantages in production or distribution, intangibles such as brand or intellectual property, etc.

The factors affecting each dimension are supported by a variety of analyses, including benchmarking. An overall rating for each dimension is derived either judgmentally or by applying defined weights to each factor.

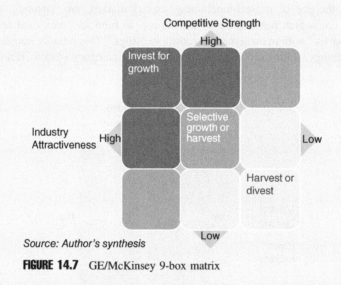

Source: Author's synthesis

FIGURE 14.7   GE/McKinsey 9-box matrix

---

[15] http://www.bcg.com/about_bcg/history/history_1968.aspx

[16] https://www.mckinseyquarterly.com/Enduring_ideas_The_GE-McKinsey_nine-box_matrix_2198

SIDEBAR 14.6: QUALITATIVE SWOT ANALYSIS

The SWOT (Strengths, Weaknesses, Opportunities, Threats) analysis represents a qualitative assessment incorporating both market attractiveness as well as competitive capabilities. The SWOT analysis is credited to Humphrey (2005) in the 1960s and 1970s.

The SWOT analysis, illustrated in Figure 14.8, begins by defining a "straw man" corporate objective – for example, to be the most profitable PC insurance company in the market or to have the broadest global retail footprint. A qualitative assessment is then undertaken to determine if the "straw man" is achievable and the issues which need to be addressed in order to achieve it. Additionally, strategies are discussed for converting threats into opportunities and for matching strengths to opportunities.

Strengths and weaknesses are influenced by internal factors (e.g., the characteristics of the business that give it an advantage/disadvantage over others) – for example, brand or distribution strengths, underwriting or capital strength, cost competitiveness, etc.

Opportunities and threats are influenced by *external* factors which affect the business – for example, profit pool growth, improving penetration rates, changes in regulation, changes in competitor behavior, changes in consumer demand, etc.

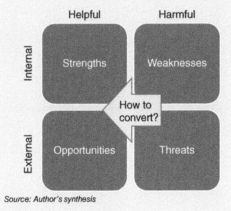

Source: Author's synthesis

FIGURE 14.8   SWOT matrix

CHAPTER 15

Balance Sheet Management

As illustrated in Figure 15.1, CFOs and CROs can significantly influence the value of their firm through three balance sheet management activities.

- First, through *asset/liability management*, managing the structural mismatch position resulting from core banking and insurance activities through improved product design, investment policy and capital markets transactions.
- Second, through *cash and liquidity management*, ensuring that all cash and funding requirements can be met even under stressed market conditions.
- Third, by managing the *capital and debt funding structure*, finding the optimum balance between different forms of equity and debt to secure the lowest-cost, most resilient funding structure within the constraints imposed by regulators and rating agencies.

BALANCE SHEET MANAGEMENT ACTIVITIES

Although introduced separately, these three activities are in fact integrally linked to one another, to the strategy of the company and to its capital budget. As such, they need to be managed in an integrated and coordinated fashion. The firm's ALCO, treasury and risk functions play a key role in managing and coordinating these activities.

Asset/Liability Management

Paradoxically, the largest financial market risk positions for most commercial and retail banks are not in their trading book but rather in the banking book, positions derived from their core customer-lending and deposit-taking activities. Most banks borrow short term from depositors and wholesale funding markets in order to lend longer term to personal and corporate borrowers. This natural mismatch (e.g., long-term assets funded by short-term liabilities) can generate positive net interest income in a steep yield curve environment – often called "riding the yield curve" – but can also expose the bank to losses in a rising rate environment as refinancing costs increase. Many banks choose to run this risk in order to earn the spread differential.

Similarly, the largest financial market risk exposure for insurance companies is their net asset/liability position: insurance companies collect premium today and invest it in order to pay

3. Better Decisions –
How to create value in Finance & Risk areas of responsibility?

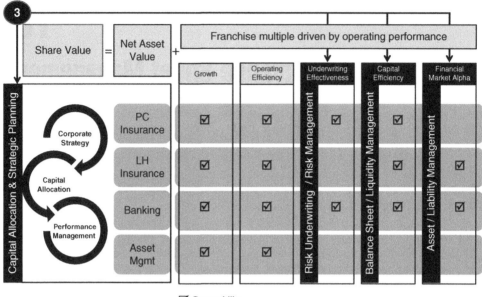

☑ Core skills

FIGURE 15.1 How to create value in the finance and risk areas of responsibility

claims in the future. A mismatch occurs if the assets are not invested in line with the risk-minimizing "benchmark" defined by their liabilities. For PC insurers, the risk-minimizing benchmark is the best-estimate future claims, equivalent to zero-coupon cash flows. Like banks, many PC insurers also "ride the yield curve," investing in longer-duration assets than their liability benchmark in order to pick up additional yield.

For LH retirement and savings products, the liability benchmark is more complicated: first, because future obligations may contain complex embedded options and guarantees and second, because the obligations can be longer in duration than the bonds available in the capital markets. As a consequence, some of the mismatch risk may be structurally "non-hedgeable," or impossible to hedge completely unless the products are redesigned. On top of this, many LH insurance companies choose to run an open mismatch position, especially if they participate in excess investment returns above the rate guaranteed to the policy holder.

The resulting mismatch positions for banks and insurers may lead to higher expected earnings, but they also lead to higher risks. It is my contention that these earnings are seldom valued at a premium by shareholders and may well lead to a discount on the firm's net asset value if they come from structurally non-hedgeable positions. As a consequence, running an open mismatch position should be done consciously and always from a value-based orientation.

Managing asset/liability mismatch risk takes place at two levels. The first is at the product level, through better product design, and the second is at the portfolio level, defining an appropriate investment and hedging strategy to manage the cumulative mismatches arising from the net customer exposures.

Several parties are involved in the A/L management process: first and foremost, the Asset Liability Committee (ALCO),[1] which defines the A/L management policy, framework and strategy; second, the Asset Liability Management (ALM), treasury and Investment Management (IM) units responsible for implementing the strategy and taking tactical decisions within the framework. The commercial or product units are also involved to the extent that product design and commercial strategy needs to be adjusted.

An important element of any ALM framework is the Funds Transfer Pricing (FTP) system used to price and transfer financial market risk embedded in a bank's loans and deposits and an insurer's policies to the ALM unit.

Cash and Liquidity Management

Effective cash and liquidity management ensures that the short-term cash and funding needs of the firm can always be met, both during "normal" times as well as during times of financial market or idiosyncratic stress.

The distinction between "normal" times and periods of stress is important. Short-term funding is normally taken for granted during normal times; however, insufficient liquidity during periods of stress can force a bank or insurer into resolution even if it is economically solvent from a net asset value perspective.

This risk is called funding liquidity risk, defined by the Bank for International Settlements (BIS, 2008) as ". . . the risk that the firm will not be able to meet efficiently both expected and unexpected current and future cash flow and collateral needs without affecting either daily operations or the financial condition of the firm."

More liquidity and long-term stable financing is generally a good thing, but it comes at an opportunity cost if very liquid but low-yielding assets such as government securities are held or if too much equity is used to finance the business.

Three parties are integrally involved in the cash and liquidity management process. First the ALCO, which is responsible for the cash and liquidity management framework and strategy. Second the treasury unit, which manages the short-term cash and funding requirements on a day-to-day basis. In most institutions, treasury reports to the third party – the CFO. In addition, the treasury function also manages the firm's corporate (as opposed to transactional) foreign exchange exposures.

Managing the Firm's Funding Structure

The firm's capital funding structure is defined by how much equity the firm has available, how far that equity is levered through senior debt or equity substitutes to finance its investment in operating subsidiaries (financial leverage) and how additional operational leverage capacity is allocated across the different businesses consistent with the overall strategy of the firm and the constraints imposed by regulators and rating agencies.

The firm's funding structure directly influences its solvency ratio, weighted average cost of capital, return on equity and dividend policy. Although the subject of spirited debate, it is through these channels that the capital funding structure has the potential to influence the value

---

[1]Given the broad role, spanning asset/liability, cash and liquidity and balance sheet funding, the ALCO is occasionally called the Finance or Finance and Capital Committee at some banks and insurance companies.

of the firm. In addition, the long-term funding structure forms the anchor point around which the treasury function conducts cash and liquidity management activities.

From a theoretical perspective, shareholders may prefer more leverage to less as it is used to finance a larger overall balance sheet and therefore a higher absolute return on equity; higher leverage also generally increases the percentage return on equity. Reality is more complicated, however, with banks and insurers typically holding more capital than the minimum required, with the quantum of excess capital driven by a variety of factors. Managing the capital structure optimally within the constraints imposed by regulators, rating agencies and the firm's own risk appetite is a critical task given the significant potential impact on value.

Three parties are integrally involved in the long-term funding decisions of the firm: first the ALCO, which typically sets the firm's long-term stable debt and funding strategy; second the CFO, who usually takes the tactical decisions; third the treasury unit, which executes the decisions.

THE ASSET/LIABILITY COMMITTEE (ALCO) MANDATE AND AGENDA

In summary, are several key players in balance sheet management: the ALCO is the governance body responsible for defining the policy and frameworks used to manage the asset/liability mismatch, cash and liquidity and the long-term funding structure of the firm as well as the strategic baseline positioning of each. The ALM, treasury and investment functions are responsible for executing those strategies and for taking tactical positions within delegated limits.

The finance and risk functions have a key role to play in these activities. In most institutions, the treasury and ALM functions report directly to the CFO and the CFO is often the Chair of the ALCO or its equivalent. Because of the potential impact on the firm's risk profile, the CRO is a key member of the ALCO and may even be Chair of the ALCO.

This section describes the balance sheet management organization and processes, beginning with the ALCO and continuing with the ALM unit and the treasury function.

The ALCO

Every bank and insurance company has an ALCO or equivalent committee. In most cases, the mandate of the ALCO is significantly broader than just asset/liability management, covering all balance sheet management activities including the management of cash and liquidity and the firm's long-term funding profile. Because it influences the allocation of financial resources and commercial strategy, the ALCO needs to be closely coordinated with the firm's strategic planning process.

The ALCO Mandate or "Rules of the Game"

Effective asset/liability management works on two levels: first, at the commercial level, coordinating activities between the product and ALM units in order to ensure that the structural mismatch from customer business is manageable; second, at the portfolio level, actually managing the mismatch through capital market transactions.

Consistent with this definition, the *American Banker*[2] describes the ALCO as "A committee, usually comprising senior managers, responsible for managing assets and liabilities to maximize income and safety over the long run. In a financial institution, the ALCO is usually responsible for asset and liability distribution, asset and liability pricing, balance sheet size, funding, spread management, and interest rate sensitivity management."

Similarly, the Society of Actuaries (2003) defines ALM for insurers as ". . . the practice of managing a business so that the decisions and actions taken with respect to assets and liabilities are coordinated . . . the ongoing process of formulating, implementing, monitoring and revising strategies related to assets and liabilities to achieve an organization's financial objectives, given the organization's risk tolerances and other constraints."

A Broader Definition   As the previous definitions from the American Banker and the Society of Actuaries imply, the ALCO typically plays a broader role than narrowly focusing on asset/ liability management. Typically, the ALCO is also the governing body for cash and liquidity management and the firm's long-term funding structure.

This broader role makes sense because all three balance sheet management activities – asset/liability management, cash and liquidity management and capital funding policy – are integrally linked, with decisions in one area influencing the others. It also makes sense because the personnel who have to deal with each of the three balance sheet management activities overlap substantially; as a consequence, firms find it easier to extend a single ALCO agenda than to create three different committees. The remainder of this Handbook is written from the perspective of a broader ALCO mandate.

The ALCO Mandate in Detail   In larger institutions, the ALCO operates at a governance level in each of the three balance sheet management areas

- asset/liability management
- cash and liquidity management
- long-term capital funding structure

by:

- defining and approving the balance sheet measurement and management frameworks;
- setting the balance sheet strategy through baseline targets and limit recommendations;
- regularly reviewing and steering the strategic baseline;
- deciding on material transactions.

These decisions may either be taken on behalf of the Board of Management or in the form of recommendations for approval by the full Board of Management. The ALM unit, treasury and investment functions work within these boundaries to manage the A/L portfolio, the cash and liquidity and long-term funding profile of the firm.

In larger organizations, the ALCO focuses on strategy and policy and may be supported by more tactically oriented sub-committees – such as a treasury or ALM committee that meets more frequently. In smaller organizations, the ALCO also undertakes more operational decisions regarding portfolio positioning. These considerations lead to the following broad ALCO mandate.

---

[2] http://www.americanbanker.com/glossary/a.html

SIDEBAR 15.1: GENERIC ALCO MANDATE

Committee objective. Optimize the financial earnings, value and risk profile of the company's structural balance sheet while ensuring adequate capital, cash and liquidity resources to support profitable growth via the following steps.

1. Approving balance sheet management frameworks.
   a. *ALM measurement and management*, including the firm's FTP system and cash flow replication approaches; accounting and value-oriented financial risk measures; associated investment and derivatives policies, guidelines and limit framework.
   b. *Cash and liquidity measurement and management*, including the firm's liquidity risk measurement framework and associated liquidity management policies, guidelines and limit framework.
   c. *Capital funding measurement and management*, including the framework for determining the firm's leverage capacity, its solvency capital targets, dividend policy and the basis for calculating the firm's cost of capital.
2. Defining the strategic baseline or target positioning in coordination with the strategic planning process and recommending concrete management limits to the Risk Committee for approval.
   a. Coordinate the firm's commercial and ALM, cash and liquidity and capital funding strategy in the strategic planning process. Define the firm's funding and liquidity risk appetite.
   b. Based on the strategic plan and risk appetite, define the
      - strategic baseline or *target asset/liability portfolio* and associated *management limits* to be delegated to the ALM unit;
      - strategic baseline or *target cash and liquidity profile* and associated *management limits* to be delegated to the treasury unit and operating business units;
      - strategic baseline or *target capital funding structure* and the associated *management limits* to be delegated to the treasury unit.
   c. Based on the strategic baseline and market conditions, determine the firm's cost of capital in aggregate and by business unit for the planning period.
   d. Allocate capital, liquidity and operating leverage resources to the business units, ALM unit and treasury unit consistent with the strategic plan.
3. Approving material transactions, based on the authorities delegated by the Board of Management.
   a. All material A/L and cash and liquidity transactions which fall between the competence of the full Board of Management and the delegated business unit limits.
   b. All external capital and financial leverage transactions, including
      - transactions which impact financial leverage, including unsecured debt and hybrid issuance, intra-group loans, etc.;
      - material cash funding decisions, including intra-group capital injections, loans and dividends, as well as acquisitions and divestitures.
4. Regular review and steering, ensuring that the management framework and limits are adhered to and making course changes as market developments warrant.

ALCO Composition

ALCO decisions have both financial and commercial implications. It is therefore important that the right people are involved, especially those who have a stake in the outcome. The typical ALCO is therefore comprised of the following.[3]

- The Chairman, a role typically played in larger organizations by the CFO or a combination of CFO and CRO. Because the ALCO influences both the commercial and financial management strategy of the firm, the bulk of the agenda should be chaired by the CFO, a member of the C-Suite with a "first line of defense" orientation. However, if the ALCO also approves limits and the control framework, this part of the agenda should be chaired by the CRO given its second line of defense orientation.
- Core members, including the CFO, CRO, Head of ALM or CIO in insurance companies (representing the execution of the strategic A/L positioning), Head of Treasury (representing the funding and liquidity management execution), Head of Products (representing the underwriting and customer origination functions) and, finally, Head of Economic Research in order to provide a forward-looking market view. Additional members may be invited on an ad hoc basis as the agenda warrants.
- An ALCO Process Manager, responsible for maintaining and coordinating the agenda and ensuring follow-up. In my experience, this role is critical and I will spend more time on this in the next subsection.

The implementation of ALCO decisions is the responsibility of the ALM, treasury and commercial units (and, in insurance companies, the investment function), with monitoring provided by the ALM Process Manager.[4]

In larger organizations, the ALCO may be supported by other, more operationally or tactically focused committees which meet more frequently.

- For insurers, as discussed later, ALM and investment management are part of the same value chain. As such, some insurers have an Investment Committee which meets more frequently (e.g., monthly or ad hoc as needed), chaired by the CIO. It is positioned between the ALCO and the asset managers and decides how to position the investment portfolio around the strategic asset allocation benchmark, approves large investment decisions within its delegated authority and monitors the activities and performance of the internal and third-party asset managers.
- A Treasury Committee for both banks and internationally active insurers, meeting monthly or ad hoc as required and chaired by the Head of Treasury. The purpose of this committee is to coordinate the operational cash and liquidity management activities of the group. Liquidity and leverage are a group resource; it may be the case, however, that different subsidiaries are better positioned to tap into specific pockets of liquidity and funding – such as commercial paper programs, securities lending and borrowing or repurchase agreements, etc. The purpose of the Treasury Committee is to coordinate these activities; it consists of those responsible for managing operating leverage and liquidity across the group.

---

[3]In smaller organizations, the ALCO may be chaired by the CEO. Occasionally, it is chaired by the Chief Investment Officer (CIO) in insurance companies, reflecting the strong integration of ALM and investment management.

[4]The remainder of this Handbook will use CIO and Head of ALM interchangeably for insurers.

Balance Sheet Management, Integration into Strategic Planning

Because of its potential to influence business strategy and the firm's capital budget, the ALCO's agenda and processes have to be well coordinated with the company's overall strategic planning process. This is accomplished by a well-defined corporate calendar and standing agenda.

As discussed earlier, the strategic planning process is divided into four phases: a direction setting phase at the beginning of the year; a bottom-up planning phase; a budgeting phase, where the plans are translated into concrete targets and financial resource allocations are finalized; and finally, ongoing execution and performance reviews during the year. Table 15.1 outlines an example corporate calendar, integrating the ALCO activities explicitly into these four phases.

Strategic Direction Setting   Normally, the Top-Down Indicators (TDIs) are defined by top-line revenue and bottom-line operating profit targets for each business unit in order to "set the bar" for the bottom-up planning phase which follows. The ALCO is involved in the process by:

- ensuring that the TDIs can be met given the projected capital, funding and liquidity resources for the group for the coming year;
- providing guidance to the businesses with regard to the availability of these resources to support their business activities;
- setting expectations with respect to cash dividends to be up-streamed, consistent with the TDIs and capital projections;
- giving guidance on individual products which might have an impact on ALM, expressed in terms of target volumes and pricing strategies – especially for products which cannot be hedged.

Bottom-up Planning   The ALCO approves the market outlook and rate scenarios to be used as the basis for planning. In addition, the ALCO develops its own ALM, cash and liquidity and capital funding strategy proposal for the coming year, including any major shifts and the associated impact on earnings and risk.

In Q3, the business units prepare plans putting detailed numbers and specific actions behind the strategy. Prior to approving the plans, the ALCO needs to: review the financial market assumptions to be used for planning purposes as well as the cost of capital to be used by the business segments; define its ALM, cash and liquidity and capital funding strategy into concrete baseline or targets; plan the associated investment or net interest income results; iteratively review the financial resources (e.g., capital, cash, liquidity and funding) requested by the business units as well as the projected ALM-relevant volumes.

Final Budgeting   In Q4, after the plans have been approved, the ALCO and Risk Committee conclude the planning process by explicitly budgeting the financial resources to be allocated to the business units and setting limits aligned with each business's approved strategy.

Balance Sheet Management, Quarterly Agenda

In addition to contributing to the strategic planning process, the ALCO takes decisions on a more frequent, operational level in three broad areas (illustrated in Table 15.2): first, reviewing (and adapting as necessary) the ALM, capital and liquidity baselines; second, approving material transactions; third, reviewing the overall ALM framework.

TABLE 15.1 Integration of ALCO into strategic planning process

	Jan	Feb	Mar	Apr	May	Jun	Jul	Aug	Sep	Oct	Nov	Dec
Activity	Strategic direction			Bottom-up planning						**Budgeting**		
Balance sheet management	Indications for capital, leverage and liquidity capacity for the group and for the operating entities.			Guidance on market rates and scenarios assumptions to be used for planning. Iterative process, from guidance to final strategy, on <ul><li>strategic asset/liability baseline;</li><li>capital, leverage and liquidity capacity for the businesses to be used for planning.</li></ul>						Final budgeting of capital and balance sheet resources. Translation into explicit limits: <ul><li>risk limits for AL unit, treasury and operating businesses;</li><li>capital, funding and liquidity resources for operating businesses</li></ul> Products impacting ALM.		
Commercial activities impacting ALM	Indications for product pricing and volumes from an ALM perspective (e.g., limits on non-hedgeable volumes, etc.).			Iterative process, from guidance to final strategy, on major ALM-relevant changes in product and product margin considerations.								

TABLE 15.2 ALCO quarterly agenda

Activity	Jan	Feb	Mar	Apr	May	Jun	Jul	Aug	Sep	Oct	Nov	Dec
Quarterly agenda: Ongoing execution and performance review												
Risk Committee	X			X			X			X		
ALCO	X			X			X			X		
Treasury and Investment Committee		X	X		X	X		X	X		X	X
ALM preparation and review of implementation		X	X		X	X		X	X		X	X
Quarterly (or monthly) ALCO agenda												
ALM baseline review and decisions (regularly)												
1. Market developments and current positions												
2. Likely scenarios, position alternatives and implications												
3. Decision and responsibilities												
Capital and liquidity baseline review and decisions (regularly)												
1. Projected solvency, cash and dividends, base case and stress scenarios												
2. Projected liquidity position, base case and stress scenarios												
3. Implications, alternatives and recommendations												
4. Decision and responsibilities												
Transaction approval (ad hoc as necessary)												
1. Own funding transactions (debt issuance, securitization, etc.)												
2. Large transactions impacting funding and liquidity positions												
ALM framework review (spread across the year or in an annual batch)												
1. Review individual product and FTP model assumptions and revise as necessary												
2. Commercial policy change proposals with high impact on ALM												

Reviewing Baseline or Target Positioning   One of the most important decisions made by the ALCO is the strategic baseline positioning of the AL portfolio, cash and liquidity and capital funding structure of the firm. The strategic positioning of each involves a trade-off between risk and return. Although the decision is complex, the process for taking the decision is characterized by four intuitive questions:

1. How did our positioning perform since the last meeting?
2. What is our current position?
3. What is the impact of likely scenarios on different alternatives?
4. Which alternative is optimal?

Committees generally are not effective at taking decisions. In order to make the ALCO more effective, recommendations should be developed, pre-syndicated and agreed *before* the meeting if possible. If no prior agreement can be reached, the syndication process will at least provide an understanding of where the issues are and the room to maneuver. In my experience there are a few common mistakes made by ALCOs which might prevent them from taking good decisions (see also Darling Consulting Group, 2007).

- An *in*effective ALCO (or any committee, for that matter) doesn't prepare beforehand, assuming that they can go through each of the decision points during the meeting.
- An *in*effective ALCO meeting will have an agenda which does *not* support decision making, but instead focuses on facts and figures.
- An *in*effective ALCO will have the goal of informing the participants, not on taking the decisions. Following the logical sequence of the four questions above, the structure of the meeting should support decisions.
- An *in*effective ALCO will be confronted with a wealth of information, none of which is specifically focused on supporting a decision.

A common symptom is the Zahlungsfriedhof or "numbers graveyard" phenomenon – reports the size of the Manhattan telephone book (for those of you who can appreciate such a dated reference), where all the information is available in principle but none is accessible. Another symptom is the "hopscotch" phenomenon – having to go from the table on page 23 to the graph in the appendix on page 47 and back to the qualitative description on page 12, etc. in order to answer the questions which need to be answered.

In contrast, an effective ALCO will have a limited number of pages for each decision (e.g., AL portfolio positioning, cash and liquidity and capital funding position), each answering the critical questions. What happened in the markets? What is our current position? What can happen in the future? What are the recommended changes to the positions? Any additional information is relegated to an appendix or backup.

- An *in*effective ALCO will either exclude representatives from the commercial businesses which are impacted by the decisions, making implementation more difficult, or include more people than absolutely necessary, complicating the decision-making process.
- Finally, an *in*effective ALCO will not follow up and track the implementation effectiveness of decisions taken.

Reviewing Commercial A/L Implications In addition to setting the strategic baseline, the ALCO will influence the institution's commercial policy both directly and through the ALM framework.

Commercial policy. The ALCO influences the bank's loan and deposit pricing policy as well as volume targets by maturity, with the objective of ensuring that margins, volumes and resulting net interest income are optimized after managing the structural mismatch.

Similarly in LH insurance companies, the ALCO influences decisions on the use of management levers for steering the profitability of existing business (e.g., crediting strategy for traditional participating products, cap and floor rates for fixed index annuities, etc.), new business pricing strategies as well as volume targets for difficult-to-hedge liabilities.

ALM framework review. The ALCO is charged with reviewing and updating the ALM and FTP framework on a regular basis. This includes, for example:

- reviewing the replicating portfolio assumptions used to represent demand deposits and other non-maturing accounts in banks and the benchmark portfolio used to represent an insurer's liabilities. Both replicating portfolios are based on models and assumptions which need to be periodically reviewed and validated;
- reviewing the FTP rates, including all the adjustments built into the framework such as any term funding premium, bid–offer spreads, etc.

ALCO Preparation: The Role of the ALM Manager

Committees are not particularly good at taking decisions, suffering from a variety of predictable ills: it is difficult to bring people up to speed and take decisions on complex issues in less than two hours; the meeting can be hijacked by special interest groups and random coalitions; tough decisions can always be delayed or avoided by a request for additional analysis; important subjects can get lost in the agenda, etc.

Nonetheless, committees do serve a valuable purpose – they build a common understanding of the issues and consensus on the solution, reinforcing the commitment needed when implementation involves cross-functional efforts.

Successful decision making by committee depends on careful preparation and the ALCO process manager plays an important role in this, before, during and after the ALCO.

Before the meeting, the ALCO process manager:

- Coordinates preparation of the discussion materials and recommendations. For example, when reviewing the strategic baseline for the AL portfolio and the cash and liquidity position, it is important to understand likely scenarios and possible alternatives. This is supported by the process manager, who brings together market and investment experts, helping them to formulate their views on potential scenarios and possible actions and then coordinating the analysis required to understand the implications for the portfolio. Similarly, the ALCO process manager should coordinate with the product areas the discussion of the product models and assumptions which influence the ALM portfolio.
- Pre-discusses and syndicates the analysis and conclusions. The process manager should ensure that the analysis and recommendations are pre-syndicated, not only to the ALCO members but also to those key individuals who provide counsel to the ALCO members, making sure that they understand the issues and have had time to think critically about the recommendations. The process manager should build a consensus on the direction before the meeting if possible and, if not possible, understand the issues and positions before the meeting commences.

During the meeting, the process manager ensures the smooth running of the agenda, moving the meeting toward decisions, and is responsible for taking the minutes.

Following the meeting, the process manager follows up with the areas responsible for implementation (e.g., ALM unit, treasury, commercial, etc.), ensuring that the committee's decisions are implemented.

In terms of the individual, the ideal ALCO process manager should have a good understanding of the technical issues in order to facilitate a content-rich discussion before, during and after the ALCO meeting. Equally as important, the individual should have a personality which allows them to coordinate and build consensus without necessarily having to "own" each individual issue or analysis. By its mandate, the ALCO brings together a diverse collection of interests and forges a consensus; the ALCO Manager should have the "soft" skills necessary to achieve this objective.

THE ASSET/LIABILITY MANAGEMENT (ALM) UNIT

The ALM unit is responsible for managing the structural market risks arising from the firm's customer business. The starting point for asset/liability management is the separation of commercial or underwriting decisions from the financial or ALM decisions.

The value of bank loans and deposits is affected by both underwriting and financial risks. The credit risk of a borrower affects the value of the loan, as does the level of interest rates through the discounting of future cash flows, the resetting of variable interest payments and the sensitivity of prepayment options. Similarly, the value of deposits is affected by interest rates, both through discounting and deposit re-pricing.

Insurance is also affected by both underwriting and financial risks. The present value of PC policies is subject to adverse claims developments, but also to changes in interest rate levels used to discount the best-estimate claims: as interest rates decline, the discounted value increases, lowering the insurer's economic net asset value. In addition to longevity, mortality and morbidity risks, the claims of LH savings and retirement products depend in a complex manner on financial markets, with policy holder obligations being directly linked to the performance of financial investments due to their embedded options and guarantees as well as the company's own participation in the returns from general account assets.

All banks and most insurers separate underwriting decisions from market risk management decisions in one way or another. Many firms implement a full, formal FTP system and ALM organization to achieve a clear and transparent separation. The reasons are straightforward.

- Both underwriting and financial risk management decisions can have significant impact on the value of the firm, but
- they are sufficiently different in terms of systems, processes and skills to warrant focused, specialized management and
- combining the two may lead to the wrong incentives, with underwriting functions tempted to "bet the market" in order to make up for lackluster underwriting results.

Put cynically, it may seem easier to "visit the (market) casino" than it is to generate solid returns based on world-class underwriting, even though the latter are more highly valued by shareholders.

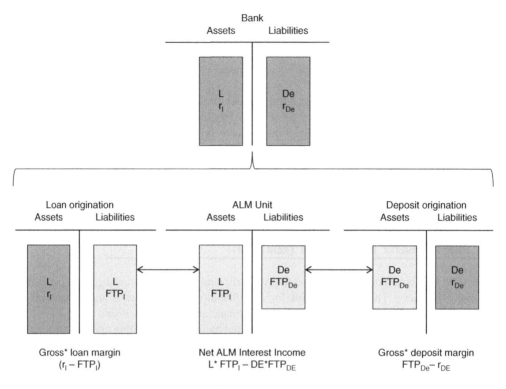

Gross margins, before the allocated cost of risk or expenses

FIGURE 15.2   FTP and the role of the ALM unit

The "Classic" Bank ALM Portfolio

Most banks have a unit which is charged with managing the A/L mismatch position, often called the ALM unit or ALM portfolio. The separation of responsibilities between the Commercial and the ALM unit requires a profit attribution framework aligned to the decision-making organization. This is accomplished using an FTP system, as illustrated in Figure 15.2.

The ALM portfolio consists of virtual risk-free loans bearing an interest rate equal to the internal FTP for loans, FTP_l. These virtual loans are at least partially funded by virtual deposits, which bear the internal FTP for deposits, FTP_{De}. As discussed later, the virtual loans and deposits in the ALM portfolio can be broadly thought of as replicating transactions which perfectly mirror the interest rate risk of the customers' products but which are priced at rates available for marginal risk-free investments and placements by the bank.

The difference between the customer loan and deposit rates (r_l and r_{De}, respectively) and their FTP surrogates is the *gross product margin* and remains the responsibility of the origination or product units. Separating the product margin from any financing and market risk considerations helps to focus the commercial and underwriting units on loan and deposit origination, underwriting and pricing.

The virtual loans and deposits transferred to the ALM unit represent the structural interest rate mismatch position of the bank. The mismatch can manifest itself in two different ways: first, in terms of differences in overall volumes as depicted in Figure 15.2, leading to a net financing (or funds placement) requirement and second, in terms of the financial characteristics of the balances, including (re-pricing) durations, currency and liquidity mismatches (discussed later in Chapter 18).

If the mismatch is left open, then small changes in interest rates can have large implications for the mark-to-market value and future net interest income margin of the bank. The ALM unit is charged with managing this structural mismatch position through investment, funding and hedging activities, all within the framework provided by the ALCO.

The "Classic" Insurance ALM Portfolio

Similar to the bank, the insurance company's overall balance sheet is divided into two centers of competence, one focused on the commercial and underwriting decisions (the technical or underwriting account) and the other focused on the investment or mismatch management decisions (the ALM account). The replicating portfolio, representing the financial risks of the liabilities, transfers the financial risk embedded in the insurance policies to the investment center of competence and provides the anchor point for liability driven investing. Associated with the replicating portfolio is an implicit funds transfer price, discussed in the next subsection. The mechanics are illustrated in Figure 15.3.[5]

The conceptual ideal for insurers is virtually identical to the bank ALM organization because it is based on the same economic principles: a separation between the investment management and underwriting functions, achieved through replicating portfolios which transfer all the financial market risk from the latter to the former.

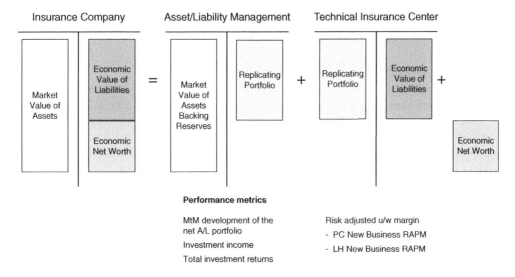

Source: Adaptedfrom Hancock, et al. (2001)

FIGURE 15.3 ALM and the replicating portfolio

---

[5]See Wilson (2004), Hancock *et al.* (2001) or Oechslin *et al.* (2004,2007) for additional descriptions of this approach.

Implementation of this ideal is more prevalent for PC insurers. However, more often it is only accomplished implicitly by attributing normalized investment returns to the PC underwriting function or by defining operating profit to exclude capital gains, both of which go some way toward separating and insulating underwriting earnings from (major) financial market movements.

Implementation at LH insurers is less frequent, primarily because the investment margin earnings from LH retirement and savings products depend implicitly or explicitly on the performance of the investment portfolio, making the separation more challenging and introducing a circularity – product profitability depends on investment margins which depend on investment decisions.

Unfortunately, this circularity can lead the technical product areas to rely heavily on financial market returns as they design and price products. It is my conviction that a clearer separation of commercial from financial market risk decisions brings greater transparency and accountability even for LH insurers, although the two do require a higher degree of coordination.

Two Complications to the "Classic" ALM Unit

The "classic" ALM portfolio for banks and insurers looks deceptively simple. However, there are two common but important complications which arise in practice.

- First, the definition of a strategic investment portfolio representing the assets backing the firm's capital, applicable to both banks and insurers.
- Second, the explicit recognition of non-hedgeable risks and product subsidies, applicable to both banks and insurers.

The Strategic Investment Portfolio for Assets Backing Capital

Both banks and insurance companies hold capital to support their business and the assets backing the firm's capital represent a substantial part of the firm's net asset value.

Managing the assets backing capital is different from managing the net asset/liability portfolio arising from customer business. Capital is a resource which is leveraged to reach the firm's full operating profit potential; as a consequence, it can be valued by shareholders at a premium to its current net asset value. A decline in the capital base can therefore represent a greater decline in market value if potential future business is foregone.

As a consequence, the assets backing capital are typically managed more for the preservation and steady growth of the capital base than for taking additional financial market risk. This strategy helps to secure the continued, steady growth of the business at an attractive valuation multiple.

The exception that proves the rule is a new class of reinsurers who are embracing a "hedge fund" mentality with regard to both the asset and liability side of the balance sheet. Ernst & Young (2013) state that "A new breed of reinsurer is evolving – those that are comfortable taking calculated risks not just on the underwriting side, but on the investment side. While reinsurers traditionally keep their assets in conservative, low-risk investments . . . these new companies are tapping into the skill of hedge fund managers to handle their investments." See also Green (2012). According to Ernst & Young, the

Insurance Company Asset/Liability Management Technical Insurance Center

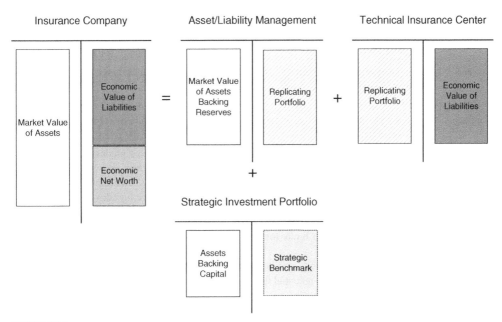

FIGURE 15.4 The ALM and strategic investment portfolio

benefits to investors include higher investment returns on capital as well as through leverage from the premiums and reserves, greater investor liquidity than a hedge fund if the reinsurer is listed and greater tax benefits. The benefits to the hedge fund include higher and more stable AUM (and AUM fees) and "free money to invest." These attributes clearly separate these companies from more traditional insurers, both in business model and target shareholders.

Because of the difference between the assets backing liabilities versus capital, many banks and insurers split the balance sheet into a portfolio representing only the customer business and a strategic investment portfolio containing the assets backing the firm's capital, as illustrated in Figure 15.4. (Although the figure is based on the insurance balance sheet, the analog for the banking balance sheet is straightforward.)

As discussed, these two portfolios have different management mandates, described in Table 15.3.

The "Model" Portfolio, for the Stuff No One Wants

The second complication arises if there are significant risks which cannot be hedged or if the products are subsidized in order to meet commercial objectives.

Risks Which Cannot be Hedged Because the performance of many ALM units is often measured on a mark-to-market or total return basis, the ALM unit may refuse to take the replicating positions at the FTP rates if the underlying risks cannot be hedged, traded or actively managed at those prices.

The reason is simple. A position which cannot be managed is like an anvil around the neck of the ALM unit and they may not want to go swimming in highly efficient and competitive capital markets with an anvil around their neck.

TABLE 15.3   Management mandates, ALM and strategic investment portfolios

	ALM portfolio	**Strategic investment portfolio**
Contents	Replicating portfolio representing net customer business and related operational transactions.	Remaining financial assets backing the firm's capital.

Mandate	■ A moderate duration *mismatch* between assets and liabilities.
	■ Risk exposure restricted to:
	  ▪ interest rate risk for banks;
	  ▪ interest rate risk and a conservative credit profile for PC insurers;
	  ▪ a combination of fixed income and limited real assets which maximizes the net asset value within limits for LH insurers.
	■ Sufficient funding capacity and liquidity in the portfolio to cover potential funding requirements and cash calls.
	■ Balance accounting earnings and mark-to-market returns.
		■ A mid- to long-term *target duration* of the assets (e.g., 5–10 years).
		■ Assets allocated predominantly to fixed-income securities with a:
		  ▪ conservative credit profile;
		  ▪ conservative liquidity profile;
		  ▪ low risk capital/risk weighted asset utilization.
		■ Sufficient liquidity in the asset portfolio to cover potential cash and capital calls from subsidiaries.
		■ Emphasis on steady interest income rather than total returns.

Common sources of non-hedgeable financial market risk include the following.

■ *The replicated cash flows are not traded at all or only in very thin markets.* For example, 30-year funding or swaption capacity to cover long-dated prepayable mortgages may not be available in some markets and, if available, only at very wide bid–offer spreads; similarly, LH retirement products may have cash flows which extend beyond the longest bond available in the market.

■ *The replicated cash flows may be highly complex or can only be hedged with significant residual basis risk.* For example, some banks re-price products based on indices for which there are no or limited derivatives (e.g., discretionary rates for deposits, prime rates), introducing a basis risk when hedging. Similarly, LH insurance products can reference managed fund indices or include complex, path-dependent options such as high water marks, cliquet or Asian averaging features or be written on underlying funds for which no derivatives are traded.

■ *The replicated cash flows are based on behavioral assumptions; actual behavior, and therefore hedge ratios, may be different.* For example, the replicating cash flows from non-maturing deposits depend on the sensitivity of withdrawals and re-pricing to interest rate changes. Similarly, LH insurance cash flows are affected by customer lapse sensitivities and the insurer's credit rating strategy. While these assumptions may hold on average, they are unlikely to hold in every period and any deviations will lead to hedge slippage.

■ *The replicated cash flows are based on models which are subject to assumption changes and parameter updates.* The replicating cash flow models for non-maturing deposits, prepayable mortgages, PC claims and LH policies depend on models and assumptions. The hedge ratios can materially change as these models and parameters are updated, typically by the commercial or product units.

Products Which Are Subsidized Alternatively, the bank or insurance company may want to subsidize specific products for commercial reasons while neutralizing the impact on both the product and ALM units simultaneously.

For example, the bank may want to raise more deposits and therefore raise deposit rates. However, the origination unit may not be thrilled by this decision if it means declining or even negative margins; it is also somehow "unfair" to pass the cost on to the ALM unit. Similarly, an insurer may want to subsidize a particular product in order to gain more "shelf space" in a distribution network or to "feed" a tied agent system. The commercial objectives of the bank or insurance company may be impossible to reach if the impact of subsidization is not neutralized somehow.

Introducing the "Model" and "Subsidy" Accounts If these issues are material then it may be desirable to create a break between the representation which the ALM unit "sees" and the actual product sold to the customer. This can be accomplished by inserting a *model account* or a *subsidization account* between the ALM and product accounts, as illustrated in Figure 15.5 for a bank (with an analogous representation for insurers being straightforward).

"Model" accounts isolate the economic impact from the ALM unit and the product manager, with the results being allocated to the commercial division at a higher level within the company. This allocation makes sense because these risks cannot be effectively managed or hedged in the financial markets but must be managed through product design and limits.

The introduction of such an account does not eliminate the underlying issue but only hides it. From a value management perspective, the account needs to be managed by limiting the

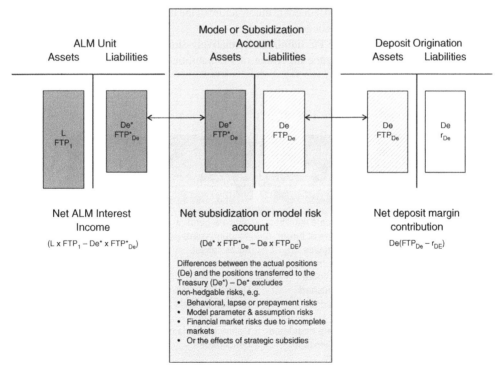

FIGURE 15.5 Introducing a model/subsidy account

volume on account (e.g., through product limits or subsidization budgets) and by triggering discussions about whether the commercial strategy makes sense in the first place.

Introducing a model or subsidization account dramatically increases complexity in terms of management reporting and decision making; as such, it is not done lightly and some institutions choose to ignore the leakage if immaterial or, better yet, reduce the leakage by changing the product features or commercial strategy.

THE INSURER ALM–INVESTMENT VALUE CHAIN

The ALM and investment management activities of insurance companies are more complicated than the ALM operations of a bank. The reason is straightforward: a bank ALM portfolio comprises both customer assets and liabilities, with the decision focused on managing gaps and implementing tactical overlays. In contrast, the insurer generates only liabilities from its customer franchise, leaving a much more fundamental investment decision to be taken (albeit a liability-driven investment decision); in addition, a significant selling point of most LH retirement and savings products comes from investment performance.

As a consequence, insurance ALM is really a chain of activities, beginning with liability modeling and ending with an investment in an individual security. The steps taken by an insurer are illustrated in Figure 15.6.

Liability-Based Benchmarks or Replicating Portfolios Insurers are liability-driven investors – they have to invest the premium collected today in a manner which allows them to meet their future claims obligations. As a consequence, the structure of the liabilities is the starting point for their investment management decisions.

The financial risk profile of PC liabilities is relatively straightforward: financial market variables generally do not influence the value of PC liabilities except through the discount

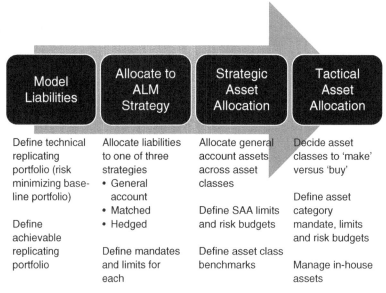

FIGURE 15.6 Insurance ALM investment value chain

effect. As such, the financial risk of PC liabilities is generally well represented by a strip of zero-coupon bonds equal to the claim's best-estimate cash flows in the currency that the claims are expected to be paid.[6,7]

The financial market risk embedded in LH retirement and savings products is more complicated. This is because the insurer's future obligations depend directly on investment decisions and financial market developments through the investment returns credited to the policy holder's account and the value of guarantees embedded in the product.

In addition, the economics on LH products depend critically on how policy holders and the company are assumed to manage their options; for example, how likely are policy holders to surrender their policies or exercise their deferred annuities in a rising or falling interest rate environment, how will your company set the crediting rate on general account products if realized returns exceed or fall below the minimum guaranteed level, etc. These behavioral assumptions can greatly influence the product's optimal hedge ratios and investment strategy.

Stochastic cash flow models are required to understand, value and manage these products. These models are used to develop a financial representation, or replicating portfolio, which characterizes the financial risk of the liabilities. The price of the replicating portfolio is the funds transfer price. Various approaches to calculating replicating portfolios for LH savings and retirement products are described in Chapter 17 on calculating FTPs.

Allocate Liabilities to ALM Strategy The next step is to allocate the liabilities, typically at the product level, to a specific asset/liability strategy.

Most PC companies manage the net asset and liability position in one general account and manage it with a single strategy. This is because zero-coupon cash flows representing best-estimate PC claims are already homogenous in their risk characteristics and because any excess investment returns accrue solely to the insurance company.

In contrast, LH companies assign their liabilities into one of three main ALM strategies (Society of Actuaries, 2003). This is necessary because different products have different risk and return characteristics. For example, it is standard to apply a strict fair value hedging strategy to the fair value elements of variable annuities, a cohort cash flow matching strategy to pay-out and deferred annuities and a general account investment management strategy to traditional profit participation products. Each of these three approaches are described in Sidebar 15.2.

Strategic Asset Allocation For products to be managed using a general account strategy, the next step is to define a liability-driven strategic asset allocation benchmark for the general account. In this context, the *strategic asset allocation benchmark* is defined as the *baseline allocation of investments between asset classes, taking into account the characteristics of the liabilities* while balancing risk and expected returns.

In contrast, *tactical asset allocation* is defined as the *active selection of individual securities, sectors, etc., within an asset class in order to take advantage of perceived short-term opportunities.*

---

[6]The exception to this rule are future claims which are subject to claims inflation, in which case the representation should also include inflation-indexed zero-coupon cash flows if they are traded.

[7]Liquidity risk considerations will also influence the investment strategy. This dimension will be covered in greater detail in Chapter 18.

SIDEBAR 15.2: THREE LIABILITY-BASED MANAGEMENT STRATEGIES

Insurance companies follow a liability-based investment strategy; however, different liabilities may require different approaches. There are three generic liability-based strategies which are used by insurers depending on the characteristics of the liabilities. Each of the three has a unique asset management mandate associated with it.

A *general account approach* is typically used by PC companies and for traditional LH profit participation policies. These liabilities and associated assets sit on the insurer's balance sheet – in the general account – and the insurance company participates, either fully in the case of PC or via contractual terms in the case of LH insurance, in any investment returns which are in excess of those needed to meet policy holder obligations.

Because the insurance company participates in the investment returns, general account strategies attempt to generate excess investment returns through both tactical and strategic asset allocation, but in a manner consistent with investment constraints and the risk characteristics of the liabilities as well as the risk appetite of the group.

The resulting general account investment mandates are generally defined by a strategic baseline allocation to asset categories (e.g., fixed income, equity, real estate, alternatives, etc.), with each category having a well-defined benchmark portfolio. Positioning decisions can be taken around the strategic baseline, subject to constraints such as aggregate portfolio risk measures – asset duration, duration mismatch and equity gearing, allowable ranges by asset class, minimum ratings for fixed-income securities and guidelines on the use of derivatives, to name but a few.

A *matched approach*, typically used for deferred and pay-out annuities and GICs (Guaranteed Investment Contracts). All these products share three common characteristics: first, their financial market risk is well represented by a strip of zero-coupon bonds; second, they tend to have relatively narrow margins at the time they are underwritten and a high exposure to interest rate risk if left unmatched; third, limited management discretion to recoup losses from "wrong" bets.

As a consequence, the matching investment strategy uses available fixed-income assets with attractive but secure spreads to closely match the liability-specific cash flows (and not just their duration) by origination cohort at the point of sale. By following this matching approach, the insurance company "locks in" a reasonably stable profit margin or investment result over the lifetime of the product and is insulated from financial market losses except in the case of default.

The investment mandate for the matching approach consists of cash flow matching criteria, minimum ratings for fixed-income securities, guidelines on the use of derivatives, limits on fixed-income securities with embedded options such as mortgage-backed securities, etc. As opposed to the general account approach, the success of a matched approach depends solely on tight A/L matching by cohort and security selection or tactical asset allocation and not at all on strategic asset allocation.

An *explicit fair value hedging approach*, used for insurance liabilities which are accounted under fair value option accounting standards, including some variable annuity benefits and the current year's equity-linked component of fixed index annuities (as opposed to the deferred annuity component). Most institutions choose to explicitly hedge these liabilities in order to avoid the high P&L volatility recognized by mark-to-market accounting if left unhedged.

Some insurance companies use a dynamic, or delta,[8] hedging strategy, rationalizing that it is too costly to structurally hedge the liabilities using static options due to the high implied volatilities charged in the market relative to historical volatilities as well as the increasing bid–offer spreads for longer-dated or more complex options. This approach leaves the net position exposed to larger market movements, or "gapping markets," as well as to changes in the level or shape of implied volatility curves.

Some companies also use short-dated options to hedge some higher-order Greeks such as gamma and vega.[9] This reduces the risk of gapping markets but leaves the exposure to implied volatility surface rotations or fundamental shifts in the curve over time. Very few hedge completely using static, structured products bought from an investment bank due to the perceived high cost of doing so.

Both dynamic and partial static hedges are governed by strict asset management and derivative mandates, including tight limits around specific hedge ratios such as delta, gamma, vega and rho, and the requirement that the hedges be rebalanced on a regular basis, typically daily.

Occasionally, business units would like to relax these relatively tight limits in order to "take advantage of trading opportunities" in option Greeks with the goal of increasing profitability. Given the competitive nature of the underlying insurance products, it is difficult to make good money even if we keep our "eye on the ball." Opening up the equivalent of a hedge fund focused on thinly traded options markets qualifies as taking our eye off the ball and should be avoided. Equally as compelling is the fact that we could always take trading positions independently from this portfolio, with greater transparency and a better alignment of incentives.

Regardless of the mandate details, hedge effectiveness will be impacted by basis risk (the risk that the liability and hedge index performance deviates) and behavioral risk (the risk that lapse and annuitization assumptions prove to be wrong, altering the effective hedge ratios). These risks can only be minimized by redesigning the products.

As opposed to both the general account and the matched strategy, the explicit hedge strategy does not rely on strategic or tactical asset allocations; rather, it relies on the accuracy of the hedge models and flawless hedge execution in order to ensure that the returns which the insurance company expected at the time of origination actually materialize. Toward this end, hedge effectiveness needs to be closely and continuously monitored, monitoring unexplained drift in the value of the "hedged" portfolio, the residual volatility of the hedged P&L, etc. and decomposing the hedge result into basis risk, behavioral risk, unhedged financial market movements, etc.

---

[8]Delta refers to the first-order effect of a change in value for a change in the risk factor, e.g. the delta of an equity-sensitive position can be expressed in the limit as $\delta = \partial P / \partial e$ or, for discrete movements in equity prices, as $\delta = \Delta P / \Delta e$.

[9]Gamma is the change in delta for a change in the underlying, e.g. $\delta = \partial(\partial P / \partial e) / \partial e = \partial^2 P / \partial e^2$, and is a measure of the position's convexity. Vega is the sensitivity of the position to a change in implied volatilities, e.g. $v = \partial P / \partial \sigma$, a measure only relevant for options or products with embedded options.

Why Separate Strategic and Tactical Asset Allocation? There are three reasons why separating strategic and tactical decisions makes sense: first, strategic asset allocation decisions have a greater impact on investment results than tactical asset allocation decisions; second, they require very different skills, information and perspectives; third, it allows for the parallel use of both in-house and third-party asset managers.

Strategic allocation decisions can have a much higher impact on realized portfolio returns than security selection. This conclusion goes back to an influential article by Brinson *et al.* (1986). The authors studied the asset allocation of 91 pension funds between the period 1974–1983, replacing the fund's actual bond, stock and cash positions with corresponding market indices for each asset category to calculate the return on the "virtual indexed" portfolio. They found that the returns based on the market indices were not only significantly correlated to the actual returns of the managed portfolio (96.7%), but the index returns were generally also higher than the returns on each of the individual managed asset classes after fund management expenses were taken into account.

A follow-up article by Brinson *et al.* (1991) confirmed the results for a broader sample of pension funds, and Ibbotson and Kaplan (2000) found qualitatively similar results for mutual funds.

The conclusions were that most of the difference in investment performance is driven by strategic asset allocation and not by security selection within a class, and that the returns on the market indices were superior to those of the managed asset classes after expenses. One of the common interpretations is that, if tactical asset allocation is to generate value after expenses, then it has to be done with sufficient focus and expertise so that it has at least a chance of generating alpha.

These observations led insurance companies to implement a *hub and spoke* or *core–satellite* investment model (e.g., Singleton, 2004). Under the core–satellite approach, the bulk of the assets are allocated to low-cost market indices (the hub or core portfolios), giving "beta" returns at low cost while maintaining flexibility to shift between asset classes strategically. The remaining assets are allocated to specialized, actively managed investment mandates (the spoke or satellite portfolios), which are perceived to generate "alpha" after the active management fees.

The SAA Benchmark Portfolio and Mandate The SAA benchmark portfolio is defined by both qualitative and quantitative aspects. In general, the ALCO should be able to express its investment strategy and philosophy in a clear, concise and descriptive manner. The qualitative statement may reference the firm's external rating and solvency targets, the role of liabilities in determining the SAA, the risk/return and income targets of the firm, and so on.

This investment philosophy is then translated into quantifiable parameters at least once a year through the strategic planning process. The most important parameters are definitions of the benchmark portfolios by asset class, their target weights and allowable "lee-ways." Most SAA mandates include a combination of fixed-income benchmarks (potentially to the level of sub-class, e.g., corporate, municipal, asset backed, emerging markets, sovereigns issues), equity benchmarks (e.g., domestic, international, emerging markets, etc.), real-estate benchmarks, alternative asset category benchmarks (private equity, hedge funds, infrastructure, etc.). For example, insurers may use the Barclays Capital Aggregate Bond or analogous index as the benchmark to measure fixed-income performance, an equity index based on S&P or Euro Stoxx, etc.

TABLE 15.4   Strategic asset allocation mandate dimensions

	Strategic asset allocation mandate description
General	Investment strategy and philosophy
	External rating and solvency targets
	Role of liabilities in determining the SAA
	Risk/return and income targets
By asset class	Benchmark index, including
	Benchmark leeways
	Tracking error VaR
Across asset classes	VaR limits
	Duration target and limits*
	Equity sensitivity limits
	Concentration limits and excluded names*
	Real asset sub-limit
	Alternative asset sub-limit
	Foreign exchange limits*
	Asset coverage ratios
Policies	Derivative policy
	Foreign exchange hedging policy
	Qualifying asset definitions

*Potentially also defined by asset class.

Around each of these benchmarks is set an allowable range or "leeways" per asset class, allowing the investment function to deviate from the SAA within predefined boundaries. Additional targets and constraints will also be imposed internally and externally, as illustrated in Table 15.4.

Tactical Asset Allocation   The final step is to invest in individual assets within each asset class. In order to measure performance, it is necessary to define explicit TAA (Tactical Asset Allocation) benchmarks per asset class and associated tracking error limits or leeways; this is done as part of the strategic asset allocation decision. Once the benchmarks and tracking error limits have been defined, security selection decisions are taken in an attempt to beat the benchmarks and create "alpha."

Some of these portfolios are managed in-house and others by third-party asset managers. Third-party managers are not only used for individual asset classes (e.g., equities, high yield, emerging markets or alternatives) but occasionally also by strategy. For example, some firms[10] and investment banks offer hedging services to variable annuity writers in the form of reinsurance contracts (but very often excluding behavioral and actuarial risks which cannot be hedged). Sidebar 15.3 gives some guidance on using and selecting third-party asset managers.

---

[10]An example is the firm White Mountain, http://secfilings.nyse.com/filing.php?ipage=4709846&DSEQ=&SEQ=28&SQDESC=SECTION_PAGE

SIDEBAR 15.3: ON SELECTING A THIRD-PARTY ASSET MANAGER

WHAT IS OUTSOURCED?

Working along the investment value chain, few insurers outsource the modeling, ALM strategy and strategic asset allocation steps.[11] However, virtually all insurers "outsource" some of their portfolio for tactical asset management, especially satellite, alternative asset portfolios and increasingly core "beta" portfolios.

WHY OUTSOURCE TACTICAL ASSET ALLOCATION?

There are two general reasons to outsource tactical asset management: lower costs and higher returns. Increasingly, firms are allocating the "core" of their portfolio to "beta" indexed strategies. These third-party funds typically have lower expenses, driven by scale economies, lower transaction costs from less portfolio "churning" and lower management fees.

The remainder of the portfolio is allocated to "satellite funds," each focused on an individual asset class where investment expertise is potentially a differentiating factor (e.g., private equity, hedge funds, infrastructure or high-yield funds, etc.). The expectation is that excess returns can be generated by specialized portfolios with "star" asset managers focusing on niche strategies requiring extensive and difficult-to-replicate skills.

WHAT CRITERIA SHOULD BE USED IN SELECTING AN ASSET MANAGER?

There are a handful of criteria which are used in practice to select a portfolio manager. Interviewing decision makers at 12 pension funds, Hababou and Martel (1998) group the criteria into four broad buckets: past performance, investment philosophy, staff and organization. Fitch (2013) uses five categories to rate fund and asset managers: company, controls, investments, operations and technologies.

The following is a synthesis based on the literature (Cogent Research, 2010; IPE, 2011) and industry practice. Decisions are generally taken by assigning weights to the individual criteria and comparing the results for different asset managers.

Investment Philosophy and Focus

- Is the strategy clearly articulated, understandable and logical? Is it supported by clearly articulated and quantifiable limits?
- Is the investment process consistent with the strategy?
- Does the fund strategy complement our overall strategic asset allocation strategy?
- Is there a clear alignment between our expectations and what the fund can deliver?

---

[11]The exception to this rule are corporate and occupational pensions, where the sponsors may lack the skills and systems in-house to model and manage their asset/liability positions and therefore seek the advice of actuarial and investment consultants.

Past Performance

- How has the fund performed relative to peers and benchmarks?
- Has the fund performed well across the cycle and in different environments? How much of the fund's performance is due to skill and how much is due to "being in the right place at the right time"?
- Has the level of performance fairly compensated the investor for the risks assumed and the expenses?
- Has the level of risk and the portfolio composition varied over time in a manner consistent with its strategy? What are the explanations for the inconsistencies?

Staff Criteria

- Does the management team have the required skills and resources? Do they have the tenure and experience that you expect?
- Is it a "star" system? What happens if the "star" gets hit by the proverbial bus? Is there a succession or contingency plan in place?
- Is it an investment "team"? What is the depth of the bench? Is there a process to develop talent over time and does the process work? Are there signs of instability (e.g., high turnover)?
- Do they have a high level of integrity? What is their track record regarding regulatory compliance? Are they disciplined in their approach?

Organizational Criteria

Investment enablers

- Does the company have access to market information, research, analysis and decision support tools which give them a potential advantage?
- What is done with the insights? Does the manager demonstrate thought leadership in leveraging the insights into alpha?

Controls and governance

- Does the company have sufficient controls, especially the segregation of duties and strict compliance with sales, trade execution and portfolio valuation requirements?
- Are the operations and processes sufficiently staffed and controlled (e.g., trade confirmations, record keeping, valuations and reconciliations, corporate actions)?
- Are there any potential conflicts of interest in terms of the structure of fees, ownership structure or other relationships?
- What other services beyond asset management are provided (e.g., in terms of accounting, reporting, risk management, etc.)?
- Is the systems support adequate in terms of data management, workflow support and security?
- Are there sufficient resources, sustainable profits and/or shareholder commitment (if applicable) to sustain future investments in infrastructure as required?

Fund investment performance is reviewed on a regular basis, for example monthly or quarterly. Fund managers and their mandates should be critically and more extensively reviewed at least annually, including an on-site visit and desk level review, and ad hoc if the stability of the fund's staff and philosophy warrant.

The Implications for ALM Portfolio Design The asset/liability management process for insurers is more complicated than the ALM process for banks: whereas bank ALM units manage the net asset/liability gaps from their core customer positions, the insurance ALM process has to build the investments from the ground up based on their liabilities, contending with strategic and tactical asset allocation decisions as well as whether to run the investments in-house or through third-party asset managers. In this sense, insurance ALM and investment management are integrally linked.

A consequence is that the resulting ALM portfolios are also more complicated. In principle, insurers should measure the performance at each step in the combined value chain, beginning with the original product design and underwriting decisions and continuing to the strategic and tactical asset allocation decisions, including asset manager selection. This requires different portfolios to be defined and aligned with the different decisions. An illustrative portfolio constellation for an insurance company can be seen in Figure 15.7.

Starting from the upper right corner, the product unit is responsible for the difference between the *actual liabilities* and the *achievable replicating portfolio*. The difference can represent the "model account," containing the non-hedgeable structural risk discussed earlier: the achievable replicating portfolio can be managed in the capital markets, whereas the actual liabilities contain features which cannot be managed (e.g., cash flows beyond the longest available bond, highly complex embedded options, etc.), unexpected developments in behavioral assumptions (e.g., lapse or annuitization propensities, the crediting strategy of the firm, etc.) and unexpected developments in actuarial assumptions (e.g., mortality and longevity rates, etc.). Because it depends on product design, it should be "allocated" to the product or commercial department.

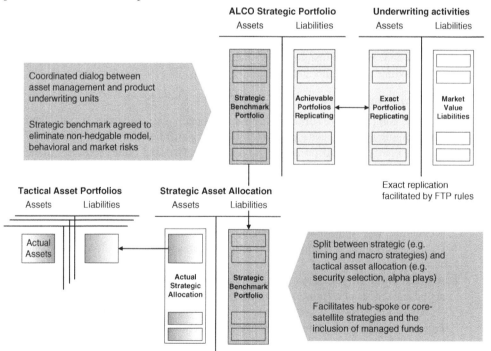

FIGURE 15.7 ALM and the replicating portfolio

Moving to the left, the ALCO defines the SAA benchmark portfolio, balancing commercial and risk/return considerations, and takes responsibility for the profit or loss arising from any mismatch between the two. Both the product and the investment functions participate in the ALCO.

Moving down, the investment management function allocates funds across the asset categories, using the SAA benchmark portfolio as guidance and staying within delegated leeways. They are responsible for any gap between the actual SAA allocation and the SAA benchmark portfolio.

Finally, moving to the lower left corner, the tactical asset managers are responsible for investing in individual securities within an asset class or strategy. They are evaluated based on their performance relative to the asset class benchmark, subject to a risk budget.

The multi-step process described here is complex, but it provides a basis for measuring the performance of the different decision makers along the insurance ALM/investment value chain.

THE TREASURY FUNCTION

The ALCO provides the governance framework for all three core balance sheet management activities, including asset/liability management, cash and liquidity management and managing the long-term funding structure of the firm.

While the ALM unit executes the ALM decisions, both cash and liquidity management and the long-term funding structure are managed operationally by the treasury unit. These two are often combined, because the capital funding strategy forms the anchor point around which cash and liquidity management takes place.

In addition to these core activities, the treasury also manages the structural foreign exchange exposure of the company and, in some smaller banks, may also engage in limited proprietary and customer trading activities. Owing to the potential conflict of interest between trading and treasury services, the two activities are separated in larger banks.

Cash and Liquidity Management

One of the core responsibilities of the treasury unit is to manage the short-term cash and funding requirements of the commercial units, ensuring that they are met on time and at low cost, as well as placing short-term excess liquidity at favorable rates.

This process begins by netting the daily cash flows within the firm and only funding or placing the net residual in the market. The netting happens not only for today's cash flows, but also the projected cash flows over short- and medium-term horizons.

By netting internally, the firm avoids the bid–offer spread on the difference between the gross and net amounts and also avoids unnecessary financial leverage with external counterparties. For firms with multiple subsidiaries, short-term surplus liquidity or financing needs can be managed through a group-wide cash pool, using inter-company loans to facilitate the netting across entities in the group before going external. Sources and uses of funds need to be monitored and managed on a currency-by-currency basis in order to ensure that sufficient liquidity is available in the face of currency-specific market dislocations.

Raising short-term funding is typically done through the central bank (if the firm has access), as well as other banks or short-term commercial paper programs managed by the treasury. Placement of short-term surplus cash is done through similar channels or invested in money market funds or corporate commercial paper.

The treasury's decision on how long to place surplus cash or how long to fund short-term cash needs is influenced by the firm's predictable cash flows over the near horizon. Liquidity risk measurement and management are discussed in detail in Chapter 18.

Implementing Capital Funding Decisions

In addition to managing the short-term cash and liquidity position of the firm, most treasury units are also responsible for implementing the group's overall capital funding strategy, including the issuance of traditional or hybrid equity as well as secured and unsecured bonds.

As discussed in Chapter 19, there are many factors which influence the firm's capital funding strategy including management's external rating aspiration, regulatory constraints and, through the capital budget, the firm's dividend and growth policy. Ultimately, the treasury is responsible for ensuring that the firm's rating aspirations are met and that there is sufficient cash to pay dividends, either from operational cash flows or funded through an increase in financial leverage, and sufficient cash remaining to fund the firm's organic and inorganic growth aspirations.

Internal loans may also be used to allow a subsidiary to upstream cash through dividend payments while leaving the subsidiary's solvency position unaltered: ignoring possible restrictions on intra-group transactions or concentrations, such internal loans substitute one asset on the subsidiary's balance sheet, cash, with another, an intra-group loan, freeing up cash so that it can be used by the group for paying dividends. Such intra-group loans do not represent financial leverage but rather dividend pre-financing if the loans are "settled" at the end of the year with the cash dividend from the subsidiary; however, if the loans remain in place over time, they represent a form of financial leverage called double leverage.

These two activities form the obvious core of all Treasuries, both in banking and insurance companies. This is confirmed in the recent BCG Treasury Survey, which concludes: "According to our survey, four out of five banks have increased the importance of funding planning in the overall planning process, fostered new long-term funding sources, and introduced new structural liquidity risk rations . . . To be sure, liquidity risk management has become a core treasury function along with . . . capital management responsibilities."

Managing Corporate Foreign Exchange Exposure

In addition, the treasury units at most banks and insurance companies also manage the firm's *corporate* foreign exchange profile. There are three primary sources of foreign exchange exposure for a bank or insurance company.

First, *customer-driven foreign exchange positions* are originated by the company's or subsidiary's core business activities. For example, a bank in a developing economy may offer foreign currency mortgages, desired by borrowers due to the lower notional interest rate, or allow a customer to make a foreign currency deposit in order to preserve value in the face of domestic inflation or currency depreciation. Similarly, insurance companies may offer LH investment products which are linked to foreign investments or, in the case of a large commercial PC program, the premium may be denominated in USD even though the claims can occur anywhere in the world.

Customer-driven foreign exchange risk is typically managed by the ALM unit. Unfortunately, this can also be a source of structural, non-hedgeable risk unless the ALM unit can access matching foreign currency funding or assets with the same tenor as the underlying customer positions. If not, then – as with any structural, non-hedgeable risk – the volumes need to be limited and the benefit from accessing the customer profit pool has to be carefully and objectively balanced against the structural non-hedgeable risk taken.

Second, *own FX trading positions* are taken tactically as part of the investment, market making or proprietary trading strategy. This risk is taken and managed by the foreign exchange trading unit responsible, whether a bank trading desk or the asset management function within an insurer, which may decide to back domestic liabilities partially with foreign currency assets.

Both these and customer-driven exposures are often referred to as *currency transaction risk*. Currency transaction risk occurs because the company has transactional exposure denominated in a currency which is different from its reporting currency. Any unhedged position leaves the individual company's balance sheet and earnings exposed to changes in foreign exchange rates (Sorensen and Kyle, 2008).

The third type of exposure is the *corporate foreign exchange or translation risk*. This risk occurs in the context of a parent and subsidiary with different reporting currencies. In such cases, the parent is exposed to a foreign exchange translation risk even if the subsidiary has no currency transaction risk on its own balance sheet. The parent's exposure is equal to the net asset value it has invested in the subsidiary: if the subsidiary's currency depreciates, then the value of the subsidiary on the parent's balance sheet, as well as the subsidiary's future earnings and dividend-paying capacity, will also depreciate.

Hedging the firm's corporate exposure or translation risk is more complex than managing transactional FX risk for two reasons. The first is that accounting and economic perspectives may be quite different. This is because accounting translation principles often contain elements of both historical and current market valuations. For example, historical exchange rates can be used for certain equity accounts, fixed assets and inventory items, while current exchange rates can be used for current assets, current liabilities, income and expense items (e.g., Eiteman *et al.*, 2003).

Corporate foreign exchange risk management is also complicated from an economic perspective by two considerations. First, investors purchase shares of an internationally diversified financial services group understanding that it is international. If 30% of your net assets and profits come from emerging markets, then shareholders should ostensibly understand and accept that your share value will be exposed to a depreciation of emerging market currencies. In fact, the emerging market exposure may be the reason why they bought your shares in the first place. This would argue for little or no hedging of the corporate foreign exchange exposure.

Second, even if you did want to hedge, the investment in the subsidiary represents a claim not only to its current net asset value but also to its future earnings. This raises two non-trivial questions.

- Should the FX management focus on the initial investment and retained earnings at historical cost or on the current net asset value of the subsidiary?
- Should the next period's earnings or dividends be hedged or should you try to hedge the expected franchise value generated over some longer time horizon?

In practice, most companies hedge the subsidiary's planned dividends or earnings to ensure that the group's short-term dividend or earnings targets can be met. In addition, to the extent allowable by double-leverage constraints, part of the initial capital invested in the subsidiary can be raised in foreign currency debt at the corporate level ("double leverage" in the subsidiary's currency), thereby lowering the subsidiary's translation risk.

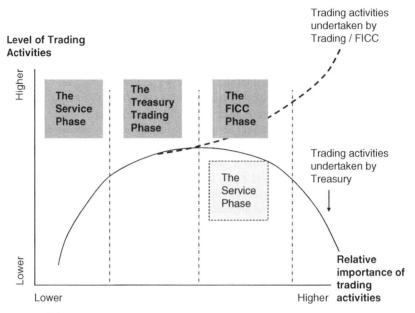

FIGURE 15.8 Generic development of treasury trading activities

Treasury Trading in Banks

Some treasury units at medium-sized banks also engage in money market and foreign exchange trading activities as a profit center. As banks become larger and trading activities become more important, the two activities are separated due to the potential conflict of interest. There is a natural progression involving three distinct phases for a bank's trading operations, as illustrated in Figure 15.8.

The Service Phase For smaller banks, foreign exchange and money market trading activities are not considered as a business for the bank but rather as a service to the rest of the bank and its customers. As a consequence, the bank executes net customer cash and foreign exchange transactions back-to-back directly with the inter-bank market without taking a trading position due to a lack of appetite, experience or scale. Most small local banks, including in particular those in emerging markets[12] which remain focused on serving domestic retail and small enterprises, choose to stay in this phase.

Customer transactions can come from the retail client network or from "sweeping" customers' investment accounts for dividends or coupons received. Because the customers are typically less price sensitive and because the positions are aggregated and closed after some delay, they are typically priced at wider bid–offer spreads.

Customer transactions which are larger than a predefined threshold are typically communicated directly to the treasury money market or foreign exchange desk, including the investment or funding horizon. This is done both because the larger transactions tend to be more price sensitive and in order to better manage the net liquidity needs of the bank in the future.

---

[12]See Asia Development Bank (2008) for a good discussion in the context of emerging and developing markets.

The Treasury Trading Phase   Depending on the bank's strategy, the next stage is the treasury trading phase for larger regional or domestic banks.

In this phase, the money market and foreign exchange desks within the treasury unit become profit centers in their own right. They are delegated intra-day and overnight limits within which to take positions, with the goal of making a trading profit and capturing customer bid–offer spreads from trades which are offsetting but asynchronous over short time horizons. In addition to this profit motive, the treasury trading desk gains credibility in execution and its profits help to defray the cost of the treasury services. Often associated with this phase are four further developments.

- First, commercial client sales desks actively develop new customer relationships based solely on trading activities and promote trading by existing customers by presenting trading and hedging ideas and strategies.
- Second, an expansion into options and other derivatives, in addition to cash money market and foreign exchange transactions, providing clients with a broader palette of solutions at higher potential margins. Against these benefits are the increased systems and personnel costs combined with the higher risks assumed by dynamically managing unbalanced trading volumes in thinly traded options markets.
- Third, splitting the activities into a service desk for the bank and a separate trading desk to eliminate the potential conflict of interest, where large corporate and high net worth customers are given direct access to the trading desk and the bundled tickets from retail clients go to the service desk.
- Finally, clear transfer pricing rules in order to mitigate the possible conflict of interest. For the anonymous, bundled and netted retail positions, the transactions are priced against mid-rates set daily with an appropriate bid–offer spread. For larger transactions, a standard bid–offer spread based on the average spot rates of predefined broker screens is used.

The FICC (or Investment Bank) Phase   At some point, the trading activities of the bank may become sufficiently large that they form the core of a broader trading strategy. This is the FICC (Fixed Income, Currencies and Commodities) phase or the investment banking phase, where the treasury function "shrinks" back to its core cash, liquidity and balance sheet management activities and the customer and proprietary trading activities go into a completely separate strategic business segment.

This generic development profile is consistent with the results of a recent treasury survey sponsored by BCG (2012), which concludes that there have been two types of bank treasury. The first is the *market-oriented model*, which "integrates the treasury function into the bank's financial-markets division, which sets profit targets . . . and oversees its running of funding, trading and derivatives desks." The second is the *CFO-oriented model*, where the treasury "focuses largely on steering tasks, reports to the bank's CFO, and does not have direct client or trading responsibility." They conclude that the larger, more complex banks tend toward the CFO-oriented model, representing 70% of global players. In contrast, roughly 66% of the smaller, regional banks follow the market-oriented model, defining the treasury as a profit center. Apparently missing in the survey are the smallest banks, which use the treasury as a service provider for executing back-to-back customer transactions.

CHAPTER 16

The Economics of Asset/Liability Management

Retail and commercial banks as well as insurers take most of their financial market risk in the asset/liability portfolio.

Banks and PC insurers typically "ride the yield curve," investing in assets with a longer duration than liabilities, in order to benefit from an upward-sloping yield curve but running the risk that the yield curve falls or flattens. In addition, PC insurers may also invest in real assets such as equities or real estate in an effort to increase earnings.

LH insurers often have the opposite rate exposure, with liabilities that have longer duration than assets available in the market, a structural mismatch exacerbated by complex embedded options and guarantees which cannot be completely hedged. In addition, LH insurers may have an incentive to invest in riskier assets when they participate in the returns from general account assets.

THE ROLE OF ALM EARNINGS

Financial market returns contribute significantly to the operating profits of banks and insurers.

PC Insurers

It is not unusual for investment returns to comprise anything from 70% to 100% of the total operating earnings of a PC insurance company, depending on market yields and underwriting results. Figure 16.1 illustrates the contribution to operating earnings by source for a stylized PC insurance company.[1]

---

[1]The stylized PC insurance company writes business in a steady state at a combined ratio of 95% or 100%. The ECI for the business is 75%, implying that the required capital is about 75% of the premium in a steady state. The average duration of claims and expenses is assumed to be 3.5 years and 0.5 years, respectively, with the latter reflecting the upfront commissions. The risk-free rate of return is assumed to be 3%. The company is assumed to match assets and liabilities. However, it is assumed to earn an additional spread on reserve assets and capital of 0.5%, which can come from a variety of sources (e.g., active A/L mismatch on the margin, corporate bond spreads or the risk premia from other investments). The tax rate is assumed to be 33%.

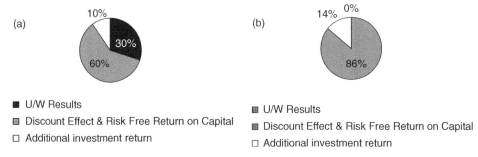

- ■ U/W Results
- ▨ Discount Effect & Risk Free Return on Capital
- ☐ Additional investment return

- ▨ U/W Results
- ■ Discount Effect & Risk Free Return on Capital
- ☐ Additional investment return

FIGURE 16.1   (a) 95% Combined ratio (b) 100% Combined ratio

As illustrated, the total investment income from the assets backing reserves and capital contributes 70% of operating profit for this stylized PC insurer at a 95% combined ratio and 100% of operating profit if the combined ratio is 100%. Capturing these earnings can expose the PC insurer to credit risk, interest rate risk and real asset price risk, to name but a few.

This stylized company is broadly consistent with Allianz results in 2012 and 2013 (Allianz, 2014c): in 2012, Allianz's PC combined ratio was 96% and underwriting results represented 31% of the IFRS operating profit; in 2014, Allianz's combined ratio improved to 94.3%, representing 42% of IFRS operating profit.

However, the conclusion that PC insurers "live from their investment results" would be incorrect: for the illustrative examples, 60–85% of operating profit is "earned" from the *risk-free* return on reserves and capital and only 10–15% from the *additional spread* from taking additional financial market risk. *The risk-free investment income represents the carry from receiving the premium in advance of paying the claims. It is correctly attributed to the PC underwriting activities (as is done in the PC New Business RAPM), as it would not exist if the company did not underwrite policies.*

LH Insurers

The contribution of financial market returns to an LH insurer's operating profit depends on its business mix. It can range from close to 0% for pure protection and unit-linked products to slightly under 100% for guaranteed savings and annuity products, where investment profits are shared between the insurer and the insured.

Table 16.1 gives the contribution to Allianz's IFRS operating profit before deferred acquisition costs by source and by product segment. In 2013, investment returns contributed 116% of the operating profit for guaranteed savings and annuities but only 3% and 8% for protection and health and unit linked without guarantees, respectively.

Capturing these investment returns exposes the LH insurer to credit risk, interest rate risk and real asset price risk. Some of the exposure is actively taken through ALM decisions; some is forced on the LH insurer by offering products with durations longer than the bonds available in the capital markets – a type of structural mismatch which cannot be actively managed.

Banking

Depending on the shape of the yield curve, "riding the yield curve" can contribute up to 20% to a retail and commercial bank's net interest income margin. OWC (2013) estimates the 2012 contribution from asset/liability mismatch for European banks and highlights the risks, saying

TABLE 16.1 2013 Allianz LH operating profit details, EUR mio

	LH Segment		Guaranteed savings & annuities		Protection & Health		Unit linked w/o guarantees	
	12M2012	12M2013	12M2012	12M2013	12M2012	12M2013	12M2012	12M2013
Loadings and fees	4293	4483	2772	3004	1210	1162	311	317
Investment margin	2913	2532	2825	2512	80	11	9	9
Technical margin	1208	1191	604	613	534	525	69	53
Expenses	−5430	−5525	−3890	−3970	−1316	−1287	−224	−269
Operating profit before DAC	2984	2681	2311	2159	508	411	165	110
Contribution, investment margin	98%	94%	122%	116%	16%	3%	5%	8%

Source: Allianz (2014c). Reproduced by permission of Allianz SE.

that the "ALM margin (defined here as the value generated by duration mismatch between assets and liabilities) is generally small and has a contribution which ranges from −10% to 10% (of total earnings)." Capturing this net interest income exposes the bank to interest rate risk.

The Risks

The old adage is that "there is no free lunch" – open asset/liability mismatch positions may be expected to generate operating earnings, but they can also lead to substantial losses from an economic perspective.

"Riding the yield curve" in banking or PC insurance can prove to be very expensive if interest rates increase or if the yield curve flattens or inverts, increasing the cost of financing and making the returns from the long-dated assets look less attractive. Similarly, taking reinvestment risk through a mismatched LH portfolio can prove to be very expensive if interest rates decline, potentially creating an earnings drag as reinvestment rates fail to meet guarantees.

While most companies manage these risks well, there are some very high-profile ALM disasters which have threatened entire industries, as discussed in the following sections. In any case, capital needs to be allocated to cover the mismatch position and returns need to be measured not on an absolute earnings basis but relative to the deployed capital.

Earnings Versus Value

When taking ALM decisions, it is important to keep in mind that shareholders are not generally willing to pay a premium relative to the firm's current net asset value for ALM earnings. The valuation framework developed in Part Two: Better Information suggests that shareholders are only willing to pay a premium if the firm generates excess returns (or "alpha") compared with a risk-equivalent portfolio. This means that the bank or insurer has to "beat the market" for its net assets to be valued at a premium multiple.

Delivering alpha or "beating the market" after expenses is challenging in an unconstrained investment portfolio.[2] Delivering alpha in the context of structural mismatch positions which cannot be hedged and within the multiplicity of accounting and regulatory constraints imposed on banks and insurers is even more challenging. It is for these reasons that shareholders and analysts view ALM mismatch results with some skepticism and generally do not ascribe a higher multiple to these positions.

The remainder of this chapter highlights the risks and returns from asset/liability management, leading to the following high-level principles to consider when setting the firm's asset/liability management strategy.

RULES OF THE GAME: ASSET/LIABILITY MANAGEMENT STRATEGY AND PHILOSOPHY

Banks and insurers take open ALM mismatch positions, either by choice or forced on them by product design. These mismatch positions can contribute significantly to the earnings of the firm; however, they generally will not improve, and may in fact negatively influence, the firm's valuation multiple to net asset value.

---

[2]See the earlier discussion which presented evidence that the tactical asset allocation decisions of pension funds and mutual funds generally did not add value compared with the benchmark returns after deducting asset management fees.

> ALM results are not a substitute for the more attractive, more highly valued technical results earned by blocking-and-tackling in the areas of sales excellence, operating efficiency, underwriting effectiveness and capital management. As such:
>
> ■ ALM risk should be consciously taken, actively managed and strictly limited, both from an earnings and a value perspective.
>
> ■ Product design should eliminate structural mismatch positions or non-hedgeable financial market risk. If accessing a profit pool requires a structural mismatch, participating in that profit pool should be consciously limited and potentially existence-threatening concentrations in unhedgeable risks should be avoided.

THE RISKS: SOME SPECTACULAR ALM FAILURES

Most banks and insurance companies take open ALM positions as a standard business practice. Very often this is based on the belief that there is a "normal" level of interest rates and that, if we ever find ourselves in a "non-normal" situation, mean reversion in rates will return rates to "normal" and the relative stability of accounting earnings allows the firm to come out of such periods unscathed.

However, there have been situations where management's assumptions of an upward-sloping, stable and mean-reverting yield curve have proven to be horribly wrong. When this happens, the same ALM mismatch which looked benign turns out to be a big, ugly, existence-threatening monster, not only for the individual firm but for entire industries.

History is littered with large-scale, system-wide failures in ALM – failures so spectacular that entire industries have been jeopardized. This section provides an overview of some of the most spectacular ALM failures in the belief that history is the best teacher.

The US Savings and Loan Crisis of the 1980s

The first case study occurred in the USA during the 1980–1990s. The victims were Savings and Loan (S&L) institutions, not-for-profit cooperative financial institutions similar to UK building societies which accept deposits and make personal loans, making financing more broadly available to members typically in the working class.

S&Ls had a strategy of "riding the yield curve": their funding, primarily deposits and interest-bearing checking accounts, were short-term while their loans were long term and fixed rate. As long as the yield curve remained upward sloping and stable, the S&Ls would post a good net interest income result. If the yield curve were to suddenly increase, then the S&L would face a loss on a mark-to-market basis but would see only part of this come through in terms of lower net interest income over time as the shorter-term deposits re-priced to higher levels relative to the longer-term fixed assets.

This "riding the yield curve" strategy unraveled when the Federal Reserve raised rates dramatically in 1979 to counteract commodity (oil) price-led inflation, with short-term Treasury bill rates peaking at 16%. As predicted, the results took some time to be recognized through accounting earnings, but the effects were also masked by the growth in the industry in

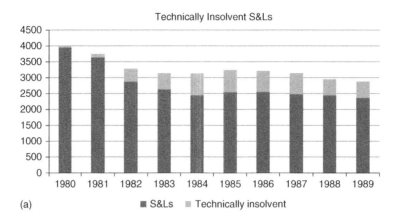

(a)

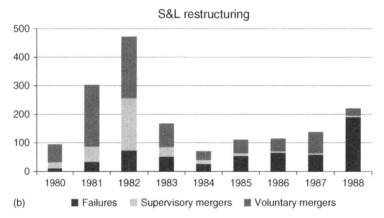

(b)

FIGURE 16.2   (a) S&L failures in the 1980s – technical insolvencies (b) S&L failures in the
1980s – restructuring actions
Source: Data from FDIC (1997).

an attempt to "evergreen"[3] the problem away, by accounting forbearance and by actions to
merge weaker institutions. In spite of these heroic efforts, the impact ultimately manifested
itself via insolvencies, as illustrated in Figure 16.2.

An important source of these failures was the systemic interest rate mismatch in the
industry:[4] "The level of thrift failures at the start of the 1980s was the largest since the Great
Depression, and the primary reason for these insolvencies was the result of losses incurred
when interest rates rose suddenly."

In his address to the Federal Reserve system, Bodie (2006) states, "Asset–liability
mismatch was a principal cause of the Savings and Loan Crisis of the 1980s. The federal
government's failure to recognize the mismatch risk early on and manage it properly led to

---

[3] An "evergreen" strategy is an analogy to a growing plant, where the outer green shoots of new growth
mask the dying or diseased old growth. In this context, the strategy is to run fast enough with (hopefully)
profitable new business so that the past doesn't catch up with you, a strategy which sounds suspiciously
like a Ponzi scheme.

[4] http://eh.net/encyclopedia/article/mason.savings.loan.industry.us

huge losses by the Federal Savings and Loan Insurance Corporation, which had to be covered by taxpayers."

However, higher interest rates triggered a secondary effect which was just as bad. In an attempt to allow the S&Ls to "grow" their way out of the situation (the "evergreen" strategy), banking regulation was relaxed, allowing S&Ls to introduce new products such as adjustable-rate mortgages (a good thing) but also to expand their business footprint in order to offer additional sources of earnings to offset the drag of the legacy business (a bad thing).

This expansion led to bad and sometimes fraudulent business decisions, which increased insolvencies even after interest rates had stabilized. "One reason for this latest round of failures was because of lender misconduct and fraud . . . (A) prominent fraud-related failure was Lincoln Savings and Loan headed by Charles Keating. When Lincoln came under regulatory scrutiny in 1987, Senators . . . (known as the 'Keating Five') questioned the appropriateness of the investigation." The Lincoln Savings case is also interesting because the company paid USD 51 mio for Michael Milken's junk bond activities, expanding its sources of earnings, even though it had negative net worth exceeding USD 100 mio at the time.

The cost to the industry was huge. "By the time the S&L crisis was over by the early 1990s, it was by most measures the most expensive financial collapse in American history. Between 1980 and 1993, 1,307 S&Ls with more than $603 billion in assets went bankrupt, at a cost to taxpayers of nearly $500 billion."[5]

In summary, an industry-wide ALM mismatch led to systemic problems for the S&L industry when rates spiked. The problem was exacerbated by the very same strategies designed to address the issue – accounting forbearance to buy the S&Ls time and deregulation offering the opportunity to "evergreen" the bad portfolio, hoping that a high enough new business growth could mask the symptoms of an ailing back book. Qualitatively, these same developments characterize all the systemic failures caused by ALM mismatches.

The Japanese Insurance Crisis of the 1990s

A second interesting case example occurred in Japan during the 1990s, spurred by the oft discussed "Japanese interest rate scenario" characterized by extremely low interest rates and sideways economic development. What may be less familiar is the specific impact on Japanese life insurance companies which had a large structural duration mismatch on their books at the time.

Market Developments and Policy Response

The seeds of the Japanese scenario were planted in the late 1980s, a period characterized by a widespread real-estate and equity market asset bubble. From 1985 to 1989, the Nikkei equity market index went up by close to 325%. It gave back close to half those gains in 1990, dropping by 30–40% in a single year. Over the next decade, the Nikkei lost most of the remaining gains, ending up at 20% of its 1989 peak (see Figure 16.3).

GDP broadly mirrored the equity market, with the average growth rates of above 3% during the late 1980s boom period being substituted by lackluster, sideways developments in the following decade. Including negative GDP developments, GDP grew by only c. 0.5% overall during the decade 1990–2000.

Monetary and fiscal authorities tried to counteract these developments, with monetary policy targeting lower and lower rates in order to spur economic growth. This was particularly

---

[5] http://eh.net/encyclopedia/article/mason.savings.loan.industry.us

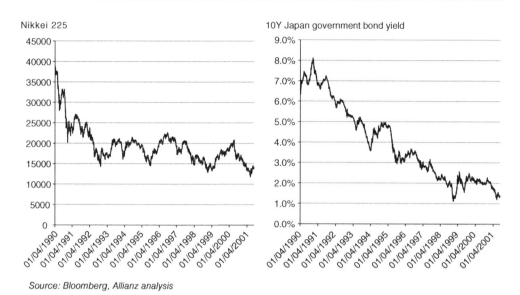

Source: Bloomberg, Allianz analysis

FIGURE 16.3   Japanese market developments in 1990–2000. Reproduced by permission of Allianz SE.

evident in the Bank of Japan uncollateralized call rate and the market rate for Japanese government bonds, which declined from above 6% during the period 1985–1993 to c. 2% after 1997, as shown in Figure 16.3.

Impact on the Insurance Industry

While the collapse of the equity and real-estate asset bubble negatively impacted Japanese LH companies, the coup de grace was delivered by the sustained low interest rate environment. During the 1980s–1990s, the Japanese LH insurance industry had written long-dated participating business, deferred and pay-out annuities promising customer rates up to 6+%, with an average in-force rate of around 3.5% (Takagi, 2005; Nieder, 2013).

Unfortunately, these policies were not matched from a duration or cash flow perspective, leaving the companies open to reinvestment risk. The impact of the sustained low rates emerged only gradually during the 1990s, leading to an increasing "negative spread" in the LH insurer's earnings as new investment returns fell below the technical or guaranteed rate on the policies. By 1999 and 2000, the "negative spread" accounted for between 30% and 40% of the industry's net profits. As shown in Table 16.2, between 1997 and 2003, eight Japanese insurers became insolvent, representing more than 10 million policies and more than 10% of the industry's reserves.[6]

Some of the firms were supported by the industry-funded policy protection fund. In addition, other actions were taken during resolution, including lowering the policy holders' reserves, lowering the guaranteed minimum rate of return and limiting withdrawals or imposing surrender penalties in order to prolong the time for the firms to recover. The risk of further insolvencies was mitigated when the rules were changed in 2003, allowing resolution through the courts as opposed to through administrative proceedings.

---

[6]Data from Kobayashi (2014) and Okubo (2014).

TABLE 16.2   Overview of Japanese insurance insolvencies, 1997–2001

Insurer	Date	Assets (yen bn)	Reduction in technical provisions	Guaranteed rate after reduction	Penalty for early withdrawal	Assistance by Policy Holder Protection Fund
Nissan	4.1997	1822	0%	2.75%	7 yrs	✓
Toho	6.1999	2190	10%	1.50%	8 yrs	✓
Dai-Hyaku	5.2000	1300	10%	1.00%	10 yrs	✓
Taisho	8.2000	154	10%	1.00%	9 yrs	✓
Chiyoda	10.2000	2233	10%	1.50%	10 yrs	—
Kyoei	10.2000	3725	8%	1.75%	8 yrs	—
Tokyo	3.2001	690	0%	2.60%	10 yrs	—
Taisei	11.2001	344	10%	1.05%	7 yrs	✓
Yamato	10.2008	194	10%	1.00%	10 yrs	✓

The Industry Response

"Negative spreads" from the legacy blocks unfortunately remained a fact of life for the next decade (Shirakawa and Ogasawara, 2011), "Yields offered on new policies have . . . lowered to reflect prevailing market interest rates, but life insurers nevertheless find themselves saddled with negative margins due to the ongoing mismatch between assumed and actual yields."

In addition to lowering new business guarantees, Japanese firms also took other actions including "evergreening" their portfolio, cutting costs and taking more investment risk.[7]

It is interesting that the second largest variable annuity market in the world developed in Japan during this period, primarily as a way to alter the product mix to products with less inherent interest rate mismatch risk.

These steps – reducing guarantees, taking more investment risk, "evergreening" the portfolio and cutting costs – are prominent in most insurance ALM disasters. To many, the "lessons learned" from the Japanese parable may seem irrelevant – after all, the "normal" risk-free rate of return in Europe and the United States since the 1970s has been more than 3.5%, almost as if there are natural forces keeping it at this "normal" level. Times and perceptions have changed since 2008, illustrated by the fact that most of the analysis which is used to develop this case study came from after 2010!

The Taiwan Insurance Near Miss in the 2000s

The Japanese case is not isolated. One high-profile case of an industry near miss can be found in Taiwan.

---

[7]According to Credit Suisse (2011), Japanese life insurers managed their profitability through a combination of: "(1) increased premium revenues from new products; (2) a decline in insurance payouts attributable to increasing longevity; (3) cuts to operating costs; and (4) an improvement in asset portfolio performance, (with) higher returns from foreign securities and stocks, while lengthening average duration of JGBs."

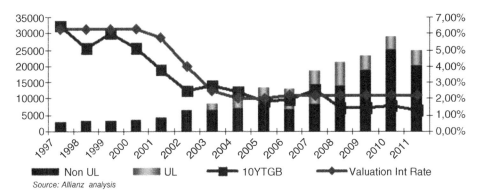

FIGURE 16.4 Taiwanese life market developments: Interest rates and new business mix. Reproduced by permission of Allianz SE.

As Figure 16.4 illustrates, interest rates in Taiwan have been almost as low as those in Japan over the past decade. The figure plots the 10-year Taiwanese government bond rate and the technical valuation rate used by the Taiwanese LH insurance industry for determining their reserve requirements. Both were well above 4% in the late 1990s, falling to or below 2% since 2003.

Figure 16.4 also illustrates that, prior to 2003, the Taiwanese LH insurance market was dominated by traditional participating and endowment policies (the non-UL (Unit Linked) products in the figure).

Of particular interest in the context of ALM are the regular premium participating products written during the late 1990s, which offered guarantees between 6% and 8% and a typical *liability duration over 30 years* due to the regular premium accumulation phase combined with a guaranteed rate for the decumulation phase, well beyond the longest-duration bonds available in the local capital markets. There was no chance to match the product, implying a structural mismatch and exposure to reinvestment risk.

As rates declined, new "legacy blocks" were created which proved to be an earnings drag for the incumbents. Similar to the Japanese case, Taiwanese insurers tried a variety of strategies for mitigating the impact of a poorly matched portfolio. Virtually all firms in the industry followed an "evergreen" strategy, growing their portfolio with more profitable new business in an attempt to outrun the legacy block, a tactic which was more feasible in Taiwan due to the low historical penetration rates for savings and retirement products.

In addition, regulators have attempted to develop a broader debt capital market (Sit, 2013), with the Financial Supervisory Commission (FSC) launching its "Bond Market Development Project" targeting a greater supply of high-yield foreign-denominated bonds and eliminating restrictions on investing in locally issued, foreign-denominated Rimimbi bonds. Regulations were further loosened over time, allowing firms to take on a more aggressive investment strategy: the domestic real-estate limit was increased from 19% to 30% in 2001, overseas investment limits were increased to 45% in 2007, overseas real estate can be purchased in 2012, etc.

Some in the industry (especially foreign-owned subsidiaries) changed their product mix, emphasizing products with lower interest rate sensitivity such as unit-linked products and structured notes as well as protection products. These product changes are encouraged by the FSC in order to build up additional sources of expense and mortality margins to offset the reinvestment drag on the back book. The FSC has also encouraged insurers to improve risk management by making the firm's contributions to the Insurance Guarantee Fund depend on its risk management practices, including its "ERM system, asset–liability management committee and Chief Risk Officer (CRO)" function.

In spite of these changes, the foreign-owned subsidiaries of large international groups such as ING, Prudential UK and AIG were sold to domestic firms. Why would international firms want to sell and domestic firms want to buy? Some assume that the decisions are influenced by the difference in accounting between local GAAP and international IFRS standards, providing the different players with a different perspective on the business. Others assume that local players may have an advantage should low rates persist, especially if regulatory forbearance or resolution becomes necessary. Finally, others might assume that local players are picking up a large interest rate option at a low premium due to their limited liability, something that a large international group may not be able to exercise due to reputational concerns.

In any case, the continued low interest rate scenario in Taiwan is causing an earnings drag which, like the gravity well of a black hole, is difficult to escape.

European Life Insurance in 2002[8]

There are three important asset/liability management decisions which traditional life insurers need to take: the positioning of assets backing liabilities and capital, the crediting strategy or profit-sharing policy for the existing book of business and the setting of new business guarantees. The equity market crash in the early 2000s served to highlight challenges in all three areas for European life insurers.

Investment Strategy

In the late 1990s, most European life insurance companies followed what would now be considered an aggressive investment policy. Spurred by the bull markets of the late 1990s and reinforced by actuaries' calculations based on "long-run" equity return expectations, insurers felt comfortable in taking large equity exposures.

According to a Fox–Pitt, Kelton European Insurance Report published in June 2003, equities comprised between 50% and 80% of UK funds in 2000. Although lower (in the region of 15–35%) for other European countries such as Germany, Switzerland, the Netherlands and Belgium, it was still significant compared with fund surplus.

In 1999, the "dotcom bubble" burst, causing a global fall in equity; the Euro Stoxx 50 fell by over 50% between 1999 and 2002 (see Figure 16.5).

Following the market crash, the value of the investment portfolio, and therefore the fund surplus, declined dramatically. In their December 2000 Insurance Sector Report, Merrill Lynch estimated that some insurers lost more than 30% of their embedded value, with a significant number losing between 0% and 20% (see Figure 16.6).

The decline in surplus was so material that it forced several life insurers to take consequent action, including:

- cutting dividends (Aviva, ING, amongst others);
- raising capital or injecting equity (Aegon, Ergo, Swiss Life, Winterthur and Zurich Financial Services, amongst others);

---

[8]This section borrows from Wilson (2003b).

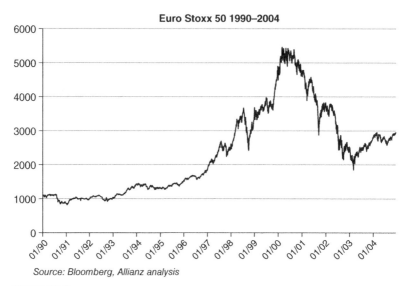

Source: Bloomberg, Allianz analysis

FIGURE 16.5 Euro Stoxx 50 index, 1986–2012. Reproduced by permission of Allianz SE.

■ selling or putting non-core businesses into run-off (Mannheimer Leben, Royal Sun Alliance, Hannover Leben, Winterthur and Zurich, amongst others).

In addition, the equity market crash was also the impetus for developing Solvency II, a more risk-based solvency regime.

Crediting Strategy

The situation was exacerbated by the insurers' crediting strategy. Insurers generally have latitude in determining how investment returns are declared and how they are split between the policy holder (through the company's crediting policy) and the insurance company (through its

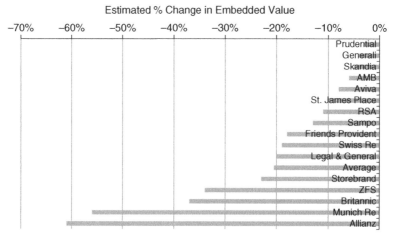

FIGURE 16.6 Merrill Lynch's December 2000 Insurance Sector Report
Source: Data from Merrill Lynch, Insurance Sector Report, December 2000.

participation rate). This discretion is intended to be used to "smooth" investment returns over time, building and leveraging unrealized gains as a "buffer" to dampen market swings.

Despite suffering massive losses on their investment portfolio between 1999 and 2002, almost all firms nonetheless elected to credit policy holders with investment returns above the minimum guaranteed return level – at the same time that some of them were asking shareholders for an equity infusion! For example, according to a JP Morgan research report, the average bonus rate in Germany for 2003 was 4.8%, well above the 3.25% minimum guaranteed rate.

New Business Guarantees

New business pricing, or setting the guaranteed rate for new business, is the third important ALM decision. Intuitively, the guaranteed minimum rate of return should be partly determined by current market conditions; if it is set higher, then the new cohort of policy holders is being subsidized either by the existing pool of customers or by the company. Table 16.3 illustrates that most companies in Belgium, Germany and Switzerland were offering guarantees with strike rates close-to-the-money and even in-the-money for Swiss Group Life business.

The Standard Response to an ALM Crisis

Suppose an insurer (or bank) finds itself with a large mismatch in a sustained low (high) interest rate environment. What can be done about it?

There is an old adage: closing the barn door after the cows have left doesn't help. If rates have developed adversely, market value losses will have already occurred; any subsequent hedging may prevent further losses, but it will also lock in the losses which have already occurred. Obviously, it is much, much better to close the barn door *before* the cows get out or, in the context of ALM practices, to *design better products which **can** be hedged and **actually** hedge the risk while the business is being written*.

But suppose that this good advice has not been followed. What does the typical firm do when confronted by rates which are not "normal," leading to the gradual emergence of a "legacy book" of business? The following is from the perspective of an insurer, but works equally well for banks as the case studies illustrate. Typically, management passes through seven distinct phases.

TABLE 16.3   New business guarantees and market rates, 2004

Country	Individual business	Group business	10-yr Bond
Belgium	3.25%	3.25%	3.80%
France	2.50%	2.50%	3.70%
Germany	3.25%	3.25%	3.60%
Italy	2.50%	2.50%	3.80%
Netherlands	3.00%	3.00%	3.70%
Switzerland	2.00%	3.25%	2.20%
UK	0.00%	0.00%	4.00%

Source: Data from JP Morgan European Insurance Update, June 2003.

1. *The "denial" phase.* Wait it out and hope for "normal" rates to re-emerge. Continue to offer attractive returns to existing and new policy holders. This phase typically lasts for the first 1–2 years.
2. *The "evergreen" phase.* After the first year, lower the guarantees and focus on growth in an attempt to outrun the drag from the legacy block. Argue that it "lowers the average guarantee level," even though the lower average only masks the loss of the legacy block while putting even more cows in the barn, with the door still open, until the products are redesigned.
3. *The "visit the casino" phase.* After a further 1–2 years, analysts become concerned. The next step is to change the asset/liability strategy in two important ways:
   - take more risk in an effort to pick up yield – invest in high-yield loans, off-shore or non-domestic assets, illiquid or real assets (e.g., equities, hedge funds, etc.) and generally lower credit quality assets;
   - increase the asset duration as much as possible, but only at yields above the average guarantee level – encourage long-dated issuance by sovereigns and corporations, originate long-dated infrastructure and real-estate loans, etc.
4. *The "closing the barn door" phase.* By about the third or fourth year, it becomes clear that "hope" may not be the best strategy. So, begin changing the products to take less structural risk, typically:
   - introduce products with lower structural exposure to interest rates, for example guarantees which reset;
   - change the product mix to avoid rate risk altogether (e.g., to more unit-linked products or structured notes and more protection-oriented products such as mortality, long-term care or health riders);
   - encourage policy loans and policy surrenders or conversions to the "new" generation of products (note that conversions in particular are likely to generate policy holder protection and sales practice concerns).
5. *The "tighten the belt" phase.* At about the same time, focus on managing distribution and administration expenses in order to compensate for the shrinking "investment margin."
6. *The "lobby" phase.* When it becomes apparent that low interest rates are likely to stay a problem, lobby for regulatory and/or accounting forbearance to lengthen the recovery period, for example by changing the technical interest rate, creating new reserves, etc.
7. *The "denouement" phase.* As last resort, exit the market, merge with a stronger entity or suffer insolvency.

From the above, there is no good solution for a "legacy block" of business. Far better in terms of creating sustainable value is to design products which can be hedged and then actually hedging them. If you have to take some structural mismatch risk to participate in a profit pool, make sure it is limited and that the cost is offset by the profit potential, objectively measured. In general, however, pricing will not make the bet on rates attractive if the bet is large and one-sided enough.

Post-2008, a Potential Crisis in the Making

The sustained low interest rate environment following the 2008 crisis presents another potential case study, albeit one which has not yet fully played out.

The "New Normal" and Low Rates

According to PIMCO, the financial crisis of 2008 was definitive, not in terms of the short-term, "cardiac arrest" which followed the Lehman bankruptcy, but rather in terms of the longer-term implications for the global economy from DDR (De-leveraging, De-globalization and Re-regulation) – see Gross (2009) and El-Erian (2010).

Of special note are the actions of governments and central banks, which were led ". . . to unconventional responses that, by definition, are uncertain in their effectiveness yet consequential in disrupting long-standing relationships" (El-Erian, 2009): Long-Term Refinancing Operations (LTROs) of the European Central Bank and TARP asset purchases in the United States, quantitative easing and, for the foreseeable future, low interest rate targets in the hope of spurring an anemic global economy through cheap credit.

Prior to 2008, rates were generally above 4% in the USA and Europe. Owing to these actions, the period after the 2008 financial crisis has seen much lower rates, as illustrated in Figure 16.7.

To put this into context, rates in September 2012 were the lowest on record in the Netherlands since 1517, the lowest in the USA since 1790 and the lowest in the UK since they began documenting rates in 1694 (*Wall Street Journal*, September 5, 2012).

Where are We Today?

PWC (2012) ranked low interest rates as one of the most significant risks facing the global insurance industry: "In 2011, life insurers started to feel meaningful effects from the low interest rate environment. If rates continue to stay low then life insurers' pain will be broader and deeper (leading to) lower investment earnings, smaller margins, loss recognition on traditional products."

Some analysts take comfort from the fact that it will take years for low investment rates to run through accounting earnings. For example, Standard & Poor's (2012) states that "Insurance companies also have some of the most significant interest rate risk, especially given their exposure to predominately fixed-income assets and the liabilities they back . . . *The full effects of persistently low interest rates would take several years to unfold, so we do not expect rating actions in the near term*" (emphasis added).

Some equity analysts share this view,[9] "Our detailed analysis highlights challenges ahead for the insurance industry . . . the most severe challenges emerge slowly and are dependent on a prolonged period of very low yields. *We believe a sustained low interest rate period would be an earnings headwind for the major stocks in our coverage and nothing else*" (emphasis added).

This is cold comfort from a market value perspective, which suggests that LH insurers' value should fall below their historical book value as the current net asset value of the firm becomes impaired due to the mismatch and the franchise value is challenged as new business margins become squeezed (lower rates mean less "pie" to share between policy holders, distributors and insurers). Once again, the economic view prevails over the accounting view: in 2012 the European LH sector was trading at 0.7–0.9× book and tangible net asset value (and only about 0.5× embedded value), representing a significant discount.

Low rates for a year or two may leave room for speculation that the "old normal" is around the corner. Low rates for four or five years begins to raise some serious doubts. In point of fact, many markets have already reached stage 6, the lobbying phase, with several European

---

[9]Barclays Capital (2011), insurance sector equity research.

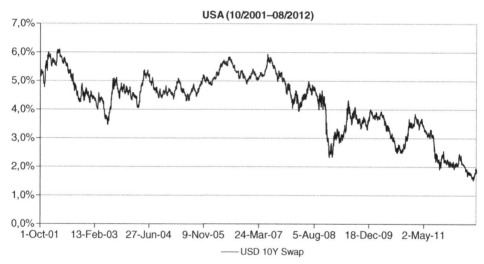

FIGURE 16.7   Global interest rate developments, 2001–2012. Reproduced by permission of Allianz SE.

countries allowing for an increase in technical discount rates for insurers and pensions (including Denmark, the Netherlands, Switzerland and Solvency II's long-term rate anchoring approach – see Schwartzkopff and Wienberg, 2012) and others creating new reserve requirements and limiting dividend payments to meet the challenges of sustained low interest rates (Reuters, 2014).

One explicit study conducted by the Bundesbank in 2013 (Dombret, 2013) predicts that under a mild, sustained low interest rate scenario up to 12 German life insurers with a market share of 14% would become insolvent by 2023 and, under a stronger scenario where other asset classes are affected, up to 32 firms representing a 43% market share could become insolvent.

The effect of the ECB's quantitative easing in 2015 has accelerated this trend; in their insurance sector report,[10] MainFirst makes a grim forecast, stating that 'We believe that about 40% of the (German life) industry will be loss-making from 2015 on . . . and the industry as a whole from 2025".

The German industry is not alone in being adversely impacted. According to Moody's,[11] Germany, Taiwan, Norway and the Netherlands are said to be at "very high risk" (defined as markets in which investment returns are below guarantee levels and where duration gaps are high and predicting that profits and capital will deteriorate if rates stay low over five years?; Switzerland, Sweden, South Korea and Japan are said to be at "high risk"; and, the United States, Italy, Hong Kong, Canada and France are "moderate risk".

Commenting further on the global low interest rate developments globally, the IMF[12] states in their 2015 Global Financial Stability Report that "The challenges facing life insurers should be tackled promptly. Regulators need to reassess the viability of guarantee-based products and work to bring minimum return guarantees offered to policy holders in line with secular trends in policy rates. Prompt regulatory and supervisory actions are needed to mitigate damaging spillovers from potential difficulties of individual insurers".

THE RETURNS: ARE SHAREHOLDERS WILLING TO PAY A PREMIUM OR A DISCOUNT?

As stated in the introductory paragraphs to this chapter, banks and insurers generate significant expected earnings by taking financial market risk in the asset/liability portfolios. However, not all expected earnings warrant a premium to today's net asset value. As demonstrated in Part Two: Better Information, at least theoretically the earnings are already fairly priced into today's net asset value; only excess returns or "alpha" will lead to a multiple expansion.

The remainder of this chapter answers two questions. First, does "alpha" exist which could lead to a valuation premium? Second, why wouldn't we believe that banks and insurers actually face a "negative alpha" from structural mismatch positions which cannot be hedged?

Does Alpha Exist? The Theory

Alpha is controversial. Many believe it impossible to consistently create alpha after expenses in efficient markets, except in some very specific circumstances. This raises the obvious question – does alpha exist?

From a theoretical perspective, there are four sources of alpha: an information advantage, a long-term investor advantage, a funding cost advantage and a customer franchise advantage.

Better Information, Leading to Market Timing and Security Selection

One potential source of alpha is *better information*. Suppose that an investment manager or trader has better information about the ex ante risk/return profile of a market or an individual asset. This advantage may come from faster access to market-relevant data, more advanced

---

[10]MainFirst, 2015, Insurance Sector Report; Dradhidy in German Life: Little strokes fell German Oaks.

[11]Moody's Investors Service, March 2015, Global Insurance Themes: Low Interest Rates are Credit Negative for Insurers Globally, but Risks Vary by Country.

[12]IMF, April 2015, Global Financial Stability Report; Navigating Monetary Policy Challenges and Managing Risks.

trading algorithms or more skilled analysis of markets, trends and individual complex transactions such as private equity, infrastructure, etc. Such an information advantage might be used to generate alpha relative to passive portfolio managers through better

- *strategic asset allocation* across different markets (e.g., fixed income, equities, etc.), overweighting "underpriced" markets and underweighting "overpriced" markets;
- *market timing*, dynamically tilting the asset allocation toward higher risk positions if market developments are deemed likely to be systemically positive and tilting more toward a conservative allocation (e.g., more into cash) when markets are likely to develop negatively;
- *security selection* within an asset class, overweighting securities which are deemed to be "underpriced" and underweighting "overpriced" securities.

Investment managers and banks make significant investments in collecting information and increasing execution speed in order to gain a competitive advantage. From a societal perspective this investment is beneficial as it promotes market transparency, efficiency and liquidity as well as promoting discipline on the issuers of debt and equity securities.[13] But can a sustainable competitive advantage be built, especially after the cost of collecting information and transaction costs to take advantage of the information?

The Academic View   There is considerable literature focused on whether investment alpha exists or, more accurately, whether investment professionals add value after deducting the additional investment expenses from an actively managed portfolio.

The academic debate is well summarized by Fama and French (2008), who argue that, by definition, passive investors will get no alpha. It therefore follows ". . . Then if some active investors have positive α before costs, it is, dollar for dollar, at the expense of other active investors. Thus, . . . active investment is in aggregate a zero sum game (and) After costs . . . active investment is a negative sum game."

The empirical results, summarized by French (2008), are profound. Investigating the fees, expenses and trading costs of an active investment strategy, he finds that ". . . the typical investor would increase his average annual return by 67 basis points over the 1980–2006 period if he switched to a passive market portfolio." This is consistent with the results of Brinson *et al.* (1986, 1991) discussed earlier. The *Financial Times* writes that UK pension funds alone are "wasting more than GBP 6 bn a year" by investing in actively managed funds rather than passive funds (Johnson, 2013).

US News and World Report (December 11, 2014) says, "The active or passive fund debate is over: At this point, the evidence is overwhelmingly in favor of passive fund". This sentiment is echoed by *The Economist* (April 25, 2015) which calls active investing over-"hyped", stating that there is new evidence to cast "more doubts about fund manager's stock picking powers".

This and subsequent academic literature indicates that consistent and lasting outperformance, after adjusting for expenses and risk, is very challenging and quite possibly illusory.

The Common-sense View   One might argue that academics who debate alpha are doing so because they cannot create alpha: in other words, those that can, do and those that cannot, research. With this in mind, let's move from the academic debate to someone who actually manages money successfully. What does Warren Buffet have to say about the value of "alpha" after fees and expenses (Loomis, 2009, 2014)? In 2008, Warren Buffet made a bet with Protégé Partners, a New York fund of hedge funds, that a passive investment in the equity markets would beat the

---

[13]See Sidebar 13.4 on whether bank trading activities add or subtract from market liquidity.

investment in a fund of actively managed hedge funds after expenses over a 10-year period. As of early 2014, the passive investment is up 40+% compared with only 10+% for the fund of funds.

Additional anecdotal evidence supports the view that it is very expensive to gain an information advantage and, even if gained, any advantage is likely to be short lived. Some firms in the market gather information so vigorously that their efforts cross the legal and ethical line: prominent examples include hedge fund insider trading cases such as SAC Capital[14] and Galleon,[15] the recent discussions regarding high-speed trading and "dark pools" (Patterson, 2014) and the apparent Libor and foreign exchange rate fixing by the trading desks of banks.[16]

In addition, any advantage will likely be short lived. The pursuit of a trading advantage leads to electronic trading strategies which offer a window of advantage measured literally in milliseconds.[17,18] The evidence suggests that a competitive advantage from information is costly to build, difficult to maintain and, even if successful, short lived.

In addition, the ability of some financial services firms to leverage an information advantage may be limited. First, you need the strategy and commitment to make the heavy investment in people, information and systems. Then, you need to actively trade based on the information – which may be challenging for highly regulated, liability-driven LH insurers as well as bank ALM portfolios and proprietary trading desks under the new Volcker Rule. This is hardly the platform for a premium multiple on a bank or insurance company's net asset value.

Long-term Investing

A second potential source of alpha often cited is through being a long-term investor. Long-term investing is defined in the World Economic Forum (2011) report as ". . . investing with the expectation of holding an asset for an indefinite period of time by an investor with the capability to do so. (Long-term) Investors . . . are less concerned about interim changes in asset prices, and instead are focused on long-term income growth and/or long-term capital appreciation . . ."

The benefits. Taking a long-term perspective can potentially lead to better performance through three channels: access to risk premia not available to short-term investors, ability to invest counter-cyclically and lower trading costs.

---

[14]". . . Criminal allegations were brought against SAC Capital Advisors . . . (which) is charged of 'systematic insider trading' . . . over an 11 year period . . . (The manager of the fund) would encourage employees to get information from analysts . . . saying, . . . 'This isn't about spreadsheets, it's about relationships'" (Jarvis *et al.*, 2013).

[15]"Raj Rajaratnam . . . Galleon co-founder . . . was found guilty of all 14 counts against him in the largest illegal stock-tipping case in a generation. A jury . . . returned its verdict . . . that (he) engaged in a seven-year conspiracy to trade on inside information . . ." (Glovin *et al.*, 2011).

[16]See the discussion on risk culture in Chapter 20 for more on these events.

[17]"An error was discovered following a systems upgrade designed to make their automated trading system 'Trading Axis' faster and better, leading to a flood of erroneous trades on the automated exchange." Krishnamurthy (2013), Gammeltoft and Barinka (2013).

[18]"On Tuesday morning at precisely 8:30, after a 10 second countdown synchronized to the Naval Observatory's atomic clock, a Labor Department flipped a master switch in the agency's battened-down pressroom and computers blurted out the monthly CPI. Until that moment, the market-sensitive data was guarded with launch-code secrecy . . ." in order to prevent a trading advantage (Cushman, 2012).

Access to Premia Relative to Short-term Investment Strategies   Long-term investment strategies may lead to higher average returns with lower volatility, often attributed to the existence of:

- *risk premia*, defined as higher expected returns relative to less risky investments, with the higher expected return dominating the short-term volatility over longer time horizons;
- *illiquidity premia*, providing a higher level of returns to those who can afford to hold illiquid investments;
- *complexity premia*, providing a higher level of returns from positions which require a higher level of due diligence – such as infrastructure investments, private equity, insurance-linked securities, structured notes, etc. – effectively a barrier to entry to all but those willing to build the skills and pay the cost of due diligence.

For example, many general account insurance asset managers and investment advisors advocate a long-term equity strategy in the belief that the long-term returns from equities will both dominate and be less volatile than other asset classes. This is supported by the analysis of Charles Schwab (schwab.com), who studied returns from the S&P 500 over different holding period horizons from 1926 and found that ". . . as you move from a one-year holding period to a three-year, 10-year and finally to a 20-year holding period, the number of negative returns goes down. In fact, there's never been a 20-year period with a negative return."

Various authors have investigated the existence of an illiquidity premium in the fixed-income market, discussed in greater detail in Chapter 17. Other authors have investigated the existence of an illiquidity premium in the context of publicly traded and private equity (see, e.g., Pastor and Stambaugh, 2003; Korajczyk and Sadka, 2008).

Less Pro-cyclical Trading   It is generally accepted that investors may be driven by behavioral biases, including:

- investing based on what you believe others are willing to pay or following others in the belief that they may know something that you don't, leading to asset price bubbles and "irrational exuberance" (Schiller, 2005);
- putting more emphasis on short-term information as opposed to long-term fundamentals, leading to increasing optimism in rising markets and increasing pessimism in falling markets (Thaler and Sunstein, 2009);
- an asymmetric bias, putting more weight on loss avoidance at the expense of potential gains (Thaler *et al.*, 1997).

These natural biases lead to pro-cyclical behavior, "following the herd" and, ultimately, to buying high and selling low. This pro-cyclical behavior can be exacerbated by leverage constraints, mark-to-market accounting rules and regulatory regimes which potentially force banks and insurers to sell assets into a declining market.

A long-term investor can in principle profit from these biases, for example taking a "risk on" position at the trough of the cycle and not selling into a falling market.

Lower Costs   Long-term investing is also potentially less expensive: saving on initial investment fees and due diligence costs by amortizing them over longer time periods; lowering average transaction costs by limiting the number of trades and the portfolio churn; eliminating the cost of acquiring short-term information; and lowering taxes to the extent that capital gains are taxed differently from investment and trading income. These expense savings can be substantial.

The prerequisites. Taking advantage of these perceived benefits is not for everyone, with some prerequisites absolutely necessary.

Stable, Predictable Funding   First, long-term investing requires long-term, stable funding: it will not work if depositors, policy holders and collateralized funding sources can pull their funds overnight, potentially forcing a sale of risk positions at depressed prices during a flight to quality or liquidity crisis.

Ability to Sustain Short-term Volatility   Second, the firm or fund must be able to sustain short-term volatility in their market-consistent net asset value. While stable funding sources are critical, the ability to weather short-term volatility is also driven by the accounting regime and regulatory framework under which the firm operates. A fully mark-to-market accounting and risk-based regulatory regime is less conducive to long-term investing as it may force sales in depressed markets.

Alignment of Interests   A final prerequisite is that managers have interests which are aligned with a long-term strategy. This may not be the case if bonuses are paid on performance measured over a shorter time horizon or if the decision makers face a higher probability of being replaced due to short-term performance deviations from the market. In this sense, there may be a natural bias toward short-term strategies for fund managers, bank traders and even A/L managers in LH insurers.

Who can take advantage of this? Long-term investing is more applicable to LH insurers which have long-term, illiquid liabilities; PC insurers generally have shorter liabilities and bank trading books and asset managers more often focus on very short-term strategies. However, the World Economic Forum study suggests that even LH insurers are being displaced as long-term investors, facing "accounting and regulatory pressures (to) reduce the risk a life insurer is willing and able to take" with "multiple stakeholders with potentially different objectives."

A more fundamental question is whether just showing up at the race is sufficient to win the prize. By definition, alpha represents excess returns relative to a risk-appropriate benchmark portfolio or investment style. Theoretically, long-term investing creates value if the strategy is difficult to replicate. If the strategy adds so much value, it is not clear what barriers to entry prevent specialized asset management firms from also meeting these needs?

Cheaper Access to Funding and Leverage

A third potential source of competitive advantage often cited is that some financial services firms, especially banks and PC insurers, may enjoy a cheaper cost of funding and leverage, increasing the return on equity from investing, trading and from carrying a trading inventory.

Funding Advantage for Banks?   Prior to 2008, it was often argued that the trading businesses of a universal or commercial bank had a funding advantage relative to pure-play investment banks due to access to cheaper customer deposit funding, greater access to inter-bank markets and fewer constraints on leveraging their portfolio.

This advantage is often attributed to the repeal of the Glass–Steagall Act in the United States (Merkley and Levin, 2012), which allowed banks to use their balance sheets to compete in trading businesses with investment banks: "The commercial banks were now free to compete with investment banks and securities firms for outsized returns in risky trading businesses. As competition intensified, the largest firms used their low funding costs, large balance sheets and implicit taxpayer backing to amass enormous, risky proprietary trading positions."

As the quote indicates, to some observers the "funding advantage" was nothing more than a subsidy from depositor protection schemes and implied backstops for "too big to fail" banks. This "advantage," if it existed at all, will be more limited in the future due to Basel III liquidity and leverage ratios, higher capital requirements on the trading book, improved internal FTP systems, as well as regulatory changes which limit proprietary trading positions such as the Volcker Rule.

Funding Advantage for PC Insurers? Another common claim is that PC insurers generate cheaper funding, which can then be used as leverage to "supercharge" the rate of return on investments. A commonly cited example is that of Warren Buffett's Berkshire Hathaway, a conglomerate which owns Geico, General Re and National Indemnity insurance firms. While ceding that Buffett also generated alpha through picking his acquisition targets, Frazzini *et al.* (2013) attribute a substantial amount of his investment performance to this funding advantage.

Summarizing the results, the *Economist* (Buttonwood, 2012) writes, "Without leverage, however, Mr Buffett's returns would have been unspectacular. The researchers estimate that Berkshire, on average, leveraged its capital by 60%, significantly boosting the company's return . . . Yet the underappreciated element of Berkshire's leverage are its insurance and reinsurance operations, which provide more than a third of its funding" as it collects premiums upfront and pays claims later on.

The *Economist* concludes that ". . . thanks to the profitability of its insurance operations, Berkshire's borrowing costs from this source have averaged 2.2%, more than three percentage points below the average short-term financing cost of the American government over the same period." As Tim Worstall writes in *Forbes* (Worstall, 2013), "If you can borrow below market and make only market returns then you're going to outperform the market in your returns on equity."

There is, however, a fundamental problem with this conclusion: it confuses the underwriting profit from Geico and General Re with a lower cost of funds to purchase other assets. Berkshire's insurance businesses generate value in their own right through operating and underwriting excellence; there are many insurers which did not turn a profit during this period. To relegate this superior business performance to an asset "funding advantage" is to confuse the real source of value creation.

Funding Advantage for LH Insurers? The funding advantage for LH insurers is not commonly cited, primarily because the cost of funding often looks unattractive under a market-consistent lens. Chapter 17 shows how to interpret the "clean" market-consistent new business margin as an option-adjusted borrowing spread. The bottom line is that, although Warren Buffett's PC insurance generated underwriting profits worth three percentage points below the Treasury rate, LH insurers often generate a cost of funds in excess of Treasury and swap rates if measured on a "clean" basis.

Market Making and Customer Franchise

The final potential source of competitive advantage is a strong customer franchise, which provides the following benefits.

High-quality customer flows generally, giving an advantage through two channels.

- First, allowing a trading desk to capture fees and the bid–offer spread between buyers and sellers by matching client orders in real time or by taking small inter-temporal positions with minimal inventory. This is often called "market making." The customer spread will depend on their access to the market, with smaller, retail customers paying a higher bid–offer spread than larger, institutional clients (see Radcliffe, 1997).

- Second, providing structural advantages to the market maker, including for example better information on trading flows, lower transaction costs, faster access to trading platforms, etc. These benefits were discussed in Sidebar 13.4.

A strong retail or wealth management customer base specifically, offering structured investment notes to retail clients with the risk managed by the bank's trading desk in the capital markets.

Professional clients whose specific investment views are met more efficiently by higher-margin, structured solutions rather than through lower-margin, commoditized products (a strategy discussed in the context of Bankers Trust in Chapter 3).

It is important to recognize that in most of these trading examples, "alpha" is created because of *the customer franchise, a defensible source of competitive advantage difficult for others to replicate, and not due to the financial risk taking*, although some risk taking is required to create value from the customer franchise.

Unfortunately, it is difficult to differentiate between proprietary trading and market making, a view shared by Senators Merkley and Levin when they discussed the Volcker Rule in the Dodd–Frank Act (Merkley and Levin, 2012): "Separating truly client-oriented trading from proprietary trading is going to be challenging . . . As one banker reportedly explained, 'I can find a way to say that virtually any trade we make is somehow related to serving our clients.'"

This inherent opacity implies that shareholders do not know whether they are paying a premium for proprietary trading or "punting" in the financial markets, or for a valuable and defensible customer franchise. Based on these observations, only the strongest customer franchises should lead to a permanent lift in a firm's market multiple.

On the Trail of a Defensible Alpha

Table 16.4 summarizes the discussion. The conclusion is that there are only a few clear sources of defendable competitive advantage available, most of which depend not on financial market risk taking but on a strong customer franchise and economies of scale.

Why Shouldn't Alpha be Negative?

The existence of alpha is a great conversation starter; an even more interesting question is *why would we believe that ALM alpha is not negative for some banks and insurers?* The answer to this question will help us understand whether shareholders shouldn't actually *discount* the net asset value of financial services firms rather than paying a premium for it.

I define *negative structural alpha* as *the performance drag from financial market exposures which cannot be hedged, traded or managed due to constraints or product design*. If it is challenging to "beat the market" with full flexibility and no constraints, the odds must surely decrease if you cannot trade the position.

Recognized Internally as Value Destroying

Banks and insurers recognize this negative structural alpha and actually discount the value of their own activities. How can I say this?

TABLE 16.4 Sources of "alpha" – a summary

Source of alpha	Description	Assessment	ALM	Trading	Asset Management
Information	Better access to market-relevant data (faster, deeper, more comprehensive), more advanced trading algorithms or more advanced analysis of individual complex transactions (e.g., private equity, infrastructure, etc.), leading to better asset allocation, market timing and security selection	Challenging in efficient markets, especially after expenses	✗	??	??
Long-term investing	Access to long-term risk, illiquidity or complexity premium Ability to avoid pro-cyclical investment bias Lowering transaction costs	Access does not guarantee outperformance Prerequisites (stable funding, limited constraints, aligned incentives) are increasingly challenging No barriers to entry – if it is so valuable, why don't funds emerge to capture the value?	?? LH only	✗	✗
Funding	Lower cost of funding, leading to higher returns on levered equity	For banks, possibly subsidized by tax payers and deposit holders For PC insurers, a confusion between underwriting profitability and funding	?? PC only	??	✗ Except specialized asset managers (e.g., private equity, with lock-up periods)
Customer franchise	Strong customer flows in market-making businesses (capturing bid–offer spreads with low risk position) and in retail/wealth management segments (leading to higher fees and margins on investment solutions)	Possible for the strongest customer franchises but difficult to distinguish from proprietary position taking	✗	✓	??

The most direct evidence is my own negotiation of FTP or performance benchmarks with asset/liability managers: *all* asset/liability managers want a benchmark against which their performance or "value added" can be measured; *none* of them are willing to accept the risk-minimizing replicating positions which represent the products their company actually sells simply because the risks from these products cannot be managed.

More specifically, every asset/liability manager I have ever met tries to exclude from their benchmarks any and all non-hedgeable risks, including long-dated cash flows which cannot be matched in the fixed-income market, complex embedded options, positions which include basis risk relative to liquid hedging markets and any behavioral risks.

This makes perfect sense from the perspective of AL managers: by negotiating the benchmarks, they are negotiating their bonuses. Who would want the albatross of a 30-year unhedgeable, highly complex embedded option hanging around their neck when it comes time to explain the investment results and argue for a higher bonus?

This logic raises a meaningful question: If your own asset/liability managers – the professionals who know the products and markets well – do not want the risk because they cannot manage it, why should we think that the positions are worth a *premium* to shareholders? Isn't it more logical that they should be valued at a discount to net asset value?

Recognized Externally as Value Destroying

Some in the insurance industry have recognized this explicitly. For example, the earliest work on market-consistent valuation frameworks for insurers included an explicit cost of capital for non-hedgeable financial market risks.

This cost is mentioned in Swiss Re's ground-breaking work on how insurers create shareholder value (Swiss Re, 2001): "It may not always be possible to find a (replicating portfolio). For example, the cash flows from certain life insurance or long-tail business may extend beyond the horizon of available fixed income investments. This *replication risk . . .* should be reflected in the frictional capital costs allocated to this product." The additional frictional capital charge advocated by Swiss Re to cover the non-hedgeable financial market risk is a direct example of a "negative alpha."

The concept of a cost of non-hedgeable financial market risk found its way into the original CFO Forum market-consistent embedded value principles and associated disclosures (CFO Forum, 2009). This is reflected in MCEV Principle 9: "An allowance should be made for the cost of non-hedgeable risks (including) the impact of non-hedgeable, non-financial risks and non-hedgeable financial risks (. . . e.g.) when market assumptions are required where there is no market or where the market is not sufficiently deep and liquid."

Unfortunately, it is no longer common practice to explicitly recognize the frictional cost or "negative alpha" of non-hedgeable financial market risk. In fact, this cost has quietly disappeared from many company's MCEV disclosures, probably because the industry realized how taking the framework to its logical conclusion sheds a negative light on the value of long-term, non-hedgeable products.

Other Factors Leading to a Negative Alpha

There are other reasons why shareholders may discount the financial market earnings of insurers and banks. The underlying question is: Would investors rather take the financial market risk on a bank or insurer's balance sheet or in their own investment account? Table 16.5 presents factors which influence the shareholders' evaluation of this important question.

TABLE 16.5   Financial market risk – through a bank or insurer or by the shareholder directly?

Advantages of taking financial market risk on a bank or insurer's balance sheet	Disadvantages of taking financial market risk on a bank or insurer's balance sheet

▪ May be the only way to access profitable customer margins which cannot be replicated directly by shareholders.
▪ Lower transaction costs and investment expenses due to economies of scale in investment or financial market transactions.
▪ Access to leverage at a lower cost.
	▪ Possibility of structural, non-hedgeable financial risk positions, leading to negative alpha performance.
	▪ Double taxation, at the corporate level and on dividends/capital gains to shareholders.
	▪ The conglomerate discount (e.g., the sum of parts) is greater than the share price, with financial market investments sharing the implicit discount.
	▪ Inherent opacity, exacerbating principle–agent problems, e.g.
	  ▪ acceptance of too much risk/"heads I win, tails you lose";
	  ▪ diversion of firm resources for management's own purposes.
	▪ Shareholders' inability to influence tactical and strategic trading strategy.

If asked directly, I believe that most shareholders would rather have the capital returned than see it invested in financial market positions which they can achieve on their own, avoiding double taxation as well as a conglomerate and opacity discount.

In general, buy- and sell-side analysts do not put much stock in active trading by insurers and retail and commercial banks, as reflected in their valuation approaches. For example, Morgan Stanley states: "We estimate a normalized return . . . , that is the return we expect to be achieved over the cycle, allowing for average . . . investment returns, using the formula Fair Value/Book Value = Normalized RoE/Cost of Capital." This practice is not unique to Morgan Stanley, nor to the insurance industry. Most analysts normalize returns in order to ensure that they are paying for sustainable operating profit as opposed to good luck on financial market bets.

Does the same argument hold true for investment banks? Here the jury is out. Certainly, prior to 2008, markets seemed willing to pay a premium to net asset value for firms with strong trading activities. However, since 2008, valuations of banks with strong trading franchises have declined, with analysts questioning whether such "outperformance" was really anything more than a chimera with the head of over-extended leverage and the tail of misaligned incentives. The BBC (Knight, 2011) comments that "(O)thers argue that much of the investment banks' reported profit is not real. Because bankers are paid such big bonuses, they seek clever ways to report higher profits while concealing the true risks from their own management or shareholders."

CHAPTER 17

The Practical Aspects of Asset/Liability Management

This chapter focuses on making the "rules of the game" for asset/liability management practical. It builds on the previous chapters on balance sheet management organization and the economics of ALM.

RULES OF THE GAME: ALM OPERATIONS

Both banks and insurers take an open mismatch position, either by choice or by product design. These mismatch positions contribute significantly to the earnings and risk of the firm, but generally not to a premium on their valuation multiple. The "rules of the game" for managing the mismatch result are straightforward.

1. The group needs to put in place the organizational prerequisites to manage asset/ liability mismatch risk.
   a. A management organization, including a governance body (the ALCO) and line management (the ALM unit, ALM process manager and selected business units) with explicit limits and delegated authorities.
   b. A risk and performance measurement framework focusing on both accounting earnings as well as market-consistent or fair values of the mismatch portfolio.
   c. A clear separation of product contribution from the mismatch result using Funds transfer Pricing (FTPs) and New Business RAPM, to provide the right incentives to product managers and the ALM function.
2. A value-oriented asset/liability management strategy.
   a. Effective asset/liability management begins with product design. There is no investment or hedging strategy which can circumvent the potential drag of a poorly designed product.
      i. Products should be designed to minimize non-hedgeable financial risk, allowing the possibility to manage the mismatch result in principle (e.g., reduce durations below the longest maturity available bonds and swaps, reduce the complexity of embedded options and guarantees, eliminate basis risk and behavioral risk, etc.).

>   **ii.** If non-hedgeable financial risk is necessary to participate in a specific profit pool, evaluate the trade-offs objectively and limit the total exposure.
>
>   **b.** When managing the ALM mismatch result through investment and derivative overlay strategies, always keep the following in mind.
>
>   **i.** "Mean reversion" or a "normal level of rates" are just assumptions – they are not physical laws comparable with Planck's constant or gravity and are heavily influenced by monetary policy.
>
>   **ii.** Even if expected to generate accounting earnings, ALM mismatch positions are generally not valued at a premium by shareholders and can represent a significant risk in terms of value.
>
>   **iii.** As such, they need to be kept within well-defined limits and managed from both an accounting and a value perspective.

ALM PERFORMANCE AND RISK MEASURES

Asset/liability mismatches can have a strong impact on both accounting earnings and the company's market value surplus. Unfortunately, the accounting and market value perspectives can differ dramatically: most banks use historical cost or accrual accounting systems for the "banking book," an approach which is disconnected from market value principles. Even more complicated, most insurers' balance sheets are split down the middle, with assets on fair value and liabilities on amortized cost, making value management even more complicated.

Because of the disconnect, optimizing one dimension will ultimately cause a problem along the other: perversely, closing an economic mismatch can introduce higher accounting earnings volatility and vice versa. As a consequence, both sets of measures need to be managed simultaneously.

ALM Measures for Banks

Table 17.1 summarizes the most common measures used by banks for measuring performance and risk in their ALM and strategic investment portfolios. The table is not meant to be comprehensive, highlighting only those measures which are most commonly used in practice.

Many of the measures have been introduced earlier. The re-pricing gap analysis and Earnings at Risk (EaR) measures are new and are discussed below in greater detail. Both provide information on the future development of the NII under different interest rate scenarios and management actions.

Specific Frameworks: Static Re-pricing Gap Analysis

The starting point for managing the NII margin is the static re-pricing gap analysis based on existing business, as illustrated in Table 17.2 on page 374.

The expected principal and interest payments of all assets and liabilities in a given currency, represented by AV and LV, are divided between the columns of Table 17.2 and allocated to their *re-pricing maturity*. For fixed-rate, fixed-term loans, the re-pricing maturity corresponds to the date on which the cash flows should be received (e.g., annual interest payments annually and the principal on its repayment date).

For floating-rate, fixed-term loans, the loan's principal and interest payments are placed at the floating rate reset date. For demand deposits which can re-price during the course of days, the entire notional volume may be allocated to the first column, although it is more likely that it will be distributed across the re-pricing ladder to the extent to which they are re-priced based on a rolling average of recent market rates.

TABLE 17.1 Bank ALM measures

Focus area and objectives	Accounting and solvency measures and tools	Value-based measures and tools
Portfolio coverage:	ALM and Strategic Investment (SI) portfolio (All measures applicable for both portfolios unless specifically mentioned.)	
ALM contribution: Describe the contribution to earnings or value attributable to the positioning of the mismatch portfolio.	**Net interest income (NII)**, compared with plan and peers (for the total). **Re-pricing gap analysis**, total projected NII over time and under different scenarios. Static and dynamic analysis.	Total MtM* returns. Investment RAPM. Return on Value at Risk (RoVaR). For SI portfolio: ▪ Absolute Tracking Error (ATE)** against a risk-appropriate, fixed-income benchmark; ▪ Tracking Error Adjusted Returns (TEAR).**
ALM risk measurement: Describe risk relative to the management objectives.	Net interest income: ▪ NII Earnings at Risk (EaR), measuring the uncertainty surrounding the future NII contribution; ▪ NII sensitivities and scenarios. Solvency (rating agency and regulatory): ▪ solvency at risk; ▪ solvency sensitivities and scenarios.	VaR. Tracking Error (TE)** for SI. Value sensitivities (e.g., basis point value, duration, convexity, etc.). Value sensitivities and scenarios (e.g., ±100 bps rate movements, implied volatility movements, etc.).

*Mark-to-Market.
**As defined in the last section in this chapter.

Many banks will have only one re-pricing gap analysis, having customer business in only one currency; however, if the bank is active in multiple currencies, then a re-pricing gap analysis needs to be done for each currency.

This static gap analysis can be used to assess specific interest rate scenarios. For example, one can calculate the total projected impact on NII of an interest rate scenario consisting of an instantaneous parallel shift in rates (ΔR), with rates remaining constant thereafter, by using Equation 17.1.

EQUATION 17.1: Calculating NII impact using static re-pricing gap analysis

$$\Delta NII = \sum_i (AV - AL)_i x \Delta T_i x \Delta R$$
$$\Delta NII = (\text{Time weighted cumulative gap})_T x \Delta R$$

where ΔT_i represents the time period represented by the bucket or column in Table 17.2 (e.g., $\Delta T_1 = 1/12, \Delta T_2 = 2/12, \Delta T_3 = 3/12, \Delta T_4 = 6/12$, etc.).

TABLE 17.2   Static re-pricing gap analysis

Volumes	< 1 mn	< 3 mn	< 6 mn	< 1 yr	Interest rate insensitive balances
Asset	AV_{1mn}	AV_{5mn}			Notional cash flows allocated to the appropriate re-pricing maturity
Liability	LV_{1mn}	LV_{3mn}			
Net	$(AV\text{-}LV)_{1mn}$	$(AV\text{-}LV)_{3mn}$			
Cumulative	$(AV\text{-}LV)_{1mn}$	$(AV\text{-}LV)_{1mn} +$ $(AV\text{-}LV)_{3mn}$			

This sensitivity measure can be translated into a rudimentary EaR measure by making an assumption about the distribution of future interest rate changes. For example, assuming that parallel shifts in interest rates are normally distributed with mean μ and volatility σ, for example $\Delta R \approx N(\mu, \sigma)$, the NII EaR for a given confidence interval is calculated using Equation 17.2.

EQUATION 17.2:   NII EaR based on static re-pricing gap analysis

$$\Delta NII = (\text{Time weighted cumulative gap})_T x(\alpha\sigma - \mu)$$

where α represents the number of standard deviations needed to produce the maximum event within the specified confidence interval of size CI (e.g., 2.33 for a 99% confidence interval, 2.58 for a 99.5% confidence interval, etc.).

A Numerical Example   Suppose that the bank balance sheet consisted of only deposits and a single loan. Further, assume that the total volume of demand deposits re-price on a monthly basis; they are therefore placed in the first column of the re-pricing gap analysis. If the loan is a fixed-rate, zero coupon loan which matures in 1 year, its notional volume would be placed in the fourth column, as illustrated in Table 17.3.

For this stylized balance sheet, the total impact on NII under an instantaneous, parallel 100 bps movement in interest rates would be equal to $-300*100$ bps$*(11/12)$, indicating that the NII is only "locked in" for the first month and thereafter would decrease as the deposits re-priced to the higher level of interest rates for the remaining 11 months.

TABLE 17.3   Static re-pricing gap example

Static re-pricing gap analysis

Volumes:	< 1 mn	< 3 mn	< 6 mn	< 1 yr	. . .
Asset				100	
Liability	100				
Net	−100	0	0	100	
Cumulative	−100	−100	−100	0	

If we further assumed that the change in rates was normally distributed with mean zero, standard deviation equal to 15% times the current rate level (e.g., $\Delta R \approx N(0, R^*15\%)$) and the current interest rate was 5%, then the NII EaR at a 99% confidence interval would be equal to 4.81, representing a worst-case change in rates within a 99% confidence interval equal to 1.75% (e.g., $2.33^*15\%^*5\%$) times the time-weighted cumulative re-pricing gap of 275 (e.g., $300^*(11/12)$).

Dynamic Re-pricing Gap Analysis

Issues with static gap analysis While giving an initial impression of the NII risk profile of the bank, the static gap analysis may be misleading for a variety of reasons.

- It assumes that all products re-price immediately to rate changes and ignores commercial policies which tend to stabilize deposit and loan rates to short-term movements in rates.
- It assumes that all products re-price based on the same reference rate, whereas in practice there may be many rates which are relevant (e.g., prime lending rates, inter-bank rates, etc.).
- It ignores more complicated rate dynamics such as falling then rising rates, a flattening or steepening of the yield curve, etc.
- It ignores behavioral dynamics such as prepayment and withdrawal propensities which have an impact on effective rate duration.
- It ignores future new business and the impact of commercial policy changes which will also impact volumes.
- It cannot be used to separate margin dynamics from reference rate dynamics, where the latter in principle can be hedged through effective ALM. This separation also requires an FTP approach.
- Finally, it focuses only on NII developments and not on the net present value of the open positions.

Solving the Issues Capturing all these effects requires a more complex analysis framework, one which is dynamic and includes the following abilities.

- *Better model the cash flows* the bank expects under different rate scenarios, for example by
  - defining behavioral rules governing future customer demand for loans and deposits as well as loan prepayment and deposit withdrawal elasticities and keeping track of volumes, customer rates and margins by origination year cohort;
  - defining behavioral rules governing the bank's own interest rate re-pricing dynamics, including the dynamic adjustment of customer margins to changing interest rates and the basis risk between customer and reference rates;
  - including new business in the analysis.
- *Generate financial market scenarios* of interest, including
  - real-world market scenarios for different management and reporting purposes (e.g., NII planning, scenario analysis and stress testing);
  - stochastic scenarios using an Economic Scenario Generator (ESG), including
    - stochastic real-world scenarios to support portfolio positioning decisions for optimizing NII risk and return, including the development of rates over the projected time horizon;
    - stochastic *risk-neutral* scenarios to value the cash flows and embedded options and guarantees within the portfolio, introducing a *fair value perspective to complement the NII perspective.*

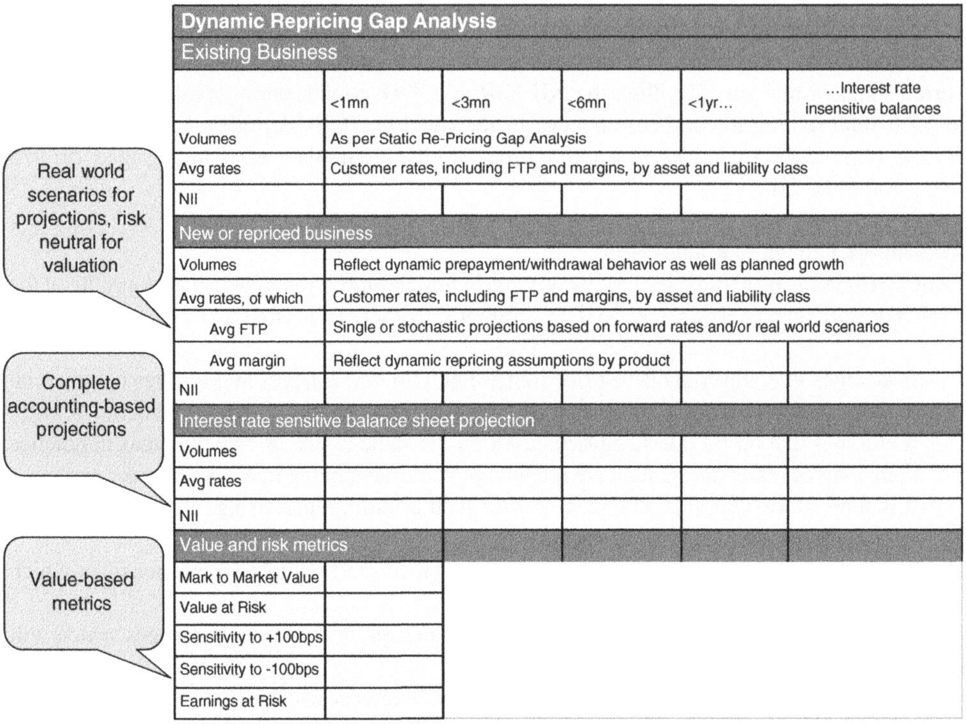

Dynamic Repricing Gap Analysis					
Existing Business					
	<1mn	<3mn	<6mn	<1yr...	...Interest rate insensitive balances
Volumes	As per Static Re-Pricing Gap Analysis				
Avg rates	Customer rates, including FTP and margins, by asset and liability class				
NII					
New or repriced business					
Volumes	Reflect dynamic prepayment/withdrawal behavior as well as planned growth				
Avg rates, of which	Customer rates, including FTP and margins, by asset and liability class				
Avg FTP	Single or stochastic projections based on forward rates and/or real world scenarios				
Avg margin	Reflect dynamic repricing assumptions by product				
NII					
Interest rate sensitive balance sheet projection					
Volumes					
Avg rates					
NII					
Value and risk metrics					
Mark to Market Value					
Value at Risk					
Sensitivity to +100bps					
Sensitivity to -100bps					
Earnings at Risk					

Callouts:
- Real world scenarios for projections, risk neutral for valuation
- Complete accounting-based projections
- Value-based metrics

FIGURE 17.1 Dynamic re-pricing gap analysis

A dynamic balance sheet projection framework incorporating these elements is illustrated in Figure 17.1. The logical progression is to include the behavioral relationships for single scenarios in the static gap analysis and then to run the analysis under both stochastic real-world and risk-neutral scenarios.

Most large banks have dynamic gap analysis, implemented either by developing their own systems or by purchasing off-the-shelf systems from third-party vendors, an option which makes sense due to the complexity of developing and maintaining a system internally. A good reference describing the functionality and decision criteria for selecting an ALM system can be found in McQuire (2006).

ALM Measures for Insurers

The measurement framework for an insurer's ALM function (Society of Actuaries, 2003) is more complicated than that used by a bank, predominantly because of the added complexity of isolating the performance of strategic asset allocation decisions from tactical asset allocation decisions; this requires multiple portfolios each with its own, specific benchmark against which performance is measured – including a benchmark representing the actual liabilities for product performance, a strategic benchmark for the SAA portfolio and asset class-specific benchmarks for each of the TAA portfolios. In addition, it also requires that risks, and returns, be measured relative to the benchmark, putting a higher emphasis on tracking errors and outperformance metrics.

TABLE 17.4 Insurance ALM measures

Focus area and objectives	Accounting measures and tools	Value-based measures and tools
Portfolio coverage:	Strategic investment portfolio (representing assets backing capital) ALCO portfolio (representing SAA benchmark versus achievable replicating portfolio) SAA portfolio (representing SAA actual versus benchmark) TAA portfolios (representing TAA actual versus asset class-specific benchmark) (All measures applicable for all portfolios unless specifically mentioned.)	
ALM contribution: Describe the contribution to earnings or value attributable to the positioning of the mismatch portfolio.	**Investment income**, compared with plan and peers in total.	MtM returns. Investment RAPM. Return on VaR (RoVaR).* Absolute Tracking Error (ATE)* against the benchmark portfolio. Tracking Error Adjusted Returns (TEAR).*
ALM risk: Describe risk relative to the management objective.	Investment income at risk. Investment income sensitivities and scenarios. Solvency (rating agency and regulatory). Solvency at risk. Solvency sensitivities and scenarios.	VaR. TE.* Value sensitivities (e.g., basis point value, duration, convexity, etc.). Value sensitivities and scenarios.

*As defined in the last section in this chapter.

An overview of performance and risk measures typically used within an insurance ALM framework is given in Table 17.4. The objective of Table 17.4 is not to be comprehensive but to provide an overview of the most common measures used in practice (see also Gilbert, 2008; Goldman Sachs, 2010).

All these measures are discussed elsewhere in this Handbook.

Insurance ALM and the Allocation of Investment Capital

The second reason why insurance ALM is more complicated than bank ALM is due to the nature of the products sold: whereas the decision to hedge a loan or deposit does not generally affect the product's stand-alone margin or economics, taking more financial risk can have a profound impact on the economics of a participating LH product. On the one hand, taking more risk may increase expected investment margins, making the product more competitive and increasing earnings, but it also increases the value of the guarantees and the risk to share-holders, deteriorating the product's economics.

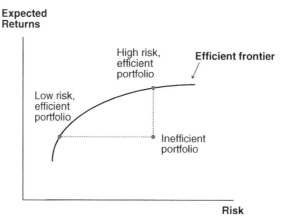

FIGURE 17.2   Efficient frontier

As a consequence, care must be taken, both in optimizing the ALM position for a given product and level of risk and in allocating investment risk capital across the different products.

Portfolio Optimization and Efficient Frontier

As its name implies, portfolio optimization tries to find the optimal investment portfolio for a given level of risk. The concept of an efficient frontier and portfolio optimization are not new, having been pioneered by Harry Markowitz in the 1950s (Markowitz, 1952). Markowitz's insight was that the risk and return of an asset cannot be evaluated in isolation but needs to be evaluated in the context of the overall investment portfolio. In this context, asset correlations and diversification also play a role and the optimal portfolio depends on the contribution of each asset to the overall riskiness of the portfolio.

An *efficient frontier* is defined generically as *the set of portfolios offering the maximum expected return for a given level of risk (or, equivalently, the minimum risk portfolio for a given level of expected return)*. The concept is illustrated in Figure 17.2, leaving open the definition of "risk" and assuming that no risk-free asset is available, or alternatively that the portfolio cannot use financial leverage. Any portfolio below the curve is inefficient in the sense that a higher return can be achieved for the same level of risk or a lower risk can be achieved for the same level of return.

Efficient frontiers and portfolio optimization techniques are used extensively in the insurance industry to support strategic asset allocation decisions (e.g., Goldman Sachs, 2010; Ernst and Young, 2014b). One framework commonly used is the original Markowitz mean–variance framework, described in Sidebar 17.1, which assumes that returns are jointly normally distributed and that "risk" can be measured by the portfolio's return variance.

As the mean–variance framework illustrates, portfolio optimization can be reduced to a formal optimization problem involving several components: an objective function, the control variables (e.g., portfolio weights), a measure of risk, constraints and an assumption about asset (liability) returns.

SIDEBAR 17.1: MEAN–VARIANCE AND MEAN–CVAR EFFICIENT FRONTIER[1]

MEAN–VARIANCE PORTFOLIO OPTIMIZATION

Markowitz investigates the case where asset returns are normally distributed or, equivalently, investors' preferences are quadratic in wealth. In these circumstances, the efficient frontier is the answer to a well-defined optimization problem: *minimize the variance of the portfolio for a given level of expected returns or maximize the expected return for a given portfolio variance.*

Equation 17.3: Efficient frontier

$$\text{Minimize } \sigma_p^2 \text{ subject to } r_p = \mu.$$

$$\text{Equivalently, maximize } r_p \text{ subject to } \sigma_p^2 = \sigma^2$$

where $\sigma_p^2 = \frac{1}{2}\sum_i^n \sum_j^n \omega_i \omega_j \sigma_{ij}$, $r_p = \sum_i^n \omega_i r_i$ and $\sum_i^n \omega_i = 1$.

Here, σ_p^2 and σ_i^2 are the portfolio's and asset i's return variance, respectively, r_p and r_i are the expected returns for the portfolio and asset i, respectively and ω_i is the weight of asset i in the portfolio. We limit the values of μ to be those that are feasible – for example, there exist some values of ω satisfying $\sum_i^n \omega_i = 1$ such that $\mu = \sum_i^n \omega_i r_i$.

The efficient frontier is found for a valid μ by solving the first-order conditions for the constrained optimization problem, a set of $n + 2$ equations in $n + 2$ unknowns in the portfolio weights and two Lagrangian multipliers representing the constraints, e.g. $(\lambda_1, \lambda_2, \omega_i)$:

$$\sum_j^n \omega_j \sigma_{ij} - \lambda_1 r_i - \lambda_2 = 0 \quad \forall i \in (1, \ldots, n)$$

$$\mu = \sum_i^n \omega_i r_i$$

$$\sum_i^n \omega_i = 1$$

The asset-only Markowitz framework can easily be adapted to support liability-based investment decisions by explicitly deducting the liabilities as the starting positions for the optimization, with implications for the first-order conditions. In addition, it is also common practice to include short-sale restrictions if required to deliver sensible results.

The efficient frontier in Figure 17.3 was calculated using data from April–September 2014 for the following fixed-income and equity indices: Barclays short-, medium- and long-term bond indices, the S&P 500 and the Euro Stoxx 50.

MEAN–CVaR PORTFOLIO OPTIMIZATION

Conditional Value at Risk (CVaR) is an alternate risk measure that is more sensitive to losses in the tail of the returns distribution. CVaR is a measure of the average of all losses which are greater than the confidence interval threshold; CVaR will be higher if the return distribution has a fatter tail, representing a higher probability of an extreme loss.

---

[1]Example and MATLAB code contributed by Jean-Frederick Breton (Jean-Frederic.Breton@mathworks.com).

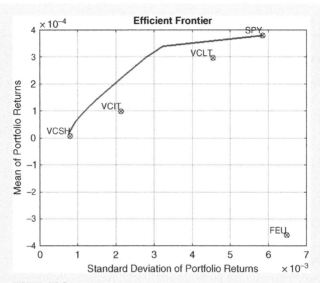

FIGURE 17.3 Efficient frontier curve
Source: Jean-Frederic Breton, reproduced with permission.

In some situations, performing mean–CVaR portfolio optimization might provide portfolios that are more robust in the face of extreme loss realizations.

One way to compare the efficient portfolios we obtain from mean–variance and mean–CVaR optimization is to look closely at the weights allocated to each asset. We visualize the weights for the CVaR and mean–variance side by side using area plots, as in Figure 17.4. This allows us to see the mix of the different assets in each of the efficient

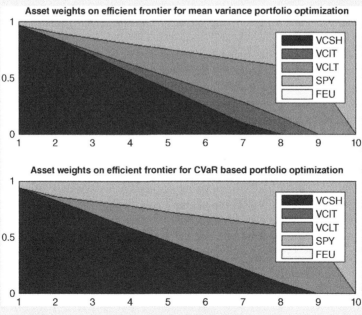

FIGURE 17.4 Mean–variance and mean–CVaR optimization
Source: Jean-Frederic Breton, reproduced with permission.

portfolios. The x-axis represents the portfolio number along the efficient frontier while the y-axis represents the asset weight in the portfolio. As we move to the right on the x-axis, the corresponding efficient portfolio moves away from the minimum-variance portfolio. Notice that the minimum-variance portfolio in both cases only allocates cash to the short-term bond index and to S&P 500. Also, neither mean–variance optimization nor mean–CVaR optimization allocates cash to the DJ Euro Stoxx 50 index. This is due to the under-performance of the index in the historical period April–September 2014.

The resulting portfolio weights produced by the two different optimization routines can be explained by the fact that the mean–variance approach assumes a normal distribution for returns while the mean–CVaR does not. We see in the histogram plot of the returns in Figure 17.5 that the normal distribution (illustrated by the curve) may

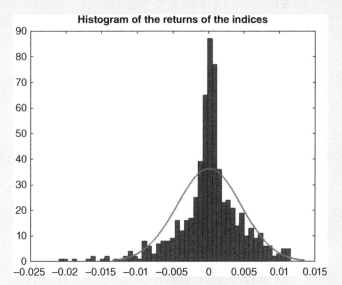

FIGURE 17.5 Histogram of the returns of the indices
Source: Jean-Frederic Breton, reproduced with permission.

not be a good assumption to represent the returns data (represented by the histogram) as the empirical data has more outliers or extreme events than would be predicted by the normal distribution. The x-axis represents the percentage returns, split into 50 buckets while the y-axis represents the number of occurrences in each of these buckets.

Given the complexity of insurance businesses, especially with regard to external constraints on assets, derivatives and solvency, various combinations are used in practice, as illustrated in Table 17.5. Many of these alternatives can only be solved using numerical techniques.

The use of portfolio optimization techniques is typically done at the SAA level, defining the strategic benchmark which is then left constant during the year (subject to major market changes). Not surprisingly, the optimal portfolio will depend heavily on the assumptions made with regard to expected returns. As such, it is important to evaluate the robustness of the efficient portfolio to different starting assumptions.

TABLE 17.5 Portfolio optimization/efficient frontier approaches used in practice

	Objective function	Control variables	Risk measures	Constraints	Asset returns
Markowitz mean–variance	Maximize single-period expected total returns.	Portfolio weights (constants).	Portfolio return variance.		Normally distributed.
Common variations	Multi-period returns.* Accounting returns, operating profit.	Portfolio response functions for multi-period dynamic problems.	Risk relative to investment and liability benchmarks.** Portfolio shortfall risk and other downside risk measures (e.g., CVaR).*** Capital measures – internal model, regulatory, rating agency.	No short sales. Reserve coverage ratios. Liquidity ratios. Solvency ratios. Duration and equity sensitivities.	Asymmetric returns for derivatives, liabilities. Mean-reverting equity and interest rate processes. Different scenarios (e.g., "bull market," "bear market").

*Panjer (1998), Gabih *et al.* (2005).
**Panjer (1998), Chow (1995).
***Harlow (1991).

Allocating financial risk capital to general account portfolios

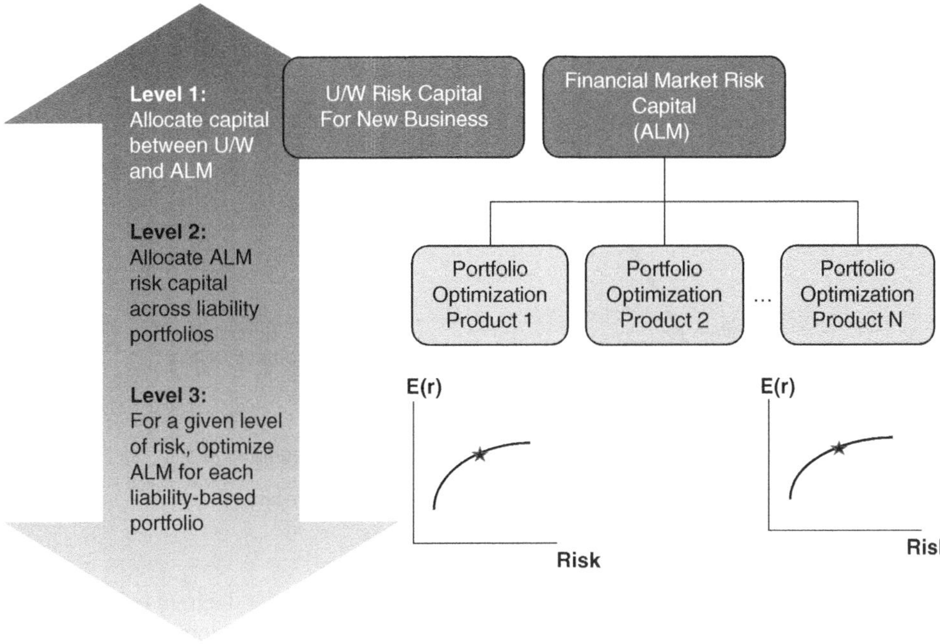

FIGURE 17.6 Optimizing financial market risk

Allocating Investment Capital

Portfolio optimization answers the following question: What is the optimal ALM position for a given level of financial risk or capital? It does not answer a more fundamental question: How much financial risk capital should be allocated to a particular product or strategy in the first place?

As illustrated in Figure 17.6, there are three levels at which capital allocation decisions need to be taken in the context of insurance ALM.

- The allocation between underwriting and ALM risks. This allocation determines the relative mix between underwriting results and financial market earnings or alpha and is done as an integral part of the corporate strategy discussion, covered in Chapter 14.
- The allocation of ALM risk capital between different liability portfolios. Assuming that we are generally willing to take more financial risk, for example by increasing equities or focusing on assets offering an illiquidity premium, should this increased risk appetite be taken in a PC company's general account or in an LH portfolio – and if so in which LH portfolio? A practical framework for taking this decision is given in the remainder of this section.
- Finally, the optimization of the ALM position at the portfolio level as part of the ALM process, as discussed in the previous section.

Assuming that the insurer wants to take more financial market risk, the question arises how to allocate that risk across different products and portfolios. The challenges are more complex for LH participating businesses because financial risk taking can have a material effect on the underlying product economics, with different products and portfolios behaving differently.

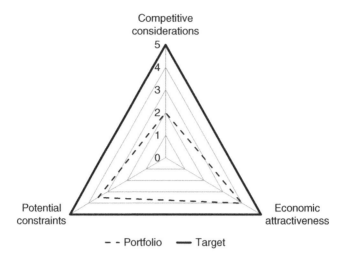

* Qualitative / quantitative criteria defined for each dimension

FIGURE 17.7   Factors affecting investment capital allocation

A practical decision support framework is illustrated by the spider diagram in Figure 17.7. In general, there are three dimensions influencing the decision: economic attractiveness, competitive considerations and potential constraints. Qualitative and quantitative benchmarks are defined for each dimension representing the target or ideal situation, with the actual situation mapped in the diagram for comparison. A weighting scheme can be defined and applied within and across the dimension to deliver an overall ordinal ranking indicating where additional financial market risk capital should be allocated.

Competitive Considerations

- Are new business demand and/or existing business lapse rates highly elastic with respect to credited investment returns?
- Are competitors in a weaker or stronger position? How will they respond to a change in crediting policy?
- What is the impact of new business volumes on expense levels? What new business volume is necessary to support expense ratios and tied-distribution channels?
- Is the new business consistent with the company's overall product strategy?

Economic Attractiveness

- Is the new business attractive without investment returns (e.g., on a New Business RAPM or new business margin basis)?
- Is the new business attractive from a real-world IRR or new business investment margin perspective, both of which reflect investment risk and returns?
- How is investment risk and return shared between policy holders and shareholders? Is the shareholders' participation asymmetric, bearing the bulk of the risk but earning a smaller percentage of the returns?

- Does the fund have sufficient unrealized gains or other buffers to absorb financial market losses? Does the profit-sharing rule effectively allow for smoothing and sharing?
- Is there flexibility in managing the economics through other management levers (e.g., adjusting the split between annual and terminal bonuses, the split between policy holder and shareholder participation, adjusting future maintenance and expense fees, caps or floors, etc.)?
- Is the allocation of investment risk optimal from a tax perspective?

Potential Constraints

- Are key constraints being met (e.g., with respect to regulatory, rating agency and internal solvency ratios? With respect to reserve coverage ratios, the use of derivatives, etc.)?
- Can accounting earnings, realized and unrealized gains and losses, be managed?

CALCULATING FUNDS TRANSFER PRICES (FTPs)

FTP systems and associated replicating portfolios are the fundamental building blocks of effective asset/liability management. They are used to separate underwriting decisions from financial market risk-taking decisions. The FTP for a specific product gives two related results.

- First, it defines the arm's-length *transfer price* of financial risk from the areas responsible for the product to the AL portfolio.
- Second, it implicitly or explicitly defines the *replicating portfolio*, or the portfolio of capital market transactions which can be used to represent the product's financial market risk in the AL portfolio.

This section discusses how FTPs are calculated in practice (for further references, see Buruc, 2008; CFO Forum, 2009; Dermine, 2015; Moody's Analytics, 2011).

Principles Defining FTPs

The FTP is the arm's-length, objective transfer price of financial risk from an individual product to the ALM portfolio. Related to each transfer price is a financial representation or replicating portfolio – a portfolio of cash and derivative instruments which "replicates" the financial risk of the underlying policy or bank product. The replicating portfolio is the position that the ALM function "sees."

Given the goal of separating underwriting from financing or investment decisions, an FTP should satisfy several principles.

- First, the FTP should be calculated using actual market prices.
- Second, the FTP should reflect the specific financial cash flow characteristics of the product as far as possible.
- Third, it should reflect the marginal cost of hedging financial risks for a highly rated financial institution in liquid, wholesale markets in the same currency as the underlying product.

- Fourth, the transfer price should in principle be able to "purchase" the replicating portfolio or hedging cash flows which neutralize the product's financial market risk.
- Finally, because it is used to calculate underwriting product contributions and will influence management decisions, the FTP should be set in a transparent and consistent manner.

The first step in designing an FTP system is to define the instruments which form the basis for the price and the replicating portfolio. The second step is to determine the replicating portfolio from those markets for each and every product.

Step 1: Defining the Reference Markets

The markets which define the FTP should have sufficient liquidity, leading to a narrow bid–offer spread, so that it is actually practical to hedge a marginal net mismatch position. In addition, they should involve no or limited counterparty risk so that the product decisions are clearly separated from all other risk considerations.

The General Case

In developed economies, most institutions use inter-bank money market and interest rate swap curves as the basis for building their FTP pricing or "risk-free" curve.

The Swap Curve as the Base Discount Curve If both on- and off-shore swap markets exist, they will typically use the on-shore swap market as a better reflection of the true cost of hedging local currency cash flows.

The use of swap curves is required under Solvency II for the valuation of technical insurance liabilities (albeit with a credit adjustment) and is supported by the CFO Forum's MCEV Principle 14: "The reference rate is a proxy for a risk free rate appropriate to the currency, term and liquidity of the liability cash flows. Where the liabilities are liquid the reference rate should, wherever possible, be the swap yield curve appropriate to the currency of the cash flows."

OTC and Exchange-traded Option Prices for Embedded Options For pricing the embedded options (e.g., lapse or prepayment options, re-pricing options, etc.), the FTP framework needs to include the option prices. Most banks and insurers use OTC (Over-The-Counter) and exchange-traded markets as the basis for their FTP framework. The use of OTC and exchange prices is consistent with the use of swap rates as the base discount curve, especially given the role that swap rates play in the valuation of OTC and exchange-traded options.

There are nine complications to this general rule, discussed in the remainder of this section.

Developing Economies without Liquid Swap Markets

Complications arise in developing markets where swap curves are not liquid or may not exist. As a consequence, financial institutions in emerging markets sometimes use a government bond curve instead. The CFO Forum MCEV Principles state: "Where companies have businesses in territories and or currencies where swap curves do not exist or do not provide a robust basis for producing reference rates then a more appropriate alternative, such as the government bond yield curve, may be used."

The use of a government curve may complicate the valuation and management of embedded options. If derivatives markets exist, they are typically quoted relative to inter-bank and swap rates. As a consequence, par swaps and options may appear to be in- or out-of-the-money depending on the spread between the government and swap curves. This will affect hedging decisions as it will distort hedge ratios, making embedded options appear more or less expensive than the cost of the hedge instrument actually available in the market.

This is also the first area of difference between bank and insurance FTPs. Banks in emerging markets typically include an additional margin above the local government bond rates to better reflect their marginal cost of funding. The rationale is summarized in Buruc (2008): "Using credit risk free market indices like a (government) treasury yield curve will encourage banks to make loans that are less profitable than they appear and to discourage deposits that can be profitable." Insurers come from a different perspective, one focused on policy holder protection, and therefore do not have an issue with discounting liabilities at the government curve even if they could never achieve the same cost of raising marginal funds.

Bid–offer Spreads to Reflect Structural Imbalances

Most banks and insurers use *mid*-rates as the basis for their FTP framework. This practice is theoretically justified under one of two conditions: either the cash flows within a specific maturity bucket are roughly "balanced" (implying that the mid-rate is a "fair rate" if we are not to explicitly give the ALM function a margin) or the bid–offer spread for the FTP curve is negligible and can be ignored.

These assumptions are likely to break down in practice: it is not uncommon for banks to have shorter-term deposit funding and longer-term assets, or even to have more assets than customer deposits, implying an asset overhang in certain maturity buckets. Similarly, LH insurers active in pension and annuity businesses, generating liabilities which can extend beyond 30 or 40 years, far beyond the tenor of most swap markets.

If the *mid*-rate is used in such situations, then the ALM unit will suffer an economic loss if it actually does hedge the mismatch: a 5–10 bps bid–offer spread means that it costs the treasury 2.5–5 bps to perfectly hedge its position relative to the mid-rate.

In cases where the mismatch or bid–offer spread is significant, some companies use the appropriate bid or offer rate by tenor bucket in order to ensure that the product origination units see the true marginal cost to the institutions of offering such cash flows.

Products with Behavioral Assumptions

The FTP for products with embedded options has to reflect the current market prices for comparable traded options. The value of these options depends on, among other things, the tenor of the option, the tenor of the underlying security (if it is an interest rate option) and the degree to which the option is in- or out-of-the-money. Implied volatility term structure and associated "smile" reflecting the "moneyness" of the options (e.g., whether the option is in-the-money or out-of-the-money compared with current market conditions) are necessary pricing inputs.

FTPs for core banking and insurance products cannot be priced or managed without making specific behavioral assumptions about how customers and management exercise the options. Intuitively, these behavioral assumptions determine hedge ratios and how many options are in the replicating portfolio.

Because the assumptions influence the perceived economics of the product, the assumptions may also represent a conflict of interest, with product managers making overly optimistic assumptions about prepayments or lapses in order to bolster the product's perceived contribution. It is important to back-test the actual versus assumed behavior and update the models or parameters if they diverge greatly.

Reflecting Own Borrowing Cost or Credit Risk

It is entirely possible that the company's marginal cost of funds is significantly higher than the swap curve. In such cases, it is common for banks to add an additional margin to the inter-bank swap rates in order to reflect their actual marginal cost of funds and provide the right incentives for loan and deposit origination. In contrast, an additional margin to reflect own credit spread is generally not made by insurers.

Recognizing the Value of Term Funding or the Illiquidity Premium

It is increasingly common for banks and insurers to adjust the reference curve to reflect the value of term funding.

Term funding is defined as financing which matches the maturity of an asset being purchased. In contrast, revolving funding is defined as financing which is shorter in tenor and which must therefore be rolled over in order to finance an asset to its maturity. Note that this definition refers only to principal cash flows and not to interest rate resetting frequency: both a 5-year floating rate note and a 5-year fixed coupon financing have the same term under this definition.

Typically, term funding costs more than revolving funding. The 2008–09 financial crisis highlighted the value of term funding – banks which did not have sufficient term funding were unable to refinance their positions, in some instances leading to a resolution scenario; examples are given in Chapter 18.

Grant (2011) criticizes bank practices before the crisis, concluding: "Probably the most striking example of poor LTP (Liquidity Transfer Pricing) practice was that some banks (before the crisis) treated liquidity as a 'free' good, completely ignoring the costs, benefits and risks of liquidity. They neglected to charge or credit respective businesses, products and/or transactions accordingly." As a consequence, Grant concludes that there was an incentive to engage in "over-aggressive" trading behavior and the "accumulation of illiquid assets in the search of revenues."

Based on these experiences, FTP systems are being adapted to recognize the value of term funding and provide appropriate incentives to minimize funding liquidity risk. For example, Principle 4 of the Bank for International Settlements' Principles for Sound Liquidity Risk Management and Supervision (BIS, 2008) states: "A bank should incorporate liquidity costs, benefits and risks in the internal pricing, performance measurement and new product approval process . . . , thereby aligning the risk-taking incentives of individual business lines with the liquidity risk exposures their activities create for the bank as a whole."

Similarly, Principle 3 of the CFO Forum's Principles (2008) states: "The cost of securing adequate liquidity should be reflected in product design and valuation. Necessary liquidity can be provided through liability product design as well as by the investment portfolio backing the products and/or through external or contingent lines." Taking it one step further, the CFO Forum's revised MCEV Principles advocate the use of an illiquidity premium for the valuation of insurance liabilities under Principle 14, which states: "a swap yield curve with the inclusion of a liquidity premium (where appropriate) should be used for liabilities which are not 'liquid'."

Sidebar 17.2 provides an overview of different methods for including illiquidity in the FTP. **Incorporating the Term Funding Premium into an Insurers FTP Framework – the Solvency II Approach**   The practice of including a term funding premium is well established in the European insurance industry; as mentioned earlier, the CFO Forum MCEV Principles (2009) outline the use of an illiquidity premium for the valuation of LH liabilities. In particular, Solvency II allows for the application of a "volatility adjuster" and "matching adjustment" (VA and MA, respectively), derived from an earlier "Counter-Cyclical Premium" (CCP), all of which attribute some portion of current bond spreads to be used to discount liabilities.

SIDEBAR 17.2: ON THE BENEFIT OF TERM FUNDING

Term funding is defined as financing which matches the principal maturity of an asset. In contrast, revolving funding is defined as financing which must be rolled over in order to finance the asset to its maturity. In general, "sticky" core deposits or life insurance policies which cannot lapse have more value because they represent longer-term funding. Financial services firms often choose to recognize the value of term funding in their FTP framework.

WHY AN ILLIQUIDITY OR TERM FUNDING PREMIUM?

Amihud *et al.* (2005) describe a set of circumstances leading to a positive value of term funding in equilibrium. Theoretically, it can arise if some individuals have a longer holding horizon than others and are faced with exogenous transactions costs, search frictions in matching buyers and sellers, or any variability in the price of short-term financing due to changing demand and supply conditions, a theoretical precondition for which there is substantial empirical evidence during times of crisis leading to a flight to quality and restricted liquidity.

Hibbert *et al.* (2009) does a good job describing the literature, both theoretical and empirical, on the term funding premium. There are several ways to calculate the additional cost or benefit of term funding, the direct approach based on wholesale financing alternatives unique to the institution and several indirect approaches which use average industry data.

DIRECT APPROACH

The direct approach for estimating the cost of term funding leverages information from the wholesale financing markets for a specific institution. It begins by recognizing that the cost of senior unsecured funding for a bank or insurance company can in principle be decomposed into three parts.

Equation 17.4: Cost of term funding, or the illiquidity premium

Unsecured term borrowing cost = Short-term inter-bank rate + CDS adjustment
+ Term funding spread

where CDS is the term-appropriate cost of a credit default swap for your company. For example, the 5-year unsecured borrowing cost for a bank or insurance company is decomposed into:

- the appropriate short-term inter-bank rate (e.g., Libor or Euribor);
- the CDS cost for the full 5-year funding term to reflect the credit risk of an unsecured borrowing;
- an appropriate term funding spread derived from the Floating Rate Note (FRN) market.

This last component represents the price of term funding for the bank or insurance company as it is the only difference between the cost of revolving funding versus term funding. In general, the term funding spread will be positive; however, the spread can be distorted by short-term demand and supply conditions for the company's CDS, the liquidity of the market and transaction costs.

Duffie (1999) shows, using an arbitrage argument in a world with no transaction costs or bid–offer spreads, that if the short-term inter-bank rate is replaced by a risk-free FRN, then this reduces down to two components, the risk-free FRN rate and the CDS.

Longstaff et al. (2005) investigate this relationship based on treasury rates and determine that ". . . the majority of the corporate spread is due to default risk. This result holds for all rating categories and is robust to the definition of the riskless curve. We also find that the non-default component (or term liquidity premium) is time varying and strongly related to measures of bond-specific illiquidity as well as to macro-economic measures of bond market liquidity." The proportion of the spread attributed to default risk averaged from 51% for AAA/AA-rated bonds to 83% for BB-rated bonds.

Gintschel and Wiehenkamp (2009) use a similar approach to estimate a global liquidity factor, which "is time-varying but persistent and drives a fair amount of the serial and cross-sectional variation in fixed income prices. Moreover, liquidity exposure varies predictably with maturity and credit rating suggesting a flight to quality phenomenon."

Although this represents the borrowing cost of term funding on a variable interest rate basis (e.g., with interest rates re-set every 6 months), it can easily be converted into fixed-rate funding through an interest rate swap. Because there is no exchange of principle, the fixed–floating interest rate swap rate in isolation can be seen as inappropriate for valuing committed term funding.

INDIRECT APPROACHES

Not every firm has on-the-run bonds in each maturity, the market in a particular name may simply not be actively traded and CDS markets are potentially also subject to liquidity and counterparty credit risk. In such cases, it is possible that the direct approach can lead to a negative implied cost of term funding.

As a consequence, indirect approaches are often used. Indirect approaches follow the same basic process but use bonds and CDS from a wide variety of issuers to estimate an "average" illiquidity premium.

There are three indirect approaches which have been investigated (the average CDS approach or negative basis approach, the covered bond approach and the proxy or structural model method), all of which are described in detail by Hibbert et al. (2009).

Indirect CDS Approach or Negative Basis Method

This is the direct approach applied to a wider universe of issuers and delivering an average term funding premium. As such, this approach will not give a specific estimate of the value to your firm but rather the average for all corporate issuers in the market.

Indirect Structural Model Method or Proxy Approach

The proxy approach replaces the market observable CDS spread with an own estimate of the credit risk in the bond. For example, one may use the Merton model (Merton, 1974) to estimate a credit risk charge (instead of the current CDS rate) and then deduct this from observable bond spreads. The use of such models is discussed in Stark (2009) but investigated extensively in Eom et al. (2004).

As the names imply, the goal of these approaches tends more toward stabilizing fair valuations for solvency calculations than as a representation of fair values directly. For example, Danielsson *et al.* (2012) commented that the 2011 Sovency II draft ". . . introduces the possibility of a countercyclical premium. Upon declaration by the regulator . . . that distressed market conditions exist, an additional wedge is to be added to the risk-free term structure to . . . reduce balance sheet stress for insurance companies in times of high illiquidity and credit spreads."

The logical disconnect between solvency stabilization and fair valuation roles becomes clear if one remembers the history behind the development of these measures: regulators and the industry found that the original illiquidity premium, needed in the 2008 financial crisis, was more difficult to rationalize for application to Italian and Spanish sovereign bonds during the 2011–12 crisis, especially since the Italian sovereign bonds were very actively traded. As a consequence, the concept morphed from an illiquidity premium to a counter-cyclical premium and was extended to also include sovereign issuers.

When motivated from a fair valuation perspective, insurance companies use a reverse logic. Many believe that, by raising long-term committed funding from policy holders, they have an advantage in buying long-term assets which should yield an additional spread or "illiquidity premium." Under this perspective, insurers are answering the question "What average additional spreads can I earn if I had long term funds available?" and attributing part of this benefit to the liabilities by using a higher discount rate. In this sense, LH insurers have a natural position in long-term liabilities and are rationalizing how they can make them "cheaper" by allocating some of the (efficient market) asset returns to discount their liabilities to justify their business model.

In contrast, banks typically have a natural long-term asset position and want to give an incentive to raise more long-term committed financing. Grant (2011) discusses two approaches used by banks, a "pool" approach (which gives the average benefit to all liabilities and the average cost to all assets) and a "liquidity term structure" approach (which calculates the benefit for different maturity buckets). The term structure approach is superior, especially if there is a large imbalance between term borrowing and lending. See also Matz and Neu (2007) and Moody's Analytics (2011) for further discussion.

Inflation-indexed Transactions

Most bank and insurance products are denominated in nominal as opposed to real terms; as such, the use of nominal interest rates and prices for the FTP is appropriate. However, some products have cash flows which are either explicitly or implicitly linked to inflation, for example:

- deposits or loans in emerging economies subject to persistent and high inflation may be explicitly linked to inflation;
- some defined benefit pension products may be explicitly linked to observed inflation rates in an effort to stabilize the purchasing power of those covered in retirement;
- finally, PC claims may be subject to implicit claims inflation (medical claims due to more expensive diagnostics and treatments and automobile claims due to higher prices of imported replacement parts).

It is not appropriate to use nominal rates for such products if a traded inflation index exists. Instead, the FTP should at least in part be based on the inflation-linked term structure of interest rates. However, using a traded inflation index may introduce basis risk if the product's cash flows are not explicitly linked to the index. For example, while one would normally expect medical claims inflation, one would not expect it to match the developments in the consumer or producer price index, the typical starting point for traded inflation indices.

Explicit recognition of inflation in the FTP (and implicitly in the replicating portfolios so that it can be effectively hedged) is practical in two cases: first, for bank and insurance products in countries with a history of high inflation with explicit indexation and the existence of inflation-linked bonds developing in parallel; second, for LH pension products which are explicitly linked to an inflation index. In both cases, the basis risk is a second-order effect relative to the baseline inflation risk.

Otherwise, it may be better to treat the embedded inflation as a non-hedgeable risk and allocate an appropriate risk capital against it; this is done, first, by including expected inflation into the pricing and, second, by including the risk capital charge for any unexpected inflation.

Adjustment for Non-interest-bearing Reserve Requirements

The FTP logic assumes that, on the margin, the deposit or insurance premium funds can be placed without restrictions in the capital markets and receive the FTP rate and that all loans or investment assets purchased can be funded, on the margin, at the FTP rate.

This is not always the case. For example, banks are sometimes required to place some fraction of their deposits as reserves in central bank accounts which do not pay interest. In this case, the deposit FTP rate may be adjusted for the frictional cost introduced by these non-interest-paying reserves. See Klein (1971) and Monti (1972) for a discussion.

Adjustment for High Credit Risk Assets

The general principle applied to FTPs is that the credit risk, both expected losses and unexpected losses, is retained and reflected in the net risk-adjusted margin earned by the product unit. As such, the ALM unit would see a €100 interest rate risk position for every €100 loan made.

Suppose, however, that expected default rates were significant, implying that the expected future repayment may be significantly less. For example, a 2.5% p.a. probability of default implies that the expected principle repayment of a 5-year €100 loan is only €88. This could lead to over-hedging of the interest rate risk if the ALM Unit uses the full notional value of €100 instead of the expected value of €88. Although the product unit should be held accountable for the expected credit losses (and the unexpected losses!), if material enough, the expected credit losses may also be represented in the ALM portfolio to ensure the appropriate interest rate risk representation.

Commercial Considerations

Finally, commercial considerations may ultimately influence adjustments to the "economically correct" FTPs. For example, a bank may want to significantly grow the deposit base in order to secure cross-sell opportunities, to take advantage of a weaker competitor, to secure more deposit funding, etc. This can be accomplished by giving an incentive to the distribution network, tilting their focus toward selling deposits. In the other direction, Dermine (2015) discusses how FTP rates might be changed to reflect a cap on loan volumes due to an inability to generate sufficient deposit funding.

Because a direct adjustment may distort the economic decisions made by the ALM unit, more often than not commercially driven adjustments are "booked" on the account of the

TABLE 17.6 FTP approaches

Approach	Description	Application
Direct, no-arbitrage approach	Define the set of replicating instruments by direct observation such that, when deducted from the underlying position, the result is a constant margin assuming no underwriting risk. Delivers the FTP, gross product margin* and replicating portfolio simultaneously.	Products with fixed best-estimate cash flows (e.g., term deposits and loans, PC best-estimate claims).
Simultaneous margin and replicating portfolio by minimizing hedge error variance	Use numerical techniques to find the set of replicating instruments and constant product margin which, when deducted from the underlying position, minimize the hedge error variance. Delivers the FTP, gross product margin* and replicating portfolio simultaneously.	Non-maturing deposits.
Option-adjusted valuation combined with portfolio replication	Use option pricing theory to value the embedded options and guarantees. The FTP and gross product margin* are calculated directly. Calculate as a second step the replicating portfolio which best matches the value and risk characteristics of the underlying portfolio.	Products with complex embedded optionality (e.g., prepayable loans, LH guaranteed savings and retirement products).

*Gross product margin is defined as the margin after deducting the cost of financial market risk or the replicating portfolio.

business unit responsible for the commercial decision. Such "subsidization" or adjustment accounts have been discussed previously.

Step 2: Calculating the FTP and Replicating Portfolio for Each Product

Once the set of market instruments has been selected, the second step is to calculate the FTP and associated replicating portfolio for each product or position. As described in Table 17.6, this can be done in one of three ways: a direct approach, a simultaneous numerical approach and a two-step option-adjusted spread approach.

Direct, No-arbitrage Replication

Simple bank products have FTP rates which can be deduced directly, as illustrated in Table 17.7.

For each of these examples, a constant gross customer margin is calculated by "deducting" a traded instrument from the original loan or deposit, "as if" the loan's cash flows were risk free. The traded instrument represents the "replicating portfolio."

TABLE 17.7 Illustrative FTP and margin calculations for simple banking products

Product	Gross underwriting margin*	ALM component**
5-year floating-rate loan paying 6-month Libor + 75 bps, no prepayment possible	75 bps	6-month Libor***
5-year fixed-rate loan paying 5-year swap rate + 75 bps, no prepayment possible	75 bps	5-year swap rate***
6-month term deposit paying Libor − 50 bps, no early withdrawal possible	50 bps	6-month Libor
6-month term deposit paying prime − 50 bps, no early withdrawal possible	50 bps + cost of basis swap, Libor prime	6-month Libor

*Gross margin, without deduction of expected loan losses, expenses and cost of underwriting capital covering unexpected loan losses.
**FTP framework based on inter-bank and swap rates excluding any own credit, term funding or other adjustment.
***5-year term funding premium could be added to FTP rate if the cost of term funding is explicitly recognized, reducing the loan margin.

The same approach is used by PC insurers, with zero-coupon bonds "replicating" the product's best-estimate cash flow profile. However, the gross margin in PC insurance is typically expressed as a present value instead of as an annualized margin. Consider a PC product with €100 of best-estimate claims, expected to run off in 5 years with a run-off profile of {50%, 25%, 12.5%, 6.25%, 6.25%}. At a 5% flat swap discount rate, this cash flow profile has a present value of €91.13, leading to a "gross margin" contribution from discounting the expected claims of €8.87. For PC products, the comparable "gross margin" from using current market rates is equivalent to the discount effect on future expected claims.

Replicating Portfolio that Minimizes Hedge Error Variance

The above examples were relatively simple because the exact replicating portfolio can be found by inspection. This direct approach will not work for products which have an indefinite maturity and whose re-pricing is subject to management actions, for example non-maturing deposits which can in principle be withdrawn overnight (but are actually much more sticky) and whose pricing follows financial market rates but with a lag. This implies that deposit margins suffer from compression relative to spot swap rates in a falling rate environment and expansion during a rising rate environment. It is difficult to identify directly a portfolio of cash bond and derivative positions which reproduces similar behavior.

The direct approach is instructive however, illustrating that the *FTP can be thought of as the return on a replicating portfolio which minimizes the hedge error variance between the replicating portfolio and the core banking product.*

Viewed in this way, the FTP represents a well-defined optimization problem which can also be applied to non-maturing accounts: simply select the optimal portfolio weights $\{\omega^*\}$ and constant customer margin $\{m\}$ such that the expected "distance" between the product offered (whose value is a function of the FTP rate and constant customer margin, $P(r + m)$) and a portfolio of admissible financial market building blocks, which also depend on the FTP rates $(\omega'A(r))$, is minimized.

EQUATION 17.5: Optimal replicating portfolio determination

$$\{\omega^*, m^*\} = \arg \min_{\{w,m\}} E\langle \|P(r + m) - \omega'A(r)\| \, | \, no\,U/W event\rangle$$

If the measure of "distance" is based on quadratic or squared deviations (e.g., $E\|\,\| = E[x - E(x)]^2$) then the optimal replicating portfolio minimizes the hedge error variance between the product and the replicating portfolio at a constant expected margin. Consistent with the examples, the expectations operator $E\langle|no\,U/W\,event|\rangle$ recognizes only financial market uncertainty and no underwriting risk events (e.g., no loan default or adverse PC claim developments around the best estimates) or behavioral risks (e.g., no unexpected lapse or prepayment dynamics, etc.). An example of this approach is outlined in Sidebar 17.3.

SIDEBAR 17.3: REPLICATING PORTFOLIOS AND NON-MATURING ACCOUNTS

Wilson (1994) developed this approach to model demand deposits or non-maturing accounts. The challenge is to develop a replicating portfolio policy which invests all the available deposits at any point in time in the FTP instruments and which mimics as much as possible the actual deposit pricing behavior of the bank. Wilson (1994) split the total volume between a "core volume" of deposits, expected to grow at a rate β, and an additional volume v_1^t that could vary, being positive in some periods or negative in others to reflect unusual withdrawal activity. The total volume of demand deposits at any point in time was therefore equal to the core volume plus the residual, e.g. $V_t + v_1^t$ where $V_t = \beta V_{t-1}$.

Replicating strategies were investigated which divided the core volume V_t such that it was invested in *portfolios* of zero-coupon bonds invested over time but with the same original durations, N, with constant weights ω_n where $\sum \omega_n = 1$. Each of these zero-coupon bond portfolios in turn comprised investments in underlying zero-coupon bonds of the same maturity but invested during previous periods, and growing at the same growth rate β.

Labeling the individual zero-coupon bond invested at time t with maturity n as v_n^t, the portfolio of two-period zero-coupon bonds outstanding at any point in time comprises $\{v_2^{t-1}, v_2^t\} = \{\beta^{-1}v_2^t, v_2^t\}$, with the first cash flow $(\beta^{-1}v_2^t)$ maturing one period from now and the second (v_2^t) in two periods. The portfolio of three-period zero-coupon bonds comprises $\{v_3^{t-1}, v_3^{t-1}, v_3^t\} = \{\beta^{-2}v_3^t, \beta^{-1}v_3^t, v_3^t\}$, with the first cash flow maturing $(\beta^{-2}v_3^t)$ in one period and so on.

The volume invested in each sub-portfolio is also growing at the rate β, as is any arbitrary sum of these sub-portfolios. Normalizing $v_n^t = 1$, the total volume of demand deposits at any point in time can be written as an arbitrary function of the portfolio weights, e.g. $V_t + v_1^t = \sum \omega_n \left(\sum_{s=1}^n \beta^{1-s} \right) V_t + v_1^t$, and the implied return on this portfolio is equal to $r_t(\omega) = \sum \omega_n \left(\sum_{s=1}^n \beta^{1-s} r_n^{t-s} \right) + \frac{v_1^t}{V_t} r_1^t$.

The optimal replicating portfolio in Wilson (1994) was selected by choosing portfolio weights so that the return on the replicating portfolio plus a constant margin, m, best matched the actual deposit pricing history, e.g. $\{\omega_n^*, m\} = \arg \min_{\{w_n, m\}} \| r_t - m - r_t(\omega_n) \|$. In general, this is done in two steps using non-linear regression techniques: first, estimate the core volume growth rate β, where the residuals can be interpreted as v_1^t and second, find the weights which minimize the distance between the actual deposit rate and the rate on the replicating portfolio.

Option-adjusted Spread and New Business Margin

The final approach for determining the FTP is a two-step process used when the product has complex embedded options which cannot easily be replicated using standard building blocks available in the capital markets.

The first step is to value the financial market risk in the product, accomplished using option-adjusted spreads for banking products and "clean" new business margins[2] for LH retirement and savings products. In the second step, the replicating portfolio is calculated explicitly.

In banking, OAS approaches are regularly used for valuing prepayable mortgages and tranches of mortgage-backed securities (Fabozzi, 1997; Miller, 2007). In the insurance industry, OAS has been used less frequently (for a direct application of OAS in insurance, see Griffin, 1990; Becker, 1991; Girard, 2001) but it has a direct analog, the MCEV-NBM, which is used much more broadly.

Step 1. Calculate the Option-adjusted FTP   In the remainder of this section, the OAS approach is motivated by considering its application to wholesale funding alternatives and then extrapolated to the valuation of bank and insurance products, following Wilson (2010).

Wholesale Funding Analogy   A bank or insurer can raise funds in the wholesale capital market through different types of bond, for example par, callable, putable or convertible bonds. Each has a very different risk and return profile from the issuer's perspective. For example, one would expect to pay a lower coupon for a convertible issue than a straight par bond. But how much less?

Option-adjusted spreads can be used to compare the different funding alternatives. The OAS is defined as the spread over the swap curve which equates the value of the principal raised to the present value of the future stochastic cash flow commitments, using the appropriate financial market techniques for the valuation of the embedded options.

The OAS is illustrated in Figure 17.8: intuitively, the OAS is the spread above or below Libor which is necessary to equate the value of the future coupons, principle repayment and embedded options (gray box) to the proceeds from issuing the bond.

---

[2]"Clean" new business margins refer to new business margins calculated according to the CFO Forum 2009 MCEV Principles, but excluding frictional cost of capital, any liquidity premium or yield curve anchoring and calculated before tax.

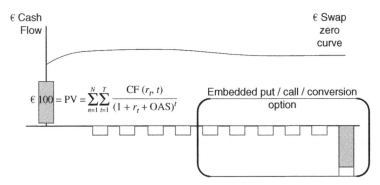

Option Adjusted Funding Spread is defined as the effective spread over-/under Libor for a financing alternative. It equates the present value of the cash received against the present value of future obligations, including any embedded options valued using financial market techniques

FIGURE 17.8 Illustration of OAS calculations

The formal definition of the option-adjusted spread is given by the following equation:

$$OAS \Big| PV = \frac{1}{N}\sum_{n=1}^{N}\sum_{t=1}^{T}\frac{CF(r_t^n, t)}{\prod_{s=1}^{t}(1 + r_s^n + OAS)}$$

where $CF(\cdot)$ is the bond's cash flow at time t, r_t^n is the risk-free rate of return at time t under scenario n, the N scenarios are risk-neutral scenarios so that the value of the embedded options is calculated correctly and OAS is the constant margin needed to equate the present value of the future cash flows with the principle of the loan.

Table 17.8 gives some example calculations. The first row of the table provides the OAS calculated for different 10-year financing alternatives if swap rates are at 4.5%, flat across the term structure.

The first column represents a 4.5% par coupon bond; the OAS for a 4.5% bond issued in a 4.5% market is 0, confirming that we are borrowing at no spread to Libor. The next column represents a 4.0% par coupon bond with an OAS of −48 bps. The interpretation is straightforward: issuing a 4% bond in a 4.5% market is the same as borrowing at Libor − 48 bps (recognizing small discount effects). Similarly, issuing a par bond with a 5% coupon is the same as borrowing at Libor + 48 bps (the fourth column).

TABLE 17.8 OA – wholesale funding alternatives (4.5% flat term structure)

	4.5% par bond	4% par bond	5% par bond	4% callable bond	4% putable bond	5% callable bond	5% putable bond
OAS (bps)	0 bp	−48 bp	48 bp	−57 bp	−10 bp	8 bp	64 bp
NBM (%)	0%	4.0%	−4.0%	4.4%	0.5%	−0.4%	−4.8%

The remaining columns represent bonds with embedded options. For example, if the bond is callable, then it is worth more to the issuer and the cost of funding is lower than for a par bond with the same coupon (e.g., Libor − 57 bps and Libor + 8 bps for the 4.0% and 5.0% coupons, respectively). If the bond could be put (or "lapsed") at the discretion of the bond holder, then the cost of funding would increase relative to the par bond with equivalent coupon (e.g., Libor − 10 bps and Libor + 64 bps for the 4.0% and 5.0% coupon bonds, respectively).

As can be seen, the OAS approach makes the different financing alternatives directly comparable by translating the product features into a comparable spread at current market rates, even for products containing embedded options. In a similar manner, the OAS can be used as the FTP to calculate the gross margin on prepayable loans. However, the optimal replicating portfolio must still be estimated.

OAS vs. NBM   Although not originally intended to be applied to wholesale financing alternatives, we can also calculate the MCEV-NBM based on the original CFO Forum MCEV Principles[3] to evaluate the same alternatives. The results are in the second row of Table 17.8.

Comparing the OAS with the NBM, we see that the two measures are related: a positive NBM is associated with a negative OAS, implying that value is created when borrowing at lower than the swap rate, including embedded options.

In fact, one can interpret the NBM as the discounted value of the OAS to be earned in the future; in other words, the NBM should be roughly equal to the OAS times the weighted average life of the funding alternative, a relationship confirmed in Figure 17.9, where WAM is defined as the Weighted Average Maturity.

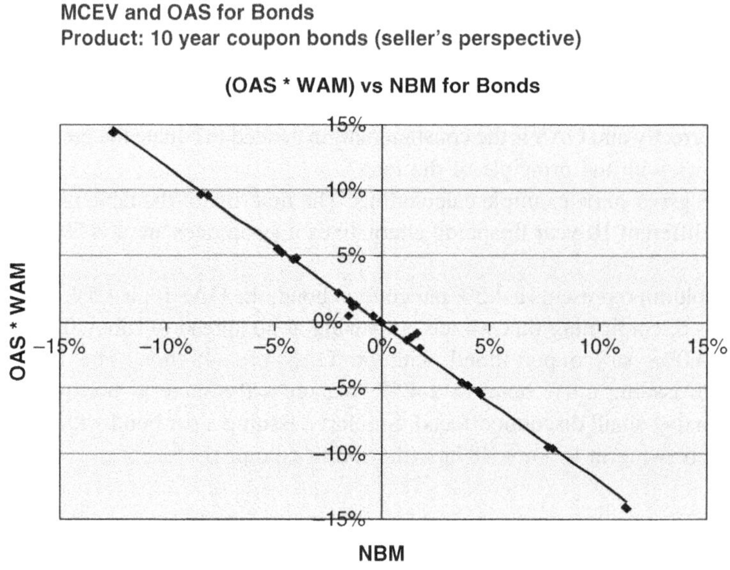

MCEV and OAS for Bonds
Product: 10 year coupon bonds (seller's perspective)

(OAS * WAM) vs NBM for Bonds

FIGURE 17.9   Comparison of OAS and NBM for bond liabilities

---

[3]In order to make it an apples-with-apples comparison, we have calculated the NBM before tax, before any frictional cost of capital and have set underwriting cost of capital to 0. In addition, the table illustrates the "clean" NBM, without any illiquidity premium, yield curve anchoring, etc.

TABLE 17.9   OAS – traditional European life products

	Annual ratchet – 0% min guarantee, no lapse	Annual ratchet – 2% min guarantee, no lapse	Annual ratchet – 3% min guarantee, no lapse	Annual ratchet – 2% min guarantee, 2% deterministic lapse	Annual ratchet – 2% min guarantee, dynamic lapses
OAS (in bp)	−100 bp	−10 bp	30 bp	−10 bp	20 bp
NBM (in %)	4.6%	0.3%	−1.3%	0.2%	−0.5%

Market conditions: 4.5% flat yield curve.
Product specifications: 10-year, 50%/50% bond/equity fund, 80/20 profit sharing.

Interpreting the LH NBM as a Cost of Funding   Both the OAS and NBM can also be applied to LH savings and retirement products. Consider the analysis of traditional European life insurance products given in Table 17.9. For these products, the insurance company purchases a portfolio of assets with the premium and participates in 20% of the investment returns above the guarantee level, with the remainder going to the policy holder. An intuitive pattern emerges: the insurer's cost of funding or OAS increases as the guarantees and lapse options become "richer"; not surprisingly, the NBM declines as well.

The OAS and NBM for LH products are also intuitively related: a positive NBM implies a negative OAS, or that the cost of borrowing funds from our insurance customers is below Libor, while a negative NBM implies a borrowing cost above Libor, or positive OAS. Second, the NBM can be seen as the discounted present value of the OAS funding spread, as illustrated in Figure 17.10, which plots the NBM against the OAS times the weighted average life for traditional and unit-linked products with different guarantee levels.

Step 2. Calculate the Replicating Portfolio   The OAS or "clean" NBM represents the appropriate *price* to transfer the financial market risk from the products to the AL unit. However,

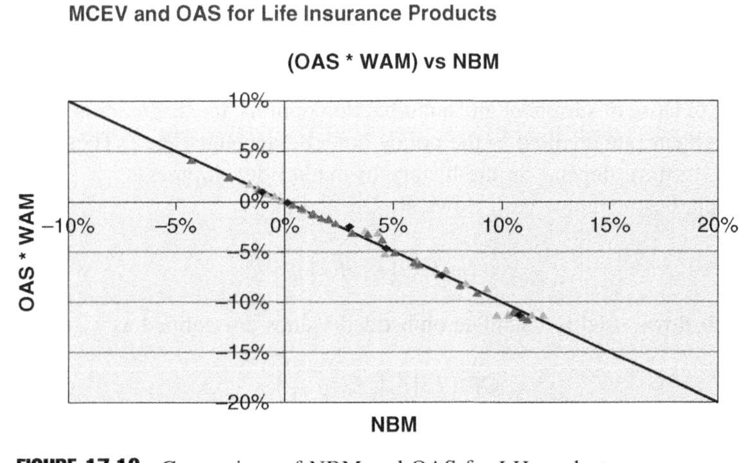

MCEV and OAS for Life Insurance Products

(OAS * WAM) vs NBM

FIGURE 17.10   Comparison of NBM and OAS for LH products

it does not give a representation of the product which can be used to manage the asset/liability mismatch. Consider €100 in an investment account; if you wanted to hedge the value of the investment account, you would have to know whether the €100 represented a fixed-income security or an equity or leveraged derivative or some combination of the three. The value itself does not tell the AL manager how to hedge the account.

The second step is therefore to define the replicating portfolio which most closely matches the OAS or NBM value under different financial market scenarios. There are various approaches to defining the replicating portfolio using FTP information, as described in Sidebar 17.4.

SIDEBAR 17.4: ON REPLICATING PORTFOLIOS AND OTHER REPRESENTATION TECHNIQUES

Liability-driven investment strategies start from the liabilities. Unfortunately, LH savings and retirement liabilities are complicated, including embedded options and guarantees with complex path-dependent features and requiring simulation approaches to value and calculate sensitivities. Accurately assessing different asset/liability strategies requires jointly modeling and simulating all assets and liabilities. This often leads to nested simulations which are computationally burdensome.

In order to reduce complexity, LH insurance companies often use proxy approaches to represent the financial market risk of their portfolios. Similarly, proxies are often used to represent portfolios of prepayable mortgages and other banking products with high option-adjusted spreads.

The most common proxy approaches include the certainty-equivalent cash flows, sensitivity instruments and replicating portfolios, described below using LH products to illustrate the concept.

CASH FLOW REPRESENTATIONS

The simplest representation of complex LH products is to use the product's best-estimate cash flows or the cash flows based on management's expected market developments (as is done in standard European embedded value approaches; CFO Forum, 2004a).

More formally, define the product's future cash flow at time t as $\mathrm{CF}_t\left(\vec{r}_t, \vec{\phi}_t\right)$, where $\vec{r}_t$ represents the history of the financial market rates which influence the cash flow (e.g., $\vec{r}_t = \left\lfloor \{r_{1,0}, r_{2,0}, \ldots, r_{n,0}\}, \{r_{1,1}, r_{2,1}, \ldots, r_{n,1}\}, \{r_{1,t}, r_{2,t}, \ldots, r_{n,t}\} \right\rfloor$) and $\vec{\phi}_t$ the history of behavioral actions taken by the policy holder and the insurance firm (e.g., the exercise of lapse or surrender and annuitization options, the discretionary component of the investment rate credited to the policy holder's accounts, etc.). These behavioral actions can, in turn, depend on the history of market developments.

Then, the best-estimate cash flows are defined as

$$E_0\left[\mathrm{CF}_t\left(\vec{r}_t, \vec{\phi}_t\right)\right]$$

and the cash flows used to calculate embedded values are defined as

$$\mathrm{CF}_t\left(E_0[\vec{r}_t], E_0\left[\vec{\phi}_t\right]\right)$$

where $E_0[x]$ is the expected value of x based on information at time 0.

Both of these lead to representations consisting solely of zero-coupon cash flows. This means that they will not correctly represent the value and sensitivities of embedded options and guarantees, nor will they correctly represent any cash flow variations coming from equity market returns, etc. As such, while useful for PC insurance portfolios and pure risk LH products, they should not be used for LH savings and retirement products.

SENSITIVITY REPRESENTATIONS

The second approach, using sensitivity instruments and hedge ratios, is slightly more complex but has the advantage of capturing the non-linear behavior of options and guarantees. The sensitivity approach begins with the value of the liability, defined as

$$V_0(r_0) = \sum_{t=1}^{T} \frac{E_0^q \left[CF_t\left(\vec{r}_t, \vec{\phi}_t \right) \right]}{1 + z_{0,t}}$$

where r_0 is the initial market conditions, $z_{0,t}$ is the risk-free discount rate at time 0 for a zero-coupon cash flow maturing at time t and $E_0^q \left[CF_t\left(\vec{r}_t, \vec{\phi}_t \right) \right]$ is expected cash flow at time t relative to the risk-neutral probability measure $E_0^q[\cdot]$.[4]

Sensitivity-based approaches calculate the sensitivity of value to changes in the different market rates which affect value. Sensitivities can be calculated either on a discrete or a continuous basis.

Discrete sensitivities are calculated by $\frac{\Delta V}{\Delta r} = V(r) - V(r + \Delta r)$ for any arbitrary Δr. Assuming that the value function is twice continuously differentiable, the continuous sensitivity called delta is the vector of first-order derivatives of the value to changes in the market rates (e.g., $\delta_V = \frac{\partial V}{\partial r}$) and Gamma that of second-order derivatives (e.g., $\gamma_V = \frac{\partial^2 V}{\partial r^2}$). Both are calculated using numerical approaches. This sensitivity information can be used to represent the value and risk profile of the liability.

Hedge-equivalent Positions

Sensitivities can be used to calculate hedge-equivalent positions. For example, if the interest rate sensitivity of the liabilities is equal to δ_V and the interest rate sensitivity of a 1-year and a 10-year bond is δ_{1y} and δ_{10y}, respectively, then the product might be represented by 1-year and 10-year bond positions which satisfy the following system of equations:

$$\delta_V = \omega_{1y}\delta_{1y} + \omega_{10y}\delta_{10y}$$
$$V = \omega_{1y}V_{1y} + \omega_{10y}V_{10y}$$

where ω_{1y} and ω_{10y} are replicating portfolio weights for the 1- and 10-year bonds used to represent the liability and the second equation represents the constraint that the value of the hedge assets has to equal the value of the liabilities.

---

[4]For a good overview on risk-neutral valuation techniques and their motivation, see Bauer *et al.* (2009) and Delcour (2012).

In general, if you want to perfectly match N sensitivities and the value constraint, then you need $N+1$ instruments which have distinct sensitivities to the same risk factors. The optimal hedge ratios are calculated by solving $N+1$ linear equations in $N+1$ unknowns of the following form:

$$\delta_{1,V} = \sum_{n=1}^{N} \omega_n \delta_{1,n}$$

$$\dots$$

$$\delta_{N,V} = \sum_{n=1}^{N} \omega_n \delta_{N,n}$$

s.t.

$$V = \sum_{n=1}^{N} \omega_n V_n$$

where $\delta_{i,V}$ is the value sensitivity to the ith risk factor, $\delta_{i,n}$ is the sensitivity of the nth hedge instrument to the ith risk factor and ω_n is the weight on the nth hedge instrument. Note that the same approach can be used to calculate hedge ratios including first-order delta and second-order gamma as well as arbitrarily defined sensitivities and scenarios, you just need enough instruments which are sufficiently independent to span the liability's sensitivities.[5]

The resulting hedge portfolio can be interpreted as a type of replicating portfolio which perfectly matches those sensitivities that are measured but which is less accurate for other sensitivities that are not measured.

Taylor Series Approximation

Similarly, you can use the sensitivities to represent the liability using a Taylor series expansion, for example

$$V(r + \Delta r) = V(r) + \delta'_{V(r)} \Delta r + \frac{\left(\Delta r' \gamma_{V(r)} \Delta r\right)}{2} + \varepsilon$$

where V_0 is the value of the liabilities at the initial market conditions, Δr is the vector of market rate changes and ε represents an error term of order 2.

Interpolation Techniques

The second-order Taylor series expansion represents a quadratic approximation to the value function based on the sensitivity of the value to small changes in market rates. Other approximation approaches can be applied if discrete sensitivities at different intervals are used. Examples include linear, polynomial and spline interpolation.

---

[5]More specifically, the solution to the system of equations is found by inverting the matrix of hedge instrument sensitivities and only exists if the hedge instrument sensitivities form a linearly independent family so that the matrix of sensitivities can be inverted.

REPLICATING PORTFOLIOS

Replicating portfolios are widely used by LH insurance companies (see, e.g., Oechslin *et al.*, 2004, 2007; Schrager, 2008; Wilson, 2007; Davidson, 2008; Della Casa and Gaffo, 2013). A good overview of portfolio replication approaches can be found in Boekel *et al.* (2009).

The end result is a portfolio of financial instruments (the "replicating portfolio") which is "close" to the actual liability. There are two benefits of the replicating portfolio approach. First, like the hedge ratio approach, it gives a representation which has an intuitive interpretation: if done properly, one can actually "see" the minimum guaranteed cash flows in the form of zero-coupon bonds, the guarantees in terms of investment portfolio put options and dynamic lapses in terms of interest rate swaptions.

Second, because a richer set of financial instruments is selected, it is hoped that the behavior of the replicating portfolio will be "better" when used to represent market scenarios which were not in the calibration set.

The replicating portfolio approach is implemented via a formal constrained optimization problem consisting of an objective function, a solution space and a constraint set.

The objective function. There are many different measures of distance (the objective function) used in practice, broadly differentiated between:

- the measure of distance (e.g., absolute deviations represented by an L_1 norm, squared deviations represented by the quadratic or L_2 norm, etc.) and
- the variables of interest (e.g., the difference in present value under different market scenarios – $V(r_0 + \Delta r)$ vs. $\sum_i R_i(r_0 + \Delta r)$, the difference in cash flows under different scenarios at different points in time – $CF_t(\vec{r}_t)$ vs. $\sum_i CF_{t,R_i}(\vec{r}_t)$, the difference in value or cash flows over certain time buckets, etc.).

The solution space and constraints. More formally, the replicating portfolio approach tries to find a set of weights (ω_i) for a set of replicating instruments (R_i) which minimizes the "distance" between the replicating portfolio and the original liabilities.

The set of replicating instruments and associated constraints represent the solution space to the replicating portfolio problem. The selection of replicating instruments will depend on the characteristics of the liabilities. In general, zero-coupon cash flows are needed to represent the minimum guaranteed cash flows; equity and interest rate options are needed to represent the asymmetric behavior of the guarantees; interest rate options are necessary to represent dynamic lapse or annuitization behavior; path-dependent, Asian averaging or constant maturity derivatives may be useful in representing management's crediting strategy; etc. The strike levels of the options will generally depend on the liability guarantee levels.

It may be logical to put some constraints on the solution space. Two of the most common constraints include non-negativity constraints on cash bonds and equities and the constraint that the value of the replicating portfolio has to equal the value of the liabilities.

In addition, it is common to include trading penalties for certain instruments (e.g., in the form of $-\alpha \omega_i^2$, where α represents the cost or penalty for taking a larger position in instrument i) in order to ensure that you do not have large, adjacent offsetting cash and derivative positions.

An example.[6] In this example we attempt to capture the risk profile of a life insurance contract with Guaranteed Minimum Withdrawal Benefit (GMWB) under all scenarios using a replicating portfolio of financial market instruments.

The objective of the replication will be to minimize the average error by the optimal choice of weights w_k:

$$\min_{w_k} \sum_{n=1}^{N} |e_n|$$

$$\text{where} \quad l_n - \sum_{k=1}^{K} w_k a_{kn} = e_n \quad \forall n = 1, \ldots, N$$

where N is the number of scenarios, l_n is the net present value of the cash flow of the target portfolio (or contract) and a_{kn} is the instrument.

Figure 17.11 gives the average cash flow profiles over all simulations for the cost of the GMWB benefit (average present value cost: \$2337), the fees collected (average present value fees: \$8340) and the probability of a loss event (27%).

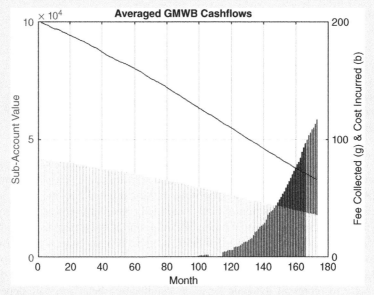

FIGURE 17.11   Average cash flow profile simulations
Source: Jean-Frederic Breton, reproduced with permission.

The allowable replicating instruments included zero-coupon bonds and equity options with different maturities and strike rates, reflecting our knowledge of the contract. The replication error can be represented in one of two different ways: either as a scatter

[6]Example and MATLAB code contributed by Jean-Frederick Breton (Jean-Frederic.Breton@mathworks.com).

diagram comparing the replication value versus the actual value under each of the scenarios or by viewing the relative sensitivities of the replicating portfolio versus the GMWB product. Both are illustrated in Figures 17.12 and 17.13.

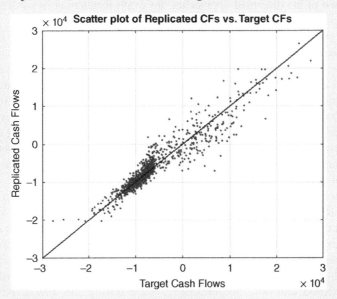

FIGURE 17.12 Scatter diagram of replication value and actual value
Source: Jean-Frederic Breton, reproduced with permission.

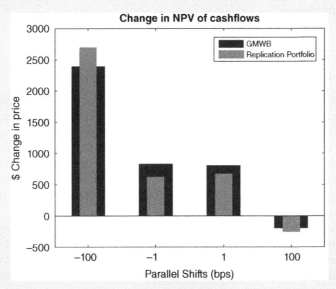

FIGURE 17.13 Relative sensitivities of the replicating portfolio and GMWB product
Source: Jean-Frederic Breton, reproduced with permission.

Rejected FTP Concepts

Different methods have historically been used to calculate product margins for banks and insurers, which have subsequently been rejected because they did not provide the right economic signals. Two of the discarded approaches are worth mentioning in particular: the single-rate pooling and cohort pooling approaches (Katafian, 2001; Buruc, 2008).

The *single-rate pooling approach* uses the average cost of financing or the average return on assets implicitly as the FTP to calculate product margins. For example, a bank may be tempted to use the average cost of financing for the bank as the FTP or funding cost for loans. Unfortunately, this would be problematic for several reasons: first, it would implicitly subsidize lending activities with the excess profits generated by deposits; second, it would give a bias toward longer-term loans in steep yield curve environments; third, the resulting loan margin would contain some residual interest rate mismatch risk to the extent that the average bank financing structure did not perfectly match the specific loan's cash flow characteristics. The same issue arises if one were to use the average loan yield to measure the profit contribution of deposits.

Another approach used historically is the *cohort pooling approach*, really a refinement of the single-rate pooling approach. Under this approach, the balance sheet is partitioned horizontally, creating cohorts or layers of assets and liabilities with similar characteristics, for example long-term deposits implicitly funding long-term loans, etc., and then assigning some fraction (e.g., ½) of the implied net interest income margin per cohort pool to each as their contribution. In German, this approach was called the "Schictenbilanz" method and was predominantly used during the 1980s. Although representing a refinement on the pool approach, the cohort approach is also flawed for the same reasons, being characterized by an arbitrary split of the net interest income margin between loans and deposits and an inexact recognition of the financial characteristics of the loans and deposits.

MEASURING ALPHA

In spite of the debate about whether alpha exists, it is important for banks and insurers to measure and attribute the performance of the asset/liability management function, the investment management department and the trading desk.

Alpha is defined as *the market returns generated in excess of risk-appropriate financial market benchmarks*. It is measured in principle by *deducting the returns from an actual or theoretical risk-appropriate benchmark portfolio from the portfolio's realized returns*. If the remainder is positive (or more often positive than negative), the conclusion might be that you have generated "alpha."[7]

Alpha is always measured on a mark-to-market basis as opposed to an accounting basis because accounting returns are not generally comparable, being influenced by decisions regarding whether and when to recognize capital gains, the implications of different impairment rules, etc. In this context, mark-to-market returns offer a common yardstick for comparing risks and returns.

---

[7]Although another common explanation is that you chosen an inappropriate risk-appropriate benchmark portfolio.

The Challenges of Measuring Alpha

Alpha is challenging to measure for two reasons: first and foremost, because you have to define the "right" risk-appropriate benchmark – selecting a treasury or investment grade bond benchmark for an actively managed portfolio including high-yield convertibles and bonds with high option adjusted spreads is setting the stage for a false positive.

It is also challenging because it is difficult to disentangle the sources of excess returns with any confidence. Generally speaking, "excess returns" in any period can come from four sources – luck, asset allocation/market timing, security selection and customer franchise – and shareholders would like to know which is the predominant source in order to assign an appropriate multiple.

Approaches for Asset-only Portfolios

There is a large academic literature focused on measuring alpha for asset managers and investment funds. Alpha measures for asset-only portfolios broadly fall into three categories: simple benchmark approaches, model agnostic approaches and model-based approaches. For a comprehensive overview of investment fund performance measurement, see Knight and Satchell (2002).

Benchmark Portfolios and Tracking Errors

The simplest approach is to compare your results against peers or against a traded index which closely matches your portfolio.

Blake and Timmerman (2001) comment that peer and index benchmarking are the most prevalent approaches used by life insurers and pension funds to measure investment performance. They cite WM Company, one of two companies along with CAPS (Combined Actuarial Performance Services) which create independent and publicly available benchmark indices: while most of the indices are asset class specific (e.g., regional equity indices, bond and real-estate indices), they also provide peer group benchmarks for pension funds (the WM50 for large funds and the WM2000 for small and medium-sized funds). WM also has a peer-group index for with-profits LH insurers.

Asset class benchmarks can also be created in-house and tailored to the company's own portfolio. For example, if the investment strategy is to select individual stocks from within the S&P 500 universe, then you might choose the S&P 500 as a benchmark. Similarly, if the investment strategy is to select individual corporate bonds, then you might select a corporate bond index which represents the investment universe.

- A composite index may need to be constructed if the investment universe is broader. For example, if equities can be selected from the S&P 500 and the Nasdaq index, then a more appropriate index can be constructed by weighting the S&P 500 and Nasdaq indices using your portfolio's strategic benchmark weights.
- Additional adjustments may be necessary to normalize returns for specific risks. For example, selecting the S&P 500 index might encourage investment in high-beta shares, a strategy which would seem to "outperform" during bull markets. A more appropriate benchmark might be an S&P 500 index weighted by the beta of the portfolio actually selected. The same can be done if the strategy focuses on small-cap equities, for example. Similarly, fixed-income benchmarks can be adjusted to reflect the actual or target duration of your portfolio.

Absolute tracking errors (ATE), defined as the difference between the actual returns and the benchmark returns, can be calculated based on the benchmarks – for example, $ATE_t = (R_t - R_t^B)$. A passive investment approach seeks to minimize the tracking error whereas an active approach may generate large tracking errors over time (ostensibly combined with a positive mean). Various statistics can be calculated based on the tracking error. For example, the *average ATE* over a long time horizon, $\varphi ATE_t = \frac{1}{T}\sum_{t=1}^{T} ATE_t$, gives an indication of the average "alpha" or outperformance relative to the benchmark. In addition, some in the industry (e.g., Stein, 1999) define the *tracking error* as the standard deviation of the absolute tracking error – for example, $TE = \sqrt{\frac{1}{T}\sum_{t=1}^{T}(ATE_t - \varphi ATE_t)^2}$. TE is on the same scale and can be compared directly with returns. If we were to assume that the TE is normally distributed, we would expect a portfolio with an annual tracking error of 1% to be within 1% of the benchmark portfolio returns two years out of three. $TE \leq 0.5\%$ generally represents an index fund, where the small tracking error standard deviation can arise due to the desire to limit transaction costs from directly matching the benchmark.

Model and Benchmark Agnostic Measures

The following gives a flavor of the approaches used in practice; interested readers are referred to Farah (2002)[8] for a more comprehensive overview of the literature.

One of the earliest and most well-known performance measures, the *Sharpe Ratio* (SR) (Sharpe, 1966), compares returns above the risk-free interest rate to the portfolio's absolute risk level as measured by its standard deviation – for example, $SR_i = (R_i - R_f)/\sigma_i$, where R_i is the portfolio's/position's realized returns, R_f is the risk-free return and σ_i the standard deviation of the portfolio's returns. Measured empirically:

$$S = \frac{\frac{1}{T}\sum_{t=1}^{T}(R - R_f)}{\sqrt{\frac{1}{T}\sum_{t=1}^{T}\left[(R - R_f) - \left(\frac{1}{T}\sum_{t=1}^{T}(R - R_f)\right)\right]^2}}$$

The *Modigliani–Modigliani risk-adjusted performance* measure (sometimes referred to as RAP, RAPA or M^2; Modigliani and Modigliani, 1997) gives the same ranking but is expressed in basis points and so can be compared with benchmark returns, where $RAPA_i = \sigma_m SR_i$. RAP is defined before the deduction of the risk-free rate of return – for example, $RAP_i = \left(\frac{\sigma_m}{\sigma_i}\right)(R_i - R_f) + R_f$, with $RAPA_i = RAP_i - R_f$.

Return on VaR measures are similar to the Sharpe ratio, but with VaR replacing the portfolio's standard deviation (e.g., $RoVaR = R_i/VaR_i$).

All of the above measure absolute returns or returns relative to the risk-free rate of return. An alternative measure, the *tracking error adjusted return*, measures the net contribution of deviating from a benchmark portfolio relative to the additional risk of deviating from the benchmark (e.g., TEAR = ATE/TE). This measure is especially appropriate for a liability-driven investor if the benchmark portfolio represents the liability; in this case, it measures the relative benefit of deviating from the liability benchmark compared with the risk of not meeting the liabilities.

---

[8]Farah also discusses parametric and non-parametric tests as well as more complicated factor-based models for building the benchmark portfolio.

Model-based Measures

Model-based measures use financial market models to define the appropriate risk-equivalent benchmark. Some of the most well known measures of excess returns are based on the CAPM model discussed in Chapter 4.

The *Treynor measure* (Treynor, 1965) rearranges the CAPM SML into a measure of excess returns – for example, defining $T_i = (R_i - R_f)/\beta_i$, where R_i is the portfolio returns, R_f is the risk-free rate of return and β_i is the portfolio's beta. Substituting in the CAPM excess return definition (e.g., $R_i = \alpha + R_f + \beta_i R_p$), we get $T_i = \alpha/\beta_i$. This is similar in principle to creating a beta-weighted benchmark portfolio as discussed above.

The *Jensen measure* (Jensen, 1968, 1969) takes a more direct approach, defined as $R_{i,t} - R_{f,t} = \alpha_i + \beta_i R_{p,t} + \epsilon_{i,t}$, where $R_{p,t}$ is the market risk premium at time t. α_i, β_i are parameters which need to be estimated, with α_i representing excess returns. Under certain simplifying assumptions, Jensen shows that α_i will be over-estimated and β_i will be under-estimated if the asset manager has market timing capabilities.

The *Treynor–Mazuy measure* (Treynor and Mazuy, 1966), defined as $R_{i,t} - R_{f,t} = \alpha_i + \theta_{i,1} R_{p,t} + \theta_{i,2} R_{p,t}^2 + \varepsilon_{i,t}$, is an attempt to separate security selection from market timing. Superior security selection is still measured by α_i while superior market timing is measured by $\theta_{i,2}$, the concept being that "market timers should make money when the market rises or falls dramatically, that is, when the squared return on the market is large" (Lehmann and Modest, 1987).

Recognizing that the CAPM does not match empirical evidence, other authors make adjustments to better match empirical data. An example is the four-factor model of Elton *et al.* (1996), which adds to the equity market return factor three additional "market return factors" for the difference between small-cap and large-cap performance, growth versus value stocks, investment grade and high-yield bond indices. Seeking to resolve similar issues, Carhart (1997) introduces new "factors" including one for high-M/B stocks and "momentum."

Approaches for Liability-driven Portfolios

A/L portfolios are liability driven to some extent. For example, a bank's A/L portfolio will consist of a portfolio of replicating assets, which mimic the market risk behavior of the actual loan portfolio, minus the replicating liabilities, which mimic the market risk of the deposits, as well as any other derivatives or securities allocated to the portfolio. The interest rate risk of this (leveraged) portfolio increases if the cash flows are not perfectly matched. Similarly, PC and LH insurers as well as pension funds also have liability-driven investment strategies because their interest rate risk profile depends on whether or not the liabilities are "matched."

Measuring alpha for liability-driven portfolios is complicated because you have to take the liabilities into account. The simplest approach is to set the benchmark portfolio equal to the replicating liability portfolio and calculate tracking errors.

Illustrative Example: Measuring Alpha in the Leveraged CAPM World

As an illustrative example, consider the CAPM discussed earlier, with excess returns (α_i) defined in the CAPM world using the SML (e.g., $R_i = \alpha_i + R_f + \beta_i R_p$). If R_i are the portfolio's actual returns and $\hat{R}_i$ the risk-appropriate benchmark returns, excess returns or alpha are measured in the CAPM world by $R_i - \hat{R}_i = (\alpha_i + R_f + \beta_i R_p) - (R_f + \beta_i R_p) = \alpha_i$.

Assuming that the investor's equity (e, where without loss of generality we assume $e = 1$) can be leveraged by short-term, risk-free debt (d), the risk-adjusted benchmark portfolio is defined by $\hat{R}_i = \gamma R_f + \beta_i R_p$, where $\hat{R}_i$ is the expected return from risk-appropriate *levered* portfolio i for one unit of investment (e.g., $(e + d) = 1$), recognizing the cost of leverage and including any expected excess returns (α); $\gamma = \frac{e}{e+d}$ is the percentage of equity financing of the total portfolio. In this case, alpha is defined by $R_i - \hat{R}_i = (\alpha_i + \gamma R_f + \beta_i R_p) - (R_f + \gamma \beta_i R_p) = \alpha_i$.

Measuring Alpha for Fixed Cash Flow Liability-driven Portfolios

Using similar logic, Babbel and Staking (1989) extend the analysis to the case where the liability funding is long term and both assets and liabilities are fixed income only. The relationship between the duration of the investor's surplus and the duration of the assets and liabilities is given by the following equation.

EQUATION 17.6: Surplus duration measure (Babbel and Staking, 1989)

$$D_s = D_l + \left(\frac{A}{S}\right)(D_a - D_l)$$

where $\{A, L, S\}$ represent the market value of the fixed-income assets, liabilities and surplus, respectively, and $\{D_a, D_l, D_s\}$ represent the duration of the fixed-income assets, liabilities and surplus, respectively. The Babbel and Staking measure can be used to define a risk-appropriate benchmark portfolio where the only risk to the net asset value of the firm is driven by duration mismatch; it does not explicitly isolate the potential alpha generated through security selection or market timing.

Remaining in the (fixed assets, fixed liabilities) world, Plantinga and van den Meer (1995) extend the analysis by isolating the investment alpha results from the maturity mismatch results. Assuming that liabilities (L) are backed by liability-driven investments (B) and that surplus (S) is backed by non-liability-driven investments (O),[9] the resulting performance attribution schema is given in the following equation.

EQUATION 17.7: Investment performance attribution (Plantiga and van den Meer, 1995)

$$r_s^a = r_0^a + \lambda\left(r_b^a - r_b^p\right) + \lambda\left(r_b^p - r_l^a\right) + \tau\left(r_b^a - r_o^a\right)$$

where

r_s^a = realized return on surplus
r_0^a = realized returns on non-liability driven investments
r_b^a = realized returns on liability-driven investments
r_b^p = realized returns on a benchmark portfolio appropriate for the liability-driven investments
r_l^a = realized returns on the liabilities
$\lambda = L/S$, the ratio of liabilities to surplus (a financial leverage ratio)
$\tau = (B - L)/S$, called the funding mismatch portfolio.

---

[9]Note that the equation and interpretation of Plantiga and van den Meer's results work also if the assets backing surplus are allowed to contain other than fixed-income securities.

Plantiga and van den Meer interpret r_0^a as the return on assets backing surplus; any outperformance on these assets can be measured using the asset-only approaches outlined earlier. They interpret $\lambda\left(r_b^a - r_b^p\right)$ as the pure asset outperformance (or alpha) on assets backing the liabilities, since the realized returns are compared with a risk-appropriate benchmark. They interpret $\lambda\left(r_b^p - r_l^a\right)$ as a "maturity mismatch" result and $\tau\left(r_b^a - r_o^a\right)$ as the "funding mismatch" result, reflecting over- or under-funding of the asset portfolio backing the liabilities.

The attribution of returns between an insurer's strategic and tactical asset allocation decisions is discussed in greater detail in Chapter 15.

CHAPTER 18

Cash and Liquidity Management

Funding and liquidity risk is defined by the Bank for International Settlements (BIS, 2008) as ". . . the risk that the firm will not be able to meet efficiently both expected and unexpected current and future cash flow and collateral needs without affecting either daily operations or the financial condition of the firm."

This risk has little to do with being economically insolvent but can be just as deadly. The distinction is important: it has been argued that some economically solvent firms were forced into resolution due to a liquidity crisis during the 2008 financial crisis (see the case examples later in this chapter) while other, insolvent firms – the "walking dead" or "zombies" – continued to function only because government liquidity support prevented their collapse.[1]

MANAGING FUNDING LIQUIDITY RISK

In contrast to other risks, managing liquidity risk is not about holding more capital: if customers do not believe that the bank or insurer can cover its obligations, then they will seek to recover their deposits and redeem their policies, representing a draw on the firm's liquidity and creating a self-fulfilling, downward spiral. Additional capital will not help once the spiral is initiated; liquidity risk management is about avoiding the spiral in the first place.

High-level principles for managing funding liquidity risk can be found for the banking industry in BIS (2008) and for the insurance industry in CRO Forum (2008). Summarizing these principles, there are three important activities which need to be taken in order to effectively manage funding liquidity risk:

- first, clearly define a *risk strategy and appetite* for funding liquidity risk;
- second, have in place the *governance framework* to manage funding liquidity risk;
- third, take steps to *pro-actively manage* the funding liquidity profile of the firm.

---

[1]Cowen (2011) writes in the *New York Times*, "If enough depositors fear frozen accounts, the banks will be emptied out, and they also will require additional government bailouts, on top of the bailouts for the bad real estate loans. The banks come to resemble empty shells, conduits for public aid but shrinking and unprofitable as businesses — and, to a large extent, that is already the case in Ireland. Portugal is moving in this same direction, toward being a land inhabited by zombie banks. It's the zombie banks that doom the current European bailout plans."

Liquidity Risk Appetite: Evaluating the Trade-offs

The ALCO is responsible for defining the firm's liquidity risk strategy and appetite. Unlike risks taken on the margin during the normal course of business, defining an appetite for liquidity risk is not as simple as balancing the expected costs and benefits because the risks and rewards are asymmetric.

The cost of having a too conservative liquidity profile is straightforward, comprising four elements.

- *Opportunity cost of liquid assets.* As discussed in Chapter 17, illiquid assets typically pay a premium compared with more liquid assets. Holding liquid assets which can be sold quickly to cover cash needs represents an opportunity cost in the form of additional yield foregone.
- *Higher cost of funding.* As discussed in Chapter 17, long-term committed financing costs more than short-term revolving financing, which may disappear during a liquidity crisis. As a consequence, the overall, weighted average cost of financing will increase as more term unsecured debt, hybrid or equity capital is added to the mix.
- *Opportunity cost of maintaining unused leverage capacity.* "Keeping some powder dry" in terms of debt issuance capacity or retaining qualifying assets for collateralized financing will improve the funding liquidity risk profile, but it will also lead to a lower level of expected operating income.
- *Direct cost of contingent funding.* Contingent funding such as committed lines of credit also have a direct and measurable cost. However, as the case examples illustrate, contingent financing should be viewed skeptically as it may not be there during times of crisis.

In contrast, the benefits are more challenging to measure because of the non-linear way in which they accrue: during "normal" market conditions, when markets are flush with liquidity, the benefits may appear negligible and it is easy to take liquidity for granted. In contrast, during periods of market dislocation, the benefits can be measured in terms of the ultimate currency – the survival of the firm.

As a consequence of the asymmetry, the trade-offs between having too much or too little liquidity need to be evaluated not based on the risk/reward analysis around the "best-estimate" or "business as usual" scenario but relative to an extreme worst-case scenario. In general, banks and insurers have little appetite for funding liquidity risk, preferring to meet their obligations with a very high degree of confidence under a wide variety of stress scenarios.

The Role of the Group versus the Business

ALCO is responsible for setting the liquidity management strategy and framework, with treasury responsible for day-to-day liquidity management activities. However, as Figure 18.1 illustrates, liquidity risk is actually managed in two distinct "pools."

The most important liquidity management activities take place day-to-day in the treasury and in operating business units within the limits set by ALCO. The remainder of this chapter focuses on these activities.

In addition, liquidity management also takes place at the group level: most groups keep a *strategic liquidity reserve* in the form of *unencumbered liquid assets held as cash and cash equivalents, including balances with banks and central banks payable on demand, cash on*

First priority: Liqudiity managed by
Treasury and within the Operating Entities

Additional liquidity buffer held at the
Group level.

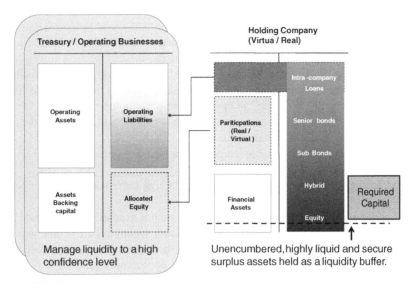

FIGURE 18.1   Capital funding structure

hand and Treasury bills or similar securities. In addition to this liquidity reserve, the group will also reserve some financial leverage capacity to meet contingencies.

Tapping into the group's strategic liquidity buffer should only be done as a last resort: *the operating businesses cannot and should not view the group as providing a liquidity backstop; they need to manage their own liquidity resources and risk profile to a high confidence level.*

Rules of the Game

Following industry practice, the rules of the game for managing funding liquidity risk are summarized below.

RULES OF THE GAME: FUNDING LIQUIDITY MANAGEMENT

Funding and liquidity are group resources which are managed within the constraints imposed by management's risk appetite, regulators and rating agencies. In order to make the most of these resources, the firm does the following.

- Clearly defines a risk appetite in terms of the ability to meet liquidity requirements under extreme stress scenarios.
- Puts in place the organizational prerequisites to manage funding liquidity risk:
  - a measurement framework consisting of funding liquidity gap profiles and coverage ratios under different scenarios and over different time horizons;
  - a management organization, including a governance body (the ALCO) and line management (the treasury and selected business units) with explicit limits and delegated authorities;

- an incentive system, including a liquidity-adjusted FTP system, to ensure that operating businesses proactively manage their liquidity resources and are aware of the costs.
- Set the firm's strategic liquidity profile.
  - Establishing a stable, long-term financing base around which cash, funding and liquidity management activities are undertaken.
  - Establishing a strategic liquidity reserve at the group level consisting of unencumbered, liquid assets and debt issuance capacity to be used to finance cash and capital calls from the operating business units.
  - Allocating funding and liquidity resources in a manner consistent with the firm's capital allocation and business strategy.
- Optimize the firm's financial leverage from a liquidity perspective.
  - Securing sufficient term funding capacity.
  - Matching funding to use (e.g., long-term foreign currency funding for foreign subsidiary participations, etc.).
  - Laddering the commitments such that they are not exposed to concentrated roll-over risk (e.g., refinancing a significant amount within a narrow time window).
  - Opportunistically retiring existing funding before it matures, replacing it and extending the duration as and when market opportunities allow.
  - Managing and diversifying the sources of financing, reducing concentrations by product (e.g., deposits, inter-bank, commercial paper, public and private notes, etc.) and by "pool" (e.g., USA, Europe, Asia and different sources – sovereign wealth funds, institutional investors, retail investors, etc.).
- Minimizing potential cash calls through product design (e.g., redemption gating, withdrawal or surrender charges, contract as opposed to calendar anniversary dates, etc.) and avoiding positions with immediate, large potential cash calls (e.g., from guarantees, rating-based collateral triggers, etc.).
- Within each liquidity portfolio, ensuring that there are sufficient unencumbered liquid assets to meet cash calls even under extreme scenarios and matching funding to use (e.g., long-term funding for long-term, illiquid assets).

WHAT HAPPENS IF IT GOES WRONG?

The need to manage funding liquidity risk is summarized by the Basel Committee on Banking Supervision (2010). Referring to the earliest "liquidity phase" of the 2007–8 financial market crisis: "(M)any banks – despite adequate capital levels – still experienced difficulties because they did not manage their liquidity in a prudent manner . . . Prior to the crisis, asset markets were buoyant and funding was readily available at low cost. The rapid reversal illustrated how quickly liquidity can evaporate . . . (lasting) for an extended period of time. The banking system came under severe stress, which necessitated central bank action to support both the functioning of money markets and, in some cases, individual institutions."

Banking Examples: Northern Rock, Bear Stearns, Lehman

The BIS summarized the issues very broadly; behind the summary are some very interesting cases, which are both illustrative and informative.

Northern Rock

One prominent example of funding liquidity risk is the case of Northern Rock.[2] Arguably, Northern Rock was well capitalized and solvent on an economic basis at the time of its failure. Unfortunately, as the crisis progressed, it failed to secure sufficient financing through normal channels due to stressed market conditions. As a consequence, Northern Rock was forced into bankruptcy.

Northern Rock was a domestic, retail mortgage bank domiciled in the UK. Mortgages were funded through a combination of customer deposits, the issuance of mortgage-backed securities and short-term, inter-bank funding. During the summer of 2007, a vicious liquidity cycle began, one which would ultimately spell the end of Northern Rock as an independent financial institution.

- First, investors became concerned about the mortgage asset class, caused by adverse developments in the sub-prime market in the USA. This sudden imbalance between demand and supply had an associated negative impact on asset values, and financing mortgages through securitization became impossible.
- Second, because of the opacity surrounding bank balance sheets and bank conduit exposures to mortgages, funding in the short-term, inter-bank market also disappeared, putting further pressure on asset values and eliminating the second pillar of Northern Rock's financing strategy.
- This in turn caused a crisis in confidence for Northern Rock's depositors, closing down the third and final pillar of their financing strategy as depositors withdrew £3 billion of deposits during a 3-day period in August 2007.

Critical for the discussion on balance sheet management: up until this cataclysmic sequence of events, Northern Rock remained solvent in terms of regulatory ratios and was profitable with an acceptable loan–loss ratio. Arguably, the failure of Northern Rock was not due to a lack of capital or net asset value, but rather to a fragile financing strategy.

Bear Stearns and Lehman Brothers

While the details are different, funding liquidity played a significant role in other high-profile bank bankruptcies during the 2008 financial crisis. For example, declining asset and derivative values led to collateral calls for Bear Stearns and its asset manager, raising concerns within the market. "In response to this Bear (Stearns) issued a press release on 10th March 2008 stating that there were no grounds for any rumours regarding their lack of liquidity saying that it has $17 billion in cash. However, the fact that a public announcement has been made was read as a signal by many Wall Street experts, that the bank was in trouble. There were also reports that a major bank had refused to lend to Bear via a repo transaction a short term loan of $2 billion and therefore rumours persisted that the bank was losing confidence among its creditors."[3] In a predictable self-fulfilling prophecy, Bear Stearns was forced into the arms of JP Morgan three days later.

---

[2]An excellent and detailed study of the Northern Rock case can be found in Llewellyn (2010).

[3]From http://financetrainingcourse.com/education/2011/02/liquidity-risk-management-case-study-the-liquidity-run-cycle-illustrated-bear-stearns-june-2007-to-16th-march-2008/ and http://www.kamakuraco.com/Blog/tabid/231/EntryId/306/Case-Studies-in-Liquidity-Risk-JPMorgan-Chase-Bear-Stearns-and-Washington-Mutual.aspx

Lehman Brothers followed a similar fate, almost in sympathy with Bear Stearns: "17th March 2008 saw Lehman's share price decline sharply by more than 48% following the collapse of Bear Stearns . . . which raised concerns in the market whether other investment banks, in particular Lehman, would meet the same fate. There were reports that on that day South Asian Bank DBS instructed its traders not to work with Lehman. These instructions were later withdrawn."[4] The "smooth" resolution of Bear Stearns may have been a mixed blessing, creating the impression that a similar action might be possible for Lehman and allowing Lehman to continue business from March until September.

Unfortunately, against the background of a deteriorating market, it became clear in early September that no "White Knight" was in the wings to support Lehman and that the government was also not willing to bail them out, either directly or in terms of a back-stop guarantee for potential saviors. "When news reports on 9th September indicated that the talks had ended the 45% fall in Lehman's stock price pushed the S&P 500 and Dow Jones down. This was exacerbated when the US government announced that it would not bail out Lehman as it had done Bear Stearns if the situation became critical. Credit Default Swaps, default insurance for Lehman's debt increased significantly, a reverse indicator of how the markets perceived Lehman's financial strength. This resulted in a run on the bank with hedge fund clients pulling out, lines of credit being withdrawn, great margin/collateral calls and trades being cancelled."

This was the last straw, breaking the market's already strained confidence. Lehman ultimately collapsed on September 15, 2008, leading to the largest bankruptcy filing in US history.

Non-traditional Insurance Examples: General American and AIG

It is generally hard to find a funding liquidity catastrophe for an insurer triggered by its core, *traditional* insurance activities. This is because traditional insurance collects the premium upfront and there is little or no opportunity for the customer to accelerate payment on their obligations.

In PC, most of the current-period claims are paid out of current-period premium. Furthermore, either an event happens or it doesn't and there is a lag in final payment while the claims are examined, adjusted and the payments made. Given the lag, the high liquidity of insurers' assets and the prospects of a hardening market following a large event, securing cash to pay the claim is typically not an issue.

In LH savings and retirement products, early surrenders may not be contractually possible and there are often tax and other incentives such as surrender charges which provide a disincentive for the policy holder to ask for their money back prematurely. Alternatively, the contracts may contain market value adjustments to the surrender value, making the whole point mute.

Nonetheless, there are some examples of a liquidity crisis stemming from *non-traditional or non-insurance* activities within an insurance group. The distinction between traditional and non-traditional activities is critical and helped the International Association of Insurance

---

[4]From http://financetrainingcourse.com/education/2011/02/liquidity-risk-management-case-study-lehman-brothers/. See also http://www.kamakuraco.com/Blog/tabid/231/EntryId/290/Case-Studies-in-Liquidity-Risk-Lehman-Brothers-Dick-Fuld-was-Right.aspx and http://citeseerx.ist.psu.edu/viewdoc/download?doi=10.1.1.186.5564&rep=rep1&type=pdf

Supervisors (IAIS) and the FSB conclude that traditional insurance activities are not systemically relevant.[5]

General American Insurance, Non-traditional Insurance Activities

A notable case from the insurance industry comes from the late 1990s. General American was a company which was arguably economically solvent but which nonetheless lost its independence because it could not meet its cash obligations in the short term. This case is interesting because it represented a wake-up call in terms of liquidity management for the insurance industry. The post mortem of General American was extensively discussed and the following is based on the Society of Actuaries' panel on the subject (SOA, 2000).

Laura Brazer of Moody's Investor Service posed the right question (SOA, 2000), "What caused a reasonably healthy $30 billion life insurance group to lose its independence in a matter of weeks? Well, as you know, the regulators did not deem this as an insolvency; rather, it was a case of inadequate liquidity." She cites three reasons for the failure.

First, General American had a major exposure to credit-sensitive funding agreements: it had issued $6.8 billion worth of GICs to institutional investors, representing 20% of the market and 400% of its statutory capital. Exacerbating the situation was the fact that the majority of the GICs were callable, with the investors able to demand their cash back within 7 business days ($5 bn), representing 60% of the 7-day market and a sizable potential liquidity call.

Second, a significant amount of this GIC business was reinsured with a smaller, less well-rated company called Integrity Life Insurance Company. As Brazer notes, "In fact, for those familiar, this was really a fronting arrangement that enabled ARM Financial (the parent of Integrity Life Insurance) to sell these products . . . ARM had the product and General American had the ratings."

Third, the great bulk of the GICs issued by General American were owned by just three savvy, institutional investors, representing not only a high concentration but also a high sensitivity to any news. As Victor Modugno pointed out during the panel, "Unlike individual policy holders, these institutional policy holders sit by Bloomberg screens and watch for the first sign of trouble to exercise their options to take money out."

The rest is history: ARM Financial (the parent of Integrity Life Insurance) announced large losses, effectively wiping out half of its capital and putting it into financial trouble. This put into serious doubt the $3.5 billion worth of contracts which Integrity Life Insurance was to have backed or "reinsured" in the next 30 days, moving General American into the front of the firing line. Rightfully, Moody's downgraded General American. This caused the institutional investors to put their 7-day GICs back to General American and demand repayment. As a consequence, General American was forced to put itself under administrative supervision, ultimately being purchased by Met Life.

As with many stories, there is often an interesting epilog. During the liquidity crisis, General American tried to draw down a $2 billion credit line from Goldman Sachs; the credit line was not honored by Goldman, raising the question whether one can count on contingent liquidity facilities. Goldman Sachs was later sued by General American, claiming both wrong

---

[5]The International Association of Insurance Supervisors (IAIS, 2013) has defined "traditional" and "non-traditional" insurance activities for the purpose of deciding the systemic relevance of insurers. Their conclusion was that "traditional" insurance (which includes PC insurance and most LH insurance) is not systemically relevant for these reasons but that "non-traditional" insurance (including LH variable annuities, GICs, mortgage insurance and credit guarantees) may be.

doing with respect to the credit line as well as the failure to disclose that Met Life was Goldman's client before it advised General American on the sale or the proposed purchase price (Brown Smith Wallace, 2008). Goldman Sachs ultimately settled the suit for $100 million.

AIG, Non-insurance Products

Another notable case during the 2008 financial crisis was AIG, the largest insurance group in the world at that time. Similar to General American, AIG's liquidity crisis did not stem from its traditional insurance activities, but rather from its non-traditional, non-insurance activities.

Prior to 2008, AIG built up a substantial derivatives position in its AIG Financial Products (AIGFP) subsidiary, accumulating over USD 440 billion worth of credit default swaps, including over USD 55 billion sold protection on lower-quality sub-prime loans. AIGFP was fully guaranteed by AIG and, because of AIG's high credit rating, normally did not have to post collateral with its derivative trading counterparties; however, collateral cash calls could be triggered if AIG was downgraded by the public rating agencies. However, concerns began to be raised with respect to AIG's credit rating due to the general deterioration in the credit markets.

According to Bloomberg (Son, 2008), AIG pro-actively took action to secure sufficient liquidity, "(AIG sought) $70–75 billion in loans arranged by Goldman Sachs and JP Morgan Chase . . . (in an attempt to) raise cash to forestall debt-rating downgrades that . . . may have 'a material adverse effect on AIG's liquidity' and trigger more than $13 billion in collateral calls from debt investors who bought swaps."

The failure to secure liquidity caused a vicious cycle and AIG was downgraded three grades by S&P on September 15, 2008, citing a "combination of reduced flexibility in meeting additional collateral needs and concerns over increasing residential mortgage-related losses."

Because AIG was considered to be systemically relevant, the Federal Reserve Bank of the United States created a credit facility of up to $85 billion secured by the shares of its operating subsidiaries. This represented the second largest bailout in history, following the previous bailout of Fannie Mae and Freddie Mac.

AIG's failure, brought about by its derivative or "shadow banking" operations, significantly damaged the reputation of the insurance industry and heavily influenced the FSB's interest in reviewing the systemic relevance of insurers.

MEASURING FUNDING LIQUIDITY RISK

In well-functioning markets, economic solvency should be sufficient to guarantee liquidity: as long as there is positive net asset value and this is transparent to the markets, it should be possible to monetize that value through asset sales or borrowing to cover the cash liability.

However, as the previous cases illustrated, economic solvency alone may not be sufficient during times of market dislocation. In such situations, unexpected cash or collateral demands combined with an inability to raise funds through borrowing prove to be a lethal combination.

Measurement Principles

Funding liquidity risk is typically measured by the ratio of the firm's liquid assets and secure borrowing capacity relative to its (expected and unexpected) cash flow commitments over predefined time horizons and under different stress scenarios.

For example, liquidity ratios for corporate borrowers are based on liquid assets relative to short-term debt obligations. Liquidity ratios for banks and insurers are more challenging given their higher leverage, more complex financing structure and higher uncertainty surrounding the liquidity of assets and the stability of their funding.

Because of these complexities, liquidity measurement for financial institutions tends to be more of an "art" than a "science," with the "art" being to define what "liquid assets," over what "time horizon" and under what "scenarios." The following sections provide some useful examples and frameworks illustrating the "art" of liquidity risk measurement (see also Duttweiler, 2009).

An Example: Basel III Ratios for Banks

Although specific to banks, the Basel III liquidity measures are nonetheless illustrative of the principals involved in answering "what liquid assets?" over "what time horizon?" under "what scenarios?," making this section of generic interest for all readers.

Following the 2008 financial crisis, the Basel Committee on Banking Supervision (BIS, 2009a) developed a proposal for updating liquidity measurement, management and reporting standards, specifically defining two new measures (the Liquidity Coverage Ratio – LCR, a measure of liquidity over a short horizon under stressed conditions and the Net Stable Funding Ratio – NSFR, representing a longer horizon under more stable conditions). In addition, the proposals also formulated a series of metrics used for monitoring the liquidity concentration and developments of the bank.

In July 2010, the Basel Committee on Banking Supervision (BIS, 2010) came out with a more detailed calibration and an implementation time line, beginning with an observation period in 2011 and leading to the introduction of the LCR in January 2015 and the NSFR in January 2018. The following discussion summarizes BIS (2009a).

Liquidity Coverage Ratio

According to BIS, the objective of the LCR is to "ensure that a bank maintains an adequate level of unencumbered, high quality assets that can be converted into cash to meet its liquidity needs for a 30-day time horizon under an acute liquidity stress scenario specified by supervisors . . . by which time it is assumed that appropriate actions can be taken by management and/or supervisor and/or the bank can be resolved in an orderly way."

The LCR is defined as follows:

$$\text{LCR} = \frac{\text{Stock of high-quality liquid assets}}{\text{Net cash outflows over a 30-day time period}} \geq 100\%$$

The Stress Scenario Banks are required to meet 100% LCR where the ratio is calculated under a stress scenario which combines idiosyncratic or firm-specific shocks and a systemic or market-wide liquidity shock. The scenarios are designed to stress the firm's ability to raise funds by borrowing or through the sale of assets, including:

- a three-notch downgrade in the institution's public credit rating;
- run-off of a proportion of retail deposits;
- loss of unsecured wholesale funding capacity and reductions in potential sources of secured funding on a term basis;

- loss of secured, short-term financing transactions for all but high-quality liquid assets;
- an increase in market volatilities that impact the quality of collateral or potential future exposure of derivatives positions, thus requiring larger collateral haircuts or additional collateral;
- unscheduled draws on all the institution's committed but unused credit and liquidity facilities;
- the need for the institution to fund balance sheet growth arising from non-contractual obligations honored in the interests of mitigating reputational risk.

The Numerator – the Stock of High-quality Assets The stock of high-quality assets in the numerator must be unencumbered[6] and should meet the following criteria.

1. Fundamental asset characteristics, including:
   a. low credit and market risk;
   b. ease and certainty of valuation;
   c. low correlation with risky assets;
   d. listed on a recognized exchange.
2. Market-related characteristics:
   a. sizable, stable and active market;
   b. presence of committed market makers;
   c. low market concentration (i.e., diverse group of buyers and sellers);
   d. flight to quality (i.e., assets that tend to be bought by the market in a crisis).

Assets which clearly meet these requirements include cash, central bank reserves (to the extent to which they can be drawn down in times of stress), claims on sovereign and other qualifying borrowers including the BIS, IMF, European Commission, multi-lateral development banks and government or central bank debt issued in domestic currencies by the country in which the liquidity risk is being taken.

Other assets also qualify for inclusion, but subject to a "haircut" relative to their current market value. For example, the original consultative document suggested a 20–40% haircut on corporate and covered bonds meeting specific criteria.

The Denominator – Net Cash Outflows Net cash outflows are defined as cumulative outflows minus inflows expected under the stress scenario. Cumulative expected outflows and inflows are calculated by multiplying outstanding balances of liabilities with roll-off factors, assets with drawdown factors and receivables with net inflow factors.

Cash Outflows For example, deposit funding is assumed to run off with a minimum factor of 7.5% for stable deposits and 15% for less stable deposits. Unsecured wholesale funding is assumed to run off at a minimum of 7.5–15% for funding from small business customers, 25% for non-financial corporations, sovereigns, central banks and public sector entities with operational relationships and 75% if no operational relationship exists. Finally, no credit (or 100% run-off assumption) is applied for unsecured wholesale funding by financial institutions such as banks, insurance companies, etc. Similarly, no credit is given for secured

---

[6]That is, not pledged explicitly or implicitly in any way to secure, collateralize or credit enhance any transaction and not held as a hedge for any other exposure.

funding transactions backed by anything except government debt in domestic currencies or similar claims.

Funding generated by asset-backed commercial paper programs or similar conduits is assumed not to roll over if maturing during the 30-day horizon or if the assets can be "put" back to the conduit (e.g., "liquidity puts"). Finally, it is assumed that committed credit facilities and liquidity facilities draw down between 10% and 100% depending on their characteristics.

The calculation of net cash outflows should reflect the impact of the idiosyncratic rating scenario, including any additional collateral required under a "downgrade trigger," as well as valuation changes on collateral posted and derivative positions. Finally, contingent liabilities also need to be included, including guarantees, letters of credit, potential repurchase of the bank's own debt, the potential purchase of notes where customers expect ready marketability, stable value funds, etc.

Cash Inflows   Cash inflows should only be considered from existing contractual arrangements which are fully performing and for which the bank has no reason to expect a default in the next 30 days. These include up to 100% of retail and wholesale performing loan inflows but 0–100% of reverse repos and secured lending which matures during the period, again depending on the characteristics. Finally, it is assumed that no line of credit can be drawn for the benefit of the bank under the stress scenario.

Net Stable Funding Ratio

The NSFR is different from the LCR in that it represents less severe market conditions over a longer-term time horizon. As such, it measures the longer-term resilience of the funding profile during more normal times rather than the survival of the company during periods of extreme stress.

The stated objective of the NSFR is to provide an incentive to secure more medium- and long-term funding for the bank, limiting the over-reliance on wholesale funding during times of buoyant market liquidity and encouraging better assessment of liquidity risk.

In addition, the NSFR should help to address the "cliff effects" of the LCR – for example, what risks are inherent after the first 30 days? Especially in focus are investment banking inventories, off-balance sheet exposures, securitization pipelines and other activities depending on their liquidity profile. The NSFR is defined by the following formula:

$$\text{NSFR} = \frac{\text{Available amount of stable funding}}{\text{Required amount of stable funding}} > 100\%$$

The Numerator – Available Stable Funding Factors   In order to calculate the firm's available stable funding, all sources of funding are mapped into one of five categories, each of which is assigned a multiplicative factor reflecting the "stability" of the funding. The Available Stable Funding (ASF) factors give longer and more stable funding sources (such as paid-in capital) more weight than less secure financing (such as wholesale, inter-bank borrowing). The categories and factors are described in Table 18.1.

The Denominator – Required Stable Funding Factors   Similarly, all potential funding requirements, both on- and off-balance sheet, are mapped into categories based on their characteristics. Table 18.2 summarizes the original proposed calibration for on-balance sheet assets.

TABLE 18.1   NSFR available stable funding factors

ASF factor	Components/description
100%	Tier 1 and 2 equity. Preferred stock with maturity greater than 1 year, recognizing embedded options. Secured and unsecured borrowings with effective maturity greater than 1 year.
85%	"Stable" retail and small business non-maturing deposits and term deposits of less than 1 year.
70%	"Less stable" retail and small business non-maturing deposits and term deposits of less than 1 year.
50%	Unsecured funding provided by non-financial corporate customers with a residual maturity of less than 1 year.
0%	All other liabilities.

The implicit prioritization of business activities is interesting in this table. For example, assets typically found in a trading book (marketable securities such as debt and equity) are given lower weight than loans to retail clients. One can interpret this either as a judgment of the underlying liquidity of the positions[7] or as a desire to continue to support the bank's core customer franchise at the expense of trading activities should liquidity become a concern.

For off-balance sheet commitments, the required stable funding factor is 10% for the undrawn amount of conditionally revocable or irrevocable credit and liquidity facilities. Factors for other contingent commitments are set at the discretion of the national supervisors.

TABLE 18.2   NSFR required stable funding factors

RSF factor	Components/description
0%	Cash, money-market instruments. Securities and loans to financial institutions of less than 1 year.
5%	Unencumbered marketable securities from sovereigns, central banks, BIS, IMF, etc., with residual maturities greater than 1 year.
20%	Unencumbered corporate and covered bonds rated at least AA with maturities greater than 1 year.
50%	Gold. Unencumbered equities listed on a major exchange. Unencumbered corporate or covered bonds rated AA− to A−. Loans to non-financial corporate clients of less than 1 year.
85%	Loans to retail clients having a residual maturity of less than 1 year.
0%	All other assets.

---

[7]Although this interpretation may be incorrect. For example, many banks in Spain created covered bonds or Cedulas during the 2012 sovereign bond crisis in Europe in order to directly place them with the European Central Bank as collateral, an activity which was possible only with the relaxation of the ECB's collateral standards. In this way, retail loans were made liquid very quickly.

Additional Metrics

In addition to the LCR and NSFR, additional metrics were prescribed to monitor the ongoing development of the institution's liquidity position. These metrics include the maturity mismatch or gap report as well as measures of the concentration of funding sources.

Contractual Maturity Mismatch or Gap Report   The objective of the gap report is to identify periods when funding gaps can be anticipated if no further action is taken. These are periods when the institution is especially vulnerable to a decrease in market liquidity. For example, it may be the case that a large part of the bank's stable funding in the form of hybrid or preferred shares needs to be redeemed at a specific date or within a narrow time window; clearly, the bank's exposure to funding risk increases during periods when the need to raise funds is concentrated.

The gap report is produced by mapping the contractual cash inflows and outflows from all on- and off-balance sheet items to defined time buckets, for example overnight, 7 day, 14 day, 1, 2, 3 and 6 months, 1, 3, 5 and >5 years. Assets should be reported based on their latest possible maturity and liabilities at their earliest possible date of outflow. This report is similar to the static re-pricing gap report discussed in Chapter 17, but buckets the cash flows based on payment dates instead of on interest rate reset or re-pricing characteristics.

Concentration of Funding   In addition to timing concentrations, the bank can also be exposed to potential concentrations on specific sources of funding. For this reason, additional metrics are recommended to monitor the concentration to specific sources of funding, including:

- the ratio of funding sourced from each significant counterparty relative to the bank's overall balance sheet;
- the ratio of funding sources from each significant product or instrument relative to the bank's overall balance sheet;
- the net funding requirement by currency.

Available Unencumbered Assets   This represents an inventory of unencumbered assets which can be potentially used as collateral in secondary markets or which are eligible for use as collateral under a central bank's standing facility. The value of these assets should reflect the haircuts which would likely be used when using them as collateral, as well as be reported by currency or any other characteristic which might segment their use as collateral.

Beyond Liquidity Ratios

The Basel III metrics are illustrative of generic liquidity measurement approaches, making explicit assumptions about the firm's expected and unexpected cash flows over specific time horizons under different scenarios. Similar concepts are used by insurers.

The benefit of these ratios is that they reduce a complex landscape into two numbers which are ostensibly comparable across institutions; the drawback is that they reduce a complex landscape into only two numbers, masking potentially important issues and observations.

In order to gain a greater insight into their liquidity position, many institutions have developed a more comprehensive and robust framework for measuring liquidity risk, one which is adapted and flexible along all the dimensions – the liquidity of assets, the stability of liabilities and the scenarios which can influence both. The following provides some additional insights.

Asset Liquidity Characteristics

The following additional criteria may influence how you categorize assets for liquidity management purposes.

- *Accounting classifications.* For example, whether the asset is held to maturity versus available for sale, whether it is held in the banking or trading book or whether it is part of a hedged accounting determination, any of which could introduce a higher hurdle on the liquidation of the assets.
- *Asset/liability management considerations.* For example, the most liquid assets may be government securities, which may also have the longest duration and be needed to manage the duration mismatch of an insurer's portfolio. Selling these off to secure liquidity may address a liquidity issue but open up reinvestment risk in a falling rate environment.
- *Implications driven by accounting, statutory or contractual treatment.* For example, some European with-profit participation policies have specific rules governing how realized investment returns are to be distributed between the policy holder and the shareholder. Selling positions to increase liquidity may have unintended consequences for the rates which need to be paid on the policy account and therefore for the overall value of the liability.

Basel III liquidity ratios assign "haircuts" per liquidity class in order to give a net liquidity position. The alternative is to construct an asset volume liquidity ladder, as is done in Figure 18.2.

Liability Liquidity Characterization

Liabilities can also be characterized by their stability and predictability. This was implicit in the LCR's higher weighting of retail deposits (supported by deposit guarantees) compared with

Projected liquidity profile of invested assets

Liquidity Profile of Invested Assets

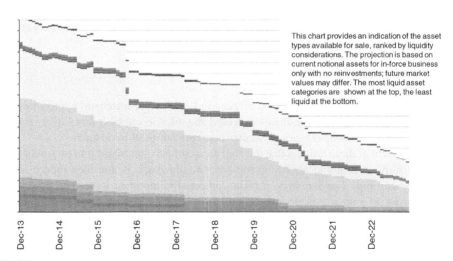

This chart provides an indication of the asset types available for sale, ranked by liquidity considerations. The projection is based on current notional assets for in-force business only with no reinvestments; future market values may differ. The most liquid asset categories are shown at the top, the least liquid at the bottom.

FIGURE 18.2   Asset liquidity profile

Best estimate cash flow projections

Projected cash-inflows and outflows (in-force only)

Net cash flows (in-force only)

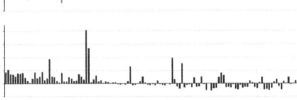

Cummulative cash flows
- In-force only
- With new business

FIGURE 18.3   Best-estimate cash flow projections

unsecured wholesale funding from financial institutions. The main factors affecting liability liquidity include contract terms (penalties, tax benefits, deferral or gating periods, etc.) and customer behavior.[8]

Another factor to consider is the behavior of the distribution channel. For example, in lieu of sensible commission structures, some distribution channels may have an incentive to "churn" accounts in order to generate more fee income. In addition, some may even have an obligation to promote early withdrawal if your institution faces an idiosyncratic shock.

Representing the Baseline Liquidity Profile

The next step is to combine the asset and liability cash flows to come up with a baseline, net cash flow liquidity or funding gap comparison. This can be done in the form of a ratio as in Basel III or, as illustrated in Figure 18.3, in graphical form.

It is critical that the baseline be done for each currency as well as in aggregate: in addition to having different supply and demand characteristics, transferability may become restricted and local markets may be affected by factors such as central bank operations, including the relaxation of collateral standards, the purchase of own sovereign debt securities, etc.

The funding and liquidity gap analysis can be extended to include new business. For example, new premiums from PC insurance policies or large single-premium LH business can be used to pay policies without liquidating assets. However, relying on new business to bridge funding requirements may be problematic as the new business may not materialize and is itself potentially dependent on the group's rating and liquidity profile.

Liquidity ratios can be defined directly based on the baseline gap information. For example, a simple liquidity ratio can be defined by dividing the cumulative available liquidity

---

[8]For a very good summary of insurance-related liquidity risk issues, see American Association of Actuaries (2000).

resources over a specific period by the cumulative liquidity requirements:

$$\text{Liquidity ratio over period } [T, T + \Delta T] = \frac{\displaystyle\sum_{t \in [T,T+\Delta T)} \text{ALR}_t}{\displaystyle\sum_{t \in [T,T+\Delta T)} \text{RLR}_t} \geq 100\%$$

where ALR_t represents the available liquidity during the period $[T, T+\Delta T)$ and RLR_t is the required liquidity resources during the same period.

More conservative, one could also take "haircuts" on both the available and required liquidity resources cumulating over the same time period, leading to an adjusted liquidity ratio illustrated by the equation below:

$$\text{Adjusted liquidity ratio} = \frac{\displaystyle\sum_{t \in [T,T+\Delta T)} \sum_{i} \omega_i \text{ALR}_{i,t}}{\displaystyle\sum_{t \in [T,T+\Delta T)} \sum_{j} \omega_j \text{RLR}_{j,t}} \geq 100\%$$

where ω_i represents "haircuts" on available liquidity resources, for example cash and government securities might have a weighting of 100%, investment grade corporate or covered bonds might have a rating of 80%, and so on. Similarly, ω_j would represent the (in)stability or (in)security of funding requirements, for example non-cancellable term deposits or non-surrenderable LH policies may have a weight of 0, retail deposits with a multi-product customer relationship or LH policies which are still under their surrender charge period may have a weighting of 20%, and so on.

Scenario Analysis

Meeting liquidity ratios during normal times may not be sufficient to ensure survival during times of stress. Management should also define coverage ratios which need to be met under relevant liquidity and funding stress scenarios. This is reflected in the FDIC requirements (FDIC, 2008) for measuring and managing liquidity risk, which state that "Contingency funding plans should incorporate events that could rapidly affect an institution's liquidity, including a sudden inability to securitize assets, tightening of collateral requirements or other restrictive terms associated with secured borrowings, or the loss of a large depositor or counterparty." In general, there are four types of stress scenario which can be considered.

- *Systemic stress scenarios.* Market-wide or systemic stress scenarios affect all institutions and all asset classes. Typically, such a stress scenario would include:
  - larger haircuts or longer time periods required to liquidate risky positions, associated with a general increase in risk aversion and a flight to quality;
  - general tightening or failure of funding alternatives, with wholesale or institutional funding becoming unavailable – this might be counteracted somewhat by a positive "flight to quality" as customers shift business to more financially secure companies;
  - assumptions with regard to the reactions of central banks and regulators in terms of liquidity provision, regulatory forbearance, etc.
- *Idiosyncratic stress scenarios.* Idiosyncratic scenarios are by definition firm specific, with funding sources "running for the exit" due to a perceived weakening in the firm's credit

quality. Idiosyncratic stress scenarios could include a firm-specific rating downgrade, events which trigger extraordinary cash calls (e.g., a natural catastrophe in an insurer's home market, a cash call from a guaranteed subsidiary, etc.).

■ *Cash flow and solvency scenarios.* Third, event scenarios which lead to a spike in cash or solvency requirements. For example, spiking interest rates may be beneficial for insurers from an economic perspective but lead to lower statutory surplus due to accounting artifacts.

■ *Combined stress events.* Finally, a combination of the above individual stress scenarios.

Firms should map each element of available and required liquidity onto underlying factors in order to see the aggregate impact of the scenario.

Based on this mapping, scenario-specific coverage ratios can be defined, some hypothetical and some historical, such as the default of a (or several) large fixed-income asset(s), under an extreme or shocked lapse scenario, with respect to asset and funding market conditions during the 2008 financial crisis, etc. Figure 18.4 illustrates how scenario-specific liquidity ratios can be displayed over different time horizons.

Making It Dynamic

At Swiss Re New Markets (SRNM), a funding liquidity risk management framework was developed similar to the one above. It began with an assessment of available and required liquidity resources, mapped the resulting cash flow profile into a static gap analysis, defined important factors which might influence the firm's liquidity profile and evaluated the liquidity gaps under different scenarios.

The issue faced was that SRNM was exposed to a wide variety of different contingent liquidity calls, including for example a large exposure to natural catastrophe risks through its

12-month rolling Cash Flow Coverage ratios
Best estimate and stress scenarios

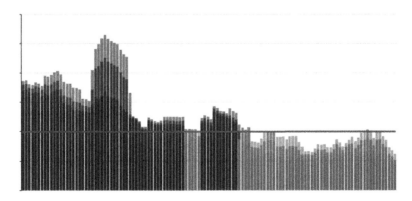

Target is a cash flow coverage ratio above 100%. The chart shows monthly cash flow coverage ratios for the next 12 months. The three shades show the best estimate (generally the highest), followed by the coverage ratio after default of the most important corporate counterparty and the coverage ratio after default of the 3 most important counterparties. The same analysis is done for other scenarios.

FIGURE 18.4 12-month rolling cash flow coverage ratios – best-estimate and stress scenarios

primary excess of loss insurance, short-term cash calls originating from derivatives positions, liquidity back stops for asset-backed commercial paper programs, etc. As a consequence, liquidity needs could pop up in many different currencies, triggered by many different events.

In order to ensure robust liquidity in the face of so many factors, a Monte Carlo simulation engine was built around the most important factors which might influence the liquidity position. By doing so, not only were the best-estimate and scenario liquidity ratios monitored, but a feeling was also obtained for the confidence intervals surrounding these ratios. In addition, a "VaR" envelope was calculated around the liquidity ratio, measuring the worst possible liquidity ratio over different time horizons.

This final step is not necessary for all institutions, especially where the liquidity profile is primarily driven by assumptions on asset liquidity and funding market availability. However, it may be desirable for those institutions which are exposed to complex contingent cash calls from a wide variety of different sources.

CHAPTER 19

Managing the Capital and Funding Structure

T he capital funding structure of a bank or insurer is defined by how much equity the group has available, how that equity is leveraged in order to finance the group's operating businesses and how capital and leverage resources are allocated and managed by the businesses.

The firm's funding structure has a direct influence on its solvency ratio, weighted average cost of capital, return on equity and shareholder dividend policy, with more equity implying higher solvency ratios and cost of capital but lower return on equity and dividend capacity. Although the subject of spirited debate, it is through these channels that the firm's funding structure has the potential to influence value. More specifically, balance sheet decisions influence both the quantum of capital required to finance the firm's operations as well as the cost of that capital. In addition, long-term funding forms the anchor around which the Treasury conducts cash and liquidity management activities.

This chapter focuses on how banks and insurers finance their investments in operating businesses along the debt-equity continuum; the allocation of economic capital from a value management perspective was discussed in Chapter 14.

There are many financing alternatives along the debt-equity continuum used to finance the firm's investment in operating businesses and as operating leverage. These alternatives include asset-backed financing (including mortgage backed securities, covered bonds, repurchase agreements), senior unsecured bonds, loans and deposits, subordinated debt, hybrid capital and shareholders' paid in capital. Appendix D: Beyond Debt and Equity describe this continuum.

CAPITAL FUNDING MANAGEMENT

Whether or not an "optimal" capital structure exists is the subject of much theoretical debate. This section presents a simple model describing how banks and insurers "optimize" their capital structure, with the rest of the chapter providing theoretical and empirical support.

Context

As illustrated in Figure 19.1, capital and funding decisions take place at two levels: at the group or holding company level and at the Treasury/operating business level.

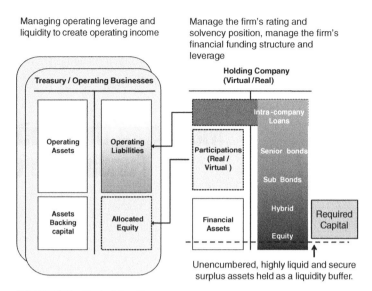

Managing operating leverage and liquidity to create operating income

Manage the firm's rating and solvency position, manage the firm's financial funding structure and leverage

FIGURE 19.1   Capital funding structure

Governance. The ALCO sets the group's target capital structure (equity and financial leverage) and allocates resources (economic capital and operating leverage) to the operating businesses through the strategic planning process. Operating businesses use economic capital and operating leverage to generate operating returns.

Difference between economic and externally defined capital. In general, the economic capital which is allocated from a strategic perspective is different from the capital defined by accountants, regulators and rating agencies for two reasons. First, because the latter are generally not defined on an economic basis: whereas economic capital represents value which can in principle be monetized and distributed to shareholders, the same cannot be said for book equity (which may include non-cash items such as goodwill, deferred acquisition costs, etc.), Tier 2 qualifying hybrid capital, etc. Second and related, because the liquidity, leverage and solvency conditions imposed by regulators and rating agencies represent constraints on value optimization and do not represent a measure of value itself. *Value managers manage value by allocating economic capital, subject to the constraints imposed by regulators and rating agencies.*

Determinants of capital structure. The group's capital structure, solvency and leverage ratios need to meet minimum regulatory requirements at all times. Banks and insurers generally target higher solvency ratios, choosing to hold more capital than the minimum required by regulators. The exact level of excess capital depends on a variety of factors specific to the firm and the industry.

The bank or insurer meets its capital and solvency target with a combination of equity and qualifying hybrid securities. As the name implies, hybrid securities lay somewhere along the debt–equity continuum; they often receive favorable treatment by rating agencies and regulators for calculating solvency ratios and have a lower after-tax cost of capital than the cost imputed to equity capital due to the deductability of coupon payments.

Financing the businesses and subsidiaries. In addition to equity, the group also finances operating businesses through *financial leverage*, defined as *hybrid capital, senior and subordinated bonds issued in the capital markets by the group or holding company.*

The total capital allocated to operating businesses is generally greater than the consolidated equity of the group. The difference between the two is called *double leverage*, defined as the difference between the *sum of the equity allocated to operating subsidiaries or businesses and the group's consolidated equity.*[1] Barring cross-holdings of equity and internal debt at the subsidiary level, double leverage is financed entirely by financial leverage and is a powerful tool for mitigating the effects of uneconomic capital or reserve requirements from a consolidated group perspective (discussed later). Financial and double leverage at the group has to be serviced by dividends from operating subsidiaries.

Accessing the capital markets to raise equity, hybrid capital and bonds is generally limited to the group or holding company for two reasons: first, because the group typically has a better rating and better access to the capital markets than the operating subsidiaries and second, because of the need to manage the group's consolidated solvency and leverage ratios.

Financial and Operating Leverage and Cash Planning

Financial leverage represents a call on future earnings and a strain on the cash flow to the group. Projected dividends from operating subsidiaries must be sufficient to cover the cash commitments to financial leverage as well as the dividend to shareholders. While leverage ratios can fluctuate to cover dividends and other contingencies, the capital budget and management policy should lead to a sustainable cash flow pattern from operating businesses.

Financing operating assets. Business units can leverage their allocated economic capital through *operating leverage*, defined as *all other forms of financing used by the Treasury and operating businesses to lever assets in the pursuit of operating returns.* Operating leverage excludes equity, hybrid capital and bonds, and includes inter-bank loans, structured notes, collateralized financing such as securities borrowing and lending, (reverse) repurchase agreements, (asset-backed) commercial paper programs, covered or asset-backed bonds, as well as derivatives such as credit default swaps if used to create a leveraged position in the underlying.

Because operating leverage adds to the group's overall leverage ratio, it needs to be monitored closely and allocated as a scarce resource by the ALCO to business units and Treasury during the strategic planning process.

On the difference between financial and operating leverage. In addition to the differences in form, the most important difference between financial and operating leverage is that *the cost of operating leverage is directly deducted as an expense from the operating business unit; in contrast, the cost of financial leverage is deducted from the corporate segment but is included in the weighted average cost of capital used as the hurdle rate when measuring the economic value added from the operating units.*

Rules of the Game for Managing the Firm's Capital Structure

Large banks and insurers[2] follow a relatively simple process for defining their own, unique "optimal" capital structure.

---

[1]Standard & Poor's (2012) defines "Double leverage (DL) holding company investments in subsidiaries divided by holding company (unconsolidated) shareholders' equity. DL renders the non-operating holding company (NOHC) dependent in part on dividends to meet interest payments on external debt . . . High DL – of 120% or more – is a sign of aggressive liquidity and capital management." See also Standard & Poor's (2013).

[2]The following discussion is relevant for large, diversified banks and insurers who are active in the capital markets. It has less relevance for mutual organizations or firms which are local in character.

First, they *define a long-term rating aspiration*, a critical decision given banks' and insurers' high reliance on leverage to create value. The rating aspiration depends on two firm-specific factors: the business model (with more credit-sensitive businesses requiring a higher rating) and managerial preferences and risk appetite (with the management of some firms simply preferring to have more balance sheet security than others). In addition, it also depends on the rating profile of competitors and the evaluation criteria applied by public rating agencies.

Second, the *rating aspiration determines a target level and ranges for solvency capital and leverage* which are generally more conservative than the minimum regulatory requirements.

Third, firms *maximize leverage within these ranges in a manner consistent with their business strategy and risk appetite*.

- All firms maximize financial leverage at the holding company level, accepting hybrid and senior debt issuance to the upper end of the range in an attempt to lower their weighted average cost of capital and recapture diversification benefits through the use of double leverage. However, some issuance capacity is kept available (e.g., for strategic acquisitions, subsidiary cash calls, dividend financing or periods of stress).
- At the operating level, businesses maximize operational leverage in a manner consistent with their strategy:
  - businesses which use leverage dynamically to increase risk assets (e.g., trading operations) will maximize operating leverage subject to the risk and operating leverage constraints imposed by ALCO, implying that leverage ratios will vary over time, leveraging/accumulating risk assets when risk capacity is available and deleveraging/decumulating risk assets when risk capacity is binding;[3]
  - businesses which do not use leverage dynamically (e.g., insurance companies and retail/commercial banks) target a stable debt/equity financing structure based on the (relatively stable) capital intensity of the business.

This simple approach leads to the following "rules of the game."

RULES OF THE GAME: CAPITAL FUNDING MANAGEMENT

Capital and leverage are group resources managed on behalf of shareholders within the constraints imposed by regulators and rating agencies.

ECONOMIC VS. EXTERNAL CAPITAL DEFINITIONS

The group distinguishes between *external capital*, defined and used by regulators and rating agencies, and *economic capital*. Economic capital, defined as the economic value invested in the operating business which can in principle be returned to shareholders, is the basis for strategic capital allocation decisions and for evaluating the value created by a business; externally defined capital measures and requirements represent constraints to capital and leverage decisions.

---

[3]This approach is consistent with the evidence presented in Chapter 13.

OPTIMAL CAPITAL STRUCTURE DRIVEN BY EXTERNAL CONSTRAINTS

1. The firm is committed to always meeting minimum regulatory capital requirements for the group and for each local operating entity and holds capital in excess of the minimum regulatory requirements in each balance sheet.
2. Management sets a target rating for the group based on *its business model, management's risk appetite and peer rating comparison.* This target rating implicitly defines its target capital structure as well as solvency and leverage ranges.
3. The firm periodically reviews its rating aspiration and can deviate from the target rating, solvency and leverage ratios in the short run (e.g., due to a strategic acquisition or an unexpected loss), but manages its dividend policy, retained earnings and risk profile so as to bring it back within the target ranges over time.

LEVERAGE CAPACITY

The leverage capacity belongs to the group and is managed as a group resource.

1. As part of the capital budgeting process, leverage capacity is first split between *group financial leverage,* used to optimize the group's weighted average cost of capital, and *operational leverage,* allocated to the businesses to finance operating income.
2. The group *optimizes its financial leverage to lower its weighted average cost of capital* within its target rating aspiration and regulatory constraints:
   a. utilizing significantly its issuance capacity for *qualifying hybrid capital* (a substitute for shareholder equity) and *senior unsecured bonds (*as double leverage to recapture diversification benefits across the group);
   b. however, some leverage capacity is kept in reserve to meet contingencies and consistent with its funding liquidity risk appetite;
   c. *only the group can raise equity and financial leverage in the form of hybrid capital and senior, unsecured bonds.*
3. *Operating leverage is allocated to the subsidiaries and business units* in a manner consistent with their business model and strategic plans. *Operating leverage* may include intra-company loans, commercial paper programs, structured note and asset-backed securities issuance capacity, inter-bank borrowing, collateralized borrowing through repurchase agreements, securities lending and borrowing arrangements, etc.

MANAGING ECONOMIC CAPITAL

Excess capital and cash resources belong to the group and are managed as a group resource.

1. Economic solvency targets are set by the group based on its risk appetite and form a binding constraint at the group level. Economic solvency targets are generally not set for operating businesses or, if they are, they are not strictly binding in order to reduce the constraints on dividend paying capacity and capital fungibility.

2. In order to retain flexibility, the firm *keeps as much as possible of the group's excess capital at the holding company level in a liquid, unencumbered and transferable form.*

3. Subsidiaries and sub-holding companies are physically capitalized to the *minimum regulatory capital requirements* (or rating agency requirements, if an external rating is needed) *plus a prudent buffer* to cover the possible volatility in local solvency ratios.

4. The number of subsidiaries with an external public rating is kept to a minimum in order to increase capital flexibility across the group; externally rated subsidiaries should be positioned strategically so as to reduce any limitations on capital fungibility.

5. Intra-group transactions are used to improve capital efficiency, fungibility and transferability, including for example reinsurance, derivatives or asset sales to improve the diversification benefits recognized at the group or circumvent uneconomic capital or serve requirements in the operating entities.

6. Most subsidiaries' growth is financed *through retained earnings*. If funding for planned growth is in excess of retained earnings, it is funded by capital allocated from the group as part of the capital budgeting and allocation process.

7. All earnings in excess of those required for planned growth *are transferred to the group as a cash dividend.*

DIVIDEND POLICY

The group's *dividend policy is set through the capital budgeting process consistent* with the group's target solvency ratio, return on equity and planned growth.

1. In general, growth and regular dividends are funded out of retained earnings. Increased financial leverage deviating from the firm's target financing structure can be used to bridge gaps, but returning to the target structure over time.

2. The firm's regular dividend policy should be predictable and progressive. Any capital accumulated in excess of the target can be returned to shareholders through share repurchases or special dividends.

DETERMINING THE OPTIMAL CAPITAL STRUCTURE

There is a long debate whether value can be created simply by changing the mix between a firm's equity and different forms of debt. This debate began in the 1950s with the seminal work by Modigliani and Miller (1958) in the context of industrial corporations and has recently been "modernized" to reflect the specifics of financial services firms.

In a nutshell, the debate is about whether dividing the firm's earnings between debt and equity (or, by extension, other forms of financing) can increase the value of one source of financing without coming at the expense of another. In other words, is capital structure nothing but a zero-sum game?

The Intuition

The Modigliani–Miller (MM) theorem states the conditions under which the capital financing structure of the firm is a zero-sum game, with changes to the capital structure representing a shift of value between shareholders and debt holders. If these conditions are met, then the capital structure of the firm is irrelevant for the aggregate value of the firm and only determines which source of financing, debt or equity, will get more of the pie.

Merton Miller, who shared the Nobel Prize in part for this work, summarized the zero-sum argument in his testimony in Glendale Federal Bank's lawsuit against the US government in 1997 (Gifford, 1998): "I have a simple explanation [for the first Modigliani–Miller proposition]. It's after the ball game, and the pizza man comes up to Yogi Berra and he says, 'Yogi, how do you want me to cut this pizza, into quarters?' Yogi says, 'No, cut it into eight pieces, I'm feeling hungry tonight.' Now when I tell that story the usual reaction is, 'And you mean to say that they gave you a [Nobel] prize for that?'"

The strong result of financing structure irrelevance depends on two strong assumptions.

- First, any financing decision by the firm can be "reversed" by investors. This implies that investors with different preferences are not willing to pay more or less for a specific financing profile because they can always achieve the profile on their own.
- Second, the financing decision does not influence the operating cash flow profile of the firm, ensuring that the "size of the pizza" is not affected by financing decisions.

The concrete assumptions needed for the MM theorem are listed below, including an assessment of whether there is an advantage to debt or equity financing if the assumptions are relaxed. In general, there is an advantage to increasing debt levels.

First, there are *no distortionary taxes*. If interest payments to debt holders are tax deductible but dividends are not, then the tax shield on debt represents additional value in terms of a lower overall tax bill. This tax distortion influences the "size of the pizza" which is distributable to shareholders and debt holders. *Advantage: debt.*

Second, *capital markets are efficient and frictionless and both investors and firms can access debt financing at the same terms.* This allows shareholders and debt holders to releverage or deleverage their positions to any desired leverage ratio which might fit their personal risk profile. As a consequence, investors do not have a personal preference for firms with different leverage but the same operating assets. *Advantage: debt* (as it is realistic to assume that shareholders may face a higher cost of leverage than large public firms).

Third, there are *no bankruptcy costs or frictional costs* which could dissipate the firm's value away from debt and equity holders in the event of an insolvency. *Advantage: equity* (as frictional bankruptcy costs represent a cost impacting the "size of the pizza" in the event of bankruptcy, a cost which is borne by all financiers of the firm and should therefore be avoided).

Fourth, there are *no information asymmetries between managers and other stakeholders*, including shareholders, depositors and policy holders, and *managers' incentives are aligned to those of both the debt and equity holders* of the firm. If there are information asymmetries, then management may have an incentive to squander resources for their own personal gain. Alternatively, if managers' incentives are not aligned with *both* debt and equity holders, then they might have an incentive to take higher risk decisions with the attitude "Heads I win, tails equity and bond holders lose." *Advantage: mixed, but leaning toward a balance between debt and equity* (as an optimal contract between managers and the firm).

Complications for Banks and Insurers

There are several additional factors which may influence the funding structure of financial services firms, including the existence of explicit or implicit guarantees, minimum regulatory capital requirements, the incentives to take risk and the ability to create value from liabilities.

Table 19.1 provides a summary of the most important factors influencing a bank's or insurer's financing decisions from a theoretical perspective; a more detailed discussion follows.

TABLE 19.1   Factors influencing capital structure for financial institutions

Factors affecting all corporations . . .	Advantage goes to . . .
Tax shield on interest payments	Debt
Differences in cost of borrowing, corporations vs. individual shareholders	Debt
Frictional bankruptcy costs	Equity
Information asymmetries	Debt
Factors specifically affecting financial service firms . . .	**Advantage goes to . . .**
Subsidized debt through implicit or explicit guarantees	Debt
Minimum regulatory requirements and associated "buffers"	Equity
Asymmetric information, principal–agent problems, moral hazard and signaling	Debt
Value created by customer liabilities	Debt
Double leverage to recapture diversification benefit	Debt
Overall advantage:	**Debt**

A quick glance at Table 19.1 leads to the conclusion that, at least theoretically, the advantage goes to debt financing. Barring other considerations (discussed later on), the consequence is that banks and insurance companies should hold the minimum capital required by regulators and maximize their use of leverage.

Implicit and Explicit Support Mechanisms

Explicit or implicit guarantees or other support mechanisms give an advantage to debt financing if debt holders become less sensitive to the credit quality of the firm and if the guarantee is provided by a third party at a subsidized (or zero) cost.

Capital structure distortions caused by implicit or explicit guarantees are summarized by Harrison (2004): "These can provide a free option to the bank owners who can increase their value by increasing leverage. At an extreme, a full government guarantee of a bank would push the optimal bank balance sheet structure to the corner solution of being totally debt funded . . ."

Implicit or explicit guarantees can generate significant economic distortions, both directly through the pricing of debt and indirectly by influencing management's behavior. This raises the obvious question: Why do such implicit or explicit support mechanisms exist? Sidebar 19.1 answers this question.

SIDEBAR 19.1: ADDRESSING EXTERNALITIES: EXPLICIT AND IMPLICIT SUPPORT MECHANISMS

Implicit or explicit support for banks or insurers can be explained as a public policy response to micro- and macro-externalities. *Externalities* are defined as *economic consequences or spill-overs on a third, unrelated party stemming from decisions taken by others operating in their own self-interest.* In other words, what you do impacts other people.

MICRO-EXTERNALITIES

Consider a bank defaulting on its deposits or an insurer on its policies. These actions may place a burden greater than the direct loss on the bank's customers to the extent that the individuals are not able to manage the consequences without some form of public support. In this case, the consequences are felt not only in the direct private costs but also as social costs through the public support mechanisms.

MACRO-EXTERNALITIES, OR SYSTEMIC RELEVANCE

Macro-externalities, as the name implies, are bigger and more systemic in their consequences. Some banks may be so large and interconnected that a bankruptcy will not only affect their own customers, but also reverberate through the banking sector and ultimately impact the broader economy. As Thomas Huertas of the FSA explained in his speech to the London School of Economics in 2010, "(Some) banks are highly interconnected with one another. The failure of one bank may weaken the banks which had exposure to the failed bank . . . that can produce losses in liquidity and/or capital that the still solvent bank(s) must be able to withstand and, if need be, offset . . . their failure would potentially give rise to a much larger social cost."

 The insolvency of a large bank may cause a "domino effect," contributing to the insolvency of other banks; this is a first-order externality. More critical are the higher-order effects, including the potential for a system-wide decrease in credit availability and the disruption in payment and settlement activities, both leading to a decrease in economic activity. Such institutions are called G or D-SIFIs, an acronym for Globally- or Domestically- Systemically Important Financial Institutions.

Examples Examples of explicit guarantees on bank liabilities include deposit insurance such as that provided by the FDIC in the USA, an independent agency created to maintain stability and public confidence in the nation's financial system by insuring deposits, as well as similar schemes in other countries.

 Schemes also exist in the insurance industry, covering at least part of any losses from failed coverage. One example is the Insurance Guarantee Fund in the USA, "When a company is found to be in poor financial condition, regulators can take various actions to try to save it. Insolvencies do occur, however, despite the best efforts of regulators. All states have procedures through which the property/casualty insurance industry covers claims against insolvent insurers" (Insurance Information Network of California, 2008).

 However, some support mechanisms may only be implicit. The financial crisis of 2008 provided examples of implicit support mechanisms for financial institutions which were deemed to be "too big to fail," summarized in Hildebrand (2008): "In the current crisis, government protection has become manifest and explicit in the form of the recent G7 and G20 communiques (which) . . . declared[4] unambiguously that they, 'agree to take decisive action and use all available tools to support systemically important financial institutions and prevent their failure'. In other words, governments imply that large banks are simply 'too big to fail'."

---

[4]G7 Finance Ministers and Central Bank Governors Plan of Action.

TABLE 19.2   Support mechanisms announced or implemented during the 2008 financial crisis

	Asset		Liabilities and capital		
	Asset guarantees	Asset purchase programs	Expand or introduce retail deposit schemes	Guarantee wholesale borrowing	Bank capital injections
Australia			✓		
Canada					
France	✓			✓	✓
Germany	✓	✓	✓		✓
Italy					✓
Japan		✓			✓
Netherlands	✓		✓	✓	✓
Spain			✓	✓	✓
Switzerland	✓	✓	✓		✓
UK	✓		✓	✓	✓
USA	✓	✓	✓	✓	✓

Note: Check marks represent measures announced and/or used (Schich, 2009, author's analysis).

Schich (2009) summarizes the actions taken by governments during the crisis, ranging from full and partial guarantees for specific financing arrangements such as deposits or senior debt, direct asset purchases or guarantees on specific blocks of assets and capital injections (see Table 19.2).

Impact on the Cost of Debt   Explicit and implicit support translates into a lower cost of debt financing as it makes debt holders less sensitive to the creditworthiness of the firm. This benefit is explicitly recognized by rating agencies, with Standard & Poor's stating (2011a): "The support framework criteria factors in the likelihood of support from a government or parent . . . For a private-sector commercial bank . . . , the criteria assess the likelihood of government support by drawing on assessments of both the bank's 'systemic importance' . . . and the government's tendency to support private-sector commercial banks."

The benefits can be substantial, as evidenced after the crisis when support was withdrawn. The *Daily Mail* (Shipman, 2011) commented: "Confidence in UK banking system rocked as agency downgrades 12 bank and building society credit ratings . . . Moody's said the downgrades followed the Government telling the banks to stand on their own two feet rather than rely in future on taxpayer bailouts. The agency said it believes the institutions are now at greater risk . . . (and the) decision will make it harder for banks to borrow and loan."

Implications for Management Behavior   Implicit and explicit support also affects managerial decisions, leading to an increase in risk taking relative to if the support was not available. This is an example of *moral hazard*, defined as a *situation where a party has a tendency to take risks because the losses are not borne solely by the party taking the risk.*

The connection between implied guarantees, financing structure and moral hazard is well summarized in a speech by Hildebrand (2008), "No sane banker will intentionally manage his bank into insolvency. But he or she has a lower incentive to avoid insolvency than if he were not insured. This sub-optimal level of caution is immediately apparent in banks' balance sheets: Banks tend to hold very low levels of capital . . . (and) have a preference for very high leverage."

There is a substantial literature on the size and distortionary effects of such implicit or explicit guarantees. Interested readers are referred to Akerloff and Romer (1993), Miller (1995), Harrison (2004), Geanakoplos (2010) and Admati *et al.* (2010).

Regulatory Response   International regulations have been reformed in an effort to address the externalities from banks which are deemed "too big to fail," described in Sidebar 19.2.

SIDEBAR 19.2: REGULATORY RESPONSE TO "TOO BIG TO FAIL" INSTITUTIONS

There are several proposals currently being debated designed to mitigate systemic risk and the negative consequences of implicit or explicit guarantees. Broadly speaking, these measures fall into three areas.

RAISE THE BAR, GENERICALLY

A natural response to systemic risk is to raise the bar for *all* market participants in order to make sure that fewer firms, large or small, go bankrupt in the next crisis.

One avenue is to increase capital requirements and the quality of capital. This is currently being done under Basel III for banks and Solvency II for European insurers. For example, the minimum Tier 1 capital requirement increased from 2% to 4.5% under Basel III and many regulators are requiring higher margins; when these new thresholds are combined with the way that required capital is measured, especially capital requirements for trading books, even "well-capitalized" banks under Basel II needed to raise capital to meet Basel II requirements. Similarly, Solvency II is likely to trigger an increase in capital requirements within some firms in the European insurance industry.

Another response is to introduce blunt, notional constraints on leverage, especially if risk is difficult to measure. The motivation for such measures is summarized in Hildebrand (2008): "In an ideal world, we would of course also want to take into account the riskiness of banks' assets . . . To compensate for differences in banks' assets, we would ideally require banks with riskier assets to hold more capital. The Basel Committee . . . has embraced precisely such a risk-weighted approach. More risk, more capital. If we lived in an ideal world, this simple principle would work well. By 'ideal', I mean a world in which risks can be observed by everybody and assessed precisely. What has become abundantly clear in recent months is that we do not live in an ideal world. Banks and the risk they incur are far from transparent . . . What Basel II needs, therefore, is a safeguard to provide the financial system with additional protection against (this opacity) . . . Which brings me back to the obvious and simple response to excessive leverage: The imposition of a limit on banks' leverage as a complement to the risk-weighted approach reflected in the current Basel framework."

RAISE THE BAR, SPECIFICALLY FOR G-SIFIs

A second response is to focus higher regulatory attention specifically on those firms who are deemed "too big to fail" while promoting economic Darwinism for all remaining firms. In this context, regulators are advocating additional capital requirements for G-SIFIs. This designation includes not only G-SIBs and G-SIIs, standing for "banks" and "insurers," respectively, but potentially also non-bank financial institutions such as asset managers. In order to accomplish this, two contentious issues are in the process of being resolved.

- First, the concrete criteria to be used to distinguish SIFIs from ordinary banks or insurance companies. These designation criteria are hotly debated[5] and include indicators of size, complexity, interconnectedness, the lack of ready substitutes and global activities. For insurance companies, the distinction between traditional insurance versus *non-traditional* and *non-insurance activities (NTNI)* is playing a role in the debate as it is generally accepted that *traditional* insurance activities are not systemically relevant (IAIS, 2013).
- Second, the implications of being categorized as an SIFI, with three areas emerging including recovery and resolution planning, higher loss absorbency (a euphemism for higher capital requirements) and increased supervision and risk management requirements, as outlined in the FSB's (2012) update: "G-SIFIs are required to meet higher supervisory expectations for risk management functions, data aggregation capabilities, risk governance and internal controls."

ISOLATE SYSTEMIC ACTIVITIES

There have been three important policy recommendations put forward, all of which have a common thread: ring fencing "core" banking activities and "non-core" trading or investment banking activities such that, if government support is needed, it is to the benefit of customers and not shareholders or managers.

The Volcker Rule

In the USA the Volcker Rule, named after the former US Federal Reserve Chairman, Paul Volcker, is a part of the Dodd–Frank Wall Street Reform and Consumer Protection Act (US Securities and Exchange Commission, 2011).[6] It was approved in December 2013 with effect in 2015 (Patterson, 2013). The proposal specifically prohibits a bank or institution that owns a bank from "speculative" activities for its own account (e.g., activities which do not benefit customers – including proprietary trading and owning or investing in a hedge or private equity fund).

The Vickers Report

In the UK, an Independent Commission on Banking chaired by John Vickers was established in June 2010 to consider reforms to the UK banking sector which would promote financial stability and competition (UK Government Policy Paper, 2012). The Commission made its recommendations to the UK government in September 2011. Similar

---

[5]See, for example, Forbes 9.04.2014, "MetLife plans to fight 'Systemically Important' Designation".

[6]For a concise summary, see also Morrison and Foerster (2010).

to the Volcker Rule, the headline was that British banks should "ring-fence" their retail banking divisions from their investment banking arms; however, it falls short of the Volcker Rule by not proscribing such activities. The government announced the same day that it would introduce legislation into Parliament aimed at implementing the recommendations.

The Liikanen Report

The Liikanen Report, published in October (2012), was prepared at the behest of the European Commission by a group led by Erkki Liikanen, Governor of the Bank of Finland and ECB Council Member. The report considered structural reforms to the EU banking sector to promote financial stability during a period of heightened uncertainty regarding EU sovereign and bank debt.

The recommendations were similar to the Volcker Rule and the Vickers Report, advocating the strict "ring-fencing" of proprietary and third-party trading activities both in terms of risk management and capital allocation: "The trading division will have to hold its own capital, meaning that it stands or falls by its own activities and cannot, in theory at least, knock over the bread-and-butter retail banking operations. The idea is to get taxpayers off the hook by ensuring that governments do not have to step in to safeguard deposits if traders blow a hole in their balance sheet." The Liikanen Report also advocates a better alignment of executive pay with long-term objectives, notably by including a long-term, "fixed-income" component in bankers' bonuses, "meaning they could be written down if short-term profits yield long-term troubles."

Similar proposals regarding the structure of pay were made by the Squam Report (French et al., 2010), discussed in the context of incentives and performance management in Chapter 14.

Minimum Regulatory Capital Requirements

Banks and insurance companies differ from industrial corporations in that they are highly regulated entities which face minimum capital requirements. Managerial risk aversion leading to capital in excess of the minimum requirements makes the possibility of regulatory intervention more remote (Carney, 2013).

In addition, Gropp and Heider (2009) point out that banks (and, by extension, other regulated financial services entities) hold a "buffer" on top of the minimum regulatory requirements in order to minimize the potential dilution and value destruction from an emergency capital raising: "Raising equity on short notice in order to avoid violating the capital requirement is costly. Banks may therefore hold discretionary capital to reduce the probability that they have to incur this cost."

This line of argument has an intuitive appeal: having the benefit of sitting in a well-capitalized firm during the 2008 crisis, my vicarious impression was that even a distant possibility of a forced capital raising was sufficient for the market to deeply discount the shares of those less fortunate. In some instances, the effect seemed discontinuous, with a small threat being sufficient to tip the scales and leading to a dramatic decline in share value.

Opaque Risk Taking Enhances the Principal–Agent Problem

As mentioned previously, the MM theory can break down if the activities of managers are opaque and if their incentives differ from those of the firm's shareholders and creditors.

The Principal–Agent Problem . . . One can consider shareholders to be the "principals" of the firm and management their "agents." If the activities of the agent are opaque to the principals, then a *principal–agent problem* can occur, defined as a situation where *management (the agents) may take actions which are in their own best interests but not necessarily in the interests of shareholders (the principals).*

In their seminal work, Jensen and Meckling (1976) assume that management has an incentive to divert profits and surreptitiously capture personal benefits. Such a situation may also occur in financial services with potential examples including overly aggressive M&A activity[7] and the inappropriate use of corporate resources.[8]

If direct monitoring is costly, a higher leverage ratio may be useful because it puts more pressure on management to "be good" (Pinegar and Wilbricht, 1989) due to the burden of a fixed expense. The conclusion, summarized in French *et al.* (2010), is that "Debt is valuable in a bank's capital structure because it provides an important disciplining force for management."

. . . Complicated by Moral Hazard The principal–agent problem becomes even more challenging in financial service firms given the limited liability nature of the firm and the potential for governmental support. Admati *et al.* (2010) suggest that "Equity holders have no interest in disciplining (excessive risk taking) and might even be complicit in undermining mechanisms to do so . . . Given the fixity of their claims, debt holders do not participate in the high returns in the event of success, but are burdened with the increased risk and increased cost of default . . . The phrase 'heads I win, tails the creditor or the taxpayer loses' captures the essence of a problem that has led to many banking crises of the past."

Paradoxically, even higher levels of debt, and especially subordinated debt whose value is more sensitive to changes in the firm's risk profile, may be part of the answer both as a disciplining and signaling device. Admati *et al.* (2010) point out, "Debt, as a hard claim that must be periodically renewed, (may) . . . provide market discipline that enhances corporate governance and prevents bank managers from taking excessive risk or mismanaging the firm." Gropp *et al.* (2004) estimate the role of subordinated bank debt in signaling the risk of the issuing bank, a subject which has also been explored in Berger *et al.* (2000), DeYoung *et al.* (2001), Bongini *et al.* (2002) and others.

Profitable Liabilities

While debt finances productive assets in industrial corporations, some bank and insurance liabilities actually create value in their own right. As a consequence, increasing customer liabilities actually increases the "size of the pie."

Customer deposits and structured investments sold to wealth management clients are products which can contribute significantly to the profitability of a bank. Oliver Wyman (OWC, 2013) estimates that 18–19% of the total European retail banking revenues came from current accounts in 2011–12 and that a further 13–15% came from associated products including small business liabilities, savings and overdrafts. In addition to generating customer

---

[7]Consider the RBS/ABN Amro acquisition, with Sir Goodwin's behavior captioned as "Hubris, over-arching vanity and how one man's ego brought banking to the brink" (*Daily Mail*, 2009).

[8]"Cue Todd Thomson, chief executive officer of Citigroup Inc.'s Global Wealth Management division . . . (who) was fired . . . for 'lapses in judgment' including 'the inappropriate use of company aircraft . . . (and installation) of a wood burning fireplace in his (Manhattan skyscraper) office'" (Lewis, 2007).

margins from deposits, information from deposit accounts can also improve asset underwriting. Similarly, the bulk of the value created by insurers originates from the liability side of the balance sheet by issuing well-underwritten policies.

Double Leverage to Recapture Diversification Benefits

Double leverage can be used to "recapture" group diversification benefits and mitigate the impact of uneconomic capital requirements.[9]

There are often restrictions which force groups to write business into different legal entities as opposed to into a single legal entity, for example restrictions on cross-border transactions and limitations on combining activities in the same balance sheet to name two of the most important.

These restrictions, and any other non-economic restrictions, artificially increase the total capital required by the group.

- Economic capital depends on risk and diversification: for example, insurers lower the economic capital required per unit of exposure through diversification. Barriers to recognizing diversification create uneconomic, "locked excess capital" from a group perspective.
- In addition, local capital and reserve requirements may reflect a level of prudence which is not economically justified; examples include equalization reserves for European PC insurers and XXX mortality reserves in the USA.

This uneconomic, locked excess capital adversely affects the value of the firm. The sum of the capital invested in all subsidiaries would be significantly more than the economic capital required to support the consolidated group on a "look-through" basis, implying lower capital efficiency, higher CERs and a lower value of excess returns.[10] In addition, locked excess capital also represents a constraint on growing profitable business if growth is to be funded from internal sources.

Double leverage can mitigate this frictional cost as long as the group's total capital requirements are determined on a "look-through" basis when rating agencies and regulators evaluate the capital requirements and debt-bearing capacity of the holding company. In this case, the holding company can raise debt equal to the diversification benefit or uneconomic reserve requirements and then downstream the proceeds as "equity participations" in the operating subsidiaries. From a consolidated view, the group holds the capital required "as if" all the business were held in a single balance sheet with no non-economic distortions.

However, a full "look through" may not be possible as it would imply that:

- the group is committed to supporting all subsidiaries in case of a local insolvency, so long as the resources are available elsewhere in the group, representing an implicit guarantee;

---

[9]An additional channel is through the tax benefits from debt issuance at the group level. See, e.g., Hsu (2000).

[10]See our earlier discussion on the CER. Theoretically, this frictional cost would not exist if shareholders had perfect information, clearly distinguishing between the minimum level of capital required and the actual required capital. Under these conditions, it might be argued that the firm's weighted average cost of capital should be lower (assuming that the excess capital was invested in riskless assets). However, financial service conglomerates are generally more complex and opaque by their nature.

■ any excess economic value is either held at the group or can somehow make its way from one subsidiary to another as needed.

These conditions will not be fully met in practice because some of the excess capital may remain locked locally. As such, it may not be possible to use double leverage to fully recapture the diversification benefit or mitigate uneconomic capital requirements. However, double leverage is not the only way to "recapture" diversification benefits. Other approaches include intra-group risk transfer arrangements such as asset sales, reinsurance and derivative transactions as well as limited or full guarantees, which unfortunately may also be limited by regulators and rating agencies.

THE EMPIRICAL REALITY: WHAT DETERMINES CAPITAL STRUCTURE?

Looking again at Table 19.1, debt seems to have the clear advantage over equity financing. As a consequence, banks and insurers should theoretically hold capital very close to the minimum regulatory requirements. However, the empirical evidence is more complex.

More Than the Minimum, Linked to Size and Risk Profile . . .

The fact is that banks and insurance companies hold capital in excess of the minimum requirements imposed by regulatory constraints, with the amount related to the size and risk profile of the firm. For example, Barth *et al.* (2005), Berger *et al.* (2008), Brewer *et al.* (2008), Flannery and Rangan (2008), Gropp and Heider (2009) and Berlin (2011) have noted that banks choose to hold capital in excess of minimum capital requirements.

Berger *et al.* (2008) state: "Since the mid-1990s, the typical large US banking organization has substantially exceeded even these highest supervisory standards . . . As of March 2008 . . . the 70 BHCs (Bank Holding Companies) with assets exceeding $10 billion had a mean Tier 1 leverage ratio of 7.04%, a Tier 1 risk-based ratio of 8.55% and a total risk-based capital ratio of 11.08%; in each of these categories, between 90–95% of these companies exceeded the well-capitalized levels."

Similar levels of over-capitalization have also been recognized in the insurance industry. For example, most insurers in the USA hold capital in excess of the minimum implied by a 100% RBC ratio, the level at which the supervisor takes control of the company, or even 200%, the level at which a management action plan is required. In fact, most insurers in the USA have solvency ratios higher than 300+% (NAIC, 2009).

Berlin (2011) lists three common observations regarding the leverage of banks. The first is that larger institutions tend to be more highly levered. This is a natural consequence if there is a fixed cost to capital market access, for example the cost of a public rating, or if the larger banks are considered by the market as being "too big to fail."

The second is that leverage tends to decrease with risk; in other words, the higher the risk of the portfolio, the lower the leverage. This is logical if bankruptcy is to be avoided. Both of these observations are also supported by Guo and Winter (1997) for the PC insurance industry; they find that leverage is increasing with firm size and decreasing with the loss ratio uncertainty, a measure of risk.

. . . But Cross-sectional Variations are Difficult to Explain . . .

Berlin (2011) states that beyond these two factors, there is a "limited understanding of the cross-sectional variation in bank capital structure choices." The same is true in the insurance industry: although the parameter estimates for risk, size and rating in Guo and Winter are all statistically significant, the adjusted R-squared of the regression is only 6.5%, suggesting that the model explains only a small part of the cross-sectional variation in capital structure for insurance companies.

In other words, *we cannot really explain firm-specific capital funding decisions beyond the observation that leverage tends to be increasing in firm size and decreasing in risk.*

Frustrated, researchers have adopted the more agnostic concept of "firm fixed effects," summarized by Berlin (2011): "We know it is there, and we know that it helps explain the firm's choice of capital structure; we just don't know what it is. This finding is a challenge for the . . . theory because it suggests that much of the variation in firms' leverage is potentially explicable by some model of firm decision making, just not the one that we have."

Under the more agnostic "fixed effects" model, individual firms somehow decide how much capital to hold and then dynamically adjust their financing to attain their target structure. Berlin (2011) comments: "(T)he empirical evidence is consistent with a dynamic trade-off model in which firms choose a target leverage ratio to which they actively adjust over some period of time."

This "agnostic" view is also supported by the empirical work of Gropp and Heider (2009), who comment: "Like non-financial firms, banks have stable capital structure targets at levels that are specific to each individual bank. These targets do not seem to be determined by standard corporate finance variables or by regulation, but rather by deeper, so far unobserved parameters that remain fixed during long periods of time for each institution."

. . . With Firm-specific Factors Explaining a Lot

In general, a firm's rating is a critical target variable for the company and the CFO. Kisgen (2006) notes generically[11] that "credit ratings are the second highest concerns for CFOs when determining their capital structure, with 57.1% of CFOs saying that credit ratings were important or very important in how they choose the appropriate amount of debt for their firm." Leverage plays an even bigger role in banking and insurance, so it is easy to see how CROs and CFOs of financial institutions pay an even higher attention to their debt rating.

However, the rating aspiration of a firm is largely driven by factors unique to the firm; in my experience, there are three firm-specific factors which determine a bank's or insurer's target rating.

Some Businesses Require a Higher Rating

The first is the firm's business strategy, with some businesses requiring a higher rating in order to serve customers. Kisgen (2006) suggests that a higher rating is a prerequisite to serving credit-sensitive customers, in addition to implying a lower cost and increased access to leverage, important for some trading businesses.

Empirical observations support these views in insurance. Kartasheva and Park (2011) find that insurance companies writing short-tail property risks tend to have a lower rating than

---

[11]Citing evidence from Graham and Harvey (2001).

writers of PC commercial, long-tail casualty and excess lines where the ability to meet large claims over longer time horizons is critical. Epermanis and Harrington (2006) find that customer demand for insurance is elastic with respect to ratings, with commercial customers in particular showing high sensitivity to rating changes. Sommer (1996) and Cummins and Danzon (1997) find evidence that higher-rated firms are able to get better prices, in effect compensating them for the higher level of capital required to serve credit-sensitive customers.

Similarly, banks which are heavily dependent on wholesale funding sources may target a higher rating in order to ensure access to funding, as will those who write long-dated derivatives, implying a level of capital in excess of regulatory minimum requirements. Jokivuolle and Peura (2006) find evidence that banks define a target rating and then hold sufficient capital to maintain that rating even in the face of market volatility. Their results reinforce the observation of Nickell *et al.* (2000) ". . . that many banks target at least the A rating can also be drawn . . . (suggesting) that banks may take extra measures to restore their capital base and hence their rating after falling below the A grade."

These observations all point to an "economic" balancing act between the costs and benefits of maintaining a higher rating, summarized in Standard & Poor's (2006) research note on the international insurance industry: "The competitive landscape, market demands, and financial challenges . . . certainly weigh heavily against their attaining, and retaining, a 'AAA' rating . . . In many cases, clear trade-offs between capital discipline and stakeholder demands argue against even trying to attain a 'AAA' rating. Nevertheless, the 'AAA' rating remains a door-opener for new business and is clearly still a competitive advantage."

Managerial Preferences

The second firm-specific factor is attributable to the managers of the firm, driven by personal preferences as opposed to economic reasoning: even adjusting for business mix, some managements are simply more conservative than others.

Allianz, for example, has been historically known as a conservatively capitalized insurance company. We discuss on a regular basis whether our rating is economically beneficial given our business mix and whether our customers are willing to pay a premium for the rating; because of (and occasionally in spite of) the discussions, Allianz management has always confirmed its commitment to maintaining their AA rating, one of the few to do so throughout the 2008 financial crisis and 2011–12 European sovereign crisis.

This commitment is recognized by analysts. Regarding Allianz, Autonomous (2012) confirms the firm-specific nature of the capital structure decision: "Allianz comes out as the strongest capitalized name within the group (of European insurers analyzed). Whilst we acknowledge the robustness of the group's balance sheet, we would observe . . . (that) Allianz holds itself against a tougher than average capital threshold so we would be a bit cautious in translating a higher economic capital ratio vs. peers into greater (dividend) distribution flexibility."

Regulatory and Rating Agency Pressure

The third firm-specific factor is the firm's interaction with rating agencies and regulators, some of which encourage firms to hold higher levels of capital than the regulatory minimum. While most discussions between firms and supervisors occur within the confidence of the confessional, a prominent public example of regulatory pressure is the so-called "Swiss finish," requiring a significantly higher level of capital imposed on banks by Swiss regulators compared with minimum requirements under Basel II/III (Letzing, 2013). Similar approaches are being explored in other jurisdictions, for example in the USA.

More Than Debt and Equity

As its name suggests, hybrid capital is a hybrid between equity and debt: it is a form of debt financing in terms of tax treatment but has loss-absorbing properties which are similar to equity. Because it is trying to be different things to different stakeholders, hybrid capital tends to be more complex than simple debt or equity. Currie (1998) says, "It must be perpetual but it doesn't have to be forever. It has to feel like equity but look – to tax authorities – like debt. Defining a banks' core capital is one of the thorniest issues facing bank regulators."

A logical question given the relative complexity of hybrid capital is why it is used at all? The answer is simple: because hybrid capital is recognized by rating agencies and regulators as a substitute for paid-in capital; as such, the use of hybrid capital improves solvency ratios defined by rating agencies and regulators but at a lower cost than equity, in part due to its seniority relative to equity and in part due to the tax deductibility of its payments, thereby improving the firm's economic profit from the shareholders' perspective.

Bentston *et al.* (2000) highlight the impact of regulatory recognition for hybrid capital. "On October 21, 1996, a ruling by the Federal Reserve pruned some thorns from the prickly issue of defining banks' core capital. As a result, bank holding companies (BHCs) were presented with a cost effective way to raise regulatory capital in the form of a debt–equity hybrid called trust-preferred securities (TPS). These instruments . . . are attractive because they generate both tax-deductible interest payments and qualify as Tier-1 (core) regulatory capital . . . Although TPS and other similar hybrids have existed since late 1993, after the Fed's ruling BHCs issued, through 1999, $31 billion of these securities across 162 filings for an average issue size of $188 million. Prior to this ruling, no BHC had announced a TPS filing."

The rapid uptake of TPS is logical from a shareholder's perspective given the tax benefits and the regulatory capital recognition. Looking at share price changes around the time of the Fed's announcement, Bentston *et al.* (2000) not surprisingly found that "The stockholders of BHCs generally benefited from the TPS issues, and those with relatively lower capital ratios benefited even more. This is a unique result, since TPS is the only security that provides clear benefits to BHC's stockholders. The positive share price reaction occurs even though almost all BHCs held more than the regulatory minimum amount of capital (relative to assets). A regulatory emphasis on Tier-1 capital appears to have given BHCs incentives to exceed the minimum required ratio. Market forces, as evidenced by the effect of uninsured sources of funds on BHCs' desired capital ratios, also encourage BHCs to hold relatively more capital. When the tax disadvantage of equity capital is removed, BHCs that can achieve greater tax benefits, have relatively lower capital, and are funded with more uninsured funds, are more likely than other BHCs to increase their capital by selling TPS. Furthermore, the stock market appears to view this increase as beneficial."

CHAPTER 20

Risk Management

Financial services firms create value for shareholders and clients by intermediating, underwriting and advising on risk. It should not come as any surprise therefore that a large part of a bank's or insurer's performance ultimately depends on how well it manages risk. As illustrated in Figure 20.1, risk underwriting is a core skill for making loans and issuing insurance policies.

However, risk underwriting has to be seen in the context of a broader Enterprise Risk Management (ERM) framework, beginning with the basic activities of risk identification, evaluation, underwriting, monitoring and management, all governed by a well-defined risk strategy and appetite. This chapter outlines the most important aspects of a comprehensive ERM framework for banks and insurers, going into greater detail in the area of risk underwriting.

ENTERPRISE RISK MANAGEMENT

CFOs and CROs need to ask, and answer, the "right" questions – questions which have the potential to substantially influence the value of their firm.

In terms of risk management, the "right" questions can be phrased as a hierarchy similar in spirit to Maslow's (1943)[1] hierarchy of needs: only by sufficiently satisfying the lower levels can a CRO begin to address those needs at a higher level. However, whereas the Maslow hierarchy comprises seven levels (beginning with the physiological needs of food and shelter and ending with spiritual self-actualization), the risk management hierarchy (illustrated in Figure 20.2) has four levels, beginning with risk underwriting and ending with risk communication.

An effective ERM framework answers these questions by developing the appropriate governance structures, processes, information and incentives.

Risk Underwriting: The Foundation of a Profitable Company

Many firms focus on risk reporting systems and complex metrics as outward signs of good risk management. The reality is that there is no amount of risk dashboards or risk-adjusted metrics which will overcome the performance drag of a poorly underwritten portfolio.

---

[1]The basis of Maslow's theory is that human beings are motivated by a hierarchy of unsatisfied needs, and that certain needs lower in the hierarchy need to be satisfied before needs further up the hierarchy can be addressed.

3. Better Decisions –
How to create value in Finance & Risk areas of responsibility?

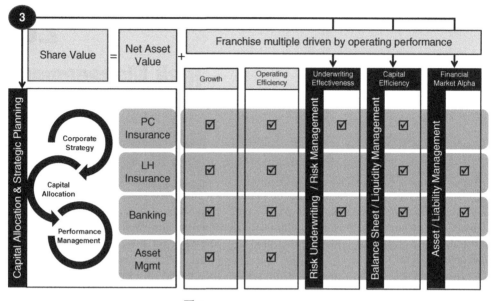

FIGURE 20.1 Better decisions – how to create value in the finance and risk areas of responsibility

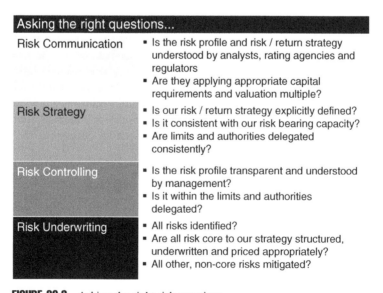

FIGURE 20.2 Asking the right risk questions

As such, the most important question for CROs and CFOs to answer is whether the organization is underwriting "good" business, day-in and day-out, every single day? This requires an affirmative in three specific areas.

Are All Relevant Risks Identified?

Before a bank or insurer can underwrite, price and manage a transaction, it first has to identify and acknowledge the underlying risk. Having made significant investments in data, systems and statistical techniques, banks and insurers are pretty good at identifying the risks from individual insurance policies and loans. Nonetheless, as frequent "surprises" have taught the industry, challenges in risk identification remain.

Some of these surprises have come from "unknowable" events, or risks with no known precedents. For example, prior to 2001 the worst-case scenario for property insurance on a Manhattan skyscraper was the loss of a few floors from fire or water damage; the terrorist events of September 11th illustrated that a previously unknown risk event can lead to much greater losses.

Other "surprises" may be the result of anticipated events but with unanticipated severity, so-called "unknown" events; for example, while it is easy to imagine a fall in equity or housing prices during a recession, the severity of the fall during the 2008 financial crisis caught many by surprise.

Still other "surprises" come from fundamental changes in the social, political, economic or legal frameworks. For example, the evolution of tort and class action law has substantially changed the risks from product liability insurance (think asbestos!) and changes in personal bankruptcy laws have affected mortgage and credit card defaults in the USA.

Are We Appropriately Underwriting the Risks That Are Core to Our Strategy?

If risk identification is the foundation of a successful balance sheet business, then risk under-writing is the cornerstone. Following after risk identification, risk underwriting begins with an assessment of the risk and then continues with transaction structuring, pricing and acceptance.

For financial services businesses, there is no return without risk. The importance of good underwriting for risk-absorption businesses such as retail and commercial lending and primary insurance is obvious: transactions underwritten today will be with the firm for a long, long time, offering only limited opportunity to take corrective action after they have been originated.

Paradoxically, as Sidebar 20.1 illustrates, risk underwriting is also the cornerstone to financial intermediation businesses such as the "originate-to-distribute" lending model and market making in banks.

SIDEBAR 20.1: WHY UNDERWRITING IS IMPORTANT FOR INTERMEDIATION BUSINESSES

Some may argue that risk underwriting has become less important given the rise of the "originate-to-distribute" or risk intermediation business model. One example is in banking, where a bank originates loans, packages them into asset-backed securities or temporarily holds them in inventory for sale on the secondary loan market and ultimately sells the risk to others, retaining limited "skin in the game." Insurance-linked securities represent the analog in the insurance industry.

The "Originate to Distribute" Model

What incentive does the bank have to underwrite a loan if it does not plan on holding it any longer than necessary? To the originators, professional underwriting might seem an archaic and superfluous skill. As for the buyer, "Caveat Emptor!" According to Lang and Jagtiani (2010),[2] "Others cite the 'originate-to-distribute' model as distorting incentives for risk taking, since lenders no longer had 'skin in the game.' . . . (Evidence supports this view: prior to 2008, there was) a pronounced decline in underwriting standards . . . median combined loan-to-value (CLTV) ratios rose (and) the share of subprime loans with piggy-back mortgages and low documentation increased substantially . . ."

However, history has shown that underwriting is also critical for intermediation businesses. Consider the fate of the mortgage originators following the 2008 financial crisis: when the real-estate bubble burst in the USA, the banks were caught with a significant amount of high-risk mortgages on their balance sheet which could not be packaged and sold.

The direct consequences were significant: of the top 10 mortgage originators at the end of 2007, only two were still operating in 2010, and these only with the support of a larger financial services firm (CitiFinancial) and/or because they emphasized good underwriting standards to begin with (Wells Fargo).[3] The other eight firms, including such once-venerable firms as Washington Mutual, Countrywide Financial and New Century Financial, were no longer operating in 2010, being driven into the arms of more solid firms or into insolvency.

The indirect consequences were also significant: the litigation initiated by those who bought the portfolios is still on-going. The list of the top 10 bank penalties (Berman, 2013) includes, at #5, the JP Morgan Chase and Credit Suisse fine of USD 417 mio for "packaging and selling troubled mortgages to investors," at #4 Goldman Sachs with USD 550 mio for "defrauding investors in a mortgage-backed security fund," and finally at #1 Bank of America and nine other lenders with USD 20 bio for "making bad mortgages and then selling them to the government."

Adding insult to injury, the failure to underwrite also imposed significant externalities on society, with the originate-to-distribute model often cited as a root cause of the 2008 financial crisis. Forbes (Denning, 2011) states, "Why did we have a financial crisis in 2008? The demand for higher-yielding paper led Wall Street to begin bundling mortgages. The highest yielding were subprime mortgages . . . These mortgagee originators' lend-to-sell-to-securitizers model had them holding mortgages for a very short period of time. This allowed them to relax underwriting standards, abdicating traditional lending metrics such as income, credit rating, debt service history and loan to value."

Positions Held in the Trading Book

Similarly, some may argue that underwriting skills are not needed for the trading book where risks are either dynamically hedged in a liquid market or warehoused briefly until

---

[2]It has been argued that underwriting standards for real-estate mortgages declined precipitously in the years leading up to the financial crisis, driven in part by the rise of mortgage originators who had limited incentives to apply appropriate underwriting standards.

[3]Top ten list, *Wall Street Journal*, March 14, 2007.

a customer with an offsetting position seeks to trade. Unfortunately, the supposedly liquid and easy to hedge trading book positions can also turn problematic during times of crisis.

Consider the loan and structured credit warehouses held in a bank's trading book, representing the raw material for packaging structured credit products such as CLOs/CDOs[4] or leveraged loans warehoused for secondary market syndication. While such positions may look like the princess at the ball during bull markets, they are likely to resemble evil witches when the secondary market dries up during bouts of illiquidity and heightened risk aversion.

As an example, CDO activities contributed substantially to the losses and eventual government support of UBS during the 2008 crisis, including the warehousing of assets which were ostensibly only to be held for 1–4 months (UBS, 2008). Because the assets were held in the trading book, they were generally not subject to the same strict level of credit underwriting and had less conservative aggregate notional limits applied.

In summary, underwriting excellence is fundamental to banking and insurance: it is impossible to sustainably create shareholder value if they do not appropriately structure, underwrite, price and manage their core products from a risk and return perspective.

Are We Mitigating Risks That Are not Core to Our Strategy?

While there may be no return without risk, the converse is not true: unfortunately for financial services firms, there are plenty of risks without compensating returns. Examples include operational and reputational events such as internal fraud or compliance failures, events which can significantly and adversely affect the value of your franchise but have limited upside potential in the eyes of shareholders.

Anyone seeking evidence need look no further than the internal fraud case at Barings:[5] "One of the most infamous tales of financial demise is that of Barings Bank. Trader Nick Leeson was supposed to be exploiting low-risk arbitrage opportunities . . . In fact, he was taking much riskier positions . . . Thanks to the lax attitude of senior management, Leeson was given control over both the trading and back-office functions. As Leeson's losses mounted, he increased his bets. However . . . the losses increased rapidly, with Leeson's positions going more than $1 billion into the red. This was too much for the bank to sustain; in March of 1995, it was purchased by the Dutch bank ING for just one pound sterling."

A further example relates to the sales and suitability issues which plagued Bankers Trust.[6] Between 1994 and 1996, Bankers Trust was sued by four of its major clients, including Gibson Greeting Cards and Procter & Gamble, who asserted that Bankers Trust had misled them with respect to the risk and value of derivatives they had purchased from the bank. Bankers Trust clients felt that it had unfairly exploited their lack of sophistication in handling these sophisticated derivative products. Due to the reputational consequences, the cases invalidated the Bankers Trust business model and ultimately cost Bankers Trust its independence.

---

[4]Collateralized Loan Obligations, Collateralized Debt Obligations are securitizations backed by loans and other forms of debt, often divided into senior-, mezzanine- and equity-components before being sold to investors.

[5]www.erisk.com/Learning/CaseStudies/Barings.asp

[6]www.erisk.com/learning/casestudies/bankerstrust.asp

These are just two examples of how operational and reputational events can destroy substantial franchise value while offering limited upside potential. Other examples include failures in financial reporting or cyber security, processing errors, business continuity management, etc.

Risk Controlling: Providing Transparency, Establishing Control

Although it is the foundation of a profitable firm, underwriting excellence is not enough: ensuring that each individual loan or policy is appropriately underwritten does not guarantee that the aggregate portfolio is optimal from a risk and return perspective. Assuming that all risks are clearly identified and appropriately underwritten, the next level in the risk management hierarchy is risk controlling. In this context, CROs and CFOs need to ask two important questions.

Is the Risk Profile of My Portfolio Transparent and Understood?

It is important that management understands the risk profile of the portfolio, both for tactical steering as well as to understand the "tall-tree" exposures (e.g., the largest risk accumulations which might materially threaten the firm's earnings, solvency or value creation objectives).

"Tall trees" can come from large, individual transactions such as underwriting commitments, leveraged loans associated with M&A transactions, strategic equity investments, individual commercial insurance policies, etc.

Alternatively, they can also build up through the accumulation of many smaller transactions. For example, a material exposure to a regional recession can be built up through a portfolio of small retail mortgages or SME loans; similarly, a dangerous accumulation of earthquake or windstorm exposure can result from a portfolio of well-underwritten homeowners' property insurance.

An understanding of the firm's risk profile is accomplished through the ubiquitous "risk dashboard" or "risk cockpit" using a combination of measures, often including portfolio Value at Risk (VaR, described in Sidebar 20.2) notional exposures and sensitivities, complemented by stress testing and scenario analysis.

SIDEBAR 20.2: ON VALUE AT RISK MEASURES[7]

Value at Risk is defined as the maximum loss for a portfolio within a pre-defined confidence interval over a pre-defined time horizon. It is often used to measure capital adequacy. For example, Basel II defined required capital for trading books based on a 99% confidence interval over a 10-day holding period and Solvency II at a 99.5% confidence interval over a 1 year horizon. More formally[8], given a confidence level $\alpha \in (0,1)$, the VaR of the portfolio at the confidence level α is given by the smallest number l such that the probability that the loss L exceeds l is at most $(1-\alpha)$, or $VaR_\alpha(L)$ is the level α-quantile, i.e.

$$VaR_\alpha(L) = inf\{l \in \mathbb{R} : P(L > l - a)\} = inf\{l \in \mathbb{R} : F_L(l) \geq \alpha\}$$

---

[7]Example and MATLAB code contributed by Jean-Frederic Breton (Jean-Frederic.Breton@mathworks. com).

[8]Definition from Artzner, et al. (1999).

Where the second equality holds if one knows the distribution for losses, e.g. $F_L(l)$ is the cumulative probability that losses are less than or equal to l.

There are many numerical approaches to calculate VaR depending on the portfolio and assumptions. VaR for a trading book requires assumptions about the distribution of financial market prices such as interest rates and implied volatilities and how assets are valued using those prices; VaR for a loan portfolio depends as well on assumptions about default and migration probabilities and correlations; and, for a PC insurance portfolio, on claims frequency and severity distributions. For a detailed discussion of VaR approaches for market and credit risks, see Wilson (1998). There are three common approaches used for financial market risk.

- **Historical simulation:** Revalue the portfolio using a set of historical financial market prices, sort the returns from worst to best and select the percentile of interest. Implicitly assumes that history will repeat itself, at least the history contained in the sample. Suitable for non-linear (e.g. option) products because they are valued exactly.
- **Delta normal:** Assumes that asset returns are normally distributed. Alternatively, that the financial instrument depends on a spot financial market price, S, where $\Delta S/S$ is a normal variable and the pricing function P(S) is well approximated by a linear function, $\Delta P = \delta \Delta S$. Under these assumptions, portfolio returns are also normally distributed. This approach is not suitable for non-linear (e.g. option) products. In addition, it may underestimate the probability of extreme events as historical returns tend to have a "fat tail" compared to the normal distribution.
- **Monte Carlos simulation:** Assumes a stochastic process for financial market prices with the choice of distributions and parameters (e.g. correlations) derived from historical data. A common assumption is that equity prices, exchange rates and interest rates are log normally distributed, e.g. LN(S) is normally distributed. A set of simulated prices are generated, the portfolio is revalued using these prices, returns are sorted from best to worst and the percentile of interest is selected. Suitable for non-linear portfolios but may underestimate the probability of extreme events.

For the following Exhibit, we use data from the S&P 500 index (10 years of daily returns from April 1993 to April 2003) and compare the VaR from the three different approaches. The Delta normal method produces the smallest VaR (-2.1%), followed by the Monte Carlo method (-2.8%) and the Historical simulation method (-3.2%). In general, we can expect the VaR figure produced by the Delta normal and Monte Carlo methods to be smaller than historical simulation as historical distributions tend to have "fatter tails" (e.g. put more probability on extreme events) than assumed distributions (normal, log-normal). For non-linear portfolios, the Delta-normal approach will generally under-estimate the VaR because of the linear representation of option values.

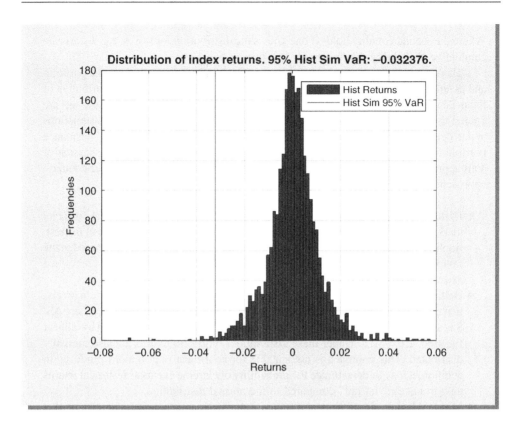

Most banks and insurers focus on risk controlling and reporting, investing substantially in data, systems and analytical techniques. While producing tangible results in terms of systems and reports, this investment must be balanced against the other dimensions in the hierarchy: the best risk dashboard cannot eliminate the losses of a poorly underwritten portfolio or a poorly aligned risk/reward strategy.

Is the Risk Profile Within Delegated Authorities?

In addition to creating transparency, risk controlling also ensures that the firm's risk profile remains within delegated authorities which define the "room to maneuver" for taking business decisions.

Risk limits range from strategic to tactical, beginning with a definition of the firm's risk appetite and culminating with operational trading desk limits or underwriting authorities. It is through these limits that banks and insurers direct focus on the risks the company wants (and avoid those that the company does not want), limit their tall-tree exposures and only allow risk taking by those professionals best positioned to underwrite and manage the portfolios.

There is a balancing act to setting limits: they should be binding enough to constrain potentially ruinous risk taking and "steer" the business in a manner consistent with the firm's strategy; on the other hand, they also need to be loose enough to promote entrepreneurial behavior and agility in responding to opportunities. Achieving the balance requires both technical frameworks as well as experienced judgment, a theme which is emphasized later in Chapter 21.

Risk Strategy: Making a Conscious Link Between Risk and Reward

Assuming that all risks are appropriately identified and underwritten and that the resulting portfolio of risks is well understood and within delegated authorities, the next level in the hierarchy is to ensure that these limits and authorities are the result of a risk/reward strategy focused on shareholder value creation. This in turn requires answering two questions.

First, where do we create value and where should we invest for growth? These are generic questions equally valid for industrial corporations. Different for banks and insurers is the role of risk in creating value in financial services, requiring risk considerations to be explicitly integrated into the business strategy.

Which risks do we want (e.g., lending or trading, retail or commercial, retirement or life) and which do we not want? How do we create value from taking the risk? Do we have the technical capabilities to underwrite the risk? To expand the firm's footprint into adjacent markets and products?

These questions must be answered explicitly in order to integrate risk and strategy, followed by an alignment of business targets, risk policies, authorities and limits.

Second, is the risk profile consistent with our risk-bearing capacity and our risk appetite? There should be a positive relationship between risk and return: the more risk, the more return. In spite of the expected returns, the cumulative risks that the firm can underwrite will be constrained by the amount of capital that is available and the appetite to leverage that capital in taking risk.

Some constraints are defined externally, for example through regulatory requirements and large exposure directives, which need to be met at all times. Other constraints are set by management, dictated by the firm's risk appetite and strategy. For example, virtually all financial services firms hold more capital than the regulatory minimum; determining how much more depends on management's risk appetite, representing a further constraint on the total risk the firm takes and the limits it is willing to grant.

Risk Disclosure: Influencing Capital Requirements and Share Value

Assume that all risks are appropriately identified and underwritten; that the resulting portfolio is well understood and within delegated authorities; and, finally, that the limits are a consequence of a well-thought-out strategy linking risks and returns.

Unfortunately, this is still not enough. The last question which management should address centers around communication with external stakeholders: Is our risk profile and risk/return strategy transparent and correctly interpreted by external stakeholders, leading to an appropriate valuation multiple and minimum solvency requirements?

External stakeholders, and especially equity analysts, shareholders, rating agencies and regulators, have a significant influence on the economics of our business, the room to maneuver and, as a consequence, the value of the firm.

For example, the ability to leverage capital to underwrite more profitable business will depend on rating agencies' and regulators' opinions: both have clear ideas about the capital needed to protect depositors, policy holders and other debt holders. But these opinions can be positively influenced, leading to lower capital requirements if the view is positive or to higher requirements for a less favorable view of the financial and managerial strength of the firm.

Improving communications about risk with shareholders and analysts is therefore important. For example, consider the possible reaction to unanticipated events: it is commonly held that earnings volatility is "bad." However, far worse are surprises which are inconsistent with the market's understanding of the firm's strategy: for example, a large trading loss at an investment bank or natural catastrophe loss at a reinsurer might well be accepted by the market as "bad luck" or an aberration with limited impact on the firm's valuation multiple; however, the same loss at a retail bank or primary insurance company may cause a fundamental revaluation of the firm's multiple.

Better communication can insulate the firm from the negative impact of "unexpected" earnings surprises: if the market understands your business strategy and how you create value by taking risk, then it should not be surprised when some of the risk materializes, leaving your franchise multiple intact. In addition, clear communication can also support a higher valuation multiple both by committing management and by helping them to establish a valuable reputation for "doing what you say you will do."

TAKING THE RIGHT DECISIONS

Asking the right questions is only the beginning: successful firms are able to take the right decisions and execute them consequently.

An ERM Framework

How can finance and risk functions help in consistently taking the right decisions? As Figure 20.3 illustrates, there are many operational levers which can be pulled, both by the

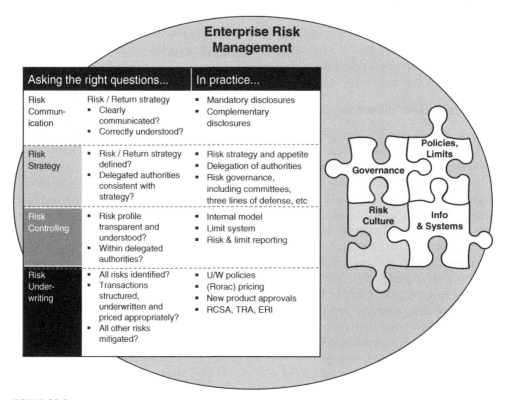

FIGURE 20.3 Elements of an ERM framework

Risk function as well as by the business. Working from the bottom of the hierarchy, the Risk function can support the following.

- Underwriting, for example by implementing a risk-based technical pricing framework (New Business RAPMs), defining underwriting guidelines and policies and approving new products before they are introduced. The Risk function can also ensure that all other risks not core to the strategy, especially operational and reputational risks, are identified and mitigated through a Risk Control Self-Assessment (RCSA), and that material risks are identified through the Top Risk Assessment (TRA) and Emerging Risk Initiatives (ERI).
- Risk reporting and controlling, for example by implementing internal models as well as risk and limit reporting systems.
- Risk strategy, for example explicitly integrating risk into the strategic planning process, aligning risk and business strategy and defining the firm's risk appetite and limits consistent with both.
- Supporting mandatory and voluntary disclosures to regulators, rating agencies, shareholders and customers in order to ensure that the risk strategy and profile are understood; ensuring that the appropriate capital requirements – not more and not less – and the right valuation multiple are applied.

Pulling these operational levers requires an appropriate risk organization, processes, information and culture. Collectively, these define an ERM framework. The remaining chapters in this part of the Handbook describe ERM in detail, grouped around four main themes.

- *Risk identification and evaluation* focuses on developing the organization, skills and processes necessary to identify and evaluate risks ranging from the strategic to the tactical, including market, credit, insurance, operational and reputational risks.
- *Risk underwriting* focuses on developing the organization, skills and processes necessary to appropriately analyze, structure and price the market, credit or insurance risks that you take to create value for shareholders when offering products and services to your customers.
- *Operational risk management* focuses on developing the organization, skills and processes needed to mitigate the operational and reputational risks which are inherent in your business system but not desired.
- *Risk and limit controlling* focuses on developing the organization, skills and processes needed to make the risk profile of the organization transparent and ensure that it remains within delegated authorities.

Integrating risk and strategy in the strategic planning process is covered in Chapters 13 and 14 and an explicit example of a risk strategy for underwriting businesses is given in Chapter 23.

Relation to Other ERM Frameworks

ERM is a term which is often used but which is defined differently by each insurer and bank. Nonetheless, all the definitions emphasize the elements of governance organization, processes, information and culture and how these influence the way that the firm manages risk, beginning with risk identification and ending with risk strategy.

One of the most influential ERM frameworks is the COSO framework, developed by the Committee of Sponsoring Organizations of the Treadway Commission (COSO, 1992, 2011). The COSO principles are designed to help companies assess and enhance their internal control systems. The framework consists of several elements, as summarized in Sidebar 20.3.

SIDEBAR 20.3: THE COSO (2004) ERM FRAMEWORK

"Enterprise risk management consists of eight interrelated components. These are derived from the way management runs an enterprise and are integrated with the management process. These components are:

- Internal Environment – The internal environment encompasses the tone of an organization, and sets the basis for how risk is viewed and addressed by an entity's people, including risk management philosophy and risk appetite, integrity and ethical values, and the environment in which they operate.
- Objective Setting – Objectives must exist before management can identify potential events affecting their achievement. Enterprise risk management ensures that management has in place a process to set objectives and that the chosen objectives support and align with the entity's mission and are consistent with its risk appetite.
- Event Identification – Internal and external events affecting achievement of an entity's objectives must be identified, distinguishing between risks and opportunities. Opportunities are channeled back to management's strategy or objective-setting processes.
- Risk Assessment – Risks are analyzed, considering likelihood and impact, as a basis for determining how they should be managed. Risks are assessed on an inherent and a residual basis.
- Risk Response – Management selects risk responses – avoiding, accepting, reducing, or sharing risk – developing a set of actions to align risks with the entity's risk tolerances and risk appetite.
- Control Activities – Policies and procedures are established and implemented to help ensure the risk responses are effectively carried out.
- Information and Communication – Relevant information is identified, captured, and communicated in a form and timeframe that enable people to carry out their responsibilities. Effective communication also occurs in a broader sense, flowing down, across, and up the entity.
- Monitoring – The entirety of enterprise risk management is monitored and modifications made as necessary. Monitoring is accomplished through ongoing management activities, separate evaluations, or both."

Later, in 1998, the Basel Committee presented the Framework for Internal Control Systems in Banking Organizations (BIS, 1998). The framework comprises five components similar to the COSO (e.g., control environment, risk assessment, control activities, information and communication, and monitoring).

Consistent with the ERM framework outlined in this Handbook, both of these frameworks comprise organization or governance, processes and information, aligned to a clearly articulated risk strategy and combined with a specific focus on risk identification, assessment and management.

THE ROLE OF CULTURE

Most large banks and insurers have implemented all the outward signs of an ERM framework, making a substantial investment in terms of governance organization, processes and systems and generating a veritable bookshelf of documentation for their quantitative models and qualitative policies and procedures. Most of these firms have had their bookshelf and models reviewed by external parties, including audit firms, rating agencies[9] and regulators.[10]

ERM "Box Ticking" Isn't the Answer

One would think that, after such a large investment and significant scrutiny, bank and insurance ERM frameworks could be relied upon to ensure the future viability of the firm. Unfortunately, this would be a wrong assumption.

The following is from the testimony of the Bear Stearns co-COO to the Senate Financial Crisis Inquiry Committee.[11] Bear Stearns was an early victim of the 2008 financial crisis, being forced into the arms of JP Morgan Chase rather than facing resolution proceedings.

As the quote illustrates, having all the outward trappings of an ERM framework is not sufficient to ensure the viability and success of the firm.

> *You have also asked me to address risk management practices. Risk at Bear Stearns was managed through a system of checks and balances. Each business unit was responsible for managing its risk, and the head of each division was then responsible for managing the aggregate risk within its units. The Executive Committee approved explicit limits for all areas of the firm – at the trading book level, and also by unit and by department – which were monitored by department heads.*
>
> *These limits were reviewed and monitored by the Risk Management Group, which was an independent unit that reported to the Executive Committee and met regularly with the Board's Risk Committee. This group, headed by Bear Stearns' Chief Risk Officer, served as an independent check on the business units' own risk management function. It distributed daily P&L statements that highlighted any significant gains and losses. It also provided daily written reports to senior management commenting on changes in exposure, any unusual trades, and any concentrated positions. The Risk Committee held weekly meetings, and the Risk Management Group made monthly presentations to the Executive Committee. At the weekly meetings, trading managers reported on their positions and their risk, and the risk management teams were present to verify the accuracy of these reports and to express their views. In this way, the Risk*

---

[9]For example, Standard & Poor's regularly undertakes an independent review of insurance companies' ERM frameworks as part of their ERM rating. See Standard & Poor's (2005).

[10]Especially the internal model and Pillar II ERM framework as part of their internal model approval process. See, for example, BIS (2009b). See also http://www.fsa.gov.uk/about/what/international/solvency/policy/governance

[11]http://www.fcic.gov

Committee and the business units served as constant checks on each other. There was an active dialogue among senior management about the firm's overall risk appetite, which we reviewed during both weekly and monthly meetings.

In my opinion, Bear Stearns' risk management practices were robust and effective. During my tenure on the Executive Committee I found the Risk Management team to be highly trained and very experienced. Overall, I thought Bear Stearns was well-managed, and I was saddened and disappointed when the firm collapsed.

What conclusions can be drawn? First, evidence of an ERM framework is not enough. Virtually all large banks and insurance companies have the outward trappings of an ERM framework – even those banks or insurance companies which failed spectacularly during the financial crisis – as if someone had gone through both industries with Copy & Paste functionality.

Second, and more importantly, there is something more than an ERM framework which differentiates "good" from "bad" firms: the real differentiating factor (the "secret sauce," so to speak) is *culture: my strong conviction is that there is no ERM framework – no reports or heat maps, no risk strategies and risk appetite statements, no controls or separation of duties, no bookshelf of documentation – which will be effective if the company has a dysfunctional risk and business culture.*

Others seem to agree. The Institute of Risk Management (2012) comments: "Over recent years significant progress has been made in developing rules, frameworks, processes and standards for managing risks. However the business press everyday confirms that these disciplines are not in themselves sufficient to make a tangible difference to the success or failure of organisations. Rules can be misunderstood and misapplied, inadvertently or deliberately. The 'missing link' . . . is the organisation's risk culture."

Regulators also agree, with the Financial Stability Board (FSB, 2014) commenting that "Weaknesses in risk culture are often considered a root cause of the global financial crisis, headline risk and compliance events. A financial institution's risk culture plays an important role in influencing the actions and decisions taken by individuals within the institution and in shaping the institution's attitude toward its stakeholders, including its supervisors."

Finally, in a wave of enlightened self-interest, senior leadership in many financial services companies – including UBS,[12] Barclays[13] and RBS[14] – also concluded that risk culture is the critical factor to the success of a firm.

The concept of "risk culture" is inherently amorphous, defying direct or quantitative measurement, as the following definitions illustrate.

- Culture is "The combined set of individual and corporate values, attitudes, competencies and behaviour that determine a firm's commitment to and style of operational risk management" (BIS, 2011).

---

[12]UBS (2010) summarizes: "As a result of the internal and external investigations, the Board of Directors concluded that not only technical and financial market specific, but also cultural factors contributed to the problems of UBS. The new management of UBS is endeavoring to create a more sustainable corporate culture within UBS."

[13]According to the Chairman of Barclays Bank, Marcus Agius, ". . . the leaders of industry must collectively procure a visible and substantive change in the culture of our institutions, so as fundamentally to convince the world once again that they are businesses which can be relied on" (*Financial Times*, 2010).

[14]The CEO of RBS, Stephan Hester, echoed the sentiment, saying "Banks must undergo a wholesale change in their culture and refocus their behavior on meeting the needs of customers to restore trust in the industry" (Reuters, 2012).

■ Culture is "The norms and traditions of behaviour of individuals and of groups within an organization that determine the way in which they identify, understand, discuss, and act on the risks the organization confronts and the risks it takes" (IIF, 2009).

It might seem as if the border between "good" and "bad" firms is inherently subjective, with the "bad" only being conclusively identified in retrospect after the damage has been done. Nonetheless, I believe that there are at least five symptoms of a dysfunctional risk culture: at one end are institutionalized failures in business judgment, cases where an invisible line is crossed into the zone of "taking too much risk" consciously or unconsciously; at the other end is behavior which is at best of questionable ethics and at worst illegal.

The five symptoms of a dysfunctional risk culture are described in the remainder of this chapter using obvious industry examples. But the sheer boldness and audacity of the examples should not bring a false sense of security: in my experience, each of these symptoms is present to some extent, at some point in time, in every bank or insurer – it is only a matter of degree.

Dysfunctional Risk Culture: "Dancing While the Music Is Playing"

This first symptom is a failure in business judgment, crossing the invisible line between the "right" amount of risk and "too much" risk. Consider the following (rhetorical) question: When is it okay for a firm to significantly reduce its risk management standards and materially increase its vulnerability? Apparently, when it is the most successful!

As history has shown, management can become so enamored of continued success during bull markets that common sense and risk discipline become the victims. If the market leaders are doing bigger and bigger deals, then so should we! If they are building bigger LBO or CDO or mortgage warehouses, then so should we! If they are relaxing underwriting standards with sub-prime, "covenant-light" and "no-documentation" loans, then so should we!

The reason? Management can become deathly afraid . . . not of the consequences when the bubble bursts, but rather of *not* participating in the excesses of a bubble economy: afraid of what shareholders will say when they see revenue growth lag that of competitors, afraid of what employees will say when they see bonus pools at other institutions fill up more rapidly and, perhaps just a little, afraid of the implications on their own incentive compensation.

This culture is illustrated succinctly by Chuck Prince's now infamous quote[15] made in 2007 before the financial crisis hit fully: "When the music stops, in terms of liquidity, things will be complicated. But as long as the music is playing, you've got to get up and dance. We're still dancing."

Unfortunately, the music stopped in 2008 with catastrophic results for Citigroup, leading to a loss of more than 90% of its market value and requiring support from the US government. After the dust settled, the vice chairman of the Congressional Financial Crisis Inquiry Commission (FCIC) compared Citigroup to "a lemming" because of the reluctance to rein in risk taking as late as mid-2007. Mr. Prince's reply was that Citigroup would have lost market share and key employees if it did not compete: "It would have been impossible to say to bankers, we're not going to participate . . . and expect to have any people left."

Citigroup was not unique in grabbing the bull market by the tail with disastrous results. In its forensic analysis published in 2010, UBS cited several contributing factors for its need for

---

[15]Chuck Prince was the CEO of Citigroup during the 2008 crisis (*Financial Times*, 2007).

government support during the crisis; one of them was clearly "dancing while the music played." "Growth strategy: In the summer of 2005, UBS had spun off a significant portion of its business in fixed income investment products into its subsidiary Dillon Read Capital Management (DRCM). At the end of 2005, the decision was made to develop, in parallel to DRCM, the same type of business inside the UBS Investment Bank, since UBS hoped to become one of the top banks in the world in this sector as well."

Another contributing factor was being over-optimistic following several years of success. "False sense of security despite warning signs: Toward the end of 2006 . . . it became apparent that the growth in the US real estate market might be turning into a speculative bubble. In spite of these signs . . . the management of UBS Investment Bank was confident. It falsely believed, on the one hand, that its investments . . . were, in fact, safe . . . (and that) the holdings of investment products held in its 'warehouse' could be sold at any time in the market. Because of these assumptions, which in retrospect turned out to be incorrect, UBS neglected to take additional measures to limit its risks in the US housing market."

If the organization is committed to "dancing while the music is playing," it runs the risk of not finding a chair to sit on once the music stops. Perversely, this risk increases the more "successful" the firm.

What can be done to combat lemming-like behavior? Is the answer to be contrarian, to bet against the rising tide? Most likely not. It is incredibly difficult to be contrarian in the face of a bull market. Arguably, "value" investors such as Warren Buffet, David Dremen, John Neff and Mark Ripple have a track record of remaining disciplined and, yes, being contrarian. However, against this handful of successful individuals are many others who could not hold on to their convictions in the face of the rising tide, a situation made worse for those working for a company driven by short-term shareholder and employee expectations.

Consider the case of Tony Dye, CIO at Phillips & Drew through the 1990s, another famous value investor who bet against the tide during the tech stock bubble in the late 1990s, earning him the nickname "Dr Doom." Unfortunately, he could not hold onto his views using his client's money, most of whom missed out on the "gains" during the tech bubble and, by 2000, he left his job. At the time of his departure, the *Financial News* wrote: "It takes a brave man to go against the consensus in the investment world and whatever one thinks about Tony Dye, he certainly had the courage of his convictions." Soon thereafter, the market collapsed and he was vindicated . . . unfortunately, too late.

Not all firms have the luxury of being contrarian. However, all firms have the ability (and responsibility) to maintain underwriting discipline, especially in the face of irrational compet-itive behavior, and to run a balanced portfolio, even in the face of a bull market and market exuberance. It is how we choose to participate in the bull markets which determine our fate when the bears come out to play.

Dysfunctional Risk Culture: "Babe Ruth" Leader

The second symptom of a dysfunctional risk culture also represents a failure in business judgment. I call it the "Babe Ruth" syndrome after the famous American baseball player. Most people admire Babe Ruth (Sinek, 2010) and there is a lot to admire: in 1923, Babe broke the record for the most home runs in a season as well as the record for the highest batting average. He was the first player to hit 60 home runs in a season, a record he held for 34 years, and he held the career home run record for 39 years until it was broken in 1974. Not satisfied with a base hit, Babe Ruth was known for "swinging for the fences," trying to hit a home run each time at bat.

However, there are less flattering facts about Babe Ruth which are not as well remembered: he broke another record in 1923, when he struck out more times than any other player; he also held the record for the most strike-outs during his career, a record he held for 29 years.

It is easy to admire someone with Babe's statistics, someone who swings for the fences each and every time at bat and who succeeds enough times to have a winning team. For Babe, the benefits outweighed the cost in terms of strike-outs. However, there is a big difference between baseball and financial services: in baseball, the game continues after a strike-out of an individual player, whereas in business it can be fatal to the team and to shareholders.

Against this high-stakes background, it can be very dangerous to have a charismatic and authoritarian leader who is willing to take bold positions and play a view regardless of the consequences, disregarding or suppressing the input of others.

The collapse of MF Global is a case in point. In March 2010, John Corzine, the ex-CEO of Goldman Sachs, took over the reins of MF Global which was at the time a struggling brokerage company with a strong presence on the Chicago Mercantile Exchange. Mr. Corzine wanted to convert the relatively unexciting but over-leveraged broker into an investment bank. He brought with him a significant amount of trading experience . . . and a desire to act on that expertise to prop up earnings in a low-rate environment. Beginning in 2010, Mr. Corzine built up $6.3 billion leveraged proprietary trading strategy on five European sovereign bond markets. This was "a trade so big it spooked the markets and led to a run on the firm," earning Mr. Corzine the sobriquet "de facto Chief Trader" in the congressional investigation following the demise of MF Global (Protess, 2012).

Although the CRO raised the alarm internally, the bells were quickly muted as Mr. Corzine moved oversight of his trading strategy to the board: "And when MF Global's chief risk officer argued that the European bet had grown too big, Mr. Corzine effectively stripped the executive of the ability to check that trade. Oversight of Mr. Corzine's trading was eventually delegated to the firm's board, which tended to support its chairman" (Protess and de la Merced, 2012). It is valid to ask whether a Board of Directors should be responsible for operational risk oversight, clearly not best practice. However, the line was crossed when MF Global used customers' segregated funds to cover the hole in its balance sheet.

Apparently bold but authoritarian leadership characteristics are a hallmark of investment banking. According to Moore (2010): "(An) authoritarian management style and culture is marked by . . . managers who require total submission from their employees, demand adherence to strict edicts that only they can issue, become enraged when challenged, and discourage the input of underlings. To most investment bankers and traders, this sounds like an average day at the office – and, unfortunately, it is. Authoritarianism, often tied in with narcissism, is probably the most common management style on Wall Street, said Dartmouth Tuck School of Business Professor Ella Bell."

Moore cites other strong personalities on Wall Street to support the assertion: Richard Fuld, ex-CEO of the defunct Lehman Brothers whose bullying earned him the nickname "the Gorilla" and former Merrill Lynch CEO E. Stanley O'Neal who apparently surrounded himself with "yes" men. According to the article, "An authoritarian doesn't want to be surrounded by the best people, because they don't like to be challenged and need to be at the center of everything."

However, the trait is not limited to investment banking. Referring to the demise of the Royal Bank of Scotland led by Fred Goodwin, the *Observer* (Kampfner, 2013) paraphrases Martin (2013) in writing that "The star of the show . . . is Fred Goodwin, aka Fred the Shred (a nickname he apparently quite liked), a man who made up for his ignorance about the complexity of banking with hubris and bullying. In 1998, Goodwin was brought in as deputy chief executive and, together with his board, set about the great aggrandisement of the Edinburgh-based bank . . . The only thing that mattered to Goodwin was growth. He was on the prowl for the next takeover. The hapless board waved through each plan (in so far as he bothered to tell them) . . . Anyone who aired doubts was shouted at or sidelined . . . One former employee tells the author 'he manufactured fear.'"

In 2007, RBS together with a consortia of Fortis and Santander made a bid for ABN Amro. The ill-timed bid – at the peak of the financial market bubble and just before the crisis – ultimately led to RBS and Fortis needing to be rescued by their respective governments. Apparently, apprehension was expressed privately by the Board about such a large and complex deal but they "felt that saying no would be seen as a de facto move to replace Sir Fred . . . once again highlighting the lack of countervailing voices in the RBS hierarchy" (Wilson *et al.*, 2011).

Dysfunctional Risk Culture: The "Golden Rule"

The third symptom of a dysfunctional culture is the "Golden Rule." As a CRO, I personally would say that this begins to take us out of the realm of poor judgment and into the realm of near negligence.

The Golden Rule states that "He who makes the gold, makes the rules." As related to risk management, it means that the independent risk function is kept from exercising its control and oversight responsibilities for business areas which produce an inordinate amount of earnings. Often, this is done either so as to not disturb the "goose that lays the golden egg" or because management is afraid that the quality and source of the earnings will not stand up to scrutiny.

History is rife with examples of the "Golden Rule" leading to disaster. Consider AIG Financial Products (AIG FP), the business unit which caused the largest insurer in the world to require government support. AIG FP was once considered the crown jewel in the AIG portfolio. However, what began as a disciplined business leveraging AIG's strong credit rating in the long-dated swaps market morphed into a "credit insurance" strategy, with AIG FP taking "premiums" for writing huge volumes of credit default swaps on increasingly more toxic underlying risks.

The management at AIG apparently liked the business because it resonated with their insurance origins: you receive a premium upfront for providing coverage of an identified risk. The management at AIG FP liked it because of the large bonuses during the benign period up until 2007 on the more than \$450 bn of notional exposure.[16]

However, as the underlying assets' credit quality deteriorated and spreads increased in 2008, AIG FP suffered mark-to-market losses and significant liquidity calls which it could not meet. The damage was not limited to the subsidiary. AIG ultimately needed to be rescued by the US government because it had guaranteed AIG FP (the AIG liquidity risk management case is discussed in detail in Chapter 18).

In the post-mortem analysis it emerged that AIG FP suffered from the "Golden Rule." Specifically (Roth, 2009), "(A)t a January 2008 meeting . . . AIG's auditor, Pricewaterhou-seCoopers, concluded that the access to AIG FP enjoyed by (AIG) risk officers 'may require strengthening.' And in March, 2008, the Office of Thrift Supervision sent a letter to AIG . . . (saying) that AIGFP 'was allowed to limit access of key risk control groups while material questions relating to the valuation of the [swap portfolio] were mounting.' One of the risk control groups named was (the AIG CRO) Lewis' team . . . AIG CEO Edward Liddy (was

---

[16]According to the Office of Thrift Supervision (OTS, 2007), AIG FP had a net exposure of USD 467 bn of super senior credit default swaps on March 31, 2006.

asked) during a congressional hearing, 'Where was the risk management of your company? Where was the failure of your own internal risk-management procedures?' Mr. Liddy's response, 'We had risk-management practices in place. They generally were not allowed to go up into the financial-products business.'"

A similar high-profile loss caused by the "Golden Rule" occurred in the equity derivative trading business at UBS[17] during the late 1990s, where it is alleged that the risk management function was impeded from executing their responsibilities for a business unit which again seemed to be the goose that was laying golden eggs.

In other cases, the blocking was passive as opposed to active. For example, consider the prominent rogue trading cases including Nick Leeson at Barings Bank, Jerome Kerviel at Societé Générale[18] and Kweku Adoboli at UBS: in each of these cases, management is alleged to have turned a blind eye to clear signals that the business was "too good to be true."

Dysfunctional Risk Culture: "Arbitraging the System"

A third clear signal of a dysfunctional risk organization is the company which tolerates or promotes the blatant arbitrage of internal or external rules. Such activities may begin innocuously, for example by condoning small actions which consciously arbitrage internal models in order to increase earnings: investment managers may select the highest-yielding bond within a rating class, traders may put on a short-term hedge expiring immediately after a reporting date, or internal models may be updated to "better reflect the economics of the business."

Although beginning innocuously, if tolerated over longer periods of time such actions can become admired and ingrained as part of the corporate culture, providing an incentive to manage the models and circumvent the rules rather than doing good business. It is at this point that the innocuous can become problematic.

Consider the case of Lehman Brothers, one of the most high-profile examples of a firm caught out in its own arbitrage activities. During the financial crisis, Lehman regularly used an accounting arbitrage, the infamous "repo 105" transactions, to temporarily move assets off its balance sheet over the quarter end only to be unwound shortly afterwards: while repos (or repurchase agreements) are normally considered as financing and therefore considered for leverage and liquidity purposes, the "repo 105" transactions were considered a sale under English law, allowing Lehman to artificially deflate its balance sheet by billions at the end of every quarter.

In the court-appointed examiner's report following Lehman's bankruptcy, these deals were said to have created "a materially misleading picture of the firm's financial condition in late 2007 and 2008" and represented "actionable balance sheet manipulation . . . (and) . . . nonculpable errors of business judgment."

The actions were understood and condoned by senior management of the firm, as the following email excerpt illustrates.

> It's basically window-dressing.
> I see . . . so it's legally do-able but doesn't look good when we actually do it? Does the rest of the street do it? Also is that why we have so much BS [balance sheet] to Rates Europe?
> Yes, No and yes.:)

---

[17]The UBS case study is described at www.derivativesstrategy.com/magazine/archive/1998/1098fea3.asp

[18]Case studies on these examples can be found at www.prmia.org

Other examples of industry-wide "arbitraging the system" contributed materially to the 2008 financial crisis, including the $400 bn worth of Structured Investment Vehicles (SIVs – non-consolidated, off-balance sheet funding vehicles which allowed banks to greatly increase leverage without showing up on the balance sheet – see Appendix D: Beyond Debt and Equity for a discussion) and the highly leveraged CDOs known as CPDOs (Constant Proportion Debt Obligations) issued just before the crisis: they paid +200 bps over Libor but still had AAA rating. Sound too good to be true? Unfortunately, it was!

The insurance industry may not be immune to a culture of arbitraging the system. Consider the AIG/General Re case, originally closed in 2006. In 2000, analysts criticized AIG for declining loss reserves; AIG and General Re entered into a loss portfolio transfer which allowed AIG to increase its reported loss reserves by $500 million because it was booked as a reinsurance contract, even though there was no material risk transfer. SEC associate director Andrew Calamari stated: "(General) Re arranged to sell financial products to AIG and Prudential for the sole purpose of enabling those companies to manipulate their accounting results and mislead investors." Ultimately, five former executives from General Re and AIG were convicted in connection with the case, including General Re's CEO and CFO and the vice president in charge of reinsurance for AIG (BestWeek, 2010).

The AIG/General Re story has an ambiguous, if not happy, ending: the convictions were "vacated in 2011 by a federal appeals court because of errors by the trial judge and the appellate judges made clear what they thought of (a star witness) Mr. Napier's testimony . . . 'Compelling inconsistencies suggest that Napier may well have testified falsely'" (*WSJ*, 2015). Unfortunately, the exculpatory evidence has been prevented from being made public by the federal government.

One would think that an arbitrage culture would be impossible today in light of such high-profile and recent experience. Apparently, this is not the case. In 2013, the *Financial Times* reported that "Some global banks are using models that let them hold one-eighth of the capital held by their competitors against the same assets, according to a study that will boost claims that lenders are manipulating the main measure of bank safety."

Around the same time, the *Wall Street Journal* (2013) reported that "Big European banks are boosting the key gauge of their financial health through largely cosmetic maneuvering even as regulators in some countries try to crack down on the practice. Banks are recalculating the risks in their loan portfolios and trading books in flattering ways, a move that has the effect of raising their (capital) ratio . . . while such maneuvering has been going on for years, analysts say it appears to be accelerating at some major European banks, which are under pressure to raise their capital ratios as . . . Basel III start phasing in this year."

Capital and valuation models in the insurance industry are also not immune. Consider, for example, the significant changes to MCEV described earlier in Chapter 7: the inclusion of an illiquidity premium to discount liabilities and the anchoring of long-term interest rates, brought into practice only after the 2008 financial crisis, have contributed tens of billions to the industry's available financial resources.

Dysfunctional Risk Culture: The "*Wall Street Journal Test*"

At the other end of the continuum is unethical and illegal behavior. There is something called the "*Wall Street Journal* test," which you might have heard about. If you ever find yourself in a situation wondering "Am I doing the 'right' thing?," one way to find the answer is to imagine seeing your picture on the cover of the *WSJ* and reading a half-page article about what you did;

if you would be comfortable with absolutely everything objectively bared to regulators, family and friends, then it passes the test.

This test is useful and should be standard operating procedure in virtually all circumstances, especially those where there are no "right" or "wrong" answers – such as for environmental and social issues. In addition to potentially influencing your decision, the *WSJ* test also prepares you if and when your decision is critically reviewed, since you would have already thought critically and prepared your rebuttal.

There are, however, situations where the *WSJ* test should not need to be invoked, situations where there is a clear black-and-white answer, where there is no ambiguity between what is right and what is wrong. Most people would agree that committing fraud by manipulating financial markets or taking advantage of unsophisticated customers such as charitable foundations and trusts do not belong on the "right" side of the divide.

Unfortunately, these truths are apparently not universally obvious across the financial services industry, an industry where the true north of individual and institutional ethical compasses may occasionally be influenced by greed. Consider the following examples of behavior which would have failed the *WSJ* test if it had been used in advance:

The Libor Fixing and FX Scandals

The Libor fixing scandal emerged in a *Wall Street Journal* article on April 16, 2008, alleging that banks were under-stating their cost of funds in the inter-bank market, apparently in an attempt to limit fears that market liquidity was drying up and that the creditworthiness of some banks was deteriorating as measured by their cost of funding.

At first the allegations were denied, with the Bank of International Settlements (Gyntelberg and Woolridge, 2008) stating that the "available data do not support the hypothesis that contributor banks manipulated their quotes to profit from positions based on fixings" and the IMF (2008) commenting: "Although the integrity of the US dollar Libor-fixing process has been questioned by some market participants and the financial press, it appears that US dollar Libor remains an accurate measure of a typical creditworthy bank's marginal cost of unsecured US dollar term funding." However, memos released later indicate that representatives of the Bank of England and the US Federal Reserve were aware of the practice.

The academic study by Snider and Youle (2010) corroborated the *Wall Street Journal* article and suggested another, far more nefarious reason for submitting incorrect rates: the manipulation of the values of derivative contracts which use Libor as the reference rate. This led to a broader investigation, surfacing some very interesting emails and telephone transcripts which implicated traders in unethical activities as far back as 2005.

- In one exchange between a banker and a broker, the banker wrote "if you keep 6s [i.e., the six month JPY LIBOR rate] unchanged today . . . I will f—ing do one humongous deal with you . . . Like a 50,000 buck deal, whatever . . . I need you to keep it as low as possible . . . if you do that . . . I'll pay you, you know, 50,000 dollars, 100,000 dollars . . . whatever you want . . . I'm a man of my word." Subsequent trades generated more than $250,000 in fees to the broker.
- And, as if they did not want to leave any doubt, a trader wrote "It's just amazing how Libor fixing can make you that much money or lose if opposite. It's a cartel now in London," to which another trader replied, "Must be damn difficult to trade man, especially (if) you (are) not in the loop."

Ultimately, there were large fines to be paid for market manipulation. The *Wall Street Journal* (Peaple, 2013) reported that "US and UK regulators have (already) hit five big banks, including Barclays and UBS, with USD 3.5 billion of penalties related to the setting of Libor . . . In Europe, antitrust regulators are set to levy penalties that could approach €1 billion each against six big banks of alleged collusion in manipulating benchmark interest rates." In addition, both the Chairman and CEO of Barclays resigned over the scandal, as did the CEO of Rabobank.

Subsequent investigations produced evidence of manipulation in other markets as well. In the same article, the *Wall Street Journal* reports that "Global regulators are now looking at potential manipulation in global foreign exchange markets." The *Wall Street Journal* (Strasburg, 2013) reported in a separate article that "The investigations are focused on chat rooms with names such as 'The Cartel' . . . Investigators have found messages in which traders joked about being able to influence currency exchange rates and appeared to inappropriately share information with competitors." The article continues by saying that banks are reviewing their policies with respect to chat rooms and other methods of communication within the industry, a classic case of addressing the symptom and not the illness. The story did not end well, with global regulators fining 6 global banks $4.3 billion (*Reuters News*, 2014).

Treating Your Customer Fairly

Taking advantage of unsophisticated customers is an age-old practice: the infamous circus leader P.T. Barnum[19] is (inaccurately) supposed to have said "There is a sucker born every minute." Unfortunately, the practice seems to have also made its way into high finance.

In one of the earliest high-profile cases, *Business Week* (Holland and Himelstein, 1995) reported that two employees of Bankers Trust discussed a leveraged deal the bank sold to Proctor & Gamble: "'They would never be able to know how much money was taken out of that,' says one employee, referring to the huge profits the bank stood to make on the transaction. 'Never, no way,' replies her colleague. 'That's the beauty of Bankers Trust.' . . . According to P&G: 'Fraud was so pervasive and institutionalized that Bankers Trust employees used the acronym 'ROF' – short for rip-off factor, to describe one method of fleecing clients' . . . P&G quotes another Bankers Trust employee saying to a colleague: 'Funny business, you know? Lure people into that calm and then just totally f---'em.'" As discussed elsewhere, public disclosure of these practices proved fatal to the Bankers Trust business model, pushing the company into the arms of Deutsche Bank.

A decade later in a *New York Times* op ed, Greg Smith (2012a) wrote: "Today is my last day at Goldman Sachs . . . I believe that I have worked here long enough to understand the trajectory of its culture, its people and its identity. And I can honestly say that the environment now is as toxic and destructive as I have ever seen it. To put the problem in the simplest terms, the interests of the client continue to be sidelined in the way the firm operates and thinks about making money."

In the op ed, Smith claims that Goldman bankers in London frequently called unsophisticated clients "muppets." Echoing the Bankers Trust scandal of a decade earlier, Smith (2012b) said during an interview that "'Getting an unsophisticated client was the golden prize . . . The quickest way to make money on Wall Street is to take the most sophisticated product and try to sell it to the least sophisticated client." The most prized unsophisticated clients are "philanthropies or endowments or teachers' retirement pension funds in Alabama or Virginia or Oregon."

---

[19]P.T. Barnum was the founder of America's most famous circus, Barnum & Baily's Circus.

What Defines a "Good" Risk Culture and How Do I Get One?

Senior leadership and regulators alike are recognizing the importance of risk culture and thinking through what can be done to shape it. The FSB (2014) comments that "Culture can be a very complex issue as it involves behaviors and attitudes. But efforts should be made by financial institutions and by supervisors to understand an institution's culture and how it affects safety and soundness."

Standard Recommendations: More of the Same . . .

Toward this end, many reports have been issued providing guidance on assessing, measuring and managing risk culture.[20] Most begin where ERM leaves off, by promoting additional measures to strengthen the ERM framework and then monitoring performance carefully.

For example, the FSB (2013a,b) references several reports to guide institutions in building the foundations in terms of structure, risk appetite and compensation,[21] providing detailed, prescriptive actions and suggesting that "A sound risk culture should emphasize throughout the institution the importance of ensuring that:

i. an appropriate risk–reward balance consistent with the institution's risk appetite is achieved when taking on risks;
ii. an effective system of controls commensurate with the scale and complexity of the financial institution is properly put in place;
iii. the quality of risk models, data accuracy, capability of available tools to accurately measure risks and justifications for risk taking can be challenged;
iv. all limit breaches, deviations from established policies and operational incidents are thoroughly followed up with proportionate disciplinary actions when necessary."

Most then continue by recommending that the controls should be tested for implementation and effectiveness and that evidence should be collected, "(including) a list of indicators . . . (which) should be treated as a starting point . . ." for assessing risk culture.

. . . But Is It Sufficient?

In summary, most recommendations for improving risk culture focus on additional controls leading to tangible indicators – tangible in the sense that evidence can be documented, collected and assessed. And herein lies the paradox.

- Do we really believe that "culture" is something that can be objectively measured, like the weight of a turnip or the sensitivity of a bond to interest rates?
- Do we believe that adding to the already voluminous ERM bookshelf of controls and evidence (which apparently failed many institutions in the last crisis) will actually resolve a "cultural" issue?

---

[20]I recommend reading FSB (2014). See also Levy *et al.* (2010), Towers Watson (2011) and Daisley (2013).

[21]See also FSB, *Principles for Sound Compensation Practices*, April 2009 and FSB, *Principles for Sound Compensation Practices: Implementation Standards*, September 2009.

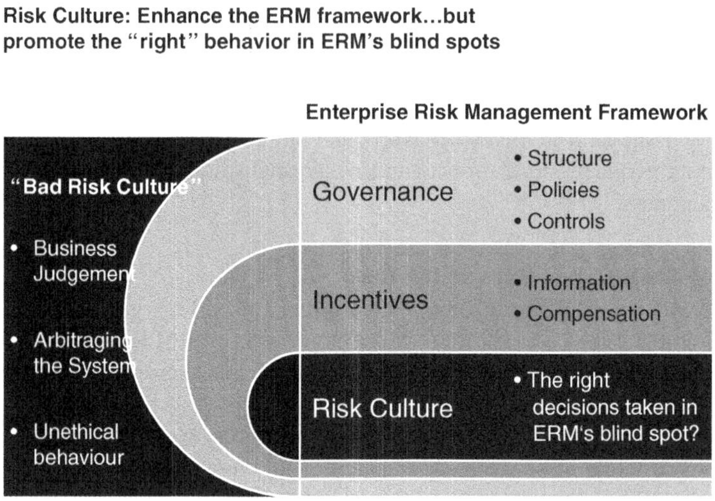

Risk Culture: Enhance the ERM framework...but promote the "right" behavior in ERM's blind spots

FIGURE 20.4 Improving ERM – what happens in ERM's blind spots

- Or, will the creation of increasingly more elaborate ERM controls simply hide the symptoms of a bad culture under additional documentation requirements[22] without actually addressing the underlying illness?

While I believe that a strong ERM framework is necessary, it is not sufficient. My strong conviction is that there is no ERM framework – no additional reports or heat maps, no risk strategies and risk appetite statements, no controls or separation of duties and no additional measurement activities – which will be truly effective in combating something as amorphous and damaging as a dysfunctional risk and business culture.

What is a "Good" Risk Culture?

My thinking leads to a different definition of a "good" risk culture (illustrated in Figure 20.4): a good risk culture is one where individuals take the decisions which are right for your company even in the blind spots of your ERM framework. More specifically, a good risk culture is one where individuals take the right decisions when they are not being controlled or when the ERM framework is silent and, especially, when the right decision goes against their own personal incentives.

There is no framework of controls that will catch all possible bad behaviors. A good risk culture is one where individuals take actions to improve the institution and its long-term franchise value, even if it goes against their short-term interests. Internal controls and the alignment of incentives help, but they are not enough.

Building a "Good" Risk Culture is a Lot Like Parenting

Just like parenting, ultimately we want individuals to act independently and take the right decisions even when no one is watching. In the case of parenting, getting this behavior is much

---

[22]In their defense, the FSB (2014) recognize this risk, stating that "Supervisors should avoid supervisory methodologies that treat these indicators as a checklist."

more challenging than adding an additional layer of controls. First, because parents cannot be around all the time and second, because adding additional controls may be counterproductive, especially if hiding behind the controls gives an excuse to not develop one's own moral compass (Markham, 2014): too many, too rigid controls prevent thinking, learning and developing, and may produce individuals incapable of independent direction in the absence of rigid guard rails.

This insight is at the heart of the *Financial Times* op ed by Hill (2014). Citing research on the successes of the Lloyd's insurance market, he comments: "These people have mastered a complex, self-regulating balancing act, governed by internal understandings that are stronger than mere regulations. The implication is that elsewhere, where regulators, lawyers and compliance officers are in charge of controlling excesses, self-discipline atrophies and people lose valuable skills . . . Self-regulation, bounded by the ethical norms and shared responsibilities that friends cultivate and observe, can work. Regulators and politicians should take note before they sling it all out with the dirty bathwater of bad behavior."

So, *in addition to making tangible ERM improvements and monitoring new indicators, firms also need to focus on the "softer" elements, developing and nurturing individuals' ethical compass.* Being overly prescriptive and relying on stultifying controls is not the answer; more important than "rewards" and "punishment" are "clarity," "consistency," "communication" and being a "role model."

- The journey starts by communicating and enforcing reasonable rules and doing so consistently.
- It continues by learning, using judgment in evaluating issues, discussing both lessons and conclusions openly and taking actions consequently. In this way, new precedents are set and the ability to openly discuss and decide between "right and wrong," even in the absence of rules or precedents, is reinforced. Valuable learning opportunities which can be institutionalized include file reviews and transaction post mortems, underwriting training, celebrating "underwriting heroes" on a par with "rainmakers," etc.
- In lieu of an actual parent, all individuals – and especially senior management – need to become role models. This includes setting a consistent "tone at the top," including a commitment to ethical principles generally, as well as:
  - an "underwriting culture" where risk is taken on behalf of the institution as if it were your own;
  - a "customer culture" where customer needs and value play a prominent role in product design and sales;
  - a stronger identification with the long-term success and reputation of the company than an individual.
- Finally, an alignment between corporate and individual goals and cultural principles.

These steps are echoed and enhanced in the context of building a "good" underwriting culture in Chapter 23.

CHAPTER 21

Risk Governance and Organization

Before embarking on a detailed description of each core risk framework (risk identification, underwriting and controlling), it is worthwhile to make a few general comments on risk governance and organization.

This chapter begins by describing the "textbook" answer to the question, "What defines 'good' risk governance?" We start with general principles and continue with the definition of the three-line-of-defense model. We then answer some common questions with regards to the organization of the risk function.

RISK GOVERNANCE PRINCIPLES

There are a few high-level principles which define good risk governance:[1]

- senior management and Board "ownership" of both risk and returns;
- an explicit articulation of the firm's risk appetite and its strategy for creating value by taking risk;
- clear accountability and incentives to take the right risk/reward decisions;
- an effective risk culture promoting transparency as well as personal integrity and ethical behavior;
- the design, implementation and testing of a comprehensive system of controls, periodically validated by independent, external personnel;
- as part of the control framework, independent checks and balances including independent risk management and audit, separation of duties and definition of the first, second and third lines of defense;
- sufficient skilled and experienced personnel in the front line as well as the risk and control functions.

Because these are principles and not detailed rules, there are as many risk organizations in practice as there are banks and insurance companies, with the differences to be found in the details of the committee structures, reporting lines, authorities, etc. The remainder of this chapter provides insights into the role of the Board and senior management in managing risks and how the risk function should be organized.

---

[1]More detailed principles can be found in PRMIA (2009).

ROLE OF THE BOARD AND MANAGEMENT

Corporate governance differs by country. For example, most Anglo-Saxon countries have a single-tier Board, combining executive and non-executive directors; the Chairman is often the CEO and there is often a Management or Executive Committee comprising only executives of the firm. In the two-tier European model, the Supervisory Board consists solely of non-executives and employee representatives and is led by a non-executive Chairman; the Management Board consists of full-time executives and is led by the CEO.

In spite of the apparent differences, the roles of the Board and executive management in managing risks are quite similar in Anglo-Saxon and European institutions. The remainder of this section does not differentiate between the two models but instead refers to the Board and management, respectively. The roles of each, and their risk-relevant committees, are discussed in detail below.

The Board of Directors and Management Board[2]

The Board, elected primarily by shareholders, is the highest body of authority in the company and oversees the company's activities. The members of the Board have a fiduciary responsibility to the shareholders but, as a matter of enlightened self-interest for the benefit of shareholders, Boards also consider the interests of other stakeholder groups such as employees, the community and the environment.

Typical duties of the Board include the establishment of broad policies and objectives for the company, selecting and reviewing the performance of the chief executive and management compensation, ensuring adequate financial resources, approving annual budgets and accounting to the stakeholders for the company's performance. For large stock companies, the Board tends to have more of a supervisory role, delegating much of the operational decision making to the executive management of the firm but retaining strategic and control responsibilities.

The committees at the Board which play a direct role in risk and finance include the Audit, Risk and Compensation Committees, described below; in addition, most firms also have a Nomination Committee to ensure adequate Board recruitment and staffing.

The Management Board or Executive Board is typically responsible for developing and recommending strategy to the Board and overseeing the daily operations of the firm. The committees at the Management Board level which play a direct role in risk and finance include the Asset/Liability Management Committee (or the Finance Committee), the Risk Committee and the Reserve Committee (for insurers).

Given the complexity of banking and insurance businesses, good corporate governance requires an appropriate level of skills and experience within the Board, especially within the risk and finance-related committees. Increasingly, candidates for Board and certain management positions are being challenged directly by regulators under a "fit and proper" test. In addition to ensuring sufficient knowledge, good corporate governance also dictates that there should be sufficient independent directors on the Board to effectively challenge management.

Audit Committee

The responsibilities of the Audit Committee include: oversight of the financial reporting and disclosure process and associated controls; monitoring of the firm's accounting policies and

---

[2]A good discussion of the role of the Board can be found in FSB (2013a).

principles; overseeing external auditor hiring and independence; reviewing the performance of internal audit; oversight of regulatory compliance and whistleblower hotlines. The Audit Committee reviews the reserves of insurance companies, complemented by a Reserve Committee at executive management level. The Audit Committee is typically chaired by a non-executive Board member.

Risk Committee

Boards at financial services companies increasingly have a Risk Committee responsible for assisting the Board in identifying, assessing and reviewing the risk profile of the firm; defining and approving the risk strategy and risk appetite of the firm; reviewing the risk policies, guidelines, models and procedures; and, finally, ensuring the independence, adequacy (in terms of staff, skills, systems, etc.) and effectiveness of the risk management function.

At the Management Board level, the Risk Committee performs the same functions. In addition, it also has the highest level of transaction approval or limit-granting authority. The Risk Committee is chaired by the CRO or occasionally the CFO; because risk and return are two sides of the same coin, both business and control functions are represented on the Risk Committee.

Compensation Committee

A Compensation Committee is typically required for a publically listed company and is responsible for developing the compensation framework for executives; establishing and reviewing CEO and executive officer compensation levels, including share or equity grants, guarantees, etc.; and responding to shareholder recommendations with regard to compensation issues. The Compensation Committee is almost always chaired by a non-executive Board member.

The Compensation Committee is also often mirrored at the Management Board level, taking decisions for senior employees below the Management Board level.

Asset/Liability Management Committee

The ALCO is discussed extensively in Chapter 15. It is responsible for decisions related to the structure of the firm's balance sheet, its overall liquidity position and the management of the firm's structural asset/liability position.

Given its operational focus, the ALCO is a management committee; because different and potentially conflicting interests need to be balanced, both business and control functions affected should be represented on this committee.

Investment Committee

Some insurance ALCOs may be more strategic in orientation. In such cases, the firm may also have an Investment Committee, as management committee, chaired by the CIO or CFO, which meets more frequently and is mandated to rebalance the asset/liability portfolio around the strategic benchmark or take tactical investment decisions within delegated competencies.

Reserve Committee

The Reserve Committee, also a management committee, comprises key stakeholders in the reserving process (e.g., finance, underwriting, claims and risk management) and is often chaired by the CFO. The Committee discusses the analysis and recommendations of the lead reserving actuary and ultimately selects reserve levels. The results are presented and discussed by the Audit Committee.

THREE-LINE-OF-DEFENSE MODEL

Management and the Board are responsible for ensuring an adequate internal control framework for running the business and ensuring that the company stays on course to achieve its objectives; in some instances, this responsibility is codified in commercial and securities law.

COSO (2011)[3] defines an adequate internal control framework as a "process, effected by an entity's board of directors, management and other personnel, designed to provide reasonable assurance regarding the achievement of objectives in the following categories:

- Effectiveness and efficiency of operations,
- Reliability of financial reporting,
- Compliance with applicable laws and regulations."

COSO defines the first category as addressing the firm's basic business objectives, including performance and profitability goals; the second and third are self-explanatory.

Risk Controlling and the Three-lines-of-defense Framework

Everyone in the firm, from the front office to the back office, has a role to play in the firm's internal control system. For example, senior executives (including the CEO) sign accountability statements with respect to the accuracy of financial statements and the adherence to internal policies; underwriters perform periodic reviews to ensure that underwriting policy is adhered to; and back-office personnel perform checks to limit internal fraud and the wasting of corporate assets.

In general, key controls are conducted by individuals who are independent, accomplished through a *segregation of duties*. As an example, in light of the Nick Leeson/Barings rogue trading experience, it is now accepted practice that an independent back office performs basic controls including trade, confirm and general ledger reconciliations.

In addition to the basic principle of segregation of duties, there is also an overarching concept of "three lines of defense" employed by all banks and insurers, as illustrated in Table 21.1.

The **first line of defense** includes the front office or business people who are *ultimately responsible for the profit and losses from taking commercial decisions*, for example with regard to ALM, trading and investments, underwriting, new product development, etc. Also included in the first line are business steering activities (e.g., strategic planning and performance management). As discussed later, a more recent trend is to also include activities which require explicit independent controls because of the potential influence on financial results and business steering (e.g., financial reporting, corporate actuarial/reserve setting).

---

[3]COSO is the Committee of the Sponsoring Organizations of the Treadway Commission, a joint initiative of five private sector organizations (American Accounting Association, American Institute of CPAs, Financial Executives International, Association of Accountants and Financial Professionals in Business, Institute of Internal Auditors) dedicated to providing thought leadership on enterprise risk management, internal control and fraud deterrence. http://www.coso.org/documents/Internal%20Control-Integrated%20Framework.pdf

TABLE 21.1   Three lines of defense

First line	Second line	Third line
Responsible for taking and steering risk/reward decisions within ERM framework.	Responsible for ▪ developing ERM framework, ▪ design and implementation of independent risk controls, ▪ risk management.	Responsible for testing adequacy of design, implementation and effectiveness of ERM framework.
Business, business steering.	Risk, compliance.	Internal audit.

The first line of defense forms a critical element of the internal control framework: if the front office does not have the right culture, incentives or skills, then no amount of additional controls will make up for the deficit. The first line of defense can and should define and implement controls in their own sphere of responsibility (e.g., performing underwriting or closed file reviews, monitoring customer complaints, monitoring and testing data security breaches, etc.) in order to ensure success in meeting their own business objectives.

The **second line of defense** consists of independent control functions, often specifically identified by regulators. Risk management and compliance are universally considered to be a second-line-of-defense function; other functions are also included, as discussed below. It is the responsibility of the second line to *define the ERM framework, to be approved by the Board, within which the front line can operate in the normal course of business.*

Second-line functions translate management's risk appetite and strategy into an ERM framework. The ERM framework is analogous to "guard rails" and speed limits found on the highway or race track: they are designed to keep the drivers (the first line of defense) within safe operating boundaries under normal conditions; however, they do not steer the car. The second line also defines and ensures the implementation of additional, independent controls; carrying the analogy further, these independent controls are analogous to traffic police, speed radar devices, etc., ensuring that the ERM framework is adhered to.

The **third line of defense** consists of internal audit, complemented by external audit. It is audit's responsibility *to test that the internal control procedures, and in particular the enterprise risk framework, is adequately designed, implemented and effective.* Activities include verifying that the risk profile and decisions are consistent with policies, delegated authorities and the risk appetite of the institution, validating internal models and escalating situations where there is a failure in the controls.

On the Difference between Risk Management and Risk Controlling

If the guard rails and speed limits are well defined, it might be tempting to conclude that the first line should be allowed to operate with relative autonomy within the guard rails. And in my experience, this is the correct approach . . . 95+% of the time.

However, the conclusion would be wrong the other 5% of the time. It is wrong because it is based on an incorrect assumption: that a risk management framework can be designed which will be effective in *all* circumstances. Personal experience has taught me that there is no such thing as an ERM framework robust to every situation. More specifically, experience illustrates the following.

- *Any risk measure and internal model* (a key component of the risk-controlling framework) *will be wrong with probability one during the next crisis*. Even worse, it will be wrong in ways that cannot be imagined. This is the reason that the industry has a love/hate relationship with models: we love them because they are useful tools for managing our businesses during "normal times" and we hate them because they will let us down during the next crisis when it really matters.
- *Any risk measurement and limit framework can and will be arbitraged* by the front line, which has the incentives, intelligence and capabilities to do so. This arbitrage can be subtle (e.g., always selecting the highest-yielding bond within a given rating band in order to pick up yield) or overt (e.g., putting on a one-week hedge one day before month-end reporting). In either case, the bank or insurer can count on its frameworks being arbitraged.
- Any framework which attempts to be comprehensive, anticipating any and all imaginable scenarios, is likely to be *overly complex and restrictive*, so tightly defined that the "guard rails" de facto end up steering the car and being incapable of keeping up with a dynamic business.

The conclusion is that, while *risk controlling* in a strict sense may work 95+% of the time, some form of *risk management* must also be undertaken by the second line for the remaining 5%. With this in mind, the second line should undertake two activities.

1. Risk controlling and oversight for the "normal business."
   - Help the Board and management to define the ERM framework and additional, independent controls within which businesses can operate on a "business-as-usual" basis.
   - Make transparent the risk profile and limit utilization of the businesses.
   - Provide technical analysis as needed to support business decisions.
2. Risk management for the exceptional circumstances when the frameworks fail.
   - Have a deep, professional understanding of the business (not just the models!).
   - Be close to the business, discussing key decisions before they are taken.
   - Exercise professional judgment, helping to find the right solution but occasionally saying "no" (representing a veto) if the risk frameworks prove inadequate or if they are being arbitraged.

At first blush, this may seem to jeopardize the independence of the second line; in reality, the risk management activities described above are an integral part of the control framework needed to deal with exceptional circumstances.

However, in order to ensure that the risk management function does not end up steering the car, their rights and limitations should be clearly defined. More specifically, the second line functions:

- should have *broad and binding "veto" rights*[4] on everything (e.g., on transactions, cumulative portfolio positions, marketing materials, etc.) without restriction as it is not clear a priori where the exceptional circumstances will arise;

---

[4]The phrase "veto right" is used here to imply a stronger form of escalation – one that cannot be over-ridden directly by a business head but must be escalated up both the first- and second-line organization for discussion.

- should *not take a commercial view*, clearly separating its risk control view (e.g., "no objection, veto which requires escalation") from any commercial view (e.g., "things to consider to improve the business but not conditions precedent for a risk approval").

The logic is that, if a "veto right" is granted to the second line of defense, then it will be kept narrowly defined but be more empowered.

Industry Trends

A survey of 14 banks and insurers conducted in 2013 provided interesting insights which support this thinking.[5] In summary, the second line of defense functions in the financial services industry are becoming fewer, more focused on control but also more empowered to say "no." With regard to the composition of the second line, the survey indicated the following.

- The risk management function is always in the second line of defense, together with compliance, which was included in all but one instance.
- The finance function (including financial and management reporting, corporate actuarial, investor relations, treasury, tax, corporate finance and corporate strategy) is in the first line in the majority of firms. This represents a significant trend: five years ago, the finance function would have been in the second line in the majority of firms. While some of these functions are independent of P&L, their designation as a first-line function reflects their role in business steering and the need for additional, independent controls over financial reporting.
- Other functions – including business continuity management, IT and data security, human relations – were occasionally included in the second line in some firms. However, the trend was clearly toward fewer but more empowered second-line functions.

With regard to the rights and limitations of the second line of defense, we have the following.

- All second-line functions had the right to define policies and controls, test controls and escalate issues identified; however, first-line functions also shared these rights when it came to their areas of responsibility.
- The second-line functions had a "veto" right in 6 out of the 14 firms. However, the right of veto was negatively correlated with the breadth of the second line: those with only risk and compliance in the second line had a higher probability of empowering the function with the right of veto.

Some Special Cases

If there is too much influence by the second line on commercial decisions, there is a risk that it will lose its independence, creating unnecessary frictions and becoming an impediment to doing good business. On the contrary, too little influence and the resulting portfolios may underperform or even present severe challenges during times of crisis.

---

[5]Thanks to Rick Lester and his team at Deloitte for providing industry insights.

Credit Portfolio Management

One illustration of this tension can be found in the evolution of credit portfolio management within banks. The objectives of the credit portfolio management function are noble: to optimize the portfolio of retained risks by promoting adequate, risk-based pricing, directing the underwriting activities of the firm and managing the retained portfolio through asset sales and credit derivatives.

During the 1990s, when banks first set up the functions, the credit portfolio management team was often located within the risk function. The reason was understandable: most of the intellectual foundations, tools and frameworks for managing the portfolio, including risk-adjusted returns, the measurement of diversification benefits, etc., were developed and implemented by the risk function.

However, as the credit portfolio management function began to live up to its mandate of optimizing the portfolio, it became apparent that it was steering the business as opposed to providing the framework within which business decisions are taken. And, by managing the portfolio, they lost their ability to remain objective in evaluating risks and returns. As a consequence, the credit portfolio management functions of most banks have subsequently migrated from the risk function to become a front-line or business function, often called the credit treasury.

The Relation between Underwriting and Risk Control

A second illustration arises in the context of the credit or insurance underwriting function and the risk management function. If the underwriters are responsible for the risk/return decision, what role does the risk function have in the credit or insurance underwriting approval process? Some institutions may relegate risk to a pure control function.

It is clear that underwriting needs a strong commercial orientation, balancing the potential rewards of accepting the loan or policy against the associated risks, and pricing the transaction so as to optimize the margin. As a consequence, most underwriting decisions are made by the first line within guidelines, defined and monitored in part by the risk function. This is the risk function's risk control role.

However, some material, complex or new transactions will not fit within the framework designed to cover 95% of the business and therefore need to be independently reviewed and underwritten from a risk perspective. This is the risk function's risk management role.

Getting the relationship between the front-line and the second-line risk activities "right," and risk control versus risk management in the second line, is important: too little risk involvement and the organization can experience unnecessary underwriting losses; too much and the organization may miss out on profitable commercial opportunities.

THE RISK FUNCTION

The role of the CRO and generic job descriptions were discussed earlier in Chapter 2. This section looks at the organizational interfaces: up, down and sideways from the position of the CRO.

The general principles are clear: the risk function should be independent, without direct P&L responsibility; it should be prominently positioned in the firm such that it can constructively influence business decisions; it should have sufficient resources and skills; it should be integrated into the core management processes of the firm, including strategic planning, balance sheet management, underwriting and compensation. The devil is in the detail, however, with four questions commonly being asked (as illustrated in Figure 21.1).

Common organizational questions

1. To whom should the CRO report?
2. Should the CRO have an enterprise scope, covering all risks, or is it possible to manage risks in silos?
3. Should the global risk network have a direct reporting line or a "dotted line"?
4. What is the internal organization of the Risk Function?

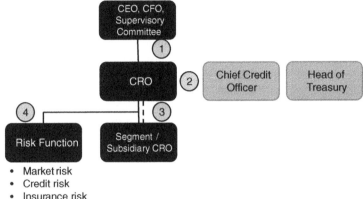

- Market risk
- Credit risk
- Insurance risk
- Operational risk

FIGURE 21.1 The design of the risk function

To Whom Should the CRO Report?

There are three prevalent CRO reporting relationships at banks and insurers: to the CEO, either directly or as a member of the Executive or Management Board; to the CFO; to the Chairman of the Supervisory Board/Audit Committee. All three reporting lines can work in principle. However, the trend at banks and insurance companies is toward a direct reporting line to the CEO as a member of the Executive or Management Board.

This trend is supported by regulators, as evidenced by the FSB's (2013a) recommendation that supervisors should "set requirements to elevate the CRO's stature, authority, and independence in the firm . . . (and that) The CRO should have a direct reporting line to the CEO and a distinct role from other executive functions and business line responsibilities (e.g., no 'dual-hatting') . . . For instance, the CRO reporting to the chief financial officer (CFO) or assuming the responsibilities of both the CRO and CFO should be avoided to preserve the independence and effectiveness of both roles."

Similarly, most major European insurance companies are migrating toward this reporting structure: whereas in the early 2000s only Swiss Re had a CRO on the Executive Board, many of the CRO Forum firms have by now elevated the CRO to the Management Board.

One might be tempted to ask for the ultimate level of independence and require the risk function to report to the Supervisory Board or the Audit Committee of the Supervisory Board. To my mind, this would be a mistake: isolating the risk function completely from the business implicitly assumes that the risk framework will be adequate to meet every eventuality, including being robust to arbitrage, market crisis, etc. Reality has illustrated time and time again that this is not the case, arguing strongly for a risk function which is both independent of the business but still sufficiently close to intercede if the framework proves inadequate. Isolating and focusing the risk function on a pure control or audit role will not accomplish this.

What is the Scope of the Risk Function?

Is it necessary to have a CRO responsible for all risks, including financial market, credit, insurance, operational, etc., as ERM implies, or is it sufficient for credit, market and insurance risk managers to operate in silos?

The Silo Approach

Some organizations, predominantly smaller, more focused institutions, have historically structured their risk functions along silos. As a consultant, I worked with one of the top 20 banks in the USA, a "pure" commercial credit institution, regional in scope. The most important risks for this bank were credit and the asset/liability management risk associated with its commercial lending business. The bank decided on two separate risk silos: a Chief Credit Officer (CCO) to run credit underwriting, portfolio management and workout functions and a Head of Market Risk, reporting to the CFO, who was also the treasurer in charge of asset/liability management.

Similarly, some PC insurance companies also split risk management roles between assets and liabilities, with a Chief Underwriting Officer (CUO) bringing a strong commercial but risk-aware focus to insurance underwriting decisions, and a Head of ALM to cover the financial market and credit investment risks.

The Enterprise Scope is Gaining

In contrast, most of the largest banks and insurers have defined a broader and more comprehensive scope for their CRO, covering all risks ranging from financial market to credit, insurance and operational. The enterprise scope is the de facto standard for the largest banks and insurance companies for four reasons.

- First, the commercial orientation of silo-based risk management structures may face a strong headwind from regulators. This is because a clear, independent risk control function is difficult to evidence in CCO/CUO/Head of Treasury roles which both take and control risk decisions. As such, many of the silo organizations still in place are based on the strength and character of individuals and often evolve into enterprise-wide risk structures when those individuals retire.
- Second, without a comprehensive, integrated perspective, it is possible for risks to "fall between two chairs." For example, many banks suffered significant losses from credit-risky positions in their trading book during the 2008 crisis. Market risk managers failed to underwrite the credit risk in the trading book due to the (faulty) assumption that market liquidity would always be there, whereas credit underwriting focused only on "banking book" exposures, leaving a gap between the traditional credit and market risk silos with respect to traded credit. Closing this gap requires a close interaction between credit and market risk management, made possible through enterprise-wide risk management.
- Third, common frameworks are needed to identify and manage risk and combining activities can lead to efficiency gains as well as better insights. For example, the generic COSO framework is used in different guises to identify, evaluate and control risks, for example through the Top Risk Assessment (TRA), operational Risk Controlled Self-Assessment (RCSA), compliance and audit risk assessments and emerging risk assessments; it is much more efficient (and appreciated by the rest of the organization) to consolidate and coordinate these analyses.

- Finally, an enterprise risk function helps to ensure uniform risk assessment and risk appetite and reduces complexity in approval processes, limit and capital allocation processes, etc. In other words, it is normally easier and more efficient to go to one second-line-of-defense function than to two or three.

Should Risk have a Direct or Dotted-line Reporting Function?

This question is relevant for diversified financial service firms which operate with a corporate center distinct from the business lines. In this context, a direct reporting line is defined by the right to directly set objectives, evaluate performance and take hire, fire and compensation-related decisions for personnel within the function. In contrast, a dotted reporting line is defined as the ability to give *input* on objectives, performance evaluations and hire, fire and compensation. These rights can be important from a positive perspective, for example in terms of setting and reinforcing the risk agenda, as well as from a defensive position, for example by protecting individuals who are doing the right risk management job but may be in conflict with line management on specific issues.

The form of the reporting line is influenced by legal structure: most banks and reinsurers use branches (where corporate governance supports a direct functional reporting line), in contrast to primary insurers which use subsidiaries (where governance supports a direct reporting line to the subsidiary's CEO). In addition, it is also influenced by the management structure of the business: most banks and reinsurers have more global lines of business, for example global trading or global specialty lines, again supporting a global, direct reporting structure for the risk function.

I have worked in both types of organization – direct reporting lines at Swiss Re New Markets and Dresdner Bank, dotted reporting lines at ING and Allianz. Both can work in practice; however, you have to work a bit harder to create an effective global risk network under the dotted line framework. Some observations on creating an effective risk network include the following.

- First, the risk (and finance) functions should *"mirror" the line management organization*. In other words, if the businesses are run with strong global reporting lines, then the risk function should mirror this organization: in my experience, it is challenging to implement a reporting line which is not aligned with line management because there is no correspondence between the business and risk leaders, making it difficult to become an effective business partner.
- Second, regardless of who has the direct reporting line, *the indirect reporting line must be able to give meaningful input on objectives, performance evaluation, hiring, firing and compensation.*
- Third, if the risk function has a dotted reporting line to the CRO, it is imperative that there are explicit *escalation procedures* put in place: the local risk functions have the right to halt with immediate effect any business activity or new product; if local management disagrees, they have the right to escalate to the next higher level, ultimately to the CRO and the Risk Committee of the Board. This "veto and escalate" procedure is critical to ensure that local risk functions can perform their second-line roles in a decentralized company.
- Finally, and most critically, the CRO who wants to develop a strong functional network around dotted reporting relationships has to *work harder* in order to build a trust-based relationship with both the CROs as well as the business leaders across the organization.

Note: Risk Management Functions are not likely to be under one manager, but are likely to
have a Head of Market Risk, Head of Credit Risk, etc.

FIGURE 21.2   The design of the risk function

For example, I set myself the target of visiting each of the largest operating entities at least
once a year and all of them at least once every two years. In addition to meeting with the local
CRO and his/her team, I also meet with senior management and try to understand the business
and market context, the company's management team and strategy and the issues that they face.
My rationale is twofold.

- First, I need to have the confidence that the local CRO "has my back" and will do the right
  thing in terms of identifying, managing and escalating risk issues, just as I need the CRO to
  understand that I "have their back" and will resolve appropriately any issue which is
  escalated.
- Second, if there is ever the need for me to discuss an issue with the CEO over the phone,
  there is enough context, understanding and relationship for us to come to the right solution.

In addition, I also structure my corporate risk function to include coverage officers
responsible for understanding the business, the risks and the management team. These
coverage officers are indispensable for building a bridge between the corporate center and
the operating entities in a dotted-line reporting function.

What Internal Organization of the Risk Function?

The final set of questions have to do with the internal organization of the risk function.
Figure 21.2 represents a "straw man" organization for the corporate risk function.

Should Risk Reporting be Separate from Risk Management?

In general, most risk functions engage in two activities: risk management and risk reporting or
controlling. In some firms, these activities are in the same team. I believe that the risk reporting
activities should be separated from risk management activities, if at all possible. I generally
expect risk reporting to be an effective, efficient and controlled "reporting factory" capable of

delivering standard risk and limit reports. Ultimately, this reporting function may even be "outsourced" to finance or "off-shored." In contrast, I expect from risk managers professional experience and judgment combined with a close proximity to the business. While not completely incompatible, these two roles are sufficiently different to warrant their separation if critical mass can be achieved.

What is the Role of Risk Management?

Risk management should be close to the business and have the professional experience required to understand the business and intercede as necessary, both at the portfolio and individual transaction levels. In addition, they should support the setting of limits for their areas through the strategic planning process, conduct ad hoc portfolio or product reviews and develop recommendations on important issues which may arise. They are also responsible for providing risk-specific management discussion and assessment for risk issues in the ORSA (Own Risk and Solvency Assessment), the annual report, etc.

What is the Role of Risk Methodology?

The risk methodology teams need sufficient technical capabilities in order to develop and maintain the firm's internal model, keeping up with business developments. However, the methodology teams should not be allowed to "run amok." The downside of a separate methodology team is that the team's raison d'être is defined by models, committing the firm to a perpetuity of model changes/improvements. This risk can be mitigated by enforcing two rules.

- First, all new models have to fit into a robust, efficient and controlled risk reporting system. This means that some "bleeding edge" model developments may never be implemented.
- Second, model changes should come only once a year (unless you are compelled otherwise by regulators or financial reporting reasons): all material model and assumption changes are incorporated in the strategic plan and then implemented at the beginning of the new plan year. In this way, the amount of "noise" introduced during the year is minimized and any model or parameter changes will not influence the assessment of current performance against plan.

What About Risk IT and Project Management?

Risk reporting is a systems-intensive activity. Systems need maintenance and development. Furthermore, the reporting process is naturally defined, enabled and controlled by systems, for example, setting up and triggering batch processes. For this reason, many risk organizations have a risk IT support team, including resources for project management. The remit of this team is the business or reporting applications, taking the IT infrastructure, hosting and standards as given.

"PowerPoint Factories"

Conspicuous by its absence in my "straw man" is a "PowerPoint factory." Some firms have a large staff devoted to turning their analysis into "management-friendly" (read: PowerPoint) exhibits, a practice which I try to avoid. While I have nothing per se against PowerPoint, my experience is that you can spend far too much time transferring information into horizontal pictures rather than supporting an effective risk dialog.

For ad hoc analysis and for management's assessment of the risk, I like the memo format and try to use horizontal exhibits only for standardized reporting – where the exhibits can be populated automatically. This means that management discussion and assessment has to be separated and put upfront in the document, where it belongs. This separation allows more time to be invested in the assessment and less in formatting (and reformatting) of each individual exhibit.

Coverage Teams

A coverage team is a necessity if there is a dotted reporting relationship between the corporate CRO and the business unit or segment CROs. The coverage team is responsible for building a relationship with the CRO and business leadership of the operating entity, understanding the market context as well as business and risk issues, providing value-added insights to the risk reporting process and supporting the local risk function in prioritizing their objectives. The coverage team should work in a coordinated manner with the specialist risk functions covering market, credit, insurance and operational risks.

The Internal Validation Unit (IVU)

The IVU is charged with maintaining the internal model inventory and performing or coordinating regular, independent model and model change reviews for all material models, assumptions and parameters as part of the internal model approval process.

The model validation unit is independent from the model developers, who typically reside in the risk methodology teams. The question of independence is occasionally raised if the IVU reports to the CRO. A common suggestion is to have the IVU report to the audit function. While this potentially strengthens the independence of the IVU, it does so at the potential expense of attracting, managing and retaining highly qualified technical resources. Recognizing this trade-off, most firms (and regulators) prefer to have the IVU report to the CRO.

The Policy and Governance Team

The policy and governance team has responsibility for maintaining the firm's risk policy framework and ensuring the adequacy of the firm's internal control environment.

The Compliance Function

Some banks and insurers combine the compliance and risk functions. The advantages of this are that many compliance failures are also operational risk events, indicating inadequate or failed internal controls, and that the risk assessments are overlapping. The potential disadvantage is in maintaining focus in addressing compliance-related issues, especially surrounding anti-money laundering, anti-corruption, anti-fraud, international sanctions, etc.

The CRO Office

The CRO office takes care of line activities (e.g., preparation and minutes for the Risk Committee; human resource planning, development and performance evaluation; cost center planning and budgeting, etc.), project work (e.g., adapting to regulatory changes such as G-SIFI, Basel III/Solvency II, internal models, specific strategic initiatives, etc.); coordinating cross-functional reporting activities (e.g., ORSA, risk contributions to the Resolution and Recovery Plans (RRPs), etc.); and, finally, coordinates ad hoc initiatives.

CHAPTER 22

Risk Identification and Evaluation

R isk identification and evaluation is the foundation of any ERM framework. Unfortunately, it is not simple: first, we have to define what "risk" is in the context of a financial services firm, then we have to identify the critical risk events and, finally, we have to evaluate or measure the likelihood of those events occurring. The remainder of this chapter is devoted to these three steps: risk definition, risk identification and risk evaluation.

FROM RISK IDENTIFICATION TO EVALUATION

Some concepts are difficult to define absolutely, depending instead on the mutable perspective of the observer. The definition of risk is similar: what is a risk for one person might very well be an opportunity for another. For example, a fall in equity markets will harm the long-term institutional investor but may represent a windfall for a long/short hedge fund. Similarly, a fall in house prices hurts the existing home owner but may make the property market accessible to those who do not currently own a home.

Defining Risk

Risk is generically defined as *the possible failure to meet your desired and expected objectives due to future, uncertain events*. Unfortunately, this definition is only slightly less vague given that banks and insurers, like individuals, have to pursue many different and possibly conflicting objectives in parallel.

Fortunately, the most important objectives, and therefore risks, facing financial services firms can be summarized by value, earnings, solvency, liquidity, strategy and operations.

Value Objectives

Increasing the value of the firm should be a top objective for any company, including both financials and non-financials. As a consequence, the most common metric used to measure risk within banks and insurers is the mark-to-market net asset value of the firm.

Mark-to-market risk metrics such as Value at Risk (VaR) (defined as the worst-case market value loss within a given confidence interval) are prevalent because they align directly with the value shareholders currently have invested in the firm.

In addition to being used internally, mark-to-market metrics are at the core of many solvency frameworks, including the definition of required capital for the trading book under Basel III and for insurance companies under Solvency II.

Earnings Objectives

Banks and insurers also focus on accounting earnings. This focus is rational because management gives market guidance with respect to accounting earnings, because accounting earnings influence analyst and shareholder views on franchise value, and because accounting values may drive other important measures such as statutory or rating agency solvency ratios.

As a consequence, Earnings at Risk (EaR) measures, defined as the worst-case earnings surprise relative to forecast or plan within a given confidence interval, are also prevalent. The scenarios driving EaR can be in conflict with the scenarios driving VaR, leading to mixed steering impulses. For example, a bank that wants to hedge the market value of the banking book will reduce its VaR but increase its EaR if the hedges fail to qualify for hedge accounting; while reducing market value risk, the hedges would introduce accounting volatility.

Solvency Objectives

A third important objective of financial services firms is to maintain an appropriate solvency position. Inadequate solvency can lead to supervisory intervention, a lower public rating, a loss of public confidence and the need to raise additional capital.

In the context of solvency ratios, risk is typically measured relative to a firm-specific solvency target and the ability of the firm to withstand stress scenarios. For example, many firms measure the impact on economic, regulatory and rating agency solvency ratios of an equity market melt-down or a dramatic decline in interest rates or a scenario combining the two.

Unfortunately, regulatory and rating agency solvency regimes also differ from accounting standards and mark-to-market values, implying that actions taken to manage solvency metrics may conflict with other objectives.

Liquidity Objectives

A fourth important objective of a bank or insurer is to maintain sufficient liquidity to meet cash obligations and funding requirements, important because an inability to meet these obligations will jeopardize the survival of the firm even if it remains economically solvent. The most often used measure in this context is the stressed liquidity ratio, reflecting the ability of the firm to meet its cash funding requirements over different time horizons under different stress scenarios.

Examples

Value, earnings, solvency and liquidity are the four most important dimensions along which financial services firms typically define risk, not surprising given that they are core to managing shareholder value. Table 22.1 illustrates some of the measures financial services firms employ.

The Risk to Other Management Objectives

However, other categories of management objectives are also important.

- *Strategic objectives*, for example in successfully building a growth platform in emerging markets, capturing synergies from a transformational acquisition or implementing a turn-key systems project.
- *Business objectives*, for example hitting expected business volumes and managing critical customer behavior (e.g., retention), with deviations potentially impacting not only revenues but also expense ratios.

TABLE 22.1 Definitions of risk measures

Measurement basis	Earnings	Value	Solvency	Cash and liquidity
Description	Potential impact on earnings due to uncertain future events.	Potential impact on value due to uncertain future events.	Potential impact on solvency ratio due to uncertain future events.	Potential impact on the availability of cash and the probability of a cash call due to uncertain future events.
Measurement basis	An accounting basis (e.g., IFRS earnings and shareholders' equity).	On a mark-to-market basis for the existing portfolio.	Solvency ratios based on ■ economic capital, ■ regulatory capital, ■ rating agency capital.	Future projected cash flows.
Example measures	Impact of predefined scenarios and sensitivities.			

■ Standardized sensitivities, e.g., (key rate) duration or VB01 (value of a basis point), convexity or gamma, etc.
■ Management-defined scenarios:
   ■ stress scenarios (e.g., 30% drop in equity markets, shock lapse or withdrawal scenarios, ±200 bp rate movements, default of the largest exposure, etc.);
   ■ multiple event scenarios (e.g., {rates down, equity markets down}, {marine hull damage, harbor warehouse property damage, business interruption});
   ■ operational risk scenarios (e.g., fraud, business continuity, etc.).
■ Historical scenarios:
   ■ financial crisis of 2011, 2008, 2001, 1997, 1992, etc.;
   ■ Northridge earthquake, Hurricane Andrew, etc.;
   ■ rogue trader events, mis-selling events, etc.

Statistical measures based on single events:

■ probability of borrower default ("scoring") or probability of a claim being filed;
■ modeled 1-in-10-year losses based on rate movements, equity market developments, lapse or withdrawal rates, etc., often used for EaR measures;
■ modeled 1-in-250-year losses, e.g., for natural catastrophes based on single events (Occurrence Exceedance Probabilities, OEP).

Statistical measures which combine events:

■ 1-in-250-year combined events such as a combined earthquake, windstorm, etc. (measured as an Aggregate Exceedance Probability, AEP);
■ maximum possible loss or expected maximum loss (e.g., VaR, tail-VaR) for market, credit, insurance, operational and other risks;
■ contribution to VaR or tail-VaR for market, credit, insurance, operational and other risks.

- *Operational objectives*, for example maintaining high-quality, continuously available and secure operations.
- *Reputational objectives*, for example avoiding events which adversely impact the trust of clients or business partners.

Financial services firms also use scenarios and define risk KPIs to cover operational, reputational, strategic and business risks, for example employee turnover and absenteeism rates, project delays, failure rate on transaction processing, press mentions, etc.

Taxonomy of Risk Events

Banks and insurers are exposed to a wide variety of events which can influence the value, earnings, solvency or liquidity of the firm. For example, equity prices can go down (or up); interest rates can spike (or go down or go inverse); a borrower or major reinsurer can go bankrupt; an earthquake or flood can cause property damage and interrupt business; litigation or regulatory sanctions can follow compliance breaches or a failure in sales practices; errors in processing, failures in business continuity or data security can cause direct losses as well as reputational damage; and on and on and on.

In fact, there are so many potential risks that it would be easy to get lost without putting some structure on the discussion. The financial services industry, including regulators and rating agencies, has converged upon a common taxonomy to classify risk events. This standard is illustrated in Table 22.2.

The categories should be relatively straightforward to interpret except for unknowable risks. Liquidity risk has been discussed in the context of balance sheet management, and the remainder of this section will discuss market, credit and operational risks in detail. This chapter concludes with some thoughts on managing unknowable risks.

On Unknowable Risks

One category – "unknowable risks" – is worthy of additional comment. "Unknowable risk" is the catch-all, covering events which fall outside the realm of experience. Introducing this concept, Diebold *et al.* (2010) distinguish between known, knowable and unknowable risks by considering the assessment of the probability of risk events separately from the assessment of the severity of the event, as illustrated in Table 22.3.

Taken literally, it is impossible to identify unknowable risks ex ante (unless you write science fiction for a living): by definition, there is nothing in human experience that would lead one to imagine such events.

The popular concept of "black swans" was coined by Taleb (2010) to describe an event which lies somewhere between unknown and unknowable risks. The phrase was motivated by the story of European visitors to Australia who had their world-view turned on its head: because the Europeans had only ever seen white swans, they assumed that all swans were white; they were therefore quite shocked to see the indigenous black swans of Australia.

In the context of financial markets, Taleb defined a black swan as an event which ". . . is an outlier, as it lies outside the realm of regular expectations, because nothing in the past can convincingly point to its possibility. Second, it carries an extreme impact. Third, in spite of its

TABLE 22.2 Risk category

Risk Category	Potential losses* due to
Market risks	Financial market movements, e.g., in interest and foreign exchange rates, equity prices, credit spread levels, traded commodities, traded inflation, etc.
Credit risks	'Credit events' reflecting a decreased ability or willingness of the borrower to meet its obligations, including
	■ Deterioration in likelihood of a credit event (e.g., increase in the prob of default, Pd).
	■ Deterioration in the amount which can be recovered in the case of default (e.g., increase in the loss given default, LGD).
	■ Inability to pay due to currency restrictions, nationalization, etc. (e.g., country or transfer risk).
Insurance risks	Unexpected adverse claims developments, including
	■ For PC insurers, premium and reserve risk encompassing unexpected frequency, severity and timing of claims, claims inflation, etc., including natural and man-made catastrophe events (e.g., NatCat, Terror).
	■ For LH insurers, unexpected developments in individual, levels and trends for mortality, morbidity, longevity rates, including pandemics.
Operational risks	Internal & external fraud; employment/workplace practices; clients, products and business practices; business disruption and systems failures; damage to physical assets.
Strategic & Business risks	Unexpectedly weak demand; unanticipated change in customer behavior, e.g., lapses or persistency; failure of strategy or implementation, e.g., strategic investments or projects, etc.
Liquidity risks	Failure to meet short-term cash obligations.
Unknowable risks	Risk scenarios which fall outside the realm of experience.

*Losses refer to measures relevant to the company's objectives (e.g., economic value, accounting earnings, regulatory or rating agency solvency ratios, etc).

TABLE 22.3 Known, knowable and unknown risks

Risk	Event	Severity	Definition
Known	√	√	Distribution of potential losses is well understood in terms of the drivers of both frequency and severity. Example, credit card or home-owner insurance losses.
Unknown	(√)	?	Recognition of the potential for an event, but difficulty in assessing the probability of occurrence or severity with any certainty. Example, systemic crisis or terrorist attack.
Unknowable	?	?	Events cannot even be imagined, although once they occur they enter into the realm of the unknown. Example, cybersecurity at the turn of the last century.

outlier status, human nature makes us concoct explanations for its occurrence after the fact, making it explainable and predictable."[1]

Whether a risk is a black swan, an unknown risk or an unknowable risk may be difficult to determine: for example, the attack on the World Trade Center on September 11, 2001 can be considered either a black swan or unknown risk, depending on your view of whether the Oklahoma City bombing in 1995[2] qualified as sufficient prior evidence of the possibility of domestic terror events.

The distinction is also somewhat pedantic. More important than the classification is the recognition that, in the words of Shakespeare (*The Tempest*), "there is more under heaven on earth than can be dreamt of by man." In other words, there will always be some events which are so unimaginable that we will never be able to fully describe them ex ante. Instead, our best management response is to build an organization which is robust to their occurrence, a topic discussed later in this chapter.

Risk Evaluation

A risk taxonomy is only useful if we can apply it in practice to identify, evaluate, measure (where possible) and manage risks. As illustrated in Figure 22.1, there are two broad

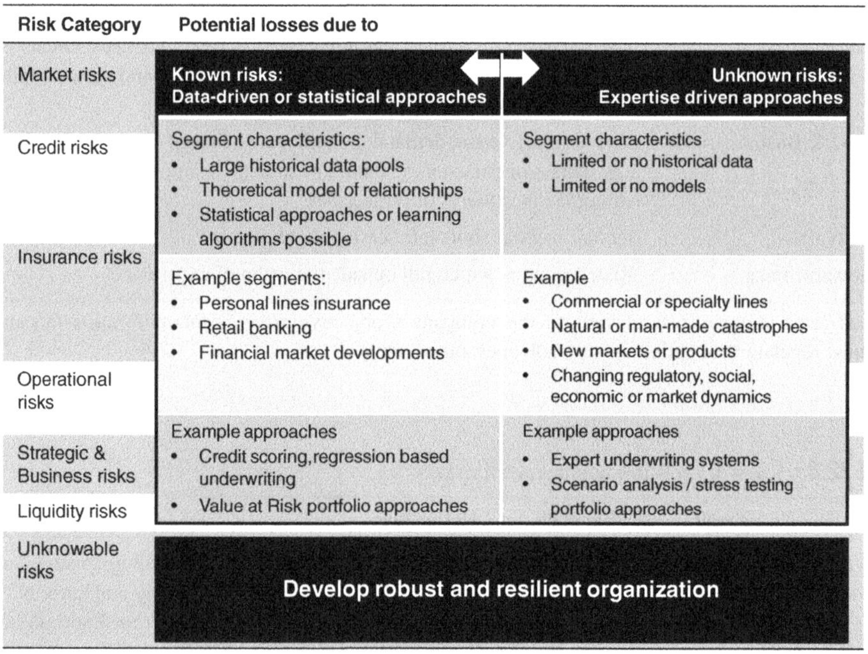

Risk Category	Potential losses due to	
Market risks	**Known risks:** **Data-driven or statistical approaches** ⬅⬆➡	**Unknown risks:** **Expertise driven approaches**
Credit risks	Segment characteristics: • Large historical data pools • Theoretical model of relationships • Statistical approaches or learning algorithms possible	Segment characteristics • Limited or no historical data • Limited or no models
Insurance risks	Example segments: • Personal lines insurance • Retail banking • Financial market developments	Example • Commercial or specialty lines • Natural or man-made catastrophes • New markets or products
Operational risks		• Changing regulatory, social, economic or market dynamics
Strategic & Business risks	Example approaches • Credit scoring, regression based underwriting	Example approaches • Expert underwriting systems • Scenario analysis / stress testing
Liquidity risks	• Value at Risk portfolio approaches	portfolio approaches
Unknowable risks	**Develop robust and resilient organization**	

FIGURE 22.1 Risk characterization along the known–unknowable continuum

---

[1] http://www.nytimes.com/2007/04/22/books/chapters/0422-1st-tale.html

[2] The Oklahoma City bombing was a domestic terrorist bomb attack on the Alfred P. Murrah Federal Building in Oklahoma City on April 19, 1995. It was the most destructive act of terrorism on American soil until the September 11, 2001 attacks. The Oklahoma blast claimed 168 lives, including 19 children under the age of 6, and injured more than 680 people. The blast destroyed or damaged 324 buildings within a 16-block radius, destroyed or burned 86 cars, and shattered glass in 258 nearby buildings.

approaches for evaluating and quantifying risks: *data-driven* approaches which work at the known end of the continuum and *evaluation-based* approaches which work at the unknown end. These two evaluation approaches are described here at a high level and revisited again in Chapter 24 in the context of risk underwriting.

By its definition, identifying and evaluating "unknowable" risks is challenging and the best defense is to build a robust and resilient firm, as discussed in the next section.

DATA-DRIVEN APPROACHES

As the name implies, data-driven approaches can be applied when there is sufficient historical data to develop statistical or other inference models. This is typically the case with financial market data as well as for customer segments such as retail segments in mature markets.

The estimated relationships are used to support risk underwriting (e.g., "scoring" models), leading to better underwriting results and more efficient processes, and to support client relationship or lifetime value management programs, capturing more value from existing clients.

In addition, data-driven approaches are at the heart of financial market VaR approaches,[3] with historical data used either directly (historical simulation) or to model the relationship between financial market developments for use in Monte Carlo simulation approaches. VaR and similar approaches form the basis of most firms' internal capital models and many regulatory solvency regimes.

Data-driven models are powerful and necessary tools, especially in the complex areas of risk underwriting and capital management. However, there is the risk of an over-reliance on models, leading in the best case to a false sense of security and in the worst case to wrong decisions with potentially disastrous results.

What can go Wrong?

There are many things which can go wrong with data-driven approaches.

Our models will be wrong in unpredictable ways. Models are a simplified abstraction of a highly complex, evolving and intractable reality. They are calibrated using historical data, analogous to driving while looking only in the rear-view mirror. The potential breakage points are intuitive:

- historical events may not be representative of future events;
- the relationships may change in ways that cannot be anticipated due to, for example, changes in *technology*, *policy* or *behavior*;
- the models are estimated with error – even if the model structure is appropriate, there is no guarantee that it will be accurate for more extreme events.

As a consequence, risk models are likely to be wrong when it matters most – not during long, sustained periods of "normal" market behavior but during crisis periods characterized by rapid and dramatic change. Diehard quants hate to hear this, because the logical conclusion is

---

[3]In addition to financial market VaR, historical data is also used to model the VaR for credit, insurance and operational risk; however, due to the relative lack of data, expert judgment very often needs to be used for modeling these segments.

that we will never be able to make risk models "right," no matter how much theory, assumptions and math we throw at them.

Myopic reliance on models can lead to missing the obvious. So prevalent are data-driven approaches in financial services that risk modeling and risk management are becoming synonymous. As a consequence, risk managers are becoming more narrowly focused on technical issues, incapable of seeing beyond the math to the bigger picture, and lacking the practical business experience and common sense necessary to use the models safely.

The more complicated the model, the more likely it is to be trusted blindly and without challenge. One explanation is the emergence of a model "cult," with technicians parading as robed priests who speak a different (and often incomprehensible) language; in such cases, challenging the model is heresy. Another is the steep learning curve necessary to understand the models, implying that those who actually understand them are seldom capable of seeing beyond the math. Another is that it may be easier to distract attention to improving models rather than taking a critical look at the business. Whatever the reason, I do know that we very often throw out common sense when we are confronted with complex models (Sidebar 22.1).

SIDEBAR 22.1: ON COMMON SENSE AND MODEL REFINEMENT

Carroll (2010) describes the aftermath of the 2008 financial crisis when banks' credit scoring models broke down, with actual defaults far in excess of those predicted by the models. Was this a failure in the model or in common sense? The response to the former would be more technical models in an effort to increase accuracy; the response to the latter would be to apply more common sense when using the models.

He concludes that it was in fact a bit of both. "Upon closer inspection, . . . credit scores actually performed quite well in terms of rank ordering risk . . . What happened in the past three years . . . is that the relative payment/default performance of the borrowers tracked very well with their score bands: people with higher scores indeed defaulted at a lower rate than those with lower scores.

In retrospect, this is not surprising. A score and its calibration are very much functions of the economic environment in which they were generated. The scores in use during the period 2004–07 were mostly developed using performance data drawn from the years that were economically 'neutral' or even somewhat 'buoyant' (albeit we might now say 'falsely buoyant')."

The modeling response would be to use both time series, through-the-cycle data as well as panel data. Common sense would suggest that we should never forget the "Credit 101" lessons – credit cycles happen! Both conclusions would be correct.

There is a love/hate relationship between risk managers and their models: on the one hand, models provide valuable insights; on the other hand, they cannot be relied on blindly. What can we do to use models more effectively?

First and foremost, use the models in a manner which mitigates the issues. Poor managers do not recognize and compensate for the inherent model failures; good managers will recognize and accommodate the limitations. For example, VaR is a useful cornerstone of any limit framework, but it makes heroic assumptions about the volatility and correlation between risk events; a mitigating control is the use of simpler measures of risk as "back stops," measures such as notional or delta-equivalent exposures, leverage ratios, etc. which do not rely on those same heroic assumptions.

Second, don't let the model substitute for common sense, as in the credit scoring example in Sidebar 22.1. Validate the models, not from a statistical sense but from an intuitive sense, questioning whether the model output matches the expectations of seasoned professionals. Having the seasoned, experienced professionals who are willing to ask the question is even more important.

EVALUATION-BASED APPROACHES

At the risk of stating the obvious, data-driven approaches work well when you have sufficient data but do not work at all for unknown risks characterized by a paucity of data.

The Ubiquity of Unknown Risks

Unfortunately, unknown risks form a significant part of a bank's or insurer's profile, as the following examples illustrate.

Underwriting in a Developing Market

Consider underwriting in an emerging economy that you have just entered. By definition there will be insufficient data available to model the risks of a personal loan until enough experience is collected. In spite of this (initial) lack of data, underwriting decisions still need to be made today in growth markets.

Underwriting in "Narrow" Segments

Consider underwriting in a narrow segment with a unique risk profile. For example, the risk of a small business may be very different depending on whether it is services or retail or manufacturing and, within the services sector, whether it is a hair salon or garage. In theory, further segmentation may improve underwriting decisions; in practice, it may be impossible to implement.

Underwriting Under Rapid Technological Change

Suppose a client asked us to underwrite the first North Sea off-shore oil drilling platform. How are we supposed to identify, measure and underwrite the risks inherent in something which has never been seen before? Equally, how can the client evaluate whether or not the risk charge is "too high" or "too low"?[4] Fast-forward to today and ask the same questions with regard to nanotechnologies, genetic modification, self-driving vehicles, etc.

Underwriting Under Social, Economic or Political Regime Changes

Even if you have a wealth of historical data, it may be invalidated by social, economic or political changes. Consider the 2005 bankruptcy reform in the USA which made personal bankruptcy more costly and reduced the amount of debt relief under bankruptcy for high net worth individuals. The positive effects on unsecured loan losses might have been predicted, but the negative impact on mortgage bankruptcies would have been much more difficult to anticipate.

Li *et al.* (2010) found that ". . . prime mortgage default rates rose by 17% and sub-prime mortgage default rates by 19% after bankruptcy reform." The reason was counterintuitive: by

---

[4]In fact, British Petroleum chose to self-insure catastrophic risks such as those which might be caused by the failure of an off-shore oil platform. For a good discussion, see Doherty and Smith (1993).

making bankruptcy on unsecured loans more difficult, borrowers had less flexibility to meet their secured borrowing obligations. Before the reform, ". . . filing for bankruptcy loosens homeowners' budget constraints and allows them to shift funds from paying credit card debt to paying their mortgages. Bankruptcy thus gives financially distressed homeowners a way to avoid losing their homes when their debts exceed their ability to pay." This flexibility was limited by the reform.

The Generic COSO Framework

Banks and insurers use expert judgment to underwrite unknown risks, having developed approaches for improving institutional judgment by capturing, reinforcing and leveraging institutional skills. These approaches are described in greater detail in Chapter 23.

For other applications involving unknown risks, banks and insurers follow the COSO (2004b) principles, tailored to the specific application. Examples include the TRA and the ERA.

The generic COSO process encompasses three steps: risk identification, risk evaluation and continual review.

Risk identification is done through formal brainstorming sessions under the following ground rules.

1. Gather experts from a variety of disciplines and experiences, both internal and external to the firm and industry, in order to broaden the insight pool and allow for greater association. Participants can come from front office, operations, investments, finance and include technical experts and management.
2. Encourage all to speak openly, introduce ideas and draw free associations. Provide positive incentives to throw out ideas, even those which may at first seem bizarre or redundant, and do not criticize. Collect and record all the ideas.
3. Launch the conversation with familiar anchor points and then branch out through free association. For example, begin with historical precedents from both internal and external loss experience, in the industry and in other industries.
4. Approach the problem from several different directions in parallel. This may yield similar results, but occasionally will lead to important incremental insights. For example:
   a. look at possible chains of events which might lead from A to B to C (e.g., the implication of sovereign debt restructuring on the balance sheets of banks and the consequences for derivative counterparty exposures);
   b. look at large, material "things" and ask what might make them vulnerable (e.g., if 50% of your business is concentrated in one product or one country or one customer, ask what makes the concentration vulnerable);
   c. look at any large positions which have a low modeled risk profile, asking what assumptions the model makes that can go wrong.

Risk evaluation places each of the identified risks in a two-dimensional matrix, the first dimension representing the frequency and the second the potential severity. These dimensions can represent a qualitative assessment (e.g., high, medium, low) or they can be tied to a concrete scale (e.g., once every year, every decade, every century, etc. for frequency and 50% earnings/5% equity, 100% earnings/10% equity, etc. for severity).

Typically, risk evaluation is done in parallel with risk identification, allowing the expert panel to jointly discuss scenarios, consequences and likelihoods and to iterate to a consensus range of outcomes.

Continual re-evaluation. By necessity, risk identification is an ongoing process, both because the world is changing and because we learn, allowing us to make new associations and draw new conclusions.

Example: Top Risk Assessment (TRA)

Most companies have a formalized process called the top risk assessment to assess their most important risk exposures.

Objectives and Scope

The TRA identifies and prioritizes the firm's top risks and assigns "ownership" to the most senior level for remediation. This process covers known and unknown risks, modeled risks and risk scenarios, including financial market, credit, insurance, operational, reputational, business and regulatory risks. It is applied across the businesses and at the group level.

Output

The output includes the top risks and risk appetite, the assignment to senior business leaders and remediation activities, as summarized in Figure 22.2. Backing up this overview are details regarding the risk scenarios and remediation plans.

Top RiskSummary Report
Entity:
Reporting date: xx.xx.xxxx

Management Assessment
- ....
- ....
- ....

Severity - Economic	< z mio	< y bio	< x bio	< X bio	> X bio
Severity - Reputational	Low		Medium		High
More than 1x year					
Once every 1-2 years				2	1
Once every 2-5 years					
Once every 5-10 years					
Less than every 10 yrs					

Event	Balance sheet risks	Changes to last quarter	Remediation	Responsible
1	Systemic market failure impacting all asset classes, reduced market liquidity, lower rates	None	Continue to reduce risk concentrations	ALCO
2...	Failure largest counterparty, inflation spike, low iterest rates, etc.	...	...	...

Event	Reputational risks	Changes to last quarter	Remediation	Responsible
1	Data security breach with third parties accessing confidential customer data	None	Penetration testing project, data encryption	Chief Information Officer
2...				

Event	Strategic risks	Changes to last quarter	Remediation	Responsible
1	Demographic changes – longevity. Failure to address needs of aging population	None	Pensions Task Force	Head of Life Insurance, Asset Management
2...	Mega-cities,disruption in distribution paradigms, relative expense performance, etc.	...	...	

FIGURE 22.2 Example of the TRA Summary Report

As illustrated, it may be desirable to separate the top risks into three categories, each with its own presentation.

- First, those risks with a sudden, *immediate economic impact* (e.g., global recession, systemic failures, large exposures, etc.).
- Second, those risks which predominantly impact the firm's *reputation* and franchise value, without an immediate balance sheet or solvency impact (e.g., data security breaches, sales practices issues, etc.). These require a different severity metric, based not on dollars and cents but on a high–medium–low qualitative assessment.
- Third, those *strategic risks* which have a longer-term opportunity cost if not appropriately addressed (e.g., technological changes impacting distribution paradigms; a failure to reduce expenses; demographic changes such as longevity, middle class in developing economies, mega-cities, etc.).

Process
The TRA is an annual, bottom-up process, building on the detailed analysis within each area. The scenarios and remediation activities are reviewed on a quarterly basis.

Technical Setup
Three technical decisions need to be taken to set up the TRA. The first is the categorization of event probabilities and severities. It is useful to set ranges rather than use point estimates, for example, event frequencies in 1-in-5, 1-in-10, 1-in-50 and 1-in-200-year buckets. In addition, a decision has to be made on how to characterize severities (e.g., based on mark-to-market or accounting terms, relative to net income or solvency).

The second relates to reporting of the risks on an *as-is* evaluation (the level of risk today, including existing controls and management actions) or on both an as-is and an *inherent* basis (the risk without current compensating controls or risk mitigation). Inherent risk provides a stable baseline against which management actions can be evaluated; the drawback is that it is artificial. For example, do we evaluate a property theft scenario under the (arguably ludicrous) scenario that there are no locks on any of the windows or doors, without a security system or security guards?

Finally, how to coordinate with other, related functions? Similar processes may be run by internal audit, legal or compliance. It is beneficial to coordinate the activities and definitions as far as possible in order to eliminate confusion and duplicate work.

Example: Scenario Analysis And Crisis Management

Scenario analysis is a valuable tool for identifying and evaluating unknown risks, in particular the risks arising from complex, interconnected events. It is also an important tool for *managing* risks. The following example, based on Wilson (2013a,b), describes scenario analysis using the 2012 European sovereign debt crisis as a practical example.

Scenario Analysis
As opposed to best-estimate forecasting, the end product of scenario analysis is a set of possible future events or "states of the world" and, in the case of scenario trees, the logical path leading to those states. For example, one may be interested in the "best" case, the "worst" case and the "expected" macroeconomic outcome, including the implications of each for the bank's or insurer's specific portfolio.

This process is in itself useful for identifying risks. The results can also be used to evaluate management actions, for example if you are willing to define a trade-off between the (scenario-weighted) expected value and some measure of risk (e.g., the scenario-weighted volatility or distance between best and worst cases, etc.). Scenario analysis proceeds generically in three steps.

Define Event Space and Factors to be Considered   In the case of the euro sovereign crisis, in early 2011 Allianz pulled together experienced professionals from the risk, investment, economics, treasury and legal departments as well as business professionals from the affected local markets. They were sequestered in a workshop with the objective of developing the scenario tree.

Materials were distributed before the workshop, including current news, economic research and a synopsis of previous historical events of a similar nature; also distributed was an overview of the portfolio to trigger connections from both directions. The workshop was facilitated, but it was done with a "light touch," allowing the conversation to range widely before reining in the discussion.

The scenario tree that emerged to describe the possible events remained relatively stable during 2011–12:

- "muddle through," characterized by financial market volatility but with growth sufficient to correct the underlying fundamentals;
- "escalation," marked by a crisis in confidence triggering a flight to quality, a precipitous decline in asset values and risk-free rates due to aggressive monetary intervention. Following "escalation," either
    - an eventual step "back from the cliff," returning to the muddle through scenario (where we still seem to be) or
    - a "United States of Europe," characterized by a stronger and more credible fiscal union addressing the underlying fundamentals, or
    - "partial or full break-up of the euro."

While these scenarios could potentially be mapped into the more traditional "best-case," "baseline" and "worst-case" scenarios, we found it useful to retain the labels as they were more descriptive.

Underlying each were more specific and detailed steps in the scenario tree. For example, we considered different possible sequences of affected countries; restructuring versus exit scenarios; possible actions of regulatory forbearance; possible legal scenarios with regard to contract redenomination, etc.

Analyze Impact and Alternatives   The next step analyzed the impact of the scenarios. In the case of the euro crisis, Allianz focused primarily on the first-order effects on economic, regulatory and IFRS balance sheets; also evaluating likely competitor behavior for both new business and M&A opportunities.

In addition, different management alternatives were analyzed, for example shifting assets to safer counterparties or jurisdictions, redrafting contracts to explicitly address potential redenomination issues, enhancing systems to include multi-currency capabilities, etc.

Management Recommendations   The final step was to discuss and decide on management actions. In order to do so, some statements about management preferences needed to be made. The high-level goals which Allianz committed to during the crisis were:

1. the group's ability to withstand up to a 50% haircut on peripheral sovereign bonds and the likely devaluing of other risk assets in sympathy;
2. the local entities' ability to continue to write profitable business from a systems and balance sheet perspective.

Meeting these objectives required Allianz to take immediate action, reducing fixed-income exposures to peripheral sovereign issuers and banks, reducing equity exposures, increasing group liquidity reserves and adapting local administration systems.

Common Challenges in Scenario Analysis During a Crisis

Scenario analysis is a useful risk tool, providing a structured approach for eliciting, interpreting and consolidating expert judgment on complex issues. However, it also has some limitations.

- Expert judgment will likely be wrong in the details during dynamically evolving crisis situations.
- It can be difficult to converge to a few scenarios. If you ask 100 experts, you will get 100 different answers. Scenario analysis multiplies this by a factor of 20, with experts disagreeing on whether it is a 1% or a 5% probability or whether there shouldn't be a fork in the tree with a different commodity price development, etc.
- It is difficult to take events seriously which fall outside our comfort and experience zone. During the first months of 2011, many pundits discounted the probability of a collapse of the euro, even though there is no immutable, physical law holding the euro together.
- Analysis is easy; taking action is difficult even in the face of consensus. Put simply, scenario analysis is not a guarantee of effective decision taking and the execution of those decisions.

Mitigating the Issues

Scenario analysis is a means to an end, and not the end in and of itself; a good scenario analysis is necessary, but not sufficient, to effectively steer through a crisis. More important is taking the right decisions and executing them consequently. This is too often forgotten, leading to more analysis and less management action. Nonetheless, there are some "tricks" which can support effective scenario analysis.

- First, consensus on details is not necessary; consensus on the "headlines" is. 100 people will have 100 opinions; nonetheless, some consensus is necessary in order to progress to the next step – management action. To resolve this paradox:
  - it is better to get consensus around something *directionally correct* (such as "things are likely to get much worse with a high probability") and to act decisively than to reach consensus in all details with no action at all;
  - *choose scenarios which "tell a story"* – the scenarios we chose ("muddle through," "escalation," "back from the cliff," "United States of Europe" and "breakup") conveyed an intuitive message that was easily understood by all;
  - *focus on ranges, not spot estimates* – it doesn't matter whether it is a 15% or a 25% probability that equity markets will plummet; what does matter is that it is a real possibility;
  - *focus on the first-order effects* – as a European insurer it was important to focus on interest rates, bond spreads, equity markets and consumer demand for liquidity; not as

important is the impact on gold or oil prices or a host of other variables which have only second-order impact.

- Recognize diminishing returns to analysis. Your scenario will be wrong in the details with absolute certainty; the key is to make sure that it is directionally correct on the major points and build organizational resilience for the remaining uncertainty.
- Avoid analysis paralysis; refresh the scenarios only periodically. While a detailed analysis at regular intervals feels more "structured," the reality is that it occupies your best resources when they could be better used actually managing the crisis. Working with ranges gives some leeway, as does regularly reviewing but not refreshing the analysis unless there are material changes.
- Be prepared to take decisions. The objective is to take the right decisions and to execute effectively. Decision taking in large organizations is inherently complex even in normal times; taking decisions under accelerated time lines and difficult circumstances even more so. The following are some things which support better decision making during a crisis.
- Adjust your behavior and expectations.
  - Singles and doubles are good; don't swing for the fences during a crisis.[5] By definition, crises are times of significant uncertainty; taking large bets during such periods may lead to great rewards, but it can also lead to ruin. Examples include John Corizine's exaggerated bet on the Eurozone and its disastrous results for MF Global[6] as well as the cost paid by RBS, Bank of America (Duhigg, 2008; Story and Dash, 2009) and others for transformational M&A deals during the 2008 financial crisis.
- During the crisis, Allianz discussed opening a USD position as a "hedge" with the idea that the USD would appreciate if the Eurozone were to fall deeper into crisis; however, the scenario of a "new Deutsch Mark" becoming a safe-haven currency similar to the Swiss franc was also considered. The conclusion was that an open USD position was a trade, having nothing to do with business fundamentals but expressing a view on correlations, and that a hedge would be better accomplished by directly closing out the positions of concern. In retrospect, the right decision was made but for the wrong reasons: the dollar did depreciate in 2013, not due to the new Deutsch Mark but due to home-grown problems in the USA from the 2013 debt ceiling crisis.
  - *Recognize what is a hedge and what is a trade and don't confuse them.* A hedge closes a position with certainty; a trade expresses a view which may or may not materialize.
  - *Don't take decisions based on the mean.* In normal times, decisions can be taken based on the best estimate, a natural inclination when worst-case scenarios are distant. More weight needs to be put on the tails during a crisis. This can be done intuitively or mechanically, for example by making an explicit trade-off between the (scenario-weighted) expected value and some measure of risk – such as the scenario-weighted volatility or the distance between best and worst cases.
- Remove impediments to taking and executing decisions.
  - *Take the actions which can be taken, not the ones you would like to but cannot.* Some actions represent immediate, no-regret moves, for example shifting deposits to safer banks

---

[5]In American baseball, the batter swings at a ball thrown by the pitcher. If successful, the batter can run, possibly taking one, two, three or four bases. Taking four bases is called a home run. Swinging for the fences is a metaphor for attempting to hit a home run, an aggressive gamble but one with a large potential pay-off if successful.

[6]*New York Times Editorial*, November 2, 2012, "Mr. Corzine's big bet."

in less affected countries, raising liquidity, etc. Others may be desired but not possible due to reduced market liquidity, for example selling GIIPS[7] subordinated bank debt or illiquid alternative assets. If your desired move is stymied due to market conditions, consider actions further afield: the sale of senior debt of non-GIIPS banks may be the best that you can do to minimize exposure to a systemic financial sector event.

- *Contingency planning to be prepared to act when required.* Because of the accelerated time lines and high uncertainty, opportunities come and go rapidly, leaving the ill prepared behind. Preparing the organization is critical and contingency planning can help by building an appropriate sense of urgency and consensus beforehand. Other steps which can help include the following.
    - *Alter traditional decision channels.* During normal times, decisions may be taken by the full ALCO. However, committees do not react quickly. Delegate authorities to individuals or to a crisis task force, on call 24/7, to execute contingent actions.
    - *Train for and test the contingency plan*, potentially under "surprise conditions," to ensure that actions become second nature and are effective. For example, at Allianz we conducted "war games," having the crisis task force react to a default scenario over the weekend and evaluating their preparedness via Monday morning conference calls.
    - *A caveat on contingency planning.* There can be situations where triggers are met, but the anticipated actions cannot be taken. Consider the hypothetical rule to "sell Cedulas or European bank subordinated debt if markets deteriorate to a specific point." In a declining market, you are likely to find yourself standing in a long queue of sellers with no one buying; it may be more reasonable to sell into a situation of temporary euphoria. If your contingency plans are to provide more than illusory comfort, think critically whether the actions can be taken in the scenario which triggers them.
- *Set the right incentives.* Selling an asset into a soft bid will likely realize a loss relative to its current carrying value. This provides a disincentive to sell if bonus targets will be missed with certainty, whereas there might still be a chance to reach targets if the position is left open. Similarly, there may be an incentive to continue to write new business even if of questionable value due to changing market conditions. The solution is to adjust targets, either implicitly or explicitly, for example by setting up an operating profit or net income "budget" to be used by the businesses to close risky positions.

Other Evaluation-Based Approaches

In addition to the TRA and scenario analysis, Allianz uses similar frameworks for other risks, including operational risk, business trend risk and emerging underwriting risks.

Risk Control Self-assessment

Allianz applies a similar process for the identification, segmentation and analysis of operational risks (discussed in detail later). Similar to the TRA, the RCSA process follows an annual cycle, beginning with cross-functional workshops designed to identify potential operational risk events and their root causes, the as-is risk, potential risk mitigation actions and the residual risks post-mitigation.

---

[7]GIIPS refers to those countries which were primarily affected by the European sovereign debt crisis: Greece, Ireland, Italy, Portugal and Spain.

Trend Assessment Committee

The objective of the TAC, which meets half-yearly, is to identify trends that may influence the economics of the industry over longer time horizons, including demographic trends, climate change and global warming, political and judicial trends such as tort reform, etc.

The risks and opportunities arising from these trends are evaluated equally, leading to new business opportunities as well as risk mitigation actions. One result has been the Allianz Center for Climate Change, a unit which develops products and services to counteract the impact of climate change for our customers and supports the development of "green" products. Another example is the Pensions and Savings Task Force, combining both insurance and asset management perspectives, launched to create products and services to meet the retirement demands of an aging population.

Emerging Risk Assessment

ERA is similar to the TAC but more narrowly focused on insurance underwriting risks. Examples include product liability for nanotechnologies and genetic modification, property losses from electromagnetic forces and climate change, and the implications of demographic changes such as longevity and obesity.

At Allianz, ERA meets twice a year and consists of a subset of CUOs. The members review and prioritize the list of emerging risks. Based on this prioritization, project teams or task forces are set up to evaluate the potential and to make recommendations with regard to mitigation steps.

The Allianz ERA has had some important business implications, including for example the inclusion of referral mechanisms in the minimum underwriting standards, the adjustment of standard contract wordings, the explicit monitoring and limitation of exposures and the development of new products to exploit opportunities.

BUILDING A RESILIENT ORGANIZATION

The only way to "manage" extreme and unimaginable events is to *build organizational resilience*. This section introduces two important topics for building a resilient organization: recovery and resolution planning and the lessons that can be learned from High-Resilience Organizations (HROs).

Recovery and Resolution Planning

Following the 2008 financial crisis, international regulators have adopted measures to increase the resilience of financial services firms and to limit the externalities should the measures fail to be successful. Broadly speaking, the new regulatory measures fall into three categories:

- higher capital and loss absorbency,
- recovery and resolution planning,
- enhanced supervision.

Recovery and resolution planning is mandated by the FSB (2011a,b) for institutions considered to be globally systemically relevant. Increasingly, local supervisors are adopting similar rules for firms considered to be domestically relevant.

Broadly speaking, increased loss absorbency and recovery planning improve resilience. The Financial Services Authority (FSA, 2011) summarizes the role of recovery planning in building organizational resilience in the following.

> *Recovery plans* aim to reduce the likelihood of failure by requiring firms to identify options to achieve recovery, to be implemented when a crisis occurs. The plans must be developed and maintained by the firm, in coordination with the FSA, but they should all have the following features:
>
> ▪ *sufficient number of material and credible options to cope with a range of scenarios including both firm-specific and market-wide stresses;*
> ▪ *options which address capital shortfalls, liquidity pressures and profitability issues and should aim to return the firm to a stable and sustainable position;*
> ▪ *options that the firm would consider in more severe circumstances such as: disposals of the whole business, parts of the businesses or group entities; raising equity capital which has not been planned for in the firm's business plan; complete elimination of dividends and variable remuneration; and debt exchanges and other liability management actions.*

Broadly speaking, resolution planning and enhanced supervision are designed to limit the externalities should a failure occur. FSA (2011) summarizes the role of resolution planning in limiting externalities in the following.

> *Resolution packs* will assist the authorities to wind-down a firm if it fails for whatever reason. The resolution data and analysis to be provided by firms is intended to identify significant barriers to resolution, to facilitate the effective use of the powers . . . and so reduce the risk that taxpayers' funds will be required to support the resolution of the firm. The information provided to the authorities will help to prepare a resolution plan with the following aims:
>
> ▪ *ensure that resolution can be carried out without public solvency support exposing taxpayers to the risk of loss;*
> ▪ *seek to minimise the impact on financial stability;*
> ▪ *seek to minimise the effect on UK depositors and consumers;*
> ▪ *allow decisions and actions to be taken and executed in a short space of time (or the 'resolution weekend');*
> ▪ *identify those economic functions which will need to be continued because the availability of those functions is critical to the UK economy or financial system, or would need to be wound up in an orderly fashion so as to avoid financial instability (critical economic functions);*
> ▪ *identify and consider ways of removing barriers which may prevent critical economic functions being resolved successfully;*
> ▪ *isolate and identify critical economic functions from non-critical activities which could be allowed to fail; and*
> ▪ *enhance cooperation and crisis management planning for global systemically important financial institutions (G-SIFIs) with international regulators.*

Recovery and resolution planning can be a valuable exercise for two reasons. First, because it forces firms to think about the possibility and nature of potential crisis events. More importantly, because it forces them to plan specific actions, both current and contingent, which would make their businesses more robust to severe shock scenarios. Ernst and Young (2012) quote one bank executive as saying, "It seems very reasonable to ponder these fundamental questions — if something happened, what businesses would we curtail or sell? What actions would we take? Where would we raise capital and liquidity? How would we communicate to our key stakeholders?"

Most G20 countries have required their global systemically relevant banks (G-SIBs) to submit a recovery and resolution plan to local regulators by the end of 2012. Systemic insurers (G-SIIs) were in the process of submitting their recovery plans in 2014. These represent a significant investment by the firms, ranging from hundreds to thousands of pages.

However, further work still needs to be undertaken, with regulators in the USA rejecting the first wave of resolution plans submitted by US banks (*USA Today*, 2014), saying that the banks "made . . . assumptions about the likely behavior of customers, counterparties, investors, central clearing facilities, and regulators (that were unrealistic, and failed to) . . . make, or even to identify, the kinds of changes in firm structure and practices that would be necessary to enhance the prospects for orderly resolution . . . (The banks must establish) a rational and less complex legal structure that would take into account the best alignment and business lines to improve the firm's resolvability."

Principles of High-Resilience Organizations

The HRO literature defines principles for building a resilient organization. An HRO is defined as one that can successfully avoid catastrophes in a risky, complex environment where "accidents" can be regularly expected.

The literature has focused on wildfire response teams, air traffic control, military personnel engaged in guerrilla warfare, operators of nuclear or large chemical plants and NASA. Important case studies include the Cuban missile crisis, the Three Mile Island nuclear incident, the Challenger explosion, the Bhopal chemical leak and the Columbia spacecraft explosion.

Banking and insurance also operate in a risky, complex environment and need to build resilience in the face of unanticipated extreme events. In general, HROs build organizational resilience through five principles (Hopkins, 2007), described below in the context of financial services firms.

Principle 1: Preoccupation with Failures Rather than Successes

First, HROs are not complacent in the face of long periods of success: just because they have been enjoying a "bull run" for the past years does not mean that they expect it to remain that way forever. Rather than "dancing while the music is playing,"[8] an HRO will question market developments, searching for the downside such as asset bubbles and "irrational exuberance."[9]

Second, HROs continually look out for signs of change, no matter how small, and pay attention to "near misses," lapses or errors which could be a weak signal of future failures. For example, an HRO will certainly raise more questions surrounding breaks in back-office closing procedures, a weak but clear signal of the potential for internal fraud.

Corollary: History has a habit of repeating itself. Learn from it. If one looks closely, most "black swans" have occurred before in one form or another . . . and will more than likely occur again! Consider Table 22.4, which provides a post mortem of a recent financial crisis.

---

[8] A reference to the quote by C. Prince, ex-CEO of Citigroup, discussed in Chapter 20.

[9] Alan Greenspan, 1996, during a speech to the American Enterprise Institute concerning the possibility of a dot-com bubble, is quoted as saying, "But how do we know when irrational exuberance has unduly escalated asset values, which them become subject to unexpected and prolonged contractions . . . ?"

TABLE 22.4   Summary of the financial crisis

Business strategy: Increase revenue velocity through intermediation, supported by low funding costs and low capital due to liquidity	"Instead of just letting the loans clutter up their own balance sheets, investment banks pooled the loans; cut the pools up into classes rated triple-A on down . . . and sold the loans (in packaged form) to institutions, including pension funds, hedge funds and mutual funds."
	Quote from a market participant: "Right now, I have $10 bn of assets on my books . . . so I'm going to sell out this $2.5 bn and . . . I'll be able to originate more". (He) kept rolling the dice; and he kept winning. (In his last year) he reportedly received a $50 m pay package from his employers.
Market dynamics: Market confidence fails, triggering liquidity crisis. Assets remain on the bank's book.	"But the market (which was) loved a few months ago is not the market of today. The real estate boom that . . . the investment banks had fueled came to a screeching halt when the global turmoil roiled the markets in late summer. The effects were sudden and drastic. Deals collapsed. Initial public offerings were called off. The 'flight to safety' that drove down stocks as investors sought comfort in Treasury bonds also decimated the market in the mortgage-backed securites that Wall Street sold to finance its real estate lending. And the sound of knees knocking could be heard at industry conferences from Houston to Boston as investors flashed back to the early 1990s when inflated property values collapsed."
	"Now though, with financial institutions demanding steeper returns on mortgage backed securities or refusing altogether to buy the loans warehoused on investment bankers' balance sheets, Wall Street has abruptly tightened the capital spigot to a mere trickle. And, as a result, the real estate deals . . . are shriveling, properties are commanding as much as 25 percent less than sellers expected in June."
The fall-out: Banks with large positions on their books are forced to take large writedowns	"Rumours abound that (the) guru of the bank's mortgage backed operation will be tossed out, that the investment bank is losing millions and that he is stuck with $2 bn high risk and $9.3 total American mortgages on the bank's balance sheet."
	"Officials (of one foreign owned company) began pouring money into the floundering American operations (and) announced that it was taking a pretax loss. Most of the losses in the United States came from market down the value of its huge inventory of real estate related loans. Currently, the company has about $10 bn on its books."
The future: Optimistic that lessons have been learned	"There is a sign of hope in this wacky market. The curent troubles are rooted in the way Wall Street financed growth, not in the supply and demand for space. That suggest that the next downturn in real estate may be less devastating than the last because the excesses of the market are being weeded out. Already, bankers are limiting loans to 70 percent of a property's value, compared with 95 percent months ago."
	"For these reasons, investors and issuers are likely to take a much more careful look at how MBS loans are underwritten and may peform far higher levels of due diligence. Issuers and investors alike will pay far greater attention to fundamental real estate market conditions, mortgage underwriting standards, property performance, additional leverage, and a wide variety of ancillary criteria."

These quotes provide a relatively concise storyline describing the financial crisis of 2008. What is thoroughly surprising is that these quotes were written between 1998 and 2000 in reference to the 1998 financial crisis.[10] The similarities between the two crises are profound, raising the obvious question: How can we better learn from the past?

An obvious step is to *first, not discount historical scenarios.* A typical response to historical scenarios is "Yeah, but that was then and this is now!" or "That was Japan, this is Europe" and "There is no way that it can happen here and now!"

It is common for people to discount rare and unpleasant events and even more common to do so during sustained bull markets. Although common, it doesn't make it right: we experience a major financial crisis more than once a decade and, although they may differ in the details, they are surprisingly similar in terms of the big picture.

Second, listen to experience. Retain risk and business professionals who have lived through a complete cycle and had to clean up the mess.

Third, act on your intuition. Risk managers may feel uneasy or unsettled about the current environment. The first response may be with the logical journalist's questions "what? where? how? why?" in an attempt to formulate a "story" around the possible event. However, sometimes the story is unclear, while the sense of unease remains acute. Building a resilient organization means acting on our sense of ill ease, filling in the "what? where? how? why?" with the benefit of hindsight.

Corollary: Balance your business profile. The natural response is to continue to expand in areas where you are successful. While taking advantage of opportunities is good, the flipside may be that your firm becomes increasingly vulnerable – what was once a strength can turn out to be a liability.

Industrial examples are prevalent: the historical strengths of Xerox and IBM in digital reproduction and mainframes turned out to be existence threatening with the advent of new technologies. Examples from the financial services industry where once successful business concentrations turned out to be a liability include securitization warehouses, tied sales channels and a single-product focus in LH insurance.

In addition to creating the right culture and incentives, firms should think carefully about their aggregate exposure to fast-growing markets. Firms with a more balanced business portfolio have the option to "sit this one out." Mono-line firms do not have this option and are therefore more vulnerable.

Principle 2: Reluctance to Simplify

HROs invest in building a "big picture" view of their environment. They task people to dig deeper and look further and broader, exploring possible interconnections, developing and testing alternative scenarios. In addition, they invest in collecting information, even if it might seem to be inconsequential at first glance, because of the potential signaling value it may contain.

Scenario analysis, TRAs, ERAs and stress testing should be "business as usual" for bank and insurers.

Principle 3: Sensitivity to Operations

HROs organize their activities so that they are capable of reacting to emerging situations. The antithesis of an HRO is a "silo" organization, where each function focuses only on its own

---

[10]Quotes sourced from the *New York Times*, November 1, 1998; *CireMagazine* 1998; *Online Insider*, week of June 26, 2000.

narrow activities and does not share information across the organization nor think about its role in terms of broad-based recovery actions.

Prior to the 2008 financial crisis, market risk "silos" focused on the trading book under the assumption that any position could be quickly liquidated; traditional credit risk "silos" focused on the banking book using traditional fundamental analysis. When liquidity dried up, it became apparent that there was significant credit risk in the trading book. Most banks now create a bridge between the two worlds, effectively breaking down the silos.

In addition to promoting thinking and activities *across* silos, HROs encourage open information flows *up and down* the organization at all levels. As noted by Hopkins (2007), "people who refuse to speak up out of fear enact a system that knows less than it needs to know to remain effective."

Principle 4: Commitment to Resilience

HROs are resilient to errors or crisis situations. This does not mean that HROs do not make errors or can prevent crisis, rather that they are acutely aware that errors and crisis will happen and therefore put in place early warning systems, preventative controls and correction mechanisms and contingency plans should the need arise. Especially through contingency planning, HROs are not immobilized by errors or crisis and are able to mobilize themselves more quickly and more effectively to respond to the situation. This is the concept underlying recovery plans.

Corollary: Pay the price for flexibility. Flexibility is an asset which can prove to have infinite value when facing the unexpected. It can be achieved in many different ways.

- Financing and liquidity flexibility (e.g., holding excess capital, unutilized debt issuance capacity, maintaining an open dialog with potential core investors, etc.).
- Cost flexibility (e.g., through a flexible labor force, outsourcing, a higher proportion of variable compensation, etc.).
- Commercial flexibility (e.g., through maintaining an open architecture with regard to sourcing products and services, etc.).
- Reaction flexibility (e.g., establishing a (generic) cross-functional crisis response team; maintaining contact details; aligning senior responsibilities for communication, decision taking and implementation in the case of an adverse event; and reinforcing this through regular tests of preparedness or "war games").
- Securing time to react (e.g., through an open dialog with supervisors and other stakeholders whose goodwill and forbearance you may need during a crisis).

Flexibility can be costly. However, the expenses can be rationalized as an "insurance premium" paid to protect the firm against unforeseen events.

Principle 5: Deference to Expertise

The final principle for HROs is that they allow those with the expertise to lead. Hopkins (2007) comments that "Researchers . . . note that even the lowest level seaman can abort a landing (on an aircraft carrier), without reference to higher authority. When the tempo returns to normal, the locus of decision making moves back up the hierarchy."

In banks and insurance companies, this can be accomplished by the delegation of decision authority from committees to a crisis task force or to individuals in the treasury or credit functions, etc.

CHAPTER 23

Risk Underwriting – Strategy and Governance

R isks are broadly divided into two categories: those which the bank or insurer chooses to manage in order to create shareholder value (most frequently market, credit and insurance risks) and those that are undesired risks but unavoidable (most frequently operational and reputational risks).

Developing best-in-class underwriting skills for the former is the foundation of good risk management: the transactions underwritten today will form the basis for the firm's earnings for many years in the future and there is no amount of risk management after the fact which can make up for the earnings drag of a poorly underwritten portfolio.

This chapter describes what a "good" risk underwriting strategy and organization looks like; Chapter 24 describes the analytical tools used for underwriting and pricing.

UNDERWRITING CONTEXT

There are many definitions of underwriting, some of which are narrowly focused, for example only on the decision to accept or decline a loan or insurance policy.

- "Underwriting refers to the process that a large financial service provider (bank, insurer, investment house) uses to assess the eligibility of a customer to receive their products (equity capital, insurance, mortgage or credit)." (Wikipedia.com)
- "To set one's name to (an insurance policy) for the purpose of thereby becoming answerable for a designated loss or damage on consideration of receiving a premium percent: insure on life or property; *also*: to assume liability for (a sum or risk) as an insurer." (Merriam-Webster.com)

A narrow interpretation misses an important lever which banks and insurers use to create value: the ability to structure and price their products in order to capture higher margins or mitigate risks.

This Handbook uses a broader definition of underwriting as *the process through which a transaction or risk position is analyzed, structured, priced and ultimately accepted or declined by a bank or insurer.*

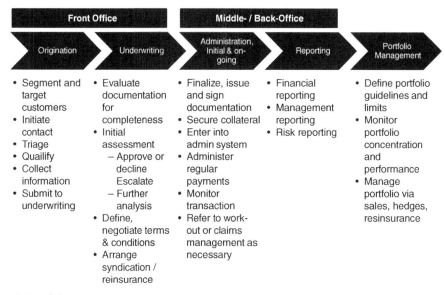

FIGURE 23.1   Example underwriting business system

Underwriting in a Business Context

"Good" underwriting must be seen in the context of the overall business strategy and operations. The underwriting process is an important and integral part of the business system, beginning but not ending with origination (see Figure 23.1). A "good" underwriting organization not only gets the transaction decision "right" in isolation, but also integrates this decision into the adjacent steps of the business system to improve efficiency and customer satisfaction.

Origination

The business system begins with the origination of qualified applicants comprising: customer segmentation and targeting; lead generation; managing the lead pipeline; qualifying potential applicants; collecting information from the customer; and, finally, submitting qualified applicants to underwriting.

Key success factors include: generating sufficient qualified leads; successfully evaluating and prioritizing the leads; optimizing the time spent on originating leads, conversion of leads and administrative or back-office activities; and, finally, ensuring a smooth interaction with the underwriting function.

Underwriting can support origination by giving guidance on acceptable risks, thereby: focusing origination and customer relationship management efforts; making it easier to collect information and submit applications; making underwriting decisions more predictable and explainable; and, ultimately, improving the success rate of submitted applications.

Underwriting

Underwriting begins with an evaluation of the submitted documentation for completeness and the qualification of the applicant within the underwriting guidelines. At this point, one of four actions are possible: direct approval or denial; a request for further documentation and analysis; and/or redirecting the file to the appropriate level or team.

The request for further documentation or analysis can be mundane (e.g., requesting missing documents or clarifications) or it can be more intensive (e.g., an on-site visit/analysis of the collateral or property in question). Escalations are made to specialist teams (e.g., due to the complexity of non-conforming transactions) or to a more senior underwriter with higher authority (e.g., based on materiality criteria).

In parallel, terms (e.g., pricing) and conditions (e.g., covenants, retention levels, sub-limits, etc.) are defined and negotiated. In addition, facultative reinsurance or syndication partners are arranged if necessary in order to meet internal risk retention limits or portfolio management objectives.

Key success factors include: the percentage of "right" decisions (profitable acceptances, unprofitable rejections); the amount of "customer surplus" captured through pricing; and the cost and time efficiency with which these decisions are taken.

Administration

Initial and ongoing administration follows an affirmative decision. It begins with the finalization, issuance and signing of the documentation; entering the contract into the administration system; securing collateral and making payments; logging and monitoring future events such as the collection of payments; monitoring the transaction for performance; and triggering risk mitigation activities.

Key success factors include cost effectiveness; the number of processing fails; monitoring the transaction for adherence to contract terms; early risk identification and intervention; and the effectiveness of the intensive care or claims management process.

Underwriting supports administration by ensuring a high proportion of conforming acceptances; verifying and aligning terms and conditions with reinsurance or syndication partners; and a continual feedback loop, especially with the intensive care or claims management departments, in order to improve underwriting guidelines based on actual experience.

Portfolio Management

The individual transactions are to be seen in the context of the broader portfolio. First, underwriting guidelines and limits are needed to ensure that the sum of all transactions is appropriate for the firm's risk appetite and business strategy; second, the net portfolio exposure needs to be actively managed (e.g., through sales, securitization, hedging, reinsurance, etc.).

Underwriting can support portfolio management by using standardized documentation, terms and conditions, allowing a transaction to be more easily sold or securitized; and by defining conditions to allow for early warning, pre-emptive management and sufficient rights in the case of a claim or a loan default.

Evaluating Underwriting Effectiveness

As the discussion illustrates, success is not narrowly defined in terms of an individual risk decision or ensuring "adequate" technical pricing; it is ultimately about maximizing the value of the business by integrating underwriting into the broader business system. Consistent with the business system, there are five criteria which are used to evaluate underwriting, as seen in Table 23.1.

Customer satisfaction. Are we providing good service to our customers and intermediaries, causing them to want to do business with us again?

Operational efficiency. In terms of the average cost and elapsed time per decision (complex or simple), the number of exceptions or escalations, etc.

TABLE 23.1   Criteria defining underwriting effectiveness

Underwriting effectiveness
Customer satisfaction
Cost efficiency
Decision effectiveness
Commercial effectiveness
Portfolio effectiveness

Decision effectiveness. How often were "Type 1 errors" made (e.g., writing business which leads to a loss) or "Type 2 errors" (e.g., not writing business which ultimately was loss free, representing an opportunity cost of foregone profits).

Commercial effectiveness. Are we maximizing value from our pricing/volume strategy? Are we systematically subsidizing or under-/over-pricing some segments? Are we charging higher prices to segments with a lower price elasticity and vice versa? Are we making the most out of discount programs and the pricing discretion delegated to the sales channel?

Portfolio management effectiveness. Are we structuring transactions and using documentation to increase flexibility and protect the interests of the firm (e.g., in terms of covenants, perfection of interest in collateral or reinsurance proceeds, etc.)? Does the documentation allow us to easily transfer, securitize or sell the transaction or portfolio?

These criteria can be in conflict. For example, customer satisfaction is not likely to increase by saying "no" or by charging a higher price, even if this is the right decision, and higher cost efficiency may lead to lower customer satisfaction and poorer decisions.

Developing an Effective Underwriting Organization

Balancing the customer satisfaction, cost efficiency and decision effectiveness becomes more complicated when recognizing that different segments require different approaches. In practice, there are three underwriting segments defined by the characteristics of the customer/product (see Table 23.2).

Personal lines[1] are characterized by a high number of transactions, low notional amounts and competitive, retail margins. Customer price discovery is facilitated by Internet comparison shopping as well as distribution channels with open platforms such as brokers, banks and independent financial advisors; however, margins reflect retail, as opposed to wholesale, volumes and risk-based segmentation is critical, made possible by the volume of business.

Managing the all-in cost per transaction is critical, implying the need for efficient, straight-through processing and rules-based acceptance, combined with standardized terms, conditions and documentation.

Commercial lines are characterized by higher notional values but fewer customers and transactions. In addition, there are greater and more recognizable differences across and between customers. In comparison with personal lines, conditions can be more competitive due to the larger notionals and independent broker or advisor support.

---

[1]These characteristics can be equally applicable in the SME segments with sufficient customers; for ease of communication, we use the term "personal lines" generically to cover any segments with similar characteristics.

TABLE 23.2 Three generic underwriting segments

Category	Personal lines	Commercial lines	Structured solutions
Segment characteristics	◾ Small ticket size, high volume, competitive margins. ◾ Abundant historical data. ◾ Standardized terms and conditions. ◾ Risk segmentation is critical.	◾ Larger ticket size, smaller volume, lower margins. ◾ Smaller quantity of historical data. ◾ Some differentiation in terms and conditions. ◾ Risk segmentation is critical.	◾ Larger, more complex transactions, fewer deals, higher margins. ◾ Small number or non-existent comparables. ◾ Transaction structuring is critical.
Examples	◾ Personal lines, direct insurance. ◾ Personal lines, credit cards, overdrafts, retail mortgage lending.	◾ Corporate loans, commercial mortgages, etc. ◾ Commercial insurance. ◾ Facultative or treaty reinsurance.	◾ Structured, asset-based, leveraged or project finance. ◾ M&A transactions. ◾ Alternative risk transfer transactions. ◾ Structured reinsurance.
Characteristics of the underwriting model	◾ Reliance on risk modeling/ segmentation. ◾ Standardized acceptance criteria. ◾ Standardized pricing. ◾ Limited exceptions. ◾ Straight-through processing.	◾ Risk modeling only partially possible. ◾ Reliance on judgment and expertise. ◾ Discretionary acceptance, decided case by case. ◾ Discretionary pricing, terms and conditions case by case. ◾ Delegated authorities for acceptance, pricing and conditions.	◾ Individual deal modeling possible. ◾ Cross-functional, team-based underwriting. ◾ Full discretion regarding acceptance. ◾ Full discretion regarding pricing, subject to individual deal RAPM calculations.

Managing the all-in cost and increasing processing efficiency is also critical. It is complicated by the fact that automated decision models are not possible and standardized terms and conditions may not be optimal from a risk/return perspective. Often, expert systems and decision support tools are used to support underwriting decisions.

Structured solutions are characterized by very low volumes, with each transaction a unique solution to a unique problem. Cross-functional teams comprising product, legal and accounting professionals are often required in order to deliver the value to the customer. As a consequence, margins should be higher and negotiated with the customer using value-based pricing rather than the cost of delivery.

UNDERWRITING STRATEGY

A clearly defined underwriting strategy produces consistent and predictable earnings over the business cycle, balancing profitability, portfolio quality, market share and growth, and is a fundamental building block for the firm's broader risk strategy and risk appetite.

The underwriting strategy will influence the products and markets you are active in, the growth you can achieve and the technical skills needed to serve that segment. *It is therefore absolutely critical to align the underwriting strategy and business plan* through the strategic planning process.

Underwriting strategy influences the business through three channels, as illustrated in Figure 23.2.

- A high-level underwriting strategy helps to keep the organization focused on the business that you want and build the skills where you need them.

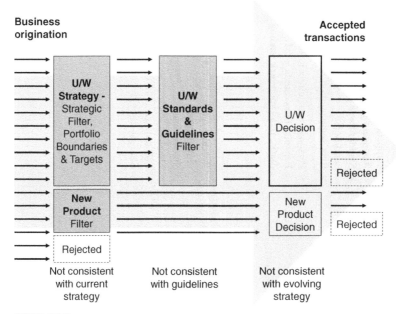

FIGURE 23.2 Three elements of an underwriting strategy

- Detailed underwriting policies and guidelines to guide technical underwriting decisions from a risk and commercial perspective.
- Finally, a new product approval process ensures that underwriting and business objectives stay aligned, even under changing market conditions.

Underwriting Strategy

An underwriting strategy comprises a high-level segmentation of the market, helping to focus resources on the business that you want and avoid business that you do not want. In addition, there has to be an explicit link between the underwriting and business strategies and associated commercial targets in order to keep the two aligned (see Table 23.3).[2] Combined, these provide a first "filter" for transactions to be considered.

Underwriting Policies and Guidelines

More detailed underwriting rules are required to steer day-to-day business. These are defined through technical minimum standards, policies and guidelines, some of which are driven by risk considerations, others by commercial considerations. Underwriting guidelines cover such things as the following.

- Maximum gross and net transaction capacity limits, where net is measured relative to anticipated sell-down, reinsurance or other hedging activity.
- Excluded business (e.g., in terms of contractual forms such as financial guarantees, trade credit insurance, credit derivatives, etc.; specific risk restrictions such as acts of war or terrorism; compliance restrictions such as business with sanctioned countries; ESG-sensitive[3] transactions, etc.).
- Conditions precedent for specific business (e.g., risk engineering requirements; physical property/collateral asset due diligence; documentation requirements; hedging or risk mitigation requirements, etc.).
- Referral conditions (e.g., the requirement to refer specific transactions to specialized underwriting teams, etc.).
- Escalation conditions, both secondary review of non-standard or material risk transactions or in case of a disagreement on a decision, terms or conditions.

New Product Approval Processes

If innovation is the siren, business entrepreneurs are the sailors: product innovation can be a major source of competitive advantage for businesses facing rapidly evolving customer needs and competitor behavior. Innovative new products can be the difference between capturing higher volumes and margins as a "first mover" or the more limited returns of a commoditized product as a "me, too" follower.

Unfortunately, no static underwriting strategy or guidelines can fully anticipate a dynamically changing market. Because innovation is inevitable, the underwriting strategy

---

[2]For broad guidance, see BIS (2001a) and FSB (2013b). For a practical example, see Strischek (2003).

[3]Environmental, Social and Governance (ESG) is a term used to refer to industries or activities which may be perceived by some parties as being inappropriate based on personal convictions. See Chapter 26 for a discussion.

TABLE 23.3   Elements of an underwriting strategy statement

Elements	Examples
High-level segmentation	A statement of the target customer/product/geographic segment. "We serve retail and corporate customers globally." "We are a regional retail/commercial bank/insurer." "We focus on specialized or niche industries/customer segments/products."
Link to commercial strategy	Statements outlining trade-offs between underwriting and commercial strategy. Overall targets "We will not sacrifice quality for volume or growth, even over the cycle." "We have a bias towards predictable earnings and pursue the lowest risk approach to achieve our target rate of return." "We balance customer satisfaction, profitable relationships, portfolio quality and prudent growth." Customer related "We are relationship driven and work to develop profitable relationships, exiting those which cannot be made profitable." Underwriting specific "We only underwrite those risks where we have the expertise, infrastructure and skills and which meet our standards." "We maintain consistent underwriting standards throughout the cycle; we do not loosen standards during hard markets, even if we don't grow as fast as competitors, nor during soft cycles to gain business."
Portfolio targets and boundaries	Specific guidance regarding excluded and targeted business. Boundary conditions ■ Willingness to write business by customer segment, product, geographic region. ■ Willingness to write business based on profitability. ■ Portfolio targets. ■ Portfolio composition/diversification targets. ■ Volume and pricing targets by segment. ■ Portfolio concentration limits.

and organization must be able to adapt. However, entering into new underwriting classes or products can also lead to deteriorating results due to a lack of experience and/or scale.

A well-designed product innovation and approval process (illustrated in Figure 23.3) mitigates these risks while at the same time providing a source of competitive advantage, allowing the company to innovate and bring new products to market faster and with more confidence. The following discussion looks at the product approval process from a risk and underwriting perspective.

The product innovation plan is the plan for developing new products and bringing them to market during the coming year; it is discussed during the strategic planning process and may be updated during the year.

Many new products represent only marginal changes to existing products, implying that only limited risk and underwriting approvals are necessary. However, some changes may represent significant innovations into uncharted water which require more formal review and prior approval.

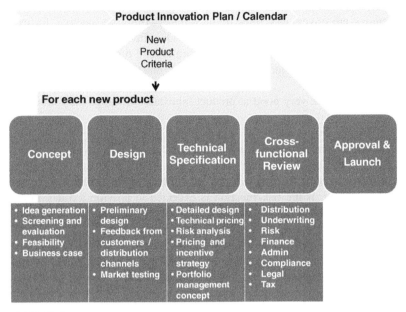

FIGURE 23.3 New product approval process

From an underwriting perspective, criteria must be clearly defined regarding what constitutes a new product. Common criteria include material differences in:

- targeted customer segment, the use of the product by the customer or the distribution channel for reaching the customer;
- changes to the risk profile (e.g., underlying risks covered by the contract, the structure of cash flows, terms and conditions, documentation, covenants, etc.);
- contractual form (e.g., derivative, security, insurance policy, special purpose vehicle, etc.).

For innovations meeting the criteria, the new product approval process specifies a minimum level of technical analysis on which to base the approval decision. From a risk perspective, the analysis is supported by a standardized template covering:

- customer needs and projected demand;
- product economics to the firm, distribution partners and the customer;
- risk profile of the product, hedging or investment strategies, critical assumptions and underwriting experience;
- capital and liquidity requirements.

Careful consideration should be given to sales practices and suitability, especially sales materials and sales incentives.

All parties in the end-to-end process need to be involved to ensure that the new product not only makes sense from an underwriting perspective and meets clients' needs, but that it can also be delivered and administered effectively. Involved in the new product approval process should be distribution, risk management, underwriting, finance and accounting, treasury, back-office administration and IT, legal, compliance, etc.

Also required are governance rules from an underwriting perspective, for example the triage process for qualifying new product ideas; the identification of "high-risk" products for additional scrutiny; the application process and turn-around times for each step; the right to "veto" or halt the new product introduction by specific functions, the escalation procedures in case of disagreement, etc.

Companies which are very good at product innovation leverage the following.

- A formalized "product champion," someone who feels personally responsible for shepherding new products through what can be a complex process involving many steps and many parties.
- A clear understanding by the participants of their responsibilities, combined with appropriate staffing: if the risk function is expected to provide a 5-day turnaround on 25 new product approvals a year, including detailed technical analysis and benchmarking, then they need to have sufficient staff dedicated to the task.
- Finally, earlier and more frequent communication. For every successful new product, there are many more which get side-lined due to pricing, risk or administration considerations. Each of these failures is costly and frustrating. Dead-ends can be avoided by earlier and more frequent communication across silos, for example through a formal, cross-functional triage process or, better yet, informal conversations early on.

UNDERWRITING GOVERNANCE

Developing an underwriting organization with the skills, processes and capabilities to execute the strategy is the second cornerstone. Underwriting governance defines who takes underwriting decisions and how. A generic governance structure is outlined in Figure 23.4.

This generic underwriting organization has the following key attributes.

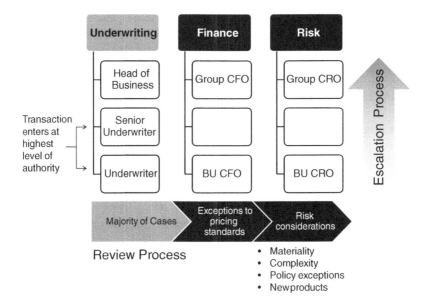

FIGURE 23.4 Underwriting decision organization

- The majority of transactions are underwritten within the business units, being assigned after triage to the most senior underwriter who has the appropriate level of authority to eliminate a duplication of efforts at lower levels.
- If a transaction requires an independent risk review due to materiality, complexity, guideline exception or new product, then it is in parallel directed to the risk function for review; in the case of a profitability review relative to the firm's pricing guidelines, it should be in parallel referred to the CUO for single transactions or to the CFO or strategic planning team for portfolio exceptions.
- If there is disagreement regarding either the risk or commercial pricing reviews, the business has the right to escalate the decision to the next level within the business and risk/finance hierarchy, where such escalations are the exception and not the rule.

Defining Underwriting Authorities

In the past, many firms took underwriting decisions by committee. It is now accepted that the majority of decisions should be taken by individuals within the normal course of business. The rationale is that individual decision making supports greater accountability for both good and bad decisions, avoids the socialization of blame or success and greatly increases efficiency, measured both by elapsed time and cost.

Delegated underwriting authorities should reflect the experience and judgment of the individual, with higher authorities granted to more senior, experienced underwriters. Underwriting authority can also be aligned with formal accreditation from internal underwriting academies, reinforcing an underwriting culture.

In order to increase efficiency, opportunities are triaged and enter the underwriting organization at the first level for which the underwriter has the competence and authority to take the decision. A transaction may be material or complex enough to require the Executive Board or Risk Committee to be informed or give a formal approve. Normally, criteria are defined by authority level so that a target percentage of interventions is achieved (e.g., define authorities and criteria such that the number of escalations are 1-in-500 or 1-in-1000 for commercial business at the level of the Risk Committee).

Who "owns" the Underwriting Decision – Risk or Business?

Some companies have a CUO (or head of the product or technical area) representing the first line of defense and a CRO representing the second line of defense. Who ultimately takes the underwriting decision? Is it a business decision, resting with the first line of defense, or a risk decision with the second?

These are not trivial questions: underwriting decisions are important, with critical implications for the revenue and earnings growth of the firm; however, a wrong call or a series of wrong calls can be the difference between profit and loss during the quarter.

The solution is a balanced application of the risk governance principles discussed earlier: the independent risk function should help the firm define an underwriting framework (including underwriting strategy, guidelines, limits and delegated authorities) within which the first line takes the majority of underwriting decisions.

However, recognizing the limitations of any framework, the risk function remains close to the business and has the professional experience necessary to occasionally intervene, halt and escalate problem cases if the framework proves inadequate.

Underwriting Referral and Escalation Processes

The most efficient solution is to have risk-aware underwriters decide the majority of applications with few escalations and referrals. Under what conditions should a transaction be referred to the next level or be reviewed independently? Normally, escalations and referrals occur because of either risk or profitability considerations or both.

Risk-Based Referrals

There are four specific instances where an independent risk function should express an explicit, independent and binding decision on individual loans or insurance policies.

- First, transactions which *exceed predefined materiality thresholds*. In other words, at some point a loan or policy exposure becomes large enough that an independent, explicit, ex ante review and approval is required.
- Second, transactions *which require an exception to the underwriting guidelines* or policies, for example the guideline specifying prohibited business activities, deviations from standard contract wordings, covenants or policy restrictions, etc.
- Third, transactions which are suitably *complex or which fall outside the "normal" range* in terms of structure, documentation, pricing, subsequent hedging or risk management activities, etc.
- Fourth, transactions which represent *"new" products or segments* for which the institution does not have extensive underwriting experience.

These criteria are valid for both retail business, which is largely automated, and commercial business, for which an underwriter is directly involved. They should not be controversial – each represents a situation where an independent review by an experienced professional is desirable, both from a business as well as a risk perspective. The critical discussions are often around how to set the materiality thresholds or escalation rules in practice so that a "reasonable" number of transactions – not too many and not too few – are reviewed.

Profitability-based Referrals

In addition to these four risk-based criteria, many institutions also use an additional criterion requiring explicit, independent approval (albeit by another function besides the risk function).

- Fifth, transactions or products which do not meet the firm's profitability targets and require cross-subsidization.

There are several commercial reasons for subsidizing a transaction, product or customer segment, for example to gain "shelf space" at a distributor, to round out a product palette, to support a broader client relationship or to increase the volume of business which is accretive on a marginal if not a full-cost basis.

These decisions should be taken in a conscious and disciplined manner as opposed to being left solely to the discretion of individual underwriters. But these are commercial and not risk decisions: trivially, there is no risk as the transaction is known to be economically loss making at inception.

Approving profitability exceptions requires a balanced view of the strategic or tactical rationale and shareholder value. Such approvals are therefore best left to the CUO for individual transactions and to the finance function and strategic planning process for large-scale, structural deviations from pricing standards.

In general, a profitability exception should only be granted if accompanied by an explicit budget and remediation plan. In other words, a maximum subsidization limit should be defined, giving the front line greater flexibility in deciding where and how to subsidize specific transactions in order to maximize the overall profitability of the business while capping the total subsidy.

Escalations

There will inevitably be disagreements between the first and second lines, whenever independent reviews and approvals are required. Because of the inevitability, it is important that the firm has a clear escalation procedure to resolve potential conflicts.

The most straightforward procedure is to allow the business sponsor to escalate a denied transaction to the next higher level of *both* the business and risk functions. For example, a commercial loan officer may escalate a denied transaction to the Head of Commercial Business *and* the CRO of the Commercial Segment, with the clear understanding that the transaction cannot be concluded until a decision is taken to reverse the earlier veto.

In order to make this feasible when decisions need to be taken in real time, it is important to define the minimum information needed for the decision (preventing a ping-pong game of information requests) and turnaround times for escalated transactions. In addition, it is important that the thresholds, processes and culture be such that the escalation of a transaction should be the exception and not the general rule: if the majority of transactions end up being escalated, then clearly the process is not well designed in the first place.

Underwriting Controls

Adhering to underwriting guidelines and processes is critical for the success of an underwriting organization. For this reason, most companies perform ex post reviews of the underwriting process. These reviews help to ensure that guidelines are followed and also represent an opportunity to build and disseminate institutional knowledge. Given the dual benefits, underwriting reviews are carried out by the underwriting function itself with the active involvement of the second (risk) or third (audit) line of defense. Underwriting reviews are described in the next chapter.

CHAPTER 24

Risk Underwriting – Technical Tools

I n addition to a clear underwriting strategy and governance organization, technical underwriting tools are valuable to evaluate, segment and price the risk of each applicant or
transaction.

Using the right underwriting tools can lead to substantial benefits, defensively in terms of
reducing average losses and the volatility of losses and offensively by giving greater
confidence in writing and growing business in higher risk segments. In addition, they can
lead to higher customer satisfaction and greater cost efficiency if appropriately integrated in the
business system.

There are three, broad technical underwriting approaches aligned with the three different
segments:

- data-driven or "scoring" approaches for segments where sufficient data exists to build
  robust predictive models (e.g., retail or personal lines);
- evaluation-based, expert judgment approaches for segments where there is insufficient
  data to build reliable models (e.g., commercial and corporate);
- transaction-specific approaches suitable for structured solution businesses.

RETAIL SEGMENT: "SCORING" MODELS

Mature retail insurance and lending businesses typically have sufficient historical data to
develop robust predictive models in support of risk underwriting ("scoring" models).

Business Uses and Benefits

Scoring models are predictive models using explanatory variables such as income, gender, etc.
to "separate" good customers from bad customers. An example, discriminant analysis, finds a
linear combination of explanatory variables which separate potentially "good" and "bad"
clients into groups but with the distance between the good and bad groups made as large as
possible, as illustrated in Figure 24.1.

The use of scoring models brings significant business benefits: they can lead to better and
less volatile loss ratios by improving underwriting decisions; they can be used to grow the
business by giving greater confidence to underwrite higher risk segments; and they can be used

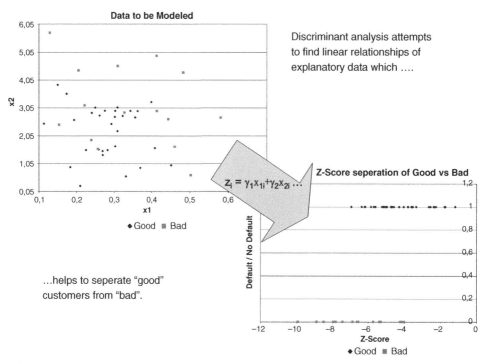

FIGURE 24.1   Discriminant analysis to separate "good" and "bad" applicants

to implement a more automated and streamlined underwriting process, leading to lower costs, faster turn-around times and more transparent decisions.

There are two types of underwriting scoring model: *application scoring*, used to evaluate the risk of a new customer, and *behavioral scoring*, used to evaluate the evolving risk characteristics of an existing customer based on additional information gained through the business relationship. The same techniques are also applied in customer relationship management and marketing applications (see Chapter 11). Limitations on the use of potentially sensitive data for underwriting is discussed in a later section of this chapter.

Example: Credit Scoring
Credit scoring is used broadly by banks. According to Fair Isaac, a company specializing in designing and implementing credit scores, over 75% of mortgage lenders and over 90% of credit card lenders in the USA use credit scoring techniques.

A credit score is a number, typically between 300 and 850; a higher number is associated with lower risk. In its simplest form, points are assigned to the answers provided by an applicant, with higher points indicating lower risk and the sum of all points being the score. While easy to use and explain, the additive approach cannot capture potential interactions between the variables; more advanced approaches introduce an "if . . . then . . . else" dependency. Statistical and non-statistical techniques are used to set the weights optimally to reflect the risk of an applicant.

Example: Risk "Scoring" in the Insurance Industry
Similar approaches are used in insurance to help the underwriter decide whether to accept a life insurance risk or write an automobile collision policy. In insurance, the risk of a claim

being filed is predicted based on such factors as age, gender, address, socio-economic background, claims history, lifestyle choices, physical characteristics, personal and family history, etc.

Overview of the "Scoring" Process

Scoring uses historical data to identify characteristics which differentiate between "good" and "bad" customers. There are a wide variety of scoring approaches and the best approach will depend on the specific application, the data available and the ease of embedding into the overall business system. However, all of the approaches rely on the same three-step process: data, modeling and embedding.

Data

Having access to the right data is critical. You need a sufficient quantity of both "good" and "bad" customers in the sample in order to estimate or "train" the model. In addition, you need to reserve sufficient data to test the model's performance "out of sample" in order to ensure that the results can be generalized reliably. The data should be representative of the segments that you are underwriting and should include not only your own experience but also data from customers that you rejected (in order to avoid an "acceptance bias") and those that went to your competitor, if possible.

A broad set of potential explanatory variables needs to be collected if you hope to find new relationships which may be complex and not readily identifiable. An example data "shopping list" is given in Table 24.1, most of which can be rationalized by some theory regarding the relationship to ultimate customer performance.

In general, data has value and more data is more valuable.[1] As a consequence, a clearly defined data strategy should be developed, supported by sufficient investment in data collection and analysis. Data can be acquired from *data suppliers* (e.g., Bloomberg, Reuters, etc. for financial market prices or from services which collect bankruptcy filings, insurance claim filings, etc.), by participating in *industry consortia* (such as RAS[2]) and by targeting new client segments to enhance the firm's proprietary data.

After collecting data, the next step is to *manage, pre-process and archive the data*. This includes correcting data for outliers, anomalies or missing observations; developing a data architecture suitable to support the archiving, use and analysis of the data; and developing analysis systems to be used by model builders, transforming data if required (e.g., from categorical data into binary data), etc.

The next step is to *analyze, understand and filter the data*. Simple analysis is used, such as: plotting/visualizing the data, looking for relationships and outliers/anomalies;

---

[1] Exceptions to this rule can arise if you include data with a different underlying relationship, for example from a different segment or from the same segment but a different time period impacted by behavioral, social, economic or judicial changes.

[2] Risk Analysis Services (RAS) is an industry-led data consortium focused on key credit risk metrics, including risk ratings (PD & LGD), non-accrual rates by industry, past-due/delinquencies, non-accrual levels and charge-offs. It provides benchmarking services.

TABLE 24.1 Examples of "scoring" data requirements

Contract data	Client-specific data	External data
Sales channel (e.g., direct, agent, broker, etc.). Type of insurance policy or loan: ■ overdraft, card, mortgage, credit line, etc.; ■ property or liability, home, auto or small business, etc.	Individual customer data ■ Age and gender. ■ Address, # years at the address. ■ Employment, # years. ■ Other insurance contracts or forms of indebtedness. ■ Actual usage, for example as measured by telematics, etc.	Geo-demographic data ■ Population density. ■ Average income levels. ■ Property mapping (e.g., relative to flood, earthquake or windstorm zones). ■ Concentration of regional employment, etc.

Contract parameters:
 	
■ amount of loan, monthly payments, loan-to-value ratio, subordination or collateral, etc.;
■ sum insured, self-insured retention/ deductibles, exclusions, etc.;
■ length of contract.
	Relationship data
	
	■ Historical performance:
	  ■ payment delinquencies, average/peak balances, etc.;
	  ■ claims filed, paid and rejected, number of claim-free years, etc.
	■ Other accounts or policies with the company and their performance.
	
	Corporate customer data
	
	■ Industry code.
	■ Number of employees.
	■ Years of establishment.
	■ Location of business, etc.
	
	Property data
	
	■ Type of property.
	■ Construction characteristics.
	■ Value of property, etc.	

calculating simple statistics (means, standard deviations and correlations); performing more advanced analysis such as regression, analysis of variance, principle components analysis, clustering, etc.

Modeling

The next step is to select the modeling approaches to be investigated. There are a wide variety of scoring approaches, including regression techniques, discriminant analysis, k-nearest neighbors, decision trees and neural networks, to name a few. Some models rely on structural or statistical assumptions; other approaches are more agnostic, with fewer preconceived structural assumptions, including neural networks and genetic learning algorithms. Sidebar 24.1 gives an overview of discriminant analysis; the table in the footnote provides general references for data-driven approaches in insurance and banking for the interested reader.[3]

More modeling approaches are now feasible due to increased computer power, data storage and software. Increasingly, the only limitations are imposed by the lack of qualified and experienced personnel who can estimate the models and ensure that the results make sense.

Initial modeling Estimating "the model" can be seen as a two-step process: first, find the best "fit" within a class of models (e.g., the best set of explanatory variables within a regression or discriminant analysis or neural network) and second, select the "champion" from across the different modeling approaches.

SIDEBAR 24.1: A DIGRESSION ON LINEAR DISCRIMINANT ANALYSIS[4]

ASSUMPTIONS

Linear discriminant analysis is a statistical technique based on the assumption that the explanatory variables are normally distributed and share the same covariance matrix conditional on whether they are "good" or "bad." For example, the explanatory variables x are distributed as $P(x|y=0), P(x|y=1)$ with mean and variance given by $N(\mu_0, \Sigma_0), N(\mu_1, \Sigma_1)$ where 0 indicates "good" and 1 indicates "bad." Linear discriminant analysis requires the further restriction that $\Sigma_0 = \Sigma_1 = \Sigma$.[5]

ESTIMATION

Under these assumptions, it can be shown that the optimal linear combination is given by the "z-score," $z_i = \sum_{j=1}^{n} \gamma_j x_{i,j}$, where $\gamma = \hat{\Sigma}^{-1}(\mu^0 - \mu^1)$ and n_0 and n_1 represent the number of "good" and "bad" customers in the sample data and $\hat{\Sigma} = \frac{(n_0-1)}{(n_0+n_1-2)}\hat{\Sigma}_g + \frac{(n_1-1)}{(n_0+n_1-2)}\hat{\Sigma}_b$.

---

[3]The following are general references for data-driven scoring approaches in banking and insurance.

Segment	General references
Banking	Altman *et al.* (1981)
	Altman and Saunders (1998)
	Abdou and Pointon (2011)
Insurance	Nyce (2007)
	Batty *et al.* (2010)
	Pozzolo (2011)

[4]Sidebar 24.1 follows Resti and Sironi (2007).

[5]Relaxing the assumption that the explanatory variables are normally distributed (as opposed to categorical – e.g., falling into discrete categories (or non-normal) – requires the use of other approaches such as the Logit or Probit approaches described later); relaxing the assumption of a common covariance matrix leads to quadratic discriminant analysis.

RESULTS AND INTERPRETATION

Under these assumptions, it can also be shown that the probability of default for customer i can be estimated as $Pd_i = \frac{1}{1+\frac{1-p_\phi}{p_\phi}\exp(z_i-\alpha)}$, where p_ϕ is defined as the average portfolio probability of default and α is defined as the z-score cut-off point which is exactly halfway between the "good" and "bad" firms, calculated as $\alpha = \frac{1}{2}\gamma'(\mu_0 + \mu_1)$.

If the firm wants to set a specific cut-off point based on the estimated probability of default, then it would define a new cut-off threshold, α_{pd}, using $\alpha_{pd} = \alpha + \ln\left(\frac{p_\phi}{1-p_\phi}\right)$.

Finally, assume that there are different costs associated with making a Type 1 error (defined as accepting a "bad" firm) versus a Type 2 error (defined as not accepting a "good" firm). Label these costs as $C(0/1)$ and $C(1/0)$, respectively. If we want to set the acceptance threshold such that the expected cost of a Type 1 error was exactly equal to the expected cost of a Type 2 error (e.g., $C(0/1)Pd = C(1/0)(1 - Pd)$), then it can be shown that the new acceptance threshold should be defined by $\alpha_{1/2} = \alpha_{pd} + \log\left(\frac{C(0/1)}{C(1/0)}\right)$.

The selection of variables to be tested will in general follow a process of elimination/inclusion: "backwards elimination" begins by including all variables and then removing them one by one based on their relative contribution; in contrast, "forward selection" begins with none and adds a new variable sequentially based on the highest contribution. Brute-force approaches, trying every combination and ranking the results, are also possible. Convergence to a good model providing sensible results is quicker for the experienced modeler using intuition, theory and an understanding of the underlying data.

As there are many approaches, some criteria need to be defined to select the "champion" across model classes. *Quantitative criteria* include an *analysis of the results* (e.g., the number or ratio of incorrectly classified cases in aggregate) for both the accepted and rejected cases; the predictive power of the model in out-of-sample tests; Relative Operating Characteristic (ROC) plots;[6] non-parametric techniques including plotting the residuals in order to visually identify outliers or patterns which require further explanation. Within a class of models, they also include *model-specific statistics* such as the R-squared and the t-statistics and F-statistics used for regression analysis, Wilks' lambda used for discriminant analysis, etc.

Qualitative criteria should also influence your selection of the final model. These include the following.

- *Intuition.* The model should make intuitive sense given its use, mitigating blind acceptance of the results and supporting the use and communication of the model. Some steps include the following.
  - Develop a hypothesis before you estimate the model and benchmark the results against your hypothesis. Do the signs and the variables make sense? If the results differ from your hypothesis, why do they differ?

---

[6]ROC illustrates the performance of the binary classification model (e.g., default/no default) as its discrimination threshold is varied by plotting the fraction of true positives out of all positives versus the fraction of false positives out of all negatives.

- Understand the sensitivity of the model to critical assumptions. Are the predictions robust to parameter estimation errors?
- Understand the sensitivity of the model to inputs. Do the results under extreme inputs still make sense? Do different combinations give reasonable outcomes? What happens if some data is missing when the model is applied?
- Test the model *out-of-sample* to validate its predictive capabilities and use new data to *back-test* the model's predictive capabilities. Are the results materially different?
- *Simplicity and robustness.* Borrowing from Occam's razor, the simpler the model the better. The model should use data which is readily available but produce results which are also robust to missing data, an issue which is certain to come up during the underwriting process.
- *Embedding in the underwriting process.* Ultimately, the model has to be integrated into an efficient underwriting process; understanding how the model fits into the process is critical. The more data is required, the more needs to be collected; the more complex the decision rule, the more difficult to explain and embed into an organization. Pragmatic trade-offs between simplicity, robustness and accuracy need to be taken.
- Finally, can the *information be legally and ethically used*? For example, in some instances the use of gender, genetic information or postal address may not be allowed to influence underwriting decisions.

After Modeling   The model needs to be fully documented, summarizing the suitability of the model for its intended purpose, the adequacy of the data, the general procedures used and the reasons for choosing those procedures. The documentation should describe the use and limitations of the model, identify key personnel and milestones in the model's construction and describe validation procedures and results. The model and documentation should be independently reviewed and validated and formally approved as required by the firm's internal control procedures.

On an ongoing basis, the model should be compared with actual experience ("back-testing"). The focus should not only be on understanding broad model slippage, but also on identifying specific segments where the model does not provide robust results. Finally, the model should be re-estimated periodically in order to account for changing relationships which could arise due to changing legislation, legal precedents, social patterns, etc.

Embedding

The final step is to embed the model into the underwriting process. Some of the critical issues to be considered when embedding include commercial, process and governance-related considerations.

From a *commercial perspective*, how conservative should you set the acceptance threshold? What are the trade-offs you are willing to make between a Type 1 error (e.g. incorrectly accepting a "bad" risk) and a Type 2 error (e.g. incorrectly refusing a "good" risk)?

From a *process support* perspective, will the model be used as a "black box" with no link between input and output for the sales rep and underwriter, or is there a need for a clear and explainable link? Related to this, will the link be made through a scorecard, assigning "points" to different attributes which the underwriter can follow or through a calculation tool? Will it be a multi-step process or a "fast quote" dependent on limited information or a combination?

From a *governance perspective*, how to integrate the model into acceptance processes and authorities? Specifically.

- How will scoring be used? Will scoring replace human underwriting? Will scoring be used to triage new applications between "fast-track," clear decline and high-touch reviews? Will different models be used at different points (e.g., one for triaging and another requiring more information for more difficult cases)?
- Whether and how to allow for overrides? Under what conditions can underwriters override the model decisions on individual cases? What are the requirements with respect to tracking over-rides and experience?

Social Limitations

The best possible scoring approaches may not be allowed due to regulatory constraints aimed at achieving social objectives or fairness considerations. For example, on April 2, 2009, the European Parliament approved the Gender Directive Article 5 (1): "Member States shall ensure that in all new contracts concluded after 21 December 2007 at the latest, the use of sex as a factor in the calculation of premiums and benefits for the purposes of insurance and related financial services shall not result in differences in individuals' premiums and benefits."

The European insurance industry raised concerns, summarized by the ABI (2010): "Risk based pricing is key to the efficient operation of the private insurance markets. There are significant gender differences in accident, morbidity and mortality risks. Gender is used when it helps the accuracy of pricing products which cover these risks."

Other examples of restrictions on the use of personal data to develop underwriting decision criteria include the following.

- "Red lining," the practice of declining an applicant for credit on the grounds that he/she lives at an address which is deemed unsatisfactory. The name derives from the practice of drawing a red line "exclusion zone" around an area on a map. Red lining is outlawed in many countries, including the USA and the UK.
- Using genetic information[7] (e.g., explicit exclusions on collecting genetic information, requiring genetic testing and the use of such information in determining eligibility requirements, risk selection or risk classification).
- Credit[8] information for the underwriting or pricing of auto or home-owner policies, etc.

Regulatory constraints need to be respected. However, the impact of such constraints in terms of the economics and potential subsidization of products and segments must be well understood in order to design optimal programs while reducing the frictional costs. As the ABI (2010) pointed out in the context of gender-neutral underwriting: "A ban on a relevant rating factor such as gender cannot be achieved without costs . . . (which) would ultimately be borne by consumers. (For example) motor insurance premiums for young females would increase (by up to 25% on average), and pension income for the majority of annuitants would fall (by 2% or more)."

---

[7]See, e.g., http://www.ncsl.org/IssuesResearch/Health/GeneticNondiscriminationinHealthInsuranceLaws/tabid/14374/Default.aspx, which gives a table outlining the restrictions on the use of genetic information for underwriting or pricing health insurance in the USA.

[8]See, e.g., http://www.pciaa.net/web/sitehome.nsf/lcpublic/402/$file/PCICreditWP021109.pdf, which describes the historical development and restrictions on the use of personal credit scores for underwriting or pricing of property insurance.

COMMERCIAL LINES: LEVERAGING EXPERT JUDGMENT

Data-driven approaches cannot be applied to segments with data insufficient to build robust predictive models or where environmental changes have invalidated historical data.[9]

Given the diversity within the segment, corporate and commercial business is typically evaluated and underwritten based on experience and judgment rather than statistical tools. The use of expert judgment is often characterized as "more art than science," for example when evaluating the "five Cs" of credit, described in Sidebar 24.2.

SIDEBAR 24.2: THE FIVE Cs OF CREDIT UNDERWRITING

It is commonly held (e.g., Strischek, 2009) that there are five Cs which must be considered during the credit underwriting process.

CHARACTER

The character of a borrower is one of the most important determinants of whether the loan will be repaid, especially during periods of adversity. Evaluating character directly is challenging, but some useful indicators include credit history (payment, early notification of problems, restructuring, default), employment history, stability of residence, connections to the community, references, management track record, existence of civil disputes or criminal allegations, etc.

CAPACITY

A borrower's capacity refers to their ability to make payments on time, which depends on the borrower's ability to generate income or cash flow to service their obligations, the level of their existing obligations and their ability to absorb any potential uncertainty surrounding their income or obligations.

CAPITAL

While capital is not directly recognized as the means by which the borrower should repay the loan, having more capital resources is nonetheless better: if capital resources are liquid, they can be used to cover cash shortfalls from operations or income and if they are tangible, they can potentially be used as collateral to gain cash for similar purposes.

CONDITIONS

Conditions refer to the external factors which might impact the ability of the borrower to repay the loan. Because loan repayment will depend on the future cash flows of the borrower, it is important to assess how those cash flows might be influenced by external

---

[9]This can include changes in the social, regulatory, judicial and economic environment. This latter is illustrated in Carroll (2010), "When losses soared in 2008 and 2009, many lenders reverted to human underwriting . . . about 90% of large banks that make small business loans had either abandoned score-based adjudication processes in favor of human underwriter, or had severely cut back the proportion of loans that were auto-adjudicated . . ."

conditions (e.g., the economic environment, regional economic concentration, any relevant regulatory or policy changes, etc.).

COLLATERAL

Collateral is any property of value which can be pledged against the repayment of the loan and which is accepted by the lender. For personal loans, collateral often takes the form of the asset being financed, whether a home, a car or a securities account.

Looking narrowly, this is not to say that technology cannot be used to make underwriters more efficient, for example at performing administrative tasks, managing data and workflow – equivalent to ordering paint and setting up the canvas – but in the end it is a human hand which will paint the Mona Lisa. This thought is reflected in the US Department of Labor annual report, which suggests that "Underwriting software will continue to make workers more productive, but it does not do away with the need for human skills. As a result, employment of underwriters will increase as a growing economy and population expands."

However, while describing the underwriting process as an "art" makes for a good sound bite, these segments are nonetheless exposed to the same commercial imperatives as personal lines: competitive margins make cost efficiency a priority, and getting consistent and effective acceptance criteria across a large number of "artists" becomes even more important.

There are three important activities used to improve the effectiveness of judgment-based underwriting decisions. The first and most important is to develop an effective and pervasive *underwriting culture*; the second is to consistently *leverage expert judgment* through the codification of the institution's underwriting experience, for example through decision support systems; the third is to *continually validate and reinforce the underwriting culture and experience*, for example through underwriting reviews. Each of these is discussed in some detail in the remainder of this section.

Building an Underwriting Culture

Commercial banks make loans and commercial insurers sell policies. Underwriting is the most important success factor for these businesses – it is what the company *does*. Unfortunately, underwriting in these segments is complicated by the fact that it needs to be done by individuals, and every individual brings their own experience (or lack thereof), personal biases and objectives to the table.

Successful firms make underwriting a significant part of the corporate DNA and a cornerstone of their culture. The results are greater consistency and effectiveness, leading to higher and more predictable profits across the cycle.

Unfortunately, it is also one of the most challenging tasks. Similar to a good "risk" culture, a good "underwriting culture" is amorphous – difficult to define, difficult to characterize and, because of this, difficult to implement.

It is difficult to define because of what it is not – it is not the policies, procedures, rules and authorities, although these complement and reinforce an underwriting culture. Rather, underwriting culture is analogous to the atomic force which keeps electrons circulating the nucleus of an atom – the invisible "glue" which nonetheless binds all the concrete bits that can be benchmarked (e.g., policies, procedures, guidelines and processes) together to deliver "good" decisions. Strischek (2002) states that "It is the way things are done around here . . . More broadly . . . (an underwriting) culture is the system of behavior, beliefs, philosophy, thought, style, and expression relating to the management of the . . . (underwriting) function."

Start with the Basics

While it is easy to measure the number of policies and rules, it is less easy to measure the mindset of the individuals who take decisions within those rules. As a consequence, there is no checklist for defining or implementing a "good" underwriting culture. Nonetheless, the concrete elements which have already been discussed are necessary but not sufficient.

- A well-defined and communicated *underwriting strategy*. This strategy needs to be realistic and aligned with the business targets: a strategy which is at odds with short-term targets will not work. In addition, it also needs to be supported by the management of the firm, including the CEO, the businesses and the finance and risk functions.
- Well-defined *underwriting policies and guidelines*. These policies need to be lived with discipline: it does no good to have policies for which "the exception is the rule" or an environment where decisions taken are consistently overruled due to commercial concerns. Discipline is reinforced by effective audit and independent review of the compliance with the standards.
- Finally, *organizational adequacy*. The underwriting function must have sufficient skilled resources, there must be clear accountability for decisions and an alignment of incentives between the underwriting and commercial functions.

Reinforce an Underwriting Culture

There are several additional factors which help to build a pervasive and effective underwriting culture.

Process is Good, a Focus on the Fundamentals is Better   Good underwriting focuses on a few qualitative points: understanding the client and their rationale for entering into the transaction, the risks which might cause the loan or policy to under-perform and whether or not it makes sense for the bank or insurer to engage in the transaction from a risk/return perspective. And, while processes and documentation may support these objectives, the two should not be confused.

To help understand the difference, consider the anecdote in Zweig (1995) describing how Citibank's underwriting culture changed "from style to substance" following management changes in response to poor credit experience: "(The old CEO) 'never looked at the business. He only looked at the process.' He said, 'If you fail the credit audit I'm going to fire you.' But he never looked at the credits."

However, the losses suffered by Citicorp in real estate and leveraged buy-outs led the new CEO to see the dangers of ". . . confusing style with results. (The old CEO . . .) was the quintessential well-organized 'process manager.' 'Just because guys have neat desks, lots of reviews and numbers, doesn't mean they will necessarily do a good job . . . it wasn't that he saw a [risk] and took the risk. He didn't see it.'" Years later Reed said, "All of us would say Larry is risk-averse, yet he produced a lot of risks."

Training and Shared Experiences   Culture is defined as a set of shared attitudes, values, goals and practices that characterize an institution, organization or group. If you step back and consider what lies at the foundation of the American, German or Chinese cultures, elements will likely include a common language and shared experiences, making the socialization of a common set of beliefs possible. The fact of the matter is that cultures are not inherited but are learned, they evolve and are reinforced through a process of socialization.

Author Ed O'Leary (2010)[10] comments that the "functional dean of students" at the Lending Officer's Training program in the Bank of New York was the head of the credit department. "He was a source of great credit experience and wisdom (and) . . . a wonderful story teller who would embellish his commentaries with personal details and anecdotes of bank officers and customers . . . (essential details that) . . . contained the rules, regulations, etiquette, and expectations of the bank."

It is not a stretch to imagine the role of a common language and the continual sharing of experiences or "story telling" in developing an underwriting culture. A common language and philosophy, up and down the underwriting function and also cutting across the organization, can be created for example by:

- cross-fertilization and job rotations between the underwriting and commercial functions;
- underwriting training programs, including levels of accreditation comparable to a "black belt" system, linked to authority levels;
- on-the-job apprenticeship or mentoring of junior underwriters by senior professionals;
- structured opportunities to share case experience (e.g., cross-staffing of file or underwriting reviews, creation of expert or specialist groups for specific products or risk types, etc.);
- standardized documentation and analysis requirements.

As an example, Allianz has a comprehensive training and apprenticeship program for its PC businesses in the form of an Underwriting University comprising modules which must be passed before attaining a higher underwriting grade. With the higher grade comes more underwriting authority and the possibility of a higher position in the underwriting organization. These courses are not taught by academics but by professionals who have gone through the same programs and who work in the trenches. The same teachers also mentor underwriting "apprentices." The purpose is to convey practical underwriting knowledge, experience and, ultimately, culture.

Making Heroes   Every culture has its heroes – ordinary people who nonetheless manage to accomplish extraordinary things. But heroes are more than that – they are also role models for others to admire and emulate and help propagate a common culture and set of beliefs. Just so, the underwriting function needs its heroes. This can be accomplished by raising the profile of the underwriting function, aligned with its value to the organization:

- acknowledging and celebrating the feats of "underwriting heroes" on a par with the front-office "rainmakers";
- requiring underwriting experience for promotion to senior line positions and rotating line managers into the underwriting function as part of their career development profile.

---

[10]http://www.ababj.com/credit-talk/training-and-credit-culture-2-part-rules-part-stories.html

It is said that the tone at the top sets the tone throughout the organization; another way to phrase this for less favorable outcomes is that "the fish begins to stink from the head." If you want to create an outstanding underwriting culture, the vision must be shared and championed by leadership.

Approaches for Codifying Expert Judgment

In addition to the softer elements of culture, technical approaches to codify and share experience are also important. Two prominent examples include Case-Based Reasoning (CBR) and expert systems. Both complement an underwriting culture by leveraging best practice across the broader organization. This is important to keep in mind when reading the following examples: the goal is not the technical approach, but rather the act of codifying, sharing and leveraging institutional underwriting experience.

Case-based Reasoning

CBR is a straightforward approach for codifying and disseminating expert judgment. In this approach, expertise is embodied in a library of past cases which set precedents that can be studied and extrapolated rather than encoded in explicit decision rules or algorithms. According to the AIAI (Watson, 1997), CBR can prove useful for applications where:

1. records of previously solved problems exist;
2. historical cases are viewed as an asset;
3. remembering previous experiences is useful;
4. specialists . . . find it difficult to articulate their thought process when solving problems;
5. experience is at least as valuable as textbook knowledge.

CBR is often used, for example, in medical diagnostics and underwriting. In the context of an underwriting organization, each case refers to a specific underwriting problem and is constructed to include a description of the problem and the solution, with the reasoning behind the solution described.

In practice, the characteristics of a new case are matched against the library, relevant cases are retrieved, differences are identified and the precedents are interpreted to derive a solution or set of solutions. The history can then be updated to include the new case, preserving institutional knowledge and making it generally available across the underwriting organization. A variety of tools are available which can be used to support the retrieval, reuse, revision and archiving of cases.

Expert Systems

Expert systems derive heuristic rules from cases and implement those rules in a decision support tool. In its simplest form, a group of senior, experienced underwriters work through and discuss specific cases and then develop a set of rules which can be implemented in a decision support system made available to the broader underwriting community. In the terminology of expert systems, *knowledge engineers* work together with *subject matter experts* in order to derive *inference rules* which are then coded into decision support systems.

This process is described more fully in Sidebar 24.3, which describes the development of the CLUES expert underwriting system by Countrywide Financial.

SIDEBAR 24.3: TACTICAL RISK IDENTIFICATION USING EXPERT SYSTEMS: THE CLUES CASE STUDY

Expert systems are used to support the risk identification and underwriting of bank loans, illustrated by the CLUES system introduced by Countrywide Financial in the 1990s:[11]

> *CLUES is an elegant solution to a complex problem. CLUES has an abstract (rule-based, expert system) decision-making model that evaluates a loan file in the same way that a human would . . . provides extensive justification for the decisions made . . . (and) recognizes when it has reached the limits of its knowledge.*

The process for developing an expert system begins by clearly and narrowly defining the problem – for example, should the loan or policy be denied, granted or referred to a senior underwriter for further review? The next step is to identify experts with a track record of success within the firm or broader industry whose experience you want to capture.

These experts are asked to provide "rules" on how they evaluate similar problems; very often, these "rules" are implicit in an underwriter's end decision, derived by a process which is complex and opaque. As such, the "rules" may need to be inferred, formulated and refined into explicit "inference rules" using a variety of methods, including interviews and workshops with explicit test cases.

The process is supported by "knowledge engineers" trained to interview the subject matter (underwriting) experts and translate the "art" of underwriting into concrete rules.

> *Underwriting is considered an art . . . It takes years of experience . . . (and the) process is intuitive rather than scientific. The challenge for the knowledge engineers was to represent the through process of an underwriter in a manner that could be implemented as a software system.*

An inference rule is a conditional statement consisting of an if–then–else clause, for example, "If (the applicant has been convicted of insurance fraud) then (the decision is to reject coverage)." An expert system is made up of many inference rules, each entered separately but collectively used to draw conclusions. Modular rules allow the use of a "core" across all segments, augmented by special rules for new and specialized segments, fraud checking, etc. Any rule may be deleted, modified or added without affecting other rules; this simplifies both the update and maintenance of the decision rules.

A rule-based system improves communication, for example by making transparent the strengths and weaknesses of an application as well as the specific rationale behind the underwriting decision.

---

[11]Sidebar 24.3 is based on Talebzadeh *et al.* (1995). For a description of expert systems applied to insurance underwriting, see Berkovsky *et al.* (2004).

> In addition to ensuring greater consistency and improving the underwriting deci-
> sions, the use of expert systems also supports other objectives including cost efficiency
> and decision efficiency:
>
> *After a year in production, CLUES has already made several significant*
> *tangible and intangible contributions (including) cost savings, consistency of*
> *underwriting, removal of human bias, training tool and improved customer*
> *service.*

UNDERWRITING STRUCTURED SOLUTIONS

Underwriting structured solutions requires a different approach. The term "structured solutions" is used broadly here, focusing on transactions which have a unique and complex risk
profile, with limited directly comparable transactions, and requiring a cross-functional team to
structure, evaluate, underwrite and close the transaction.

In the insurance industry, examples include Alternative Risk Transfer (ART) transactions,
structured or finite reinsurance programs, loss portfolio transfers. In banking, examples include
M&A transactions, large and unique asset-based financing transactions and customized or
structured client derivative solutions.

Underwriting Principles

There are a few key factors which contribute to the successful underwriting of structured
solutions.

- First, *align origination and structuring/underwriting teams*. Closing structured solutions
  involves significant investment of skilled (and expensive) resources with few deals
  concluded during a year due to resource constraints. Profitability is highly dependent
  on the success rate of closing deals and less on the volume of doors opened.
  - Clearly define and communicate underwriting guidelines to the origination team so that
    they limit the number of trips down dead-end alleys.
  - Involve underwriting and structuring resources early in industry/customer segmentation
    exercises, individual account planning, etc.
  - Manage and triage the deal pipeline rigorously, focusing on potential value added and
    the probability of closing, including clear decision points to grant "license to hunt" and
    "license to invest."
- Second, the underwriting and structuring teams need to be *appropriately staffed and*
  resourced.
  - Designate a "deal captain" who is charged with building the underwriting team and,
    together with origination, closing the transaction.
  - A well-defined staffing process, allocating from specialist pools (e.g., capital markets,
    legal, accounting, industry specialists, etc.) to be staffed on deal teams and make clear
    their time commitment.

- Leverage external resources with specific industry, accounting, tax, legal or other expertise as needed.
- Separate closing and documentation specialists from underwriting and structuring resources, which may require a more innovative, solutions-oriented perspective.

- *Price relative to value-added.* These are bespoke solutions which *cannot* be bought off-the-shelf. They involve significant investment in understanding the client, designing and structuring the solution. They are custom-made, Saville Row suits, not off-the-rack suits available at the local department store, and their pricing should reflect this. In terms of pricing:
  - understand, quantify and demonstrate the benefit to the client and negotiate fees accordingly;
  - secure confidentiality agreements regarding the structure and exclusivity or lock-in periods in order to ensure that the intellectual capital developed is not given to a competitor.

- Develop and implement a well-structured *risk-modeling framework*. In general, each structured solution requires a deal-specific model, data and assumptions. Recognizing this, the firm should:
  - clearly define risk analysis standards (e.g., cash-flow modeling standards, when to use scenario-based or full stochastic analysis, performance and risk metrics such as RAPM, VaR, etc.);
  - use risk identification and evaluation approaches suitable for unknown and unknowable risks (e.g., cross-functional, team-based assessments);
  - maintain standardized assessment tools with well-defined structures – a clear separation of data, calculations and assumptions and reusable libraries;
  - document and archive the model, assumptions and sensitivities.

- *Monitor performance regularly* and be prepared to take remedial action if the transaction deteriorates. Ongoing monitoring should be done by an independent "product control" unit, but it is important to keep the original client and underwriting team accountable. If the transaction deteriorates, bring together the original deal team under the leadership of a work-out or intensive care specialist to discuss alternatives and strategies.

- *Align incentives to the long-term profitability of the portfolio.* There are some critical points in the business system where extra care may need to be taken in order to ensure that all involved work toward the best interests of the firm:
  - ensure that deal resources do not become "stuck" in the pipeline but are dynamically allocated to those deals which offer the highest expected contribution;
  - ensure that the right underwriting decisions are taken based on a long-term view of the economics, as opposed to a short-term earnings view;
  - ensure that deteriorating transactions are quickly identified and actively managed.

UNDERWRITING CONTROLS, VALIDATION AND LEARNING

An underwriting organization learns from its successes . . . and from its mistakes. As a consequence, continuously reviewing and validating underwriting effectiveness is the third and final cornerstone of a high performing underwriting organization.

Ex-post Review

Analyzing and evaluating the ex-post performance of the underwriting process across all dimensions is critical for both data-driven and expert-based approaches, answering such questions as the following.

- *Decision effectiveness.* What was the actual experience of Type 1/Type 2 errors compared with expectations? Did the error cases have common characteristics which can be used to improve the process? How did the process perform on new segments?
- *Operational effectiveness.* What were the average resources required to underwrite the portfolio (e.g., in terms of elapsed time, personnel and costs)? What was the exception rate and characteristics of cases which fell out of the standard process? What lessons can be learned in terms of adjusting the triage and acceptance criteria?
- *Customer satisfaction.* How was the customer experience during the entire process, covering qualification, information collection, underwriting decision and communication? Where can the experience be improved?
- *Commercial effectiveness.* How did our pricing and acceptance criteria compare with competitors? When did overrides to pricing guidelines occur? What were the characteristics and were they justified? Did we retain/grow the accounts that we wanted at the rates we targeted? Where did we "leave money on the table" and where were we non-competitive?
- *Portfolio management.* How many exceptions or non-conforming contracts were concluded? How have the conditions evolved, affecting the ability to manage the transactions (e.g., in terms of covenants, perfection of interest in collateral or reinsurance proceeds, etc.)? Does the documentation allow us to easily transfer, securitize or sell the transaction or portfolio?

File Reviews

File reviews are a powerful tool for validating underwriting effectiveness and reinforcing an underwriting culture. The principles are simple: independent and experienced underwriters review the files of other underwriters (or the results of automated underwriting processes) in order to identify what works, what doesn't and how to improve. This simple practice has several immediate benefits.

- First, it supports discipline across the underwriting function, especially important given that bad underwriting decisions emerge only much later, if at all: by the time deteriorating underwriting standards show up in the claims or loss statistics, it is already too late. Because of this, it is important to test the effectiveness and adherence to underwriting standards and policies regularly and frequently.
- Second, it allows experienced underwriters to discuss challenging cases with peers and to give systematic feedback to less experienced underwriters using concrete case examples.
- Finally, it allows the firm to more rapidly identify changing market conditions and practices.

While simple in concept, there are several important details which the firm should keep in mind when designing an underwriting review process – especially in the areas of selecting files and reviewers, conducting the reviews and following up on the results.

Selecting the Files

There are several approaches for selecting files depending on your objectives.

- *Randomly selected files* will reinforce broader adherence to underwriting policies and increase the possibility of identifying emerging but latent trends.
- *Risk-based selection criteria* (e.g., focusing on a class of business, distribution channel or underwriting unit experiencing deteriorating losses) are useful for diagnosing the root causes of specific problems. Other common criteria include a newly introduced and rapidly growing business, segments with regular exceptions to underwriting standards, etc.
- Similarly, reviewing files from *different stages in the transaction's lifecycle* may also yield useful information. For example, reviewing files from cases which:
  - were lost to competitors helps to identify where standards, pricing or other factors are "out of sync" with market conditions;
  - generated a loss will help to identify both systematic underwriting deficiencies and/or emerging adverse trends.

Selecting the Reviewers

There are three approaches for selecting reviewers which can be used simultaneously.

- *A dedicated review team* with global scope, increasing the consistency across time and across the organization and the dissemination of best practices.
- *Rotating experienced underwriters*. This approach reinforces multi-lateral knowledge or specialist networks and a broader exchange of experience inherent through cross-pollination.
- *Independent specialists* from consulting firms, risk engineering firms, etc., which can be used to broaden the experience pool even further and to "buy in" learning.

In practice, a combination of all three is used. Regardless of which, a high level of underwriting experience and skills needs to be seeded into the review team; this represents a significant investment given the opportunity cost of qualified underwriters. In order to leverage this investment, it is advantageous to have more junior underwriters participate in the reviews as a form of apprenticeship.

Conducting the Review

Depending on the specific circumstances, the reviews can be performed on-site and/or remotely via desk-top reviews. Several factors influence the balance between on-site or desk-top reviews, for example the role played by management judgment versus an underwriting decision support system; the effectiveness of the document archiving system; the breadth and completeness of the documentation; and, finally, the specificity and complexity of the market and line of business.

The reviews typically cover two dimensions: transaction or file-oriented elements and a broader review of the overall underwriting organization. Each of these dimensions is supported by a standardized questionnaire. Examples of key themes to address in each type of review are given in Sidebar 24.4.

SIDEBAR 24.4: UNDERWRITING REVIEW CONTENT

There are two types of underwriting reviews: one focusing on individual files and the other on the broader underwriting organization and strategy. This sidebar outlines some of the themes which can be covered during the reviews.

UNDERWRITING ORGANIZATION AND STRATEGY REVIEWS

For each underwriting function, a general assessment of the following themes using a standardized set of questions/approach.

Strategy, Policies and Guidelines

1. Is the underwriting strategy clearly articulated? Is it aligned with the business strategy?
2. Are underwriting policies and guidelines adequate for the business? Are underwriting authorities and referral criteria explicitly delegated based on experience and skills?
3. Are policies and guidelines effectively communicated and being followed? Is the control framework adequate?
4. Are the policies, incentives, organization and culture aligned with the strategy?

Systems and Infrastructure

5. Are underwriting decisions and operations supported adequately by front office and underwriting systems? In terms of risk evaluation and pricing formation? Automated controls? Referral and exception tracking?
6. Is the quality of data high? Is data ownership clearly defined?
7. Are underwriting information and KPIs being systematically collected and reported? Are trends being identified and acted on early enough?

Organization and Culture

8. Is the underwriting organization adequately staffed in terms of experience, skills and resources? Is the turnover excessive?
9. Is there an adequate segregation of duties? Are underwriters too closely linked to origination, work-out or claims management?
10. Are the efforts to build an underwriting culture in evidence and effective? For example, through trainings, "apprenticing"/mentoring, succession planning, staffing on file reviews, etc.
11. Do the incentives adequately balance risk and returns? Cost and decision effectiveness? Are the incentives aligned with the underwriting strategy?

Business Impact

12. Is the pricing risk-adequate for all segments? Is there room to increase margin on specific segments?

13. Are discounts within delegated authorities and budgets? Are they being optimally applied and tracked?

14. Is the portfolio reviewed regularly, with actions taken to cancel or reprice under-performing segments?

TRANSACTION FILE REVIEWS

For every file selected for review, the following type of information should be collected/assessed through the use of a standardized questionnaire/approach.

General Account Information

1. Documentation of review reference file, general information.
   a. Transaction details (e.g., type of transaction, terms and conditions, etc.).
   b. Customer details (e.g., segment/industry/region, size, etc.).
   c. Customer relationship (e.g., renewal, cross-sell, distribution channel, etc.).
   d. Status (e.g., not bound, bound but open, bound with negative result – defaulted/claims filed, etc.).

Underwriting Information

2. Application and supplemental information: completeness, adequacy and verification.
   a. Overall completeness of required information with missing information resolved satisfactorily. Information is line specific (e.g., credit history, building age and condition, cars and number of drivers, etc.).
   b. Critical information verified relative to standards (e.g., ownership interest, value, condition and location of collateral or property, SIC code, etc.).
   c. Additional information as appropriate based on standards (e.g., for referral cases, loss/credit history from government/industry statistics or private bureau, website searches, risk engineering survey, etc.).
   d. Appropriately signed and dated.
3. Evaluation: completeness, adequacy and benchmarking.
   a. Underwriting analysis: was the required analysis done appropriately?
      i. For insurance contracts: verification of loss experience, root cause analysis, loss trend identification, exposure and hazard identification, likelihood of additional losses estimated, etc.
      ii. For credit contracts: evaluation of the five Cs (e.g., character, capacity, capital, conditions, collateral), balance sheet and cash flow projections, analysis of key ratios (interest leverage, coverage and liquidity ratios, etc.), identification of relevant scenarios and sensitivities, etc.
   b. Additional risk evaluations as per guidelines (e.g., site visits, increased deductibles/higher collateralization, etc.).
   c. Referrals or escalations made as per guidelines.
   d. Sufficient benchmarking of risk analysis and indicative pricing relative to segment peers and underwriting experience.
   e. Evaluation of underwriter's decision.

4. Documentation and administration.

   a. Conformity of transaction documentation to guidelines and standards based on evaluation (e.g., standard forms and wordings, additional clauses or attachments as required, etc.). Supporting rationale clearly documented.

   b. Conformity of terms and conditions to guidelines and standards based on evaluation (e.g., discounts, commissions, limits, fees, pricing, coverage). Supporting rationale clearly documented.

   c. Conformity of documentation with requirements of servicers, syndication, guarantor or reinsurance partners.

   d. Exceptions to the above clearly documented and approved.

   e. Written quotation and final contract signed at appropriate time and subsequently archived.

   f. Additional documentation evidencing client eligibility and suitability, "kyc" know your customer, customer acknowledgment/understanding of terms and conditions, etc.

   g. Data input into systems accurately: exposure information, concentration indicators (e.g., by industry, for natural catastrophes, terrorism, etc.).

5. Overall evaluation of the underwriter's performance.

Review Follow-up

Some common issues which emerge from underwriting reviews are the consistency with which guidelines are followed, the depth and quality of analysis and documentation and the appropriateness of subjective evaluations.

More often than not, the improvement potential rests with the underwriting organization and not with the individual. For example, there may be a lack of sufficient training, poorly defined guidelines or ambiguity with regard to underwriting strategy. This is an important distinction to send if the underwriting reviews are to be seen as something constructive rather than as a "witch hunt." It is easier to build a good underwriting culture if the institution is also part of the solution rather than narrowly blaming individuals.

However, less frequently, the issue lies with an individual, for example a lack of willingness or ability to perform the required tasks to the required standards. In these cases, personnel implications must follow.

Just as for any formal review, after the issues have been identified and management actions defined, the organization has to follow up, tracking implementation of mitigating controls, training programs, etc.

CHAPTER 25

Risk Underwriting – From Technical Pricing to Value Maximization

It is important to ensure not only an *adequate technical price* but also an *optimal commercial price*. This chapter outlines considerations and techniques for ensuring adequate and optimal pricing.

Setting the appropriate price is one of the most important underwriting tasks. If the price is set too low, the company faces an opportunity cost at a minimum, leaving money on the table; in the worst case, it destroys value if pricing does not cover the technical cost of production. If the price is set too high, the firm again suffers an opportunity cost, being uncompetitive in the market; in the worst case, it destroys value due to adverse selection, with only the highest risk clients willing to pay the price.

Just like Goldilocks in the story of the three bears, an effective underwriting organization must set a price which is just right, neither too high nor too low. There are three activities needed to set the optimal price.

- First, understand the *technical cost* of production, including the cost of risk and expense loadings. In the absence of commercial decisions to subsidize some business, the technical price sets the "floor" or the minimum price which the company should charge. This is typically referred to as New Business RAPM pricing.
- Second, understand the *optimal price*, or the price which captures the most economic surplus. The ability to capture surplus depends on a variety of factors, including competitors' pricing, product features, brand recognition, the elasticity of demand and supply, etc.
- Finally, put in place the appropriate *pricing processes and authorities* such that the optimal price is consistently quoted to clients.

TECHNICAL PRODUCTION COST: RAPM PRICING

The first step in pricing is to understand the cost of production. This is referred to as the "technical price" in the industry, where we have used the term New Business RAPM in this Handbook.

Determining the cost of goods sold for a financial product can be challenging for many reasons: one is that the ultimate performance is unknown at the time the product is sold and depends on future (risky) events outside the control of the firm; another is that not all the ingredients or financial building blocks can be "sourced" in the capital markets, implying that some of the risks have to be priced against the firm's own balance sheet. In short, the technical or RAPM price has to reflect the unique role that risk and capital play in financial services.

In order to address these challenges, the financial services industry has settled on a technical pricing approach which is intuitive: price the components that you can using capital market prices and, for those components which do not have a market price, ensure that the pricing is sufficient to cover the firm's cost of capital and target profit margin for the risks underwritten.[1]

This is the New Business RAPM approach discussed and motivated in detail earlier in Chapter 3. Together with other metrics, it is used for new business pricing and customer relationship management.

Loan New Business RAPM

The following describes the New Business RAPM pricing framework in greater detail.

A Static Spread Approach

The simplest loan New Business RAPM approach is the static spread or margin approach, which risk-adjusts the loan's expected operating margin and then divides it by the annualized capital requirements to support the underwriting risk, as illustrated[2] in Figure 25.1.[3]

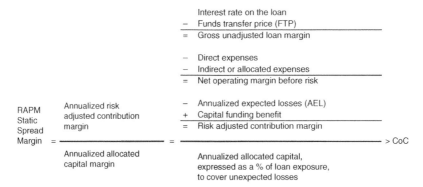

FIGURE 25.1 Static spread RAPM for technical loan pricing

---

[1]Although the most common approach used, there are theoretical issues associated with RAPM pricing of non-hedgeable risks. These issues can be addressed using either an explicit preference/utility-based approach or an assumed risk premium appropriate for the type of risk being underwritten. See, e.g., Wang (2002, 2003, 2004); Kleinow and Pelsser (2009).

[2]See, e.g., Ong (1999), Jameson (2001), Matten (2008). A discounted cash flow or option-adjusted spread approach may need to be used instead if the loan is amortizing or has embedded prepayment options, discussed later.

[3]For simplicity, the following example is before taxes; including the impact of taxes is done by deducting expected taxes from the numerator, adjusting allocated capital for any contingent deferred tax assets in the denominator and, finally, using an after-tax hurdle rate.

The Risk-adjusted Contribution Margin

Beginning with the numerator, the first step is to calculate the *unadjusted gross loan margin* by subtracting the appropriate Funds Transfer Price (FTP) from the contractual customer rate. Doing so in effect bifurcates the loan into a market-based funding component, which can be hedged at current market prices, and a credit-risky component, which cannot. As discussed in Chapter 17, the FTP is calculated based on the loans specific cash flows, "as if" they were credit risk free. The gross loan margin represents the margin available after funding costs to cover credit risk, allocated expenses and the cost of capital to support the transaction.

An *operating margin* is calculated by deducting the annualized direct and allocated expenses. Direct expenses may include amortized expenses associated with the origination and underwriting of the transaction as well as future contract administration, payment processing, etc. Allocated expenses may include the cost of the corporate center and shareholder services, etc. Full cost allocation implies that all the firm's expenses are allocated across all transactions; marginal cost allocation implies that only expenses which are directly associated with the transaction are allocated.

The *risk-adjusted contribution margin* reflects an adjustment to effectively "price" the non-traded credit risk of the loan. Loan losses are expected as a normal part of the business, and technical pricing needs to at least cover expected losses. This is done via two adjustments to the operating margin, the first deducting the Annualized Expected Losses (AEL) given by the following formula.

Equation 25.1: Expected AEL

$$AEL = APd^*EAD^*LGD$$

- The annualized expected *probability of default* (APd) depends on the borrower's rating, the anticipated tenor of the loan and the probability that the rating will deteriorate or improve during the lifetime of the loan. For example, a triple-A borrower has nowhere to go but down, implying that its APd will increase with tenor. The APd is calculated as the solution to the following equation, where p_t is the probability of the default at time t and calculated reflecting expected credit migrations in previous periods.

Equation 25.2: Expected APd

$$p_1 + (1 - p_1)p_2 + (1 - p_1)(1 - p_2)p_3 \ldots = APd + (1 - APd)APd + (1 - APd)$$
$$\times (1 - APd)APd \ldots$$

- The expected Exposure At Default (EAD) depends on the amount of principal drawn as well as an assumption regarding the future utilization of any undrawn amounts and prepayments.
- The expected Loss Given Default (LGD), which depends on the loan's seniority and collateralization.

The second adjustment is to add back the capital funding benefit. In calculating the unadjusted margin, we subtracted the FTP rate, equivalent to the assumption that 100% of the loan is "financed" by debt. Banks also hold capital to cover a loan's risk contribution to the portfolio, implying some equity funding. In order to reflect the implied equity funding, a capital funding benefit is credited to the loan.

Allocated Capital

Economic capital is required to cover unexpected defaults in excess of the expected loss burden (covered by loan loss reserves and already deducted from the margin). The technical pricing of the loan should reflect the cost of this capital. Attributing capital to a loan in a static spread model is complicated by three considerations.

- First, only default risk should be covered: deducting the FTP rate implies matched funding, eliminating all first-order market risks.[4]
- Second, allocated capital needs to be expressed representing the lifetime commitment using an annualized rate and not based just on the current year's capital requirements. The rationale is that the single-period capital requirements change over time in a predictable manner depending on the borrower's initial rating (e.g., a triple-A borrower has nowhere to go but down and so will have a higher expected capital charge in the second year).
- Third, diversification benefits need to be recognized. If capital is allocated on a stand-alone basis, then the bank will be priced out of the market for borrowers with a worse credit rating than itself as the loan would require full equity funding. However, the capital for a well-diversified portfolio is less than the sum of the capital required for each transaction, making lending to lower-rated borrowers feasible from a portfolio perspective. There are different methods for attributing capital to transactions and one has to be selected.[5]

Most firms select capital allocation keys based on the transaction's risk characteristics. One of the most common allocation keys is the transaction's Unexpected Loss (UL), defined (see, e.g., Ong, 1999) as the 1-year standard deviation of loan losses, given by the following equation.

Equation 25.3: Loan UL

$$UL = \sqrt{APd\sigma_{LGD}^2 + APd(1 - APd)LGD^2}$$

where APd and LGD are defined as before and σ_{LGD}^2 is the variance of the loss given default.

UL is a useful allocation key but is not sufficient because it ignores portfolio diversification: UL measures only the transaction's *stand-alone* loss volatility and not its contribution to the diversified portfolio. The contribution will also depend on the debtor's country and sector or segment (reflecting the debtor's "beta" relative to the total portfolio), the size of transaction (reflecting the debtor's contribution to concentration risk) and LGD characteristics (e.g., the value of real-estate collateral may be correlated with credit quality).

---

[4]Operational risk can also be considered (e.g., sales practice risks, documentation, securing collateral, etc.), although these are not the primary drivers of New Business RAPMs. Second-order or residual market risk arises if the loan's actual experience deviates from expectations with regards to the timing and level of defaults, prepayments, etc. In this case, the bank would be exposed to an open market risk position relative to the assumed funding structure.

[5]The methods include marginal methods, diversified or covariance methods and game-theoretic approaches such as Shapely and Aumann–Shapely approaches. For details, see Koyluoglu and Stoker (2002) or Smithson (2003).

As such, capital is typically allocated using a look-up table keyed to sector/exposure/ rating/tenor/collateral with the capital multipliers being recalibrated regularly to reflect the existing portfolio's diversification.

Validating the Metric

The static spread RAPM is used to determine the technical price of loans for which no market value exists. However, there is no guarantee that the results will be "reasonable" if it is applied to actively traded loans or bonds of similar characteristics and credit quality. Applying it to traded bonds or loans offers an excellent opportunity to "validate" and calibrate the RAPM for pricing of loans which are not traded. Any large deviations between the modeled price and the market price should be analyzed and understood, with the model calibrated according to the extent that there is a fundamental bias as opposed to time-varying risk premia. This calibration will give confidence in applying the model to less liquid segments and will help to eliminate internal arbitrage around the classification of the loan.

In terms of calibration to correct for a fundamental bias, the bank typically has two important degrees of freedom. The first is a capital allocation table or formula. The second is the appropriate hurdle rate or cost of capital. As discussed earlier, the allocation of risk capital is not a guarantee that returns will be normalized appropriately relative to traded markets.

Extensions

While a good starting point, the static spread approach suffers from two limitations. First, it cannot be applied to arbitrary loan repayment or amortization schedules. Second, it does not take into account the value of prepayment options. For this reason, some banks have extended the framework to risk-adjusted present value or "option-adjusted spread" frameworks similar to the stochastic MCEV framework used for LH insurance.

PC New Business RAPM

The PC New Business RAPM follows a similar approach to that used for bank loans, but is done on a discounted cash flow as opposed to a period margin basis (e.g., Nakada *et al.*, 1999). In the case of PC insurance, as shown in Figure 25.2, the numerator represents the present value of the policy's expected economic cash flows to shareholders while the denominator represents the present value of the expected allocated capital to cover technical underwriting losses.

Here, the discounted CR is the ex-ante, discounted expected combined ratio, defined as the sum of the discounted projected expenses and claims, divided by the net earned premium. Using the definition of Economic Capital Intensity (ECI[6]), the PC New Business RAPM can be rewritten as

$$PC.RAPM = \frac{\text{Discounted CR} + r_f \text{ECI}}{\text{ECI}}$$

RAPM Technical Pricing Decision Rule

In general, the decision rule is to accept business as long as PC New Business RAPM is greater than the cost of capital for underwriting risks. It is also possible to rearrange the New Business

---

[6]$\text{ECI} = \frac{\sum c_t/(1+r_f)^t}{P}$ = ratio of present value of future capital requirements to premium.

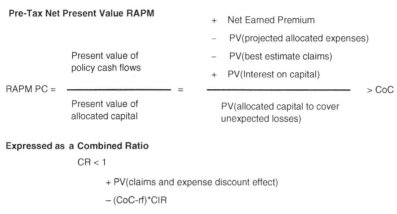

FIGURE 25.2 PC RAPM technical pricing framework

RAPM into a combined ratio decision rule. More specifically, the evaluation criteria for the PC New Business RAPM can be expressed in the following manner.

Equation 25.4: PC combined ratio RAPM

$$CR < 1 + PV(\text{discount effect}) - rp_{uw}\text{ECI}$$

where CR is the *ex-ante* expected undiscounted combined ratio for the policy on an underwriting year basis, PV(discount effect) is the difference between discounted and undiscounted expected ultimate claims and expenses using the risk-free rate of return, rp_{uw} is the risk premium above the risk-free rate of return needed to compensate for underwriting risk.

The primary differences between this formula and the "normal" combined ratio acceptance criteria (e.g. accept if the CR < 100%) are that: it is a prospective or *ex-ante* calculation, with the expected claims and expenses only for the policy being evaluated; it is based on discounted rather than undiscounted claims and expenses, putting the future claims and expenses on a comparable basis to the premium collected today; and, finally, it includes the cost of capital to compensate for uncertainty around the best-estimate claims, represented by rp_{uw} *ECI (where we have used the relationship $(CoC-r_f) = rp_{uw}$).[7]

The Numerator

The numerator of PC RAPM represents the net present value of all future cash flows associated with the policy. Two deductions are made from the policy's net earned premium.

- First, the present value of allocated expenses to ensure that the policy is priced to cover future expected administration, claims management and overhead costs.
- Second, the present value of best-estimate claims to reflect the expected claims burden and the time value of money as claims are paid in the future while premium is collected today.

---

[7]Note, under Solvency II, this term is called the "market value margin," representing the additional margin on reserves that a company of comparable diversification would need to be induced to take over the insurance policy and cover their cost of capital.

Capital is held against the uncertainty around best-estimate claims and this capital will in general be invested until it is needed. Because the capital earns a return during the period in which it is "tied up," the individual policy is allocated the discounted value of notional risk-free investment returns on the tied capital. This is called the "capital benefit."

The financial component of the liability is represented by the zero-coupon cash flows equal to the best-estimate expense and claims. The resulting numerator is not subject to any residual financial market or credit risk because we use the risk-free rate for discounting expected claims and for calculating the return on assets backing capital. This implicitly assumes that the best-estimate claims are matched by risk-free zero-coupon investments.

A brief comment: The numerator depends on the *discounted best-estimate* ultimate claims. This may not be equal to the reserves held on the statutory or accounting balance sheet. In addition to the discounting effect, reserves may be set higher than the expected ultimate claims level, for example if a prudency margin or non-economic reserves (e.g., equalization reserves) are required.

The Denominator

Insurers need to hold capital to cover the risk of unexpected losses and the technical price needs to cover the cost of that capital. Attributing capital to an individual policy for RAPM technical pricing is complicated by three considerations.

- Only actuarial risk, or the risk that the ultimate level and timing of claims does not line up with the best estimates, should be considered. Both capital and reserves are assumed to be invested in risk-free assets and match the liability cash flows, eliminating all first-order market risks.[8]
- The present value of allocated capital needs to reflect the profile of expected future annual capital requirements. Most policies have a decreasing profile: as time progresses, claims are paid and experience gained, implying a declining capital requirement. However, this pattern can be reversed in lines such as product liability, where the late emergence of latent claims as well as changes in future claims litigation practices can add significant uncertainty in later years. The profile of expected capital requirements is estimated for each line of business because they can differ dramatically (e.g., for natural catastrophe, short-tail property and long-tail liabilities). A practical solution is to define an "annuity factor" for each line of business which gives the present value of capital requirements based on the first year's capital requirement and standard capital run-off profile.
- Allocating capital on a stand-alone basis ignores diversification, one of the most important tools available to PC insurers: the capital required to support a well-diversified portfolio of policies is less than the sum of capital needed to support each in isolation. There are different methods for attributing diversification benefits and capital to transactions and one has to be chosen.[9]

---

[8]Any operational risk capital associated with the policy (e.g., for claims fraud, documentation, administration or claims adjustment errors, etc.) can be allocated based on simple rules if necessary. Second-order or residual market risk will arise should the policy's actual claims deviate substantially from expectations with regard to timing and levels. In this case, the insurer would be exposed to an open market risk position relative to the assumed investment structure for the technical reserves.

[9]These include marginal methods, diversified or covariance methods and game-theoretic approaches such as Shapely and Aumann–Shapely approaches. For details, see Koyluoglu and Stoker (2002) or Smithson (2003).

In practice, most firms select capital allocation keys based on the policy's characteristics (e.g., line of business, stand-alone risk capital or standard deviation of losses, exposure value, etc.) and then allocate capital based on a look-up table keyed to line of business/sector/ exposure, etc., with the capital multipliers being calibrated to reflect diversification relative to the existing portfolio.

Why the Combined Ratio is not Sufficient

A common rule of thumb is that an insurance business creates value if its combined ratio is below 100%, implying that the premium is greater than claims and expenses. This rule is not satisfactory for evaluating PC businesses for two reasons.

First, it ignores the time value of money. In PC insurance, premium and acquisition expenses are paid in advance, while claims and administration expenses are paid later. The combined ratio mixes present values (the premium) with future values (the claims and expenses), hiding the benefit from being able to earn investment income on the premium in the interim, a benefit which is stronger the longer the "tail" of the business.

The "carry" earned on PC premium can be a substantial motivator for both good and bad underwriting decisions. The "good" side is explained by Warren Buffett (*Insurance Journal*, 2005), who suggests that collecting premium in advance ("float") " . . . is wonderful – if it doesn't come at a high price. Its cost is determined by underwriting results . . . When an underwriting profit is achieved . . . float is better than free. In such years, we are actually paid for holding other people's money."

On the "bad" side, too strong a focus on investment returns can lead to higher asset risk, undisciplined underwriting and irrational market pricing. Once again from Mr. Buffett: "For most insurers, however, life has been far more difficult: In aggregate, the property–casualty industry almost invariably operates at an underwriting loss. When that loss is large, float becomes expensive, sometimes devastatingly so."

More importantly, the combined ratio explicitly recognizes neither the risk inherent in the business nor the capital tied up by the business. A 95% combined ratio may seem attractive, and it would be attractive for low-volatility lines of business. However, it might not be attractive for lines with very high ECI, for example highly volatile short-tail lines such as natural catastrophe or long-tail lines which ties up capital for long periods such as workers compensation.

LH New Business RAPM

Chapter 9 presents a comprehensive discussion of the LH New Business RAPM (used for protection and non-guaranteed products) and the LH Investment Margin RAPM (used for guaranteed products), comparing them against VNB, IRR and other measures in the industry. This section presents a high-level conceptual overview.

As shown in Figure 25.3, the LH New Business RAPM technical pricing measure is also calculated using "discounted" cash flows comparable with the PC New Business RAPM. In the case of LH insurance, the numerator represents the *market-consistent* present value of all cash flows attributable to shareholders, a calculation which is made challenging due to embedded options and guarantees in savings and retirement products. Identical to the PC New Business RAPM, the denominator represents the present value of the projected capital to cover the technical underwriting or non-hedgeable risks.

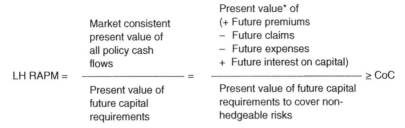

$$LH\ RAPM = \frac{\text{Market consistent present value of all policy cash flows}}{\text{Present value of future capital requirements}} = \frac{\text{Present value* of}\ (+\ \text{Future premiums}\ -\ \text{Future claims}\ -\ \text{Future expenses}\ +\ \text{Future interest on capital})}{\text{Present value of future capital requirements to cover non-hedgeable risks}} \geq CoC$$

FIGURE 25.3   LH RAPM technical pricing framework

LH RAPM vs. MCEV-VNB

The LH New Business RAPM and MCEV-VNB are similar, as a comparison of Figures 25.3 and 25.4 illustrates. The present value is calculated using market-consistent option pricing techniques.

In Figure 25.4, the VNB is calculated as the present value of future profits after acquisition expenses and taxes minus the time value of options and guarantees. This is the same value that is in the numerator of the LH New Business RAPM. The only additional term in the numerator of the LH New Business RAPM is the "capital benefit," equal to the risk-free return on capital backing underwriting risk.

VNB then subtracts the residual non-hedgeable risk (CNHR), equal to the underwriting risk premium times the present value of underwriting risk capital; this should be equal to the present value of underwriting risk capital in the denominator of the LH New Business RAPM if underwriting capital and the cost of capital are defined consistently.

The only term which is different is the deduction of the (frictional) cost of holding the required capital (FCReC), which arguably does not belong in the calculation (see Chapter 7 for a discussion). If we ignore this frictional cost, we can express the LH New Business RAPM as a function of the new business margin (NBM) and VNB:[10]

$$LH.RAPM = \frac{NBM}{ECI} + CoC_{uw}$$

where $NBM = VNB/\left[\sum p_t/(1 + r_f)^t\right]$ and the relationship was developed in Chapter 9.

$$VNB = \begin{vmatrix} +\ PVFP \\ +\ TVOG \end{vmatrix} \begin{matrix} \text{Market} & +\ \text{Premiums} \\ \text{consistent} & -\ \text{Claims} \\ \text{present} & -\ \text{Expenses} \\ \text{value* of} & -\ \text{Taxes} \end{matrix}$$
$$-\ CNHR \quad -rp_{uw}*\ PV(capital_{uw})$$
$$-\ FCReC \quad -1\%*Capital$$

* Without non-economic distortions, e.g. Ultimate Forward Rate, asset-based risk premia in the discount rate

FIGURE 25.4   MCEV-VNB framework

---

[10]The MCEV-NBM is calculated by dividing VNB by the present value of all current and future premium. As such, it represents the margin to shareholders, after taxes and the cost of capital, per unit of premium for the policy assuming that financial market risks are fully hedged.

All these ignore financial market earnings and associated risk capital. As such, they are not as useful in evaluating guaranteed products where earnings emerge as investment margins. Chapter 9 develops a new measure, the LH Investment Margin RAPM, and compares this against other measures used in the industry such as IRR, payback period, etc.

FROM TECHNICAL PRICING TO OPTIMAL PRICE

By definition, the technical cost of production only covers the firm's cost of capital on average. Any firm following this strategy will be valued at best at 1× market-consistent net asset value – shareholders will just "break even" on any capital invested in the business, with share price appreciation coming only from the growth in retained earnings (assuming of course that the embedded value emerges).

The "glass half empty" perspective would say to give the money back to shareholders – it creates the same value as growing your business and possibly even more if your firm suffers from a conglomerate discount. The "glass half full" perspective would say that your share price has tremendous potential to re-rate to a higher multiple if you can improve risk-adjusted margins. But, in order to earn that higher multiple, you have to price to more than the technical cost of production.

Product pricing is a key lever in increasing margins, along with lowering expenses and improving underwriting risk selection. Unfortunately, a higher price is not always the best price: for example, higher prices are not better if they lead to substantially lower demand (high elasticity of demand) or if you only attract the worst risks at higher prices (adverse selection). What considerations should banks and insurers keep in mind when developing a pricing strategy focused on shareholder value? There are four, summarized in the associated Rules of the Game and discussed in greater detail in the remainder of this chapter.

RULES OF THE GAME: OPTIMAL PRICING POLICY

The optimal pricing policy:

- makes clear the risk appropriate technical cost of production to ensure a minimum of unintentional adverse selection and cross-subsidization, accomplished through effective customer segmentation and product design;
- must be sensitive to demand elasticity and competitive conditions so that the total risk-adjusted contribution measured in euros is optimized and not just the contribution margin measured as a percentage;
- allows some discretion at the point of sale in order to extract the most consumer surplus, but reduces "leakage" by closely monitoring the use of delegated price authorities and promotions;
- reacts quickly and intelligently to pricing cycles and changing financial market conditions.

Risk-appropriate Pricing and Customer Segmentation

All else being equal, higher prices are better . . . but not if higher prices cause adverse selection or force cross-subsidization!

Adverse selection can be defined as situations where higher prices attract customers with a disproportionately higher risk profile. This is the case if only the riskiest customers are willing to pay the high price, possibly because your competitors are doing a better job at underwriting, pricing and risk selection. Cross-subsidization refers to earnings from profitable customers being eroded by the losses from unprofitable segments (see Chapter 11).

Adverse selection and cross-subsidization often occur simultaneously. Consider a bank offering loans to individuals of different but indistinguishable credit quality. If the bank increases the price for every borrower in order to maximize profits, at some point only the riskiest borrowers are willing to take the loan and the less risky borrowers would either delay borrowing or borrow from a competitor (for a current overview of the literature, see Phillips and Raffard, 2008). An insurer faces the same consequences by raising premiums uniformly (Dahlby, 1983). In both cases, the results are higher concentrations to lower-quality customers, subsidized by the excess profits from the few remaining high-quality customers.

The problem facing the fictitious bank or insurer is that their pricing is not sufficiently differentiated based on risk profile, as illustrated in Figure 25.5.

The bank in Figure 25.5 charges an "average price" (represented by the dashed horizontal line) sufficient to cover the "average risk." The vertical axis is the price level expressed in contribution margin, the horizontal axis the riskiness of the customers ranked in terms of their total cost of risk (TCR, expected losses and additional cost of capital deployed).

Assuming the company had a 50/50 share of the customer pool, the profits from lower-risk customers (the area below average price but above technical price) would subsidize the losses from higher-risk customers (the area above average price but below technical price) and the firm would earn the cost of capital on average; the netting of the areas represents the degree of cross-subsidization.

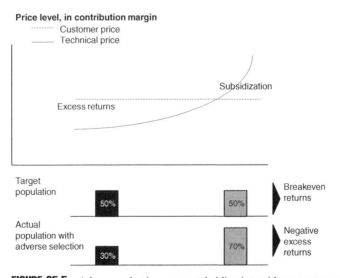

FIGURE 25.5 Adverse selection, cross-subsidization without customer segmentation

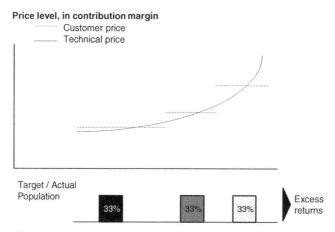

FIGURE 25.6   Adverse selection and cross-subsidization with customer segmentation

However, if the bank loses some of its high-quality customers to competitors who are better able to segment the market, they would be below break-even profitability and generate negative economic returns. This could lead to a vicious spiral, where increasing prices lead to a declining portfolio quality.

Customer Segmentation and Risk-based Pricing
Cross-subsidization and adverse selection can be mitigated by segmenting customers based on risk and pricing each segment appropriately, as illustrated in Figure 25.6. In addition, potential adverse selection can also be mitigated as low-quality customers get less in subsidies and high-quality borrowers become more difficult to poach by competitors with better segmentation capabilities.

The Limits to Customer Segmentation and Risk-based Pricing
In principle, the firm should price each and every customer based on their risk characteristics. As logical as it sounds, there are practical limits to segmentation.

First, the firm may not have sufficient information to segment the pool of customers (e.g., because the firm has not or cannot ask the right questions during underwriting or because the potential customer will not answer truthfully). For example, a potential borrower may have been given a low job performance rating or told his/her employer was in trouble, both of which might have a bearing on the lender's underwriting decision. Such information is difficult to capture and almost impossible to verify.

Second, the firm may be prohibited from using information by practical considerations, regulations or social norms. From a regulatory perspective, firms may be prohibited from using gender, credit history, etc. in the underwriting process.

Third, the increased granularity and increased expense of administering more granular pricing schemes may be decisive. In either case, some practical steps can be taken.

- Help customers to "self-select" products which are best suited to their profile. For example, insurers offer products with different deductibles, coverage features, co-insurance, bonus/malus conditions or use-based premiums. Banks offer products with different loan-to-value ratios, price differently for co-signed loans, consolidate banking activities with the lender, financial covenants, etc.

- Target marketing and sales efforts (e.g., through affinity programs providing services to individuals in retirement, pre/post-natal, etc.).

Maximizing Value, not Margins

All else being equal, higher prices are better . . . but not at the expense of significantly lower volumes.

Firms should work toward higher excess profits, measured in euros, and not on risk-adjusted contribution margins: at a 10% cost of capital, a business earning a 50% RAPM on €10 capital yields an economic profit of €4 whereas a 30% RAPM business with €100 invested capital yields €20. Clearly, shareholders would prefer both businesses; but if they had to choose only one, they would prefer the second more.

The relationship between price and demand is measured by the *elasticity of demand*, defined as the absolute percentage change in the volume demanded by customers for a percentage change in price (e.g., $\eta = |(\Delta V/V)/(\Delta P/P)|$).

Increasing prices for products with a high elasticity of demand (e.g., $\eta > 1$) will lead to a loss in total shareholder value (assuming the products are profitable in the first place): the increase in price will not be large enough to offset the loss in volume. Conversely, increasing prices for products with a low elasticity of demand (e.g., $\eta < 1$) creates value because the loss in volume is more than compensated by the increased price.

Insurers and banks regularly estimate demand elasticity by customer/channel segments. They do this by looking at actual consumer acceptances and renewals during periods when competitors are offering different rates; intuitively, this represents the outcome of only one possible "experiment."

In order to gain more "experimental data," banks and insurers also design "experiments" by offering different prices to similar pools of new and renewing customers, noting how the different pools react and then estimating the elasticity of demand. In addition, with sufficient date, one can also estimate the probability of accepting an offer or renewing the contract if the experiment is structured appropriately; this estimation is done using techniques similar to the "scoring" techniques used in underwriting. The "scoring" results are then used to build pricing or discounting tables or rules which maximize total risk-adjusted profits.

There have been a number of studies which investigated the demand elasticity of banking and insurance products. In banking, Karlan and Zinman (2005) investigate the elasticity of demand for consumer credit and Bell and Young (2010) estimate the elasticity of demand for corporate credit. In insurance, Babbel (1985) provides results for the US whole life insurance market, CBO (2005) provides results for private non-group health care in the USA and Barker and Tooth (2008) provide results for home-owners' property insurance in Australia.

Demand elasticity is not only of interest to the industry, but also to regulators and policy makers: an understanding of the elasticity of loan demand with respect to the level of interest rates can in theory be used to set optimal monetary policy following a recession. Similarly, the elasticity of demand for private health care insurance may be useful in designing an optimal public health care program.

Generic Strategies for Improving the Pricing Power of the Firm

Even if they do not undertake an empirical analysis, all banks and insurers make implicit trade-offs between price and volume based on experience and heuristic rules of thumb. In addition, many firms think carefully about strategies for increasing their pricing power vis à vis customers.

Obviously, having the lowest unit cost is the best offensive when competing in a market with elastic demand, simply because it allows greater room for maneuver relative to competitors.

How else do firms use the concept of price elasticity to improve margins? Some of the factors, and strategies, which can influence demand elasticity include the following.

Availability of Substitutes   Demand elasticity will be higher if close substitutes exist: capturing excess returns is more difficult simply because consumers have more choices.

As a consequence, banks and insurers often employ a strategy of *product differentiation*: by providing a unique feature set focused on specific customer segments, banks and insurers can reduce the substitutability of their products and potentially earn higher margins. Differentiation can manifest itself along different dimensions, including contract terms such as additional coverage, loan to value ratios or deductibles and additional services such as "friendliness" and speed, etc.

A note of caution, however: greater differentiation may lead to exponentially increasing expenses as the product portfolio becomes more complex; "mass customization" and modular products, discussed in Chapter 11), can be used to mitigate this risk.

Another potential downside of product differentiation is from opaque products with questionable value propositions, leading to sales suitability or consumer protection challenges; it is important that each product be understood by the customer, suited to their needs and fairly priced relative to the customers' needs.

Key to implementation is a clear understanding of what customers want and their willingness to pay for the feature or service. This is often accomplished through customer demand or conjoint analysis, evaluating the relative trade-offs a consumer is willing to make between feature sets or services and price (see Sidebar 25.1 later).

Income or Wealth Effect   In general, the higher the product cost relative to disposable income or wealth, the higher the demand elasticity. This is because consumers will be willing to invest more to investigate, compare and decide between alternatives.

This concept also relates to complementary products or services, which are marketed along with the primary product. For example, a consumer may have a higher elasticity of demand with regard to the big ticket item (e.g., a home mortgage or LH investment product) but exhibit less elasticity with regard to the complementary home-owner's insurance policy or health care riders offered at the same time.

As a consequence, a common strategy is for banks and insurance companies to offer *complementary products* or to *bundle* the primary product with complementary riders; consumer decisions are less sensitive to the riders, with the potential to capture a higher margin. A note of caution, however: given the increasing emphasis on consumer protection, it is important that each product and rider be well suited and understood by the customer and fairly priced relative to the customer's needs.

Information Efficiency of the Market   Consumers will have a lower elasticity of demand and be less likely to switch if they face significant costs of getting information on substitute products.

This implies that customer segments and channels with easy access to information (e.g., Internet or direct channels, consumers supported by independent financial advisors or brokers, etc.) will exhibit more demand elasticity than those with lower access to information (e.g., segments accessed through tied agents).

The strategies used to address this issue include *differentiated pricing* based on the distribution channel, *differentiated products* to appeal to a specific segment, making a direct comparison of features and prices more challenging and *differentiated incentives by channel*, compatible with lower elasticity of demand (e.g., retention or persistency-based incentive programs, etc.).

Competitor Behavior In physics, every action prompts an equal and opposite reaction. The same may (or may not) be true with regard to product pricing: if a price increase is matched by competitors, then demand elasticity will be lower, potentially even tending to zero with negative earnings impact as competitors fiercely defend their share . . . leading to a price war. If competitors do not follow, then the demand elasticity may be higher, allowing you to potentially capture more share at reasonably stable margins.

Banks and insurers anticipate how competitors will react to any change in prices. Typically, competitors behave differently depending on the structure of the industry (e.g., competitive or oligopoly, whether there is a clear market leader, your position relative to the leader, etc.), the cost structure of the industry and the potential for new entrants and their penetration strategy.

Just as your strategy will depend on how you think the competition will react, they will anticipate how you will respond. Taking decisions where circular expectations are important requires a game-theoretic approach.[11] However, game-theoretic approaches tend to be more theoretical than practical in implementation. As a consequence, heuristic approaches to competitive behavior are used more often. For example, Coyne and Horn (2009) suggest that the answers to three questions are important.

- Are your competitors likely to react? This will depend on whether your actions are noticed by the competition, whether they feel threatened by them and whether they are institutionally capable of reacting.
- What options do they have to react? Do nothing, follow suit, differentiate or launch a new product, increase promotion or marketing, etc.
- Which option are they likely to select? This depends on what the "right" move is from a shareholder's perspective as well as based on the competitors' internal performance metrics and the preferences of the management team.

Banks and insurers acquire information to better understand market conditions and the trends which affect their pricing power. This includes information on products, channels, pricing, promotions and marketing (e.g., through industry associations, trade shows or market intelligence firms); customers that your firm is in the process of or has already quoted; distribution channels (e.g., from originating brokers on lost transactions and other non-proprietary distribution networks, etc.); and "mystery shopping," by visiting competitors' branches or agents, through comparison websites and services, etc.

---

[11]Game theory is the study of conflict and cooperation between intelligent decision makers, often represented using mathematical models. The salient feature of any game theory problem is that the optimal strategy of a participant will depend on their beliefs of how others will respond.

Conjoint Analysis: Experiments to Understand Product Demand

Most managers use market intelligence and their own experience to set pricing strategy. Unfortunately, past experience represents only one possible "experiment," based on actual products and consumer behavior, as opposed to the multiplicity of "experiments" possible for a broader range of potential products and pricing strategies.

In order to acquire more information about consumer behavior under different product/ pricing strategies, financial services firms also conduct customer demand or *conjoint analysis* (e.g., Green *et al.*, 1990; Orme, 2005; Wittink and Cattin, 1989; Kuhfeld *et al.*, 1994), an experimental approach using statistical techniques to predict how people "value" products with different features and prices, described in Sidebar 25.1. The benefit of conjoint analysis is that one does not have to experiment by launching and managing different pricing and product feature strategies with real customers.

SIDEBAR 25.1: CONJOINT ANALYSIS

Conjoint analysis is a structured experiment designed to learn about customer preferences. It begins by asking representative consumers to evaluate and rank different combinations of product features such as price, customer service, environmental impact, ease of purchase, deductibles, etc. It is not necessary that all combinations be tested and some may in fact not reflect marketable product combinations; rather, the combinations are designed to elicit preferences along the different dimensions. The participants need not be limited to current customers, but can also include new potential customers and segments. With an appropriate design, the firm can gain far broader experience than would be possible by sponsoring specific product campaigns, a strategy which is anyway limited by production, marketing and other constraints.

The direct results of conjoint analysis are an estimate of the average "value" of the attributes and the trade-offs consumers are likely to make between features. This information can then be used in designing feature bundles and pricing strategies to capture more consumer surplus. If an additional assumption is made regarding the consumers' purchasing behavior,[12] then the results can be used for predicting potential market share (and cannibalization effects) caused by introducing a new product.

Once data has been collected, analysis of variance models are used to assign values to the attributes and predict consumer behavior. A utility or partial worth utility is assigned to each attribute. For example, the data may demonstrate that consumers have a preference for direct customer service over call centers over Internet; as a consequence, the conjoint analysis should assign a higher utility to direct customer service. If a second dimension, for example price or deductibles, is included then it is possible to estimate the consumer's relative preference between customer service, price, etc.

---

[12]The two most common assumptions are the maximum utility model, which assumes that the consumer will always purchase the product with attributes representing the highest utility value to the consumer and the Logit model, which assumes that the consumer's probability of purchasing a product will increase as their estimated utility increases.

A NUMERICAL EXAMPLE

An example is the metric conjoint analysis which estimates the consumer's utility directly from the data.[13] Suppose that we asked consumers to rank on a scale of 100 a loan or insurance product which was differentiated only along two dimensions, price and deductibles (for insurance) or points (for loans). In setting up the experiment, we might have two different price levels and two different levels of deductibles or points, leading to four products for the consumers to rate. The different levels and the hypothetical "empirical" rankings by two consumers are given in Table 25.1.

TABLE 25.1 Levels and rankings of two different consumers

	Features				Consumer rating	
Product	Price (€200 difference)		Deductible (€5000 difference)		Cons. 1	Cons. 2
1	Low	1	Low	1	99	90
2	Low	1	High	0	89	60
3	High	0	Low	1	55	75
4	High	0	High	0	25	12

This data could then be translated into a *metric, part worth conjoint analysis* comparing the two sets of attributes by estimating the following equations using ordinary least squares:

$$d_{ij}^k = \beta_0 + \beta_{1i} + \beta_{2j} + \varepsilon_{ij}^k$$

where d_{ij}^k are the kth consumer's stated preference on a scale of 100 for the bank or insurance product with two attributes, in our example the ith level of price and the jth level of deductible or points with $i = j = 2$. The parameters to be estimated represent the average or mean level (β_0) and an estimate of the relative preferences or utility (β_{1i}, β_{2j}) with ε_{ij}^k representing the error term.

For our simple example, the results of the conjoint/regression analysis are given in Table 25.2.

The objective is to get an understanding of how much the average consumer values each feature: the estimated coefficients can be interpreted as the partial worth of a specific attribute. In the simplistic example, consumers put a "value" of 34.5 utility points by going from a high price to a low price and a "value" of 33.0 utility points by going from a low deductible to a high deductible.

---

[13]For an excellent overview of conjoint analysis, see Hauser (n.d.), which was used as a basis for this example.

TABLE 25.2   Conjoint/regression analysis results

	Coefficient	Standard error	t-statistic
Constant	22.8	7.7	
Price	34.5	8.9	12.5
Deductible	33.0	8.9	0.9

Because we have included price as one dimension in the analysis, we can in principle imply what the consumer is willing to pay for other features. The first step is to be able to describe the value of a utility point. For example, if the difference between the low and the high price for the policy was €200, then the fact that the price reduction provides an estimated 34.5 utility points would indicate that the value of each utility point is €5.97. If we then wanted to know what the consumer was willing to pay per €1000 deductible, we could infer that it would be €38.80 (a €5000 difference in deductible is estimated to be worth 33 utility points, implying that a €1000 difference is worth 6.70 utility points at an average cost of €5.97 per point).

EXTENSIONS

There are many different ways to extend this simple analysis. For example, the linear equation can be modified by introducing non-linear transformations to the response variable (e.g., $\phi(d_{ij})$), cross-product terms (e.g., $\beta_{ij}d_{1i}d_{2j}$), etc. In addition, the experiment can be set up to be based on rankings rather than ratings (something which consumers may find easier to interpret), or based on pre-packaged (full or partial) profiles representing standard products (thereby limiting the number of dimensions, but also the granularity of the results). Finally, there are a wide variety of statistical methods which may be better suited to the specific experiment, including hierarchical Bayes' estimation, monotonic regression, linear programming methods or ranked-logit methods.

Two elements of the experimental design must be carefully considered. First, the set of survey respondents should be representative of the firm's target segment, rich enough to distinguish between different types of consumer and deep enough to ensure reliable results. Second, the number of dimensions and associated attributes must be carefully considered or else the potential number of questions will explode: if the questionnaire is to cover n dimensions with each having two attributes, then the total number of questions is of the order of 2^n. While there are different approaches to reducing this number (e.g., selecting questions which address each dimension independently, the so-called orthogonal approach, or profile ratings as discussed earlier), they do so at the risk of not capturing significant cross-dimensional effects.

Managing "Leakage" Due to Pricing Decisions

Most firms set pricing guidelines by product/segment/channel designed to achieve their commercial objectives, balancing risk and reward. The guidelines can take many forms, including for example standard tariffs, minimum pricing thresholds based on technical cost, recommended or average pricing levels needed to meet the company's RoE targets, etc.

In virtually all cases, some pricing authority is delegated to the origination or underwriting function. This delegation supports value-added pricing when customer characteristics are not easily recognized or not easily codified in explicit rules. For example, more information is available at the point of sale (e.g., client interest, the possibility of a cross-sell opportunity, evidence of competitive shopping, a "human" or "eyeball" underwriting judgment, etc.) and this information can help in setting the optimal price.

Delegating pricing authority is not without its own risks, however. One is that the discretion is used not to capture more of the consumer surplus but to make an easier sale and meet top-line targets. Put plainly, if sales has discretion to give a discount relative to the standard tariff and if they are primarily driven by top-line targets, then they may give discounts too often to reach their targets.

Uncontrolled concessions can represent a significant source of profitability "leakage." Some of the most common mechanisms to prevent this "leakage" include:

- setting explicit targets (e.g., minimum pricing thresholds such as the technical price) and the average target level for the portfolio, and measuring performance relative to those targets;
- defining explicit discounting or promotion "budgets" and allocating the budgets according to potential, for example giving more "budget" to the sales channels which produce the highest net value added;
- aligning incentives (e.g., by reducing the emphasis on top line or number of customers and focusing more on total value contribution);
- adhering to the pricing guidelines and discounting budgets, monitoring results and tracking pricing decisions at the underwriter, channel and customer level.

Managing a Cyclical Business

Businesses which suffer recurring pricing cycles offer their own challenges. A pricing cycle refers to situations where risk-adjusted margins increase or decrease in a cyclical manner due to competitive behavior or external market factors. The change in risk-adjusted margins can be driven directly by changing prices or indirectly by a change in non-price terms and conditions.

The Existence of Pricing Cycles

Many financial services businesses exhibit cyclical behavior of one form or another.

Example 1: Credit Pricing Cycles   Consider how the underwriting and pricing standards in credit markets changed before and after the 2008 financial crisis. During the "benign" period from 2002 to 2007, many factors helped to promote low risk-adjusted pricing of corporate and personal loans, including the sustained low interest-rate policy of central banks; the public policy agenda to increase home ownership, including intervention in the markets by Fannie Mae and Freddie Mac; global exchange rate disparity which promoted debt-funded consumption in the developed world; the apparent strength of the "originate to distribute" (as opposed to "originate to hold") model in banking; and a stable economic environment leading to a false sense of security and generally low risk premia.

As a result, the risk-adjusted margins for credit steadily declined, leading to all time low lending margins. Adding insult to injury, with limited room to decrease prices, banks relaxed underwriting standards, leading to "covenant-lite" and PIK (Payment in Kind) loans as well as Alt-A and sub-prime, "no documentation" and no down-payment mortgages, etc.

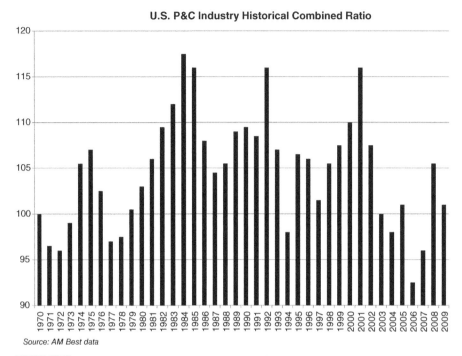

Source: AM Best data

FIGURE 25.7   US PC industry historical combined ratio

Following the crisis of 2008, many of these factors reversed, leading to higher credit spreads and tighter underwriting standards across the industry. Unfortunately, in 2013–14 the trend again reversed itself, with global low interest rates spurred by loose monetary policy ("quantitative easing") bringing again lower risk premia and relaxed underwriting standards.

Example 2: PC Underwriting Cycle   As a second example, the PC underwriting cycle in the (re-)insurance markets is well recognized and documented (e.g., Witt, 1978, 1981; Meier and Outreville, 2003, 2004; Leng *et al.*, 2004). The PC cycle manifests itself both in terms of loss ratios as well as in terms and conditions as well.

The effects of a PC cycle are readily apparent in retrospect. Figure 25.7 gives the average PC combined ratio for US companies from 1970 to 2011; in addition to volatility caused by, for example, natural catastrophes, evident in the figure are periods with deteriorating or softening conditions over many years, followed by abruptly hardening markets, repeated over time.

A softening PC market is often attributed to a combination of factors, including industry over-capitalization, sustained low loss ratios and competition for growth by individual firms in markets which are in aggregate growing only slightly faster than real GDP; in contrast, hardening PC markets typically follow large underwriting losses or investment crises which deplete the capital base of the industry. In either case, the combined ratio (and risk-adjusted margin) changes over time in a predictable manner, causing a "boom or bust" result in technical underwriting profits.

Example 3: LH Pricing Cycle   Although not often considered a "cyclical" business, in fact LH insurance is also highly cyclical. Concerning the US variable annuity market, OWC (2007) points to intense competition on price and features prior to the 2008 crisis, with complex new guarantees ". . . primarily supplier driven, aimed at capturing intermediaries' attention, rather than explicitly demanded by end-consumers. Successful players have spent heavily to build their wholesaling network, pushing up initial commissions in the fight for market share. The key success factors have been a rapid product development . . ."

Following the 2008 financial crisis, terms and conditions in the US variable annuity market have become more rational, including better pricing, simpler and easier-to-hedge features and the inclusion of levers to better manage the in-force book of business (such as management fees that can be changed).

Another example of an LH market cycle is related to the secular lower interest rate trend beginning in 2008. While most players lowered guarantees in response, it has not been enough to compensate for the lower investment rates, leading to spread compression. This can be seen in the development of the new business margins of European firms, as well as the IRRs for US companies.

The Rules of the Game for Managing Cyclical Businesses

Managing the underwriting cycle is challenging. On the one hand, keeping margins stable in a softening market can lead to adverse selection as well as to declining volumes, exacerbated by fixed costs. On the other hand, following the market will not only lead to lower revenues with certainty but also potentially to a vicious cycle as firms "race to the bottom" in order to protect share. The following lists some of the rules of the game for managing cyclical businesses (see also Lloyd's of London, 2006).

RULES OF THE GAME: MANAGING CYCLICAL BUSINESSES

Remain disciplined, redeploy capital. Monitor and manage each line of business and reduce share if prices fall below the technical cost, redeploying capital in other lines or returning to shareholders.

Develop better risk-based pricing tools. Improve technical pricing platforms, leading to greater segmentation, and use them to communicate pricing and coverage decisions.

Take action at the bottom. The bottom 20% of customers are often subsidized by the top 80%. You have more information on your customers; let your competitors suffer from the "winner's curse" as you clean your portfolio and increase the retention of attractive accounts during the soft cycle. Forced customer ranking into A, B and C categories with an explicit retention budget for the A and B categories helps this process.

Monitor the market. One of the reasons why firms are not able to manage the cycle is because they only recognize changes after the fact. Actively monitor new business and renewal terms, understand the decisions of customers you have won and lost and elicit information from brokers and intermediaries.

Position yourself for the rebound. In addition to writing less unprofitable business during the soft period, grow faster than the competition when prices harden. Some firms cannot react because they are not monitoring the market; others cannot react because:

- they have not "kept some powder dry," wasting capital resources to keep share and underwriting unprofitable business in the soft cycle rather than saving some to support an aggressive rebound;

- there are internal "psychological" challenges, with a dramatic increase of new capital into a business which has been producing sub-standard returns for a long period being a challenging sell to the corporate center.

Regardless of the source, the best way to address the issue of unavailable capital is by having a clear understanding of the cyclical nature of the business, the consequences for allocating capital over the cycle and integrating this into the firm's funding and business strategy. In other words, plan ahead and build the cycle and your response into your Capital Budget as opposed to reacting to the changing market conditions.

Don't compensate asset/liability mismatch results. Investment returns cannot replace disciplined underwriting; manage insurance and investment decisions separately and hold each accountable.

Have a resilient cost structure. Many would like to reduce new business volumes during soft markets, but are unable to do so because of tied agents which need to be "fed" and fixed expenses that need to be levered or else face a significant expense overrun. In other words, they have to write at a loss in order to prevent a bigger loss. Building flexibility through a more variable cost structure is a competitive advantage in a cyclical business.

Align incentives and manage expectations. Shareholders, analysts and the corporate center, as the shareholder surrogate, should understand that contributions and top-line growth may be lower during the soft cycle. Set and clearly communicate the strategy to make excess returns and grow faster than the industry *over the cycle*, but not necessarily by fiercely protecting share in the trough. Reinforce the efficient deployment of capital by linking rewards to shareholder value and not volume.

CHAPTER **26**

Managing Operational and Reputational Risks

B anks and insurers actively seek some risks in order to create value; there are other risks which they don't want, but unfortunately they come with the business. Operational and reputational risks fall into the latter category.

Operational risks are the cause of some of the most high-profile failures and "near misses" in financial services: internal fraud and rogue trading ultimately caused the failure of Barings Bank and severely impacted the reputation of UBS and Societé Générale; operational errors in option valuation contributed to the demise of NatWest and consumer protection concerns materially impacted the Dutch LH insurance market; internal trading practices had a significant impact on the fortunes of Putnam Investments . . . the list could go on and on.

It takes more than capital to mitigate operational risks: as the examples illustrate, the impact on the net asset value or solvency, which capital can protect, can be small while the impact on the firm's reputation and franchise value, which capital cannot protect, can be large. This is an important point: in contrast to credit, insurance and market risks, a more conservative capital level is not the best strategy to deal with operational risks.

This chapter begins by defining operational and reputational risks and then outlines a framework for managing them.

DEFINING OPERATIONAL RISK

Basel II (BIS, 2001b) defines operational risk as the *risk of financial or business loss* resulting from *inadequate or failed internal processes, people and systems, or from external events.* For reporting purposes, loss recognition is restricted to direct losses (e.g., settlements, fines, etc.).

In order to make this broad definition useful for risk management and reporting purposes, banks and insurers classify operational losses according to a taxonomy of root causes. Over time, industry definitions have converged with regulatory frameworks, leading to the now prevalent operational risk taxonomy used in Basel II/III and Solvency II, illustrated in Table 26.1.

In addition to what *is* included in the table, it is also interesting to note what *is not* included.

First, it is interesting to note that there is no separate category for "legal and compliance" risks. The reason is that legal proceedings are typically not the root cause of a loss, but rather how the loss is manifested. For example, customer or employee practices can lead to legal proceedings and settlements but the root cause is found under the customer or employee

TABLE 26.1 Basel II/Solvency II operational risk classification

Category	Sub-category	Description	Examples
External fraud		External fraud involves any theft (of assets or information), fraud, hacking damage and/or forgery executed intentionally by a third party without the assistance of an internal party.	
	External theft and fraud	Events arising due to acts intended to defraud, misappropriate property or circumvent the law by a third party without the assistance of an internal party, excluding malicious damage, with the following characteristics: ■ an intention to defraud; ■ the perpetrator seeks a personal benefit (or benefit for a close friend or relative); ■ the act violates public laws of general conduct and usually carries criminal penalties; ■ damage to the company, either directly or through the impairment of customer assets.	■ Robbery, extortion or embezzlement. ■ Theft of assets. ■ Forgery. ■ Check fraud. ■ Impersonation (i.e., deliberately assuming a client/customer identity). ■ Fraudulent claims.
	Systems security	All events relating to unauthorized access to electronic data files by non-employees for profit, excluding malicious damage.	■ Unauthorized appropriation of confidential information. ■ Computer malevolence (e.g., viruses, file destruction, hacking, etc.).
Internal fraud		Current employees or employees working under a contract are knowingly involved in a theft or fraud, including unauthorized activity where there is no legal recourse.	
	Internal theft and fraud	Events intended to defraud or to misappropriate property or circumvent regulations or company policy with the following characteristics: ■ at least one current employee, including temporary employees, must be involved; ■ the employee must use his/her position or special access to assets or information; ■ the act violates public laws of general conduct, usually carrying criminal penalties.	■ External theft or fraud events involving an employee. ■ Receipt of bribes or kickbacks. ■ Smuggling. ■ Insider trading for own account.

Unauthorized activity	Unauthorized activities should have one or more of the following characteristics: <ul><li>an intention to avoid controls, rules, minimum standards or guidelines governing conduct or limits on individuals' permitted activities;</li><li>personal benefit to a friend or relative, which may be non-financial (e.g., hiding bad performance);</li><li>no legal recourse against the individual(s);</li><li>the company is the victim, either directly or indirectly.</li></ul>	<ul><li>Transactions intentionally not reported.</li><li>Unauthorized transaction types.</li><li>Intentional mis-marking of positions.</li><li>Invalid authorization of exposures or expenditures.</li></ul>
Systems security	All events relating to unauthorized access of electronic data files by employees for profit or which cause damage to the firm.	<ul><li>Unauthorized appropriation of confidential information.</li><li>Computer malevolence (e.g., viruses, file destruction, hacking, etc.).</li><li>Data theft and disclosure.</li></ul>
Employment practices, workplace safety	This category covers operational risk events resulting from incidents connected to employment agreements, human resource processes and health and safety laws.	
Employee relations	Risk events arising due to specific mistakes or impermissible actions occurring during termination processes and events due to organized labor disruptions even if they are conducted legally in accordance with applicable employee relations statutes.	<ul><li>Compensation, benefit or termination events.</li><li>Strikes, other organized labor activity events.</li><li>Employee litigation/staff indemnification.</li></ul>
Workplace safety	Risk events related to mandatory worker insurance programs and workplace safety regulations.	<ul><li>Workers' compensation events (e.g., workplace accidents, occupational diseases).</li><li>Civil liability (i.e., accidents of customers, partners or suppliers).</li></ul>
Equality and discrimination	Risk events related to workplace equality and discrimination which arise under employee/employer laws or internal company rules. Distinguished from events involving clients or citizens in general, which are recorded under the "Improper business or market practices" sub-category.	Inappropriate behavior (i.e., discrimination or harassment).

(continued)

TABLE 26.1 (*Continued*)

Category	Sub-category	Description	Examples
Human resources management		Risk events arising from inappropriate human resources management. Human resource management issues are often identified as a contributory factor in operational risk events. Poorly trained or over-worked employees may cause processing errors, "key person risk" combined with the unavailability of itsemployees may lead to interruptions in key processes, etc. This sub-category should only be used if these issues cover the root cause of the loss event.	■ Inappropriate recruitment, training. ■ Inappropriate remuneration policy. ■ Inadequate staff assessment, management of poor performers. ■ Excessive staff turnover. ■ Departure/absence of a key staff resource. ■ Breach of regulations (labor rights, collective conventions).
Clients/third party, productsand business practices	An operational risk event may arise due to an unintentional or negligent failure to meet a professional obligation (including fiduciary and suitability requirements), or from the nature or design of a product. Events under this category typically have the following characteristics: ■ events are generally related to front-office activity; ■ the liability is often driven directly to a client driven by company behavior; ■ in most cases, the beneficiary is the company in terms of selling more products, getting or maintaining business, improving the terms of a transaction, or avoiding competition; ■ these activities generally violate either contractual covenants or laws governing conduct in the financial or commercial marketplace.		
	Suitability, information disclosure and fiduciary duty	Risk events arising from regulatory breaches or failures that impact customers, clients or trading partners.	■ Fiduciary breaches/guideline violations. ■ Suitability/disclosure issues. ■ Breach of privacy, misuse of confidential information. ■ Overly aggressive sales activities, account churning.
	Improper business or market practices	Risk events arising due to alleged improper business practice, including events arising due to retroactive changes in laws/regulations that generate losses.	■ Anti-trust behavior, market manipulation. ■ Improper external reporting practices. ■ Improper trade/market practices. ■ Insider trading (for the company's benefit). ■ Unlicensed activities. ■ Money laundering activities. ■ Discrimination events to customers or general public.

Category	Description	Examples
		Inappropriate contract disputes
Defective products	Events where the product was not correctly designed or priced (e.g., due to model errors).	■ Inadequate model implementation. ■ Breach of pricing policy. ■ Non-compliant products with internal, external requirements. ■ Inadequate approval of new products/activities. ■ Inadequate processes, complex, sensitive operations.
Trade counterparty	Events arising due to third-party actions.	■ Non-client counterparty performance. ■ Miscellaneous non-client counterparty disputes.
Sponsorship exposure	Events arising due to unplanned costs (e.g., authorized limits are exceeded).	■ Losses incurred due to exceeding client exposure limits (i.e., in asset management, wealth management).
Selection	Events arising due to a failure to properly investigate a client in accordance with internal guidelines.	■ Client fact-finding failures. ■ Insufficient checks prior to contracting.
Advisory activities	Events arising due to a failure to meet obligations.	■ Inappropriate performance or advisory activity.
Damage to physical assets	This category should be used to cover events arising due to natural/industrial disasters and malicious damage of OE property.	■ Natural disaster (floods, earthquakes, windstorms, etc.). ■ External losses (acts of terrorism, vandalism, etc.). ■ Industrial disaster losses.
Business disruption and system failures	This category covers operational risk events arising due to disruption of business operations or system failures.	
Systems failures	Events arising due to a system or infrastructure failure, often identified as a contributory factor in operational risk events.	■ Hardware or telecommunications failures. ■ Software failures. ■ Utility outages/disruptions.
Transportation and other disruption	Events arising due to a transport or other disruption that impacts the OE and results in a loss.	■ External strikes or blockades. ■ Disruption due to man-made hazards. ■ Weather, natural catastrophe or pandemic disruption.
Execution, delivery and process management.	An operational risk event may arise due to failed transaction processes or process management failures in general. Operational risk events arising in back-office areas fall within this category. These events will often be unintentional and could involve failure to properly document and/or complete business transactions.	
Transaction capture, execution and maintenance	Events arising due to failure to capture information or failure to document.	■ Data miscommunication, entry, maintenance errors.

(continued)

TABLE 26.1 *(Continued)*

Category	Sub-category	Description	Examples
			■ Missed deadlines or responsibilities. ■ Model/system misapplication/operation. ■ Accounting error/entity attribution error. ■ Delivery failure.
	Client account management	Events arising due to incorrect client records or incorrect payments within existing business.	■ Missing client permissions and/or disclaimers. ■ Missing or incomplete legal documents. ■ Unapproved access given to accounts. ■ Errors causing incorrect client records. ■ Negligent loss or damage of client assets.
	Monitoring and reporting	Events arising due to inaccurate mandatory external/internal reporting.	■ Failure to comply with mandatory reporting obligations. ■ Inaccurate external reporting leading to losses. ■ Inadequate internal reporting resulting in losses.
	Suppliers and outsourcing	Events arising due to vendor or service partner delivery failure or disputes. Outsourcing may reduce or increase the level of operational risk. The loss of control over the quality of outsourced activity; the loss of ability to conduct the activities in-house if staff and expertise are lost, creating a dependency on the external provider and creating a threat to the continuity of its operations if these providers were to fail.	■ Inadequate service level agreements (e.g., for IT services). ■ Inadequate investment mandate definitions. ■ Other outsourcing failures. ■ Inappropriate vendor disputes.
	Contractual customer documents	Events arising due to poor or inadequate data capture while taking on new business.	■ Legal documents missing/incomplete. ■ Client permissions/disclaimers missing.

practice categories; the fact that the loss manifested itself through a legal settlement is interesting, but does not provide a unique characterization useful in designing compensating controls to avoid the loss in the first place.

Reputational and ESG Risks

Second, there is no explicit category for "reputational risks," defined as a loss of franchise value due to customer reaction to changes in the firm's reputation or standing as perceived by the public. This is in contrast to the direct losses covered by the regulatory taxonomy, including fines and settlements. Managing reputational risk is important from a shareholder's perspective because franchise value can represent a large part of the firm's market capitalization and because it also reflects on management's reputation.

Reputational Risk with Operational Risk Root Causes

Similar to legal and compliance risks, the root causes of some reputational risks are already captured by operational risk events. For example, it was the employee fraud of Nick Leeson which caused the downfall of Barings; similarly, it was the risks associated with the customer practices of Putnam and Bankers Trust which caused the substantial loss in shareholder value and their ultimate takeover by other firms.

Managing these reputational risks is straightforward: the controls mitigating the operational risk root cause will be just as effective minimizing direct losses as potential indirect losses that would be suffered from a loss in reputation.

Reputational Risk and ESG Concerns

However, there are also reputational risks whose root cause does not fall conveniently into the taxonomy defined above. More specifically, a loss in franchise value can be caused by business activities which some customers or stakeholders feel strongly enough about that they withhold their business or investment in your firm. For example, there may be some customers or investors who will not do business with any firm which has dealings with non-conventional weapons manufacturers.

This is an example of an *ESG risk*, standing for Environmental, Social and Corporate Governance. Additional examples of ESG risks include being associated with companies active in "adult" or vice industries such as gambling, pornography, tobacco or alcohol; hydroelectric dams, strip mining and off-shore oil exploration which might impact the eco-system and indigenous populations; agricultural commodity trading which might be seen causing volatility in food prices in developing economies; or business activities in countries with mixed human rights practices.

In addition to withholding business from the directly involved firms, activists are increasingly challenging banks, asset managers and insurers who have business relationships with or invest in the "offending" firms.

Meeting the demands of ESG activists can be challenging for three reasons. First and foremost, because they cannot be measured against an objective yardstick or moral compass but are instead "in the eyes of the beholder": business practices will be judged differently by different individuals according to their norms and values. In addition, different stakeholders, including customers, shareholders, investors, special interest groups, etc., may hold different and potentially conflicting views of what is important. Second, because cultural norms are not static – they change and evolve as society evolves. Finally, because there may be no practical materiality thresholds associated with highly contentious ESG risks. For example, investing passively in an equity index which has a 0.01% share in an "offending" firm can be sufficient for activists to claim significant time at your AGM and in the press.

Although not covered by standard operational risk categories, reputational risks are sufficiently large to warrant another category in the framework and implementing a complete risk identification, evaluation and remediation program. A reference for the definition of ESG risks and management practices relevant to the insurance, banking and asset management industry can be found in UNEPFI (2009a,b). In these documents, the advice to the industry is to undertake four principles, paraphrased in Sidebar 26.1.

SIDEBAR 26.1: MANAGING ESG RISKS

The following paraphrases UNEPFI recommendations for managing ESG-related reputational risks.

PRINCIPLE 1: INTEGRATE ESG INTO BUSINESS DECISION MAKING

- Establish a strategy to identify, assess, manage and monitor ESG issues.
- Integrate ESG issues into risk management, underwriting and capital adequacy decision-making processes, including research, models, analytics, tools and metrics.
- Develop products that reduce ESG risks. Develop literacy programs and educate sales and marketing staff, integrate ESG into sales strategies and campaigns.
- Integrate ESG into investment decision-making and ownership practices.

PRINCIPLE 2: WORK TOGETHER WITH CLIENTS AND PARTNERS TO RAISE AWARENESS OF ESG ISSUES, MANAGE RISK AND DEVELOP SOLUTIONS

- Discuss the benefits of managing ESG issues and the company's expectations. Integrate ESG issues into tender and selection processes for suppliers.
- Encourage clients and suppliers to disclose ESG issues and to use relevant disclosure or reporting frameworks.

PRINCIPLE 3: WORK TOGETHER WITH GOVERNMENTS, REGULATORS AND OTHER STAKEHOLDERS TO PROMOTE WIDESPREAD ACTION ACROSS ESG ISSUES

- Support prudential policy, regulatory and legal frameworks that enable risk reduction, innovation and better management of ESG issues.
- Dialog with inter-governmental and non-governmental organizations, business and industry associations, academia and the scientific community and the media to support sustainable development.

PRINCIPLE 4: DEMONSTRATE ACCOUNTABILITY AND TRANSPARENCY IN REGULARLY DISCLOSING PUBLICLY PROGRESS IN IMPLEMENTING THE PRINCIPLES

- Assess, measure and monitor the company's progress in managing ESG issues; pro-actively and regularly disclose this information publicly.
- Dialog with stakeholders to gain mutual understanding on the value of disclosure through the principles.

It is interesting that the first and fourth principles are consistent with the ERM framework outlined earlier, especially risk identification, evaluation and underwriting and a clear risk strategy and transparent disclosures surrounding material risks. As such, these principles are "defensive" in nature and always implemented by firms driven by "enlightened self-interest."

However, there is much in Principles 2 and 3 which goes beyond "enlightened self-interest" and toward active proselytizing and championing of ESG issues. Moving from "enlightened self-interest" to active proselytizing may not be desirable for all ESG issues, especially as the evaluation of "what is right" can be vague and mutable, based on opinions which can and will differ. Careful consideration should be given to whether the firm wants to be an active agent for social change, on what issues and how this benefits all stakeholders, including shareholders, customers and the broader society. Championing all possible issues is neither desirable nor possible; selecting those which are more than tangentially related to the primary purpose of the company and pursuing them actively reflects enlightened self-interest.

Categorizing Loss Amounts

Operational risk events can cause two types of loss, direct and indirect.

Direct Losses

Direct losses are those which are directly quantifiable and attributable to the underlying operational risk event and which have a direct impact on the firm's financial accounts. In general, such losses are reported both gross and net of recoveries – such as insurance claims or other sources of compensation (e.g., from settlements, judgments, business partners, customers, etc.).

Examples include any charges to the profit/loss or balance sheet accounts; market losses or gains caused by incorrectly settling trades or implementing hedge positions; expenses associated with repairing the damage, including legal or professional fees, remediation fees, fines, settlements or judgments following compliance, regulatory and litigation events, etc.; direct opportunity costs associated with an operational risk event, including the time value of money, compensation for overpayment, etc.; direct losses in the case of internal fraud or processing errors; higher claims ratios or default rates in the case of external fraud or operational failures, etc. These direct losses are typically broken down into effect categories, as described in Table 26.2.

Indirect Losses

Indirect losses represent an opportunity cost, for example in the form of lost future business due to reputational damage or a lack of customer confidence, limitations put on business expansion by supervisors, failure of services and business interruption, etc. As the examples illustrate, indirect losses cannot be directly quantified but must be estimated as there is no clear path from the event(s) to an accounting entry in the general ledger. What is equally obvious is that the indirect losses can be a multiple of the direct loss, especially if the business franchise of the firm is materially impaired.

The distinction between direct and indirect losses is important. It is common practice to focus data collection and risk quantification efforts only on direct losses. This focus is

TABLE 26.2   Operational loss effect classifications

Loss impact effect	Description/examples
Write-down	Depreciation of assets due to the occurrence of an operational risk event (e.g., theft, internal or external fraud).
Compensation	Payments made to third parties for which the firm is legally responsible (e.g., claims from clients due to business interruption loss, pricing errors resulting in claims for compensation, net interest due to delays in settlement).
Loss of recourse	Losses resulting from inability to enforce claims on a third party. Loss may be incurred when a third party does not or cannot meet its obligations due to an operational risk event (e.g., duplicate payments made to third parties cannot be recouped, funds transferred by mistake to incorrect party).
Legal liability	Costs incurred in connection with litigation in a court proceeding or arbitration, including external attorney's fees, settlements, judgments paid, etc.
Regulatory action	Regulatory fines or any other sanctions imposed by regulatory bodies as a result of actions taken by the firm (e.g., fines paid for regulatory violation, costs imposed by exchanges or professional bodies).
Tax expenses	Losses occurring due to additional tax payments that the firm must cover (e.g., tax penalties or additional taxes).
Loss/damage to physical assets	Depreciation in the value of physical assets due to the occurrence of an operational risk event (e.g., replacement costs of physical assets that have been stolen or damaged, cost of immediate business resumption, costs associated with repairs to assets, loss of intangible property).
Other losses and/or costs	Losses and/or costs not covered above (e.g., cost of external consultants/temporary staff to investigate or resolve issue).

reinforced in regulatory standards, which limits loss recognition to only direct losses, and in part by a natural tendency to put lower emphasis on values which cannot be directly tied back to audited financial statements.

Limiting management focus only to direct losses is short-sighted, especially for events which can impact the firm's reputation and the confidence of its fiduciary clients, as illustrated in Sidebar 26.2.

The indirect losses associated with operational risk events can far outweigh the direct losses. Recognizing this potential is an important part of the risk identification, evaluation and management process. In addition to assessing direct losses for regulatory purposes, firms should also include indirect losses when collecting loss event data and when evaluating the potential impact of operational risk events.

SIDEBAR 26.2: PUTNAM INVESTMENTS CASE STUDY: WHY INDIRECT LOSSES ARE IMPORTANT

Putnam Investments was caught up in the market timing scandal of 2003, where it was alleged that Putnam gave preferential treatment to some of its customers when executing trades. With the agreement of the Securities and Exchange Commission (SEC) and the Commonwealth of Massachusetts, Putnam settled the charges, paying a USD 193 million fine. On top of this fine, Putnam also agreed to compensate fund investors by an approximately equal amount (Luxenburg, 2008): "Now the case is ending quietly . . . as fund shareholders receive payments designed to compensate for their losses. In the first batch of checks, 600,000 investors in Putnam funds will receive a total of $40 million. During the next six months, another $110 million will go to Putnam shareholders." These payments, along with the legal and professional fees in Putnam's defense, represent the direct losses associated with the market timing scandal.

However, the indirect losses caused by a loss of trust by its customers were far greater for both management and the value of the fund. CEO Lawrence J. Lasser, "who over the last 18 years helped to build Putnam into the nation's fifth largest mutual fund company," departed the company "in the wake of civil fraud allegations against the company and decisions by several big state pension funds to take money out of the firm's funds" (MSNBC, 2012).

The impact on the fund was also substantial, as "Public pension funds in six states . . . pulled more than $4 billion from Putnam last week." Ultimately, Putnam lost half its assets under management during a period when other funds were accumulating assets rapidly: Putnam had c. $190 billion AUM in 2006, down from nearly $400 billion at the start of 2000. Putnam was later sold by its parent to a Canadian firm for USD 3.9 billion, a substantial discount to its pre-scandal value.

MANAGING OPERATIONAL RISK

Compared with the other risks, operational risk is the most difficult to manage effectively. Although the market, credit and insurance risk models may require a PhD to understand, the management of operational risk is made more complex because of the following.

- The *diverse and ubiquitous nature of operational risk*, ranging from front-office customer practices to back-office processing errors . . . and everything in between!
- The *tenuous link between management actions and operational risk controls*: while cutting a trading position will have a direct and measurable impact on the firm's VaR, the same is more challenging in the case of implementing a diversity training program.
- Finally, because *risk capital is less useful as a tool to manage operational risks*. Operational risk capital frameworks are less mature and more subjective, making them less accepted by management and more difficult to use in risk-adjusted compensation schemes. In addition, managing operational risks requires detailed internal controls and operational block-and-tackling, not more capital. As a consequence, it is difficult to get operational risk capital to drive behavior.

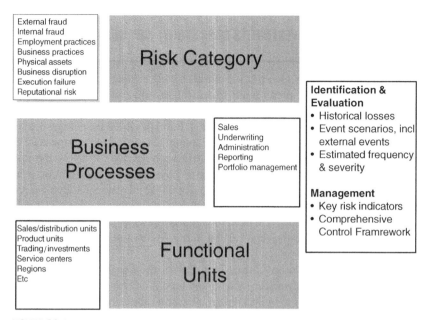

FIGURE 26.1 Operational risk identification, evaluation and management cube

Risk Identification and Evaluation

Consistent with the COSO framework, operational risk management begins with the identification and evaluation of the root causes or potential events which can cause an operational loss.

Describing and Evaluating Loss Potential by Segment, Product and Region

Banks and insurers use a three-dimensional structure, defined by business process, business area and risk category (illustrated in Figure 26.1), to structure their risk identification and evaluation process. Business processes are defined within each of the "cells," helping managers to understand what can go wrong, where and why.

This representation is necessary given the diversity and pervasiveness of operational risk: for example, administration and settlement processes will be quite different between trading, loan and insurance businesses; it would be impossible to understand what can go wrong and then implement appropriate controls in each without a clear understanding of the underlying business processes.

Risk managers need to develop a clear understanding of which risks are relevant for each cell and then combine this with an evaluation of the potential severity of the relevant events. Given data challenges, some combination of qualitative (or evaluation-based) and quantitative (or data-driven) approaches is needed. The FSA (2002) comments: "Due to both data limitations and lack of high-powered analysis tools, a number of operational risks cannot be measured accurately . . . So we use the term risk assessment in place of measurement, to encompass more qualitative processes, including for example the scoring of risks as 'high', 'medium' and 'low'."

As illustrated in Figure 26.2, data-driven approaches, supported by internal loss data capture, are used to understand and evaluate high-frequency (and, hopefully) low-severity risk events.

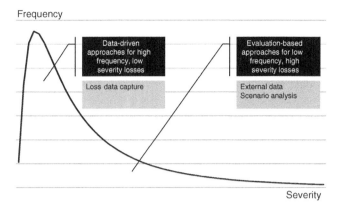

FIGURE 26.2 Identifying and evaluating the operational risks

Low-frequency, high-severity risks are captured through evaluation-based techniques, including the use of external data sources, industry case studies such as Barings, etc., combined with scenario analysis and risk identification workshops. In general, firms are encouraged to collect more internal data, shifting from qualitative assessments to direct quantification approaches where possible.

Consistent with this approach, the FSA (2002) comments: "we would still encourage firms to collect data on their operational risks and to use measurement tools where this is possible and appropriate. We believe that using a combination of both quantitative and qualitative tools is the best approach to understanding the significance of a firm's operational risks."

Data-driven Approaches

Historical losses are the starting point for evaluating high-frequency, low-severity risks once sufficient data has been collected, at which point techniques similar to those used by PC underwriters can be used to estimate the frequency and severity distributions of individual loss events as well as the cumulative loss distribution. Allianz began systematically collecting loss information across the group in 2004. Data is collected consistent with the risk taxonomy and loss representation schema presented earlier.

While loss data capture sounds simple, as with most things the "the devil is in the detail". The following can be kept in mind when designing a process to capture operational loss events.

First, loss data capture is not a "risk" activity – all departments have to contribute to capturing the data and then the losses have to be attributed to the originating unit. Operational risk can be originated in any function, but is often identified by a different function; for example, sales practice losses can first be seen by the customer call center, complaint department or legal department due to civil, arbitration or ombudsperson proceedings.

Second, the individual responsible for reporting losses may not perceive it to be in their best interest and therefore under-report. A culture of transparency has to be developed (not one of "shooting the messenger"), the responsibility explicitly defined within each function, the personnel trained to identify and classify loss events and the effectiveness validated through periodic audits.

Third, minimize inefficiencies or redundancies in data collection, leveraging existing reporting processes as much as possible. For example, most firms already collect litigation and arbitration cases in the legal department; fraud cases in the claims or loan workout department; employee practices in the human resources department; and so on. In order to ensure efficiency and consistency, use these sources as the primary data source, expanding the scope of information collected if necessary.

Fourth, the loss data to be collected should be broadly defined.

- More specifically, the loss data should be collected as soon as the potential for loss is identified, with the severity of loss estimated and updated over time. If estimates are used, capture both the best estimate as well as a "worst-case" outcome and track loss updates over time.
- Collect "near misses," defined as *events which could have caused a loss but which did not*. Although no loss occurred, near misses represent a failure in existing controls and recognition helps to better understand the potential frequency of loss events. Examples include trade settlement errors which were to your benefit once corrected.
- Capture both direct losses as well as the indirect consequences (e.g., due to reputational damage). While important to keep these separate for regulatory reporting purposes, it is also important to capture an estimate of the latter for management purposes.

Fifth, take care when capturing information for events which might later lead to litigation or regulatory action. Some categories of losses should be reviewed by in-house counsel and all descriptions should be kept to the standard of the WSJ test – that is, the manner in which the event is described is objective, factual and sensitive to potential discovery. Simply assume that all entries and associated emails will be discovered later as part of a regulatory, civil or criminal investigation or will end up on the cover of the *Wall Street Journal*.

Finally, include claims or loan default losses where the root cause can be traced to an operational risk event. In many cases, a customer default or insurance claim is the unpredictable and unfortunate consequence of a well-functioning underwriting process; in some cases, however, a failure in the underwriting process itself leads to the acceptance of a customer which ultimately files for bankruptcy or submits an insurance claim.

Examples of operational risk in the underwriting process include: a failure to collect or validate all necessary documentation prior to loan or policy approval; a failure to conduct on-site verification of the property or collateral value or the failure to conduct a risk engineering review of the property insured; a failure to perfect the collateral; etc. Similarly, operational errors in claims settlement or credit workout processes can lead to higher claims and lower loan recoveries than necessary.

Evaluation-based Approaches

Banks and insurers employ evaluation-based approaches in parallel. For example, Allianz uses a Risk Control Self-Assessment (RCSA) which is qualitatively similar to the TRA process described earlier, except the focus is on operational risk events. The differences worth highlighting include the following.

First, use external data when defining operational risk scenarios, at a minimum to trigger a discussion. Fortunately, many institutions have not experienced large-scale losses due to rogue trading or consumer protection action; however, this does not mean that such events could not happen. External information is a useful way to vicariously leverage the experience of others. External data can also be used as input for frequency and severity estimates, although care must be taken when "scaling" the information given differences in business, processes, organization and mitigating controls between firms.

Second, the number of expert workshops tends to be much higher and more focused because of the pervasiveness of operational risks. Cross-functional workshops can be organized for combined cells within the "cube" (e.g., by business/process, with representatives from the front, middle and back-office functions) in order to lessen the burden.

Third, the process should help the company design controls as well as quantify its loss exposure. In particular, the following should be collected during the workshops.

- *Frequency and severity estimates* for each loss scenario – for example, expressed as the average number of events per unit "allocation key" or Key Risk Indicator (KRI) specific to the scenario. The severity distribution is often represented using limited information, for example the minimum, average and maximum expected loss amounts or the expected and 95th-percentile loss amount, with the full distribution being filled in by a distributional assumption.
- *Allocation keys or KRIs*, such as number of transactions, error rate statistics, employee absenteeism, call or complaint center turnaround, customer satisfaction statistics, etc. There is a tendency to define too many metrics, some of which are only tangentially predictive of the scenarios. It is therefore important to evaluate the cost/benefit of additional KRIs, including an objective assessment of the predictive capability of each and to leverage KPIs already collected, especially those defined for the operations areas, call centers, etc.
- An *as-is assessment* of the control environment and the identification of *potential mitigating controls.*
- The definition of a *risk owner* and *control owners*. The "control owner," the person who executes the control, may be different from the "risk owner," the function which takes the realized economic loss. For example, losses from a failed trade may be attributed to the trading business, but some controls will be located in the back office or service center. It is important that both the risk owner and the control owners are clearly identified and understand and accept their role.

Managing Operational Risks

Managing operational risk is challenging for the same reason that identifying and evaluating operational risk is challenging: it can come from anywhere and it is very easy to get lost in the forest for the trees. Another challenge arises because the risk function is rarely responsible for remediating the issues, with the ultimate responsibility being embedded in the business directly.

The Textbook Recommendation

The textbook answer is to combine regular loss and KRI reporting with an internal control framework covering operational, compliance and reputational risks, ensuring that key controls are designed, implemented, tested and monitored for all material risks.

Designing an effective control environment begins with *identifying existing controls and any gaps to best practices* in the current control environment. Gaps in the control environment can be identified by comparison with best practices, using independent experts and exploring alternative process definitions.

It is important to use common sense when designing controls: it may not be desirable to implement 100% effective controls from a cost/benefit perspective. For example, the only sure way to absolutely ensure cyber security is to get rid of your computers completely; slightly less secure is to isolate all IT systems, making them accessible to customers, internal personnel and service providers only when sitting in an isolated Faraday cage. Obviously, a reasonable trade-off between the risks and returns needs to be made.

Once controls have been designed, *implementation needs to be periodically tested*. Some common implementation issues include a change in personnel without sufficient documentation of the control or training, ignoring controls because of a lack of consequences, the cost of implementation, etc.

Controls may be implemented perfectly but nonetheless prove ineffective in preventing operational losses. It is therefore important to *test whether the controls are effective as designed and implemented*. One approach, similar to the back-testing of internal models, involves the collection and analysis of actual loss events and understanding the specific circumstances which made the controls ineffective. In addition to analyzing loss events, testing is also done by regular variance reporting of actual versus benchmark KRI performance.

A *test plan* should be prepared for each key control for each in-scope process. The test plan should include the method of testing, the determination of the sample size, timing, responsibility for testing, etc. The testing of key controls should be delegated to an independent function, either within the area responsible or to internal or external audit.

Testing of control design, implementation and effectiveness identifies potential deficiencies, leading to remediation plans and active monitoring of actions against the plan in order to ensure implementation. However, once again common sense needs to be used: the SOX experience[1] taught us that testing a control framework can take on a life of its own, generating extensive documentation but little added value. Again, a risk-based approach should be used in testing, focusing on material risks so as not to devolve into an inflexible and crushingly burdensome "box-ticking" exercise. This extends to simple things such as the form of documentation required, the frequency of explicit testing or whether the ex-post review of realized losses is sufficient, etc.

Finally, it is important to *test whether or not loss events have actually been reported*. Operational loss data capture takes time and resources and may not always be perceived to be in the best interests of the person responsible for reporting the loss. On the one hand, the function may be afraid of the consequences should the loss be traced to their (in)actions and, on the other hand, they may also fear the additional burden by an enhanced set of controls. Either can lead to the loss not being reported or being incorrectly reported, misclassified or misrepresented.

Because the external and internal environment of the firm can be expected to change over time, managing operational risks using a system of internal controls is a dynamic exercise, requiring the process of identification, control definition, testing and remediation to be repeated regularly.

A Practical Amendment

While giving a sense of progress, the "textbook" operational risk management may not always be effective, with too much focus put on process mapping and reporting and too little on

---

[1]Sarbanes–Oxley (SOX) was enacted in 2002 for US listed companies in response to some of the more egregious accounting mis-statements, such as Worldcom, Tyco and Enron. It was also known as the "Public Company Accounting Reform and Investor Protection Act" in the US Senate and the "Corporate and Auditing Accountability and Responsibility Act" in the US House of Representatives. Similar laws were subsequently rolled out in other countries.

business impact. This is manifested by long reports in size 6 font and tiny red/amber/green (RAG) traffic lights for each risk type and process, none of which does much to spur behavior.

The risk function can add value and achieve significant impact if it prioritizes the battles which are worth fighting and then engages in those areas in a focused manner. This is done, for example, by prioritizing the two or three issues from the 20+-page report to be "championed" and raising awareness at the Risk Committee on these issues; getting the responsible line manager to acknowledge that they have an issue and accept responsibility to fix it; and, finally, reporting back six months later with their accomplishments.

This requires the risk function to have business professionals able to exercise judgment in selecting the two or three battlegrounds from the forest of potential issues. This skill set may be missing in organizations which give a preference to internal model quants and process and control-oriented audit professionals. The operational risk team should have a well-rounded skill set, including technical modeling, control and business experience.

CHAPTER 27

Risk and Limit Controlling

Two of the most important questions which CROs need to answer are: Is our risk profile transparent and understood by management? And is it within delegated authorities?

Answering these questions lies at the heart of an effective *risk and limit controlling* framework, one of the four elements of an effective *enterprise risk management* framework. I emphasize this point because risk controlling is too often confused with risk management. Reiterating a common theme, having the right information is an important and necessary precondition to creating value, but it is not sufficient – the information has to lead to business impact through better decisions and execution.

Given the complexity of most banking and insurance businesses, answering these questions typically leads to very large systems investment, in capturing the underlying data, applying the technical approaches necessary to characterize a complex risk landscape and making the results available and relevant to managers.

This chapter outlines the fundamentals of a risk and limit controlling framework.

RISK REPORTING

That a bank or insurer needs to understand its risk profile and ensure that it is within delegated limits is a bit like "Motherhood and Apple Pie" – it is compelling on an emotional level, offering nothing to disagree with, but there is not a lot of depth behind it. This section goes a little deeper in order to better understand and motivate why financial services firms typically spend so much on risk reporting systems.

In my experience, an effective risk and limit controlling framework can add value in four distinct ways, as outlined in Figure 27.1.

- *Govern the business.* Management and Supervisory Board Risk Reports are comprehensive and exhaustive, answering "What is the risk profile of the firm and is it within delegated limits?" These are "need to have" governance reports; however, they are seldom used to "run the business." Rather, they are primarily used to evidence an internal control.
- *Run the business.* "Flash reports" are designed by the business to support decision making, reflecting the way that the business is managed. Aligning business risk reports is critical for ensuring that the risk function and the business are talking the same language and working from the same information basis.

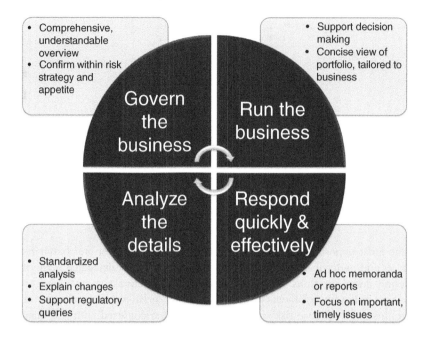

FIGURE 27.1   How does risk and limit reporting add value?

- *Analyze the details.* Standardized, detailed risk reports support technical analysts and subject matter experts in understanding portfolio developments and answering most questions from analysts, rating agencies and regulators. Similar to Board Risk Reports, these are "need to have" reports, but are nonetheless not likely to drive business decisions.
- *Respond to current issues.* Ad hoc analysis in the form of memoranda or presentations focusing on important and timely issues has the greatest potential to impact business decisions because it is focused on specific issues requiring a decision or action given the current market situation.

Further motivation for each of these objectives, as well as concrete report examples, are given in the remaining sections of this chapter.

Objective 1: Govern the Business

Consider the responsibilities of the Management and Supervisory Board Risk Committees outlined earlier: amongst others, the Risk Committee needs to regularly

- review and approve the risk strategy and risk appetite of the firm and its logical expression in terms of risk limits, capital allocations and delegated authorities;
- review the risk profile of the firm, covering all risks but focusing especially on risk concentrations which are material at the level of the firm;
- verify that the firm's current risk profile is within limits and delegated authorities.

Accomplishing these objectives requires what I call a "Board Risk Report," a cornerstone of risk governance for the modern financial services firm. Board Risk Reports are designed to be *comprehensive*, covering *all relevant risks* (including financial market, credit, insurance and operational risks) and *all relevant risk metrics* used to manage the risks and define risk appetite, including for example Earnings at Risk (EaR) measures geared to IFRS/accounting earnings; economic value and capital metrics such as Value at Risk (VaR); solvency measures based on regulatory, rating agency and internal model perspectives; liquidity measures, etc.

Board Risk Reports have to be comprehensive in order for the Supervisory and Management Boards to fulfil their governance responsibilities. Somewhat more cynically, it is also a "CYA" strategy: if a material, adverse event should occur, it is better to be able to point to the report and say that the Board was pre-informed, even if the event was buried in a footnote on page 83.

A good Board Risk Report is *designed specifically for governance purposes*, allowing quick access and understanding of the information which is important for risk governance. For example, they are in a *standardized format, quarter after quarter*, allowing readers to quickly access the information although they may not have seen the report in a while. Furthermore, the information is *presented in a manner tailored to answering the important risk governance questions*. For example, they will typically

- begin with an Executive Summary & Management Assessment, summarizing the relevant messages upfront;
- use visual cues and aggregated risk metrics (e.g., heat maps or VaR metrics) in order to make the risk profile readily accessible;
- bring all relevant limits and their utilization onto one page, clearly identifying any breaches.

An example Table of Contents for a Board Risk Report is given in Sidebar 27.1.

SIDEBAR 27.1: EXAMPLE BOARD RISK REPORT

Board Risk Reports are designed to meet two important governance objectives: first, to ensure that the risk profile is understood by senior management and second, to ensure that the firm's risk profile is consistent with its business strategy, risk strategy, risk appetite and delegated authorities.

As a consequence, Board Risk Reports are comprehensive, covering all sources of risk, utilizing the different metrics which reflect the firm's risk appetite, and communicating both the exposure profile and limit utilization. Given the breadth of the issues covered, they tend to be at a high level of aggregation, for example relying on "heat maps" or VaR aggregation approaches, in order to make the risk profile immediately accessible and understandable.

Table 27.1 shows an example of the Table of Contents for a generic Board Risk Report, including a brief summary of the contents within each chapter.

TABLE 27.1   Generic Board Risk Report table of contents

Chapter	Description
Executive Summary & Management Assessment	A summary of: ■ important market developments; ■ the firm's risk concentrations and developments; ■ limit utilization; ■ management actions. Management's assessment of the current market conditions, risk profile and solvency position.

Overview, Solvency Capital Profile	An overview of the firm's solvency position:
	
	■ based on the internal model, regulatory and rating agency capital regimes;
	■ for management units (e.g., group, business segments, business unit) and regulated legal entities, as appropriate;
	■ covering
	  ■ current solvency position,
	  ■ comparison with previous period,
	  ■ reverse, historical and standardized stress tests,
	  ■ whether or not solvency position is consistent with target ranges,
	
	Management's assessment of the solvency position and actions.

Economic Risk Profile – Overview	Overview of the firm's risk profile based on the internal model: ■ summarized by major risk categories, allocated to management units; ■ comparison with previous period. Overview of stress test results, including historical and standardized stress tests. Limit utilization for the above, as appropriate. Management assessment and actions.
Overview, Limit Utilization	An overview of all limits which define strategic risk appetite and their utilization. Description and management actions in case of limit breaches.
Economic Risk Profile – Financial Market Risk	Overview of the firm's financial market risk based on internal model: ■ summarized by market risk categories* and allocated to management units; ■ comparison with previous period. Other relevant risk measures by market risk type (e.g., key exposure indicators, including standardized sensitivities,** position equivalents, stress scenarios, etc.). Limit utilization as appropriate. Management assessment and actions.
Economic Risk Profile – Credit Risk	Overview of the firm's credit risk profile based on internal model: ■ summarized by credit risk categories (e.g., credit, country risk) and allocated to management units; ■ comparison with previous period. Other relevant risk measures: ■ top concentrations, by notional or mark-to-market exposure, risk capital utilization;

	▪ exposure profile by rating, sector, product type, maturity, etc.; ▪ watch list of critical exposures; ▪ stress scenarios. Limit utilization as appropriate. Management assessment and actions.
Economic Risk Profile – Insurance Risk	Overview of the firm's insurance risk profile based on internal model: ▪ summarized by insurance risk categories (e.g., premium, reserve, natural catastrophe, man-made catastrophe, etc.) and line of business, allocated to management units; ▪ comparison with previous period. Other relevant risk measures: ▪ top natural and man-made catastrophe risk concentrations, by return period exposure and risk capital utilization; ▪ stress scenarios. Limit utilization as appropriate. Management assessment and actions.
Economic Risk Profile – Operational Risk	Overview of the firm's operational risk profile based on internal model: ▪ summarized by operational risk categories*** and allocated to management units; ▪ comparison with previous period. Other relevant risk measures: ▪ operational risk events since previous reporting period; ▪ stress scenarios. Management assessment and actions.
Earnings at Risk Profile	Overview of the firm's EaR[†] profile: ▪ allocated to management units, comparison with previous period; ▪ combined stress tests and limit utilization. Management assessment and actions.
Liquidity Risk Profile	Overview of the firm's liquidity profile:[††] ▪ overview of current funding structure; ▪ overview of liquidity requirements and resources; ▪ combined stress tests and limit utilization. Limit utilization as appropriate. Management assessment and actions.

*For example, equity, interest rate, foreign exchange rate, real estate, commodities, credit spread risk, implied volatilities, correlations, etc.

**Sensitivities might include delta (the impact for a small change in market rates, including duration, key rate sensitivities for interest rates), gamma or convexity (the change in delta for a small change in market rates), vega (the impact of a small change in implied volatilities, relevant for option positions), etc.

***See Chapter 26 for a description of operational risk categories.

[†]EaR is typically defined as the impact on IFRS or local accounting earnings of predefined scenarios calibrated to a 1-in-10-year worst-case event.

[††]See Chapter 18 for a more detailed description of liquidity risk and examples of liquidity risk reporting.

Running at 50+ pages, most Board Risk Reports have only limited use by those who manage the business or portfolio. The reason is simple: they are designed to answer the governance questions (e.g., what is our risk profile and is it within limits?), not to be used for the active management of the business.

Objective 2: Run the Business

Managing the risks and returns from a credit portfolio, investment portfolio or trading book takes information. As opposed to Board Risk Reports, "run the business" reports do not try to be comprehensive, nor do they try to provide all possible detail which might potentially be required. Rather, *they provide a concise overview of the positions in an easy-to-understand manner consistent with the way that the business is managed on a day-to-day basis.*

As an example, consider a daily flash report received by bank trading desk managers or asset managers. These flash reports provide a concise representation of the portfolio's risk profile, limited to only one or two pages, with the positions either illustrated graphically for a quick interpretation of those elements which can change rapidly or expressed in terms of equivalent positions for a quick calculation of hedge ratios. The reports mimic the trade blotters or position-keeping systems which are used by the traders on an intra-day basis; similar to the trade blotters, they are tailored to specific trading strategies. For example, interest rate risks are represented in position equivalents using exchange traded futures contracts for short-term money market desks but swap notional equivalents for derivative or cash bond trading desks and duration gaps for liability-based investment portfolios.

As discussed later, operational limits are defined in a manner consistent with the way that management views the risks in their specific portfolio. Because flash reports present the risk profile of the unit in a concise manner tailored to the specific business, it is common to provide limit utilization information in the same format, in the same report.

Sidebar 27.2 illustrates a flash report used for an investment function following a liability-based investment strategy.

SIDEBAR 27.2: EXAMPLE FLASH REPORT TO SUPPORT LIABILITY-BASED ASSET ALLOCATION DECISIONS

Flash reports are designed to support daily decision making. They convey information specific to the business and relevant to its strategy in a concise manner; they are not designed to be comprehensive, covering all potential risks, nor do they provide a level of detail necessary to answer all potential questions.

They use position and hedge ratio information consistent with the trading strategy and limits are presented next to their corresponding exposure information to indicate available limit capacity and constraints. As much emphasis is put on how the report is integrated into management processes as on the design of the report itself.

Table 27.2 shows an example of a two-page flash report used to support general account strategic asset/liability management for an insurer. The first page provides a

TABLE 27.2 Strategic ALM flash report

Financial limit report - 3Q 2014 - Sxxx Dummy OE - exemplary figures
(CUR mn, before tax)

Risk limits (99.5% c.i.)	3Q 2014	Limit	Utilization	2Q 2014
Financial VaR	+1,430	+2,319	61.7%	+1,424
Market VaR	+1,192			+1,185
FX VaR	+45			+44
Credit VaR	+485			+485

For information only	3Q 2014			2Q 2014
Non-financial VaR	+424			+424
Total VaR before tax	+1,505			+1,500
Total VaR after tax	+1,174			+1,500

Equity sensitivity limit	3Q 2014	Limit	Utilization	2Q 2014
Total impact of EQ -30%	-126	-243	51.8%	-129
Impact on financial assets	-141			-142
Impact on financial liabilities	+15			+13

Interest rate sensitivity limit	3Q 2014	Limit	Utilization	2Q 2014
Total impact of IR -100bps	-440	-705	62.4%	-403
Impact on financial assets	+578			+558
Impact on financial liabilities	-1,017			-961

ECBS duration (parallel shift)	Total		Excluding UL business	
	3Q 2014	2Q 2014	3Q 2014	2Q 2014
ECBS duration gap	-1.1	-1.0	-1.3	-1.2
Duration financial assets	7.8	7.7	8.2	8.1
Duration financial liabilities [3]	8.9	8.7	9.5	9.3

Asset allocation limits [1]	MM	Exposure 3Q 2014	Allocation	Lower limit	Upper limit	Exposure 2Q 2014
Fixed income	13,882	13,882	93.4%	85.9%	97.9%	13,583
Cash / short-term	165	165	1.1%			165
Government	9,806	9,806	65.9%			9,601
Securitized	2,105	2,105	14.2%			2,063
Financials	586	586	3.9%			581
Non-financials	1,120	1,120	7.5%			1,104
Fixed income derivatives	104	104	0.7%			78
FX derivatives	-5	-5	-0.0%			-8
Equity / equity derivatives	261	261	1.8%		4.5%	264
Equity securities	261	261	1.8%			264
Equity derivatives	-0	-0	-0.0%			0
Real estate	518	518	3.5%		5.7%	518
Alternative investments	209	209	1.4%		4.0%	209
Alternative investments	209	209	1.4%			209
Participations L/H [2]	-	-				-
Others (not part of SAA)						
Sensitivity instruments	-	-				-
Participations P/C [2]	-	-				-
Total investments	14,869	14,869				14,574

1) Excluding unit linked business, excluding non-financial B/S items
2) Participations are part of the SAA only for OEs in the L/H segment, not for OEs in the P/C segment
3) Liability duration adjusted to the market value of fixed income assets

Sensitivity report – 3Q 2014 – Sxxxx Dummy OE – exemplary figures

(CUR mn, before tax)

Sensitivities – total portfolio including unit linked business – exemplary figures

EQ P/L	-30%	-10%	+10%	+30%
3Q 2014	-126	-40	+39	+116
2Q 2014	-129	-41	+40	+117

RE P/L	-30%	-10%	+10%	+30%
3Q 2014	-62	-18	+17	+50
2Q 2014	-64	-18	+17	+49

EQ/REVOL P/L	+1%-p
3Q 2014	-5
2Q 2014	-5

IR P/L	-200bps	-100bps	+100bps	+200bps
3Q 2014	-1.063	-440	+268	+428
2Q 2014	-1.028	-403	+239	+384

ECBS duration gap[1]	Total	Ex UL
3Q 2014	-1,1	-1,3
2Q 2014	-1,0	-1,2

CS P/L	-100bps	-50bps	+50bps	+100bps
3Q 2014	+193	+92	-85	-165
2Q 2014	+161	+76	-70	-137

IRVOL P/L	+1%-p
3Q 2014	-16
2Q 2014	-16

1) based on parallel shift of yield curve

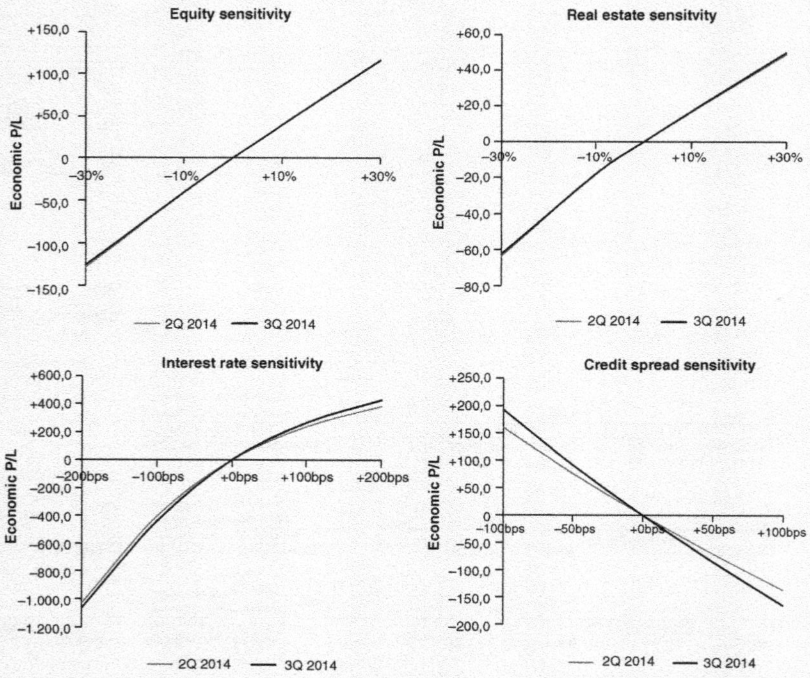

FIGURE 27.2 Sensitivity report

concise overview of the risk positions (and limits) in a form consistent with the way that asset/liability managers "think," while the second page provides greater detail on position and risk measures specific to the portfolio and strategy.

This table focuses on the most important directional positions and risk limits. The top section provides an overview of the unit's VaR limit utilization, covering only those risks which can be managed by asset managers (e.g., market and credit risks). It also provides the portfolio's net equity sensitivity and asset/liability duration mismatch, including all assets, liabilities and derivatives, with options represented in delta or cash equivalent form. The bottom section focuses on the asset side of the balance sheet, comparing the actual asset allocation (on a cash-equivalent basis) against the strategic asset allocation benchmark and limit "leeways" available to the investment manager.

Figure 27.2 provides a deeper analysis, with additional measures increasingly relevant from both a management and a Solvency II perspective.

These measures include the following.

- Additional directional risk measures, including the portfolio's sensitivity to changes in the average level of credit spreads and implied volatilities (vega).
- Measures of the portfolio's convexity (gamma) which describe how the directional risk of the portfolio changes as market conditions change. Convexity measures are particularly important for portfolios with a material exposure to options and guarantees.
- Key rate sensitivities, providing detail on how the portfolio value will evolve under non-parallel interest rate movements.

Integrated into Business Decision-making Processes

Equally important is the use of the reports in supporting decision making. Flash reports should be used by trading desks or asset managers as an integral part of their morning (or Monday morning) meetings, where the entire team goes through a well-defined agenda. For example:

1. review positions and limits;
2. discuss recent developments or news coming out during the day and the likely implications;
3. discuss any large, complex or new transactions or positions which have evolved in an unexpected manner;
4. conclude by discussing the coordinated trading strategies for the day.

The risk function participates in the morning meetings, giving them an understanding of the positions and intentions of the business unit as well as the ability to discuss and share opinions before decisions are taken.

In summary, flash reports can facilitate daily decision making or "run the business" *only if* they are structured to clearly and concisely represent the business and its strategy *and if* they are integrated into the daily decision-making processes.

Objective 3: Analyze the Details

"Govern the business" and "Run the business" reports present only the tip of the iceberg; they need to be complemented with more detailed risk reports to help experts analyze the portfolio, identify emerging issues and respond to external stakeholders.

In the interests of being concise, both Board Risk Reports and flash reports rely on assumptions. For example, duration and Value of a Basis Point (VB01) represent the portfolio's sensitivity to small, parallel shifts in interest rates, ignoring the possibility of steepening or flattening rates or larger shifts which might affect convex positions. Similarly, credit spread sensitivities assume that all credit spreads move together and the diversification calculated by VaR measures is based on recent correlations and experience. Although these assumptions may be counted on during "normal times," they can break down during times of crisis, sometimes spectacularly, shattering the risk representation to expose hidden concentrations.

It is especially important during these times of crisis to have more detailed information available in order to react quickly and communicate effectively with shareholders, rating agencies and regulators, all of whom may assume the worst and heavily discount your share price or require overly prudent capital buffers in the absence of clear guidance.

Detailed reports are also used by analysts to understand, reconcile and explain the development of the portfolio and identify trends which may influence the portfolio in the future. Finally, detailed reports also help to respond quickly to external information requests during conversations with regulators, rating agencies and analysts.

Because it is impossible to anticipate all potential information needs, a two-prong strategy is required: first, develop reports which are reasonably detailed to support most likely analysis requirements and second, ensure that your reporting systems are sufficiently robust and granular to answer additional questions through an ad hoc query. Sidebar 27.3 gives some examples of detailed reports supporting credit and natural catastrophe risks, both of which can cumulate to peak exposures.

It should be clear from the discussion that the target audience for these detailed reports consists of analysts and not senior management: the reports can run into high double-digit pages and the information is typically only accessible to the highly trained. Bringing this type of report to business leaders is a bit like offering a steak sandwich to a vegetarian: even if they do take a tentative bite, no one is going to like the result.

SIDEBAR 27.3: EXAMPLE DETAILED CREDIT AND NATURAL CATASTROPHE REPORTS

Detailed risk reports complement "Govern the risk/Board Risk Reports" and "Run the business/flash reports" and are designed to provide a reference to conduct more detailed scenario analysis, respond quickly during times of crisis, analyze portfolio movements in detail and respond to external stakeholders.

This sidebar provides the Table of Contents for two detailed risk reports, credit and PC catastrophe risks. Both of these risk categories are unique in that they accumulate across business units and products, ultimately posing concentration risk.

TABLE 27.3 Credit risk detailed report table of contents

Chapter	Description
Executive Summary & Management Assessment	Summary of: ■ highlights, key developments and issues; ■ management assessment and planned actions.
Portfolio Profile, Portfolio Aggregates	An overview of firm's current exposures and recent developments, by business unit or portfolio, expressed in terms of: ■ gross notional exposure; ■ internal model capital; ■ expected loss. Stress test results and limits.
Portfolio Profile, Detailed Composition	An overview of firm's current exposure profile and recent developments: ■ notional exposure, allocated capital and expected loss; ■ presented in two-dimensional tables, reflecting the following dimensions – country of domicile, industry sector, rating, maturity, product, etc.
Single Exposures of Interest	■ Overview of material rating changes. ■ Overview of the top risk concentrations, measured by notional exposure and contribution to risk capital, overall and for specific segments (e.g., sovereign, corporate, financials, country). ■ Watch list (e.g., restricted trading) and black list (managed reduction in exposures).

CREDIT RISK DETAILED REPORT

A credit risk report, like the one shown in Table 27.3, covers the credit exposures from all products (e.g., bonds or loans, cash deposits, derivatives, reinsurance receivables and off-balance sheet exposures) for all borrowers and counterparties, including corporations, financial institutions and sovereign entities. In addition, it also covers exposure to country risk.

PC CATASTROPHE RISK DETAILED REPORT

Catastrophe events, defined as *loss event which are larger than a predefined materiality threshold*, can arise from many sources: natural catastrophes such as earthquakes, windstorms, etc.; man-made catastrophes such as acts of terrorism, war, etc.; clash scenario accumulations, such as an air disaster near a harbor, triggering aviation, marine hull, warehouse property and business interruption claims simultaneously under different contracts.

Some of these events will be modeled, as in Table 27.4, including frequency and severity distributions, while others will be characterized based on stress scenarios or MPLs (Maximum Probable Losses).

TABLE 27.4   NatCat detailed report table of contents

Chapter	Description
Executive Summary & Management Assessment	Summary of: ■ highlights and key developments; ■ management assessment and actions.
Portfolio Profile, Portfolio Aggregates	An overview of firm's modeled natural and man-made catastrophe exposures, current and recent developments, by business unit or portfolio: ■ potential losses from single events (OEP) and in aggregate (AEP) at different return periods;* ■ MPLs for perils not explicitly modeled; ■ expected annual loss. A qualitative assessment of the firm's non-modeled risks. Limit utilization.
Single Exposures of Interest	Overview of top modeled single peril exposures (OEP): ■ gross and net of reinsurance compared with limits; ■ based on different return periods (e.g., 1-in-250 years, 1-in-1000 years, etc.); ■ include MPLs for material non-modeled perils. Overview of top clash scenarios and stress tests for non-modeled risks, compared with limits.
Gaps in Reinsurance Program	Overview of gaps in reinsurance program: ■ overview of second event exposures and scenarios without reinsurance reinstatements; ■ overview of net impact of extreme events above reinsurance limits.

*Single event exposures are often described by an Occurrence Exceedance Probability (OEP), which measures the loss to a single event on a 1-in-10-yr (100-yr, 250-yr) horizon. In contrast, an Annual Exceedance Probability (AEP) measures the potential loss from multiple events across the portfolio at different return periods.

Objective 4: Respond to Current Issues

Important risk issues arise unpredictably, issues which are not well covered by standard risk reports. These represent an opportunity for the risk and finance functions to add significant value by providing analysis and insights specific to important and timely events.

As examples, consider some of the agenda items which have appeared on Allianz's Group Risk Committee agenda between 2008 and 2014.

■ How should exposures to the global banking industry be managed following the demise of Lehman Brothers in 2008? The sovereign crisis of 2012? The European Central Banks'

Asset Quality Review (AQR) of 2014? What banks and what instruments (e.g., sub-ordinated or senior debt) should be managed?

■ What is an optimal strategic asset allocation strategy given the uncertain impact of fiscal and monetary policy, leading to sustained low interest rates or potentially spiking rates in the future? What are the potential implications of an inflationary scenario on PC reserves? On lapse risk for LH traditional products?

■ What is the optimal asset allocation and liquidity position in the face of a potential European sovereign default? Where are we exposed to critical asset classes which might deteriorate in a crisis and what should be our strategy for each asset class?

■ How should we adapt our risk appetite, limits, underwriting and reinsurance strategies in the face of historically high levels of natural catastrophe claims impacting non-peak perils in 2010–11? The sustained softening of the reinsurance market in 2013–14 due to capacity from the capital markets in the form of insurance linked securities? Are we being adequately compensated for the risks we are taking?

While information from standardized reports is useful, answering these questions requires not only data but also analyst judgment to identify the emerging issues and develop the scenarios; to understand second- and third-order implications; to define possible management actions; to evaluate the impact and trade-offs in terms of earnings, capital and liquidity; and, finally, to develop and syndicate recommendations and actions.

To be successful, the risk function must have a sufficiently broad understanding of the business and current environment and be in a position to use independent judgment to identify the issues which are worth pursuing. In addition, the first and second lines of defense have to work closely together on the analysis and recommendations. I have seen some institutions which have so narrowly defined the remit of risk to pure controlling that they are incapable of expressing an independent, business-oriented view needed to identify and carry out analysis of the issues.

AN EFFECTIVE RISK LIMIT FRAMEWORK

Limit systems perform two important functions. The first is to *allocate scarce resources.* Banks and insurers create value for shareholders and customers by absorbing and intermediating risk which can accumulate: a bank cannot finance the broader economy without assuming some credit risk and exposure to the broader economy; an insurer cannot provide a home-owner's policies without assuming some exposure to natural catastrophes. In this context, credit and natural catastrophe limits can be considered as scarce resources which need to be managed in order to create more value; in contrast to the resources necessary for an industrial corporation, too much of the "resource" can be a bad thing.

The second important role is to *ensure that decisions are within the risk strategy and risk appetite defined by management.* For example, it is illogical for a bank's money market desk to engage in commodity or equity transactions, just as it may be illogical for a personal lines PC company to write financial guarantees; nonetheless, in lieu of explicit constraints, some business leaders may be tempted to expand into these "distant adjacencies" to meet top-line growth targets. Keeping a business in their strategic "sweet spot" is accomplished through a combination of limits, guidelines, new product approval and strategic planning processes.

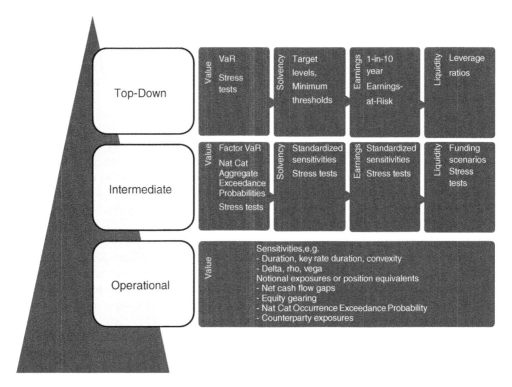

FIGURE 27.3 Limit structure

The Structure of Limits

Figure 27.3 gives a framework for thinking about the limit structures typically implemented by banks and insurers.

A limit framework should be comprehensive and aligned with the way that management defines its risk appetite, covering value, solvency, earnings and liquidity/funding. It should represent a hierarchy, with an aggregated and comprehensive view across all risks at the top. Since aggregate risk measures rely on assumptions which can break down and do not reveal the underlying factors or scenarios that are relevant, a good limit structure continues by providing further, more granular operational limits such as sensitivities and gross exposures which are not as heavily reliant on assumptions.

There are three common questions with regard to limit frameworks, addressed in the remainder of this section. Should the operational limits be "coherent" with the VaR limit? Given their extreme nature, should stress test results be used as the basis for limits? And, finally, should limit breaches be tolerated and, if so, under what circumstances?

The Coherence of a Limit System

As Figure 27.3 illustrates, VaR limits are used at the "top of the pyramid." The reason is intuitive: VaR is a comprehensive measure, capable of covering all risks, and is useful in making direct comparisons across diverse business activities given its interpretation as required capital.

Many institutions desire an operational limit framework which is "coherent" with their VaR measures. For some, the "holy grail" is a set of operational limits which allocate VaR across business units on an inter-day basis but which *do not in themselves pose additional restrictions beyond those imposed by the VaR limit*. Conceptually, the operational limit system collapses to a single point and provides no further restriction on the business beyond those implied by VaR. For instance, equity and rate sensitivity limits for trading desks would be defined such that the aggregate VaR limit will not be breached if each desk's operational limits are fully utilized.

Like the "holy grail," a coherent limit system may or may not exist (I have yet to see one in practice). More importantly, it my belief that a "coherent" limit framework should *not* be the goal.

First, VaR measures are calculated using a wide range of assumptions, especially regarding market liquidity, correlations and the tail of the distribution; assumptions that will fail in the next crisis. A good limit framework is robust to these failures; a "coherent" limit system is not. Extra care should be taken, especially for portfolios where the distance between modeled risk and notional exposure grows "large."

Second, regardless of how good the VaR model is, it can and will be arbitraged by the first line of defense; having a limit structure that does not collapse down to a single number is a safeguard against the most blatant forms of arbitrage.

Limits and Stress Testing

As discussed in Chapter 22, extreme events seem to happen with alarming frequency. Many firms use stress tests to measure the institution's exposure to extreme events.

There are three types of stress test, described in Sidebar 27.4. Two of them start with events or scenarios and then recalculate the value of the portfolio: *historical stress tests* are based on actual, historical events and *event stress tests* stress individual parameters and combinations of parameters by specific, predefined amounts.

The third, known as the reverse stress test, starts with a specific loss amount (e.g., to the point of insolvency, equivalent to 50% of planned earnings, etc.) and then works backwards to find representative scenarios which can cause a loss of that magnitude. Reverse stress tests are useful because they help understand what it takes to make the firm insolvent.

Stress tests are useful for defining limits. For example, it is important to learn from the past, saying that we do not want to become insolvent if we see the same financial crisis again. Similarly, it is intuitive to want to have a minimum level of surplus following a 30% drop in equities or a 100 bps decrease in rates or both. However, when considering the use of stress tests as limits, my experience is that they

- should be kept simple, stable in definition and few in number;
- represent large but not outrageous events;
- should be consistently applied across the organization;
- should be associated with hard limits as opposed to only triggering a discussion, given their extreme nature.

SIDEBAR 27.4: STRESS TESTS, DESCRIPTIONS AND EXAMPLES

Stress tests come in many forms, briefly described and illustrated with examples in Table 27.5.

TABLE 27.5   Stress test

Stress tests	Examples
Historical stress tests "Those who do not learn from the past are doomed to repeat it." George Santayana The portfolio's value (earnings or liquidity position, etc.) is evaluated under historical stress events. Looking at the examples, "stress" events seem to happen with great frequency, more than once a decade. Historical stress tests are complementary as they are based on correlations and events which go beyond those predicted by VaR models. Historical stress tests reinforce institutional memory and remind management that things have gone seriously wrong in the past and can potentially again in the future. In addition, they are more difficult to challenge as being "beyond belief" or "incredible in today's market" – a frequent complaint made by managers who have only experienced a bull market.	*Market events* 2011 European sovereign debt crisis 2008 Global credit and liquidity crisis 2001–02 Dotcom bubble 1998 Russian/LTCM crisis 1997 Asian crisis 1994–95 Mexican peso crisis 1992 European currency crisis 1990 Nikkei stock market crash 1987 October market crash *Natural catastrophes* 2011 Fukushima 2010 Haiti EQ 2008 Cyclone Nargis 2008 Sichuan EQ 2005 Hurricane Katrina 2005 Kashmir EQ 2004 Indian Ocean tsunami 1994 Northridge EQ *Other events* 2014 Ebola 2013 MERS 2003 SARS 1918 Spanish influenza 2001 September 11th NY terrorist attack
Event stress tests Event stress scenarios measure the impact of predefined single events or combinations which are judged to occur only rarely. They become a useful communication tool and control limit when kept simple, extreme but not outrageous and constantly used in risk communication. Event stress scenarios are also useful as limits to ensure that not too much reliance is put on correlations and other assumptions which might break down during crisis.	Single events (e.g., −30% equity market crash, −100 bps interest rate increase/decline, 200 bps increase in credit spreads, 1:250-year natural catastrophe, liquidity scenario, etc.). Combinations of single events. Stresses on more opaque assumptions (e.g., correlations, volatility term structures and smiles, etc.).

Reverse stress test	The combination of rate and equity price
Reverse stress scenarios start from a quantum of loss and answer the question, "What combination of events can lead to a loss of this magnitude?" Reverse stress tests are typically conducted with respect to the firm's solvency ratio. The more realistic the scenarios seem, the more thinly capitalized the firm is intuitively. Similar approaches can be applied to VaR measures, AEP* and other risk measures based on confidence intervals and affected simultaneously by multiple sources of risk.	movements, lapses, etc. from the Monte Carlo scenarios around the regulatory solvency confidence interval. Single events (e.g., equity market crash, interest rate decline, natural catastrophe, etc.) which would cause the predefined loss threshold. Combined events, with the same frequency of occurrence, which would cause the predefined loss threshold.

* Aggregate Exceedance Probability (AEP), a measure of the annual aggregate expected losses from natural catastrophes within a specified return period.

Responding to Active Versus Passive Limit Breaches

There are two types of limit breach, active and passive.

Active Limit Breaches

An *active limit breach* occurs *when a limit is exceeded because of a conscious decision*. In general, *active limit breaches should **not** be tolerated*, triggering disciplinary action: if the limit is in place, it needs to be respected. The reasons are intuitive.

- First, under an intelligent design of the limit framework, escalation and exception approval processes should be in place so there is no reason for a trader or underwriter to actively breach their limit without prior discussion and approval. If an exception request is approved too often then either the limits need to be redefined to align it with the institution's revealed risk appetite or to align behavior with its explicitly defined appetite. One or the other needs to take place, but not active limit breaches.
- More important is the signal that an un-reprimanded active limit breach sends to the organization. It is like a child or pet running rampant and uncontrolled in a public space with the parent "tsk-tsking" but smiling complacently and taking no corrective action; the parent is reinforcing disruptive behavior, which may prove to be a liability at some time. Risk-taking organizations also need well-defined boundaries in order to ensure a mature risk culture.

Depending on the culture of the organization, punitive action may include a reprimand from the boss's boss's boss, a direct hit to the bonus, a formal note to the employee's file, notification of audit/compliance or more formal action.

Passive Limit Breaches

Most breaches are passive limit breaches, which are not consciously triggered but are triggered by external risk events. Passive limit breaches can occur for the following reasons.

- An event is so large that it falls outside the boundary assumed by the limit. For example, VaR is based on a confidence interval; unfortunately, there is no guarantee that more extreme events will not occur, causing a loss in excess of the VaR limit.
- Some limits assume that management will take action, which may not be possible in an extreme event. For example, *stop loss limits* require management to close positions after a certain loss threshold has been breached. In addition to raising the question of time consistency (e.g., will management actually follow through and reduce the positions when the event occurs?), there is no guarantee that actual losses will not be larger than those specified by the stop loss or that the positions can in fact be unwound in a volatile market following an extreme event.
- Some limits will be exceeded by market movements without generating a loss. Consider a highly convex trading position which is delta hedged. A large market movement may increase the position's delta, causing a passive delta limit breach, with either a gain or a loss on the position.

The response to passive limit breaches is different, due to the fact that they are by definition caused by events outside management's control.

- Before such events occur, the risk function needs to clearly manage the expectations of the Board that losses in excess of the limit are possible and outline the situations when they may occur.
- Following a significant breach or a repeating series of breaches, the risk function should review the appropriateness of the limit framework.
- In addition, limit utilization may be expressed as "Red, Amber, Green" (RAG). Limits should not be expressed in a binary fashion – for example, you are either below it (the "green" zone) or above it (the "red" zone). Analogous to a traffic light, define a middle or "amber" zone as a buffer within which management discussions can take place.

RAG limit frameworks improve the frequency and quality of dialog between decision-making levels and also lower the frequency of observing passive "red" limit breaches.

FINAL THOUGHTS ON RISK AND LIMIT REPORTING

A common theme is that information by itself is necessary but not sufficient; more important for creating value is taking the right decisions and executing them effectively. It is especially easy to forget this fact in the areas of risk reporting and limit controlling, both of which focus a lot of effort on providing the necessary information. This chapter concludes by making explicit some of the principles which have been implicit in the discussion so far.

Integrate the reports and limits into the decision processes. Many times I have seen risk functions produce volumes of reports and send them into the ether with only limited follow-up.

Information by itself will not drive behavior. It is better to champion and answer the one important question right than produce a hundred pages that can answer all the wrong questions and fall on deaf ears.

Similarly, I have also spent hours in Risk Committees, reverentially going through each and every page of a report when real business issues might have been discussed. Don't make the discussion of the reports an obligation; if there is nothing important to be discussed, take note of the report and move on to the issues which require discussion.

Bring the important messages to the fore. "Zahlungsfriedhof" is a German phrase which translates as "numbers graveyard" and can be used for many risk reports. Do not assume that issues will emerge in a transparent and compelling manner from the wealth of numbers, tables, pie charts and heat maps that are produced.

There are two different communication approaches: deductive (building to the conclusion, step-by-step) and inductive (asserting the conclusion and backing it up with analysis as required). Technical specialists prefer deductive reasoning and therefore present information that way. However, an inductive communication style forces us to think through what the important messages are and how to address them, shortcutting the process for messages which are already accepted. I prefer an inductive communication style.

Simple tricks can be used to lead to an inductive communication style, for example, always include a Management Discussion & Assessment (MD&A) section upfront. Importantly, understand that an MD&A is not a movement analysis! A colleague once told me that you do not describe the temperature of the water to a drowning man; instead, you help him. Instead of describing the numbers in the MD&A, we should provide an interpretation and recommendations leading to impact.

Do not change the format or measurement approaches too frequently. It takes time and practice to understand which questions are answered by which graph and how to interpret the information. Changing the format and measures will cause confusion and, in the worst case, cause management to give up completely.

Align the reporting and limit framework with the business and its strategies. If you expect the front office to take ownership and use the numbers, then they have to represent the business "through their eyes."

Use a reporting "pyramid structure" to present the information and structure the reports at different levels of management. Start top-down with measures such as VaR and visual communication devices such as heat maps to present the aggregated view. Present details in later chapters or in appendices so that you have the information available if needed. Similarly, the Supervisory Board report is a synthesis of the Management Board report, which is a synthesis of the more detailed management reports.

Produce the reports efficiently, freeing up valuable resources to actually manage risks and interact with the business. Produce the main body of the reports through automated, batch-reporting processes, separating the analysis and commentary into a section upfront or memorandum format. Some firms employ legions of people in PowerPoint production departments to translate the information into horizontal exhibits "digestible" by senior management, often reaching mid-double-digit versions before the "storyline" is perfect. In my experience, iterating on the action titles of PowerPoint slides each and every reporting period diverts resources away from analysis and recommendations; resources better invested in risk analysis than report formatting.

Market Multiple Approaches

I t has been argued that using market multiple valuation approaches to set strategy and manage a business is fundamentally flawed as they fail to explicitly recognize the unique role that risk and capital play in risk-based, capital-intensive businesses. Nonetheless, as discussed in Chapter 5, market multiple approaches are very useful in triangulating internal valuations. This appendix outlines the generic steps to valuing businesses using a market multiple approach.

STEP 1: DEFINE THE PEER GROUP FOR COMPARISON

Select companies which have similar businesses as your own. Select enough comparables for the results to be robust, preventing individual, firm-specific valuation issues from dominating the analysis.

Get a balance between diversified, global peers as well as more focused competitors, since the latter will both sharpen the estimated sectoral multiples and give an indication of valuations without a "conglomerate discount." As an example, Table A.1 lists some diversified peers as well as more focused competitors.

Finally, eliminate those firms from the list which may be strongly influenced by idiosyncratic events. For example, firms such as AIG, ING, Royal Bank of Scotland and Citigroup, amongst others, may not be representative due to the government support they received in 2008, the volatility of large write-downs or the prospect of further losses and potential future lawsuits, etc.

STEP 2: ESTIMATE SECTORAL MULTIPLES

Estimate sector-specific valuation multiples using ordinary regression techniques based on the following equations.

EQUATION A.1 Estimation of sector valuation multiples

$$\frac{P}{E_{i,t}} = \sum_{j} \left(\varphi \frac{P}{E_j} \right) * \frac{E_{i,j,t}}{E_{i,t}} + \varepsilon_{i,t}$$

$$\frac{M}{B_{i,t}} = \sum_{j} \left(\varphi \frac{M}{B_j} \right) * \frac{B_{i,j,t}}{B_{i,t}} + \varepsilon_{i,t}$$

TABLE A.1 Example comparables list

	Insurers	**Banks**
Global generalists	Aegon	Bank of America
	AIG	Barclays Bank
	Allianz	BNP Paribas
	Aviva	Citigroup
	Axa	Credit Suisse
	Generali	Crédit Agricole
	Zurich Financial Services	Deutsche Bank
		JP Morgan
		Royal Bank of Scotland
		Banco Santander
		Union Bank of Switzerland
Specialists and local players	ACE – Commercial	Bank Julius Baer – Private banking
	Manulife – Life	Goldman Sachs – Investment banking
	MetLife – Life	HSBC – Growth markets
	Munich Re – Commercial, reinsurance	LGT Bank – Private banking
	Ping An – Life, growth markets	Morgan Stanley – Investment banking
	Prudential UK – Life, growth markets	Standard Chartered – Growth markets
	Prudential US – Life US	Bank of New York – Custody, investment services
	Swiss Re – Commercial, reinsurance	State Street – Custody, investment services
	Travelers Insurance – Commercial US	Northern Trust – Custody, investment services
	XL Capital – Commercial	

where i indicates the ith comparable firm, j indicates the jth segment, t indicates time, $\left(\varphi_{Ej}^{P}, \varphi_{Bj}^{M} \right)$ are the regression coefficients representing the jth sector's specific valuation multiple and $\left(\frac{E_{i,j,t}}{E_{i,t}}, \frac{B_{i,j,t}}{B_{i,t}} \right)$ are the relative contributions of sector j's earnings or book value to the total forecasted earnings or book value of firm i at time t.

You will need to collect time series, cross-sectional information with sufficient observations to estimate the sectoral multiples robustly. Extending the time series to include previous years may give a sense of the steady-state relationships but will also expose the analysis to systematic or market-related changes in multiples.

STEP 3: CALCULATE THE IMPLIED SUM-OF-PARTS VALUATION USING THE FOLLOWING FORMULAE

EQUATION A.2 Using market multiples to value your firm

$$V = \sum_{j} \left(\varphi \frac{P}{E_j} \right) * E_j^{Est}$$

$$V = \sum_{j} \left(\varphi \frac{M}{B_j} \right) * B_j^{Est}$$

where V is the sum-of-parts value of the firm and E_j^{Est}, B_j^{Est} are the forecasted earnings and adjusted book values for segment j.

Gain additional insights by looking at the ratio of implied sum-of-parts valuation to actual market capitalization as well as comparing the individual segment valuations against those implied for peers, identifying and explaining any outliers.

Derivation of Steady-State Valuation Multiples

hree different theoretical steady state valuation approaches are discussed in Chapter 5. This appendix provides a concise derivation and discussion of the three, e.g., the accounting approach, the discounted free cash flow approach and the market consistent approach.

THE ACCOUNTING APPROACH

The most common steady state valuation formula originates in the accounting literature, often called the residual income or Edwards–Bell–Ohlson (EBO) approach.[1] This approach expresses the steady-state value of a firm in terms of accounting earnings and the book value of equity directly. Its starting point is the Dividend Discount Model (DDM).

The DDM assumes that the value of the firm to shareholders is equal to the sum of the discounted expected dividends the firm will generate for shareholders in the future.

EQUATION B.1 Dividend discount model

$$V_0 = D_0 + \frac{\hat{D}_1}{(1 + \mathrm{CoC})} + \frac{\hat{D}_2}{(1 + \mathrm{CoC})^2} + \frac{\hat{D}_3}{(1 + \mathrm{CoC})^3} + \cdots$$

where V_0 is the current market value of equity (or market capitalization) of the firm, $\hat{D}_t$ is the expected dividend to be received at time t and CoC is the firm's cost of capital, assumed constant.

The EBO is a transformation of the DDM requiring that all balance sheet changes first flow through earnings. In this case, the book value of the firm evolves according to the following formula: $B_{t+1} - B_t = E_{t+1} - D_{t+1}$. Making the appropriate substitutions:[2]

$$V_0 = B_0 + \frac{\hat{E}_1 - \mathrm{CoC}^* B_0}{(1 + \mathrm{CoC})} + \frac{\hat{E}_2 - \mathrm{CoC}^* \hat{B}_1}{(1 + \mathrm{CoC})^2} + \frac{\hat{E}_3 - \mathrm{CoC}^* \hat{B}_2}{(1 + \mathrm{CoC})^3} + \cdots$$

---

[1] See Edwards and Bell (1961), Ohlson (1995), Lee *et al.* (1999), Gebhardt *et al.* (1999), Claus and Thomas (2001). A prerequisite for this approach is that all changes to the balance sheet must flow through the income statement, something which is violated in practice (e.g., for "available for sale" assets which impact shareholders' equity through OCI).

[2] Note, without loss of generality, we have also assumed that $D_0 = 0$.

where $\hat{B}_t$ is the expected book equity at the end of year t and $\hat{E}_t$ is the expected after-tax earnings in year t. This equation should be intuitive: it expresses the value of the firm as the sum of its current book value and the flow of expected future excess returns that it is expected to generate.

Defining return on equity[3] as $\mathrm{RoE}_t = E_t/B_{t-1}$ and rearranging, the expected future excess returns can be rewritten as $B_{t-1}(\mathrm{RoE}_t - \mathrm{CoC})$. Upon substitution and rearranging, we get:

$$V_0 = B_0 + \frac{B_0(\mathrm{RoE}_1 - \mathrm{CoC})}{(1 + \mathrm{CoC})} + \frac{\hat{B}_1(\mathrm{RoE}_2 - \mathrm{CoC})}{(1 + \mathrm{CoC})^2} + \frac{\hat{B}_2(\mathrm{RoE}_3 - \mathrm{CoC})}{(1 + \mathrm{CoC})^3} + \cdots$$

Expressing dividends as a percentage of earnings, book equity evolves according to the following difference equation:

$$B_t = B_{t-1} + E_t(1 - d)$$
$$B_t = B_{t-1}{}^*(1 + \mathrm{RoE}_t{}^*(1 - d))$$

where d is the dividend pay-out ratio. Upon substitution and rearranging terms, this leads to the following representation for the value of the firm:

$$V_0 = B_0 + B_0 \sum_{t=1}^{\infty} \left[\prod_{s=1}^{t-1}(1 + \mathrm{RoE}_s(1 - d)) \right] \frac{\mathrm{RoE}_t - \mathrm{CoC}}{(1 + \mathrm{CoC})^t}$$

This complicated formula reduces to a more manageable form under steady-state assumptions – for example, assume that $\mathrm{RoE}_t = \mathrm{RoE}$ for all t, and a constant expected rate of growth financed through retained earnings net of dividends (e.g., $g = \mathrm{RoE}^*(1 - d)$). Substituting, we get the following expression for the M/B multiple[4] of a firm expressed in terms of steady-state returns and growth.

EQUATION B.2 EBO steady-state M/B multiple

$$\frac{V_0}{B_0} = 1 + \frac{(\mathrm{RoE} - \mathrm{CoC})}{(\mathrm{CoC} - g)}$$

where V/B represents the firm's theoretical steady-state M/B multiple. Oftentimes, the term $(\mathrm{RoE}-\mathrm{CoC})^*B$ is called economic profit; it is interpreted as the net value creation above and beyond the firm's cost of capital. The term $(\mathrm{RoE}-\mathrm{CoC})/(\mathrm{CoC}-g)$ is the formula for the discounted present value of a growing perpetuity which promises to pay the holder (in this case, the shareholder) a growing amount of excess returns equal to $(\mathrm{RoE} - \mathrm{CoC})^*(1 + g)^t$ at time t where CoC is the discount rate.

The interpretation of the steady-state M/B multiple is straightforward: the value of the company only exceeds its book value if it creates returns in excess of its cost of capital (e.g.,

---

[3]Defining RoE in terms of the ratio of current-year earnings to previous-period or "inherited" book equity is slightly at odds with conventional practice in banking, which is to use current average-in-year equity. However, this is essentially definitional and the measure employed here is more tractable in the context of the multi-period discrete-time model with which we are working.

[4]In order for the infinite series to be defined, we need that the growth rate, g, be less than the cost of capital: $g = \mathrm{RoE}^*(1-d) < \mathrm{CoC}$.

only if RoE−CoC > 0). It gets an even higher multiple if it can grow the business at the same level of excess returns.

Similarly, a steady-state P/E multiple can be derived. Using the definition that $E_t = B_{t-1}{}^*\text{RoE}_t$ or, in a steady state, $E = B^*\text{RoE}$ and substituting into the equation, we get an expression for the firm's price/earnings ratio.

EQUATION B.3   EBO steady-state P/E multiple

$$\frac{V_0}{E_0} = \frac{V_0}{\text{RoE}^*E_0} = \frac{1}{\text{RoE}}\left(1 + \frac{\text{RoE} - \text{CoC}}{\text{CoC} - g}\right) = \frac{d}{\text{CoC} - g}$$

where we have used the fact that $g = \text{RoE}(1 - d)$. The interpretation of the steady-state P/E multiple is also straightforward: the value of the firm is related to the growing stream of cash dividends thrown off by the business. The higher the dividend rate and the higher the growth rate, the higher the earnings valuation multiple.

Although the derivation is intuitive to follow, there are three challenges to applying this approach in practice. The first is the necessary condition that accounting balance sheet changes are reflected in earnings (and vice versa), which is not often met by many accounting systems. The classic example is OCI, a balance sheet line item used to capture market value changes which do not flow through the income statement.

The second is that it is difficult (if not impossible!) to calculate the current value of a portfolio of assets and liabilities by using a single cost of capital to discount the net expected cash flows. It is challenging enough to value a single derivative in a bank trading book or a single variable annuity insurance policy; assuming that this valuation becomes easier or more accurate if one tosses a wide variety of transactions into a common pot and then discounts the net expected cash flows emerging from the pot with a single discount rate is a tremendous leap of faith. In fact, as discussed in Chapter 7 in the context of the insurer's market Consistent Embedded Value, there will in general only be one unique discount rate which gives the actual market value of the portfolio and this unique discount rate needs to be determined by back-solving, starting from the actual market value of the portfolio.

Third, it is complicated by the fact that there are a multitude of different local accounting regimes, making it virtually impossible to get consistent figures without translating to another, consistent basis beforehand.

THE DISCOUNTED FREE CASH FLOW ENTITY APPROACH

The Discounted Free Cash Flow (DFCF) approach also yields a comparable steady-state valuation formula and is the more prevalent approach for valuing *industrial* corporations. There are two reasons why the DFCF approach is more often used for industrial corporations.

The first is that the necessary condition for the EBO approach is violated in practice – that is, that all changes to the balance sheet are reflected through earnings (and vice versa). This condition is required to express the evolution of book equity as $B_{t+1} - B_t = E_{t+1} - D_{t+1}$. The DFCF approach solves this issue by redefining both earnings and the balance sheet so that they are consistent, focusing on actual cash flows instead of accounting variables.

The second reason is the mantra "Cash is King"[5] – a simple way of saying that following cash is more likely to lead to better valuations and decisions than following accounting

---

[5]"Cash is King" is the title of a chapter in Copeland *et al.* (2000).

earnings. Copeland *et al.* (2000) comments that accounting earnings are useful for valuation ". . . only when earnings are a good proxy for the expected long-term cash flow of the company. Not all companies generate the same cash flow for each dollar of earnings . . . The DCF approach captures all the elements that affect the value of the company in a comprehensive yet straightforward manner."

The remainder of this section summarizes the adjustments to accounting earnings made in the DFCF approach. Readers interested in a more thorough treatment of the valuation of industrial corporations should turn to Stewart (1991), Copeland *et al.* (2000), Rappaport (1998).

Using the notation in Copeland (2000), the Intrinsic Value (IV) of the firm – interpreted as the value which can be split between the equity and debt financiers of the firm – is represented by the discounted distributable free cash flows of the firm before interest expenses.

EQUATION B.4   DFCF intrinsic value

$$IV_0 = FCF_0 + \frac{FCF_1}{(1 + WACC)^t} + \frac{FCF_2}{(1 + WACC)^2} \cdots$$

where FCF_t represents the distributable free cash flow to the financiers of the firm,[6] including both equity and debt holders, at time t and WACC is the after-tax weighted average cost of capital for financing the business. In general, changing the debt/equity ratio will not affect the free cash flows generated by the operating assets of an industrial corporation and will only influence the WACC. However, this will generally not be the case for a bank or insurer which also creates value through deposits and insurance liabilities.

Defining NOPLAT as the net cash operating profit (excluding non-cash items and debt servicing charges) less adjusted taxes, IC_t as the invested capital at time t and $ROIC_t$ as the return on invested capital (e.g., NOPLAT/IC), and ensuring that the system is "closed" (e.g., all cash flows are accounted for and IC evolves according to the following formula: $IC_{t+1} - IC_t = NOPLAT_{t+1} - FCF_{t+1}$), then the identical substitutions used to generate the EBO valuation formula can be used to generate the DFCF formula given below.

EQUATION B.5   DFCF M/B ratio

$$\frac{IV}{IC} = 1 + \frac{(ROIC - WACC)}{(WACC - g)}$$

This steady-state valuation formula is similar to the EBO M/B ratio derived in the last section and is interpreted in a similar manner. The differences are due to the change in basis, from accounting to cash: book equity (*E*) is replaced by invested capital representing the

---

[6]This approach is sometimes called an *entity* valuation approach because it values the distributable free cash flows to the financiers, both debt and equity, of the firm's operating assets. It therefore focuses on earnings before interest expenses and uses a weighted average cost of capital reflecting the cost (and benefits) of both debt and equity funding. It differs from an *equity* valuation approach which focuses on cash flow that can be distributed to shareholders, net of debt servicing costs and discounting using a cost of equity. It is commonly held that an entity approach is more appropriate for valuing industrial corporations as it helps to separate operating from financing decisions.

TABLE B.1 DFCF valuation metrics

Metric	EP	TVA	IV
Acronym	Economic Profit, also known as Annual Value Added (AVA) or Economic Value Added (EVA^{TM}).	Total Value Added, also known as Shareholder Value Added (SVA^{TM}).	Intrinsic Value, also known as Intrinsic Shareholder Value.
Description	The annual amount of value being added by the business or activity in excess of its cost of capital.	The present value of all future expected economic profits from the business or activity.	The theoretical value of the business or activity.
Formula	EP = IC*(ROIC−WACC)	TVA $= \sum_{t=1} EP_t /$ $(1 + WACC_t)_t$	IV = TVA + adjusted invested equity.
Use	Used for determining current-year contribution.	Used for strategic planning and business evaluation purposes.	Used for corporate finance decisions.

tangible, cash value invested in the firm (IV), return on equity (RoE) is replaced by return on invested capital (ROIC) and the cost of capital (CoC) is replaced by the weighted average cost of capital (WACC).

The corporate finance literature uses a variety of different terms, such as economic profit, total value added and intrinsic value. Table B.1 puts ROIC, economic profit, total value added and intrinsic value into context.

THE MARKET-CONSISTENT VALUATION APPROACH

A third valuation approach is the market-consistent value approach. Similar to the EBO accounting approach, it values distributable free cash flows to shareholders only and is therefore also an equity approach as opposed to an entity approach. However, like the entity DFCF approach, the market value approach uses a different "accounting" basis for earnings and equity in order to ensure that the evolution of "equity" is consistent with the current market values of assets and liabilities.

If the mantra of the DFCF approach is "Cash is King!" then the mantra of the market value approach is "Market Values are King!" To see the difference, consider that the DFCF approach values a portfolio of bonds, derivatives and insurance policies by using one unique risk-adjusted cost of capital to discount the future net expected distributable free cash flows from all positions. If the DFCF approach is to give the correct current value of a traded bond, equity or derivative, then the unique discount rate would have to change every time the portfolio or current market rates change.

In contrast, the market value approach values each individual instrument separately, implying that each bond or derivative is valued consistent with their current market value. As it turns out, this is a tremendous advantage for valuing financial services firms given the complexity of the financial instruments they sell.

In the market value approach, earnings are redefined as Market Value Earnings (MVE) including the realized and unrealized gains and losses on existing positions as well as the

TABLE B.2 Change in accounting basis underlying different valuation approaches

	Accounting approach	DFCF approach – entity approach	Market value approach
Description	Focus on dividend distribution to shareholders, funded out of accounting earnings. Discounted using the cost of equity. Track accounting earnings and book equity.	Focus on cash distributable to financiers of the firm, including shareholders and debt holders. Discounted using the weighted average cost of capital, including debt and equity. Adjust accounting earnings to reflect operating cash flows, independent of financing decisions.	Focus on dividend distribution to shareholders, which can be funded out of operating profit or net asset value. Discounted using the cost of equity. Track mark-to-market earnings and market value balance sheet.
Distribution basis to shareholders	D = Dividends to shareholders.	FCF = Free cash flow to financiers.	D = Dividends to shareholders.
"Earnings" basis	E = Accounting earnings.	NOPLAT = Net operating income less adjusted taxes.	MVE = Market value earnings, including value of new business + realized and unrealized gains/losses.
"Balance sheet" basis	B = Book equity.	IC = Invested capital (in operating assets).	MVS = Market value surplus.
"Balance sheet" evolution	$B_{t+1} - B_t = E_{t+1} - D_{t+1}$	$IC_{t+1} - IC_t = NOPLAT_{t+1} - FCF_{t+1}$	$MVS_{t+1} - MVS_t = MVE_{t+1} - D_{t+1}$
Cost of capital	CoC = Cost of equity capital.	WACC = Weighted average cost of capital, including leverage.	CoC = Cost of equity capital.
Steady-state valuation equation	$\dfrac{V}{B} = 1 + \dfrac{RoE - CoC}{CoC - g}$	$\dfrac{IV}{IC} = 1 + \dfrac{(ROIC - WACC)}{(WACC - g)}$	$\dfrac{IV}{MVS} = 1 + \dfrac{(RoEC - CoC)}{(CoC - g)}$

market value of new business at inception. In addition, book equity is replaced by the Market Value Surplus (MVS), or the difference between the Market Value of Assets (MVA) and the Market Value of Liabilities (MVL) (e.g., MVS = MVA − MVS). Finally, returns are also defined on a market value basis, leading to RoMVS = MVE/MVS.

Beginning with the DDM, substituting these definitions and rearranging, we get the following steady-state valuation formula.

EQUATION B.6   MV M/B PE ratios

$$\frac{V}{\text{MVS}} = 1 + \frac{(\text{RoMVS} - \text{CoC})}{(\text{CoC} - g)} \quad \text{and} \quad \frac{P}{\text{MVE}} = \frac{d}{\text{CoC} - g}$$

A BRIEF DIGRESSION ON CHANGING THE ACCOUNTING BASIS

The EBO approach depended upon several key elements: first, that the balance sheet evolves according to a closed system relating earnings, dividends and the evolution of book equity; second, that cash dividends can be expressed as a percentage of accounting earnings; third, that all growth is internally funded by retained earnings. The DFCF and market value approaches follow similarly after a change in accounting basis (e.g., following the definition of internally consistent measures of earnings, returns, invested capital and risk-adjusted discount rates). Table B.2 provides an overview of this change in accounting basis.

In theory, the EBO, DFCF and market value approaches should yield the same valuation if applied "correctly." The question is which approach is easier and more accurate to apply for a financial services firm in practice? For the reasons outlined in Chapter 5, I believe that the market value approach is superior for the valuation of banks and insurers.

Valuing Banks and Insurers: The Link Between Value and New Business and Investment RAPM

Chapter 5 asserts that RAPMs provide a clear link between risk, capital and the value of the firm. This appendix provides simple examples linking the market valuation formulae developed in the previous appendix to the New Business and Investment RAPMs defined in Chapter 3, using notation specific to the banking and insurance segments.

VALUATION OF INSURERS

In this section, we demonstrate the link between the market-consistent valuation framework and the New Business and Investment RAPMs specific to the PC and LH insurance businesses.

Period Earnings

Without loss of generality, imagine a world with no taxes and all insurance contracts settled within the period that they are contracted: insurance premiums (P) are collected immediately at the start of the period and are invested as reserves to cover claims (C) and expenses (E) which are paid at the end of the period.

The premium is assumed to be invested to perfectly match the claim's best-estimate financial cash flow profile: zero-coupon cash flows are held against PC best-estimate claims and LH policy financial claims are similarly matched using a combination of financial market instruments, potentially including derivatives, so as to replicate the liability's cash flows and embedded options and guarantees in every state of the world.

The company enters the period with their Market Value Surplus (MVS) representing the net shareholder value in the balance sheet. The MVS is conceptually split between the Required Capital (RC) to cover unexpected claims and expense developments during the period and Excess Capital (EC) which represents additional assets held by the company in excess of those needed to cover underwriting or non-tradable risks. Without loss of generality, it is assumed that the RC required to support insurance risks is invested in risk-free assets but that the EC can be invested in risky assets; however, the EC must be sufficient to cover the financial market risk from the surplus

TABLE C.1 MVE for insurers

MVE = Market value earnings during the period	Earnings from insurance underwriting operations	Investment earnings on market value surplus
	$P(1 + r_f) - C - E$	r_{mvs} MVS
	P = Premium collected, beginning of period.	MVS = Market value surplus.
	r_f = Risk-free return on assets held as reserves funded from premiums.	MVS = RC + EC
		RC = Required economic capital to support underwriting activities, assumed to be invested in risk-free assets.
	C = Claims paid, end of period.	EC = Excess capital, defined as market value which is surplus to underwriting RC requirements. This value can potentially be invested in financial market risky assets but it is assumed that the risk-based solvency and leverage constraints are satisfied during each period.
	E = Expenses paid, end of period	
		r_{mvs} = Return on market value surplus, r_{mvs} = r_f(RC/MVS) + r_s(EC/MVS).
		r_s = Return on assets backing excess capital which is net of investment costs.
		r_f = Risk-free return on assets backing required capital to support the underwriting business.

assets as well as any asset/liability mismatch risk. These definitions and notation can be found in Table C.1. All these assumptions can be relaxed, but doing so complicates the exposition and notation without adding any further insights.

For this stylized example, the Market Value Earnings (MVE) and the Return on MVS (RoMVS) would be given by the following formula.

EQUATION C.1 Insurance MVE and RoMVS

$$MVE = [P(1 + r_f) - C - E] + r_f RC + r_s EC = [P(1 + r_f) - C - E] + r_{mvs} MVS$$

$$RoMVS = \frac{[P(1 + r_f) - C - E]}{MVS} + r_{mvs}$$

where I have suppressed the time subscript.

The market value surplus of the insurance firm develops according to the following equation.

EQUATION C.2 Insurance MVS development

$$MVS_t = MVE_t + MVS_{t-1} - D_t$$

$$MVS_t = [P(1 + r_f) - C - E] + (1 + r_{mvs})MVS_{t-1} - D_t$$

where D is the dividend payment.

From Earnings to Value

The next step is to go from period earnings to the value of the company. In order to do that, substitute the definition of earnings in the same manner used to derive the EBO valuation formula. The steady-state valuation equation for an insurance company in this fictitious world is given by the following.

EQUATION C.3 Insurance steady-state valuation

$$V = \text{MVS} + \text{MVS}\frac{[\text{RoMVS} - \text{CoC}]}{\text{CoC} \quad g}$$

$$V = \text{MVS} + \frac{[[P(1 + r_f) - C - E] + r_{mvs}\text{MVS} - \text{MVSCoC}]}{\text{CoC} - g}$$

Where PC.EP and LH.EP represent the PC and LH New Business Economic Profit and Investment.EP represents the Investment Economic Profit defined in Chapter 3. This can be simplified by recognizing that the cost of capital for the firm is the weighted average of the cost of capital to support the underwriting activities (CoC_{uw}) and the cost of capital to support the additional financial market risks assumed in the investment of excess capital (CoC_s), if any.

EQUATION C.4 Insurance cost of capital

$$\text{CoC} = \text{CoC}_{uw}\frac{\text{RC}}{\text{RC} + \text{EC}} + \text{CoC}_s\frac{\text{EC}}{\text{RC} + \text{EC}}$$
$$\text{CoC}_{uw} = r_f + rp_{uw}$$
$$\text{CoC}_s = r_{bm} = r_f + \beta_s(r_m - r_f)$$
$$r_s = \alpha + r_{bm} = \alpha + r_f + \beta_s(r_m - r_f)$$

where CoC_{uw} is the cost of underwriting capital, r_f is the risk-free rate of return and rp_{uw} is the additional return over the risk-free rate of return to compensate for underwriting risks. CoC_s is the return on the risk-appropriate benchmark portfolio (r_{bm}) representing the firm's financial mismatch position. In a CAPM world, $r_{bm} = r_f + \beta_s R_p$ and $r_s = \alpha + r_{bm}$, where α represents any excess returns above the risk-appropriate benchmark portfolio. Using these definitions, substituting in the definition of MVS and return on MVS (r_{mvs}) and rearranging, we get the following.

EQUATION C.5 Insurance steady-state valuation

$$V = \text{MVS} + \frac{[[P(1 + r_f) - C - E] + (r_f - \text{CoC}_{uw})\text{RC} + (r_s - \text{CoC}_s)\text{EC}]}{\text{CoC} - g}$$

For PC insurance, this reduces to

$$\text{PC}|V = \text{MVS} + \frac{[P[(1 + r_f) - \text{CR}] - rp_{uw}\text{RC} + \alpha\text{EC}]}{\text{CoC} - g}$$

$$\text{PC}|V = \text{MVS} + \frac{[\text{PC.EP} + \text{Investment.EP}]}{\text{CoC} - g}$$

For LH insurers, this reduces to

$$\text{LH}|\,V = \text{MVS} + \frac{[P^*\text{NBM} + \alpha\text{EC}]}{\text{CoC} - g}$$

$$\text{LH}|V = \text{MVS} + \frac{[\text{LH.EP} + \text{Investment.EP}]}{\text{CoC} - g}$$

Explanation of PC Valuation Formula

The equation for property and casualty products uses the definition of the Combined Ratio ($\text{CR} = (C + E)/P$) as the sum of the claims or Loss Ratio ($\text{LR} = C/P$) and the Expense Ratio ($\text{ER} = E/P$).

By definition, in this simplified world the term $P\big[(1 + r_f) - \text{CR}\big] - rp_{uw}\text{RC}$ is equal to the PC new business economic profit (PC.EP) and the term αEC is equal to the Investment Economic Profit defined earlier in Chapter 3.

Explanation of LH Valuation Formula

The equation for life products is derived by substituting the definition of new business margin, suitably adapted to this simplistic, single-period model. More specifically, VNB is defined as the present value of new business after all expenses and cost of risk and NBM as the VNB divided by premium:[1]

$$\text{VNB} = \big[P(1 + r_f) - C - E\big] - rp_{uw}\text{RC}$$

$$\text{NBM} = \frac{\text{VNB}}{P} = \left[(1 + r_f) - \frac{C}{P} - \frac{E}{P}\right] - rp_{uw}\frac{\text{RC}}{P}$$

Substitution gives the equation for LH products. Using the notation from Chapter 3, we can also rewrite $P^*\text{NBM} = \text{LH.EP}$ and $\alpha\text{EC} = \text{Investment.EP}$, respectively.

The Implied Rate of Return on the Economic Surplus

Focusing on the return to economic surplus, if the liability cash flows are completely matched and no financial risk is taken in the economic surplus, then $r_s = r_f$. If there is some financial risk taken in the economic surplus (e.g., either because of an asset/liability mismatch or through investment risk from assets in excess of RC), then $r_s = \alpha + r_{bm}$, where r_{bm} stands for the appropriate benchmark portfolio returns for the investment of the economic surplus and α represents any excess returns above the appropriate benchmark portfolio. If the CAPM assumptions hold true, then $r_s = \alpha + r_f + \beta_s(r_m - r_f)$.

Interpreting the Valuation Equations

Inspection of the valuation formulae leads to the conclusion that an insurer can create value from three primary sources.

---

[1] Note that the VNB and NBM defined here differ from the definitions in the CFO Forum MCEV Principles (2009), in two important respects: they do not include a frictional cost of capital term (defined as CReC in the CFO Forum Principles), nor does it include an illiquidity premium or other non-economic distortion to the valuation of new business. Both are discussed in Chapter 7. A third, less critical difference is that this formula does not include taxes.

- First, from earning excess risk-adjusted operating profits through superior technical underwriting and expense management capabilities:
  - for PC companies, if the technical new business economic profit PC.EP $= P[(1 + r_f) - \text{CR}] - rp_{uw}\text{RC} \geq 0$;
  - for LH companies, if the technical new business economic profit LH.EP $= P^*\text{NBM} \geq 0$ (where NBM is calculated without economic distortions).
- Second, from earning "alpha" or excess investment returns on the asset/liability mismatch and investment risk on assets backing capital, e.g. if $\alpha = r_s - r_{bm} \geq 0$ or, in a CAPM world, $\alpha = r_s - \left(r_f + \beta_s(r_m - r_f)\right) \geq 0$.
- Third, through profitable growth (g), assuming that the company is generating returns in excess of its cost of capital in the first place.

VALUATION OF BANKS

In this section, we demonstrate the link between the market-consistent valuation framework and the New Business and Investment RAPMs using notation specific to banking and focusing on loans and deposits as well as the asset/liability management activities needed to support them.

Period Earnings

Without loss of generality, imagine a world where there are no taxes and all banking products settle within the period that they are originated: deposits are collected and loans granted at the start of the period and repaid (with interest) at the end of the period, subject to any credit losses. We assume that all deposits and loans are matched by risk-free assets (and derivatives, in the case of embedded interest rate-sensitive prepayment/withdrawal options) based on the Funds Transfer Pricing (FTP) mechanism, discussed in greater detail in Chapter 17.

The bank enters the period with its Market Value Surplus (MVS) representing the net shareholder value contained in the balance sheet excluding any new business. This value is conceptually split between the Required Capital (RC) to cover unexpected loan losses during the period and the Excess Capital (EC) representing additional assets held by the company for shareholders but which are not needed to cover the underwriting or non-tradable risks.

It is assumed that the required capital is invested in risk-free assets but that the excess capital can be invested in risky assets; as such, any asset/liability mismatch risk is found in the assets representing excess capital. Finally, it is assumed that the excess capital is sufficient to cover any capital requirements arising from the financial market risks assumed, if any. These definitions and notation can be found in Table C.2. All these assumptions can be relaxed, but doing so complicates the exposition and notation without adding any further insights.

For this stylized example, the Market Value Earnings (MVE) and Return on MVS (RoMVS) given by the following formula.[2]

---

[2]Extension to include fee income businesses is straightforward.

TABLE C.2   MVE for banks

MVE = Market value earnings	Return on banking operations	Investment returns on surplus
	$[L(r_l - \text{FTP}_l - llp) + De(\text{FTP}_{de} - r_{de}) + F - E]$	$r_s\text{MVS}$
	NLM = Net expected loan margin.	MVS = Market value surplus.
	NLM = $L(r_l - \text{FTP}_l - llp)$	MVS = RC + EC
	L = Loan volume.	RC = Required capital to support loan
	r_l = Nominal loan return.	underwriting activities, assumed to be
	FTP_l = Funds transfer pricing rate for loans.	invested in risk-free assets.
	llp = Expected loan loss provisions.	EC = Excess capital, potentially
	NDM = Net deposit margin.	invested in financial market risky assets.
	NDM = $De(\text{FTP}_{de} - r_{de})$	r_{mvs} = Return on market value surplus.
	De = Deposit volume.	$r_{mvs} = r_f(\text{RC/MVS}) + r_s(\text{EC/MVS})$
	r_{de} = Return on deposits.	r_s = Return on assets backing excess
	FTP_{de} = Funds transfer pricing rate for deposits.	capital.
	F = Fee income.	r_f = Risk-free return on assets backing
	E = Expenses.	required capital to support the underwriting business.

EQUATION C.6   Insurance MVE and RoMVS

$$\text{MVE} = [L(r_l - \text{FTP}_l - llp) + De(\text{FTP}_{de} - r_{de}) + F - E] + r_s\text{MVS}$$

$$\text{RoMVS} = \frac{[L(r_l - \text{FTP}_l - llp) + De(\text{FTP}_{de} - r_{de}) + F - E]}{\text{MVS}} + r_s$$

where I have suppressed the time subscript.

Substitution into the previous formulae shows that the MVS for banks would develop according to the following.

EQUATION C.7   Bank MVS development

$$\text{MVS}_t = \text{MVE}_t + \text{MVS}_{t-1} - D$$

$$\text{MVS}_t = [L(r_l - \text{FTP}_l - llp) + De(\text{FTP}_{de} - r_{de}) + F - E] + (1 + r_S)\text{MVS}_{t-1} - D$$

where D is the dividend payment.

From Earnings to Value

Substituting these definitions into the market-consistent framework developed earlier and rearranging delivers the following steady-state valuation equation for a bank in this simplified world.

EQUATION C.8 Bank steady-state valuation

$$\frac{V}{MVS} = 1 + \frac{\text{RoMVS} - \text{CoC}}{\text{CoC} - g}$$

$$\frac{V}{MVS} = 1 + \frac{[L(r_l - \text{FTP}_l - llp) + De(\text{FTP}_{de} - r_{de}) + F - E] + r_S MVS - MVS^* \text{CoC}}{\text{CoC} - g}$$

This can be further simplified by recognizing that the cost of capital for the firm (CoC) is the weighted average of the cost of capital to support the underwriting activities (CoC$_{uw}$) and the cost of capital to support the additional financial market risks assumed in the investment of excess capital (CoC$_s$), if any.

EQUATION C.9 Bank cost of capital

$$\text{CoC} = \text{CoC}_{uw} \frac{\text{RC}}{\text{RC} + \text{EC}} + \text{CoC}_s \frac{\text{EC}}{\text{RC} + \text{EC}}$$

$$\text{CoC}_{uw} = r_f + rp_{uw}$$

$$\text{CoC}_s = r_{bm} = r_f + \beta_s (r_m - r_f)$$

$$r_s = \alpha + r_{bm} = \alpha + r_f + \beta_s (r_m - r_f)$$

where CoC$_{uw}$ is the cost of underwriting capital, r_f is the risk-free rate of return and rp_{uw} are the additional returns over the risk-free rate of return to compensate for underwriting risks. CoC$_s$ is the return on the risk-appropriate benchmark portfolio (r_{bm}) representing the firm's financial mismatch position. In a CAPM world, $r_{bm} = r_f + \beta_s R_p$ and $r_s = \alpha + r_{bm}$, where α represents any excess returns above the risk-appropriate benchmark portfolio. Using these definitions, substituting in the definition of MVS and RoMVS (r_{mvs}) and rearranging, we get

EQUATION C.10 Bank steady-state valuation

$$\frac{V}{MVS} = 1 + \frac{[L(r_l - \text{FTP}_l - llp) + De(\text{FTP}_{de} - r_{de}) + F - E] - rp_{uw}\text{RC} + \alpha\text{EC}}{\text{CoC} - g}$$

Using the definitions of loan new business and investment economic profit, e.g. Loan.EP = $[L(r_l - \text{FTP}_l - llp) - E_l] - rp_{uw}\text{RC}$ and Investment.EP = αEC, respectively, and defining economic profit for deposits and fee business analogously, Deposit.EP = $De(\text{FTP}_{de} - r_{de}) + F - E_{de},$[3] we can rewrite the steady-state valuation multiple in the following form:

$$\frac{V}{MVS} = 1 + \frac{\text{Loan.EP} + \text{Deposit.EP} + \text{Investment.EP}}{\text{CoC} - g}$$

where E_l and E_{de} represent the expenses attributable to loans and deposit (+ fee-based) businesses, respectively.

---

[3]This definition assumes that there is no economic capital required for deposit and fee-based businesses. This overly restrictive assumption can easily be relaxed by defining RC for both lending and deposit/fee-based businesses and applying an appropriate cost of capital for the deposit/fee-based businesses.

Interpreting the Results

The term $L(r_l - \text{FTP}_l - llp) + De(\text{FTP}_{de} - r_{de})$ represents the single-period loan and deposit margins measured against the appropriate matched FTP defined in Chapter 17. All contributions to NII from any asset/liability mismatch are subsumed into the investment alpha measured relative to the replicating portfolio. The present value of all future fees and expenses, loan loss provisions and capital would be discounted in a more generalized multi-period model.

There are many different ways to view the sources of value creation. One intuitive way is to divide the sources of contribution between three sources.

- Loan underwriting margins with full cost loadings. This margin can be expressed as Loan.EP = $L(r_l - \text{FTP}_l - llp) - E_l - rp_{uw}\text{RC}_l$, where E_l represents the full expense allocation to the loan product and $rp_{uw}\text{RC}_l$ represents the cost of the required capital above the risk-free return to support the business. This is equivalent to the loan new business economic profit for loans first presented in Chapter 3.
- Branch business contributions from deposits and fee businesses, which can be expressed as Deposit.EP = $De(\text{FTP}_{de} - r_{de}) + F - E_{de}$. Here, E_{de} represents the full cost expense allocation to the deposit and fee-based business.
- Excess returns from treasury's management of asset/liability mismatch and surplus capital, which can be expressed as Investment.EP = αEC.

The bank is clearly creating value if the risk-adjusted contributions from all these activities are positive; at a minimum, the sum of the three has to be positive.

Beyond Debt and Equity

As described in Chapter 19, CFOs and CROs must help their firm choose the right mix of financing on the equity-to-debt continuum, beginning with shareholders' invested funds and continuing on through hybrid, subordinated, senior and collateralized funding, ultimately reaching client-based funding alternatives such as bank deposits or insurance reserves.

Each of these alternatives offers advantages and disadvantages, illustrated by the following important questions.

- To what extent does the alternative *qualify as a substitute for shareholder capital under regulatory and rating agency solvency regimes*? Related to this, to what extent are *external limitations* put on the use of different funding alternatives?
- What is the *all-in after-tax cost of funding* for the different alternatives, including interest and tax considerations, structuring and credit-enhancement expenses and, especially for securitized financing alternatives, additional effects in the form of reducing risk capital requirements and the ability to increase volumes by relaxing other leverage restrictions.
- Finally, how *sustainable is the source of funding* under different scenarios, for example a crisis in confidence or "run on the bank," a shock to inter-bank funding liquidity due to a flight to quality or other systemically relevant event? Liquidity and funding risk considerations are examined in greater detail in Chapter 18.

The remainder of this appendix provides a brief overview of some alternatives. A good overview of many of the fixed-income financing alternatives involving securities can be found in Fabozzi (2012).

SOURCES OF CUSTOMER AND INTERNAL FINANCING

Customer Financing

The customers of a bank or insurance company are a natural source of financing. For example bank deposits and insurance premiums are both sources of cash which can be invested in other financial assets.

An additional source of customer funding, becoming more important to banks, are structured notes sold to retail and wealth management clients. A *structured note* is essentially an unsecured, medium-term note issued by a bank but "pumped up on derivative steroids" and sold as an investment alternative. In the context of securities' prospectuses, the US SEC Rule 434 defines structured securities as "securities whose cash flow characteristics depend upon one or more indices or that have embedded forwards or options or securities where an investor's investment return and the issuer's payment obligations are contingent on, or highly sensitive to, changes in the value of underlying assets, indices, interest rates or cash flows."

Some structured notes can be thought of as pre-packaged investment strategies, for example allowing the purchaser to participate in equity or rate or commodity or credit markets, with additional benefits such as a "principal guarantee." Structured notes sold by banks to their retail and wealth management clients are a form of financing as the note is internally bifurcated into its funding and derivative components; the embedded derivatives are managed by a trading desk, leaving the funding available to finance other (potentially illiquid) assets that the bank may have on its book.

Insurers often wrap bank structured notes with life or mortality protection and sell the combination to their LH clients as a unit linked investment policy. In addition, insurer's Guaranteed Investment Contracts (GICs) can also be thought of as "funding sources" rather than insurance contracts, in the sense that more of the economics to the insurer come from buying credit-risky assets and participating in the investment returns rather than from mortality or morbidity risk transfer. Because of this, GICs are seen by rating agencies operating leverage, such as A.M. Best (see A.M. Best, 2006).

Internal Dividend and Loan Financing

Consistent with the capital budget, the company's earnings provide a significant source of internal financing; earnings are augmented by capital which is released from businesses that are not growing. Both are used to finance organic growth within the existing business portfolio.

Any earnings or capital released which is excess to the operating business's needs is transferred to the holding company in the form of *internal dividends*.

Also useful are *internal loans*, loans between legal entities within a group. There are broadly three types of internal loans, two of which should not be considered as leverage.

- Inter-company loans and deposits in the *cash pool* are used to manage cash and liquidity through the netting of short-term cash requirements with available cash across the group and placing the excess at attractive rates in the market. In general, insurers have a net positive balance on the cash pool, implying that it is not a source of net funding for the institution. The cash pool can be done on balance sheet (increasing the appearance, but not the reality, of leverage) or through a bank in order to reduce the group's balance sheet.
- Inter-company loans are also used to finance dividend payments. They are loans made by the subsidiary to the holding company which are equal to the future expected dividend payment and self-liquidating: the loan is extinguished as the cash dividend is paid.

Other inter-company loans from the subsidiary to the holding company or between subsidiaries which represent more permanent financing arrangements are double leverage.

UNSECURED FINANCING FROM THE WHOLESALE MARKETS

Unsecured financing represents a direct obligation which is not collateralized by a lien on specific assets of the borrower. In the event of bankruptcy, the unsecured creditors will collectively have a general claim on the assets of the borrower, after any specifically pledged assets have been assigned to the secured creditors.

One obvious form of unsecured borrowing is a *bank loan*. When liquidity is readily available, banks are in principle willing to provide short-term loans to other banks and insurance companies; however, they are loathe to make longer-term loans to other banks or insurers because it ties up their own funding and capital for assets which provide little margin. As a consequence, bank lending to other financial institutions is predominantly short term in nature.

The alternative to short-term bank financing is capital market financing, which can be done through a variety of different channels.

- *Commercial Paper (CP)* is a short-term unsecured promissory note or security which can be issued by financial institutions and large corporations. It has a fixed maturity typically between 1 and 270 days. CP can either be sold directly by the issuing entity or through a dealer, typically a bank or securities firm. CP is issued as part of a program, with one registration to the relevant regulator (e.g., the SEC in the USA) required as opposed to a separate registration for each issuance. At the end of 2007, there was approximately USD 1 trillion CP outstanding, with greater than 80% having been issued by financial institutions.
- *Medium-Term Note (MTN)* is an unsecured note or security that usually matures in 5–10 years, although they can also be issued with any term, for example below 1 year and up to 50 years. Like CP, MTN is issued as a program, with one registration required to the relevant regulator. They are typically straightforward in their structure, offering fixed or floating interest payments.
- *Senior, unsecured bonds* are securities which are "longer" in duration than money market instruments. Bonds are typically used to provide financial leverage at bank or insurance holding companies.

SECURITIZED FINANCING

Securitized financing alternatives all share a common characteristic: the creditors of the firm have recourse to specific collateral. In spite of this commonality, there are many variations as discussed below.

Asset-backed Securities, Including MBS and ILS

Securitized funding is collateralized by a lien on specific assets of the company, for example a portfolio of loans or mortgages or other assets or emerging profits held in a collateral account.

ABS and the Banking Industry

Asset-backed securities are backed by specific assets, for example a pool of loans, credit card or other short-term receivables, student loans, royalties, etc. One of the most interesting and innovative asset-backed securities issued was the "Bowie Bond," a bond collateralized by the future royalties generated by the music library of David Bowie.[1] More mundane but more important sub-sectors of the ABS market include mortgage-backed securities, backed by residential or commercial mortgage loans (RMBS, CMBS) and collateralized loan obligations, which are backed by senior, unsecured bank loans.

ABS are used predominantly in the banking industry to facilitate their "originate to distribute" strategies: by securitizing loan assets, banks can free up additional capital and funding to generate new loans while retaining origination and servicing fees and reduce their risk profile at the same time.

Against these benefits for both banks and society are potentially very large moral hazard issues: by reducing the bank's exposure to the performance risk of the pool of assets, they may no longer have an incentive to provide the same level of underwriting care or due diligence, focusing on volume as opposed to underwriting. This moral hazard is often cited as one of the driving forces behind the financial crisis of 2008–09. For example, Keys *et al.* (2008) comment: "A central question surrounding the current sub-prime crisis is whether the securitization process reduced the incentives of financial intermediaries to carefully screen borrowers. We empirically examine this issue . . . Our findings suggest that existing securitization practices did adversely affect the screening incentives of lenders."

The perception of moral hazard has led regulators to propose minimum retention requirements to better align the interests of banks and investors. For example, in the USA, proposed changes to the Securities Exchange Act define explicit risk retention rules for ABS while in Europe, the European Council and Parliament amended the Capital Requirements Directive (CRD) that similarly mandates risk retention.

ABS and the Insurance Industry

There are fewer ABS issued by insurance companies, not surprising given that the insurance industry is a liability-driven business with limited need for additional operating leverage beyond that provided by policy holder premiums. Nonetheless, ABS are issued by insurance companies, for example in the form of embedded value securitizations in the LH sector.

First appearing in 1988, embedded value securitizations monetize the rights to emerging profits from blocks of life insurance asset accumulation and annuity products. Cummins (2004) provides a good overview of life embedded value securitizations. One of the challenges of embedded value securitizations is the complexity and unfamiliarity of the underlying risks, leading to increased due diligence and underwriting costs for the end investor and a narrower target investor base as well as higher structuring costs for the issuer.

Other insurance-linked securities, for example so-called catastrophe bonds, are not directly relevant for the issuer's leverage profile. Catastrophe bonds hold assets against uncertain catastrophe claims sufficient to collateralize the issue against a full limit loss on the underlying book of insurance business or insurance derivative.

---

[1] "Bowie Bonds" were issued in 1997 and backed by the future royalties from 25 albums that David Bowie recorded before 1990; they also had some credit enhancement from Bowie's record label, EMI Records. The bonds were bought by Prudential Insurance Company for USD 55 mio and priced to yield approximately 1.5% above the comparable return on a Treasury bond.

The Structure of ABS

The first step in issuing an ABS is for a bankruptcy-remote Special Purpose Vehicle (SPV) to purchase a pool of suitable assets. The SPV can either be managed by the originating institution or by a third party. This step converts assets to cash, frees up capital requirements and eliminates the performance risk of the pool from the originating firm's book. It also eliminates the credit risk of the originator from the ABS purchaser's perspective as the performance of the ABS is only dependent on the performance of the underlying asset pool. The SPV then typically sells the pool to a trust which issues the ABS with the interest and principal payments derived from the cash flows generated by the underlying pool of assets.

The underlying cash flows can be tranched in different forms in order to meet the preferences of different investor classes, for example offering different levels of seniority/ subordination, different interest rate and prepayment risk profiles through interest-only or principal-only tranches, etc. Depending on the form of ABS, further credit enhancement can come from over-collateralization or higher-equity participation in the SPV, third-party credit enhancement or other mechanisms.

Covered Bonds

A covered bond is an ABS in the sense that the bond holder has recourse to a specific collateral pool, but with one important difference: the collateral remains on the balance sheet of the issuer, implying that the bond holder also has recourse to the issuer. Further, the issuer typically must maintain the pool of collateral – for example, by replacing non-performing loans or loans which prepay earlier than expected, providing an additional level of security. In addition to the higher level of security, a further important difference is that covered bonds may eliminate some of the moral hazard inherent in securitizations because the bond holder has recourse to the issuer/originator of the collateral pool. A good overview of European covered bonds can be found in Packer *et al.* (2007).

More specifically, according to the European Covered Bond Council (2012): "Covered bonds are debt instruments secured by a cover pool of mortgage loans (property as collateral) or public-sector debt to which investors have a preferential claim in the event of default. While the nature of this preferential claim, as well as other safety features (asset eligibility and coverage, bankruptcy-remoteness and regulation) depends on the specific framework under which a covered bond is issued, it is the safety aspect that is common to all covered bonds . . . Covered bonds are characterised by the following common essential features that are achieved under special-law based frameworks or general-law based frameworks:

1. The bond is issued by – or bondholders otherwise have full recourse to – a credit institution which is subject to public supervision and regulation;
2. Bondholders have a claim against a cover pool of financial assets in priority to the unsecured creditors of the credit institution;
3. The credit institution has the ongoing obligation to maintain sufficient assets in the cover pool to satisfy the claims of covered bondholders at all times;
4. The obligations of the credit institution in respect of the cover pool are supervised by public or other independent bodies."

Covered bonds are primarily issued by European banks. The first issuance of covered bonds occurred in Prussia and Denmark in the 18th century. The issuance of covered bonds is also being promoted in the USA following the 2008–09 financial crisis to mitigate the potential moral hazard inherent in securitizations.

Asset-backed Commercial Paper Conduits

Asset-Backed Commercial Paper (ABCP) programs or "conduits" are similar to asset-backed securities in the sense that a bankruptcy-remote SPV issues promissory notes backed by a specific pool of collateral. However, they differ in that the pool of collateral and the level of note issuance is not static, with the notes issued increasing as the underlying collateral assets requiring funding increases.

Typically, ABCP conduits are used to fund only short-term assets such as trade receivables. These programs were originally designed to provide a liquid source of short-term working capital to corporate clients. They can be set up either by banks or large corporations and they may accept assets from a single originator or multiple originators. The ABCP will typically receive some credit enhancement in the form of over-collateralization and a first loss or equity investment.

In addition, a bank will typically provide liquidity support to the conduit in order to ensure the orderly funding of the assets as it is impractical to match the commercial paper issuance exactly with the term of the underlying assets. If a bank provides full liquidity support for the conduit, it may be treated as a direct credit substitute, in which case the assets held by the conduit are consolidated for regulatory capital purposes with those of the bank.

Structured Investment Vehicles

A Structured Investment Vehicle (SIV) is (or, was) essentially an ABCP conduit with a major difference in strategy: whereas the intention behind the ABCP conduit is to provide funding and liquidity to the issuer secured by short-term assets, the intention behind the SIV was to be a leveraged investment vehicle in its own right. SIVs accomplished this by borrowing short term to finance long-term securities or assets such as corporate bonds, mortgage-backed securities, other asset-backed securities, etc. The difference between the asset returns and the funding cost accrued to the equity investors of the SIV. I use the past tense when referring to SIVs because the last of their breed died out in 2009 during the financial crisis.

The first two SIVs, the Alpha and Beta Finance Corporations, were created in 1988–89 by two Citigroup bankers based in London, Nicholas Sossidis and Stephen Partridge-Hicks. They left Citigroup in 1993 to set up Gordian Knot, an SIV. Other SIV management firms followed suit, each with the intention of staying in business indefinitely, with the management of the SIV able to exchange assets in order to retain their rating and purchase new assets to replace maturing assets.

In addition to independent SIV management firms, many SIVs were sponsored by banks. The rationale for banks to sponsor SIVs was that it allowed them to take advantage of leverage which would have been impossible if the assets had been held on balance sheet; for example, the first SIVs had 5–10× leverage with subsequent leverage ratios around 20× for SIVs not sponsored by banks and up to 40× for SIVs sponsored by banks. Furthermore, because they were not consolidated, this leverage did not count on the bank's balance sheet.

SIVs were highly rated issuers for a variety of reasons, including their capital structure, which included junior and senior debt as well as equity, their collateralization and the apparent quality of the assets they held. This allowed them to fund at comparatively low rates. Similar to ABCP programs, SIVs also required liquidity support from banks.

The SIVs profits were attributable to the difference between short-term borrowing rates and the returns on their long-term investments and a credit arbitrage between their low collateralized borrowing costs versus the credit-risky yields on the assets that they held. Put differently, SIVs seemingly "created value" in much the same way as banks (e.g., collecting the spread between assets and liabilities generated by accepting both credit and maturity transformation as well as liquidity and funding risks).

SIVs were popular before the 2008–09 financial crisis. They typically ranged in size from USD 1–30 bn and had over USD 400 bn in assets under management in July 2007. Unfortunately, they did not fare so well during the 2008–09 crisis as a general flight to quality restricted the availability of short-term funding and prevented the liquidation of the underlying assets except at a deep discount; by the end of the crisis, all SIVs were shut down (Neate, 2009). Most banks involved in SIVs took substantial losses as their liquidity support was called and they took over the assets rather than allowing the vehicles to fail.

SIVs are often referred to as part of the "shadow banking system" and are credited with playing an important role in bringing about the crisis. The *Financial Times* reported the closure of the last SIV, Sigma Finance, on October 2, 2008, thereby closing the chapter on one part of the "shadow banking system."

Repurchase Agreements and Securities Lending and Borrowing

Both repurchase agreements and securities lending and borrowing is a forms of collateralized borrowing; because the mechanics are similar, only repurchase agreements will be discussed in this section. Under a repurchase agreement, the "borrower" agrees to sell securities to the "lender" and then repurchase them at a later date at a predetermined price. The difference between the sales and repurchase prices can be thought of as the interest rate charged on the loan and is often called the repo rate. The underlying security can be considered the collateral backing the loan as the "lender" has legal title of the asset during the term of the repurchase agreement.

In order to ensure that the collateral is sufficient to mitigate the borrower's credit risk, repurchase agreements are often kept short term, for example rolling over every night: with the "loan" value changing daily to reflect the value of the collateral, the risk that the collateral is insufficient to cover the loan value is minimized.

In addition, the collateral is often subject to a market value "haircut," with higher volatility collateral requiring a higher "haircut." For example, the haircut for Treasury bills may be only 1% but higher for equities (e.g., up to 20%). To make this concrete, suppose that the "borrower" posts €1000 collateral subject to a 20% haircut. Then the cash received would be only €800 and the interest paid, or repo rate, would be applied only to €800.

The general repo rate tends to track the short-term inter-bank borrowing rate but be a few basis points lower, reflecting the collateralization. However, if there is significant demand for the underlying security used as collateral, a "special" rate well below the general money market rate can be observed. Such circumstances may occur if there is a large maturing short interest in the specific security.

Impact on Leverage   The use of repurchase agreements by insurance companies and pension funds can generate cash which is then invested in additional securities. In the past, rating agencies would implicitly define a threshold below which repurchase agreements were considered operational leverage and above which repurchase financing would begin to be considered as financial leverage and impact the firm's rating.

Similarly, banks use repurchase agreements to fund their trading portfolios with historically no or limited impact on leverage. For example, RMI (2010): "(T)raditional repos . . . have no effect on the balance sheet – since traditional repos requires (the firm) to record (credit) a repo liability before recording an increase in cash assets."

However, the use of repurchase agreements as a form of leverage becomes clearer when the practice is abused, as it was by Lehman Brothers with their now infamous "Repo 105" transactions, which were classified as short-term repurchase agreements in the accounts of Lehman Brothers but were actually used to flatter the balance sheet over the quarter-end reporting period. RMI (2010) says, "The main motivation behind using Repo 105 was to mislead the credit rating agencies by lowering net leverage . . . Repo 105 allowed Lehman to increase sales without any increase in liabilities. Lehman could then use the cash it had received from the 'sales' to pay down its liabilities, understating its leverage." The use of repurchase agreements as a source of leverage in the banking sector will naturally come under increasing pressure due to the limits on overall leverage under Basel III described in Chapter 18.

Central Bank Financing

Eligible banks (and some non-bank financial institutions) can arrange short-term financing from the central bank. In the USA, this is called accessing the Federal Reserve Bank's "discount window" and, in Europe, the European Central Bank's standing or marginal lending facility. Both require collateral and are therefore a form of repurchase agreement described earlier.

In "normal" times, accessing central bank funding is done to smooth out short-term liquidity requirements. As such, the facilities are typically overnight. However, the Fed's discount window does offer seasonal funding up to 9 months and the ECB does offer Main Refinancing Operations (MROs) and Long-Term Refinancing Operations (LTROs) lasting beyond 3 months.

Linzert *et al.* (2004) provides a summary of the ECB's short-term lending practices, stating "Repo auctions are the predominant instrument for the implementation of monetary policy of the European Central Bank (ECB). Repo rates govern short-term interest rates and the availability of repo credit determines the liquidity of the European banking sector. The ECB conducts repo auctions as weekly main refinancing operations (MRO) with a (bi)weekly maturity and as monthly longer term refinancing operations (LTRO) maturing after three months. Although MROs are the ECB's primary policy instrument, LTROs are far from negligible. In 2003, refinancing via LTROs amounts to 45 bln Euro which is about 20% of overall liquidity provided by the ECB."

During Times of Crisis   As pointed out in Chapter 18 earlier, the banking system has become increasingly reliant on wholesale financing from the inter-bank and capital markets, leaving it with potentially fragile balance sheets if liquidity should dry up.

During such turbulent times, central banks can provide a valuable and stabilizing source of short/medium-term liquidity to the banking system through their collateralized lending operations. These actions prove invaluable during a financial crisis, especially when inter-bank lending markets freeze up due to a lack of confidence.

During the 2008–09 crisis, central banks reacted by providing valuable liquidity in the market: On August 17, 2007, they announced a temporary change to lending terms, cutting the discount rate and extending the tenor of the repos to up to 30 days (Federal Reserve, 2007). Later, on March 16, 2008, following the rescue of Bear Stearns, the Federal Reserve announced further changes, extending the maximum term from 30 to 90 days and further cutting the discount rate for primary credits (Federal Reserve, 2008). Both actions provided valuable liquidity in the market.

Similarly, during the European sovereign debt crisis of 2011–12, the ECB announced details of an extended LTRO operation (ECB, 2011a), "one with a maturity of approximately 12 months, to be conducted in October 2011, and the other with a maturity of approximately 13 months, to be conducted in December 2011." Noting that this was not effective in supporting the banking system, the ECB announced some fundamental and important changes on December 8, 2011 (ECB, 2011b): "The Governing Council of the European Central Bank (ECB) has today decided on additional enhanced credit support measures to support bank lending and liquidity in the euro area money market. In particular, the Governing Council has decided: To conduct two longer-term refinancing operations (LTROs) with a maturity of 36 months and the option of early repayment after one year . . . (and) To increase collateral availability by (i) reducing the rating threshold for certain asset-backed securities (ABS) and (ii) allowing national central banks (NCBs), as a temporary solution, to accept as collateral additional performing credit claims (i.e. bank loans) that satisfy specific eligibility criteria. These two measures will take effect as soon as the relevant legal acts have been published."

In total, close to EUR 1 trillion LTRO financing was provided to eligible banks by the ECB during 2011–12, some of which was used to purchase higher-yielding sovereign debt or immediately deposited back with the ECB in order to ensure sufficient short- and medium-term liquidity.

Market Perception   How does the market perceive firms which borrow from the central bank? It depends on the circumstances. From the perspective of rating agencies, the ability to borrow from the central bank is beneficial but there comes a point when it is too much. According to Standard & Poor's (2011a), "If a bank does not have access to a central bank's funding mechanism, the funding assessment is limited to below average at best. That's because the (rating) criteria consider this mechanism to be an important source of contingent liquidity, but not for funding ordinary business operations on an ongoing basis . . . The main differentiators for liquidity are a bank's relative dependence on central bank funding and its ability to access other liquidity sources. Liquidity becomes progressively weaker as an institution increasingly relies on funding support from the monetary authorities."

The potential stigma of relying on central bank funding caused several banks to not participate during the 2008–09 crisis. The potential stigma was raised again with the ECB's LTRO extension, as illustrated by the following from the *Wall Street Journal* (2012): "It's clear Mario Draghi sees the European Central Bank's decision to add a big dose of long-term liquidity to the financial system as a crucial component of his campaign to avert a devastating credit crunch in the euro zone. So it's no surprise he didn't take too kindly to recent suggestions by Deutsche Bank chief Josef Ackermann and other big-shot European bankers that tapping the ECB's long-term refinancing operations carries some sort of stigma. . . . So far Deutsche Bank and Barclays have said they declined to borrow from the LTRO. 'The fact that we have never taken any money from the government has made us, from a reputation point of view, so attractive with so many clients in the world that we would be very reluctant to give that up,' Ackermann recently told analysts."

HYBRID CAPITAL

Hybrid capital is a form of debt that has "equity-like" or loss absorption characteristics. Under certain conditions, it can be considered as a (partial or limited) substitute for shareholder's equity by rating agencies and/or regulators when evaluating the financial strength of the firm. As such, qualifying hybrid capital is seen as strengthening the balance sheet from the debt holder's perception without increasing shareholders' invested capital.

As Standard & Poor's defines: "Hybrid capital instruments include – but are not limited to – preferred stock, deferrable subordinated notes, trust preferred securities, and mandatory convertible securities. The equity content of a hybrid capital instrument (or hybrid) can affect the rating on a bank by influencing the measurement of the bank's capitalization." The equity content "refers to the extent to which a bank hybrid capital instrument can function as equity and therefore – via features such as coupon nonpayment or deferral, a principal write-down, or conversion into common equity – absorb a portion of a bank's losses. The criteria classify the equity content of bank hybrids into one of three categories: (i) high, (ii) intermediate, or (iii) minimal. To qualify for inclusion in total adjusted capital (TAC), subject to certain limits, a bank hybrid capital instrument must qualify for inclusion in regulatory capital and contain features consistent with the criteria for classification in either the high equity content category or the intermediate equity content category."

As the previous quote illustrates, the criteria for determining the eligibility of hybrid capital are complicated and changing rapidly. The most common forms of hybrid capital are preference shares, trust preferred securities and contingent capital or "CoCos."

Preference Shares

Preference shares are non-voting shares which are senior to normal, common shares but subordinated to other forms of debt in liquidation, they are senior to ordinary shares in that they promise to pay a fixed, non-fluctuating dividend before any dividends can be paid to normal shareholders, but typically only if the firm is in a financial position to pay the dividend.

In general, there are four different types of preferred stock: cumulative preferred stock (where unpaid dividends cumulate in the event of a temporary delay in dividend payment), non-cumulative preferred stock, participating preferred stock (where an additional dividend payment is made if the dividend on the common shares exceeds a given threshold) and convertible preferred stock (which can be converted into common shares at defined conditions).

Trust-preferred Securities

A trust-preferred security has characteristics of both preferred stock and subordinated debt. The trust-preferred security is created by a bank holding company, by creating a trust and issuing debt to the trust and then the trust issuing the trust-preferred securities. Generally, trust-preferred securities are long-term securities, callable by the issuer and offer periodic fixed or variable interest payments with the possibility to defer interest payments under certain conditions. In addition to historically being recognized as Tier 1 capital for bank holding companies, the interest payments on trust-preferred securities are also tax deductible.

Contingent Convertibles

Contingent convertibles, or "CoCos," are debt instruments which convert into ordinary shares of the issuing institution when one or more trigger events occur. The main purpose of CoCos is to increase the institution's capital or solvency ratio in times of distress. As an example, "(Credit Suisse) announced it would issue CHFbn ($6.2bn) of **Co**ntingent **Co**nvertible securities — or debt that will convert into equity once a certain trigger is reached. In this case the trigger is if Credit Suisse's reported Basel III common equity Tier 1 ratio falls below 7 per cent, or if the Swiss regulator thinks that the bank requires public support. The CoCos therefore look like they satisfy both Finma and Basel's ideas of when CoCos should convert. Qatar Holding LLC and Saudi Arabian conglomerate, the Olayan Group, are the investors in the new CoCo issue" (Alloway, 2011). As another example, Allianz issued a CoCo in 2011 through a private placement with Nippon Life; the CoCo converts to equity if Allianz's regulatory solvency ratio under Solvency II breaches a specific floor.

While potentially attractive to regulators, CoCos have had a mixed reception in the market. Oswald Gruebel, ex-CEO of UBS, commented to the *Financial Times* in March 2011 that "(contingent convertibles are) a very dangerous instrument . . . As soon as you get near these trigger levels – you don't have to hit them – what do you think shareholders will do? They will get the hell out of that stock, so fast, because you know it will halve in value if it's triggered." Similar concerns have been expressed by those who are expected to buy the bonds; as one institutional investor put it, "Let me get this straight: they (the regulators) want CoCos to count as equity for banks but as fixed income investments for insurance companies and pension funds. How is that supposed to work?"

Glossary

Absolute Tracking Error (ATE) – defined as the difference between the actual investment portfolio returns and the returns on the benchmark portfolio (e.g., $\text{ATE}_t = \left(R_t - R_t^B\right)$). A passive investment approach seeks to minimize the tracking error whereas an active approach may generate large tracking errors over time. Various statistics can be calculated based on the tracking error. For example, the *average ATE* over a long time horizon ($\varphi\text{ATE}_t = \frac{1}{T}\sum_{t=1}^{T}\text{ATE}_t$) gives an indication of average "alpha" or outperformance relative to the benchmark. Some define *tracking error* as the standard deviation of the absolute tracking error (e.g., $\text{TE} = \sqrt{\frac{1}{T}\sum_{t=1}^{T}(\text{ATE}_t - \varphi\text{ATE}_t)^2}$). $\text{TE} \leq 0.5\%$ generally represents an index fund, where small tracking errors can arise due to the desire to limit transaction costs from directly matching the benchmark.

Accumulation Phase – defined as the period of time when an annuity investor is in the early stages of building up the cash value of the annuity.

Acquisition Expense Ratio – the ratio of acquisition expenses to the premium earned.

Acquisition Expenses – the direct and indirect costs of selling, underwriting and initiating a product or service. Acquisition expenses include sales commissions and sales staff expenses (salaries, facilities and equipment costs), advertising and underwriting expenses (including appraisals, contract issuance expenses).

Active Limit Breach – occurs when a limit is exceeded because of a conscious decision by an individual. Most breaches are passive limit breaches which are not consciously triggered but are triggered by external risk events.

Activity-Based Costing (ABC) – a costing methodology that identifies activities in an organization and assigns the cost of each activity with resources to all products and services according to the actual consumption by each. This model assigns more indirect costs (overhead) into direct costs compared with conventional costing.

Adjusted R-Squared – a measure of the goodness of fit between the data and the regression line.

Administration Expense Ratio – the ratio of all operating expenses excluding acquisition and claims management expenses to the premium earned for a PC insurer.

Adverse Selection – defined as situations where higher prices attract customers with a disproportionately higher risk profile. This can be the case if only the riskiest customers are willing to pay the higher price.

Agency Costs – arise when the managers of a firm do not always take decisions in the best interests of shareholders.

Aggregate Exceedance Probability (AEP) – a measure of the annual aggregate expected losses from natural catastrophes within a specified return period.

Alpha – defined as realized investment returns generated in excess of the risk-appropriate financial market benchmark. A positive alpha can be interpreted as investment performance which "beats the market."

Annualized Premium Equivalent (APE) – the sum of annualized recurring premium plus 10% of single premium product sold during the year. APE is designed to make different regular/single premium mixes comparable.

Asset/Liability Management (ALM) – the management of the structural mismatch between the firm's assets and liabilities.

Basel II – the second of the Basel Accords, recommendations on banking regulations issued by the Basel Committee on Banking Supervision. Basel II was intended as an international standard for capital requirements. Basel II uses a "three pillars" concept – (1) minimum capital requirements, (2) supervisory review and (3) market discipline.

Basel III – the third of the Basel Accords as a global, voluntary regulatory standard on bank capital adequacy, stress testing and market liquidity risk, agreed upon by the members of the Basel Committee on Banking Supervision in 2010–11. Basel III should strengthen bank capital requirements, increase liquidity and decrease leverage.

Basis Risk – the risk associated with imperfect hedging. It arises because of a difference between the price of the asset to be hedged and the price of the asset serving as the hedge, or because of a mismatch between the expiration date of the hedge asset and the actual selling date of the asset (calendar basis risk), or due to the difference in the location of the asset to be hedged and the asset serving as the hedge (locational basis risk).

Behavioral Risk – the uncertainty surrounding management's assumptions about the policy holder's decision to lapse or surrender the policy, convert the policy into an annuity, etc. Analogously, the uncertainty surrounding a borrower's decision to prepay their loan, withdraw funds from a savings or deposit account, etc.

Bid–Offer Spread – the difference between the prices quoted for an immediate sale (bid) and an immediate purchase (offer). The size of the bid–offer spread in a security is one measure of the liquidity of the market and of the size of the transaction cost.

Black Swan Event – an event which is an outliner,[1] ". . . as it lies outside the realm of regular expectations, because nothing in the past can convincingly point to its possibility. Second, it carries an extreme impact. Third, in spite of its outlier status, human nature makes us concoct explanations for its occurrence after the fact, making it explainable and predictable."

Business Process Outsourcing (BPO) – a subset of outsourcing that involves the contracting of the operations and responsibilities of specific business functions (or processes) to a third-party service provider. BPO is typically categorized into back-office outsourcing, which includes internal business functions such as human resources or finance and accounting, and front-office outsourcing, which includes customer-related services such as contact center services.

Business Process Re-engineering (BPR) – the analysis and redesign of workflows and business processes to improve costs and customer service.

Business RAPMs – a measure of the risk-adjusted return for an entire business covering all the sources of risk and return.

Capital Asset Pricing Model (CAPM) – first introduced by Sharpe (1964) and Lintner (1964), describing how an individual security or portfolio is theoretically valued in the market.

Capital Efficiency Ratio (CER) – defined as the ratio of actual capital to minimum required capital. Normally >1, the CER can reflect the capital and leverage constraints imposed by regulators and rating agencies or excess prudence.

CAPM-RAPM – a risk-adjusted performance measure based on the CAPM.

Catastrophe Event – defined as a loss event which is larger than a predefined materiality threshold. Natural catastrophes include, for example, earthquakes, windstorms, cyclones, typhoons, flooding, hail, etc.; man-made catastrophes include, for example, acts of terrorism, war, etc.; man-made clash

---

[1] http://www.nytimes.com/2007/04/22/books/chapters/0422-1st-tale.html

catastrophe accumulations include, for example, an air disaster near a harbor, triggering aviation, marine hull, warehouse property and business interruption claims simultaneously under different contracts.

CNHR – cost of residual non-hedgeable risks, defined as the "mark-to-model" price of non-traded financial and non-financial risks such as mortality and longevity risks, operational risks, expense risks, etc. In Solvency II, it is the cost of the economic capital necessary to support the non-hedgeable risk over the life of the transaction.

CoC – cost of capital, defined as the cost of equity funding from a shareholder's perspective.

Co-insurance Rate – the proportion of the loss retained by the policy holder between the deductible and the limit.

Combined Ratio – the sum of the expense ratio, defined as non-claims operating expenses divided by premium, and the loss ratio, defined as the sum of claims and claims adjustment expenses divided by premium.

Cost Income Ratio (CIR) – defined as the ratio of operating expenses to operating income. It can be decomposed into three parts: the cost per unit of input; the cost per unit of output; the income per unit of output.

Cost of Double Taxation – represents the additional corporate taxes compared with those payable if the assets are distributed directly to shareholders today. Corporate taxes have to be paid on corporate income (e.g., coupons and gains generated by assets backing required capital); shareholders also have to pay taxes on corporate distributions (through dividends) or capital gains on their shares if earnings are retained.

Cost of Financial Distress – arises when firms go into insolvency proceedings, incurring additional costs which dilute the value available to settle policy holder, debt holder and shareholder claims.

Credit Default Option – an option to buy protection (payer option) or sell protection (receiver option) as a credit default swap on a specific reference credit with a specific maturity. The option is usually European, exercisable only at one date in the future at a specific strike price defined as a coupon on the credit default swap.

Cross-subsidization – refers to earnings from profitable customers being eroded by the losses from unprofitable segments.

Crowding-Out Effect – situations where increased government borrowing (e.g., to finance an expansionary fiscal policy) reduces or "crowds out" private investment.

Culture – defined as a set of shared attitudes, values, goals and practices that characterize an institution, organization or group.

Customer Attrition – defined as customers ending their relationship with the firm.

Customer Lifetime Value (CLV) – defined as the discounted present value of all (expected) future profits obtained from a customer over the life of the relationship.

Decumulation Phase – the period during which assets accrued in the accumulation phase are paid out to the pension scheme member in a funded scheme.

Decumulation Products – annuities which pay regular, fixed payments over the policy holder's remaining lifetime, or the joint lifetime with their spouse, or until the contract matures.

Deductible – also called retention level; the first loss amount to which the policy holder is exposed before the insurance policy begins to pay.

Deferred Acquisition Costs (DAC) – deferral of costs associated with acquiring a new customer or product over the duration of the product. DAC is treated as an asset on the balance sheet and amortized over the life of the insurance contract.

Deferred Annuities – blended retirement and savings products. Initially, they are savings and investment products which allow the account value to appreciate during the accumulation phase; later, the policy holder can either elect to take a lump sum payment or convert the account into an immediate annuity. Examples include fixed indexed annuities and variable annuities.

Defined Benefit Pension Plan – a pension plan in which an employer/sponsor promises a specified monthly benefit on retirement, predetermined by a formula based on the employee's earnings history, tenure of service and age rather than depending on investment returns. The investment risk and portfolio management are entirely under the control of the company.

Defined Contribution Pension Plan – a retirement plan in which the employer, employee or both make contributions on a regular basis. Individual accounts are set up for participants and benefits are based on the amounts credited to these accounts plus any investment earnings in the account. Only employer contributions to the account are guaranteed, not the future benefits. Investment risk and portfolio management are entirely assumed by employee.

De-globalization – the process of diminishing interdependence and integration between certain units around the world, typically nation-states. It is widely used to describe the periods when economic trade and investment between countries decline. It stands in contrast to globalization, in which units become increasingly integrated over time.

Delta – defined as the change in a security's or derivative's value for a small change in the risk factor (e.g., an interest rate delta is defined as $\delta = \partial V / \partial r$ and is related to its DV01 or VB01).

Direct Cost – defined as a cost which can be accurately traced to a cost object with little effort.

Direct Reporting Line – defined by the right to set objectives, evaluate performance and directly take hire, fire and compensation-related decisions for personnel within the function.

Dividend Payout Ratio – a financial ratio that determines how much a company pays out in dividends each year relative to its net income. It measures how much of the return is retained and reinvested into the business, and how much is returned to shareholders.

Dormant Customers – inactive customers. Economically similar to customer attrition, representing a loss in revenues, they are more expensive in terms of ongoing administration costs. Dormancy can occur when customers leave a limited amount in a savings account without other compensating business or when they discontinue regular premium payments.

Dotted Reporting Line – defined as the ability to give input on objectives, performance evaluations and hire, fire and compensation.

Double Leverage – defined as the difference between the sum of the equity allocated to operating subsidiaries or businesses and the group's consolidated equity.

DV01 – a measure of bond price sensitivity. It is the change in bond price for 1 basis point change in interest rates.

Earnings at Risk (EaR) – defined as the worst-case change in expected earnings within a given confidence interval. EaR differs from and can be in conflict with VaR. For example, a bank that wants to hedge the market value of the banking book will reduce its VaR but increase its EaR by introducing accounting volatility if the hedges do not qualify for hedge accounting.

Economic Capital (EC) – the amount of capital, assessed on a realistic basis, which a firm requires to cover its risks within a given confidence interval. EC typically covers market risk, credit risk, insurance risk and operational risk; EC typically does not include strategic risks, liquidity risk and reputational risk. It is the amount of money needed to secure survival in a worst-case scenario.

Economic Capital Intensity (ECI) – defined as the present value of the minimum economic capital required to support the business in run-off from an economic perspective.

Economic Profit (EP) – also known as Annual Value Added (AVA) or Economic Value Added (EVA^{TM}); the annual amount of value being contributed by the business in excess of its cost of capital.

Economic Scenario Generator (ESG) – generates consistent multi-dimensional scenarios of all the financial economic and macro-economic variables necessary for risk management and valuation; produces a forward-looking simulated global economy of financial markets including the pricing of derivatives and alternative assets.

Efficient Frontier – defined generically as the set of portfolios offering the maximum expected return for a given level of risk (or, equivalently, the minimum risk portfolio for a given level of expected return).

Elasticity of Demand – defined as the absolute percentage change in the volume demanded by customers for a percentage change in price (e.g., $\eta = |(\Delta V / V)/(\Delta P / P)|$).

Embedded Value (EV) – a measure of the consolidated value of shareholders' interests in the covered business. EV is the present value of shareholders' interests in the earnings distributable from assets allocated to the covered business after sufficient allowance for the risk.

Endowment Policy – designed to pay a lump sum upon maturity or on the death of the policy holder. Maturities can range from 3 years up to 20 or more years. Shorter-term endowment policies compete directly with bank deposits.

Enterprise Risk Management (ERM) – enterprise risk management is a framework for risk management, including organization and governance, internal controls, key processes, systems and information and risk culture. ERM begins by identifying events or circumstances relevant to the organization's objectives (risks and opportunities), assessing them in terms of likelihood and magnitude of impact, determining a response strategy and monitoring progress.

Environmental, Social and Governance (ESG) risks – represent reputational risks coming from activities which may be perceived by some as undesirable based on their own personal convictions (e.g., "adult" or vice industries such as gambling, pornography, tobacco or alcohol; hydroelectric dams, strip mining and off-shore oil exploration which might impact the ecosystem and indigenous populations; agricultural commodity trading which might be seen to cause volatility in food prices in developing economies; or business activities in countries with mixed human rights practices).

Equity Indexed Annuity (EIA) – a general account savings product whose crediting rate is based on an equity index return, subject to a minimum guaranteed rate of return, or floor, and a maximum return, or cap. After the accumulation phase, the policy holder has the option to take the account value as a lump sum or to convert it into an annuity.

European Embedded Value (EEV) – developed by the CFO Forum to standardize the calculation of the embedded value. It allows greater consistency in embedded value calculations and disclosures between companies.

Excess Capital (EC) – defined as market value which is surplus to underwriting risk capital requirements. This value can potentially be invested in financial market-risky assets or distributed to shareholders.

Excess of Loss (XL) Reinsurance – a form of reinsurance whereby the reinsurer indemnifies the cedant for the amount of loss above a stated excess point, usually up to an upper limit. XL reinsurance can be defined on a per risk basis (providing coverage and eliminating the risk of a single, large commercial exposure), per event basis (providing coverage for catastrophic events such as hurricanes, earthquakes, etc.) or aggregate portfolio basis (providing coverage for a larger than expected number of large losses and sometimes called a stop-loss cover).

Exclusions – perils that are not covered by the insurance contract.

Expense Ratio – for insurers, the ratio of non-claim operating expenses for the calendar year to the premium earned in the calendar year. For banks, the ratio of operating expenses to total operating revenues. It measures a company's operational efficiency in producing, underwriting and administering its business.

Expense Risk – the uncertainty surrounding future expenses relative to best-estimate expense assumptions.

Externalities – defined as economic consequences or spillovers on a third, unrelated party stemming from decisions taken by others operating in their own self-interest. In other words, what you do impacts other people.

Facultative Reinsurance – a form of reinsurance whereby each exposure is offered to the reinsurer and the separate submission, acceptance and resulting agreement is required for each individual risk that the ceding company seeks to reinsure.

FASB – Financial Accounting Standard Board; a private, not-for-profit organization whose primary purpose is to establish and improve GAAP within the USA. The FASB's mission is to establish and improve standards of financial accounting and reporting, providing decision-useful information to investors and other users of financial reports.

FCReC – frictional costs of required capital, measures the frictional cost to shareholders of capital "locked" into the business, typically calculated as the projected corporate taxes on the investment returns and the investment management expenses for the assets backing the locked-in capital.

Financial Leverage – defined as hybrid capital and bonds issued in the capital markets by the group or holding company, used to finance their operating subsidiaries or activities. It is different from operating leverage in that the expense of financial leverage is recognized as part of the weighted average cost of capital that the operating business has to meet. In contrast, operating leverage expenses are deducted from the operating profits of the business.

Franchise Value – value created from future new business and profitable growth.

Free Surplus (FS) – the market value of any capital and surplus allocated to, but not required to support, the in-force covered business at the valuation date.

FSB – Financial Stability Board; an international body that monitors and makes recommendations about the global financial system. It was established after the 2009 G-20 London Summit as a successor to the Financial Stability Forum (FSF).

FTSE4Good Index – a series of ethical investment stock-market indices launched in 2001 by the FTSE Group. A number of stock-market indices are available, for example covering UK shares, US shares, European markets and Japan, with inclusion based on a range of corporate social responsibility criteria.

Funding Liquidity Risk – the risk that a firm will not be able to meet its expected and unexpected current and future cash flow and collateral needs without affecting either daily operations or its financial condition.

Funds Transfer Price (FTP) – the theoretical market price of perfectly match funding a financial asset (e.g. bank loan) or match investing a financial liability (e.g. bank deposit or insurance liability) as if the asset or liability had no underwriting risk (e.g. no loan default risk and no insurance risk).

GAAP – generally accepted accounting principles, referring to the accounting standards or guidelines for financial accounting used in a jurisdiction. These include the standards, conventions and rules that accountants follow in recording and summarizing and in the preparation of financial statements.

Gamma – the rate of change or convexity of the value of a security or a derivative to a specific risk factor (e.g., interest rate gamma is calculated as $\gamma = \partial^2 V / \partial r^2$).

General Account Products – the assets backing general account savings or investment products are held on the balance sheet of the insurance company with returns credited by the insurance company to the policy holder's "account." The crediting rate is often at the discretion of the insurance company, subject to a minimum guaranteed crediting rate, and an insolvency of the insurance company may reduce the value that the policy holder receives relative to their account balances.

Goodwill – an intangible asset that arises when one company acquires business from another but pays more than the fair net asset value. The goodwill can be thought of as representing the future franchise value acquired. It is classified as an intangible asset on the balance sheet.

GMAB – guaranteed minimum accumulation benefit, typically for variable annuity products, for example based on return of premium, roll-up of premium at minimum rate of return, maximum anniversary value, etc.

GMDB – guaranteed minimum death benefit for variable annuity products.

GMIB – guaranteed minimum income benefit upon conversion into a pay-out annuity for variable annuity products.

GMWB – guaranteed minimum withdrawal benefit, similar to an income benefit but without triggering a conversion into an annuity, for variable annuity insurance products.

Gross Product Margin – defined as the margin after deducting the FTP cost of financial market risk or the replicating portfolio.

G-SIFI – globally systemically important financial institutions. A SIFI is a bank, insurance company or other financial institution whose failure might trigger a financial crisis. As the 2007–2012 global financial crisis has unfolded, the international community has moved to protect the global financial system through preventing the failure of SIFIs (or, if one does fail, limiting the adverse effects of its failure). Related to G-SIFIs are G-SIBs (globally systemically important banks) and G-SIIs (globally systemically important insurers) with the list of G-SIFIs being updated annually.

Guaranteed Investment Contracts (GICs) – offer a guaranteed investment return, either fixed or floating, over the term of the contract. They are more often sold to institutional clients and offer direct competition for bank deposits and certificates of deposit.

Health, Accident and Disability Insurance – indemnifies the beneficiary in the event of illness, accident or disability during the coverage period. As with term life insurance, medical examinations may be required and exclusions. Typically, these are annually renewable contracts with premium levels specific to the individual covered.

High-Reliability Organization (HRO) – one that can successfully avoid catastrophes in a risky, complex environment where "accidents" can be regularly expected (e.g., wildfire response teams, air traffic controllers, military personnel engaged in guerrilla warfare, operators of nuclear or large chemical plants and NASA). Case studies include the Cuban missile crisis, the Three Mile Island nuclear incident, the Challenger explosion, the Bhopal chemical leak and the Columbia spacecraft explosion.

IBES – a system that gathers and compiles the different estimates made by stock analysts on the future earnings for the majority of US publicly traded companies.

ICT – information and communications technology.

Idiosyncratic Risk – risk that is specific to an asset or a small group of assets. Idiosyncratic risk has little or no correlation with market risk, and can therefore be substantially mitigated or eliminated from a portfolio through diversification.

IFRS – International Financial Reporting Standards, originally called IAS (International Accounting Standards); designed as a common global language for business affairs so that company accounts are understandable and comparable across international boundaries.

Indirect Cost – defined as a cost which cannot easily and accurately be attributed to specific cost objects, typically benefiting multiple cost objects such as individual products, activities or departments, etc.

Inorganic Growth – the rate of growth driven by acquiring new business by way of mergers, acquisitions and take-overs.

Insurable Risk – a risk that meets the following characteristics. (1) Risks which diversify to some extent when pooled with other risks. (2) The loss to the policy holder can be calculated and is definite in terms of time, place and cause. (3) A loss which is accidental or outside the control of the policy holder. (4) A meaningful or material loss to the policy holder which can be covered at a premium deemed acceptable as a substitute for self-insurance.

Insurance Claims Risk – the uncertainty surrounding the best-estimate level and timing of claims, including claims inflation.

Insurance-Linked Securities (ILS) – defined as financial instruments whose values are driven by insurance loss events, including so-called catastrophe bonds, embedded value securitizations, etc.

Internal Rate of Return (IRR) – defined as the discount rate for which the discounted present value of all expected cash flows, including the initial investment and return of capital, is identically equal to zero.

Intrinsic Value (IV) – also known as intrinsic shareholder value; the theoretical value of the business or activity.

Invested Capital (IC) – represents economic investment (as opposed to a regulatory or rating agency definition of capital).

Investment RAPMs – a measure of risk-adjusted returns from taking financial market risk using a cost of capital based on a risk-appropriate benchmark portfolio available in the market.

Iso-value Lines – combinations of expected returns and growth which give the same implied market multiple under steady-state assumptions. For example, those combinations of RoIC and g where $P/\text{IC} = (\text{RoIC} - \text{CoIC})/(\text{CoIC} - g) = \kappa$, with IC the invested capital, P the theoretical price of the business, RoIC the steady-state return on invested capital and g the steady-state growth rate.

Key Performance Indicator (KPI) – a set of metrics directly linked to the desired corporate objective (e.g., shareholder value) and explicitly integrated into the firm's incentive compensation system.

LH Investment Margin RAPM – the ratio between the present value of future profits from all sources to the present value of capital tied up in the product, where profits and capital are measured including underwriting as well as financial market risk taking.

LH New Business RAPM – the ratio between the present value of future profits from underwriting to the present value of capital tied up for the underwriting risk in the product, where profits are measured as if no financial market risk is taken.

Limited Liability Put Option (LLPO) – given the limited liability nature of stock companies, shareholders are not obligated to make up any deficit if the firm's assets prove insufficient to cover its liabilities. The option to default has value to shareholders and in principle reduces the value of liabilities.

Liquidity Coverage Ratio (LCR) – a measure of liquidity funding risk with

$$\text{LCR} = \frac{\text{Stock of high-quality liquid assets}}{\text{Net cash outflows over a 30-day time period}} \geq 100\%$$

Net cash outflows are defined as cumulative outflows minus inflows expected under stress scenarios.

Loan New Business RAPM – the ratio of the present value of future profits from underwriting to the present value of capital tied up for the underwriting risk in the product, where profits are measured as if no financial market risk is taken.

Long-Term Investing – defined as investing with the expectation of holding an asset for an indefinite period of time by an investor with the capability to do so.

Loss Ratio – defined as the ratio of the sum of actual and expected claims and claims adjustment expenses for the calendar year to the premium earned in the calendar year.

Market Capitalization (MC) – the total value of the shares outstanding of a publicly traded company; equal to the share price times the number of shares outstanding.

Market-Consistent Embedded Value (MCEV) – a measure of the consolidated value of shareholders' interests in the existing, covered insurance business, including earnings distributable from assets allocated to the covered business after sufficient allowance for the aggregate risks in the business.

Market-to-Book (M/B) Multiple – a financial ratio used to compare a company's current market price to its book value. It shows the "price" (premium or discount) the market is willing to pay for the book equity invested in the company.

Market Value Earnings (MVE) – defined as period earnings expressed on mark-to-market basis. Typical differences to accounting earnings include unrealized gains/losses as well as the present value of new business originated during the period.

Market Value Surplus (MVS) – the difference between the Market Value of Assets (MVA) and the Market Value of Liabilities (MVL), e.g. $\text{MVS} = \text{MVA} - \text{MVL}$.

Material Risk Takers – defined as individuals that through decisions or influence can expose the organization to material risk.

Minimum Required Eligible Liabilities (MREL) – defined as financial leverage or funds for banks which can be "bailed-in" in case resolution measures need to be taken.

Modigliani–Miller Theorem – a theorem on capital structure which states the conditions under which the value of a firm is unaffected by how that firm is financed (e.g., the total value of the firm to debt and equity financiers is independent of how operating assets are financed by issuing stock or selling debt). The Modigliani–Miller theorem is also often called the capital structure irrelevance principle.

Moral Hazard – occurs under information asymmetry when the party with more information has a tendency or incentive to behave inappropriately from the perspective of the party with less information. With respect to insurance, it can be summarized as "the tendency of insurance protection to alter an individual's motive to prevent loss."

Near Misses – defined as events which could have caused a loss but did not.

Net Asset Value (NAV) – the value of an entity's assets minus the value of its liabilities.

Net Promoter Score (NPS) – a metric ranging between $[-100\%, +100\%]$ used to gauge the loyalty of a firm's customers. It is defined as (the number of respondents promoting the firm minus the number of detractors)/(the total number of respondents).

Net Stable Funding Ratio (NSFR) – a measure of liquidity funding risk, with

$$\text{NSFR} = \frac{\text{Available amount of stable funding}}{\text{Required amount of stable funding}} > 100\%$$

New Business Margin (NBM) – the ratio between the present value of future excess profits to shareholders (including the cost of underwriting capital) divided by the present value of future premiums, where profits are measured as financial market risk transferred to the market at current market prices. Calculated as the Value of New Business (VNB) divided by the Present Value of New Business Premium (PVNBP).

New Business RAPMs – a measure of the expected risk-adjusted excess returns from non-traded credit or insurance risk as if the loan or policy is held to maturity and financed/invested on a perfectly matched basis (e.g., excluding any financial market risks and returns).

Newly Acquired Customers – defined as new customers for which no previous business relationship existed, often the primary focus of sales-oriented companies and an important driver of revenue growth.

NFCL – non-financial component of liabilities, representing the value or cost of insurance underwriting risks. NFCL is valued using a mark-to-model approach.

Non-proportional Reinsurance – reinsurance contract indemnifying the insurer only if the loss is above a specific threshold, called the retention level, and up to a specific limit. The main form of non-proportional reinsurance is excess of loss (XL) reinsurance.

NOPLAT – net cash operating profit (excluding non-cash items and debt servicing charges) less adjusted taxes.

Operating Leverage – defined as all financing used by the Treasury and operating businesses to lever assets in the pursuit of operating returns. A key characteristic differentiating operating leverage from financial leverage is that the interest expense for operating leverage is deducted when calculating the business unit's operating profit whereas the cost of financial leverage is only recognized in the weighted average cost of capital the operating businesses need to meet.

Option-Adjusted (Funding) Spread (OAS/OAFS) – defined as the effective spread over/under Libor for a financing or investment alternative. It equates the present value of the cash received against the present value of the future obligations including embedded options, evaluated using financial markets techniques.

Over-The-Counter (OTC) – trading done directly between two parties and not through an exchange. An exchange has the benefit of facilitating liquidity, mitigating all credit risk concerning the default of one party in the transaction, providing transparency and maintaining the current market price but at the price of product or trade standardization.

Passive Limit Breach – defined as a limit breach not caused by a management action but rather by factors outside of the control of management, e.g. extreme market movements, etc.

Pay As You Drive (PAYD) – also known as Usage-Based Insurance (UBI); a type of vehicle insurance whereby the insurance premium is dependent upon the type of vehicle used, measured against time, distance, behavior and place.

Policy Limits – defined as the maximum amount of insurance coverage.

Present Value of Future Profits (PVFP) – defined as the present value of future profits which are expected to emerge from the covered block of insurance liabilities and associated statutory reserve assets; used in calculating LH Traditional and European Embedded Values (see Chapter 7).

Price-to-Book Ratio (P/BV) – a valuation ratio used to compare a company's current market price to its accounting book value.

Price-to-Earnings Ratio (P/E) – a valuation ratio used to compare a company's current share price relative to its per-share earnings.

Proportional Reinsurance – defined as a contract whereby the reinsurer takes a stated percentage share of the premium and claims for each covered policy that an insurer writes. In addition, the reinsurer allows a "ceding commission" to the insurer to cover the costs incurred by the insurer (marketing, underwriting, claims, etc.). The arrangement can be "quota share" or "surplus reinsurance."

PVIF – present value of the in-force business. The present value of future cash flows projected to emerge from the assets backing liabilities of the in-force covered business; part of an insurer's MCEV.

Quota Share Reinsurance – identical to proportional reinsurance, under a quota share arrangement, a fixed percentage of each insurance policy is reinsured.

Reputational Risks – defined as a loss of firm value due to damage to its reputation or standing as perceived by the public, where firm value refers to both direct losses as well as the opportunity cost of a potential loss in future business or franchise value.

Reserve Run-off – defined as "unexpected" claims developments from prior years relative to the carried reserves. A positive run-off means that prior year reserves were set "too high" relative to actual developments, a negative run-off means that reserves were insufficient and need to be strengthened.

Resolution and Recovery Planning – so-called "living wills" required for all G-SIFIs and any other firm assessed by national authorities as potentially having an impact on financial stability in the event of its failure.

Return on Equity (RoE) – represents the ratio of accounting net income divided by accounting shareholders' equity.

Revolving Funding – defined as financing which is shorter in tenor and which must therefore be rolled over in order to finance an asset to its maturity. The opposite of term funding.

Risk – defined as the possible failure to meet your desired and expected objectives due to future, uncertain events.

Risk-Adjusted Performance Measure (RAPM) – any of the generically defined profitability measures which divide risk-adjusted contributions by a measure of risk-adjusted required capital.

Risk-Adjusted Return on Capital (RAROC) – a risk-based profitability measure belonging to the RAPM measures.

Risk Premium – the minimum by which the expected return on a risky asset (or liability) must exceed the known return on a risk-free asset in order to induce an individual to hold the risky asset rather than the risk-free asset.

Roll-Forward – the systematic establishment of new accounting period balances by using (rolling forward) prior accounting period data, adjusted for current market conditions.

Security Market Line (SML) – the expected rate of return of an individual security as a function of systematic, non-diversifiable risk or "beta" (β) under the CAPM.

Separate Account Products – separate account insurance products hold the assets backing the savings or wealth component of the policy in a separate, segregated account on behalf of the policy holder; an insolvency of the insurer generally does not influence the separate account value. The returns to the policy holder are determined to a large extent by the returns on the separate account assets, typically invested in investment funds, subject to any additional fees or guarantees provided by the insurance company.

Service Level Agreement (SLA) – a contract for formally defined services. Particular aspects of the service (scope, quality, responsibilities) are agreed between the service provider and the service user. A common feature of an SLA is a contracted delivery time of the service or performance.

Shareholder Surrogate Model – a model of corporate governance where the corporate center applies market discipline internally to each of the business segments which is no longer feasible for external shareholders to apply due to the increased complexity, opacity and diminishing effectiveness of shareholder rights for a diversified financial services conglomerate.

Solvency II – the prudential regime for insurance and reinsurance undertakings in the European Union scheduled to come into effect as of January 1, 2016. It is modeled after the Basel II/III three-pillar approach to supervision.

Strategic Planning and Performance Management – defined as the process of setting goals; defining actions to achieve the goals; allocating and motivating resources to execute the actions; directing and monitoring performance to ensure successful execution.

Superannuation – the risk that assets are depleted before the death of an annuity investor.

Surplus Reinsurance – under a surplus share arrangement, the ceding company decides on a "retention limit" (e.g., $100,000). The ceding company retains the full amount of each risk, with a maximum of $100,000 per policy or per risk, with the remainder of the risk transferred or reinsured.

Swap – a derivative in which two counterparties exchange cash flows. Swaps can be used to hedge certain risks such as interest rate risk, or to speculate on changes in the expected direction of underlying prices. The five generic types of swap are interest rate swaps, currency swaps, credit swaps, commodity swaps and equity swaps.

Systematic Risk – the risk inherent to the entire market or an entire market segment, often referred to as "non-diversifiable risk." This type of risk is both unpredictable and impossible to avoid completely. It cannot be mitigated through diversification, only through hedging.

Tactical Asset Allocation – defined as the active selection of individual securities, sectors, etc. within an asset class in order to take advantage of perceived short-term opportunities.

Tactical Bolt-on Acquisitions – defined as acquisitions which fall within a business's current product/ market/geographical footprint, conducted by an experienced management team and executed in order to gain synergies.

Tangible Net Asset Value (TNAV) – represents IFRS net asset value or equity less intangibles such as goodwill, deferred acquisition costs (DAC) or value of business acquired (VOBA).

Term Funding – defined as financing which matches the maturity of an asset being purchased or financed. The opposite of revolving funding.

Term Insurance – provides a payment to the policy's beneficiary upon the death of the individual covered by the policy. Premiums are paid and the policy pays only during the term; the policy has no residual value after the term has expired. Term policies often require a medical examination as part of the underwriting process. They tend to be annually renewable at premium levels which can be adapted over time and which are specific to the individual covered. Various exclusions (e.g., for suicide, war, terrorism, etc.) are standard.

Time Value of Financial Options and Guarantees (TVOG) – used in calculating MCEV; the difference between the deterministic PVFP and a full stochastic PVFP calculated using financial option pricing techniques.

Total Cost of Risk (TCR) – defined as the discounted sum of expected losses (e.g., loan losses or insurance claims) and the discounted cost of the minimum capital needed to cover unexpected losses with reasonable confidence. The present value cost of the minimum capital requirements is determined by the product's Economic Capital Intensity (ECI).

Total Shareholder Return (TSR) – defined as the total return of a stock to an investor (capital gain plus dividends).

Total Value Added (TVA) – also known as Shareholder Value Added (SVA^{TM}); the present value of all future expected economic profits from the business or activity.

"Traditional" and "Non-traditional" Insurance Activities – defined by the International Association of Insurance Supervisors in the context of systemic relevance. "Traditional" insurance includes PC insurance and most LH insurance and is not systemically relevant. "Non-traditional" insurance (including variable annuities, GICs, mortgage insurance and credit guarantees) may be.

Treaty Reinsurance – a form of reinsurance in which the ceding company makes an agreement to cede certain classes of business to a reinsurer. The reinsurer, in turn, agrees to accept all business qualifying under the agreement, known as the "treaty."

Type 1 Assets – financial assets and liabilities whose values are based on unadjusted, quoted prices for identical assets or liabilities in a deep and liquid market.

Type 2 Assets – financial assets and liabilities whose values are based on their quoted prices in inactive markets, or whose values are based on models, but the inputs to those models are observable either directly or indirectly for substantially the full term of the asset or liability.

Type 3 Assets – financial assets and liabilities whose values are based on prices or valuation techniques that require inputs that are both unobservable and significant for the overall fair value measurement.

Underwriting Effectiveness – defined as the ratio of the Total Cost of Risk (TCR) to revenues or operating income.

Unit-Linked Products – insurance products investing part of the premium in a segregated investment fund such as a mutual fund, after the deduction of any fees. In the absence of any guarantees, the return on the policy holder's account directly matches the return on the fund less any applicable expense loadings or asset management fees. Unit-linked products typically do not offer a guarantee beyond a GMDB in order to qualify as insurance for tax purposes. Unit-linked products compete directly with mutual funds.

Universal Life Insurance – combination of death benefits and a savings component where the cost of the death benefit, as well as other expense loadings, are deducted from the premium every period and any remaining premium is credited to the cash value of the policy. The premium charged for protection is reset annually. The cash value of the policy grows with investment returns credited by the insurance company, subject to a minimum guaranteed level of return.

Usage-Based Insurance – defined as insurance whose premium and coverage depends upon the usage characteristics of the policy holder. Example, Pay As You Drive (PAYD) motor insurance based on telematics.

Utility Function – a theoretical construct used to compare the relative "value" of something to an individual. A utility function defines a person's willingness to pay an amount for different goods or services, also when the outcomes are uncertain.

Value at Risk (VaR) – measures the maximum possible loss for a portfolio within a predefined confidence interval over a predefined horizon. Commonly defined as the maximum losses at a 99% confidence interval over a 10-day holding period for trading books, whereas Solvency II defines minimum capital requirements at a 99.5% confidence interval over a 1-year horizon.

Value of New Business (VNB) – defined as the value of new business after all expenses and cost of risk, used in calculating MCEV.

Variable Annuity Products – separate account insurance products which are like unit-linked products during the saving or investment phase but allowing the client to select from a variety of different fund alternatives. They differ from unit-linked products in that they offer a wider range of guarantees or "riders," including the option to convert the account balances into an annuity during the decumulation phase.

Vega – a measure of an option's sensitivity to the implied volatility of the underlying asset (e.g., $\nu = \partial V / \partial \sigma$).

Whole-Life Insurance – products are similar to a universal life product but the premiums, as well as death benefits and cash surrender values, are set in advance for the whole life of the individual. As such, there is more mortality risk for the insurer.

References

Abdou, H. and Pointon, J. (2011) Credit scoring, statistical techniques and evaluation criteria: A review of the literature. *Intelligent Systems in Accounting, Finance & Management*, 18, 59–88.

Accenture (2008) A strategic approach to cost reduction in banking: Achieving high performance in uncertain times.

Adrian, T. and Shin, H.S. (2008) Procyclical Leverage and Value-at-Risk. Federal Reserve Bank of New York Staff Reports #338, revised March 2012.

Admati, A.R., DeMarzo, P.M., Hellwig, M.F. and Pfleiderer, P. (2010) Fallacies, irrelevant facts and myths in the discussion of capital regulation: Why bank equity is not expensive, Preprints of the Max Planck Institute for Research on Collective Goods, Bonn 2010.42.

Akerlof, G.A. and Romer, P.M. (1993) Looting: The economic underworld of bankruptcy for profit. Brookings Papers on Economic Activity.

Allen, J. and Zook, C. (2001) *Profit from the Core: Growth Strategy in an Era of Turbulence*. Harvard Business School Press, Boston, MA.

Allianz (2012) Q4 analyst presentation and 2012 Annual Report, https://www.allianz.com/en/investor_relations/results_reports/results.html#!me66bbef7-bcc4-46c8-a9db-7226f59a70a4

Allianz (2013) Capital Markets Day, Berlin, June 25, https://www.allianz.com/v_1372138505000/media/investor_relations/en/conferences/capital_markets_days/documents/2013_allianz_cmd.pdf

Allianz (2014a) Group Financial Results, https://www.allianz.com/v_1415339918000/media/investor_relations/en/results/2014_3q/3q14_analysts_presentation.pdf

Allianz (2014b) Capital Markets Day, London, July 4, https://www.allianz.com/v_1404469099000/media/investor_relations/en/conferences/capital_markets_days/documents/2014_Allianz_CMD.pdf

Allianz (2014c) Allianz 2013 and outlook 2014, https://www.allianz.com/v_1393480817000/media/investor_relations/en/results/2013_fy/fy13_analyst_presentation.pdf

Alloway, T. (2011) Credit Suisse's $6.2bn Swiss finish. FT.com, February 14.

Almezweq, M. and Liu, G. (2012) The value relevance of voluntary European embedded value disclosures: Evidence from UK life insurance companies. *International Journal of Accounting and Finance*, 3 (4), 343–366.

Altman, E. and Saunders, A. (1998) Credit risk measurement: Developments over the past 20 years. *Journal of Banking and Finance*, 21, 1721–1742.

Altman, E., Avery, R., Eisenbeis, R. and Sinkey, J. (1981) *Application of Classification Techniques in Business, Banking and Finance*. JAI Press, Greenwich, CT.

A.M. Best (2006) A.M. Best's perspective on operating leverage. Methodology Paper, http://www.fhlbc.com/Members/Documents/AMbestpersp.pdf

American Academy of Actuaries (2010) Common practices relating to FASB Statement 133, Accounting for derivative instruments and hedging activities as it relates to variable annuities with guaranteed benefits. A public policy practice note, http://cv.actuary.org/pdf/life/fas133_feb10.pdf

American Association of Actuaries (2000) Report of the Life Liquidity Work Group.

American Productivity and Quality Centre (1997) *Benchmarking Benchmarking*, APQR Report.

Amihud, Y., Mendelson, H. and Pedersen, L. (2005) *Liquidity and Asset Prices*, Foundation and Trends in Finance. Now Publishers Inc., Hanover, CT.

Amir, E. (1993) The market valuation of accounting information: The case of post-retirement benefits and other pensions. *The Accounting Review*, 68, 703–724.

Applebaum, Y. (2012) Have insurance companies forgotten the meaning of insurance? *The Atlantic*, May 7, http://www.theatlantic.com/business/archive/2012/05/have-insurance-companies-forgotten-the-meaning-of-insurance/256677/

Arnott, R.D. and Asness, C.S. (2003) Surprise! Higher dividends = Higher earnings growth. *Financial Analysts Journal*, 59 (1), 70–87.

Artzner, P., Delbaen, F., Eber, J.-M. and Heath, D. (1999) Coherent Measures of Risk, *Mathematical Finance*, 9 (3), 203–228.

Asia Development Bank (2008) TA-6454 (REG): Supporting Regional Capacities for Financial Asset and Liability and Risk Management: Risk Management and Asset and Liability Management in Banks.

Association of British Insurers (ABI) (2010) The use of gender in insurance pricing. Research Paper No. 24, Report from Oxera.

Athene Holding (2013) Presentation to AAA investors on Athene, February, http://www.apolloalternativeassets.com/ViewDocument.aspx?f=MHAR_AAA_Presentation_2_6_13.pdf

Autonomous (2012) In the loop: Taking stock after January's run. Research Report Issue 29, Sector: Insurers.

Babbel, D.F. (1985) The price elasticity of demand for whole life insurance. *The Journal of Finance*, 40 (1), 225–239.

Babbel, D.F. and Staking, K.B. (1989) The market reward for insurers that practice asset/liability management, Goldman Sachs.

Bacidore, J.M., Boquist, J.A., Milbourn, T.T. and Thakor, A.V. (1997) The search for the best financial performance measure. *Financial Analysts Journal* 53 (3), 11–20.

Baghai, M. and Chan, J. (2000) Three horizons of growth: Companies need to balance present operations against future possibilities to ensure success. *National Post*.

Balasumgramanyan, L. and Van Hoose, D.D. (2012) Bank balance sheet dynamics under a regulatory liquidity-coverage-ratio constraint. Working Paper 12-09, Federal Reserve Bank of Cleveland, April.

Barclays (2011) European insurance: Quality of life – Generali and Allianz stand out. *Equity Research*, June 8.

Barclays Capital (2011) Interest in Insurance: Turning to Japan, European Insurance Equity Research, 12 October 2011.

Barker, G. and Tooth, R. (2008) An analysis of house and contents insurance in Australia. ANU Center for Law and Economics Working Paper #1, Australia National University.

Barth, J., Caprio, G. and Levine, R. (2005) *Rethinking Banking Regulations: Till Angels Govern*. Cambridge University Press, Cambridge.

Barth, M. (1994) Fair value accounting: Evidence from investment securities and the market valuation of banks. *The Accounting Review*, 69 (1), 1–25.

Barth, M. and Beaver, W.H. (2001) The relevance of the value relevance literature for financial accounting standard setting: Another view. Kenan-Flagler Business School, University of North Carolina – Chapel Hill, Working Paper, January.

Barth, M.E., Beaver, W.H. and Landsman, W.R. (1996) Value relevance of banks' fair value disclosures under SFAS 107. *The Accounting Review*, 71 (4), 513–537.

Barth, M.E., Beaver, W.H. and Landsman, W.R. (1997) Are banks' SFAS 107 fair value disclosures relevant to investors? *Bank Accounting and Finance*, 10, 9–15.

Barth, M.E., Beaver, W.H. and Landsman, W.R. (2000) The relevance of value relevance research. Working Paper, Stanford University.

Bartov, E., Goldberg, S. and Kim, M. (2001) The valuation-relevance of earnings and cash flows: An international perspective. *Journal of International Financial Management and Accounting*, 12 (2), 103–132.

Basel Committee on Banking Supervision (BIS) (1998) Framework for internal control systems in banking organizations, September.

Basel Committee on Banking Supervision (BIS) (2001a) Principles for the management of credit risk, http://www.bis.org/publ/bcbsc125.pdf

Basel Committee on Banking Supervision (BIS) (2001b) Consultative document on "operational risk," January.

Basel Committee on Banking Supervision (BIS) (2008) Principles for sound liquidity risk management and supervision, September.

Basel Committee on Banking Supervision (BIS) (2009a) International framework for liquidity risk measurement, standards and monitoring. Consultative document, December, http://www.bis.org/publ/bcbs165.pdf

Basel Committee on Banking Supervision (BIS) (2009b) Proposed enhancements to the Basel II framework.

Basel Committee on Banking Supervision (BIS) (2010) Basel III: International framework for liquidity risk measurement, standards and monitoring, December, http://www.bis.org/publ/bcbs188.pdf

Basel Committee on Banking Supervision (BIS) (2011) Principles for the sound management of operational risk.

Basel Committee on Banking Supervision (BIS) (2012) Composition of capital disclosure requirements: Rules text, http://www.bis.org/publ/bcbs221.pdf

Batty, M., Tripathi, A., Kroll, A., Wu, C.-S.P., Moore, D., Stehno, C., Lau, L., Guszcza, J. and Katcher, M. (2010) Predictive modeling for life insurance: Ways life insurers can participate in the business analytics revolution. Deloitte Practitioner Series.

Bauer, D., Bergmann, D. and Kiesel, R. (2009) On the risk-neutral valuation of life insurance contracts with numerical methods in view. Working Paper, http://www.actuaries.org/AFIR/Colloquia/Rome2/Bauer_Bergmann_Kiesel.pdf

Baumgarten, P. and Heywood, S. (2011) Reinventing the corporate center. *McKinsey Quarterly*, September.

BCG (2004) Transforming retail banking processes. White Paper.

BCG (2012) In the center of the storm: Insights from BCG's Treasury Benchmarking Survey 2012.

BCG (2013) Beyond cost cutting: Six steps to achieving competitive advantage through cost excellence.

Beal, R., Weisgerber, W., Poster, C. and Becker, E. (2013) Incentive compensation/risk management – integrating incentive alignment and risk mitigation. Working Paper.

Beattie, A. (n.d.) The evolution of banking. Investopedia, www.investopedia.com/articles/07/banking.asp

Becker, D.N. (1991) A method for option-adjusted pricing and valuation of insurance products. Society of Actuaries, *Product Development News*, 30 (Nov), 1–6, http://rmtf.soa.org/option_spread.pdf

Bell, V. and Young, G. (2010) Understanding the weakness of bank lending, Research and Analysis, Bank of England Quarterly Bulletin, Q4.

Bennett, S.G. (2002) How to structure incentive plans that work. *EVAluation*, April.

Bentston, G., Irvine, P., Rosenfeld, J. and Sinkey, J.F. (2000) Bank capital structure, regulatory capital and securities innovation. Working Paper 2000-18, October, Federal Reserve Bank of Atlanta, http://citeseerx.ist.psu.edu/viewdoc/download?doi=10.1.1.200.4469&rep=rep1&type=pdf

Berger, A., Davies, S. and Flannery, M. (2000) Comparing market and supervisory assessments of bank performance: Who knows what when? *Journal of Money Credit and Banking*, 32, 641–647.

Berger, A., De Young, R., Flannery, M., Lee, D. and Oztekin, Ö. (2008) How do large banking organizations manage their capital ratios? *Journal of Financial Services Research*, 34, 123–149.

Berger, A.N. and Humphrey, D.B. (1994) Bank scale economics, mergers, concentration, and efficiency: The US experience. Wharton Business School Working Paper 94-25, University of Pennsylvania.

Berger, A.N., Hancock, D. and Humphrey, D.B. (1993) Bank efficiency derived from the profit function. *Journal of Banking and Finance*, 17, 317–348.

Berkovsky, S., Eytani, Y., Furman, E. and Makov, U. (2004), Developing a framework for insurance underwriting expert systems, International Conference on Informatics, Cesme, Turkey.

Berlin, M. (2011) Can we explain bank's capital structures? *Business Review*, Q2, Philadelphia Fed.

Berman, D. (2013) Top 7 biggest bank fines. *AdvisorOne*, January 11, http://www.advisorone.com/2013/01/11/top-7-biggest-bank-fines

BestWeek (2010) Gen Re to pay $92.2 million, dissolve Dublin subsidiary to settle finite re charges, January.

Biddle, G.C., Bowen, R.M. and Wallace, J.S. (1999) Evidence on EVA. *Journal of Applied Corporate Finance*, 12 (2), 69–79.

Binder, J. (2014) *Online Channel Integration: Value creation and customer reactions in online and physical stores*. Springer-Verlag, Berlin.

Blake, D. and Timmerman, A. (2001) Performance benchmarks for institutional investors: Measuring, monitoring and modifying behavior. Discussion Paper PI-0106, The Pensions Institute, Birkbeck College, The University of London.

Bloomberg (2014) Did bank rules kill liquidity? Volcker, Frank respond, October 20, http://www.bloomberg.com/news/2014-10-20/did-bank-rules-kill-liquidity-volcker-frank-respond.html

BNP Paribas (2003) European Retail Banking Report, March.

Bodie, Z. (2006) On asset liability matching and Federal deposit and pension insurance. *Federal Reserve Bank of St. Louis Review*, 88 (4), 323–329.

Boekel, P., Delft, L.v., Hoshino, T., Ino, R., Reynolds, C. and Verheugen, H. (2009) Replicating portfolios: An introduction, analysis and illustrations. Milliman Research Report, November, http://milliman.ie/documents/replicating_portfolios.pdf

Bongini, P., Laeven, L. and Majnoni, G. (2002) How good is the market at assessing bank fragility? A horse race between different indicators. *Journal of Banking and Finance*, 26, 1011–1028.

Bowyer, C. (2014) What's happened to the 'Bitcoin Revolution'? Adam Smith Institute, September 29, http://www.adamsmith.org/blog/money-banking/whats-happened-to-the-bitcoin-revolution/

Brav, A., Graham, J.R., Harvey, C.R. and Michaely, R. (2005) Pay out policy in the 21st century. *Journal of Financial Economics*, 77 (3), 483–527.

Brealey, R.A., Myers, S.C. and Allen, F. (2011) *Principles of Corporate Finance, Global Edition*, 11th edn. McGraw-Hill, New York.

Brewer, E., Kaufmann, G. and Wall, L. (2008) Bank capital ratios across countries: Why do they vary? *Journal of Financial Services Research*, 34, 177–201.

Bright, C., Visbal, J. and Young, N. (2008) Ten lessons for all companies from private equity, Spencer Stuart Point of View.

Brinson, G.P., Singer, B.D. and Beebower, G.L. (1986) Determinants of portfolio performance. *Financial Analysts Journal*, 42 (4), 39–44.

Brinson, G.P., Singer, B.D. and Beebower, G.L. (1991) Determinants of portfolio performance II: An update. *Financial Analysts Journal*, 47 (3), 40–48.

Brown Smith Wallace (2008) Thought Leadership Case Studies, General American, http://www.bswllc.com/case-studies-general-american

Buruc, J. (2008) Thoughts about employing Funds Transfer Pricing. International Finance Corporation.

Business Week (2009) The curious paradox of 'optimism bias,' August 13 http://www.businessweek.com/magazine/content/09_34/b4144048821798.htm

Buttonwood (2012) The secrets of Buffett's success. *The Economist*, September 29, http://www.economist.com/node/21563735

Cai, J., Cherny, K. and Milbourn, T. (2010) Compensation and risk incentives in banking and finance. Economic Commentary, Federal Reserve Bank of Cleveland, http://www.clevelandfed.org/research/commentary/2010/2010-13.cfm

Carhart, M. (1997) On persistence in mutual fund performance. *The Journal of Finance*, 52, 57–82.

Carney, J. (2013) Everything you ever wanted to know about bank leverage rules, CNBC explains. CNBC, July 12, http://www.cnbc.com/id/100880857

Carroll, P. (2010) Rethinking underwriting. *RMA Journal*, December 2010–January 2011.

Carroll, T., Linsemeier, T. and Petroni, K. (2003) The reliability of fair value versus historical cost information: Evidence from closed-end mutual funds. *Journal of Accounting, Auditing and Finance*, 18, 1–23.

Casserly, D. (1991) *Facing up to the Risks: How Financial Institutions can Survive and Prosper*. John Wiley Inc., New York.

Cassidy, J. (2010) What good is Wall Street? Much of what investment bankers do is socially worthless. *The New Yorker*, Annals of Economics, November 29, http://www.newyorker.com/magazine/2010/11/29/what-good-is-wall-street

CEA (2009) CEA Statistics No. 44: European insurance in figures, December.

CFA Institute, http://www.cfainstitute.org/learning/products/publications/inv/Documents/corporate_finance_chapter6.pptx

CFA (2006) Breaking the short-term cycle: Discussions and recommendation on how corporate leaders, asset managers, investors and analysts can refocus on long-term value. Proceedings of the CFA Centre for Financial Market Integrity and the Business Roundtable Institute for Corporate Ethics Symposium Series on Short-Termism.

CFO Forum (2004a) EEV Principles, www.cfoforum.eu, http://www.cfoforum.nl/letters/eev_principles.pdf

CFO Forum (2004b) EEV Basis for Conclusions, www.cfoforum.eu

CFO Forum (2005) EEV Disclosures and Sensitivities, www.cfoforum.eu

CFO Forum (2008) Market Consistent Embedded Value Principles and Basis for Conclusions, June.

CFO Forum (2009a) Market Consistent Embedded Value Principles, http://www.cfoforum.nl/downloads/MCEV_Principles_and_Guidance_October_2009.pdf

CFO Forum (2009b) Market Consistent Embedded Value - Basis for Conclusions, October.

Chae, J. and Wang, A. (2003) Who makes markets? Do dealers provide or take liquidity? Working Paper, Sloan School of Management, MIT, http://web.mit.edu/finlunch/Fall03/AlbertWang.pdf

Chasteen, L.G. and Ransom, C.R. (2007) Including credit standing in measuring the fair value of liabilities – let's pass this one to the shareholders. *Accounting Horizons*, 21, 119–135.

Chee, S. (2011) The information content of commercial banks' fair value disclosures of loans under SFAS 107. Job Market Paper, U.C. Berkeley, January.

Chen, S. and Dodd, J.L. (1997) Economic Value Added (EVA^{TM}): An empirical examination of a new corporate performance measure. *Journal of Managerial Issues*, 9 (3), 318–333.

Choi, B., Collins, D.W. and Johnson, W.B. (1997) Valuation implications of reliability differences: The case of non-pension post-retirement obligations. *The Accounting Review*, 27, 351–383.

Chow, G. (1995) Portfolio selection based on return, risk and relative performance. *Financial Analysts Journal*, 51 (2), 54–60.

CIMA (2008) Activity Based Costing: Topic Gateway Series No. 1.

Claus, J. and Thomas, J. (2001) Equity premia as low as three percent? Evidence from analysts' earnings forecasts for domestic and international stock markets. *The Journal of Finance*, 56 (5), 1629–1666.

CNN (2009) Mergers fail more often than marriages, http://edition.cnn.com/2009/BUSINESS/05/21/merger.marriage/

Cogent Research (2010) Institutional Investor Brandscape: 2010.

Coleman, W.H. and Fortier, K.E. (2002) Understanding and using long-term incentives, www.salary.com/hr

Collis, D.J. and Rukstad, M.G. (2008) Can you say what your strategy is? *Harvard Business Review*, April, 1–10.

Congressional Budget Office (CBO) (2005) The Price Sensitivity of Demand for Non-Group Health Care.

Contessi, S., Li Li and Russ, K. (2013) Bank vs. bond financing over the business cycle. Economic Synopses, Federal Reserve Bank of St. Louis, No 31.

Cooper, M.J., Gulen, H. and Schill, M.J. (2008) Asset growth and the cross-section of stock returns. *The Journal of Finance*, 63 (4), 1609–1651.

Copeland, T.E., Koller, T. and Murrin, J. (2000) *Valuation: Measuring and Managing the Value of Companies*, 3rd edn. John Wiley Inc., New York.

Corbett, M.F. (2004) The outsourcing revolution: Why it makes sense and how to do it right, http://www.economist.com/media/globalexecutive/outsourcing_revolution_e_02.pdf

COSO (1992) Committee of Sponsoring Organizations of the Treadway Commission, Internal Control – Integrated Framework.

COSO (2004) Committee of Sponsoring Organizations of the Treadway Commission, Enterprise Risk Management – An Integrated Approach.

COSO (2011) Committee of Sponsoring Organizations of the Treadway Commission, Internal Control – Integrated Framework.

Cotteleer, M. and Gorman, T. (2013) Making risky growth choices. Deloitte White Paper.

Couto, V. and Neilson, G. (2007) Headquarters: Irrelevant or irreplaceable? Booz Allen Hamilton.

Couto, V., Divakaran, A. and Galgar, D. (2012) Seven value creation lessons from private equity, http://www.strategy-business.com/article/00102?gko=6a378

Cowen, T. (2011) Euro vs. invasion of the zombie banks. *New York Times*, April 16.

Coyne, K.P. and Horn, J. (2009) Predicting your competitor's reaction. *Harvard Business Review*, April, 90–97.

Craig, V.V. (2001) Merchant banking: Past and present. FDIC Banking Review, September, https://www.fdic.gov/bank/analytical/banking/2001sep/article2.html

Credit Suisse (2011) What has happened under Japan's zero interest rate regime? Part 2: How has Japan's life insurance industry adapted to the low interest rate climate? Japan Economic Adviser, Economics Research, 29 September 2011.

CRO Forum (2004) European Embedded Value Principles.

CRO Forum (2008) Liquidity risk management: Best risk management practices. Working Paper, October.

CRO Forum (2009) Market value liabilities for insurance firms: Implementing elements for Solvency II, www.croforum.org

CRO Forum (2012) Investor Relationship Group: 2012 Project summary and conclusions.

Crouhy, M., Turnbull, S.M. and Wakeman, L. (1999) Measuring risk-adjusted performance. *Journal of Risk*, 2 (1), 5–35.

Cummins, J.D. and Danzon, P.M. (1997) Price, financial quality, and capital flows in insurance markets. *Journal of Financial Intermediation*, 6, 3–38.

Cummins, J.D. (2004) Securitization of life insurance assets and liabilities. Wharton Financial Institutions Center Working Paper.

Currie, A. (1998) Bank capital structure, regulatory capital and securities innovations. *Euromoney*, December, 47–50.

Cushman Jr. J.H. (2012) U.S. tightens security for economic data. *New York Times*, July 16.

Dahlby, B.G. (1983) Adverse selection and statistical discrimination: An analysis of Canadian automobile insurance. *Journal of Public Economics*, 20, 121–130.

Daily Mail Online (2009) Hubris, overarching vanity and how one man's ego brought banking to the brink, 20 January.

Daisley, M. (2013) Let's stick together: How risk and the business can learn to get along. Oliver Wyman.

Danielsson, J., Laeven, R., Perotti, E., Wüthrich, M., Ayadi, R. and Pelsser, A. (2012) Countercyclical regulation in Solvency II: Merits and flaws. VOX: CEPR's Policy Portal: Research-based policy analysis and commentary, June 23, http://www.voxeu.org/article/countercyclical-regulation-solvency-ii-merits-and-flaws

Darling Consulting Group (2007) Power up your ALCO, seven simple strategies to boost your ALCO performance.

Davidson, C. (2008) The replicating game. *Risk Magazine*, April. http://www.risk.net/insurance-risk/feature/1514564/the-replication-game

Delcour, G. (2012) On the use of risk free rates in the discounting of insurance cash flows. Master's Thesis, Faculty of Business and Economics, Katholieke Universiteit Leuven.

Della Casa, F. and Gaffo, M. (2013) Portfolio optimization via replication. *Insurance Risk*, October, http://www.risk.net/insurance-risk/technical-paper/2302844/portfolio-optimisation-via-replication

Deloitte (2014) Forward look: Top regulatory trends for 2014 in banking. Center for Regulatory Strategies, http://www.deloitte.com/assets/Dcom-UnitedStates/Local%20Assets/Documents/AERS/us_aers_dcrs_forward_look_banking_2014_020714.pdf

Denning, S. (2011) Lest we forget: Why we had a financial crisis. *Forbes*, http://www.forbes.com/sites/stevedenning/2011/11/22/5086/

Dermine, J. (2010) Bank valuation with an application to the implicit duration of non-maturing deposits. Working Paper.

Dermine, J. (2015) *Bank Valuation and Value-Based Management: Deposit and loan pricing, performance evaluation and risk management.* McGraw-Hill, New York.

Deutsche Bank (2013) Corporate bond issuance in Europe: Where do we stand and where are we heading? EU Monitor: Global financial markets, January 31 https://www.dbresearch.com/PROD/DBR_INTERNET_EN-PROD/PROD0000000000300834/Corporate+bond+issuance+in+Europe%3A+Where+do+we+stand+and+where+are+we+heading%3F.PDF

DeYoung, R., Flanner, M.J., Lang, W.W. and Sorescu, S.M. (2001) The information content of bank exam ratings and subordinated debt prices. *Journal of Money, Credit and Banking*, 33, 900–925.

Diebold, F.X., Doherty, N.A. and Herring, R.J. (eds) (2010) *The Known, the Unknown and the Unknowable in Financial Risk Management: Measurement and Theory Advancing Practice.* Princeton University Press, Princeton, NJ.

Dividend.com (2012) Dividends vs. share buybacks: It's a no brainer, November 14, http://www.nasdaq.com/article/dividends-vs-share-buybacks-its-a-no-brainer-cm189925

Doherty, N.A. and Smith, C.W. (1993) Corporate insurance strategy: The case of British Petroleum. *Journal of Applied Corporate Finance*, 6 (3), 4–15.

Dombret, A. (2013) Deutsche Bundesbank's 2013 Financial Stability Review.

Doran, G.T. (1981) There's a S.M.A.R.T. way to write management's goals and objectives. *Management Review*, 70 (11), 35–36.

Duffie, D. (1999) Credit swap valuation. *Financial Analysts Journal*, 55 (1), 73–87.

Duhigg, C. (2008) Bank of America's chief makes big bet. *New York Times*, January 12, http://www.nytimes.com/2008/01/12/business/12bank.html?pagewanted=all

Duttweiler, R. (2009) *Managing Liquidity in Banks – A top down approach.* John Wiley & Sons, Chichester.

Dye, R. and Sibony, O. (2007) How to improve strategic planning. *McKinsey Quarterly*, 3, 40–49.

Eccher, A., Ramesh, K. and Thiagarajan, S.R. (1996) Fair value disclosures of bank holding companies. *Journal of Accounting and Economics*, 22 (1), 79–117.

Economist (2002) Holey Cow! An opaque financial conglomerate out to repair its image and share price, June 27.

Edwards, E.O. and Bell, P.W. (1961) *The Theory and Measurement of Business Income.* University of California Press, Berkeley, CA.

EIOPA (2011) CP 009/2011 – Draft proposal on quantitative reporting templates and Draft proposal for guidelines on narrative public disclosure and supervisor reporting, predefined events and processes for reporting and disclosure, https://eiopa.europa.eu/consultations/consultation-papers/2011-closed-consultations/november-2011/draft-proposal-on-quantitative-reporting-templates-and-draft-proposal-for-guidelines-on-narrative-public-disclosure-supervisory-reporting-predefined-events-and-processes-for-reporting-disclosure/index.html

Eiteman, D.K., Stonehill, A.I. and Moffett, M.H. (2003) *Multinational Business Finance.* Pearson, New York.

El-Erian, M.A. (2009) A new normal. PIMCO Investment Outlook.

El-Erian, M.A. (2010) Navigating the new normal in industrial countries. Paper presented at the Per Jacobsson Foundation Lecture. http://www.imf.org/external/np/speeches/2010/101010.htm

El-Gazzar, S.M. and Jacob, R.A. (2013) The valuation effects of embedded value disclosure by life insurers. *International Journal of Economics and Accounting*, 4 (1), 26–53.

Elton, E.J., Gruber, M.J. and Blake, C.R. (1996) The persistence of risk-adjusted mutual fund performance. *Journal of Business*, 69 (2), 133–157.

England, P.D. and Verrall, R.J. (2002) Stochastic claims reserving in general insurance. Institute of Actuaries and Faculty of Actuaries, www.actuaries.org.uk/system/files/documents/pdf/sm0201.pdf

English, W.B., Van den Heuval, S.J. and Zakrajsek, E. (2012) Interest rate risk and bank equity valuations. Finance and Economics Discussion Series, Divisions of Research & Statistics and Monetary Affairs, Federal Reserve Board, Washington, D.C. 2012-26.

Eom, Y.H., Helwege, J. and Huang, J. (2004) Structural models of corporate bond pricing: An empirical analysis. *Review of Financial Studies*, 17, 499–544.

Epermanis, K. and Harrington, S.E. (2006) Market discipline in property/casualty insurance: Evidence from premium growth surrounding changes in financial strength ratings. *Journal of Money, Credit and Banking*, 38 (6), 1515–1544.

Ernst & Young (2012) Progress in financial services risk management: A survey of major financial institutions.

Ernst & Young (2013) Leading the way: Hedge fund-backed reinsurers generate AUM and permanent capital for asset managers. http://www.ey.com/Publication/vwLUAssets/EY_-_The_growth_of_hedge_fund-backed_reinsurers/$FILE/EY-Leading-the-way.pdf

Ernst & Young (2014a) Increasing authority and higher organizational profiles: 2014 insurance CRO survey.

Ernst & Young (2014b) Strategic asset allocation for Asia-Pacific life insurers: How optimized is your portfolio? http://www.ey.com/Publication/vwLUAssets/EY-Strategic-asset-allocation-for-Asia-Pacific-Life-Insurers/$FILE/EY-Strategic-asset-allocation-for-Asia-Pacific-Life-Insurers.pdf

Euramet (2013) Mega Cities, January, http://www.emrponline.eu/call2013/docs/MegaCities.pdf

Eurofi (2012) Summary of Discussions: What role and evolution for the financial system and its regulation to ensure sustainable financing of the EU economy?

European Central Bank (2011a) ECB announces details of refinancing operations from October 2011 to 10 July 2012. Press announcement, October 6.

European Central Bank (2011b) ECB announces measures to support bank lending and money market activity. Press announcement, December 8.

European Covered Bond Council (2012) http://ecbc.hypo.org/Content/Default.asp?PageID=311

Fabozzi, F.J. (1997) Advances in fixed income valuation, modeling and risk management. Frank J. Fabozzi Associates, New Hope, PA.

Fabozzi, F. (2012) *The Handbook of Fixed Income Securities*, 8th edn. McGraw-Hill, New York.

Fama, E.F. and French, K.R. (2010) Luck versus Skill in the Cross-Section of Mutual Fund Returns, *The Journal of Finance*, LXV(5 October).

Farah, N. (2002) The financial economics of performance measurement. In Knight, J. and Satchell, S. (eds), *Performance Measurement in Finance*. Butterworth-Heinemann, Oxford.

Faulkner, D., Teerikangas, S. and Joseph, R.J. (eds) (2012) *The Handbook of Mergers and Acquisitions*. Oxford University Press, Oxford.

Federal Deposit Insurance Corporation (FDIC) (1997) *History of the Eighties - Lessons for the Future, Vol 1: An examination of the banking crisis of the 1980s and early 1990s*, https: www.fdic.gov/bank/historical/history/.

Federal Deposit Insurance Corporation (FDIC) (2008) Liquidity risk management, Financial Institution Letters, FIL-84-2008, http://www.fdic.gov/news/news/financial/2008/fil08084.html

Federal Reserve Bank (2007) Press Release, http://www.federalreserve.gov/newsevents/press/monetary/20070817a.htm

Federal Reserve Bank (2008) Federal Reserve announces two initiatives designed to bolster market liquidity and promote orderly market functioning. Press Release, March 16, http://federalreserve.gov/newsevents/press/monetary/20080316a.htm

Federal Reserve Bank (2013) Payment system improvement – public consultation paper, September 10.

Federal Reserve Board (2013) Consumers and mobile financial services.

Financial Accounting Standards Board (FASB) (1991) Financial Accounting Standards No 107: Disclosures about fair value of financial Instruments, December, http://www.fasb.org/cs/BlobServer?blobkey=id&blobnocache=true&blobwhere=1175820920706&blobheader=application%2Fpdf&blobheadername2=Content-Length&blobheadername1=Content-Disposition&blobheader value2=

277095&blobheadervalue1=filename%3Dfas107.pdf&blobcol=urldata&blobtable=MungoBlobs
&cancel=Reject.

Financial Services Authority (FSA) (2011) Recovery and Resolution Plans, CP11/16, August.

Financial Services Authority (FSA) (2002) Operational risk systems and controls, Consultation Paper 142, http://www.fsa.gov.uk/pubs/cp/cp142.pdf.

Financial Times (2007) Citigroup's Chuck Prince wants to keep dancing, and can you really blame him? July 10.

Financial Times (2010) Bad actions stick, archbishop tells city, October 4.

Financial Times (2013) Risk models fuel fears for bank safety, February 1.

Fitch (2013) Asset manager rating criteria: Master criteria report.

Flannery, M. and Rangan, K. (2008) What caused the bank capital buildup of the 1990s? *Review of Finance*, 12 (2), 319–429.

Flannery, M.J. and James, C.M. (1984) The effect of interest rate changes on the common stock returns of financial institutions, *Journal of Finance*, 1141–1153.

Franzoni, F. and Plazzi, A. (2012) Do hedge funds provide liquidity? Evidence from their trades. Working Paper, University of Lugano and Swiss Finance Institute.

Frazzini, A., Kabiller, D. and Pedersen, L.H. (2013) Buffet's alpha. Working Paper, Yale University, http://www.econ.yale.edu/~af227/pdf/Buffett's%20Alpha%20-%20Frazzini,%20Kabiller%20and %20Pedersen.pdf

French, K.R. (2008) The cost of active investing. *The Journal of Finance*, 63 (4), 1537–1573.

French, K.R., Baily, M.N., Campbell, J.Y., Cochrane, J.H., Diamond, D.W., Duffie, D., Kashyap, A.K., Mishkin, F.S., Rajan, R.G., Scharfstein, D.S., Shiller, R.J., Shin, H.S., Slaughter, M.J., Stein, J.C. and Stulz, R.M. (2010) Squam Lake Report: Fixing the financial system.

Froot, K.A. and Stein, J.C. (1998a) Risk management, capital budgeting, and capital structure policy for financial institutions: An integrated approach. *Journal of Financial Economics*, 47, 55–82.

Froot, K.A. and Stein, J.C. (1998b) A new approach to capital budgeting for financial institutions. *Journal of Applied Corporate Finance*, 11 (2), 59–69.

FSB (2011a) FSB issues International Standard for Resolution Regime. Press Release, November.

FSB (2011b) Key Attributes of Effective Resolution Regimes for Financial Institutions, October.

FSB (2012) Update of group of global systemically important banks (G-SIBs), November 1.

FSB (2013a) Thematic Review on Risk Governance: Peer Review Report. Financial Stability Board.

FSB (2013b) Principles for an effective risk appetite framework. Consultative Document, July 17, http://www.financialstabilityboard.org/publications/r_130717.pdf

FSB (2014) Guidance on supervisory interaction with financial institutions on risk culture (a framework for assessing risk culture).

G.A. Kraut & Company (2008) What makes a great CFO? Does CFO quality impact valuation? Eleven investment professionals provide their insights.

Gabih, A., Grecksch, W. and Wunderlich, R. (2005) Dynamic portfolio optimization with bounded shortfall risks. *Stochastic Analysis and Applications*, 23, 579–594.

Gammeltoft, N. and Barinka, A. (2013) Goldman's options error shows peril persists after Knight. Bloomberg Business, August 21.

Garbade, K. (1986) Assessing risk and capital adequacy for Treasury securities. In *Topics in Money and Securities Markets*, No. 22. Bankers Trust, New York.

Geanakoplos, J. (2010) Solving the present crisis and managing the leverage cycle. FRBNY *Economics Policy Review*, 101–113.

Gebhardt, W.R., Lee, C.M.C. and Swaminathan, B. (1999) Toward an ex ante cost-of-capital. Cornell University, Working Paper.

Gifford, D. (1998) After the revolution. *CFO Magazine*, July 1, http://pages.stern.nyu.edu/~adamodar/New_Home_Page/articles/MM40yearslater.htm

Gilbert, C. (2008) Asset Liability Management: Performance metrics and risk attribution. Presentation to the 18th Annual CAA Conference, December, http://www.caa.com.bb/2008_Presentations/ALM_Performance_Metrics_and_Risk_Attribution_(Charles_Gilbert).pdf

Gintschel, A.C. and Wiehenkamp, C. (2009) A global liquidity factor for fixed income pricing, http://www.actuaries.org/Munich2009/papers/AFIR/Fri_12.00_AFIR_Gintschel_Asset_pricing_Paper.pdf

Girard, L.N. (2001) Market value of insurance liabilities: Reconciling the actuarial appraisal and option pricing methods. *North American Actuarial Journal*, 4 (1), 31–62.

Glovin, D., Hurtado, P. and Van Voris, B. (2011) Rajaratnam guilty on all counts in US insider trading case, Bloomberg, May 11.

Goldman Sachs (2010) Revisiting the role of insurance company ALM within a risk management framework. White Paper, October, http://www.goldmansachs.com/gsam/docs/instgeneral/general_materials/whitepaper/wp_revisiting_role_of_ins_co_alm.pdf

Golsby-Smith, T. (2011) Is your budgeting process killing your strategy? *Harvard Business Review*, January 18.

Goodman, J.A. (2009) *Strategic Customer Service: Managing the Customer Experience to Increase Positive Word of Mouth, Build Loyalty, and Maximize Profits*. AMACOM Books, New York.

Gounaris, S. (2005) Introduction of the guest editor. *International Journal of Bank Marketing for the Financial Services Sector*, Special Issue on Product Portfolio Management and Corporate Performance in the Banking Sector, 23 (1).

Graham, J.R. and Harvey, C.R. (2001) The theory and practice of corporate finance: Evidence from the field. *Journal of Financial Economics*, 60, 187–243.

Graham, J.R., Harvey, C.R. and Rajgopal, S. (2005) The economic implications of corporate reporting, SSRN, http://ssrn.com/abstract=491627

Graham, J.R., Harvey, C.R. and Rajgopal, S. (2006) Value destruction and financial reporting decisions. *Financial Analysts Journal*, 62 (6), 27–39.

Grant, J. (2011) Liquidity Transfer Pricing: A guide to better practice. APRA (Australian Prudential Regulation Authority) Working Paper, March.

Green, M. (2012) The nature of Bermuda: Reinsurers are tapping into hedge fund skills, http://www.highbeam.com/doc/1G1-292373830.html

Green, P.E., Krieger, A.M. and Srinivasan, V. (1990) Conjoint analysis in marketing: New developments with implications for research and practice. *Journal of Marketing*, 54, 3–19.

Griffin, M.W. (1990) An excess spread approach to non-participating insurance products. *Transactions of the Society of Actuaries*, 42, 231–258.

Gropp, R. and Heider, F. (2009) The determinants of bank capital structure. European Central Bank Working Paper Series No. 1096.

Gropp, R., Vesala, J. and Vulpes, G. (2004) Market indicators, bank fragility and indirect market discipline. FRBNY Economic Policy Review, September.

Gross, B. (2009) On the course to the "new normal," http://www.pimco.com/EN/Insights/Pages/Gross%20Sept%20On%20the%20Course%20to%20a%20New%20Normal.aspx

Groupe Consultatief Actuariel Europeen (2012) Market consistency. Working Paper.

Guill, G.D. (2009) Bankers Trust and the birth of modern risk management. Working Paper, Financial Institutions Center, Wharton School, March, http://fic.wharton.upenn.edu/fic/case%20studies/Birth%20of%20Modern%20Risk%20Managementapril09.pdf

Guo, D. and Winter, R.A. (1997) The capital structure of insurers: Theory and evidence. Working Paper.

Gupta, S., Hanssens, D., Hardie, B., Kahn, W., Kumar, V., Lin, N. and Sriram, N.R.S. (2006) Modelling customer lifetime value. *Journal of Service Research*, 9 (2), 139–155.

Gyntelberg, J. and Woolridge, P. (2008) Interbank rate fixings during the recent turmoil. *BIS Quarterly Review*, March, http://www.bis.org/publ/qtrpdf/r_qt0803g.pdf

Hababou, M. and Martel, J.M. (1998). A multicriteria approach for selecting a portfolio manager. *Information Systems and Operational Research*, 363, 161–176.

Haenlein, M. and Kaplan, A.M. (2011) Evaluating the consequences of abandoning unprofitable customers: A comparison of direct and indirect abandonment strategies. *Zeitschrift für Betriebswirtschaft.*

Hall, S., Huyett, B. and Koller, T. (2012) The power of an independent corporate center. *McKinsey Quarterly*, March.

Hall, E.A., Rosenthal, J. and Wade, J. (1993) How to make reengineering really work? *Harvard Business Review*, November–December.

Hammer, M. (1990) Reengineering work: Don't automate, obliterate. *Harvard Business Review*, July.

Hammer, M. and Champy, J.A. (1993) *Reengineering the Corporation: A manifesto for business revolution*. Harpert Business Books, New York.

Hancock, J., Huber, P. and Koch, P. (2001) The economics of insurance: How insurers create value for shareholders. Swiss Re Technical Paper, Swiss Reinsurance Company, Zurich.

Hardak, P. (2012) Acquisition Graph – Bank Mergers in USA (SVG).

Harlow, W. (1991) Asset allocation in a downside risk framework. *Financial Analysts Journal*, Sept–Oct, 28–40.

Harrison, I. (2004) Banks, capital and regulation: Towards an optimal capital regime for a small open economy. Working Paper, Financial Stability Department, Reserve Bank of New Zealand.

Hart, C., Heskett, J. and Sasser Jr. W.E. (1990) The profitable art of service recovery. *Harvard Business Review*, 68 (4), 148–156.

Hauser, J.R. (n.d.) Note on conjoint analysis. MIT Sloan Courseware.

Hendrick, B.J. (1907) *The Story of Life Insurance*. McClure, Philips & Co., New York.

Heppelmann, S. and Wrona, K. (2009) Holding structure – from conglomerate discount to management value added. *SCCO Research*, 36.

Hibbert, J., Krichner, A., Kretzschmar, G., Li, R. and McNeil, A. (2009) Liquidity Premium: Literature review of theoretical and empirical evidence. Barrie Hibbert Research Report.

Hildebrand, P. (2008) Is Basel II enough? The benefits of a leverage ratio. Financial Markets Group Lecture, London School of Economics, December 15, http://www.bis.org/review/r081216d.pdf

Hildreth, R. (2001) *The History of Banks*. Batoche Books, Kitchener, Ont.

Hill, A. (2014) Rules alone will not stop bad behavior. FT.com, June 16.

Hirst, D.E., Hopkins, P.E. and Wahlen, J.M. (2004) Fair values, income measurement and bank analysts risk and valuation judgments. *The Accounting Review*, 79, 453–472.

Hodder, L.D., Hopkins, P.E. and Wahlen, J.M. (2006) Risk relevance of fair value income measures for commercial banks. *The Accounting Review*, 81, 337–375.

Hoggson, N.F. (1926) *Banking Through the Ages*. Dodd, Mead & Company, New York.

Holland, K. and Himelstein, L. (1995) The Bankers Trust tapes. *Business Week*, http://www.businessweek.com/1995/42/b34461.htm

Holton, G.A. (2002) History of Value at Risk: 1922–1998. Working Paper, Contingency Analysis, Boston.

Hopkins, A. (2007) The problem of defining high reliability organizations. Working Paper, Australian National University.

Hoppe, K. (2012) The value of insurance to society. The Geneva Association Risk Management Newsletter #51, May, https://www.genevaassociation.org/media/185156/ga2012-rm51-hoppe.pdf

Horton, J. (2007) The value relevance of realistic reporting: Evidence from UK life insurers. *Accounting and Business Research*, 37 (3), 179–197.

Houltram, A. (2003) Reserving judgment: Considerations relevant to insurance liability assessment. Institute of Actuaries of Australia, http://actuaries.asn.au/Library/GI03paperhoultramV3.pdf

Hsu, C. (2000) Capital budgeting analysis in wholly owned subsidiaries. *Journal of Financial and Strategic Decisions*, 13 (1), 1–6.

Humphrey, A. (2005) History Corner: SWOT analysis for management consulting. SRI International.

IAIS (2013) Global systemically important insurers: Policy measures, July 18, http://www.iaisweb.org/supervisory-material/financial-stability-macroprudential-policy-surveillance-988

Ibbotson, R.G. and Kaplan, P.D. (2000) Does asset allocation policy explain 40%, 90%, or 100% of performance? *Financial Analysts Journal*, 56 (1), 26–33.

IIF (2009) *Risk Culture*. Institute of International Finance, Washington, D.C.

IMF (1998) Financial Derivatives. Prepared for the Eleventh Meeting of the IMF Committee on Balance of Payments Statistics, https://www.imf.org/external/bopage/pdf/98-1-20.pdf

IMF (2008) Global Financial Stability Report, World economic and financial surveys.

Incisive Media (2014) Summary report: Survey: How effective is the industry when it comes to financial planning and forecasting?

Information Technology Infrastructure Library (ITIL) v3, http://www.itil-officialsite.com/home/home.asp

ING (2013) Balance sheet management. ING Investor Day, March 31.

Insurance Information Network of California (2008) Insurance guarantee funds, September 16, http://www.iinc.org/articles/275/1/Insurance-Guaranty-Funds/Page1.html

Institute and Faculty of Actuaries (1997) Claims Reserving Manual, http://www.actuaries.org.uk/research-and-resources/pages/claims-reserving-manual

Institute of Risk Management (2012) Risk culture: Under the microscope. Guidance for Boards, http://www.theirm.org/documents/Risk_Culture_A5_WEB15_Oct_2012.pdf

Insurance Journal (2005) Berkshire Hathaway Chairman Warren Buffett on insurance economics and 2004 results, http://www.insurancejournal.com/news/national/2005/03/08/52382.htm

Investment & Pensions Europe (2011) IPE European Institutional Asset Management Survey 2011.

James, C. (1996) RAROC-based capital budgeting and performance evaluation: A case study of bank capital allocation. Working Paper, Wharton Financial Institutions Center.

Jameson, R. (2001) Between RAROC and a hard place. ERisk.com, February.

Jarrar, Y.F. and Zairi, M. (2010) Internal Transfer of Best Practice for Performance Excellence: A Global Survey, European Center for Best Practice Management Research Paper: RP-ECBPM/0019.

Jarvis, R., Katersky, A. and Kim, S. (2013) Indicted hedge fund SAC Capital 'magnet for market cheaters.' abcNews.com, July 25.

Jensen, M.C. (1968) The performance of mutual funds in the period 1945–1964. *Journal of Finance*, 23 (2), 389–416.

Jensen, M.C. (1969) The pricing of capital assets and the evaluation of investment portfolios. *Journal of Business*, 42, 167–247.

Jensen, M.C. and Meckling, W.H. (1976) Theory of the firm: Managerial behavior, agency cost and ownership structure. *Journal of Financial Economics*, 3 (4), 305–360.

Johnson, S. (2013) UK pension funds 'turn gold into lead.' FT.com, October 27.

Johnson, G., Scholes, K. and Whittington, R. (2008) *Exploring Corporate Strategy*, 8th Edition, Prentice Hall.

Jokivuolle, E. and Peura, S. (2006) Rating targeting and the confidence levels implicit in bank capital. Bank of Finland Research, Discussion Papers 27/2006.

Junus, N., Wang, D. and Motiwalla, Z. (2012) Report on pricing using market consistent embedded value (MCEV). Prepared for the Society of Actuaries, Product Development Section, Committee on Life Insurance Research, June.

Juran, J.M. (1951) *Quality Control Handbook*. McGraw-Hill, New York.

Kampfner, J. (2013) Book Review – Making it Happen. *Observer*, September 16.

Kaplan, R.S. and Norton, D.P. (1992) The Balanced Scorecard – Measures that drive performance. *Harvard Business Review*, February.

Kaplan, R.S. and Norton, D.P. (1993) Putting the Balanced Scorecard to work. *Harvard Business Review*, September.

Kaplan, R.S. and Norton, D.P. (1996) *The Balanced Scorecard: Translating strategy into action*. Harvard Business School Press, Boston, MA.

Karlan, D. and Zinman, J. (2005) Elasticities of demand for consumer credit. Economic Growth Center Discussion Paper 926, Yale University.

Kartasheva, A.V. and Park, S. (2011) Real effects of changing rating standards for catastrophic risks.

Katafian, R.E. (2001) Keys to community bank success: Utilizing management information to make informed decisions – Funds transfer pricing (FTP). *Journal of Bank Cost & Management Accounting*, 14 (1), 30.

Kaye, C. and Yuwono, J. (2003) Conglomerate discount or premium? How some diversified companies create exceptional value. Marakon Associates Research.

Keller, P. (2010) Some comments on the illiquidity premium. Working Paper, Swiss Actuarial Association.

Keys, B., Mukherjee, T., Seru, A. and Vig, V. (2008) Did securitization lead to lax screening? Evidence from subprime loans. Working Paper.

Khurana, I.K. and Kim, M-S. (2003) Relative value relevance of historical cost vs fair value: Evidence from bank holding companies. *Journal of Accounting and Public Policy*, 22, 19–42.

Kindleberger, C.P. (2006) *A Financial History of Western Europe*. Oxford University Press, Oxford.

Kisgen, D.J. (2006) Credit ratings and capital structure. *The Journal of Finance*, 61 (3), 1035–1072.

Klein, M. (1971) A theory of the banking firm. *Journal of Money Credit and Banking*, 3 (2), 205–218.

Kleinow, T. and Pelsser, A. (2009) Utility maximization under solvency constraints and unhedgeable risks. University of Amsterdam Working Paper.

Knight, J. and Satchell, S. (2002) *Performance Measurement in Finance*. Butterworth-Heinemann, Oxford.

Knight, L. (2011) What do investment banks do? BBC News, http://www.bbc.co.uk/news/business-11211776

Kobayashi, S. (2014) How should regimes for insurers be established? Experiences in Japan and implications for global standard setting. Geneva Association, Regulation and Supervision Newsletter.

Korajczyk, R. and Sadka, R. (2008) Pricing the commonality across alternative measures of liquidity. *Journal of Financial Economics*, 87, 45–72.

Koyluoglu, H. and Stoker, J. (2002) Honor your contribution. *Risk Magazine*, April, 90–94.

KPMG (2012) The power of procurement: A global survey of procurement functions, https://www.kpmg.com/US/en/IssuesAndInsights/ArticlesPublications/Documents/the-power-of-procurement-a-global-survey-of-procurement-functions.pdf

Kratochvil, M. and Carson, C. (2005) *Growing Modular: Mass customization of complex products, services and software*. Springer-Verlag, Berlin.

Krishnamurthy, K. (2013) Goldman puts four on leave after fallout from trading glitch. Reuters.com, August 25.

Kruger, M. (2011) A goal programming approach to strategic bank balance sheet management. Working Paper, Centre for BMI, North-West University, South Africa.

Kuhfeld, W.F., Randall D.T. and Garratt, M. (1994) Efficient Experimental Design with Marketing Research Applications, *Journal of Marketing Research*, (November), 545–557.

Laeven, L. and Levine, R. (2005) Is there a diversification discount in financial conglomerates? Working Paper.

Lai, I. (2012) UK's Prudential approaches Asia market with multichannel strategy, February 12, http://insurancenewsnet.com/oarticle/2012/02/28/uks-prudential-approaches-asia-markets-with-multichannel-strategy-a-331972.html?topnews

Landsman, W. (1986) An empirical investigation of pension fund property rights. *The Accounting Review*, 61 (4), 662–691.

Landsman, W. (2005) Fair value accounting for financial instruments: Some implications for bank regulation. Workshop on Accounting Risk Management and Prudential Regulation, Bank for International Settlement, Basel, Switzerland, November 11–12.

Lang, W.W. and Jagtiani, J.A. (2010) The mortgage and financial crises: The role of credit risk management and corporate governance. *Atlantic Economic Journal*, 38, 295–316.

Lawrie, G.C.G. and Cobbold, I. (2004) Third-generation Balanced Scorecard: Evolution of an effective strategic control tool. *International Journal of Productivity and Performance Management*, 53 (7), 624–633.

Leary, M.T. and Michaely, R. (2011) Determinants of dividend smoothing: Empirical evidence. *Review of Financial Studies*, 24 (10), 3197–3249.

Lee, C.M.C., Myers, J. and Swaminathan, B. (1999) What is the intrinsic value of the Dow? *Journal of Finance*, 54, 1693–1741.

Lee, P. (1991) BT looks to Sanford's sorcery. *Euromoney*, January.

Lehmann, B.N. and Modest, D.M. (1987) Mutual fund performance evaluation: A comparison of benchmarks and benchmark comparisons. *Journal of Finance*, 42 (2), 233–265.

Lehman Brothers (2000) Risk-Adjusted Capital: An Emerging Positive Secular Trend. Insurance Industry Research Report, September.

Leng, C., Powers, M.R. and Venezian, E. (2004) The relationship between underwriting profit margin and investment income: Changes in competitiveness in property and liability insurance. *Journal of Insurance and Risk Management*, 3, 35–62.

Letzing, J. (2013) Swiss politicians push for stricter bank capital rules. *Wall Street Journal Online*, November 3.

Levine, L. (2012) Offshoring (or offshore outsourcing) and job loss among US workers. Congressional Research Service, https://www.fas.org/sgp/crs/misc/RL32292.pdf

Levy, C., Lamarre, E. and Twining, J. (2010) Taking control of organizational risk culture. McKinsey Working Papers on Risk No. 16, 1–11.

Lewin, C.G. (2004) *Pensions and Insurance Before 1800: A Social History*. Tuckwell Press, East Linton.

Lewis, M. (2007) Thomson, Bartiromo and Victorian Wallstreet. Bloomberg, February 13.

Li, X., Becker, Y. and Rosenfeld, D. (2010) Asset growth and future stock returns: International evidence. *Financial Analysts Journal*, 68 (3), 51–62.

Liikanen Report (2012) High-level expert group on reforming the structure of the EU banking sector, October 2, http://ec.europa.eu/internal_market/bank/docs/high-level_expert_group/report_en.pdf

Lim, C.Y., Lee, E., Kauser, A. and Walker, M. (2011) Bank risk and the value relevance of fair value gains/losses. Working Paper, Manchester Business School.

Lintner, J. (1965) The Valuation of Risk Assets and the Selection of Risky Investments in Stock Portfolios and Capital Budgets, *Review of Economics and Statistics*, 47(1), 13–37.

Linzert, T., Nautz, D. and Bindseil, U. (2004) The longer term refinancing operations of the ECB. Working Paper No. 359, May.

Little, A.D. (2008) Five habits of highly efficient banks: How banks ride the cost curve. Financial Services Insight, August.

Llewellyn, D. (2010) The Northern Rock crisis: A multi-dimensional problem waiting to happen, http://www.prmia.org/pdf/Case_Studies/Northern_Rock_Case_Study_v_1_1.pdf

Lloyd's of London (2006) Seven steps to managing a soft cycle, December.

Lobo, D. (2012) Aviva restructure could see 15 divisions axed, http://citywire.co.uk/new-model-adviser/aviva-restructure-could-see-15-divisions-axed/a600796

Longstaff, F., Mithal, S. and Neis, E. (2005) Corporate yield spreads: Default risk or liquidity? New evidence from the credit default swap market. *The Journal of Finance*, 60 (5), 2213–2253.

Loomis, C.J. (2009) Buffett's big bet. *Fortune*, June 9.

Loomis, C.J. (2014) Buffett widens lead in $1 million hedge fund bet. *Fortune*, February 5.

Luxenburg, S. (2008) Putnam, Janus pay for market timing scandal, August 20, http://wealthmanagement.com/news/putnam-janus-pay-market-timing-scandal-did-anyone-really-lose-any-money

Mabberley, J. (1996) *Price Waterhouse Guide to Activity Based Costing for Financial Institutions*. Irwin Professional Publishing, Chicago.

Maklan, S. and Wilson, H. (2006) Developing multi-channel strategy. Cranfield Customer Management Forum Report, University of Cranfield.

Maklan, S., Knox, S. and Ryals, L. (2008) New trends in innovation and customer relationship management: A challenge for market researchers. *International Journal of Market Research*, 50 (2), 221–240.

Markey, R. and Reichheld, F. (2011) Introducing the net promoter system, Bain Briefing, http://www.bain.com/publications/articles/introducing-the-net-promoter-system-loyalty-insights.aspx

Markham, J.W. (2002) *A Financial History of the United States*, Vol. III. M.E. Sharpe Inc., New York.

Markham, L. (2014) What's wrong with consequences to teach kids lessons? Parenting.com.

Markowitz, H.M. (1952) Portfolio selection. *The Journal of Finance*, 7 (1), 77–91.

Marshall, A. (1920) *Principles of Economics: An introductory volume*. Macmillan Press, London.

Martin, I. (2013) *Making it Happen: Fred Goodwin, RBS and the men who blew up the British economy*. Simon & Schuster, London.

Martin, J.D. and Sayrak, A. (2001) Corporate diversification and shareholder value: A survey of the recent literature. *Journal of Corporate Finance*, 9, 37–57.

Masaharu, K. (2008) US and European financial conglomerate organizations and their implications for Japan and other large diversified financial firms in Asia. Working Paper, Ritsumeikan Asia Pacific University.

Maslow, A. (1943) A theory of human motivation. *Psychological Review*, 50 (4), 370–396.

Matten, C. (2000) *Managing Bank Capital: Capital Allocation and Performance Measurement*. John Wiley & Sons, Ltd.

Matten, C. (2008) *Managing Bank Capital: Capital Allocation and Performance Measurement*, 3rd edn. John Wiley & Sons, Chichester.

Matz, L. and Neu, P. (2007) *Liquidity Risk Management: A Practitioner's Guide*. John Wiley & Sons, Chichester.

Mauboussin, M.J. (2006) Clear thinking about share repurchase: Capital allocation, dividends and share repurchase. *Mauboussin on Strategy*, January 10.

Mauboussin, M.J. (2011) Share repurchase from all angles: Assessing buybacks, no matter where you sit. *Mauboussin on Strategy*, June 11.

Mawad, M., Porzecanski, K. and Jagadeesh, N. (2012) Vivendi punishes shareholders seeing need for breakup: Real M&A. Bloomberg, May 4, http://www.bloomberg.com/apps/news?pid=conewsstory &tkr=MMB:FP&sid=aOHAcBVxznec

McKinsey (2006) Improving strategic planning: A McKinsey survey. *McKinsey Quarterly web exclusive*, September.

McKinsey (2009) McKinsey Global Survey Results: How finance departments are changing.

McKinsey (2010) Banking on multi-channel. Financial Services Report.

McKinsey (2013a) Disruptive technologies: Advances that will transform life, business and the global economy. McKinsey Global Institute Report and A gallery of disruptive technologies, http://www .mckinsey.com/tools/Wrappers/Wrapper.aspx?sid={21F95813-D665-4176-80BD-3823144E3FE2} &pid={A1D4B928-3A7B-4073-AFFA-6AD78525CDB1

McKinsey (2013b) Breakaway: How leading banks outperform through differentiation. McKinsey Global Banking Annual Review.

McQuire, W. (2006) *Choosing the Right Asset/Liability Management System and Keeping it Verified!* Financial Managers Society Publication.

McTaggart, J.M., Kontes, P.W. and Mankins, M.C. (1994) *The Value Imperative*. The Free Press, New York.

Mehr, R.I., Cammack, E. and Rose, T. (1985) *Principles of Insurance*. R.D. Irwin, Homewood, IL.

Mehrdad, B., Coley, S. and White, D. (1999) *The Alchemy of Growth*. Perseus Publishing, New York.

Meier, U.B. and Outreville, J.F. (2003) The reinsurance price and the insurance cycle. Paper presented at the 30th Seminar of the European Group of Risk and Insurance Economists (EGRIE), Zurich, September 15–17.

Meier, U.B. and Outreville, J.F. (2004) (Why) is there an insurance cycle in the USA? Draft for the 31st Seminar of the European Group of Risk and Insurance Economists (EGRIE), Marseille, September 20–22.

Merkley, J. and Levin, C. (2012) Making the Dodd–Frank Act restrictions on proprietary trading and conflicts of interest work. The Roosevelt Institute's Project on Global Finance.

Merton, R.C. (1974) On the pricing of corporate debt: The risk structure of interest rates. *Journal of Finance*, 27 (3), 449–470.

Merton, R.C. and Perold, A.F. (1993) Theory of risk capital in financial firms. *Journal of Applied Corporate Finance*, 6 (3), 16–32.

Mider, Z.R. (2013) Apollo-to-Goldman embracing insurers spurs state concerns. Bloomberg News, April 22, http://www.bloomberg.com/news/2013-04-22/apollo-to-goldman-embracing-insurers-spurs-state-concerns.html

Miller, M.H. (1995) Do the M&M propositions apply to banks?, *Journal of Banking & Finance*, 19, 483–489.

Miller, T. (2007) *Introduction to Option Adjusted Spread Analysis*. Revised and expanded third edition of the OAS classic by Tom Windas. Bloomberg Press, New York.

Milne, A. and Omato, M. (2009) Risk-adjusted measures of value creation in financial institutions. Bank of Finland Research Discussion Papers 25.

Mintzberg, H. (1973) Strategy-making in three modes. *California Management Review*, 16 (2), 44–53.

Mittal, V., Sarkees, M. and Mursched, F. (2008) The right way to manage unprofitable customers. *Harvard Business Review*, April.

Modigliani, F. and Miller, M. (1958) The cost of capital, corporation finance and the theory of investment. *American Economic Review*, 48, 261–297.

Modigliani, F. and Modigliani, L. (1997) Risk-adjusted performance. *Journal of Portfolio Management*, Winter, 45–54.

Monti, M. (1972) Deposit, credit and interest rate determination under alternative bank objective functions. In Shell, K. and Szego, G. (eds), *Mathematical Methods in Investment and Finance*. North-Holland, Amsterdam.

Moody's Analytics (2011) Implementing high-value funds transfer pricing systems.

Moore, H. (2010) Bad boss: Authoritarians in finance.

Morgan Stanley (2011a) Insurance Fat Tail Friday, March 4.

Morgan Stanley (2011b) Composite insurers: The Famous Five. Equity Research, June 28.

Morgan Stanley & Oliver Wyman (2011) Wholesale & Investment Banking Outlook: Reshaping the model. Morgan Stanley Blue Paper.

Morningstar Fund Course 205, Gauging Risk and Return Together.

Morrison & Foerster (2010) The Dodd–Frank Act: A cheat sheet, http://www.mofo.com/files/uploads/images/summarydoddfrankact.pdf

MSNBC (2012) Putnam mutual fund chief to resign, http://www.nbcnews.com/id/3340968/ns/business-corporate_scandals/t/putnam-mutual-fund-chief-resign/

Nabi, M.K. and Saeed, M. (2012) Dynamics of business strategy: A case study of City Group. *IIM Journal*, 1 (1).

Nakada, P., Shah, H., Koyluoglu, H. and Collignon, O. (1999) P&C Raroc: A catalyst for improved capital management in the property & casualty insurance industry. *The Journal of Risk Finance*, Fall.

Nakada, P. and Kapitan, J. (2004) How small banks are using economic capital to compete more effectively. *The RMA Journal*, 86, 32–37.

National Association of Insurance Supervisors (NAIC) (2007) Uniform Property & Casualty Product Coding Matrix, http://www.naic.org/documents/industry_rates_pc_matrix.pdf

National Association of Insurance Supervisors (NAIC) (2009) Risk Based Capital: General Overview, July 15, www.naic.org/documents/committees_e_capad_rbcoverview.pdf

Neate, R. (2009) $400bn SIV market sold off in two years. *The Daily Telegraph*, July 7, http://www.telegraph.co.uk/finance/newsbysector/banksandfinance/5769361/400bn-SIV-market-sold-off-in-two-years.html

Nelson, K. (1996) Fair value accounting for commercial banks: An empirical analysis of SFAS 107. *The Accounting Review*, 161–182.

Nickell, P., Parraudin, W. and Varotto, S. (2000) Stability of ratings transitions. *Journal of Banking Finance*, 24, 203–227.

Nieder, D. (2013) 10 years of low interest rate experience – Experiences from the Japanese Life Insurance Market. Insurance Issues, Gen Re, April.

Nissim, D. and Ziy, A. (2001) Dividend changes and future profitability. *Journal of Finance*, 56 (6), 2111–2134.

Nolop, B. (2007) Rules to acquire by. *Harvard Business Review*, September.

Nyce, C. (2007) Predictive Analytics White Paper, American Institute for Chartered Property Casualty Underwriters & Insurance Institute of America.

O'Brien, J. (2005) Relevance and reliability of fair values: Discussion of the issues raised in 'Fair value accounting for financial instruments: Some implications for bank regulation' prepared for the BIS Accounting, Risk Management and Prudential Regulation Workshop, Basel, November 11–12, http://www.bis.org/events/armpr05/obrien.pdf

Oechslin, J., Aubry, O., Aellig, M., Käpelli, A., Brönnimann, D., Tandonnet, A. and Valois, G. (2004) Incorporating policyholder expectations into asset liability management. *Risk Magazine*, November.

Oechslin, J., Aubry, O., Aellig, M., Käppeli, A., Brönnimann, D. and Tandonnet, A. (2007) Replicating embedded options in life insurance. *Life & Pensions Magazine*, February.

Office of Thrift Supervision (OTS) (2007) Targeted Review: American International Group, Inc.

Ohlson, J.A. (1995) Earnings, book values and dividends in equity valuation. *Contemporary Accounting Research*, 11 (Spring), 661–687.

O'Keeffe, P.J.L., Desai, A.J., Foroughi, K., Hibbitt, G.J., Maxwell, A.F., Sharp, A.C., Taverner, N.H., Ward, M.B. and Willis, F.J.P. (2005) Current developments in embedded value reporting. *British Actuarial Journal*, 11, 407–496.

Okubo, M. (2014) Japan life insurers insolvencies and resolution case studies. In Geneva Association (2014) U. S. and Japan Life Insurers Insolvencies Case Studies: Lessons learned from resolutions, Geneva Association Research Report, edited by E. Baranoff, https://www.genevaassociation.org/media/913756/ga2015-insurance-resolution.pdf?utm_source=Resolution+Report&utm_campaign=030bd7ad12-Insurance_Resolution_Report1_19_2015&utm_medium=email&utm_term=0_3f77d2afd8-030bd7ad12-49610913

Ong, M.K. (1999) *Internal Credit Risk Models: Capital Allocation and Performance Measurements.* Risk Books.

Orme, B. (2005) *Getting Started with Conjoint Analysis*. Research Publishers, Madison, WI.

OWC (2003) The Evolving Role of the CFO and CRO: An International Survey. Oliver Wyman & Company.

OWC (2007) Va Va Voom: Variable annuities are in a pole position, industry report.

OWC (2013) European retail banking: An opportunity for a renaissance. http://www.oliverwyman.com/content/dam/oliver-wyman/global/en/files/archive/2013/EuropeanRetailBankingReport_FINAL.pdf

Packer, F., Stever, R. and Upper, C. (2007) The covered bond market. *BIS Quarterly Review*, September.

Panjer, H. (ed.) (1998) *Financial Economics: With applications to investments, insurance and pensions.* Actuarial Foundation, Schaumburg, IL.

Parsley, M. (1995) The Rorac revolution. *Euromoney*, October.

Pastor, L. and Stambaugh, R. (2003) Liquidity risk and expected stock returns. *Journal of Political Economy*, 111, 642–685.

Patrik, G., Bernegger, S. and Ruegg, M.-B. (1999) The use of risk adjusted capital to support business decision-making. Working paper presented at the Casualty Actuarial Society and Casualty Actuaries in Reinsurance Meeting, Baltimore, June 6–8.

Patterson, S. (2013) Volcker rule sets new hurdles for banks. *Wall Street Journal*, December 10, http://online.wsj.com/news/articles/SB10001424052702303560204579248584111312074

Patterson, S. (2014) SEC Chairman targets dark pools, high speed trading. *Wall Street Journal*, June 6, http://www.wsj.com/articles/sec-chairman-unveils-sweeping-proposals-to-improve-markets-1401986097

Peaple, A. (2013) Heard it on the street: Banks are in a fine mess, and face tough choices. *Wall Street Journal*, November 11, http://online.wsj.com/articles/SB1000142405270230467240457918576054 8017716

Perold, A.F. (2001) Capital allocation in financial firms. Harvard Business School Working Paper No. 98-072.

Peters, T. (1987) The customer as appreciating asset, http://www.tompeters.com/column/1987/005084.php

Peterson, P.P. and Peterson, D.R. (1996) Company performance and measures of value added. The Research Foundation of the Institute of Chartered Financial Analysts.

Petroni, K. and Wahlen, J. (1995) Fair values of equity and debt securities and share prices of property casualty insurers. *Journal of Risk and Insurance*, 62, 719–737.

Pfetsch, S., Poppensieker, T., Schneider, S. and Serova, D. (2011) Mastering ICAAP: Achieving excellence in the new world of scarce capital. McKinsey Working Papers on Risk No. 27.

Phillips, R. and Raffard, R. (2008) Theory and empirical evidence for price-driven adverse selection in consumer lending. Columbia University Working Paper.

Picker, I. (1992) Bankers Trust's amazing risk machine. *Euromoney*, August 1, http://business.highbeam. com/435607/article-1G1-13272482/bankers-trust-amazing-risk-machine

Pinegar, M. and Wilbricht, L. (1989) What managers think of capital structure theory: A survey. *Financial Management*, Winter, 82–91.

Plantiga, A. and van den Meer, R. (1995) Liability-driven performance attribution. *The Geneva Papers on Risk and Insurance*, 20 (74), 16–29.

Pokutta, S. and Schmaltz, C. (2012) Optimal bank planning under Basel III regulations. Cass-Capco Institute Paper Series on Risk Management #34, 03. 2012.

Porter, M. (1978) How competitive forces shape strategy. *Harvard Business Review*, 56 (2), 137–145.

Pozzolo, A. (2011) Comparison of data mining techniques for insurance claim prediction. Doctoral Thesis, University of Bologna.

Pratley, N. (2013) Asian century has already arrived for Prudential, *Guardian*, http://www.guardian.co. uk/business/nils-pratley-on-finance/2013/mar/13/asia-growth-prudential

Prefontaine, J., Desrochers, J. and Godbout, I. (2009) The informational content of voluntary embedded value (EV) financial disclosures by Canadian life insurance companies. *International Business & Economics Research Journal*, 8 (12), 1–13.

Prefontaine, J., Desrochers, J. and Godbout, I. (2011) The informational content of voluntary embedded value (EV) financial disclosures by Canadian life insurance companies during the recent period of market turmoil. *International Business & Economics Research Journal*, 8 (4), 1–13.

PricewaterhouseCoopers (PWC) (2007) Banking in 2050: How big will the emerging markets get? http:// www.pwc.com/en_GX/gx/banking-capital-markets/pdf/banking2050.pdf

PricewaterhouseCoopers (PWC) (2009) Re-engineering the organization: Managing talent in the day after tomorrow.

PricewaterhouseCoopers (PWC) (2012) Top Issues, An Annual Report.

Protess, B. (2012) House Report says Corzine's risky bets aided MF Global's fall.

Protess, B. and de la Merced, M.J. (2012) House Report faults MF Global regulators.

Proudfoot Consulting (2009) Sales Effectiveness: A study of international sales force performance. Productivity Report.

PRMIA (2009) Principles of good governance.

Prudential Insurance Company of America (1915) *The Documentary History of Insurance: 1000 B.C.– 1875 A.D.* Panama-Pacific Exposition Memorial Publications of the Prudential Insurance Company of America.

Puts, J. (2012) Bank balance sheet optimization under Basel III. Master's Thesis, VU University Amsterdam.

Radcliffe, R.C. (1997) *Investment Concepts, Analysis, Strategy.* Addison-Wesley, Reading, MA.

Rangaswamy, A. and van Bruggen, G.H. (2005) Opportunities and challenges in multichannel marketing: An introduction to the special issue. *Journal of Interactive Marketing*, 19 (2), 5.

Rankine, D. (2001) *Why Acquisitions Fail: Practical advice for making acquisition succeed.* FT/Prentice Hall, New York.

Rappaport, A. (1998) *Creating Shareholder Value: A guide for managers and investors.* The Free Press, New York.

Rappaport, A. (2005) The economics of short-term performance obsession. *Financial Analysts Journal*, 61 (3), 65–79.

Redburn, (2012) Insurance: Behavioral change in action. Fundamental Research Report, January 23.

Reichheld, F.F. (1993) Loyalty-based management. *Harvard Business Review*, March–April.

Reichheld, F.F. (2003) One number you need to grow. *Harvard Business Review*, December.

Resti, A. and Sironi, A. (2007) *Risk Management and Shareholders' Value in Banking.* John Wiley & Sons, Chichester.

Reuters (2012) CEO says banks need culture change to regain trust.

Reuters (2014) German cabinet signs draft life insurance law.

Reuters News (2014) Regulators fine global banks $4.3 billion in currency investigation, November, 12.

RMI (2010) Repo 105: True sales or massaging the balance sheet? Risk Management Institute, National University of Singapore, May.

Roth, Z. (2009) Did risk team look at Cassano's deals? AIG execs offer contradictory claims.

Sako, M. (2005) Outsourcing and offshoring: Key trends and issues. Background paper prepared for the Emerging Markets Forum, Said Business School, Oxford University, http://www .emergingmarketsforum.org/wp-content/uploads/pdf/2005%20EMF%20Outsourcing.pdf

Sandoval, E. (2001) Financial performance measures and shareholder value creation: An empirical study for Chilean companies. *The Journal of Applied Business Research*, 17 (3), 206–225.

Satmetrix (2013) Net promoter score and system, http://www.netpromoter.com/why-net-promoter/know/

Schich, S. (2009) Expanded guarantees for banks: Benefits, costs and exit issues. *OECD Journal: Financial Market Trends*, 2.

Schiller, R.J. (2005) *Irrational Exuberance*. Random House, New York.

Schrager, D. (2008) *Replicating Portfolios for Insurance Liabilities*, AENORM 59, April 2008.

Schrand, C.M. (1997) The Association between Stock-Price Interest Rate Sensitivity and Disclosures about Derivative Instruments, *The Accounting Review*, 72(1 January), 87–109.

Schwartzkopff, F. and Wienberg, C. (2012) Denmark to ease pension rules to reduce liability burden. Bloomberg News, June 13.

SCOR (2005) Bancassurance: Analysis of Bancassurance and its status around the world. Focus document, October.

Seschadri, S. (2011) Six myths of customer loyalty, https://www.executiveboard.com/blogs/6-myths-about-customer-loyalty/

Shaffer, S. (2012) Evaluating the impact of fair value accounting on financial institutions: Implications for accounting standards setting and bank supervision. Working Paper, Federal Reserve Bank of Boston QAU 12-01.

Shah, D. and Kumar, V. (2012) The dark side of cross-selling. *Harvard Business Review*, December.

Sharpe, W. (1964) Capital asset prices: A theory of market equilibrium under conditions of risk. *Journal of Finance*, 19 (3), 425–442.

Sharpe, W.F. (1966) Mutual fund performance. *Journal of Business*, 39 (1), 119–138.

Shavell, S. (1979) On moral hazard and insurance. *The Quarterly Journal of Economics*, 93 (4), 541–562.

Shin, H.S. and Adrian, T. (2008) Liquidity and leverage. Paper presented at the IMF Financial Cycles, Liquidity and Securitization Conference, April 18.

Shipman, T. (2011) Confidence in UK banking system rocked as agency downgrades 12 bank and building society credit ratings. *Daily Mail*, October 8, http://www.dailymail.co.uk/news/article-2046342/Moodys-downgrades-credit-ratings-12-UK-banks.html#ixzz1kN7a7z00

Shirakawa, H. and Ogasawara, S. (2011) How has Japan's life insurance industry adapted to the low interest rate climate? *Japan Economic Advisor*, September 29.

Sinek, S. (2010) *Re:Focus*, http://sinekpartners.typepad.com/files/babe.pdf

Singleton, J.C. (2004) *Core–Satellite Portfolio Management: A Modern Approach for Professionally Managed Funds*. McGraw-Hill, New York.

Sit, D. (2013), Life insurance: Ready and raring to go, *Asia Insurance Review*, October.

Small, R.C. (2013) Aligning incentives at systemically important financial institutions. Harvard Law School Forum on Corporate Governance and Financial Regulation, June 11, https://blogs.law.harvard.edu/corpgov/2013/06/11/aligning-incentives-at-systemically-important-financial-institutions/

Smith, G. (2012a) Why I am leaving Goldman Sachs. *New York Times*, March 14.

Smith, G. (2012b) Goldman Sachs 'muppet' trader says unsophisticated clients targeted. *The Guardian*, October 22.

Smithson, C. (2003) Economic capital – measurement and attribution. *Risk Magazine*, November, 61–63.

Snider, C. and Youle, T. (2010) Does the Libor reflect banks' borrowing costs? *Social Science Research Network*, July 22.

Society of Actuaries (2000) Liquidity Management for Life Insurers with Institutional Business, Session 64PD, Record 26(2).

Society of Actuaries (2003) Asset–Liability Management, Society of Actuaries Professional Actuarial Specialty Guide BB-1-03, https://www.soa.org/library/professional-actuarial-specialty-guides/professional-actuarial-specialty-guides/2003/september/spg0308alm.pdf

Sommer, D.W. (1996) The impact of firm risk on property-liability insurance prices. *Journal of Risk and Insurance*, 63 (3), 501–514.

Son, H. (2008) AIG's ratings cut by S&P, Moody's, threatening fund raising. Bloomberg, September 15, http://www.bloomberg.com/apps/news?sid=aq6ZlNtItdj4&pid=newsarchive

Sorensen, S.M. and Kyle, D.L. (2008) Currency translation adjustments. *Journal of Accountancy*, July 1.

Standard & Poor's (1999) Bank Ratings Criteria.

Standard & Poor's (2005) Criteria: Insurance: General: Evaluating the Enterprise Risk Management Practices of Insurance Companies.

Standard & Poor's (2006) Lonely at the Top: Why so few 'AAA' US life insurers remain.

Standard & Poor's (2011a) Banks: Rating methodology and assumptions.

Standard & Poor's (2011b) Banks: Bank hybrid capital methodology and assumptions.

Standard & Poor's (2012) Interest Rate Risk in 2012, Special Report.

Standard & Poor's (2013) Group Rating Methodology, http://www.standardandpoors.com/spf/upload/Ratings_US/Group_Rating_Methodology_5_7_13.pdf

Stark, J. (2009) A simple proxy for the liquidity premium. Barrie Hibbert Insights.

Stein, D. (1999) Introducing tracking error. Parametric Research Brief, http://www.parametricportfolio.com/wp-content/uploads/2012/02/Research-Brief-Introducing-Tracking-Error.web_.pdf

Stewart III G.B. (1991) *The Quest for Value: A guide for senior managers*. HarperCollins, New York.

Stone, M. (1947) A short history of life insurance. Insurance Research and Review Service, Indianapolis.

StoneRidge Advisors LLC (2012) Does size matter for property casualty insurers?

Story, L. and Dash, E. (2009) Bank of America chief to depart at year's end. *New York Times*, October 1, http://www.nytimes.com/2009/10/01/business/01bank.html

Strasburg, J. (2013) Banks may close door to chat rooms. *Wall Street Journal*, November 11, http://online.wsj.com/articles/SB10001424052702304868404579189861293808726

Strischek, D. (2002) Credit culture I. *RMA Journal*, November.

Strischek, D. (2003) Credit culture III. *RMA Journal*, March.

Strischek, D. (2009) The 5 C's of credit. *RMA Journal*, July–August.

Strumpf, J.G. (2012) The vision & values of Wells Fargo, https://www08.wellsfargomedia.com/pdf/invest_relations/VisionandValues04.pdf

Stulz, R.M. (1996) Rethinking risk management. *Journal of Applied Corporate Finance*, 9 (3), 8–25

Stulz, R.M., Opler, T., Pinkowitz, L. and Williamson, R. (1999) The determinants and implications of corporate cash holdings. *Journal of Financial Economics*, 52, 3–46.

Stulz, R.M., Bong-Chan, K. and Lee, D. (2000) U.S. banks, crises, and bailouts: From Mexico to LTCM. *American Economic Review*, 90, 28–31.

Swiss Re (2001) The Economics of Insurance: How insurers create value for shareholders. Technical Publication, http://media.swissre.com/documents/pub_economics_of_insurance_en.pdf

Swiss Re (2005) Insurers' cost of capital and economic value creation: Principles and practical implications. Swiss Re Technical Publishing, Sigma No. 3.

Swiss Re (2012) Sigma: Understanding profitability in life insurance, No 1.

Takagi, S., (2005) Reorganization of insurance companies, banks and others based upon the law regarding special reorganization proceedings for financial institutions. *Chuo Law Review*, 1.

Taleb, N., (2010) *The Black Swan: The impact of the highly improbable*. Penguin, New York.

Talebzadeh, H., Mandutianu, S. and Winner, C.F. (1995) Countrywide loan-underwriting expert system. *AI Magazine*, 16 (1), 51–64.

Taylor, G. (2000) *Loss Reserving: An actuarial perspective*. Kluwer Academic Publishing, Dordrecht.

Thaler, R. and Sunstein, C. (2009) *Nudge: Improving decisions about health, wealth and happiness*. Penguin, New York.

Thaler, R., Tversky, A., Kahneman, D. and Schwartz, A. (1997) The effect of myopia and loss aversion on risk taking: An experimental test. *The Quarterly Journal of Economics*, 112 (2), 647–661.

Tillinghast-Towers Perrin (2004) Market Consistent Embedded Value: Allowing for risk within an embedded value framework. Discussion document.

Tillinghast-Towers Perrin (2005) Market Consistent Embedded Value: Dispelling the myths. Discussion document.

Todaro, E. (2007) Introduction to embedded value. Presentation to the Society of Actuaries, September 17.

Towers Watson (2011) Measuring risk culture: A powerful approach to demonstrate embedding of risk management within an organization.

Towers Watson (2013) EEV/MCEV – Recent Market Trends. Presentation by Dominique Lebel, June, http://www.actuary.com/seac/handouts/201306_03b_MCEV.pdf

Traxler, D. (2013) 21 Key performance indicators for ecommerce businesses, http://www.practicalecommerce.com/articles/3906-21-Key-Performance-Indicators-for-Ecommerce-Businesses

Trenerry, C.F. (2009) *The Origin and Early History of Insurance*. The Lawbook Exchange, Clark, NJ.

Treynor, J.L. (1965) How to rate management of investment funds. *Harvard Business Review*, 43, 63–75.

Treynor, J.L. and Mazuy, F. (1966) Can mutual funds outguess the market? *Harvard Business Review*, 44, 131–136.

Turnbull, S.M. (2000) Capital allocation and risk performance measurement in a financial institution. *Financial Markets, Institutions & Instruments*, 9 (5), 325–357.

UBS (2008) Shareholder report on UBS's write-downs, April, http://www.alternatives-economiques.fr/fic_bdd/article_pdf_fichier/1213187130_Shareholder_Report_on_UBS_Write_Downs.pdf

UBS (2010) Transparency report to the shareholders of UBS AG.

UK Government Policy Paper (2012) Banking reform: Delivering sustainability and supporting a sustainable economy, June 14, https://www.gov.uk/government/publications/banking-reform-delivering-sustainability-and-supporting-a-sustainable-economy

United Nations Environmental Program Finance Initiative (UNEPFI) (2009a) The Global State of Sustainable Insurance: Understanding and integrating environmental, social and governance factors in insurance.

United Nations Environmental Program Finance Initiative (UNEPFI) (2009b) Fiduciary Responsibility: Legal and practical aspects of integrating environmental, social and governance issues into institutional investment.

USA Today (2014) Fed, FDIC call banks' "living wills" inadequate, August 5, http://www.usatoday.com/story/money/business/2014/08/05/fed-bankruptcy-plans/13641127/

US Securities and Exchange Commission (2011) Notice regarding Volcker Rule.

Vaughn, E.J. (1997) *Risk Management*. John Wiley & Sons, Chichester.

Venkatachalam, M. (1996) Value-relevance of banks' derivatives disclosures, *Journal of Accounting and Economics*, 22, 327–355.

Vo, J. (2013) Allianz Discussion Document, Royal Bank of Canada.

Volcker, P.A. (2012) Commentary on the restrictions on proprietary trading by insured depositary institutions, http://online.wsj.com/public/resources/documents/Volcker_Rule_Essay_2-13-12.pdf

Wall Street Journal (2008) Libor fog: Bankers cast doubt on key rate amid crisis, April 16.

Wall Street Journal (2012) ECB's Draghi mocks 'virile' bankers, February 9, http://blogs.marketwatch.com/thetell/2012/02/09/ecb%E2%80%99s-draghi-mocks-%E2%80%98virile%E2%80%99-bankers/

Wall Street Journal (2013) Banks find new ways to weight risk. February 21.

Wall Street Journal (2015) Another rigged prosecution? January 7.

Walter, J.S. (2004) Economic capital, performance evaluation and capital adequacy at Bank of America. *RMA Journal*, 86 (6), 20–26.

Wang, S. (2002) A universal framework for pricing financial and insurance risks. *ASTIN Bulletin: Journal of the International Actuarial Association*, 32 (November), 213–234.

Wang, S. (2003) Equilibrium pricing transforms: New results using Buhlmann's 1980 economic model. *ASTIN Bulletin: Journal of the International Actuarial Association*, 33 (May), 57–73.

Wang, S. (2004) Cat bond pricing using probability transforms. The Geneva Papers on Risk and Insurance – Issues and Practice.

Warsh, K. (2007) Financial intermediation and complete markets. Speech at the European Economics and Financial Centre, London, June 5, http://www.federalreserve.gov/newsevents/speech/warsh2007 0605a.htm

Watson, I. (1997) *Applying Case-Based Reasoning: Techniques for Enterprise Systems*. Morgan Kaufmann, San Francisco, CA.

Wicks, D. (2010) Putting strategy to work for you. *Progress Magazine*, 17 (5), http://www .progressmedia.ca/article/2010/09/putting-strategy-work-you

Wilson, H., Aldrick, P. and Ahmed, K. (2011) RBS investigation: Chapter 2 – the ABN Amro takeover. *The Telegraph*, December 11.

Wilson, T.C. (1992) Raroc remodeled. *Risk Magazine*, 5 (8), 112–119.

Wilson, T.C. (1998) Value at Risk. In C. Alexander (ed.), *Risk Management and Analysis, Volume 1: Measuring and Modelling Financial Risk*. John Wiley & Sons, Ltd.

Wilson, T.C. (2003a) Overcoming the hurdle. *Risk Magazine*, July.

Wilson, T.C. (2003b) Is ALM at European life insurers broken? *Risk Magazine*, September.

Wilson, T.C. (2004) Presentation at the 2004 PRMIA/Oliver Wyman Conference on Managing the Value of Financial Institutions.

Wilson, T.C. (2007) ING insurance risk capital framework. Presentation to Kent University, September 5, http://www.kent.ac.uk/casri/news/news-archive/pdf/TomWilson.pdf

Wilson, T.C. (2010) Consistency is King. *Life & Pensions Magazine*, January.

Wilson, T.C. (2013a) Risk management lessons learned from the financial crisis. *Journal of Risk Management in Financial Institutions*, 6 (2).

Wilson, T.C. (2013b) Risk management in the face of risky sovereign debt: Four observations, http://www.bis.org/publ/bppdf/bispap72.pdf

Wilson, T.C. and Hristova, Y. (2014) Value relevance of market consistency: A useful management tool or a volatile distraction? Working Paper.

Witt, R.C. (1978) The competitive rate regulatory system in Illinois: A comparative study. *CPCU Journal*, 31 (3), 151–162.

Witt, R.C. (1981) Underwriting risk and return: Some additional comments. *Journal of Risk and Insurance*, 48 (4), 653–661.

Wittink, D.R. and Cattin, P. (1989) Commercial use of conjoint analysis: An update. *Journal of Marketing*, 91–96.

World Economic Forum (2011) The future of long term investing, http://www3.weforum.org/docs/ WEF_FutureLongTermInvesting_Report_2011.pdf

Worstall, T. (2013) Explaining the secret of Warren Buffett's success: Double leverage, August 2, http:// www.forbes.com/sites/timworstall/2013/02/08/explaining-the-secret-of-warren-buffetts-success-double-leverage/

Wüthrich, M. (2003) Claims reserving using Tweedie's compound Poisson model, *ASTIN Bulletin*, 33 (2), 331–346.

Wüthrich, M.V. (2011) An academic view on the illiquidity premium and market consistent valuation in insurance. *European Actuarial Journal*, 1, 93–105.

Zaik, E., Walter, J., Kelling, G. and James, C. (1996) Raroc at the Bank of America: From theory to practice. *Journal of Applied Corporate Finance*, 9 (2), 83–92.

Zairi and Jarrer (2010) Employee Empowerment – A UK Survey of Trends and Best Practices. European Centre for Best Practice Management.

Zook, C. and Allen, J. (2003) Growth outside the core. *Harvard Business Review*, December.

Zweig, P.L. (1995) *Wriston: Walter Wriston, Citibank, and the Rise and Fall of American Financial Supremacy*. Crown Publishers: New York.

Index

Printed and bound by CPI Group (UK) Ltd, Croydon, CR0 4YY

23/04/2025

14660970-0005